MW01097612

LIFT

TAKE YOUR STUDYING
TO THE NEXT LEVEL.

This book comes with 1-year digital access to the
Examples & Explanations for this course.

Step 1: Go to **www.CasebookConnect.com/LIFT** and redeem your access code to get started.

Access Code:  EESR233571132113

Step 2: Go to your BOOKSHELF and select your online *Examples & Explanations* to start reading, highlighting, and taking notes in the margins of your e-book.

Step 3: Select the STUDY tab in your toolbar to access the questions from your book in interactive format, designed to give you extra practice and help you master the course material.

Is this a used casebook? Access code already scratched off?

You can purchase the online *Examples & Explanations* and still access all of the powerful tools listed above. Please visit CasebookConnect.com/Catalog to learn more about Connected Study Aids.

PIN: 9111149622

14220

Family Law in Focus

Focus Casebook Series

Family Law in Focus

Marlene A. Pontrelli
J. Shoshanna Ehrlich

Wolters Kluwer

To contact Customer Service, e-mail customer.service@wolterskluwer.com, call 1-800-234-1660, fax 1-800-901-9075, or mail correspondence to:

Wolters Kluwer
Attn: Order Department
PO Box 990
Frederick, MD 21705

Printed in the United States of America.

1 2 3 4 5 6 7 8 9 0

ISBN 978-1-4548-6804-0

Library of Congress Cataloging-in-Publication Data

Names: Pontrelli, Marlene A., author. | Ehrlich, J. Shoshanna, author.
Title: Family law in focus / Marlene A. Pontrelli, J. Shoshanna Ehrlich.
Description: New York: Wolters Kluwer, 2017. | Series: Focus casebook series
Identifiers: LCCN 2016027984 | ISBN 9781454868040
Subjects: LCSH: Domestic relations—United States. | LCGFT: Casebooks.
Classification: LCC KF505 .P66 2017 | DDC 346.7301/5 — dc23
LC record available at https://lccn.loc.gov/2016027984

About Wolters Kluwer Legal & Regulatory US

Wolters Kluwer Legal & Regulatory US delivers expert content and solutions in the areas of law, corporate compliance, health compliance, reimbursement, and legal education. Its practical solutions help customers successfully navigate the demands of a changing environment to drive their daily activities, enhance decision quality and inspire confident outcomes.

Serving customers worldwide, its legal and regulatory portfolio includes products under the Aspen Publishers, CCH Incorporated, Kluwer Law International, ftwilliam.com and MediRegs names. They are regarded as exceptional and trusted resources for general legal and practice-specific knowledge, compliance and risk management, dynamic workflow solutions, and expert commentary.

*To Matthew, Megan, Max, and Michael who helped me remember
what it was like to be a law student.*

—MAP

Summary of Contents

Table of Contents

The Focus Casebook Series

Help students reach their full potential with the fresh approach of the Focus Casebook Series. Instead of using the "hide the ball" approach, selected cases illustrate key developments in the law and show how courts develop and apply doctrine. The approachable manner of this series provides a comfortable experiential environment that is instrumental to student success.

Students perform best when applying concepts to real-world scenarios. With assessment features, such as Real Life Applications and Applying the Concepts, the Focus Casebook Series offers many opportunities for students to apply their knowledge.

Focus Casebook Features Include:

Case Previews and Post-Case Follow-Ups — To succeed, law students must know how to deconstruct and analyze cases. Case Previews highlight the legal concepts in a case before the student reads it. Post-Case Follow-Ups summarize the important points.

Case Preview

In re Hlavin

As the hypothetical of Mary Jones and her loaves of bread illustrates, the number of potential disputes about the kinds of debt that are or are not to be considered consumer debts is simply limitless. The lawyer has to recognize when the issue matters and can be contested. As you read In re Hlavin, a case involving the 11 U.S.C §707(b) dismissal for abuse provision, consider the following questions:

1. Why is it the debtors and not the bankruptcy trustee who are arguing that their home mortgage is not a consumer debt?
2. What does this court s
   gage is or isn't a consu

Post-Case Follow-Up

Is this opinion making a distinction between the repossessor himself disturbing the peace and his committing an act that motivates another to disturb the peace once the repossessor is gone? Would the result in this case have been different if the activities of the repossessors had awakened the debtor or the neighbor and the one awakened had shouted at them out of a window something like, "Stop, thief! I've called the police"? See Robinson v. Citicorp National Services, Inc., 921 S.W.2d 52 (Mo. Ct. App. 1996), and Chrysler Credit Corp. v. Koontz, 661 N.E.2d 1171 (1996). If the debtor's husband had raced outside with a firearm while the repossessors were pulling away from the property? If he or the neighbor had fired a firearm at the fleeing repossessors? If a sleeping child had been in the car unseen by the repossessor when the car was driven off? See Chapa v. Traciers & Associates, 267 S.W.3d 386 (Tex. App. 2008)? If the repossessor had violated a driving ordinance in the course of repos-

The Focus Casebook Series

Real Life Applications — Every case in a chapter is followed by Real Life Applications, which present a series of questions based on a scenario similar to the facts in the case. Real Life Applications challenge students to apply what they have learned in order to prepare them for real-world practice. Use Real Life Applications to spark class discussions or provide them as individual short-answer assignments.

> *In re Hlavin: Real Life Applications*
>
> 1. Would the result in *Hlavin* have been different if the loans secured by their home had originally been taken out to fund a failed business venture? What if they had been taken out for home improvement or a vacation but then actually used to fund a business venture? Would it matter if they told the bank the money was being borrowed for home improvement or vacation but intended it to be used to fund a business venture? What if the home loans had been taken out for mixed personal/business reasons?
> 2. If the debtors in *Hlavin* had 30 different consumer debts totaling $75,000 and only one business debt totaling $76,000, would that court find that they had "primarily consumer debts" under §707(b)(1)? What would be the result if a court utilized one of the alternative approaches to this question mentioned in *Hlavin*?

Applying the Concepts — These end-of-chapter exercises encourage students to synthesize the chapter material and apply relevant legal doctrine and code to real-world scenarios. Students can use these exercises for self-assessment or the professor can use them to promote class interaction.

Applying the Concepts

1. Assume you are consulted by the following potential bankruptcy clients. Which of these appear at first blush to be candidates for a consumer bankruptcy filing as opposed to a non-consumer or business filing?

   a. The individual owners of an unincorporated video rental store whose business has plummeted due to the popularity of Internet movie-streaming services.

   b. A married couple both employed but who have abused their credit card spending and now owe more than they make together in a year.

   c. A recently divorced woman with two children whose ex-husband is unemployed and not contributing child support and who is having trouble paying her monthly living expenses.

   d. A married couple, one of whom has suffered major health problems resulting in medical expenses in excess of what they can expect to earn in ten years.

Preface

Ensure student success with the Focus Casebook Series.

THE FOCUS APPROACH

In a law office, when a new associate attorney is being asked to assist a supervising attorney with a legal matter in which the associate has no prior experience, it is common for the supervising attorney to provide the associate with a recently closed case file involving the same legal issues so that the associate can see and learn from the closed file to assist more effectively with the new matter. This experiential approach is at the heart of the *Focus Casebook Series*.

Additional hands-on features, such as Real Life Applications, Application Exercises, and Applying the Concepts provide more opportunities for critical analysis and application of concepts covered in the chapters. Professors can assign problem-solving questions as well as exercises on drafting documents and preparing appropriate filings.

CONTENT SNAPSHOT

Chapter 1 sets the stage with a review of the historical antecedents of family law and cases that shaped the foundations of the current law in this area. **Chapter 2** builds upon these historical foundations and reviews the recent law with respect to marriage equality and recognition of same sex marriages, as well as the recognition of rights for non-marital couples.

Chapters 3 through 10 build, in order, the law with respect to family relationships and of legal separation and divorce. **Chapter 3** begins with the law of premarital and post-marital agreements that may form the basis for how assets are divided. **Chapter 4** explores the basic divorce, annulment and legal separation process. Each of the subsequent chapters takes an area of the law and details the statutory and case law that the courts must use in defining rights and responsibilities of each individual. **Chapter 5** addresses child custody and explores the best interest standard judges must use in deciding parenting rights and visitation. **Chapter 6** looks to the financial aspect of child custody decisions and how to set child support and enforce child support orders. **Chapters 7 and 8** provide in-depth coverage of spousal support and division of marital property, issues that exist in all divorce cases. The procedural aspects of family law cases are discussed in **Chapter 9** covering the divorce process, and in **Chapter 10** on jurisdiction.

Chapters 11 through 15 focus on individual aspects of family law that may not arise in every case but are important areas for practitioners to understand and to address. Thus, Domestic Violence (**Chapter 11**), Parentage issues (**Chapter 12**), Child Abuse and Neglect (**Chapter 13**), Adoption (**Chapter 14**) and Assisted Reproductive Technology (**Chapter 15**) are covered, tracing developments from the historical underpinnings to the current law applied by family courts.

RESOURCES

Casebook: The casebook is structured around text, cases, and application exercises. Highlighted cases are introduced with a *Case Preview,* which sets up the issue and identifies key questions. *Post-Case Follow-Ups* expand on the holding in the case. *Real Life Applications* present opportunities to challenge students to apply concepts covered in the case to realistic hypothetical cases. *Application Exercises* offer a mix of problem solving and research activities to determine the law of the state where the student plans to practice. State law application exercises better prepare the student to actually handle cases. The *Applying the Concepts* feature demands critical analysis and integration of concepts covered in the chapter.

Other resources to enrich your class include: Practice Skills Exercises, or supplementary material such as Examples & Explanations: Family Law 4E, by Robert E. Oliphant and Nancy Ver Steegh. Ask your Wolters Kluwer sales representative or visit the Wolters Kluwer site at *wklegaledu.com* to learn more about building the product package that's right for you.

Acknowledgments

No textbook is ever written without the help and guidance from numerous individuals. A special thank you to the students we have been privileged to teach over the years. Your thoughts and comments on developing materials that are straightforward but also challenging were invaluable. Thank you to Elizabeth Kenny at Wolters Kluwer who assisted in developing the text and seeing the project through to completion. Thank you to Tom Daughhetee, Director of Production at The Froebe Group, who kept everything moving along, oversaw all the proofreading, and added his guidance and thoughts along the way. Finally, thank you to the entire team at Wolters Kluwer who saw the need for a series of books for law students that focused on the law and learning, rather than the traditional hide-and-seek approach. As educators we appreciated the opportunity to be a part of this important series of books.

Family Law in Focus

The Law of the Family

The primary goal of this chapter is to provide you with a historically grounded understanding of the role the law plays in the structuring of family relationships. Focusing first on marriage and then on the parent-child relationship, this introductory chapter explores evolving understandings of the dynamic, and at times, contentious relationship between the regulatory authority of the state and the rights of individuals within the domestic realm. Closely aligned with this central theme, it also traces how women's evolving demands for equality have challenged the historically presumed authority of states to assign marital rights and responsibilities based upon deeply gendered assumptions regarding the rightful place of husbands and wives within the domestic order. This same theme is also applicable to same-sex gender assumptions and the shift in the law toward the constitutional right to equality in all relationships, which will be examined in more detail in Chapter 2.

Over the course of this book, we will return to many of the topics that are introduced in this chapter. So for now, your focus should be on the broad narrative arc of legal change within the domestic realm. Pay particular attention to the entwined themes of the relationship between state power and individual rights and evolving understandings of equality that over time disrupted the inequitable distribution of power between husbands and wives, and more recently between same-sex partners and heterosexual couples. As you will see, not only have these meta-themes shaped the historic contours of the field of domestic relationships, but enduring questions regarding the dynamic relationship between the permissible scope of state regulatory authority over family relationships, rights of individual autonomy and privacy, and gender roles continue to animate many contemporary debates in the family law field.

Key Concepts

- The historical evolution of the marital relationship
- The constitutional limits of the state in controlling the marital relationship
- The right of privacy in family relationships
- The legal frameworks of the parent-child relationship

This chapter cannot begin to account for all of the complexities and variations of domestic relations law, particularly as applied to families who occupy dramatically different places in the social and economic order. That being said, it is important to bear in mind that formal recognition of family bonds was withheld from certain classes of people. For example, slave marriages were not accorded legal status, and children, parents, and partners were forcibly separated from one another without regard for the ties that linked them together. While times have changed, we will see throughout the readings the role the state plays in shaping community standards in the area of domestic relations.

A. MARRIAGE: EVOLVING LEGAL FRAMEWORKS

When people think about marriage, they usually think of it as a private, intimate relationship shaped by the love, commitment, and needs of two individuals. However, this understanding of marriage as an essentially private relationship fails to account for the fact that the state also has an interest in the relationship — an interest that is grounded in the belief that the exclusivity, permanence, and procreative potential of the marital bond promote social cohesion and stability. Accordingly, states have traditionally exercised considerable control over the institution of marriage, including the relationship between spouses, in order to advance this public interest.

In order to buttress the importance of marriage as a vital social institution, states have historically drawn a bright line between marriage and other forms of intimate association. Placed outside the realm of sanctioned family life, unwed couples have been excluded from the rights, benefits, and privileges of marriage so as to not dilute the advantage of entering into a marital relationship. Tangible benefits provided to married couples under state and federal law are quite extensive. By some counts, married persons have over 1,138 benefits and protections that are provided to them based upon their marital status. Benefits include Social Security entitlements, beneficial tax treatment, immigration and residency rights for a noncitizen spouse, and veterans' benefits. Important state benefits include automatic inheritance rights in the absence of a will, medical and family leave rights, and joint property rights upon divorce.

As discussed in Chapter 2, one consequence of the gradual transition toward a more privatized understanding of marriage is that the law has begun to move away from a strict reliance on the existence of this legal bond as the exclusive marker for determining family status and the corresponding entitlement to benefits. However, as we will see, although a bit more permeable, the bright line between marriage and other forms of intimate associations remains relatively intact.

1. The Peculiar Nature of the Marriage "Contract"

Although we often speak of the marriage "contract," and a valid marriage clearly requires the consent of the potential spouses, as the Supreme Court made clear in the early case of *Maynard v. Hill*, 125 U.S. 190 (1887), marriage is also what is often referred to as a status relationship. The contours of this status have traditionally been determined by the regulatory authority of the state. Thus, while marriage is a private relationship, it is also subject to the control of the legislature. This control does not constitute interference by the government of an impairment of contract, which was a question decided in *Maynard v. Hill*. This decision sanctioned the ability of the state to control and oversee the existence of the marital relationship, including dissolving the relationship. A brief summary of the facts explain the far-reaching implications this historical decision had on the ability of states to define the status of the marriage relationship.

Maynard v. Hill involved a couple — David and Lydia Maynard — who were married in the state of Vermont in 1828, and lived there as husband and wife until they moved to Ohio in 1850. Shortly after moving, David left his family and eventually moved to Oregon, while promising either to return to Ohio or to send for Lydia and their two children. Instead, he fell in love with another woman whom he married after being granted a divorce by the Oregon legislature. The Court in *Maynard* was faced with a challenge to the validity of the Oregon divorce, which had been obtained without the knowledge of his first wife Lydia. At stake in the case was Lydia's claim to a portion of a tract of land that had been settled upon David as part of a public land grant program. Thus, the issue was whether the divorce granted David by the legislature was valid and defeated any claim by Lydia to the land after David's death. *Id.* at 216. The action was brought by Henry C. Maynard and Frances J. Patterson, the children of David and Lydia Maynard. David Maynard died intestate in 1873, and Lydia Maynard in 1879.

The Court considered the argument that the divorce impaired the "obligation of the contract of marriage" in violation of the "prohibition of the federal constitution against the impairment of contracts by state legislation." The Court explained that although "marriage is often termed by text writers and in decisions of courts as a civil contract," this characterization simply serves "to indicate that it must be founded upon the agreement of the parties, and does not require any religious ceremony for its solemnization." *Id.* at 210-211. However, the Court continued, marriage is in fact "something more than a mere contract," and thus does not come "within the meaning of this prohibition" against the state impairment of contracts. *Id.*

Expounding upon the peculiar nature of the marriage contract, the Court went on to state that

> when the contract to marry is executed by the marriage, a relation between the parties is created which they cannot change. Other contracts may be modified, restricted, or enlarged, or entirely released upon the con-

Legislative Divorce

Following the English practice prior to the mid-nineteenth century of granting parliamentary divorces, many colonial and early state legislatures were empowered to dissolve marriages by way of a special legislative enactment. While ecclesiastical courts, and later the judiciary, were able to give divorces from bed and board (referred to as *divorce a mensa et thoro*), in order to have an absolute divorce with the ability to remarry, a legislative act was often required. *Maynard v. Hill* provides an example of such a legislative act that was used to attempt to dissolve the bonds of marriage. The legislative bill in *Maynard*, typical of other legislative divorce bills, was "[a]n act to provide for the dissolution of the bonds of matrimony heretofore existing." Thus, once passed, the dissolution of marriage was complete.

> sent of the parties. Not so with marriage. The relation once formed, the law steps in and holds the parties to various obligations and liabilities. It is an institution, in the maintenance of which in its purity the public is deeply interested, for it is the foundation of the family and of society, without which there would be neither civilization nor progress.

Id. at 211.

Buttressing this understanding of marriage as a status relationship whose terms are set by law rather than by the agreement of the parties, the Court cited with approval *Adams v. Palmer*, 51 Maine 481, 483 (1863), which stated that marriage is "a social relation like that of parent and child, the obligations of which arise not from the consent of concurring minds, but are the creation of the law itself . . . [and accordingly] they can neither be modified nor changed by any agreement of parties." *Maynard v. Hill*, 125 U.S. at 211.

In speaking of marriage as a "creation of the law," the *Maynard* Court was referring to the authority that states, as distinct from the federal government, have over domestic relations based upon the Tenth Amendment edict that "the powers not delegated to the United States by the Constitution, nor prohibited by it to the States, are reserved to the States respectively, or to the people." U.S. Const. amend. X. In spite of that authority, the Supreme Court noted in 1890 that "the whole subject of the domestic relations of husband and wife, parent and child, belongs to the laws of the states, and not to the laws of the United States." *In re Burrus*, 136 U.S. 586, 593-594 (1890). However, as we will see in subsequent chapters, the federal government has increasingly made its presence felt in the realm of domestic relations through both the growing constitutionalization of the field and a variety of modern statutory schemes, such as those related to child support and child welfare.

2. The Relationship of Husband and Wife

Although the modern legal approach to marriage is to permit spouses to shape the contours of their own relationship, this is a fairly recent development. Historically, based upon the state's authority over the "rights, duties, and obligations" of marriage, the law defined the nature of the marital relationship based upon highly gendered understandings of appropriate spousal conduct.

Common Law Origins

The original marriage laws of the states in most of the country were based upon English **common law**. As eloquently expressed by William Blackstone, a famed English legal commentator, a defining aspect of this tradition was the legal subordination of married women:

> By marriage, the husband and wife are one person in law; that is, the very being or legal existence of the woman is suspended during the marriage, or at least is incorporated and consolidated into that of the husband; under whose wing, protection, and *cover*, she performs everything. . . . Upon this principle, of a union of person in husband and wife, depend almost all the legal rights, duties, and disabilities, that either one of them acquire by the marriage.

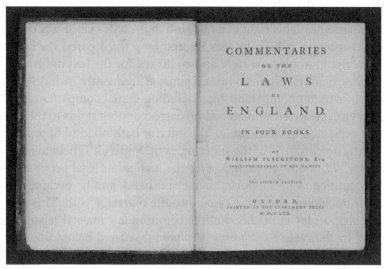

William C. Blackstone, Commentaries
Library of Congress, Washington, D.C.

William C. Blackstone, Commentaries, abridged, 82 (9th ed. 1915) (citations omitted).

This foundational doctrine of **marital unity**, by which a husband and wife were regarded as a single legal person, was outwardly manifested by the common law requirement that a wife take her husband's last name as her own. Marriage further altered a woman's legal status, and the rights that she possessed as a single woman were transferred to her husband in exchange for his support and protection. Upon marriage, a woman lost the right to own personal property (assets other than real property), and property that she owned at the time of marriage or subsequently acquired became her husband's. As owner, he could sell, destroy, or bequeath it, just as he could his separately acquired property. This property could also be taken by a husband's creditors in order to satisfy his debts. In short, as her person merged into her husband's so too did her property merge into his.

Real property — land and whatever is grown on or fixed to it — was treated differently, as title did not pass to the husband. The husband did, however, acquire the exclusive right to manage and control the realty together with the right to all rents and profits derived from it. Although the nominal owner, a married woman could not convey her realty without the consent of her husband.

Since a married woman lacked authority to act as an autonomous legal person, she lost the right to perform a variety of legal functions. Any contracts that she entered into were null and void. She also lost her testamentary capacity — the ability to make a will — and any wills she had made prior to marriage were automatically revoked. She could not sue or be sued in her own name. As the owner of her legal claims, her husband had to be joined as a party and was entitled to collect any damages that might be awarded.

Of profound consequence, a married woman also lost the right to her own labor. A husband acquired the right to his wife's services both at home and as performed for third parties. Because her labor belonged to him, he acquired an interest in the fruits of her labor, and monies paid to her for her services rendered became her husband's monies. This right of a husband to his wife's labor was characterized as a property interest. If his wife was injured by a third party, the husband was considered a victim in his own right and could sue for the loss of his wife's ability to perform her marital responsibilities. Damages frequently included compensation for the loss of her companionship, including sexual companionship, and her domestic services. Married women had no corresponding rights to their husband's services. As explained by Blackstone, "the inferior hath no kind of property in the company, care, or assistance of the superior, as the superior is held to have in those of the inferior." *Id.* at 332. In exchange for the loss of her legal persona, a married woman was entitled to be supported by her husband, and he became responsible for her debts, including those she came into the marriage with. This exchange of services for support lay at the heart of the common law marital relationship, and, as illustrated by the case of *Graham v. Graham*, discussed below, this core feature of marriage survived well into the twentieth century, long after other common law marital requirements had been replaced by more modern rules.

The Civil Law Tradition

Eight states did not follow this English common law model. These states, known as **community property** or civil law states, are Arizona, California, Idaho, Louisiana, Nevada, New Mexico, Texas, and Washington. Based upon patterns of colonization and territorial acquisitions, these states were influenced by Spanish civil law and, in the case of Louisiana, by Spanish and French law. Although it does not share this history, the state of Wisconsin is now considered a community property state based upon the enactment of a modern marital property statute that effectively tracks the modern approach of community property states to the ownership and division of assets (this approach is discussed in Chapter 8). Wis. Stat. ch. 766.

At least in theory, the status of married women was different in these states. Here, a wife's legal identity did not merge into her husband's. Instead, each spouse retained his or her separate identity, and marriage was viewed as a partnership. Subject to limited exceptions, property acquired during marriage was considered community property and belonged equally to both partners. However, even though the property was considered to belong equally to both parties, the marital partners were not regarded as equals. A husband was still given complete authority over the community property, including his wife's earnings; he could spend community assets freely, potentially leaving his wife with nothing to show for her contribution. Accordingly, in terms of her daily reality, the difference for a married woman between the common law and the civil law approaches would not have been as great as the doctrinal distinctions suggest.

3. Married Women's Property Acts

Beginning in the late 1830s, states began passing laws known as the **Married Women's Property Acts**, which led to a gradual and incremental improvement in the legal status of married women.[1] The first such Acts were enacted in the South and appear to have been motivated by economic concerns, rather than by a desire to emancipate married women. Prompted by the economic panic of 1837, in which many Southern plantation owners faced bankruptcy and loss of property — including slaves — to their creditors, legislators passed laws giving married women rights of ownership over their own property, which served to protect it from being seized by their husbands' creditors. Husbands, however, retained their common law right of management and control over their wives' property.

In other regions of the country, most notably the Northeast, the passage of these Acts responded more directly to concerns being voiced by the newly emerging women's rights activists about the legal subordination of married women. Although winning the vote soon became their focus, the reformers also sought legal equality for women within the domestic sphere.

Seeking to change the common law of marriage, reformers insisted that married women were entitled to "(1) full control over their property with the powers to contract, will, and sue regarding it; (2) the right to their own wages; (3) recognition of the wife's joint right to the earnings of the co-partnership; and (4) equal guardianship of their children." Warbassee, *supra* note 1, at 273. Thus, over the last half of the nineteenth century, states began responding to these demands. Bit by bit, laws were passed extending property rights to married women and lifting many of the common law disabilities. By the turn of the century, married women had many more rights than they had previously possessed, and in some states, they could own property, enter into contracts, and sue and be sued in their own name. Some states also passed "earnings" laws, giving a married woman a property right in the labor she performed outside the domestic realm, thus entitling her, rather than her husband, to the earnings; however, husbands retained a property right in their wives' domestic services.[2]

4. Protecting the Marital Relationship

The historic strength of the state's interest in marriage was not simply expressed in laws regulating the rights and obligations of husbands and wives, but was also evident in laws that aimed to protect the integrity and the longevity of the marital relationship. Like the state's historic insistence upon a strict gender-based allocation of marital rights and obligations, these aims were also challenged in the modern era as an inappropriate intrusion of the state into the increasingly privatized marital realm (see Modernizing Trends, below).

---

[1]This section is based mainly on the works of Norma Basch, In the Eyes of the Law: Women, Marriage, and Property in Nineteenth Century New York (1982), and Elizabeth Bowles Warbassee, The Changing Legal Rights of Married Women 1800-1861 ch. 1 (1987).

[2]*See* Riva Siegel, The Modernization of Marital Status Law: Adjudicating Wives' Rights to Earnings, 1860-1930, 82 Geo. L. Rev. 2127 (1994); Riva Siegel, Home as Work, 103 Yale L.J. 1073 (1994).

"Heart Balm" Laws

Historically, a trilogy of legal causes of action, namely, the breach of promise to marry, alienation of affections, and criminal conversation (similar to adultery), were available to "balm" the heart of those who had been wronged by a fiancé or spouse, hence their common designation as "heart balm" remedies.

These actions also helped to reinforce the state's interest in protecting the marital relationship from disruption, and buttressed its oversight of appropriate male and female behavior in the domestic realm.

An action for a breach of the promise to marry was perhaps the most common of these actions, and was intended to enforce the "responsibility of every individual to fulfill voluntarily assumed responsibilities," which in this instance involved a promise to wed. *See* Michael Grossberg, Governing the Hearth: Law and the Family in Nineteenth Century America 37 (1985).

Although sounding in contract, this cause of action was actually hybrid in nature, as a jilted party was entitled to tort-like damages for injuries suffered, such as harm to one's reputation, humiliation, and emotional distress.

The action was not formally restricted to women; however, in practice, it effectively functioned as "a remedy for respectable, mostly middle-class women," many of whom "had been seduced and abandoned." *Id.* at 90. These actions were intended to promote the state's interest in holding a man to his premarital promise in order to protect the social and financial well-being of a woman.

In contrast to the female-identified cause of action for the breach of promise to marry, tort claims for the alienation of affection and criminal conversation (despite the name, this was a civil action) were closely identified with male plaintiffs. In like manner, however, this gendered pattern of redress also reflected normative understandings of the marital relationship, which in this instance entailed the interest that a husband had in the companionship, affection, and sexual services of his wife. Accordingly, a husband was entitled to compensation if he could establish that a third party had come between him and his wife, with proof of sexual intercourse being required in an action for criminal conversation, thus depriving him of what some have characterized as his "proprietary" interest in his wife's person. This pattern began to change following the passage of the Married Women's Property Acts when many states began allowing women to bring suits against those who disrupted their marital relationships.

During the 1930s, heart balm laws began to fall into disrepute due mainly to concerns about the potential for blackmail, excessive damage awards, and the

---

The Tort of Seduction

In addition to other causes of action, the tort of seduction, which provided damages to a woman who had been induced to give up her purity based on a false promise of marriage, is sometimes also characterized as a heart balm action. The tort arose in the nineteenth century as a father's right to his daughter's chastity and was characterized as a property right. The father's damages were for loss of the working services of his daughter. Later, in the twentieth century, the tort also became a personal injury tort for the woman who lost her chastity as a result of misrepresentations made by the seducer. However, a father still maintained the right to sue for property damages. Today, the tort has been abolished in most jurisdictions.

flurry of media attraction that these cases garnered, and many state legislatures abolished these causes of action through "anti-heart balm" measures. Heart balm laws again came under a wave of criticism in the latter part of the twentieth century given contemporary shifts in understanding regarding gender equality and marital privacy (see Section B.4, below). Most, although certainly not all, of the remaining states have "repealed" the laws by way of either legislative or judicial action.

5. Marital Dissolution

The subject of divorce and dissolution of a marriage will be taken up in much greater detail in later chapters. However, as part of this introductory chapter, a basic overview of the relationship between the state's interest in the institution of marriage and the law of divorce merits consideration.

Until the no-fault revolution of the 1970s, states fiercely limited the ability of spouses to formally dissolve their marriages unless they could show marital fault. Paralleling the assumed right of states to both structure the marital relationship and protect it from third-party disruption in order to advance the public good, states sought to bind spouses to their lifetime commitment to each other. Accordingly, at least as a matter of legal principle, until the no-fault revolution, divorce was cast as a remedy for an innocent spouse who was the victim of marital misconduct such as cruelty, infidelity, or desertion. Rather than being regarded as an individual choice available to either party as it is today, divorce was regarded as an evil that was made necessary by the frailties of human nature.

Reading this understanding of divorce back into the regulatory structure of marriage makes it apparent that the fault requirement privileged marital permanence over individual wants and desires. By framing divorce as a remedy for an innocent spouse who had been injured by the other's wrongful conduct, rather than as a vehicle by which an unhappy spouse could free him- or herself from marriage that was no longer fulfilling, the goal of marital permanence clearly trumped the rights of individual spouses to decide for themselves when a marriage was over. (See Chapter 4 for further detail.)

6. Modernizing Trends

Although, as discussed in the next chapter, marriage continues to be a highly privileged form of association, it is no longer regarded as solely a status relationship whose terms are set by law in order to advance the state's interest in maintaining social order, including the reinforcement of normative gender roles. Legally, marriage now more closely resembles a contractual relationship in which rights and obligations are chosen according to the needs and desires of the individual couple, rather than assigned by the state.

This transformation is a complex one, and reflects a complex myriad of interrelated social and cultural developments that originated in the 1960s and 1970s, including the introduction of the birth control pill, the sexual revolution, the

Mildred Jeter and Richard Loving
© Bettmann/CORBIS

civil rights movement, the women's and the gay rights liberation movements, the rise of expressive individualism, and the transition to a post-industrial economy with expanding employment opportunities for women. However, there are three crucial constitutional law developments that emerged out of the social change ethos of the 1960s and 1970s and in turn contributed to the reconfiguration of the state's regulatory interest in marriage: establishing marriage as a fundamental right, the move toward equality, and the constitutional recognition of a right to privacy.

Establishing Marriage as a Fundamental Right

In 1967, the United States Supreme Court, in the case of *Loving v. Virginia*, 388 U.S. 1 (1967), struck down Virginia's anti-miscegenation law, which prohibited marriages between different races. Anti-miscegenation laws date back to the time of slavery and were once in effect in a majority of states. At the time *Loving* was decided, Virginia was one of 16 states that still prohibited interracial marriages.

Case Preview

Loving v. Virginia

Mildred Jeter and Richard Loving, an interracial couple, were residents of Virginia. Virginia had a law that banned marriages between parties of different races. Accordingly, the couple went to the District of Columbia where they were legally married. Shortly thereafter they returned to Virginia where they established their marital residency. A grand jury in Virginia indicted them for violating Virginia's law. The Lovings pleaded guilty and were given a one-year jail sentence, which was suspended on the condition that they leave Virginia and not return for 25 years. The Lovings brought suit to challenge the Virginia statute as an unconstitutional infringement on their right to marry.

As you read *Loving v. Virginia*, consider the following:

1. On what grounds did the state of Virginia seek to justify its anti-miscegenation laws?
2. What is the relationship between the Court's due process and its equal protection analysis?
3. How central to the Court's result is the fact that the challenged law involved a race-based classification?
4. On what basis does the United States Supreme Court find that racial classifications are unlawful?
5. How does the Court characterize the right to marry?

Loving v. Virginia
388 U.S. 1 (1967)

Mr. Chief Justice WARREN delivered the opinion of the Court.

This case presents a constitutional question never addressed by this Court: whether a statutory scheme adopted by the State of Virginia to prevent marriages between persons solely on the basis of racial classifications violates the Equal Protection and Due Process Clauses of the Fourteenth Amendment. For reasons which seem to us to reflect the central meaning of those constitutional commands, we conclude that these statutes cannot stand consistently with the Fourteenth Amendment.

In June 1958, two residents of Virginia, Mildred Jeter, a Negro woman, and Richard Loving, a white man, were married in the District of Columbia pursuant to its laws. [After returning to Virginia, the parties were indicted and sentenced to one year in jail. The trial judge suspended the sentence for a period of 25 years] on the condition that the Lovings leave the State and not return to Virginia together for 25 years. He stated in an opinion that:

> "Almighty God created the races white, black, yellow, malay and red, and he placed them on separate continents. And, but for the interference with his arrangement, there would be no cause for such marriage. The fact that he separated the races shows that he did not intend for the races to mix. . . ."

After their convictions, the Lovings took up residence in the District of Columbia. . . . [T]hey filed a motion in the [Virginia] state trial court to vacate the judgment and set aside the sentence on the ground that the statutes which they had violated were repugnant to the Fourteenth Amendment. [After the conviction was affirmed by the state trial court and Virginia's Supreme Court of Appeals, this appeal to the United States Supreme Court followed.]

. . .

The two statutes under which appellants were convicted and sentenced are part of a comprehensive statutory scheme aimed at prohibiting and punishing interracial marriages. The Lovings were convicted of violating [the prohibition of a "white person" marrying anyone other than another "white person" and leaving the state to evade the law with the intent of coming back to the state to reside as husband and wife.]

. . .

I.

In upholding the constitutionality of these provisions . . . , the Supreme Court of Appeals of Virginia referred to its 1955 decision in *Naim v. Naim,* 197 Va. 80, 87 S.E.2d 749. . . . In *Naim,* the state court concluded that the State's legitimate purposes were "to preserve the racial integrity of its citizens," and to prevent "the corruption of blood," "a mongrel breed of citizens," and "the obliteration of racial pride," obviously an endorsement of the doctrine of White Supremacy. *Id.,* at 90, 87 S.E.2d, at 756. The court also reasoned that marriage has traditionally been subject to state regulation without federal intervention, and, consequently, the regulation of marriage should be left to exclusive state control by the Tenth Amendment.

While the state court is no doubt correct in asserting that marriage is a social relation subject to the State's police power, *Maynard v. Hill*, 125 U.S. 190, the State does not contend in its argument before this Court that its powers to regulate marriage are unlimited.... [T]he State contends that, because its miscegenation statutes punish equally both the white and the Negro participants in an interracial marriage, these statutes, despite their reliance on racial classifications, do not constitute an invidious discrimination based upon race.

. . .

Because we reject the notion that the mere "equal application" of a statute containing racial classifications is enough to remove the classifications from the Fourteenth Amendment's proscription of all invidious racial discriminations, we do not accept the State's contention that these statutes should be upheld if there is any possible basis for concluding that they serve a rational purpose ....

[T]he Equal Protection Clause requires the consideration of whether the classifications drawn by any statute constitute an arbitrary and invidious discrimination. The clear and central purpose of the Fourteenth Amendment was to eliminate all official state sources of invidious racial discrimination in the States. (citations omitted).

There can be no question but that Virginia's miscegenation statutes rest solely upon distinctions drawn according to race.... Over the years, this Court has consistently repudiated "distinctions between citizens solely because of their ancestry" as being "odious to a free people whose institutions are founded upon the doctrine of equality." *Hirabayashi v. United States,* 320 U.S. 81, 100 (1943).... [I]f they are ever to be upheld, they must be shown to be necessary to the accomplishment of some permissible state objective, independent of the racial discrimination which it was the object of the Fourteenth Amendment to eliminate.

. . .

There is patently no legitimate overriding purpose independent of invidious racial discrimination which justifies this classification. The fact that Virginia prohibits only interracial marriages involving white persons demonstrates that the racial classifications must stand on their own justification, as measures designed to maintain White Supremacy. We have consistently denied the constitutionality of measures which restrict the rights of citizens on account of race. There can be no doubt that restricting the freedom to marry solely because of racial classifications violates the central meaning of the Equal Protection Clause.

II.

These statutes also deprive the Lovings of liberty without due process of law in violation of the Due Process Clause of the Fourteenth Amendment. The freedom to marry has long been recognized as one of the vital personal rights essential to the orderly pursuit of happiness by free men.

Marriage is one of the "basic civil rights of man," fundamental to our very existence and survival. *Skinner v. Oklahoma,* 316 U.S. 535, 541 (1942). See also *Maynard v. Hill,* 125 U.S. 190 (1888). To deny this fundamental freedom on so unsupportable a basis as the racial classifications embodied in these statutes, classifications so directly subversive of the principle of equality at the heart of the Fourteenth Amendment, is surely to deprive all the State's citizens of liberty without due process of law. The Fourteenth Amendment requires that the freedom of choice to marry not be restricted by invidious racial discriminations. Under our Constitution, the freedom to marry, or not marry, a person of another race resides with the individual and cannot be infringed by the State.

These convictions must be reversed.

Post-Case Follow-Up

Loving holds that state laws prohibiting marriages based upon racial classifications violate the Equal Protection Clause of the Fourteenth Amendment. However, the importance of *Loving* was not limited to this holding. Rather, *Loving* confirmed that marriage is a fundamental right under the Due Process Clause of the Fourteenth Amendment. Flowing directly from this proposition, the decision thus paved the way for legal challenges to state laws regulating marriage and divorce generally, based on the argument that they encroached upon fundamental freedoms or imposed gender-based classifications on spouses in contravention of the Due Process and/or Equal Protection Clauses of the Fourteenth Amendment.

As we will see in the next chapter, 48 years later, in *Obergefell v. Hodges*, the United States Supreme Court relied on *Loving v. Virginia*, 388 U.S. 1, 12 (1967), in invalidating state laws limiting marriages to one woman and one man.

Loving v. Virginia: Real Life Applications

1. Pierre and Dominique are first cousins. They live in a state that prohibits marriages between first cousins. Pierre has come to you asking whether he has grounds to challenge the law. On what grounds could you potentially challenge the law prohibiting such marriages?

2. Carla and Carlos are both teachers who work at the same school in the same school district. The school district has a policy that prohibits husbands and wives from working at the same school. Carla and Carlos intend to marry at the end of the current school year. You represent the school district. The superintendent has asked you whether it is permissible for him to advise Carla and Carlos that one of them must leave the school at the end of the school year and transfer to a different school within the district. What do you tell the superintendent?

3. Would your answer to Question 2 change if there were no other teaching positions available at another school within the district? How does this case differ from *Loving v. Virginia*?

The Move to Legal Equality

Loving v. Virginia started a movement that demanded equality not just between races, but between all individuals. Gradually, cases seeking to eliminate all remaining common law marital restrictions between genders, such as the requirement that a married woman take her husband's last name or follow him in his choice of domicile, or that limited her ability to freely dispose of her property or carry on a trade began making their way to a generally sympathetic Supreme Court.

In 1973, the Court decided *Frontiero v. Richardson*, which involved a successful challenge to a federal law that made it more difficult for service women than service men to obtain benefits for a spouse based upon a presumption of female economic dependency. The Court commented in a now-famous passage that "our Nation has had a long and unfortunate history of sex discrimination . . . that has been justified by an attitude of 'romantic paternalism,' which, in practical effect, put women not on a pedestal, but in a cage." 411 U.S. 677, 684 (1973).

Several years later, in the case of *Orr v. Orr*, 440 U.S. 268 (1979), the Court faced a challenge to Alabama's alimony laws, which provided that husbands, but not wives, could be held responsible to pay alimony upon divorce. In *Orr*, a divorced husband argued that these laws "effectively announc[ed] the State's preference for an allocation of family responsibilities under which the wife plays a dependent role, and [sought] for their objective the reinforcement of that model among the State's citizens." *Id.* at 279.

Agreeing with his position, the Court announced:

> [T]he "old notion" that "generally it is the man's primary responsibility to provide a home and its essentials," can no longer justify a statute that discriminates on the basis of gender. "No longer is the female destined solely for the home and the rearing of a family, and only the male for the marketplace and world of ideas. . . ."
>
> Legislative classifications which distribute benefits and burdens on the basis of gender carry the inherent risk of reinforcing stereotypes about the "proper place" of women and their need for special protection. Whereas here, the State's . . . purposes are well-served by a gender-neutral classification . . . the State cannot be permitted to classify on the basis of sex.

Id. at 279-280, quoting *Stanton v. Stanton*, 421 U.S. 7, 14-15 (1975).

In making it clear that states did not have the authority to assign marital rights and obligations based upon fixed understandings of appropriate gender roles, the *Orr* decision ended the long historic shadow of the marital unity doctrine. As with *Loving*, the Court's invalidation of Alabama's alimony laws based upon gender classification likewise demonstrates that there are federal constitutional limits on state laws concerning domestic relations.

The Right to Privacy

In considering what is often referred to as the "constitutionalization" of family law, namely, the imposition of federal limits on the authority of states to regulate marriage in favor of granting spouses more autonomy to shape the contours of their intimate lives, the Supreme Court's decision in *Griswold v. Connecticut*, 381 U.S. 479 (1965), is important to consider. In *Griswold*, the Court speaks directly to the constitutional right of privacy in marital relationships.

Case Preview

Griswold v. Connecticut

A Connecticut statute prohibited anyone from using "any drug, medicinal article or instrument for the purpose of preventing contraception" and further made it a crime if any person "assists, abets, counsels, causes, hires or commands another to commit any offense," and provided that that person may be prosecuted and punished "as if he were the principal offender." Appellants, the executive director of the Planned Parenthood League of Connecticut, and its medical director, a licensed physician, were convicted as accessories for giving married persons information and medical advice on how to prevent conception and prescribing a contraceptive device or material for the wife's use. The appellants were found guilty as accessories and fined $100 each. Appellants claimed that the accessory statute, as applied, violated the Fourteenth Amendment. An intermediate appellate court and the state's highest court affirmed the judgment.

As you read *Griswold*, consider the following:

1. What right is the Court is trying to protect?
2. How does Justice Douglas explain the right of privacy as a right guaranteed by the Constitution even though such a right is not specifically stated?
3. How does the concurring opinion differ from the analysis given by Justice Douglas?

Griswold v. Connecticut
381 U.S. 479 (1965)

Mr. Justice DOUGLAS delivered the opinion of the Court.

. . .

[W]e are met with a wide range of questions that implicate the Due Process Clause of the Fourteenth Amendment. Overtones of some arguments suggest that *Lochner v. New York,* 198 U.S. 45, should be our guide. But we decline that invitation. . . . We do not sit as a super-legislature to determine the wisdom, need, and propriety of laws that touch economic problems, business affairs, or social conditions. This law, however, operates directly on an intimate relation of husband and wife and their physician's role in one aspect of that relation.

The association of people is not mentioned in the Constitution nor in the Bill of Rights. The right to educate a child in a school of the parents' choice — whether public or private or parochial — is also not mentioned. Nor is the right to study any particular subject or any foreign language. Yet the First Amendment has been construed to include certain of those rights.

By *Pierce v. Society of Sisters* . . . the right to educate one's children as one chooses is made applicable to the States by the force of the First and Fourteenth Amendments. By *Meyer v. Nebraska,* . . . the same dignity is given the right to study the German language in a private school. In other words, the State may not, consistently with the spirit of the First Amendment, contract the spectrum of available knowledge. The right of freedom of speech and press includes not only the right to utter or to print, but the right to distribute, the right to receive, the right to read . . . and freedom of inquiry, freedom of thought, and freedom to teach . . . — indeed, the freedom of the entire university community. . . . Without those peripheral rights, the specific rights would be less secure. And so we reaffirm the principle of the *Pierce* and the *Meyer* cases.

In *NAACP v. Alabama,* 357 U.S. 449, 357 U.S. 462 we protected the "freedom to associate and privacy in one's associations," noting that freedom of association was a peripheral First Amendment right. Disclosure of membership lists of a constitutionally valid association, we held, was invalid "as entailing the likelihood of a substantial restraint upon the exercise by petitioner's members of their right to freedom of association." *Ibid.* In other words, the First Amendment has a penumbra where privacy is protected from governmental intrusion. . . .

The foregoing cases suggest that specific guarantees in the Bill of Rights have penumbras, formed by emanations from those guarantees that help give them life and substance. Various guarantees create zones of privacy. The right of association contained in the penumbra of the First Amendment is one, as we have seen. The Third Amendment, in its prohibition against the quartering of soldiers "in any house" in time of peace without the consent of the owner, is another facet of that privacy. The Fourth Amendment explicitly affirms the "right of the people to be secure in their persons, houses, papers, and effects, against unreasonable searches and seizures." The Fifth Amendment, in its Self-Incrimination Clause, enables the citizen to create a zone of privacy which government may not force him to surrender to his detriment. The Ninth Amendment provides: "The enumeration in the Constitution, of certain rights, shall not be construed to deny or disparage others retained by the people."

. . .

The present case, then, concerns a relationship lying within the zone of privacy created by several fundamental constitutional guarantees. And it concerns a law which, in forbidding the use of contraceptives, rather than regulating their manufacture or sale, seeks to achieve its goals by means having a maximum destructive impact upon that relationship. Such a law cannot stand in light of the familiar principle, so often applied by this Court, that a "governmental purpose to control or prevent activities constitutionally subject to state regulation may not be achieved by means which sweep unnecessarily broadly and thereby invade the area of protected freedoms."

. . .

We deal with a right of privacy older than the Bill of Rights — older than our political parties, older than our school system. Marriage is a coming together for better or for worse, hopefully enduring, and intimate to the degree of being sacred. It is an association that promotes a way of life, not causes; a harmony in living, not political faiths; a bilateral loyalty, not commercial or social projects. Yet it is an association for as noble a purpose as any involved in our prior decisions.

Reversed.

Mr. Justice GOLDBERG, whom THE CHIEF JUSTICE and Mr. Justice BRENNAN join concurring.

I agree with the Court that Connecticut's birth control law unconstitutionally intrudes upon the right of marital privacy, and I join in its opinion and judgment. Although I have not accepted the view that "due process," as used in the Fourteenth Amendment, incorporates all of the first eight Amendments . . . I do agree that the concept of liberty protects those personal rights that are fundamental, and is not confined to the specific terms of the Bill of Rights. My conclusion that the concept of liberty is not so restricted, and that it embraces the right of marital privacy, though that right is not mentioned explicitly in the Constitution, is supported both by numerous decisions of this Court, referred to in the Court's opinion, and by the language and history of the Ninth Amendment.

. . .

The Ninth Amendment reads, "The enumeration in the Constitution, of certain rights, shall not be construed to deny or disparage others retained by the people."

. . .

While the Ninth Amendment — and indeed the entire Bill of Rights — originally concerned restrictions upon federal power, the subsequently enacted Fourteenth Amendment prohibits the States as well from abridging fundamental personal liberties. And the Ninth Amendment, in indicating that not all such liberties are specifically mentioned in the first eight amendments, is surely relevant in showing the existence of other fundamental personal rights, now protected from state, as well as federal, infringement.

. . .

I agree fully with the Court that . . . the right of privacy is a fundamental personal right, emanating "from the totality of the constitutional scheme under which we live."

Mr. Justice STEWART, whom Mr. Justice BLACK joins, dissenting.

Since 1879, Connecticut has had on its books a law which forbids the use of contraceptives by anyone. I think this is an uncommonly silly law. As a practical matter, the law is obviously unenforceable, except in the oblique context of the present case. As a philosophical matter, I believe the use of contraceptives in the relationship of marriage should be left to personal and private choice, based upon each individual's moral, ethical, and religious beliefs. As a matter of social policy, I think professional counsel about methods of birth control should be available to all, so that each individual's choice can be meaningfully made. But we are not asked in this case to say whether we think this law is unwise, or even asinine. We are asked to hold that it violates the United States Constitution. And that I cannot do.

Post-Case Follow-Up

The *Griswold* decision clearly extends privacy rights to married couples as a *unit* based on the Court's assessment of the importance of the marital relationship and the "sacred" nature of the marital bedroom. A few years later, in the case of *Eisenstadt v. Baird*, 405 U.S. 438 (1972), which involved a challenge to a Massachusetts criminal statute that prohibited the distribution of contraceptives to unmarried persons, the Court held that the right of privacy extends to unmarried persons based on the rationale that the marital couple is not an independent entity with a mind and heart of its own, but an *association of two individuals* each with a separate intellectual and emotional makeup. Justice Brennan, writing for the majority, explained: "If the right of privacy means anything, it is the right of the individual, married or single, to be free from unwarranted governmental intrusion into matters so fundamentally affecting a person as the decision whether to bear or beget a child." *Id.* at 453.

Griswold v. Connecticut: Real Life Applications

1. You are staff attorney for a state representative who was just about to introduce into your state's legislature a law identical to the Connecticut statute that was held unconstitutional in *Griswold v. Connecticut*. Is there any way to revise the statute to make it constitutional under the holding of *Griswold*? How would you revise the statute?

2. Assume a state law provides that, absent an emergency situation, a woman seeking an abortion must give her informed consent prior to the procedure, and an informed consent document must be provided to her by the doctor performing the abortion and signed and delivered to the doctor at least 24 hours in advance of the procedure. The state law makes it a crime for any doctor to perform an abortion where informed consent has not been provided at least 24 hours in advance, absent an emergency. Terry is a doctor who has been charged with performing abortions without obtaining informed consent for the procedure at least 24 hours in advance. Using *Griswold v. Connecticut*, is there a basis to invalidate the law?

3. Based on the same facts as in Question 2, what arguments can be made to defend the law?

B. THE PARENT-CHILD RELATIONSHIP: EVOLVING LEGAL FRAMEWORKS

In this section, we focus on the evolving nature of the legal relationship between parent and child. In some ways, this story has much in common with the historic narrative of the marital relationship. For example, just as formal recognition of adult intimate partnerships has required the formalization of that bond through marriage, marriage has also been a prerequisite to state recognition of the parent-child relationship. Moreover, the legal contours of this relationship have also been shaped by federal constitutional doctrine. However, as we will see, legal narratives are far from identical, as each is shaped by the particular nature of the relationship under consideration.

In reading the following section, it is worth keeping the following traditional assumptions in mind, as they have shaped the legal structuring of the parent-child relationship:

- Parenthood is achieved through biology or adoption.
- Parental status is exclusive in that rights and duties for the child are reserved for a child's parents; third parties generally do not have the same rights.
- Parents will act in the best interest of their children and are accordingly entitled to an automatic "parental preference" in disputes with "third parties."

1. The Historical Patriarchal Household

In the colonial era, the well-ordered family was the foundation of community life, and it served as a "model for all other social relations." Elizabeth Pleck, Domestic Tyranny, The Making of American Social Policy from Colonial Times to the Present 17 (1987). This well-ordered family was hierarchical in nature, and each member occupied a specific place in its internal structure based upon age, gender, and the nature of the relationship to the family. The husband/father was the "governor" of the household. His wife and children occupied well-defined subordinate positions and were subject to his authority and control.

The Right of Privacy Extended to Strike Down Sodomy Laws

In 2003, relying in part on *Griswold v. Connecticut* and *Eisenstadt v. Baird*, the United States Supreme Court struck down a Texas anti-sodomy law that prohibited certain forms of sexual conduct with another individual of the same sex. *Lawrence v. Texas*, 530 U.S. 558 (2003). Justice Kennedy, delivering the opinion of the Court in *Lawrence*, explained: "Liberty protects the person from unwarranted govern intrusion into a dwelling or other private places. In our tradition the State is not omnipresent in the home. And there are other spheres of our lives and existence, outside the home where the State should not be a dominant presence. Freedom extends beyond spatial abounds. Liberty presumes an autonomy of self that includes freedom of thought, belief, expression, and certain intimate conduct."

The *Lawrence v. Texas* decision thus invalidated the laws in all states that banned same-sex sexual activity. While the Court did not explicitly use the term "privacy" in the decision, the use of the term "liberty" infers at least that the Court was protecting a fundamental right under the Fourteenth Amendment. For further discussion, see Laurence Tribe, *Lawrence v. Texas*: The Fundamental Right That Dare Not Speak Its Name, 117 Harv. L. Rev. 1893 (2004).

A father had complete command over the education, training, and discipline of his children. He also owned their labor, which was a valuable right in an agrarian society where the world of work and home were essentially one and the same. In turn, he was charged with the responsibility of supporting his children and preparing them, particularly his sons, for passage into the world.

Similar to the manner in which the law drew a bright line between married and unmarried couples, the common law likewise drew a sharp distinction between children born to married parents and those born to an unmarried woman in order to reinforce the moral and social primacy of marriage and deter promiscuous behavior. A child born outside of marriage was regarded as a "filius nullius" — a child of no one. As a "bastard," the child had no legally cognizable bond with either parent, and the parents had no enforceable obligations or rights in relationship to the child.

Children Born During Marriage

Certain presumptions, discussed in later chapters in the book, arise when children are born during a marriage. The children are presumed to be the offspring of the marriage, and there is legal attribution of fatherhood to a husband when a child is born during the marriage or within a period of time before the marriage or after the marriage has terminated.

Except as concerns children born to unmarried heterosexual parents, this chapter will not take up the question of *who else* might be considered a legal parent, such as in the case of a lesbian co-parent, or where a child is born to a surrogate mother. (These other issues are addressed elsewhere in the book.)

2. The Erosion of the Patriarchal Domestic Order

As discussed earlier in this chapter, the enactment of the Married Women's Property Acts granted women some rights in relationship to their husbands during the latter half of the nineteenth century. Although legal equality would not be realized until almost a century later, these reformist measures contributed to the gradual erosion of the patriarchal family structure.

Also relevant in this regard was the nation's gradual shift from an agrarian to a burgeoning industrial economy. As production moved off the family farm into the factory, the world of work became increasingly identified with men, and the world of home with women. The emerging middle class view of the home was that it served as sanctuary from the burdens of the harsh world in which women's gentle influence could flourish.

Children, who had been seen both as economically valuable assets and as in need of a father's stern corrective influence, began, at least within the dominant middle-class narrative, to be portrayed more as innocent beings in need of protection and nurture, and mothers soon replaced fathers as "the most powerful agent in developing a child's character." Pleck, *supra*, at 39. Rooted in this change, the favored legal status of fathers gave way to a clear maternal preference. By the end of the nineteenth century, the common law doctrine of paternal rights had been replaced by the **tender years presumption**, which embodied the belief that young children naturally belonged with their mothers. In turn, this shift further enhanced the status of married women and curtailed male authority over the domestic realm, thus making clear that the maternal bond was entitled to more weight than simply "reverence and respect."

The softening of attitudes toward children coupled with the growing emphasis on the mother-child bond contributed to improvements in the legal status of children born to unwed mothers. Most significantly, formal legal recognition was extended to the mother-child relationship. No longer a *filius nullius*, a child born to an unmarried woman became entitled to her care and support, and she in turn had reciprocal obligations toward her child. Additionally, most states amended their laws to allow for the legitimation of a previously "illegitimate" child in cases where the parents married subsequent to his or her birth, and a few states went as far as to recognize the father-child bond based on an acknowledgment of paternity.

3. Investing Parenthood with Constitutional Status

As the new middle class conception of childhood began to take hold, this stage of life was reconceptualized as a distinctive period during which time young people needed to be sheltered from the burdens and strains of the adult world. This "new normative ideal of the child as an exclusively emotional and affective asset" who belongs "in a domesticated, nonproductive world of lessons, games, and token money"[3] was incorporated into a variety of legal reforms, including compulsory school attendance requirements, child labor and child protection laws, and the creation of a separate juvenile court system.

These reforms made inroads into the historic freedom that parents had enjoyed to direct the upbringing of their children without interference from the state, which helped set the stage for two landmark Supreme Court rulings that cast a net of constitutional privacy around the nuclear family. Propelled largely by anti-immigrant sentiment and a strong desire to promote the rapid assimilation of the newly arrived, in 1919 Nebraska, among other states, enacted a law banning elementary school teachers from teaching in any language other than English, while Oregon enacted a compulsory education law, which, subject to limited exceptions, required students to attend public (as distinct from private) schools presumably to "prevent foreign-born American parents, and the private schools they utilized, from teaching children 'un-American' languages and ideas."[4]

In the rulings of *Meyer v. Nebraska*, 262 U.S. 390 (1923), and *Pierce v. Society of Sisters*, 268 U.S. 510 (1925), the Supreme Court invalidated these laws as unwarranted state encroachments upon the constitutionally protected liberty interest of parents to direct the education of their children, which might include having them learn a foreign language or attend a private school. In a clear articulation of the principle underlying this conclusion, the *Pierce* Court explained that "[t]he Child is not the mere creature of the State; those who nurture him and direct his destiny

---

[3]Viviana A. Zelizer, Pricing the Priceless Child: The Changing Social Value of Children 11 (1994).
[4]Erik M. Zimmerman, Defending the Parental Right to Direct Education: *Meyer* and *Pierce* as Bulwarks Against State Indoctrination, 17 Regent U. L. Rev. 311, 318 (2005). *See also* Barbara Bennett Woodhouse, "Who Owns the Child?": *Meyer* and *Pierce* and the Child as Property, 33 Wm. & Mary L. Rev. 995 (1992).

have the right, coupled with the high duty, to recognize and prepare him for additional obligations." *Id.* at 535.

In short, these seminal rulings served to carve out a constitutionally protected realm of familial privacy within which parents are entitled to direct the upbringing of their children.

4. Modernizing Trends

As with marriage, the fixed nature of the relationship between parent and child has been altered by constitutional developments that took hold in the latter half of the last century. Although profound in nature, unlike the radical transformation of the marital relationship, for the most part, the relationship between parent and child within the domestic realm has retained its traditional hierarchal structure "within which rights and obligations [follow] automatically from status." *See* Janet L. Dolgin, The Fate of Childhood: Legal Models of Children and the Parent-Child Relationship, 61 Alb. L. Rev. 345, 360 (1997).

Children of Unmarried Parents

As discussed, at common law, a child born to an unmarried mother was a *filius nullius* with no legally cognizable relationship with either parent. Although, as we have seen, the harshness of this approach was modulated by early nineteenth-century reforms, children of unmarried parents remained a distinct legal category of persons until the mid-twentieth century. Referred to as "bastards" or "illegitimates," they suffered a variety of legal disabilities. For example, children born to unmarried parents were frequently excluded as beneficiaries under statutory benefit programs, such as workers' compensation; they lacked inheritance rights under state intestacy laws; and they were denied standing in wrongful death actions for the loss of a parent. These legal disabilities were often most marked with respect to a child's relationship with his or her father.

In a dramatic break from this past, in 1968, in the case *of Levy v. Louisiana*, 391 U.S. 68 (1968), the Supreme Court held that the state had violated the Equal Protection Clause by denying children the right to recover for the death of their mother under the state's wrongful death law because of their "illegitimate" status:

> Legitimacy or illegitimacy of birth has no relation to the nature of the wrong allegedly inflicted on the mother. These children, though illegitimate, were dependent on her; she cared for them and nurtured them; they were indeed hers in the biological and spiritual sense; in her death they suffered wrong in the sense that any dependent would.

Id. at 72.

By recognizing that the significance of the parent-child relationship does not depend on the marital status of the parents, the *Levy* decision went a long way toward erasing the historic bulwark that the law had erected between children born within and outside of marriage. Put succinctly, post-*Levy* all children are considered to be legitimate and entitled to a legal relationship with their parents. However, as we will see in later chapters, the law is murkier when it comes to the parental rights of unmarried fathers and the rights of co-mothers in same-sex relationships.

The Recognition of Adolescents as Constitutional Persons

As indicated previously, children have not been thought of as distinct persons with legally cognizable rights. In short, their dependent and subordinate status within the household has been regarded as incompatible with the assertion of an autonomous legal self. As a result, the relationship of a child to the state has long been mediated through his or her parents.

Challenging this conception of childhood, a children's rights movement was inaugurated in this country during the 1960s. Inspired by the civil rights struggles of other disenfranchised groups, advocates sought to have children recognized as juridical persons who possessed an identity that was separate and apart from their families. Supporting this position, they argued that the failure to recognize children as constitutional beings divested them of meaningful control and decisional authority over important dimensions of their lives, which interfered with their right to self-determination.

In 1967, in the seminal *In re Gault* decision, which involved a 15-year-old boy who had been committed by the juvenile court to a youth facility for making lewd phone calls to a neighbor for a longer period of time than he would have been confined if tried as an adult, the Supreme Court expressed the concern that the juvenile court system, which had been intended to provide minors with "careful, compassionate, individualized treatment," had instead resulted in a system that lacked "fair, efficient, and effective procedures." 387 U.S. 1, 18 (1997). Explicitly stating that "neither the Fourteenth Amendment nor the Bill of Rights is for adults alone," the Court held that the "fundamental fairness" requirement of the Due Process Clause applies to juveniles as well as adults. *Id.* at 13. Two years later, in *Tinker v. Des Moines*, which involved a challenge to the suspension of high school students for wearing armbands to school in protest against the Vietnam War, the Court again affirmed that young people "are 'persons' under our Constitution . . . [who] are possessed of fundamental rights which the state must respect." 393 U.S. 503, 511 (1969).

It is important to recognize that neither *Gault* nor *Tinker* involved a dispute between a parent and child. Accordingly, the Court did not have to consider the potential for conflict between a child's assertion of the right to self-determination and the discussed historically constitutional right of parents to direct the upbringing of their children. However, the possibility of this clash of rights was raised by Justice Douglas in his dissenting opinion in the equally important case of *Yoder v. Wisconsin*, 406 U.S. 205 (1972). In *Yoder*, the Court, in reliance upon *Meyer* and *Pierce*, held that the application of a state law that required children to attend school until age 16 to Amish parents was an impermissible encroachment upon their "fundamental belief that salvation requires life in a church community separate and apart from the world and worldly influence." *Id.* at 210.

Of paramount concern to Douglas was that the "Court's analysis assume[d] that the only interests at stake in the case are those of the Amish parents on the one hand, and those of the State on the other," which, he pointedly noted, failed to account for the fact that it was "the future of the student, not the future of the parents," that was at issue in the case. *Id.* at 241, 245 (Douglas, dissenting in part). Directly challenging the view that parents have an essentially unqualified right to speak for their children, citing *Gault* and *Tinker*, Justice Douglas reminded the Court that children were now clearly constitutional persons, which, he argued, entitled them to be heard on the matter of their education.

The conception of minors as autonomous persons has perhaps been most fully realized by the Court in the abortion context. In the landmark *Bellotti v. Baird* decision, although invoking the right of parents to direct the upbringing of their children, the Court also recognized that teens have rights as child-bearing persons for whom "unwanted motherhood may be exceptionally burdensome." 443 U.S. 629, 643 (1979). Although not holding that the rights of teens to make the abortion decision are co-equal to those of an adult woman, the Court nonetheless divested parents of the authority to make this decision for their daughters by requiring states to include a confidential alternative to parental involvement in their abortion consent laws.

Despite these changes in the constitutional status of minors, it is important to recognize that when it comes to family law proceedings, children are not generally regarded as autonomous actors who have standing to assert their own legal claims. However, frequently drawing on the above-discussed as well as other landmark children's rights cases, many experts in the field have argued that minors should be afforded greater rights in family-related contests that directly implicate their well-being. Thus, for example, as discussed in Chapter 6, increasing attention has been paid to the importance of allowing children to be heard, and perhaps even represented by their own counsel, in the context of contested custody cases. *See generally* Stephen R. Arnott, Family Law: Autonomy, Standing, and Children's Rights, 33 Wm. Mitchell L. Rev. 807 (2007).

Case Preview

Parham v. J.R.

The courts have struggled with the issue of whether children have standing to assert rights on their own behalf. *Parham v. J.R.* highlights some of the issues that courts have grappled with when confronted with a young person's assertion of a right and the issue of who has authority to assert the right on behalf of a minor.

Parham v. J.R. was a class action brought by children who were being treated in a mental health hospital in Georgia. The action sought a declaratory judgment that Georgia's procedures for voluntary commitment to state mental hospitals of children under the age of 18 violated the Due Process Clause of the

Central State Hospital
Library of Congress, Washington, D.C.

Fourteenth Amendment. The Georgia statute permitted admission upon application by a parent or guardian, and the superintendent of the hospital could then temporarily admit any child for "observation and diagnosis." If the superintendent finds "evidence of mental illness," the child may be admitted "for such period and under such conditions as may be authorized by law." A child may be discharged upon the request of a parent or guardian, or the superintendent can release the child if it is determined the child has recovered from the mental illness. The District Court found the statute unconstitutional because it failed to protect adequately the children's due process rights and found that the process should include the right after notice to an adversary-type hearing before an impartial tribunal.

As you read *Parham*, note what the Court says about the following:

1. What interest was the lower court trying to protect?
2. Who has the duty to protect the minor children's interests?
3. Why did the Court find that minor children do not have an independent right to a hearing before an impartial tribunal?

Parham v. J.R.

442 U.S. 584 (1979)

Mr. Chief Justice BURGER delivered the opinion of the Court.

The question presented in this appeal is what process is constitutionally due a minor child whose parents or guardian seek state administered institutional mental health care for the child and specifically whether an adversary proceeding is required prior to or after the commitment.

. . .

Appellee J.R. was declared a neglected child by the county and removed from his natural parents when he was three months old. He was placed in seven different foster homes in succession prior to his admission to Central State Hospital at the age of 7.

Immediately preceding his hospitalization, J.R. received outpatient treatment at a county mental health center for several months. He then began attending school where he was so disruptive and incorrigible that he could not conform to normal behavior patterns. Because of his abnormal behavior, J.R.'s seventh set of foster parents requested his removal from their home. The Department of Family and Children Services then sought his admission at Central State. The agency provided the hospital with a complete sociomedical history at the time of his admission. In addition, three separate interviews were conducted with J.R. by the admission team of the hospital.

[After determining that J.R. suffered from an unsocialized aggressive reaction of childhood, it was recommended that he be admitted to the hospital to be in a more structured environment.]

J.R.'s progress was re-examined periodically. In addition, unsuccessful efforts were made by the Department of Family and Children Services during his stay at the hospital to place J.R. in various foster homes. On October 24, 1975, J.R. filed this suit requesting an order of the court placing him in a less drastic environment suitable to his needs.

. . .

Georgia's mental health statute . . . provides for the discharge of voluntary patients. Any child who has been hospitalized for more than five days may be discharged at the request of a parent or guardian. . . . Even without a request for discharge, however, the superintendent of each regional hospital has an affirmative duty to release any child "who has recovered from his mental illness or who has sufficiently improved that the superintendent determines that hospitalization of the patient is no longer desirable."

. . .

[There are no state-wide] regulations defining what specific procedures each superintendent must employ when admitting a child under 18. Instead, each regional hospital's superintendent is responsible for the procedures in his or her facility. There is substantial variation among the institutions with regard to their admission procedures and their procedures for review of patients after they have been admitted.

. . .

In holding unconstitutional Georgia's statutory procedure for voluntary commitment of juveniles, the District Court first determined that commitment . . . constitutes a severe deprivation of a child's liberty. The court defined this liberty interest in terms of both freedom from bodily restraint and freedom from the "emotional and psychic harm" caused by the institutionalization. Having determined that a liberty interest is implicated by a child's admission to a mental hospital, the court considered what process is required to protect that interest. It held that the process due "includes at least the right after notice to be heard before an impartial tribunal."

. . .

The District Court also rejected the argument that review by the superintendents of the hospitals and their staffs was sufficient to protect the child's liberty interest. The court held that the inexactness of psychiatry, coupled with the possibility that the sources of information used to make the commitment decision may not always be reliable, made the superintendent's decision too arbitrary to satisfy due process. The court then shifted its focus drastically from what was clearly a procedural due process analysis to what appears to be a substantive due process analysis and condemned Georgia's "officialdom" for its failure . . . to provide more resources for noninstitutional mental health care. The court concluded that there was a causal relationship between this intransigence and the State's ability to provide any "flexible due process" to the appellees. The District Court therefore ordered the State to appropriate and expend such resources as would be necessary to provide nonhospital treatment to those members of appellees' class who would benefit from it.

For a ward of the state, there may well be no adult who knows him thoroughly and who cares for him deeply. With natural parents there is a presumed natural affection to guide their action. . . . [H]owever, we cannot assume that when the State of Georgia has custody of a child it acts so differently from a natural parent in seeking medical assistance for the child. No one has questioned the validity of the statutory presumption that the State acts in the child's best interest. Nor could such a challenge be mounted on the record before us. There is no evidence that the State, acting as guardian, attempted to admit any child for reasons unrelated to the child's need for treatment. Indeed, neither the District Court nor the appellees have suggested that wards of the State should receive any constitutional treatment different from children with natural parents.

Once we accept that the State's application for a child's admission to a hospital is made in good faith, then the question is whether the medical decisionmaking approach of the admitting physician is adequate to satisfy due process. We have already recognized that an independent medical judgment made from the perspective of the best interests of the child after a careful investigation is an acceptable means of justifying a voluntary commitment. We do not believe that the soundness of this decisionmaking is any the less reasonable in this setting.

Indeed, if anything, the decision with regard to wards of the State may well be even more reasonable in light of the extensive written records that are compiled about each child while in the State's custody. In J.R.'s case, the admitting physician had a complete social and medical history of the child before even beginning the diagnosis. After carefully interviewing him and reviewing his extensive files, three physicians independently concluded that institutional care was in his best interests.

Since the state agency having custody and control of the child in loco parentis has a duty to consider the best interests of the child with respect to a decision on commitment to a mental hospital, the State may constitutionally allow that custodial agency to speak for the child, subject, of course, to the restrictions governing natural parents. On this record, we cannot declare unconstitutional Georgia's admission procedures for wards of the State.

. . .

The judgment is therefore reversed, and the case is remanded to the District Court for further proceedings consistent with this opinion.

Post-Case Follow-Up

The *Parham* decision, while recognizing that children have due process rights, transfers such rights to the parents and guardians (or in this case the state) to protect the best interest of the children. Thus, while a parent's decision, especially to commit a child to a mental hospital, may result in a child's loss of liberty, such loss does not violate the Fourteenth Amendment. Thus, like other decisions a parent makes on behalf of a child, the court will not interfere with such decisions so long as there is no evidence that a child is being abused or neglected, and sufficient safeguards are present to protect the child.

There are many cases where a child's liberty may be curtailed by parental action. Children who are punished by being confined to their room, prohibited from attending a sleep-over with friends, or forced to take piano lessons, may believe their liberty is being curtailed. However, each of these instances represents actions that a parent has a constitutional right to take in raising a child. The state will not become involved unless the actions of a parent cross the line from appropriate deprivation of liberty to actions that cause harm to the child.

Parham v. J.R.: Real Life Applications

1. A statute in your state provides that a parent or guardian may commit a minor child to a state hospital if the child is deemed to be drug or alcohol dependent, until such time as he or she is no longer dependent. Kelly is a single mom who has her 16-year-old son Casey committed to the state hospital claiming that he is a regular drug user, that he steals, and that she can no longer manage him. When interviewed by authorities, Casey admits that he uses marijuana on a regular basis and has stolen beer from the homes of friends. Casey is admitted to the hospital and now seeks to challenge the commitment claiming he has a right to a hearing before being committed. Based on *Parham v. J.R.*, how should the judge rule and why?

2. The law in your state provides that prior to being involuntarily committed to a mental hospital a minor over the age of 14 is entitled to a preadmission hearing on the issue of whether hospitalization is appropriate. The hearing shall be before the superintendent of the admitting hospital. Does the setting of an age limit pass constitutional muster?

3. Roberto and Delia are the parents of 16-year-old child Mason. Mason does not suffer from a mental illness, but is very disobedient and makes statements of wanting to take action that will cause damage to the world around him. His parents are concerned for his safety and the safety of others. The local state mental hospital generally only takes individuals who have been diagnosed with mental illness, but is willing to take Mason for a seven-day observation period without a preadmission hearing. Does *Parham* give the parents and the state mental hospital authority to restrict Mason's liberty interest?

4. Barry and Kate are the parents of six-year-old Mallory. Mallory has become uncontrollable at times. She constantly takes all the clothes out of her dresser drawers when left alone in her room, she throws food on the floor when she does not like what is served, and lately she has started pulling her three-year-old brother's hair and biting him. Her parents have had her tested and have been advised that she suffers from no mental illnesses but is likely just going through a stage. She does not have the same behavioral issues at school. Barry and Kate have asked you if they can simply lock her in her room when she comes home from school and continue to do so until she learns to behave properly. Does the *Parham* Court give any guidance as to what limits parents have on restricting a child's liberty interest? What would you tell Barry and Kate in response to their question?

Chapter Summary

- Although marriage is a private contract between two parties, states have traditionally exercised considerable control over the marriage relationship.

■ Legal causes of action to help protect the institution of marriage and balm the broken heart, such as breach of promise to marry, alienation of affection, and criminal conversation, have largely been repealed in favor of the more modernizing trend of privacy in marital relationships.

■ In *Loving v. Virginia*, the United States Supreme Court struck down a Virginia state law that prohibited marriage based upon racial classification, on the basis of the Equal Protection and Due Process Clauses of the Fourteenth Amendment. The case represents the first time that the Court invalidated a state law restricting entry into marriage, and it still dominates legal debates over the validity of contemporary restrictions on marriage.

■ *Griswold v. Connecticut* stands for the proposition that there is a right of privacy in the context of marital relationships into which state authority cannot intrude.

■ The constitutional right of privacy extends to the right of parents to direct the upbringing of their children. This right, however, is not without constitutional limits when considering the interests of the child.

■ While children have constitutional rights, parents and guardians are assumed to act in the minor child's best interest in asserting those constitutional rights, and children will generally not be considered autonomous individuals who have standing to assert their own rights.

Applying the Rules

1. James and Mary live in a state that prohibits both parties from marrying if either party has been convicted previously of an act of domestic violence, unless the party has gone through a 12-week anger management program. Mary was previously convicted of an act of domestic violence, but James and Mary are anxious to get married and do not want to wait until Mary goes through the mandated 12-week program. Accordingly, Mary and James get married in a neighboring state that does not have such a prohibition and then return to their home state. Mary has come to your office asking for legal advice. Answer the following questions for Mary:

    a. Do James and Mary have grounds to challenge the law in their state?
    b. What grounds would you argue for them in trying to overturn the law?
    c. What arguments can they anticipate will be made on behalf of the state?

2. You are clerking for a local trial judge who is preparing a ruling on a case challenging the state law prohibiting marriage of first cousins. Based upon your readings, what statements from the cases would you provide to the judge that may assist in the ruling?

3. Assume that you are writing a law review article on the history of family law in the United States. Explain the concept of marital unity and how the rights of individuals in a marriage developed over time.

4. You represent Ursula after the *Griswold v. Connecticut* case is decided, but before *Eisenstadt v. Baird*. Ursula has distributed contraceptives to fellow students on campus regardless of whether the students are married or unmarried. She has been convicted under a state statute that makes it a crime "for any person to distribute any drug, medicinal article or instrument for the purpose of preventing contraception to any unmarried person." What arguments can you use from *Griswold* to invalidate the state statute? What arguments will likely be made against extending the rule of law to unmarried persons?

Family Law in Practice

1. As indicated in this chapter, state law, within constitutional limits, largely defines who can marry. For example, there may be age restrictions or prohibitions against certain relatives marrying. Find your state's marriage statutes and answer the following questions:

   a. What restrictions are placed on who can be married within your state?
   b. Are there any laws (case law or constitutional amendments) that invalidate any part of your state's law?

2. While parents generally have the right to govern the upbringing of their children, such rights are not without constitutional limits. Research the case law in your state and determine whether there are any cases addressing the issue of control by the child over his or her own medical decisions. Does the child have standing in your state to bring a claim against his or her parents if the child disagrees with a medical decision that a parent wants to enforce?

3. Select a major employer in your community. Develop a set of questions and then interview the appropriate person in the human resources department regarding the company's policy in providing benefits to unmarried partners. (Note: Most companies do not presently offer such benefits, so be sure to include questions regarding any future plans and the impact that extending benefits could have on the company.)

4. Assume you are a legal advisor to a state senator who has asked you to prepare a briefing memo on an upcoming vote on a bill that would allow transgender couples to marry. The senator would like you to set out some of the major arguments in support of both sides of the issue and to conclude by recommending how the senator should vote and why. Write the briefing memo for the senator.

5. Find the law in your state on involuntary commitment of minors to state mental hospitals. What procedural safeguards are in place for the minor child? Are there due process considerations given to the minor? Does the minor have a right to a hearing or a right to counsel?

Marriage and the Legal Regulation of Nonmarital Couples

The modern trend has been away from state control over marriage in favor of giving spouses greater freedom to shape the contours of their relationship. This shift is closely linked to the Supreme Court's willingness, starting with its decision in *Loving v. Virginia*, 388 U.S. 1 (1967), to invalidate state marriage laws on the grounds that they divest individuals of federally protected constitutional rights. Accordingly, since *Loving*, the Fourteenth Amendment has operated as a check on the historic power of states to regulate marriage as a status relationship whose rights and obligations are fixed by law.

The "constitutionalization" of domestic relations law certainly does not mean that marriage is now viewed as a purely private relationship that exists outside of the regulatory power of the state. As will be discussed in this chapter, within federal constitutional limits, state laws continue to structure the relationship by determining who is eligible to marry; what the rights, entitlements, and obligations of spouses are during the marriage; and what their continuing responsibilities toward each are in the event a marriage should fail.

Marriage thus continues to be a legally transformative event:

- With marriage, each partner becomes formally connected to the family of the other. One literally acquires a "family-in-law." Mirror relationships are created such that the mother of one spouse becomes the mother-in-law of the other.

Key Concepts

- State regulations regarding who can marry
- Solemnization and licensing requirements for marriage
- The legal changes that occur as a result of being married
- The constitutional limits on state regulation of marriage
- Legally recognized nonmarital relationships

- Upon marriage, spouses automatically acquire the right to a wide range of entitlements, such as Social Security and workers' compensation benefits, health insurance coverage, beneficial immigration status, and statutory rights of inheritance.
- With marriage, each spouse acquires a legal obligation to support the other. Historically, this obligation was imposed only upon husbands, but this obligation is now mutual.
- If a marriage ends, rights to property and support are automatically triggered, and state law provides a structured framework within which competing claims can be resolved. Although one does not usually think of divorce as a "benefit" that comes with marriage, it is important to recognize that divorce provides married couples with a structured dissolution process that is not available to unmarried couples.

Reflecting the continued public and highly privileged nature of the marital relationship, the law continues to draw a clear line between marriage and nonmarital unions. As will be discussed in the final section of this chapter, now that same-sex marriages are legal in every state, the controversies of the past concerning the right to federal and state benefits for same-sex couples, and the lack of recognition in some states of same-sex marriages no longer exist. Accordingly, every married couple has the ability to take advantage of the federal and state benefits the law affords to married persons. Whether a couple chooses to marry and obtain the benefits the law affords them, or whether they wish to forgo such benefits in favor of a non-marital union is now a personal choice based on other considerations. Thus, while there may be some "marital-like" benefits in terms of alimony and support available in some states for non-married couples, there is no automatic constitutional right to these benefits outside the marriage relationship.

A. STATE REGULATION OF ENTRY INTO MARRIAGE: THE CHOICE OF A MARITAL PARTNER

If someone wishes to marry, the choice of *whom* to wed has typically been a private decision. Accordingly, even when the authority of the state over marriage was more robust than it is today, most people did not have to stop to consider whether their choice of a marriage partner lay outside the bonds of the law. However, up until 1967, if you lived in one of the 16 states in the country with an anti-miscegenation law, and your intended marriage crossed a prohibited racial barrier, the state would have had a lot to say about your plans. Not only would you have been barred from marrying in your home state, it may also have been a crime for you to leave your state and marry in another state in order to evade this prohibition.

As discussed in Chapter 1, in 1967, in the case of *Loving v. Virginia*, the Supreme Court held that under the Due Process Clause of the Fourteenth Amendment the freedom to marry is a fundamental right that is "essential to the orderly pursuit of happiness by free men" and that the denial of such a right "on so unsupportable a basis as the racial classifications embodied in" the anti-miscegenation laws was an unconstitutional exercise of state authority over marriage. *Id.* at 12.

The *Loving* Court was unequivocal that "the freedom to marry, or not marry, *a person of another race* resides with the individual and cannot be infringed by the State." *Id*. However, a looming question presented itself in the wake of this landmark decision: Were other state restrictions on the freedom to marry a person of one's choosing, such as those barring an individual from marrying a relative or a same-sex partner, also unwarranted intrusions into the fundamental right of marital choice, or would *Loving* be read more narrowly to apply only to invidious race-based restrictions on this fundamental right?

The answer as to same-sex partners came almost 50 years later with the historic decision of *Obergefell v. Hodges*, 576 U.S. ___ (2015), in which the Supreme Court held that states must recognize marriages of same-sex couples and a state must issue marriage licenses to same-sex couples who want to marry in the state. Thus, the case law makes clear that the fundamental right to choose one's marital partner extends well beyond the crossing of racial lines. However, at the same time, it is equally clear that the right is not absolute, and that some state barriers, such as those prohibiting marriages to multiple partners or to close relatives, remain in place in all states and have attracted very little controversy.

1. *Loving* and Beyond: The Fundamental Right to Marry

In order to truly understand how far the right to marriage has come, and the constitutional limits on states in regulating marriage, some historic analysis is appropriate. Eleven years after *Loving*, in the case of *Zablocki v. Redhail*, 434 U.S. 374 (1978), the Court faced a challenge to a Wisconsin law that prohibited noncustodial parents who were behind in child support payments from marrying. This case directly raised the question left open by *Loving* as to whether restrictions on the right to marry other than race-based classifications would likewise be regarded as an impermissible intrusion on the fundamental right to choose a marital partner.

Case Preview

Zablocki v. Redhail

The Wisconsin state law at issue in *Zablocki* prohibited residents who were behind in child support from marrying absent a court order or judgment. In addition, the state statute provided that court permission will not be granted unless the applicant showed proof that the support obligation had been paid and demonstrated that the children covered by the support order are not then and not likely thereafter to become public charges. Roger Redhail was ineligible to marry under the statute because he was behind on his child support obligations, and his child had been receiving benefits under a public program. Accordingly, when he applied for a marriage license, his application was denied because he did not have a court order or judgment. Redhail challenged the denial on the grounds that it violated the Equal Protection Clause of the Fourteenth Amendment. The case represents an important extension of the Court's view of the fundamental right to marry and the limits that state law may place on a person's right to marry.

As you read *Zablocki*, look for the following:

1. How does the Court describe the right to marry?
2. What cases from Chapter 1 are used by the Court here to support its decision? How does the Court use these cases to reach its result?
3. What was the sufficiently important state interest that Wisconsin was trying to protect? Why is this interest not persuasive to the Court?

Zablocki v. Redhail
434 U.S. 374 (1978)

Mr. Justice MARSHALL delivered the opinion of the Court.

After being denied a marriage license because of his failure to comply with [the state statute], appellee brought this class action under 42 U.S.C. 1983, challenging the statute as violative of the Equal Protection and Due Process Clauses of the Fourteenth Amendment and seeking declaratory and injunctive relief. The United States District Court for the Eastern District of Wisconsin held the statute unconstitutional under the Equal Protection Clause and enjoined its enforcement. We noted probable jurisdiction, and we now affirm.

I

. . .

The facts, according to the stipulation filed by the parties in the District Court, are as follows. In January 1972, when appellee was a minor and a high school student, a paternity action was instituted against him in Milwaukee County Court, alleging that he was the father of a baby girl born out of wedlock on July 5, 1971. After he appeared and admitted that he was the child's father, the court entered an order on May 12, 1972, adjudging appellee the father and ordering him to pay $109 per month as support for the child until she reached 18 years of age. From May 1972 until August 1974, appellee was unemployed and indigent, and consequently was unable to make any support payments.

On September 27, 1974, appellee filed an application for a marriage license with appellant Zablocki, the County Clerk of Milwaukee County, and a few days later the application was denied on the sole ground that appellee had not obtained a court order granting him permission to marry, as required by [the state statute]. Although appellee did not petition a state court thereafter, it is stipulated that he would not have been able to satisfy either of the statutory prerequisites for an order granting permission to marry. First, he had not satisfied his support obligations to his illegitimate child, and as of December 1974 there was an arrearage in excess of $3,700. Second, the child had been a public charge since her birth, receiving benefits under the

Aid to Families with Dependent Children program. It is stipulated that the child's benefit payments were such that she would have been a public charge even if appellee had been current in his support payments.

[A three-judge federal district] court held the statute invalid and enjoined the county clerks from enforcing it.

. . .

II

In evaluating [the statute] under the Equal Protection Clause, "we must first determine what burden of justification the classification created thereby must meet, by looking to the nature of the classification and the individual interests affected." *Memorial Hospital v. Maricopa County,* 415 U.S. 250, 253 (1974). Since our past decisions make clear that the right to marry is of fundamental importance, and since the classification at issue here significantly interferes with the exercise of that right, we believe that "critical examination" of the state interests advanced in support of the classification is required. *Massachusetts Board of Retirement v. Murgia,* 427 U.S. 307, 312, 314 (1976); see e.g., *San Antonio Independent School Dist. v. Rodriguez,* 411 U.S. 1, 17 (1973).

The leading decision of this Court on the right to marry is *Loving v. Virginia,* 388 U.S. 1 (1967). In that case, an interracial couple who had been convicted of violating Virginia's miscegenation laws challenged the statutory scheme on both equal protection and due process grounds. The Court's opinion could have rested solely on the ground that the statutes discriminated on the basis of race in violation of the Equal Protection Clause. But the Court went on to hold that the laws arbitrarily deprived the couple of a fundamental liberty protected by the Due Process Clause, the freedom to marry.

. . .

Although *Loving* arose in the context of racial discrimination, prior and subsequent decisions of this Court confirm that the right to marry is of fundamental importance for all individuals. Long ago, in *Maynard v. Hill,* 125 U.S. 190 (1888), the Court characterized marriage as "the most important relation in life," and as "the foundation of the family and of society, without which there would be neither civilization nor progress." In *Meyer v. Nebraska,* 262 U.S. 390 (1923), the Court recognized that the right "to marry, establish a home and bring up children" is a central part of the liberty protected by the Due Process Clause, and in *Skinner v. Oklahoma ex rel. Williamson,* marriage was described as "fundamental to the very existence and survival of the race," 316 U.S., at 541.

More recent decisions have established that the right to marry is part of the fundamental "right of privacy" implicit in the Fourteenth Amendment's Due Process Clause. In *Griswold v. Connecticut,* 381 U.S. 479 (1965), the Court observed:

> "We deal with a right of privacy older than the Bill of Rights — older than our political parties, older than our school system. Marriage is a coming together for better or for worse, hopefully enduring, and intimate to the degree of being sacred. It is an association that promotes a way of life, not causes; a harmony in living, not political

faiths; a bilateral loyalty, not commercial or social projects. Yet it is an association for as noble a purpose as any involved in our prior decisions."

. . .

It is not surprising that the decision to marry has been placed on the same level of importance as decisions relating to procreation, childbirth, child rearing, and family relationships. As the facts of this case illustrate, it would make little sense to recognize a right of privacy with respect to other matters of family life and not with respect to the decision to enter the relationship that is the foundation of the family in our society.

. . .

By reaffirming the fundamental character of the right to marry, we do not mean to suggest that every state regulation which relates in any way to the incidents of or prerequisites for marriage must be subjected to rigorous scrutiny. To the contrary, reasonable regulations that do not significantly interfere with decisions to enter into the marital relationship may legitimately be imposed. The statutory classification at issue here, however, clearly does interfere directly and substantially with the right to marry.

Under the challenged statute, no Wisconsin resident in the affected class may marry in Wisconsin or elsewhere without a court order, and marriages contracted in violation of the statute are both void and punishable as criminal offenses. Some of those in the affected class, like appellee, will never be able to obtain the necessary court order, because they either lack the financial means to meet their support obligations or cannot prove that their children will not become public charges. These persons are absolutely prevented from getting married. Many others, able in theory to satisfy the statute's requirements, will be sufficiently burdened by having to do so that they will in effect be coerced into forgoing their right to marry. And even those who can be persuaded to meet the statute's requirements suffer a serious intrusion into their freedom of choice in an area in which we have held such freedom to be fundamental.

III

When a statutory classification significantly interferes with the exercise of a fundamental right, it cannot be upheld unless it is supported by sufficiently important state interests and is closely tailored to effectuate only those interests. . . . Appellant asserts that two interests are served by the challenged statute: the permission-to-marry proceeding furnishes an opportunity to counsel the applicant as to the necessity of fulfilling his prior support obligations; and the welfare of the out-of-custody children is protected. We may accept for present purposes that these are legitimate and substantial interests, but, since the means selected by the State for achieving these interests unnecessarily impinge on the right to marry, the statute cannot be sustained.

. . .

First, with respect to individuals who are unable to meet the statutory requirements, the statute merely prevents the applicant from getting married, without delivering any money at all into the hands of the applicant's prior children. More importantly, regardless of the applicant's ability or willingness to meet the statutory requirements, the State already has numerous other means for exacting compliance with support obligations, means that are at least as effective as the instant statute's and yet do not impinge upon the right to marry. Under Wisconsin law, whether the children are from a prior marriage or were born out of wedlock, court-determined support obligations may be enforced directly via wage assignments, civil contempt proceedings, and criminal penalties. And, if the State believes that parents of children out of their custody should be responsible for ensuring that those children do not become public charges, this interest can be achieved by adjusting the criteria used for determining the amounts to be paid under their support orders.

There is also some suggestion that [the statute] protects the ability of marriage applicants to meet support obligations to prior children by preventing the applicants from incurring new support obligations. But the challenged provisions . . . are grossly underinclusive with respect to this purpose, since they do not limit in any way new financial commitments by the applicant other than those arising out of the contemplated marriage. The statutory classification is substantially overinclusive as well: Given the possibility that the new spouse will actually better the applicant's financial situation, by contributing income from a job or otherwise, the statute in many cases may prevent affected individuals from improving their ability to satisfy their prior support obligations. And, although it is true that the applicant will incur support obligations to any children born during the contemplated marriage, preventing the marriage may only result in the children being born out of wedlock, as in fact occurred in appellee's case. Since the support obligation is the same whether the child is born in or out of wedlock, the net result of preventing the marriage is simply more illegitimate children.

The statutory classification created . . . thus cannot be justified by the interests advanced in support of it. The judgment of the District Court is, accordingly,

Affirmed.

Post-Case Follow-Up

While *Loving v. Virginia* left open the question of whether its holding was to be narrowly construed to racial classifications, subsequent Supreme Court cases clearly showed that the holding was not so limited. Thus, the Court in *Zablocki* holds that marriage is a fundamental right and that Wisconsin's law violated the Equal Protection Clause by denying a class of people (those residents behind in child support) from being able to marry either within the state or outside the state. Relying on its previous decision of *Loving v. Virginia*, the Court explained that the right to marry was a fundamental liberty interested protected by the Due Process Clause. The Court also considered the right to marry to be part of the right to privacy found in the Fourteenth Amendment, citing *Griswold v. Connecticut*.

Subsequently, in *Turner v. Satley*, the Court invalidated a Missouri law prohibiting inmates from marrying, finding that the state's interest in rehabilitation and security did not justify this limitation on an individual's fundamental right to marry. Rather, the Court found that inmate marriages, like other marriages, are expressions of "emotional support and public commitment." The Court explained that these are "an important and significant aspect of the marital relationship."

Zablocki v. Redhail: Real Life Applications

1. Your law firm has been asked to handle a case seeking to overturn a state law that provides that prior to being married the parties must have a blood test to verify that neither party has any communicable diseases. The test results must be submitted to the county clerk, who will verify that the test results are negative prior to issuing a license. Is there any reasoning from *Zablocki* that you can use in arguing that the state law is unconstitutional?

2. Would your answer to Question 1 be stronger if the law said that test results had to be submitted to the intended spouses but the actual results were not a condition to a license being issued?

3. Would your answer to Question 1 change if the law provided that both parties are allowed to waive in writing the required blood test?

4. Assume that Roger Redhail was a wealthy individual who simply refused to pay child support instead of an individual who could not afford to pay. Would the decision of the Court have been different? What arguments would you make for the state in such a case?

2. Fundamental Is Not Absolute: State Restrictions on the Choice of a Marital Partner

Although the right to marry is constitutionally protected, all states still have laws in effect that restrict an individual's choice of marriage partner. Most common are those that ban marriage between relatives, impose a "one-spouse-at-a-time" limitation, and limit the decisional autonomy of teens. Where challenged as impermissible restrictions on the right to marry, these types of restrictions have typically been upheld on the grounds that they promote important state interests. After looking at these restrictions, we turn to the topic of the marital rights of same-sex partners who, until the Supreme Court took up the issue in 2014, were subjected to state laws defining marriage as between one man and one woman.

Incest Restrictions

All states have criminal incest laws that make it a crime for family members within a certain degree of kinship to engage in sexual relationships with one other. In some, marriage within these prohibited degrees is also a crime. Running along parallel lines, all states also have civil marriage restriction laws that generally prohibit these same relatives from marrying each other; however, there may well be variability between the criminal and the civil prohibitions. Marriages contracted in violation of these laws are void. (See Chapter 4 regarding the distinction between void and voidable marriages.)

At one time, based on the view that a husband and wife were a single person, incest laws applied equally to persons related by marriage (affinity) and those related by blood (consanguinity); in effect, the blood relatives of one spouse were treated as the blood relatives of the other. Today, a majority of states no longer ban most affinity relatives from marrying; however, bans on marriage between a stepparent and stepchild remain more prevalent in order to protect children from sexual exploitation. These bans may continue through adulthood. Although this ban as between consenting adults has been challenged as an impermissible restriction on the right to marry, it is generally regarded as necessary to safeguard children from being seen as potential sexual partners while they are growing up so that households are not disrupted by sexual jealousies. Further, as the Supreme Court of Ohio explained in upholding its criminal incest law against the claim by a stepfather that he had a fundamental right to engage in a consensual sexual relationship with his adult stepdaughter, "parents do not cease being parents — whether natural parents, stepparents, or adoptive parents — when their minor child reaches the age of majority." *State v. Lowe,* 112 Ohio St. 3d 507, 861 N.E.2d 512, 518 (2007).

In terms of specific prohibitions, all states forbid marriage between a parent and child, a grandparent and grandchild, and a brother and sister of whole or half blood. Most states treat sibling relationships created through adoption as a blood relation and prohibit marriage between adopted siblings, and most, if not all, states prohibit marriage between an uncle and a niece and between an aunt and a nephew. With respect to first cousins, the trend is in favor of lifting this restriction, and currently about half the states now permit marriage between first cousins, although a handful of these states only allow these marriages under certain circumstances such as where the parties are over procreative age or provide proof of genetic counseling.

Given that marriage is categorized as fundamental right, some scholars have questioned the appropriateness of state laws that prevent consenting adults from marrying one another based on ties of affinity *or* consanguinity. As expressed by one author on the topic:

Marriage Between First Cousins

First cousins currently can marry in Alabama, Alaska, California, Colorado, Connecticut, Florida, Georgia, Hawaii, Maryland, Massachusetts, New Jersey, New Mexico, New York, North Carolina, Rhode Island, South Carolina, Tennessee, Vermont, Virginia, and the District of Columbia without restrictions. First cousins over a certain age or under certain conditions may marry in Arizona, Illinois, Indiana, Maine, Utah, and Wisconsin.

The trend toward abolishing the prohibition between marriages of first cousins reflects the fact that concerns about the genetic risks of "inbreeding" have turned out to be less significant than once believed, at least where first cousins are concerned. According to a report of the National Society of Genetic Counselors, studies indicate that "the increased risk for a significant birth defect in offspring of a first cousin union range between 1.7 and 2.8% above the risk of the general population." Robin L. Bennett et al., Genetic Counseling and Screening of Consanguineous Couples and Their Offspring: Recommendations of the National Society of Genetic Counselors, 11 J. Genetic Counseling 97 (2002).

> All too often . . . society is merely trying to save the individual from conduct that society finds repulsive. State intervention into adult decision-making must be restricted to those instances where the danger of imminent bodily harm is readily demonstrable and marriage between adults related by consanguinity or affinity does not meet this requirement.

See Carolyn Bratt, Is Oedipus Free to Marry?, 18 Fam. L.Q. 267, 288-289 (1984) (citations omitted). Although, as discussed, there has been some loosening of marriage restrictions on adults related by affinity, this has not been the case with respect to laws prohibiting marriages between adults related by blood. Although thoughtful scholars have called for a reappraisal of the "extent to which disgust motivates" the continued application of the ban to these relationships, this suggestion has yet to gain much traction. *See* Courtney Megan Cahill, Same-Sex Marriage, Slippery Slope Rhetoric, and the Politics of Disgust: A Critical Perspective on Contemporary Family Discourse and the Incest Taboo, 99 Nw. U. L. Rev. 1543 (2005).

Multiple Marriages

All states prohibit a person from having more than one spouse at any given time (however, see the discussion below of *Brown v. Buham*). A marriage contracted in violation of the "more than one spouse at a time" prohibition is void and may subject the participants to criminal prosecution.

Like incest prohibitions, these laws have religious underpinnings as monogamy is a central tenet of the Judeo-Christian belief structure. However, the prohibition on multiple spouses has been justified on a number of other grounds. For instance, it has been regarded as essential to preserving the integrity of families by limiting an individual's financial and emotional commitments to a single spouse and their offspring. Another important consideration includes safeguarding women and girls from the sexual, emotional, and physical exploitation that some studies have shown is widespread in polygamous households. Of particular concern is the practice of older men taking underage girls to be their wives. *See generally* Hema Chatiani, In Defense of Marriage: Why Same-Sex Marriage Will Not Lead Us Down the Slippery Slope Towards the Legalization of Polygamy, 6 Appalachian L.J. 101 (2006), and Thomas Buck, Jr., From Big Love to the Big House: Justifying Anti-Polygamy Laws in an Age of Expanding Rights, 26 Emory Intl. L. Rev. 939 (2012).

Since the Court's decision in *Zablocki*, some commentators have questioned the validity of the state's interest in prohibiting individuals from having more than one spouse at a time. It is argued that these laws do not actually promote the state's interest in protecting the integrity of families, since the same concerns about financial and emotional instability are present with remarriage (or as it is sometimes called, sequential polygamy) and no limits are placed on the number of times a person can remarry and reproduce with each successive spouse. Others challenges focus more on the First Amendment freedom of religion implications of this continued ban in light of the fact that polygamy in this country is generally associated with religious beliefs. *See* Kenneth E. Sealing, Polygamists Out of the Closet:

Statutory and State Constitutional Prohibitions Against Polygamy Are Unconstitutional Under the Free Exercise Clause, 17 Ga. St. U. L. Rev. 691 (2001).

Polygamy moved into the spotlight as the result of two popular television shows — TLC's *Sister Wives* and HBO's *Big House*, which both represent plural families in a generally positive light. In the case of TLC's *Sister Wives*, Kody Brown and his "wives" Meri Brown, Janelle Brown, Christine Brown, and Robyn Sullivan were featured. After the airing of the first episode of this reality-based show, an official investigation by the local police was launched. A state statute provided that a "person is guilty of bigamy when, knowing he has a husband or wife or knowing the other person has a husband or wife, the person purports to marry another person or cohabits with another person." The criminal investigation was dropped, but the Browns had filed a constitutional challenge to Utah's bigamy law, which prohibits a married person from marrying or cohabiting with another person. They argued that this prohibition interfered with their fundamental rights of privacy and religious freedom.

As is commonly the case in polygamous households, Mr. Brown was only formally wed to the first of his four "wives." Thus, although the other relationships were viewed as marriages by the participants, "there [was] only one recorded marriage." *Brown v. Buhman*, 947 F. Supp. 2d 1170, 1178-1181 (D. Utah 2013). The court accordingly characterized the other relationships as constituting "religious cohabitation," which it defined as a "private 'spiritual' marriage not licensed or otherwise sanctioned by the state." *Id.* at 1181.

The central issue in the case boiled down to whether the inclusion of the cohabitation ban was a valid exercise of the state's regulatory authority. Although recognizing that it is within the power of a state to "protect marriage, as a legal union, by criminalizing the act of purporting to enter into a *second legal union*," through a ceremonial marriage, the court held that the state's criminalization (or selective prosecution) of religious, but not "ordinary" adulterous, cohabitation, impermissibly violated the Browns' right to religious freedom as well as the "longstanding principle that, in order to 'secure individual liberty, . . . certain kinds of highly personal relationships' must be given 'a substantial measure of sanctuary from unjustified interference by the State.'" *Id.* at 1218. In reaching this result, the court was clearly influenced by the nation's long history of animosity toward the practice of polygamy, which it pointed out the Supreme Court had characterized as a "'return to barbarism'" that was "'contrary to the spirit of Christianity.'" *Id.* at 1187, quoting *Late Corp. of the Church of Latter-Day Saints v. United States,* 136 U.S. 1, 49 (1890).

The court ultimately permitted the "[s]tatute to remain in force as prohibiting bigamy in the literal sense" as meaning "the fraudulent or otherwise impressible possession of two purportedly valid marriage licenses for the purpose of entering into more than one purportedly legal marriage." *Id.* at 1234. The decision, however, is nonetheless quite noteworthy. By investing "religious cohabitation" with constitutional protection, the *Brown* decision effectively sanctions polygamous arrangements in which the participants regard themselves as married in accordance with their spiritual beliefs, although only one marriage is actually sanctioned by the law.

Marital Age

Complex rules govern the ability of young people to marry. Most states set a minimum age, referred to as the **age of capacity**, below which a young person may not marry. Commonly, this age is 14. Some laws contain exceptions for circumstances such as pregnancy, but the exception usually confers a conditional rather than an absolute right of marriage since most states require a minor to first obtain parental and/or judicial consent. Most states also set an **age of consent** at which a person becomes eligible to consent to his or her own marriage. The age of consent is usually set at 18 — the age of majority.

For young people below the age of consent and, where applicable, above the age of capacity, the right to marry is usually conditional upon obtaining parental and/or judicial consent. Generally, states allow minors over the age of capacity to marry with the consent of a parent, but for minors younger than the age of capacity, the consent of both a parent and a judge is necessary. In some states, if a parent withholds permission, a minor may petition the court for approval. These laws were designed to serve at least two state interests. First, by requiring parental participation and approval, the law supports the traditional authority of parents over their children. Second, and perhaps more important, they are thought to protect minors from making ill-advised decisions with potentially long-term harmful consequences for themselves and future offspring.

Although, as discussed in Chapter 1, there has been a growing trend toward granting minors greater legal autonomy, challenges to these laws have not generally been successful. One important reason is that unlike other decisions, such as whether to terminate a pregnancy, the marriage decision can be postponed without any lasting, negative consequences. Moreover, unlike anti-miscegenation laws, or laws prohibiting marriage between same-sex partners, age-restriction laws do not operate as an absolute barrier to marrying one's chosen partner; they simply require deferral of the marriage date. *See, e.g., Moe v. Dinkins*, 669 F.2d 67 (2d Cir.), *cert. denied*, 459 U.S. 827 (1982).

Same-Sex Couples

The recognition of same-sex marriages by the Supreme Court represents the biggest federal change in the family law area in recent years. However, the *Obergefell v. Hodges* decision, which put an end to same-sex marriage restrictions in all states, was preceded by a number of other cases that paved the way for the Court's landmark decision. To truly understand the basis for the *Obergefell* decision, it is important to look at the decision within the historical context.

Marriage equality
Kobby Dagan / Shutterstock.com

Same-sex couples have been fighting for the right to marry since the early 1970s, when a number of couples who were denied marriage licenses brought lawsuits challenging the fairness of restricting marriage to heterosexual couples. Citing *Loving*, they argued that with marriage now firmly established as a fundamental right, states no longer had a valid basis for excluding same-sex couples who, like their heterosexual counterparts, were seeking both the social acceptance and the benefits that flow from marriage.

Early court decisions had little trouble dismissing the challenges. Courts on the state level consistently concluded that the fundamental right to choose one's marital partner did not extend to same-sex partners. Since marriage was traditionally between a man and a woman, same-sex partners were placed outside the reach of the Due Process Clause. The courts similarly concluded that because same-sex couples are critically different from male-female couples, particularly with respect to procreative potential, the denial of marital rights did not violate the Equal Protection Clause, which only requires the like treatment of persons who are similarly situated. Courts also made clear that a number of important state interests — such as encouraging procreation and protecting the traditional family — were of sufficient magnitude to offset any potential limitation of rights.

Efforts for Marriage Recognition at the State Level

In the late 1980s, prompted in part by the AIDS epidemic and bolstered by gains in civil rights protections for gay men and lesbians, activists again began to focus on securing equal marriage rights. Once again, same-sex couples who were denied marriage licenses, this time in Hawaii and Alaska, brought lawsuits arguing that the denial deprived them of the right to privacy and equal protection under their respective state constitutions.[1] For the first time, the courts in both states appeared on the brink of extending marital rights to same-sex couples; however, while the cases were winding their way through the courts, opponents waged successful campaigns to amend their respective state constitutions to define marriage as being between one man and one woman, thus effectively bringing potentially successful court challenges to an end.

Efforts at the Federal Level to Restrict Marriage

Perhaps the most distinctive legislation at the federal level to define marriage was the Defense of Marriage Act (DOMA), enacted by Congress in 1996. As enacted, DOMA had two key sections. Section 2 of DOMA sought to avoid the potential effect of the Full Faith and Credit Clause and the common law "place of celebration" rule. Under the Full Faith and Credit Clause, a state generally must honor an out-of-state marriage that is valid in the state where entered into. However, DOMA allowed states to deny recognition to marriages between same-sex partners. Section 2 of DOMA read in part that "[n]o State . . . shall be required to give effect to any public act, or judicial proceeding of any other state . . . respecting a relationship between persons of the same sex that is treated as a marriage under the laws of such other State." Defense of Marriage Act, 28 U.S.C.S. §1738(c).

---

[1] *See Baehr v. Miike*, 852 P.2d 44 (1993), and *Baehr v. Miike*, Civil Action No. 91-1394 (Haw. Cir. Ct. Dec. 3, 1996); and *Brause & Dugan v. Bureau of Vital Statistics* (Alaska Super. Ct. Feb. 27, 1998).

The second key aspect of DOMA was found in Section 3, which declared that, for purposes of federal law, "the word 'marriage' means only a legal union between one man and one woman as husband and wife, and the word 'spouse' refers only to a person of the opposite sex who is a husband or wife." 1 U.S.C.S. §7. Accordingly, even if a couple were validly married under state law, under DOMA they would not be regarded as married in the eyes of the federal government. As a result, they would be denied the many federal benefits that are available to married heterosexual couples, including Social Security spousal benefits, immigration protections, and rights under the Family and Medical Leave Act. As discussed below, in 2013, Section 3 of DOMA was declared unconstitutional by the United States Supreme Court.

Following the lead of the federal government, a majority of states enacted statutes or amended their constitutions to define marriage as being exclusively between one man and one woman. In addition to banning same-sex marriage, these "mini-DOMAs," as they were frequently known, also generally denied recognition to marriages between same-sex partners that were validly entered into in a state permitting such unions. For example, if a same-sex couple was married in New Hampshire and then traveled to visit their families in Vermont and Georgia, they would be considered married in Vermont (which recognized same-sex marriages), but not in Georgia (which did not recognize same-sex marriages).

Marriage Recognition

In 2003, in the groundbreaking case of *Goodridge v. Department of Public Health*, the Massachusetts Supreme Judicial Court ruled that same-sex couples have a constitutional right to marry. Focusing on the tangible benefits and obligations of marriage as well as its symbolic value, the court held that the arbitrary exclusion of same-sex couples from this cherished institution was at odds with constitutional principles of privacy and equality.

Case Preview

Goodridge v. Department of Public Health

Goodridge was the first high court decision to hold that same-sex partners have a constitutional right to marry. The plaintiffs were 7 same-sex couples in Massachusetts who were in committed relationships of durations ranging from 4 years to 30 years. Two of the couples were raising children together. In March and April 2001, each of the couples attempted to obtain a marriage license and were denied the license. On April 11, 2001, the plaintiffs filed suit alleging that the denial of the license, and therefore the denial of the legal and social status of civil marriage, as well as the "protections, benefits and obligations of marriage," violated the rights afforded under the Massachusetts Constitution. The lower court judge held that there was no fundamental right to marry a person of the same sex. The judge concluded that the legislature may rationally limit marriage to opposite-sex couples because those couples are capable of procreation.

While reviewing *Goodridge*, consider the following:

1. Why did the court find that the Massachusetts statute treated some individuals as second-class citizens?
2. What access to the protections, benefits, and obligations of civil marriage were denied to same-sex couples?
3. What was the Department of Public Health's rationale for arguing that same-sex marriages should be prohibited?

Goodridge v. Department of Public Health
798 N.E.2d 941 (Mass. 2003)

. . . Marriage is a vital social institution. The exclusive commitment of two individuals to each other nurtures love and mutual support; it brings stability to our society. For those who choose to marry, and for their children, marriage provides an abundance of legal, financial, and social benefits. In return it imposes weighty legal, financial, and social obligations.

The question before us is whether, consistent with the Massachusetts Constitution, the Commonwealth may deny the protections, benefits, and obligations conferred by civil marriage to two individuals of the same sex who wish to marry. We conclude that it may not. The Massachusetts Constitution affirms the dignity and equality of all individuals. It forbids the creation of second-class citizens. . . .

We are mindful that our decision marks a change in the history of our marriage law. Many people hold deep-seated religious, moral, and ethical convictions that marriage should be limited to the union of one man and one woman, and that homosexual conduct is immoral. Many hold equally strong religious, moral, and ethical convictions that same-sex couples are entitled to be married. . . . Neither view answers the question before us. Our concern is with the Massachusetts Constitution. . . .

Barred access to the protections, benefits, and obligations of civil marriage, a person who enters into an intimate, exclusive union with another of the same sex is arbitrarily deprived of membership in one of our community's most rewarding and cherished institutions. That exclusion is incompatible with the constitutional principles of respect for individual autonomy and equality under law.

. . .

A

The . . . question is whether, as the department claims, government action that bars same-sex couples from civil marriage constitutes a legitimate exercise of the State's authority to regulate conduct, or whether, as the plaintiffs claim, this categorical marriage exclusion violates the Massachusetts Constitution. We have recognized the long-standing statutory understanding, derived from the common law, that "marriage" means the lawful union of a woman and a man. But that history cannot and does not foreclose the constitutional question.

The plaintiffs' claim that the marriage restriction violates the Massachusetts Constitution can be analyzed in two ways. Does it offend the Constitution's guarantees of equality before the law? Or do the liberty and due process provisions of the Massachusetts Constitution secure the plaintiffs' right to marry their chosen partner? In matters implicating marriage, family life, and the upbringing of children, the two constitutional concepts frequently overlap, as they do here . . . .

We begin by considering the nature of civil marriage itself. Simply put, the government creates civil marriage. In Massachusetts, civil marriage is, and since pre-Colonial days has been, precisely what its name implies: a wholly secular institution. . . .

In a real sense, there are three partners to every civil marriage: two willing spouses and an approving State. . . .

Without question, civil marriage enhances the "welfare of the community." It is a "social institution of the highest importance." *French v. McAnarney*, 90 Mass. 544, 546 (1935). . . . Civil marriage anchors an ordered society by encouraging stable relationships over transient ones. . . . Marriage also bestows enormous private and social advantages on those who choose to marry. Civil marriage is at once a deeply personal commitment to another human being and a highly public celebration of the ideals of mutuality, companionship, intimacy, fidelity, and family. "It is an association that promotes a way of not political faiths; a bilateral loyalty, not commercial or social projects." *Griswold v. Connecticut*, 381 U.S. 479, 486 (1965). Because it fulfils yearnings for security, safe haven, and connection that express our common humanity, civil marriage is an esteemed institution, and the decision whether and whom to marry is among life's momentous acts of self-definition.

Tangible as well as intangible benefits flow from marriage. The marriage license grants valuable property rights to those who meet the entry requirements, and who agree to what might otherwise be a burdensome degree of government regulation of their activities.

The benefits accessible only by way of a marriage license are enormous, touching nearly every aspect of life and death. The department states that "hundreds of statutes" are related to marriage and to marital benefits. . . .

Where a married couple has children, their children are also directly or indirectly, but no less auspiciously, the recipients of the special legal and economic protections obtained by civil marriage. Notwithstanding the Commonwealth's strong public policy to abolish legal distinctions between marital and non-marital children in providing for the support and care of minors, . . . the fact remains that marital children reap a measure of family stability and economic security based on their parents' legally privileged status that is largely inaccessible, or not as readily accessible, to non-marital children. Some of these benefits are social, such as the enhanced approval that still attends the status of being a marital child. Others are material, such as the greater ease of access to family-based State and Federal benefits that attend the presumptions of one's parentage.

It is undoubtedly for these concrete reasons, as well as for its intimately personal significance, that civil marriage has long been termed a "civil right." . . .

Without the right to marry — or more properly, the right to choose to marry — one is excluded from the full range of human experience and denied full protection of the laws for one's "avowed commitment to an intimate and lasting human relationship." *Baker v. State*, 170 Vt. 194, 229 (1994). Because civil marriage is central to the lives of individuals and the welfare of the community, our laws assiduously protect the individual's right to marry against undue government incursion. . . .

B

For decades, indeed centuries, in much of this country (including Massachusetts) no lawful marriage was possible between white and black Americans. That long history availed not when the Supreme Court of California held in 1948 that a legislative prohibition against interracial marriage violated the due process and equality guarantees of the Fourteenth Amendment, *Perez v. Sharp*, 32 Cal. 2d 711, 728 [198 P.2d 17] (1948), or when, nineteen years later, the United States Supreme Court also held that a statutory bar to interracial marriage violated the Fourteenth Amendment, *Loving v. Virginia*, 388 U.S. [1 (1967)]. As both *Perez* and *Loving* make clear, the right to marry means little if it does not include the right to marry the person of one's choice, subject to appropriate government restrictions in the interests of public health, safety, and welfare. See *Perez v. Sharp*, supra at 717 ("the essence of the right to marry is freedom to join in marriage with a person of one's choice").

The Massachusetts Constitution protects matters of personal liberty against government incursion as zealously, and often more so, than does the Federal Constitution, even where both Constitutions employ essentially the same language. . . . That the Massachusetts Constitution is in some instances more protective of individual liberty interests than is the Federal Constitution is not surprising. Fundamental to the vigor of our Federal system of government is that "state courts are absolutely free to interpret state constitutional provisions to accord greater protection to individual rights than do similar provisions of the United States Constitution." *Arizona v. Evans*, 514 U.S. 1, 8 (1995).

The individual liberty and equality safeguards of the Massachusetts Constitution protect both "freedom from" unwarranted government intrusion into protected spheres of life and "freedom to" partake in benefits created by the State for the common good. . . . The liberty interest in choosing whether and whom to marry would be hollow if the Commonwealth could, without sufficient justification, foreclose an individual from freely choosing the person with whom to share an exclusive commitment in the unique institution of civil marriage. . . .

The department's first stated rationale, equating marriage with unassisted heterosexual procreation, shades imperceptibly into its second: that confining marriage to opposite-sex couples ensures that children are raised in the "optimal" setting. Protecting the welfare of children is a paramount State policy. Restricting marriage to opposite-sex couples, however, cannot plausibly further this policy. . . .

The department has offered no evidence that forbidding marriage to people of the same sex will increase the number of couples choosing to enter into opposite-sex marriages in order to have and raise children. There is thus no rational relationship between the marriage statute and the Commonwealth's proffered goal of protecting the "optimal" child rearing unit. Moreover, the department readily concedes that people in same-sex couples may be "excellent" parents. These couples (including four of the plaintiff couples) have children for the reasons others do — to love them, to care for them, to nurture them. But the task of child rearing for same-sex couples is made infinitely harder by their status as outliers to the marriage laws. . . . Excluding same-sex couples from civil marriage will not make children of opposite-sex marriages more secure, but it does prevent children of same-sex couples from enjoying the immeasurable advantages that flow from the assurance of "a stable family structure in which children will be reared, educated, and socialized." Post at 381 (Cordy, J., dissenting).

No one disputes that the plaintiff couples are families, that many are parents, and that the children they are raising, like all children, need and should have the fullest opportunity to grow up in a secure, protected family unit. Similarly, no one disputes that, under the rubric of marriage, the State provides a cornucopia of substantial benefits to married parents and their children. The preferential treatment of civil marriage reflects the Legislature's conclusion that marriage "is the foremost setting for the education and socialization of children" precisely because it "encourages parents to remain committed to each other and to their children as they grow." Post at 383 (Cordy, J., dissenting). . . .

It cannot be rational under our laws, and indeed it is not permitted, to penalize children by depriving them of State benefits because the State disapproves of their parents' sexual orientation.

The third rationale advanced by the department is that limiting marriage to opposite-sex couples furthers the Legislature's interest in conserving scarce State and private financial resources. The marriage restriction is rational, it argues, because the General Court logically could assume that same-sex couples are more financially independent than married couples and thus less needy of public marital benefits. . . .

An absolute statutory ban on same-sex marriage bears no rational relationship to the goal of economy. First, the department's conclusory generalization — that same-sex couples are less financially dependent on each other than opposite-sex couples — ignores that many same-sex couples, such as many of the plaintiffs in this case, have children and other dependents (here, aged parents) in their care. . . . Second, Massachusetts marriage laws do not condition receipt of public and private financial benefits to married individuals on a demonstration of financial dependence on each other; the benefits are available to married couples regardless of whether they mingle their finances or actually depend on each other for support.

The department suggests additional rationales for prohibiting same-sex couples from marrying. . . . It argues that broadening civil marriage to include same-sex couples will trivialize or destroy the institution of marriage as it has historically been fashioned. Certainly our decision today marks a significant change in the definition of marriage as it has been inherited from the common law, and understood by many societies for centuries. But it does not disturb the fundamental value of marriage in our society.

Here, the plaintiffs seek only to be married, not to undermine the institution of civil marriage. They do not want marriage abolished. They do not attack the binary nature of marriage, the consanguinity provisions, or any of the other gate-keeping provisions of the marriage licensing law. Recognizing the right of an individual to marry a person of the same sex will not diminish the validity or dignity of opposite-sex marriage, any more than recognizing the right of an individual to marry a person of a different race devalues the marriage of a person who marries someone of her own race. If anything, extending civil marriage to same-sex couples reinforces the importance of marriage to individuals and communities. That same-sex couples are willing to embrace marriage's solemn obligations of exclusivity, mutual support, and commitment to one another is a testament to the enduring place of marriage in our laws and in the human spirit.

It has been argued that, due to the State's strong interest in the institution of marriage as a stabilizing social structure, only the Legislature can control and define its boundaries. . . . We owe great deference to the Legislature to decide social and policy issues, but it is the traditional and settled role of courts to decide constitutional issues. . . .

The marriage ban works a deep and scarring hardship on a very real segment of the community for no rational reason. The absence of any reasonable relationship between, on the one hand, an absolute disqualification of same-sex couples who wish to enter into civil marriage and, on the other, protection of public health, safety, or general welfare, suggests that the marriage restriction is rooted in persistent prejudices against persons who are (or who are believed to be) homosexual. "The Constitution cannot control such prejudices but neither can it tolerate them. Private biases may be outside the reach of the law, but the law cannot, directly or indirectly, give them effect." *Palmore v. Sidoti*, 466 U.S. 429, 433 (1984). . . .

IV

Here, no one argues that striking down the marriage laws is an appropriate form of relief. . . . We face a problem similar to one that recently confronted the Court of Appeal for Ontario, the highest court of that Canadian province, when it considered the constitutionality of the same-sex marriage ban. . . . In holding that the limitation of civil marriage to opposite-sex couples violated the Charter, the Court of Appeal refined the common-law meaning of marriage. We concur with this remedy, which is entirely consonant with established principles of jurisprudence empowering a court to refine a common-law principle in light of evolving constitutional standards. . . .

We construe civil marriage to mean the voluntary union of two persons as spouses, to the exclusion of all others. This reformulation redresses the plaintiffs' constitutional injury and furthers the aim of marriage to promote stable, exclusive relationships. It advances the two legitimate State interests the department has identified: providing a stable setting for child rearing and conserving State resources. It leaves intact the Legislature's broad discretion to regulate marriage. . . .

. . . We declare that barring an individual from the protections, benefits, and obligations of civil marriage solely because that person would marry a person of the same sex violates the Massachusetts Constitution. . . . Entry of judgment shall be stayed for 180 days to permit the Legislature to take such action as it may deem appropriate in light of this opinion. . . .

So ordered.

Post-Case Follow-Up

In order to remedy the discrimination, the court in *Goodridge* concluded that the common law definition of marriage should be modified to mean "the voluntary union of two persons, as spouses, to the exclusion of all others," thus making Massachusetts the first state in the nation to permit same-sex couples to marry. Subsequent to *Goodridge*, the high courts in several other states concluded that denying same-sex couples the opportunity to marry deprives same-sex couples their right to equal protection under their respective state constitutions — an injury that, as stated by the Supreme Court of Connecticut, cannot, given "the history of pernicious discrimination faced by gay men and lesbians," be remedied by the "segregation of heterosexual and homosexual couples into separate institutions," thus effectively "relegating [same-sex couples] to an inferior status."

Goodridge v. Department of Public Health: Real Life Applications

1. Assume that shortly after the decision in *Goodridge* you have been asked by your state legislature how you believe that statute could have been worded to avoid the result in *Goodridge*, but still avoid recognizing the right of same-sex partners to marry. What are the statutory arguments that were successful with the court? How would the statute have to change to avoid those arguments?

2. Would your response to your state legislature be different if a state statute provided that all tangible benefits afforded married couples are also available to same-sex couples?

3. Katrina and Ulla are same-sex partners living in Massachusetts after the *Goodridge* decision. Katrina's employer provides health insurance to the spouse of married employees but not to domestic partners. Katrina and Ulla live in the same household and can demonstrate that they share expenses and are living in a marital type of relationship. They have no intention of getting married, but Ulla would still like to obtain the health insurance benefits. Is there any support in *Goodridge* to argue that Ulla is entitled to health insurance? What would be the employer's strongest arguments against extending benefits to non-married partners?

Ten years after *Goodridge*, the Supreme Court took up the issue of whether same-sex couples who were validly married under state law could constitutionally be denied federal benefits. In 2013, in *United States v. Windsor*, the Supreme Court invalidated Section 3 of DOMA, which, as discussed previously, defined marriage for purposes of federal law as being exclusively between a man and a woman. The decision thus paved the way for couples validly married under state law to receive federal benefits.

Case Preview

United States v. Windsor

Edith Windsor and Thea Spyer married in Canada in 2007. They resided in New York, which gave full faith and credit to same-sex marriages validly entered into in other states or foreign countries. When Thea Spyer died in 2009 and left her entire estate to Edith Windsor, Windsor attempted to claim a federal estate tax exemption for the surviving spouse. Her claim, which would have been available for marriages between opposite-sex couples, was denied. As a result, Edith Windsor paid $363,053 in estate taxes. She sought a refund from the Internal Review Service, which was denied.

As you read *Windsor*, consider the following:

1. Why does the Court find that Section 3 of DOMA violates the Equal Protection Clause?
2. How did DOMA treat differently relationships that the states treated as being the same?
3. Why does the Court limit its holding to marriages that are lawful under state law?

United States v. Windsor
570 U.S. 12 (2013)

Justice KENNEDY delivered the opinion of the Court.

Two women then resident in New York were married in a lawful ceremony in Ontario, Canada, in 2007. Edith Windsor and Thea Spyer returned to their home in New York City. When Spyer died in 2009, she left her entire estate to Windsor. Windsor sought to claim the estate tax exemption for surviving spouses. She was barred from doing so, however, by a federal law, the Defense of Marriage Act, which excludes a same-sex partner from the definition of "spouse" as that term is used in federal statutes. Windsor paid the taxes but filed suit to challenge the constitutionality of this provision. The United States District Court and the Court of Appeals ruled that this portion of the statute is unconstitutional and ordered the United States to pay Windsor a refund. This Court granted certiorari and now affirms the judgment in Windsor's favor.

In 1996, as some States were beginning to consider the concept of same-sex marriage and before any State had acted to permit it, Congress enacted the Defense of Marriage Act (DOMA), 110 Stat. 2419. DOMA contains two operative sections: Section 2, which has not been challenged here, allows States to refuse to recognize same-sex marriages performed under the laws of other States. See 28 U.S.C. §1738C.

Section 3 is at issue here. It amends the Dictionary Act in Title 1, §7, of the United States Code to provide a federal definition of "marriage" and "spouse." Section 3 of DOMA provides as follows:

"in determining the meaning of any Act of Congress, or of any ruling, regulation, or interpretation of the various administrative bureaus and agencies of the United States, the word 'marriage' means only a legal union between one man and one woman as husband and wife, and the word 'spouse' refers only to a person of the opposite sex who is a husband or a wife." 1 U.S.C. §7.

The definition provision does not by its terms forbid States from enacting laws permitting same-sex marriages or civil unions or providing state benefits to residents in that status. The enactment's comprehensive definition of marriage for purposes of all federal statutes and other regulations or directives covered by its terms, however, does control over 1,000 federal laws in which marital or spousal status is addressed as a matter of federal law.

Spyer died in February 2009, and left her entire estate to Windsor. Because DOMA denies federal recognition to same-sex spouses, Windsor did not qualify for the marital exemption from the federal estate tax, which excludes from taxation "any interest in property which passes or has passed from the decedent to his surviving spouse." 26 U.S.C. §2056(a). Windsor paid $363,053 in estate taxes and sought a refund. The Internal Revenue Service denied the refund, concluding that, under DOMA, Windsor was not a "surviving spouse." Windsor commenced this refund suit in the United States District Court for the Southern District of New York. She contended that DOMA violates the guarantee of equal protection, as applied to the Federal Government through the Fifth Amendment.

When at first Windsor and Spyer longed to marry, neither New York nor any other State granted them that right. After waiting some years, in 2007 they traveled to Ontario to be married there. It seems fair to conclude that, until recent years, many citizens had not even considered the possibility that two persons of the same sex might aspire to occupy the same status and dignity as that of a man and woman in lawful marriage. For marriage between a man and woman no doubt had been thought of by most people as essential to the very definition of that tem and to its role and function throughout the history of civilization. That belief, for many who long have held it, became even more urgent, more cherished when challenged. For others, however, came the beginnings of a new perspective, a new insight. Accordingly some States concluded that same-sex marriage ought to be given recognition and validity in the law for those same-sex couples who wish to define themselves by their commitment to each other. The limitation of lawful marriage to heterosexual couples, which for centuries had been deemed both necessary and fundamental, came to be seen in New York and certain other States as an unjust exclusion.

State laws defining and regulating marriage, of course, must respect the constitutional rights of persons, see, e.g., *Loving v. Virginia*, 388 U.S. 1 (1967); but, subject to those guarantees, "regulation of domestic relations" is "an area that has long been regarded as a virtually exclusive province of the States." *Sosna v. Iowa*, 419 U.S. 393, 404 (1976).

The recognition of civil marriages is central to state domestic relations law applicable to its residents and citizens. See *Williams v. North Carolina*, 317 U.S. 287, 298 (1942) ("Each state as a sovereign has a rightful and legitimate concern in the marital status of persons domiciled within its borders"). The definition of marriage is the foundation of the State's broader authority to regulate the subject of domestic relations with respect to the "[p]rotection of offspring, property interests, and the enforcement of marital responsibilities." Ibid. "[T]he states, at the time of the adoption of the Constitution, possessed full power over the subject of marriage and divorce . . . [and] the Constitution delegated no authority to the Government of the United States on the subject of marriage and divorce." *Haddock v. Haddock*, 201 U.S. 562, 575 (1906); see also *In re Burrus*, 136 U.S. 586, 593-594 (1890) ("The whole subject of the domestic relations of husband and wife, parent and child, belongs to the laws of the States and not to the laws of the United States").

Consistent with this allocation of authority, the Federal Government, through our history, has deferred to state-law policy decisions with respect to domestic relations.

Federal courts will not hear divorce and custody cases even if they arise in diversity because of "the virtually exclusive primacy . . . of the States in the regulation of domestic relations." Id., at 714 (Blackmun, J., concurring in judgment).

The significance of state responsibilities for the definition and regulation of marriage dates to the Nation's beginning; for "when the Constitution was adopted the common understanding was that the domestic relations of husband and wife and parent and child were matters reserved to the States." *Ohio ex rel. Popovici v. Agler*, 280 U.S. 379, 383-384 (1930). Marriage laws vary in some respects from State to State. For example, the required minimum age is 16 in Vermont, but only 13 in New Hampshire. Compare Vt. Stat. Ann., Tit. 18, §5142 (2012), with N.H. Rev. Stat. Ann. §457:4 (West Supp. 2012). Likewise the permissible degree of consanguinity can vary (most States permit first cousins to marry, but a handful — such as Iowa and Washington, see Iowa Code §595.19 (2009); Wash. Rev. Code §26.04.020 (2012) — prohibit the practice). But these rules are in every event consistent within each State.

Against this background DOMA rejects the long-established precept that the incidents, benefits, and obligations of marriage are uniform for all married couples within each State, though they may vary, subject to constitutional guarantees, from one State to the next. Despite these considerations, it is unnecessary to decide whether this federal intrusion on state power is a violation of the Constitution because it disrupts the federal balance. The State's power in defining the marital relation is of central relevance in this case quite apart from principles of federalism. Here the State's decision to give this class of persons the right to marry conferred upon them a dignity and status of immense import. When the State used its historic and essential authority to define the marital relation in this way, its role and its power in making the decision enhanced the recognition, dignity, and protection of the class in their own community. DOMA, because of its reach and extent, departs from this history and tradition of reliance on state law to define marriage. "'[D]iscriminations of an unusual character especially suggest careful consideration to determine whether they are obnoxious to the constitutional provision.'" *Romer v. Evans*, 517 U.S. 620, 633 (1996) (quoting *Louisville Gas & Elec. Co. v. Coleman*, 277 U.S. 32, 37-38 (1928)).

The Federal Government uses this state-defined class for the opposite purpose — to impose restrictions and disabilities. That result requires this Court now to address whether the resulting injury and indignity is a deprivation of an essential part of the liberty protected by the Fifth Amendment. What the State of New York treats as alike the federal law deems unlike by a law designed to injure the same class the State seeks to protect.

DOMA seeks to injure the very class New York seeks to protect. By doing so it violates basic due process and equal protection principles applicable to the Federal Government. See U.S. Const., Amdt. 5; *Bolling v. Sharpe*, 347 U.S. 497 (1954). The Constitution's guarantee of equality "must at the very least mean that a bare congressional desire to harm a politically unpopular group cannot" justify disparate treatment of that group. *Department of Agriculture v. Moreno*, 413 U.S. 528, 534-535 (1973). In determining whether a law is motived by an improper animus or purpose, "'[d]iscriminations of an unusual character'" especially require careful consideration. Supra, at 19 (quoting *Romer*, supra, at 633). DOMA cannot survive under these principles. The responsibility of the States for the regulation of domestic relations is an important indicator of the substantial societal impact the State's classifications have in the daily lives and customs of its people. DOMA's unusual deviation from the usual tradition of recognizing and accepting state definitions of marriage here operates to deprive same-sex couples of the benefits and responsibilities that come with the federal recognition of their marriages. This is strong evidence of a law having the purpose and effect of disapproval of that class. The avowed purpose and practical effect of the law here in question are to impose a disadvantage, a separate status, and so a stigma upon all who enter into same-sex marriages made lawful by the unquestioned authority of the States.

When New York adopted a law to permit same-sex marriage, it sought to eliminate inequality; but DOMA frustrates that objective through a system-wide enactment with no identified connection to any particular are of federal law. DOMA writes inequality into the entire United States Code. The particular case at hand concerns the estate tax, but DOMA is more than a simple determination of what should or should not be allowed as an estate tax refund. Among the over 1,000 statutes and numerous federal regulations that DOMA controls are laws pertaining to Social Security, housing, taxes, criminal sanctions, copyright, and veterans' benefits.

DOMA's principal effect is to identify a subset of state-sanctioned marriages and make them unequal. The principal purpose is to impose inequality, not for other reasons like governmental efficiency. Responsibilities, as well as rights, enhance the dignity and integrity of the person. And DOMA contrives to deprive some couples married under the laws of their State, but not other couples, of both rights and responsibilities. By creating two contradictory marriage regimes within the same State, DOMA forces same-sex couples to live as married for the purpose of state law but unmarried for the purpose of federal law, thus diminishing the stability and predictability of basic personal relations the State has found it proper to acknowledge and protect. By this dynamic DOMA undermines both the public and private significance of state-sanctioned same-sex marriages; for it tells those couples, and all the world, that their otherwise valid marriages are unworthy of federal recognition. This places same-sex couples in an unstable position of being in a second-tier marriage.

The differentiation demeans the couple whose moral and sexual choices the Constitution protects, see *Lawrence*, 539 U.S. 558, and whose relationship the State has sought to dignify. And it humiliates tens of thousands of children now being raised by same-sex couples. The law in question makes it even more difficult for the children to understand the integrity and closeness of their own family and its concord with other families in their community and in their daily lives.

What has been explained to this point should more than suffice to establish that the principal purpose and the necessary effect of this law are to demean those persons who are in a lawful same-sex marriage. This requires the Court to hold, as it now does, that DOMA is unconstitutional as a deprivation of the liberty of the person protected by the Fifth Amendment of the Constitution.

The class to which DOMA directs its restrictions and restraints are those persons who are joined in same sex marriages made lawful by the State. DOMA singles out a class of persons deemed by a State entitled to recognition and protection to enhance their own liberty. It imposes a disability on the class by refusing to acknowledge a status the State finds to be dignified and proper. DOMA instructs all federal officials, and indeed all persons with whom same-sex couples interact, including their own children, that their marriage is less worthy than the marriages of others. The federal statute is invalid, for no legitimate purpose overcomes the purpose and effect to disparage and to injure those whom the State, by its marriage laws, sought to protect in personhood and dignity. By seeking to displace this protection and treating those persons as living in marriages less respected than others, the federal statute is in violation of the Fifth Amendment. This opinion and its holding are confined to those lawful marriages.

The judgment of the Court of Appeals for the Second Circuit is affirmed.

Post-Case Follow-Up

Although *Windsor* only addressed the validity of the federal definition of marriage as contained within Section 3 of DOMA, and did not speak directly to the constitutionality of state marriage bans, the decision nonetheless accelerated the pace of change as state and federal courts relied upon the language in *Windsor* to strike down state marriage bans. Thus, for example, in concluding that "Virginia's same-sex marriage bans impermissibly infringe on its citizens' fundamental right to marry," the Fourth Circuit relied on *Windsor* for the proposition that laws that evince "disrespect for the 'moral and sexual choices' that accompany a same-sex couple's decision to marry" are constitutionally infirm. *Bostic v. Schaefer*, United States Court of Appeals for the Fourth Circuit, No. 14-1167, 20 & 37 (2014).

In a similar vein, in striking down that state's marriage ban, the federal trial court in Colorado cited *Windsor* for the underlying principle that laws that "degrade or demean" same-sex couples by withholding recognition of their marriages violate the constitutional guarantee of equal protection. *Geiger v. Kitzhaber*, United States District Court for the District of Oregon, Case No. 6:13-cv-01834-MC, 12 (2014).

The importance of *Windsor* cannot be underestimated. *Windsor* signaled a major change in the legal atmosphere as it considered the institution of marriage and the acknowledgment of legal rights by same-sex couples.

United States v. Windsor: Real Life Applications

1. You are an attorney in a small firm. The law in your state provides that marriage is between a man and a woman. The *United States v. Windsor* case has just been decided, and a client wishes to challenge the law because he wishes to marry his partner. The managing partner has asked you to advise her if there are grounds to challenge the law based upon *Windsor*. What arguments from *Windsor* can be used to challenge the law? In what ways is *Windsor* limited in its holding?

2. Would your answer to Question 1 change if the client was legally married in another state and now wants to know if the marriage will be recognized in your state based upon *Windsor*?

Building upon the cases of *Windsor* and *Perry*, challenges to state laws that prohibited marriages between same-sex partners began to mount. However, the results were often mixed, and even successful challenges in the lower courts were overturned on appeal. Thus, it would take the Supreme Court to determine the constitutionality of state laws denying same-sex couples the right to marry or to have their marriages recognized if lawfully performed in another state. The opportunity for the Supreme Court to address this issue came in 2014 when the Sixth Circuit held that states did not have a constitutional obligation to recognize same-sex marriages. The Sixth Circuit's ruling was directly adverse to the rulings in the Fourth, Seventh, Ninth, and Tenth Circuits, which had either recognized the constitutional rights of same-sex couples, or had allowed, as in *Hollingsworth v. Perry*, state court rulings to stand.

Case Preview

Obergefell v. Hodges

Fourteen same-sex couples and two men whose same-sex partners were deceased brought actions against state officials in their respective home states (Michigan, Kentucky, Ohio, and Tennessee) claiming the state officials violated the Fourteenth Amendment by denying them the right to marry or to have their marriages, lawfully performed in another State, recognized. State law in Michigan, Kentucky, Ohio, and Tennessee defined marriage as between a man and a woman.

The United States District Court in each of their home states ruled in their favor. The cases were consolidated before the Sixth Circuit Court of Appeals. The Sixth Circuit reversed holding that a state does not have a constitutional obligation to license same-sex marriages or to recognize same-sex marriages lawfully performed in another state.

As you read *Obergefell v. Hodges*, consider the following:

1. What is the liberty interest of same-sex couples that the Court seeks to protect?
2. How does the Court use *Loving v. Virginia* to justify its decision?
3. Why does the Court dismiss the assumption that the right to marry is presumed to require a relationship between opposite-sex partners?
4. What are the four principles used to demonstrate that marriage as a fundamental right applies to same-sex couples?

Hollingsworth v. Perry

In 2013, at about the same time as the *Windsor* case, the Supreme Court decided *Hollingsworth v. Perry*, 133 S. Ct. 2652 (2013). The case has an interesting procedural history. Proposition 8 was passed by voters in California in 2008. Proposition 8 defined marriage as the union between a man and a woman, thereby barring same-sex marriages in California. In 2009, two same-sex couples filed suit challenging the constitutionality of Proposition 8. The United States District Court held that Proposition 8 violated the Equal Protection and Due Process Clauses of the Fourteenth Amendment. When the state refused to appeal the ruling, the ruling was appealed by proponents of Proposition 8 to the Ninth Circuit. The Ninth Circuit affirmed the District Court's ruling. The proponents appealed to the United States Supreme Court. The Court ruled that the plaintiffs lacked standing to challenge the ruling of the Ninth Circuit Court of Appeals. The result meant that the previous decision, which ruled that it was unconstitutional to limit marriage to heterosexual couples, was allowed to stand.

Obergefell v. Hodges
576 U.S. ___, 135 S. Ct. 2584 (2015)

Justice KENNEDY delivered the opinion of the Court.

The Constitution promises liberty to all within its reach, a liberty that includes certain specific rights that allow persons, within a lawful realm, to define and express their identity. The petitioners in these cases seek to find that liberty by marrying someone of the same sex and having their marriages deemed lawful on the same terms and conditions as marriages between persons of the opposite sex.

[The Court addressed procedural history of these particular cases as well as the history of marriage in the United States.]

III

Under the Due Process Clause of the Fourteenth Amendment, no State shall "deprive any person of life, liberty, or property, without due process of law." The fundamental liberties protected by this Clause include most of the rights enumerated in the Bill of Rights. See *Duncan v. Louisiana*, 391 U.S. 145, 147-149 (1968). In addition these liberties extend to certain personal choices central to individual dignity and autonomy, including intimate choices that define personal identity and beliefs. See, e.g., *Eisenstadt v. Baird*, 405 U.S. 438, 453 (1972); *Griswold v. Connecticut*, 381 U.S. 479, 484-486 (1965).

. . .

Applying these established tenets, the Court has long held the right to marry is protected by the Constitution. In *Loving v. Virginia*, 388 U.S. 1, 12 (1967), which invalidated bans on interracial unions, a unanimous Court held marriage is "one of the vital personal rights essential to the orderly pursuit of happiness by free men." The Court reaffirmed that holding in *Zablocki v. Redhail*, 434 U.S. 374 (1978), which held the right to marry was burdened by a law prohibiting fathers who were behind on child support from marrying. The Court again applied this principle in *Turner v. Safley*, 482 U.S. 78, 95 (1987), which held the right to marry was abridged by regulations limiting the privilege of prison inmates to marry. Over time and in other contexts, the Court has reiterated that the right to marry is fundamental under the Due Process Clause.

It cannot be denied that this Court's cases describing the right to marry presumed a relationship involving opposite-sex partners. The Court, like many institutions, has made assumptions defined by the world and time of which it is a part. This was evident in *Baker v. Nelson*, 409 U.S. 810 , 93 S. Ct. 37, 34 L. Ed. 2d 65, a one-line summary decision issued in 1972, holding the exclusion of same-sex couples from marriage did not present a substantial federal question.

. . .

This analysis compels the conclusion that same-sex couples may exercise the right to marry. The four principles and traditions to be discussed demonstrate that the reasons marriage is fundamental under the Constitution apply with equal force to same-sex couples.

A first premise of the Court's relevant precedents is that the right to personal choice regarding marriage is inherent in the concept of individual autonomy. This abiding connection between marriage and liberty is why *Loving* invalidated interracial marriage bans under the Due Process Clause. See 388 U.S., at 12, 87 S. Ct. 1817, 18 L. Ed. 2d 1010; see also *Zablocki*, supra, at 384, 98 S. Ct. 673, 54 L. Ed. 2d 618 (observing *Loving* held "the right to marry is of fundamental importance for all individuals"). . . .

The nature of marriage is that, through its enduring bond, two persons together can find other freedoms, such as expression, intimacy, and spirituality. This is true for all persons, whatever their sexual orientation. See *Windsor*, 570 U.S., at ___- ___, 133 S. Ct. 2675, 186 L. Ed. 2d at 828. There is dignity in the bond between two men or two women who seek to marry and in their autonomy to make such profound choices. Cf. *Loving*, supra, at 12, 87 S. Ct. 1817, 18 L. Ed. 2d 1010 ("[T]he freedom to marry, or not marry, a person of another race resides with the individual and cannot be infringed by the State").

A second principle in this Court's jurisprudence is that the right to marry is fundamental because it supports a two-person union unlike any other in its importance to the committed individuals. This point was central to *Griswold v. Connecticut*, which held the Constitution protects the right of married couples to use contraception. 381 U.S., at 485, 85 S. Ct. 1678, 14 L. Ed. 2d 510. Suggesting that marriage is a right "older than the Bill of Rights," *Griswold* described marriage this way: "Marriage is a coming together for better or for worse, hopefully enduring, and intimate to the degree of being sacred. . . ."

A third basis for protecting the right to marry is that it safeguards children and families and thus draws meaning from related rights of childrearing, procreation, and education. See *Pierce v. Society of Sisters*, 268 U.S. 510 (1925); *Meyer*, 262 U.S., at 399. The Court has recognized these connections by describing the varied rights as a unified whole: "[T]he right to 'marry, establish a home and bring up children' is a central part of the liberty protected by the Due Process Clause." *Zablocki*, 434 U.S., at 384. Under the laws of the several States, some of marriage's protections for children and families are material. But marriage also confers more profound benefits. By giving recognition and legal structure to their parents' relationship, marriage allows children "to understand the integrity and closeness of their own family and its concord with other families in their community and in their daily lives." *Windsor*, supra, at ___, 133 S. Ct. 2675, 186 L. Ed. 2d at 828. Marriage also affords the permanency and stability important to children's best interests.

. . .

Fourth and finally, this Court's cases and the Nation's traditions make clear that marriage is a keystone of our social order.

. . .

[J]ust as a couple vows to support each other, so does society pledge to support the couple, offering symbolic recognition and material benefits to protect and nourish the union. Indeed, while the States are in general free to vary the benefits they confer on all married couples, they have throughout our history made marriage the basis for an expanding list of governmental rights, benefits, and responsibilities. These aspects of marital status include: taxation; inheritance and property rights; rules of intestate succession; spousal privilege in the law of evidence; hospital access; medical decisionmaking authority; adoption rights; the rights and benefits of survivors; birth and death certificates; professional ethics rules; campaign finance restrictions; workers' compensation benefits; health insurance; and child custody, support, and visitation rules. . . .

There is no difference between same- and opposite-sex couples with respect to this principle.

. . .

The right to marry is fundamental as a matter of history and tradition, but rights come not from ancient sources alone. They rise, too, from a better informed understanding of how constitutional imperatives define a liberty that remains urgent in our own era.

. . .

These considerations lead to the conclusion that the right to marry is a fundamental right inherent in the liberty of the person, and under the Due Process and Equal Protection Clauses of the Fourteenth Amendment couples of the same-sex may not be deprived of that right and that liberty. The Court now holds that same-sex couples may exercise the fundamental right to marry. No longer may this liberty be denied to them. . . .

. . .

No union is more profound than marriage, for it embodies the highest ideals of love, fidelity, devotion, sacrifice, and family. In forming a marital union, two people become something greater than once they were. As some of the petitioners in these cases demonstrate, marriage embodies a love that may endure even past death. It would misunderstand these men and women to say they disrespect the idea of marriage. Their plea is that they do respect it, respect it so deeply that they seek to find its fulfillment for themselves. Their hope is not to be condemned to live in loneliness, excluded from one of civilization's oldest institutions. They ask for equal dignity in the eyes of the law. The Constitution grants them that right.

The judgment of the Court of Appeals for the Sixth Circuit is reversed.

Post-Case Follow-Up

Obergefell made national news the minute the decision was handed down. Across the country, couples stood in line to obtain marriage licenses in the states that previously would not issue them to same-sex couples. The decision now raises, however, a number of other issues, such as whether couples who had previously entered into civil unions must now confirm that union by marriage in order to obtain the same benefits as married parties, and how premarital agreements, adoptions, and divorces are affected. We will explore these topics in subsequent chapters.

In addition, the case of Kim Davis, the county clerk in Rowan, Kentucky who refused to issue marriage licenses to same-sex couples due to her religious beliefs, made headlines in 2015. When Ms. Davis refused to issue licenses, an action by the ACLU was brought. The Eastern District of Kentucky, in *Miller v. Davis* (Civil Action No. 15-44-DLB), ordered her to issue the licenses. When she refused she was jailed for contempt. The matter was ultimately resolved by Ms. Davis agreeing to not interfere with the deputy clerks who were following the court order to issue licenses. The Davis case is another example of some of the constitutional issues (freedom to marry versus freedom of religion) that remain unresolved after *Obergefell*.

Obergefell v. Hodges: Real Life Applications

1. Margo and Maria live in a state that prior to *Obergefell v. Hodges* did not recognize same-sex marriages. They did, however, enter into a civil union and registered their civil union with their county clerk as civil unions were recognized. They have now come to you to seek your legal advice. They would like to know if their civil union is still valid, or do they have to go through a marriage ceremony to be considered legally married. What do you tell Margo and Maria?

2. Kasper and Bryce were married in New York before their home state of Arizona, where they lived before and after the New York marriage ceremony, recognized

same-sex marriages under *Obergefell v. Hodges*. Bryce has come to you and wants to know if they need to perform another ceremony now in Arizona?

3. Your firm represents a local legislator who would like to advance the idea that, based on *Obergefell v. Hodges*, the state law prohibiting marriage between first cousins should be abolished. Is there any part of the Court's reasoning in *Obergefell* that can be used to support abolishment of the law?

B. STATE REGULATION OF ENTRY INTO MARRIAGE: PROCEDURAL REQUIREMENTS

Although, as we have seen, the historic role of states in structuring marriage has been diminished over time, state law still sets the procedural requirements that must be satisfied in order for a marriage to be valid. Accordingly, it is actually the compliance with state licensing procedures, rather than saying "I do," that makes one married in the eyes of the law.

1. Obtaining a Marriage License

Although the requirements for obtaining a license vary from state to state, the differences are generally fairly minor. Allowing for variation, the following discussion provides an overview of the steps a couple must typically follow in order to establish a valid marriage.

First, a couple must obtain a marriage license. See Exhibit 2.1.

Licenses are usually issued by a county or municipal officer, such as a clerk. Application is made by providing information under oath about age, prior marriages, and possibly also the legal relationship between the intended spouses. In some states, the clerk simply approves or denies the license based on the information as it appears on the face of the application. In other states, the clerk has some responsibility to assess whether the information provided is correct — for example, by requiring the production of a birth certificate or a divorce decree. This application process is a mechanism for enforcing a state's substantive restrictions on who can marry, as the information enables a clerk to determine if, for example, the applicants are underage, married to someone else, or close relatives. Disclosure of these circumstances would result in denial of the license. It also enables a state to collect vital statistics about its citizens as it does with birth and death certificates. Additionally, all states now require both parties to provide their Social Security numbers, which, in the event of divorce or separation, can be used to track down an absent parent for child support collection purposes.

Most states impose a waiting period, ranging from 24 hours to 5 days, between the time of application and the issuance of the license, although in some states, the waiting period is between issuance of the license and performance of the ceremony. It is hoped that this pause will deter couples from rushing into marriage, as it gives them time to reflect on the seriousness of their decision.

EXHIBIT 2.1   **Marriage License**

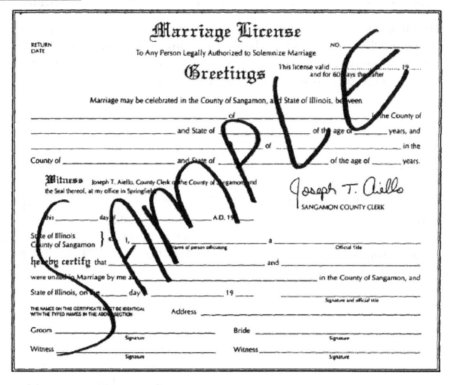

Although most states no longer require blood testing for venereal disease, or premarital physical examinations to address eugenic concerns about the transmission of hereditary defects, these kinds of requirements became very common at the turn of the nineteenth century as a way to "dramatically circumscribe who was eligible to participate in the institution of marriage."[2] States thus barred the "feeble minded," the "insane," and those suffering from a variety of aliments including epilepsy and venereal disease from marrying in order to safeguard the genetic fitness of the nation's citizenry.[3] As eugenic-based laws faded into disrepute toward mid-century, these types of premarital requirements came to function more as a way to alert a spouse to medical facts that he or she might not know about the intended spouse rather than as actual marriage bars. As of today, most states have eliminated these requirements altogether, due, at least in part, to the recognition that they serve little purpose in an era in which premarital sex is not uncommon. However, some states have instituted other types of premarital procedures, such as the provision of educational material regarding birth control, counseling for couples under a certain age, and information regarding the availability of HIV/AIDs testing.

---

[2]Mathew J. Lindsay, Reproducing a Fit Citizenry: Dependency, Eugenics, and the Law of Marriage in the United States, 1860-1920, 23 Law & Soc. Inquiry 541, 542 (1998).
[3]*Id.* at 563-578.

2. The Marriage Ceremony and Proxy Marriages

Once the license is issued, a marriage ceremony must be performed by an authorized person. States usually authorize religious leaders as well as civil officers, such as justices of the peace, to perform marriage ceremonies. Beyond perhaps requiring an oath or acknowledgment of consent to become husband and wife, the presence of witnesses, and a statement by the officiator to the effect that the parties are now lawfully wed, states do not generally regulate the form, content, or manner of the ceremony. Following the ceremony, the license must be recorded in a timely manner. This is usually done by the person who officiated at the wedding.

In a variant on the typical wedding ceremony at which both spouses are required to be present, a handful of states permit what are known as proxy marriages, where one party is represented by an agent rather than being physically present, with Montana permitting double proxy marriages if one party is a Montana resident or a member of the armed services. Although proxy marriage has a long history in the United States, it has mostly been used during times of war — perhaps most commonly when a woman finds that she is pregnant after her fiancé has been deployed. *See* Andrea B. Carroll, Reviving Proxy Marriage, 76 Brook. L. Rev. 455, 493 (2011).

If valid in the state where entered into, proxy marriages are generally recognized as valid by other states, and the couple is regarded as married under federal law. Based on a longstanding suspicion that proxy marriages may be used for the purpose of evading immigration laws, federal law requires post-marriage consummation in order for a proxy marriage to be recognized as valid for immigration purposes.[4] Thus, if an U.S. citizen is marrying a foreign national by proxy, the couple must meet the requirements under the Immigration and Nationality Act that they physically be together after the proxy marriage. In addition, they must attest to the consummation of the wedding in their immigration application.

Proxy Marriage Wedding Planning Services

With so many members of the armed forces currently stationed overseas, a growing number of business offer to provide a full range of proxy marriage wedding

Proxy marriage website
Courtesy of Proxy Marriage / A Big Sky Event

planning services in states where they are allowed. These are usually offered at a flat fee, and it is not uncommon for active-duty members of the United States military to receive a discount. In addition to providing and reviewing all forms to ensure that state requirements are met, the fee includes the services of an officiant, often a nondenominational minister or judge, and a stand-in proxy for the bride or groom.

---

[4]*See* Lucas I. Quass, Proxy Marriages and the Widow Penalty: Excluding Alien-Widows of Fallen Soldiers, 20 S. Cal. Rev. L. & Soc. Just. 501 (2011).

3. Consequences of the Failure to Comply with a Licensing Requirement

On occasion a question arises as to the validity of a marriage where there has been a technical failure to comply with a preliminary requirement, such as that the parties failed to obtain a proper marriage license or that the ceremony was performed by an individual who turns out not be qualified to do so under state law. In many states where there is no express statutory language to the contrary, the public policy in favor of upholding marriages will override the irregularity, as occurred in the following case.

Case Preview

Carabetta v. Carabetta

In *Carabetta*, the court addressed the issue of whether the parties had a valid marriage. The parties did not dispute that they had exchanged marital vows before a priest at their church and admitted that they had never obtained a marriage license. The lower court dismissed the wife's petition for dissolution of marriage on the grounds that there was never a valid marriage. The wife appealed this decision. The decision is an example of how courts view the requirement of a marriage license. All states have laws relating to a license. However, whether the failure to obtain a license is requirement that voids the marriage or a formality that is purely regulatory in nature and will not void the marriage may differ from state to state. *Carabetta* represents the rule followed in the majority of the states.

As you read *Carabetta*, consider the following:

1. What were the two requirements under Connecticut state law to have a valid marriage?
2. Why did the plaintiff believe the court should ignore one of the requirements?
3. Why did the court believe the requirement for a license did not invalidate the marriage?

Carabetta v. Carabetta
438 A.2d 109 (Conn. 1980)

Neither the plaintiff nor the defendant presently disputes the facts found in the trial court's memorandum of decision, which establish the following. The plaintiff and the defendant exchanged marital vows before a priest in the rectory of Our Lady of Mt. Carmel Church of Meriden, on August 25, 1955, according to the rite of the Roman Catholic Church, although they had failed to obtain a marriage license. Thereafter they lived together as husband and wife, raising a family of four children, all of whose birth certificates listed the defendant as their father. Until the present action, the defendant had no memory or recollection of ever having denied that the plaintiff and the defendant were married.

The issue before us is whether, under Connecticut law, despite solemnization according to an appropriate religious ceremony, a marriage is void where there has been noncompliance with the statutory requirement of a marriage license. This is a question of first impression in this state. The trial court held that failure to obtain a marriage license was a flaw fatal to the creation of a legally valid marriage and that the court therefore lacked subject matter jurisdiction over an action for dissolution. We disagree with the court's premise and hence with its conclusion.

The determinants for a legally valid marriage are to be found in the provisions of our statutes. "At least since *Maynard v. Hill*, 125 U.S. 190, 210-14, 8 S. Ct. 723, 31 L. Ed. 654 (1888), it has been clear that the legislature has plenary power to determine the circumstances under which a marital relationship is created and terminated. *Morgan v. Morgan*, 103 Conn. 189, 195, 130 A. 254 (1925); *Starr v. Pease*, 8 Conn. 541, 546-47 (1831)." *Joy v. Joy*, 178 Conn. 254, 256, 423 A.2d 895 (1979). Although a marital relationship is in its origins contractual, depending as it does upon the consent of the parties, "a contract of marriage is *sui generis*. It is simply introductory to the creation of a *status*, and what that *status* is the law determines." *Gould v. Gould*, 78 Conn. 242, 245, 61 A. 604 (1905); *Hames v. Hames*, 163 Conn. 588, 592-93, 316 A.2d 379 (1972); *Perlstein v. Perlstein*, 152 Conn. 152, 156, 204 A.2d 909 (1964).

In determining the status of a contested marriage, we are bound therefore to examine with care the relevant legislative enactments that determine its validity. Such an examination must be guided by the understanding that some legislative commandments, particularly those affecting the validity of a marriage, are directory rather than mandatory. "The policy of the law is strongly opposed to regarding an attempted marriage . . . entered into in good faith, believed by one or both of the parties to be legal, and followed by cohabitation, to be void." *Hames v. Hames*, supra, 599.

The governing statutes at the time of the purported marriage between these parties contained two kinds of regulations concerning the requirements for a legally valid marriage. One kind of regulation concerned substantive requirements determining those eligible to be married. Thus General Statutes (Rev. 1949) §7301 declared the statutorily defined degrees of consanguinity within which a "marriage shall be void." As this court has indicated in *Hames v. Hames*, supra, 598, this substantive condition is not necessarily exclusive; lack of consent to a marriage, for example, would also be a substantive defect, derived from the common law, sufficient to avoid a marriage. For present purposes, it is enough to observe that, on this appeal, no such substantive defect has been alleged or proven. The other kind of regulation concerns the formalities prescribed by the state for the effectuation of a legally valid marriage. These required formalities, in turn, are of two sorts: a marriage license and a solemnization. In *Hames v. Hames*, supra, 599, we interpreted our statutes not to make void a marriage consummated after the issuance of a license but deficient for want of due solemnization. Today we examine the statutes in the reverse case, a marriage duly solemnized but deficient for want of a marriage license.

As to licensing, the governing statute in 1955 was a section entitled "Marriage licenses." It provided, in subsection (a): "No persons shall be joined in marriage until both have joined in an application . . . for a license for such marriage." Its only provision for the consequence of noncompliance with the license requirement was contained in subsection (e): ". . . any person who shall join any persons in marriage without having received such [license] shall be fined not more than one hundred dollars." General Statutes (Rev. 1949) §7302, as amended by §1280b (1951 Sup.) and by §2250c (1953 Sup.). Neither this section, nor any other, described as void a marriage celebrated without a license.

As to solemnization, the governing section, entitled "Who may join persons in marriage," provided in 1955: "All judges and justices of the peace may join persons in marriage . . . and all ordained or licensed clergymen belonging to this state or any other state so long as they continue in the work of the ministry may join persons in marriage and all marriages attempted to be celebrated by any other person shall be void; but all marriages which shall be solemnized according to the forms and usages of any religious denomination in this state shall be valid." General Statutes (Rev. 1949) §7306, as amended by §1281b (1951 Sup.) and by §2251c (1953 Sup.). Although solemnization is not at issue in the case before us, this language is illuminating since it demonstrates that the legislature has on occasion exercised its power to declare expressly that failure to observe some kinds of formalities, e.g., the celebration of a marriage by a person not authorized by this section to do so, renders a marriage void. We have enforced the plain mandate of this injunction. *State ex rel. Felson v. Allen,* 129 Conn. 427, 431, 29 A.2d 306 (1942).

In the absence of express language in the governing statute declaring a marriage void for failure to observe a statutory requirement, this court has held in an unbroken line of cases since *Gould v. Gould,* 78 Conn. 242, 247, 61 A. 604 (1905), that such a marriage, though imperfect, is dissoluble rather than void. *Hames v. Hames,* supra, 598; *Perlstein v. Perlstein,* 152 Conn. 152, 157-58, 204 A.2d 909 (1964); *Vendetto v. Vendetto,* 115 Conn. 303, 305, 161 A. 392 (1932). We see no reason to import into the language «[n]o persons shall be joined in marriage until [they have applied for] a license,» a meaning more drastic than that assigned in *Gould v. Gould,* supra, to the statute that then provided that "[n]o man and woman, either of whom is epileptic . . . shall intermarry." Although the state may well have a legitimate interest in the health of those who are about to marry, *Gould v. Gould* held that the legislature would not be deemed to have entirely invalidated a marriage contracted in violation of such health requirements unless the statute itself expressly declared the marriage to be void. Then as now, the legislature had chosen to use the language of voidness selectively, applying it to some but not to all of the statutory requirements for the creation of a legal marriage. Now as then, the legislature has the competence to choose to sanction those who solemnize a marriage without a marriage license rather than those who marry without a marriage license. In sum, we conclude that the legislature's failure expressly to characterize as void a marriage properly celebrated without a license means that such a marriage is not invalid.

The plaintiff argues strenuously that our statutes, far from declaring void a marriage solemnized without a license, in fact validate such a marriage whenever it has been solemnized by a religious ceremony. The plaintiff calls our attention to the language of §7306, as amended, that "all marriages . . . solemnized according to the forms and usages of any religious denomination in this state shall be valid." To the extent that this language suggests greater validity for a marriage solemnized by a religious ceremony than for one solemnized by a civil ceremony, it is inconsistent with other provisions of the statutes with regard to solemnization and licensing. It has long been clear that, under our laws, all authority to join parties in matrimony is basically secular. In *Hames v. Hames,* supra, 594-95, we recently reaffirmed the holding of *Goshen v. Stonington,* 4 Conn. 209, 218-19 (1822), that "[a] clergyman in the administration of marriage, is a public civil officer, and in relation to this subject, is not at all distinguished from a judge . . . or a justice of the peace, in the performance of the same duty." Neither counsel nor this court has been able to discover the legislative history attending the enactment of this puzzling language. Whatever may be its antecedents, for present purposes it is sufficient to note that §7306 at the very least reinforces our conclusion that the marriage in the case before us is not void.

The conclusion that a ceremonial marriage contracted without a marriage license is not null and void finds support, furthermore, in the decisions in other jurisdictions. . . . In the majority of states, unless the licensing statute plainly makes an unlicensed marriage invalid, "the cases find the policy favoring valid marriages sufficiently strong to justify upholding the unlicensed ceremony. This seems the correct result. Most such cases arise long after the parties have acted upon the assumption that they are married, and no useful purpose is served by avoiding the long-standing relationship. Compliance with the licensing laws can better be attained by safeguards operating before the license is issued, as by a more careful investigation by the issuing authority or the person marrying the parties." Clark, Domestic Relations, p. 41 (1968).

Since the marriage that the trial court was asked to dissolve was not void, the trial court erred in granting the motion to dismiss for lack of jurisdiction over the subject matter. We need not decide whether the plaintiff's cause of action should have been an action for annulment rather than an action for dissolution. That question should have been raised by a motion to strike; see Practice Book, 1978, §152; not by a motion to dismiss for lack of subject matter jurisdiction. *Hames v. Hames,* supra, 598-99; *Perlstein v. Perlstein,* supra, 155. In either case the trial court had subject matter jurisdiction.

There is error, the judgment is set aside and the case is remanded for further proceedings in accordance with this opinion.

Post-Case Follow-Up

The plaintiff in *Carabetta* sought a dissolution of a marriage that the lower court felt never existed. Although it may have been easy for the plaintiff to simply agree that the marriage was invalid, this may have caused other problems for the plaintiff. For example, we are not told whether there are children of the marriage, whether alimony or child support is being sought, or whether there is substantial property that was acquired during the "marriage" that needs to be divided. As we have seen in the context of equality for same-sex couples, marriage bestows a number of benefits that are not available to unmarried couples. Accordingly, there may have been economic reasons why the plaintiff wanted to have the marriage dissolved, versus just voided.

The court in *Carabetta* does not address these issues, but instead focuses on the fact that the license is merely a formality that does not void a marriage. The court finds support in the fact that the statute does not specifically declare the marriage invalid, but merely requires a fine for non-compliance. The court also appears to find persuasive the fact that the parties acted on the assumption that there was a marriage and that no purpose is served by voiding a marriage.

Carabetta v. Carabetta: Real Life Applications

1. Harvey and Wanda started dating in 2005. In 2007, Harvey learned that his company was transferring him overseas for a six-month assignment and that he had to leave within one week. The law in their state requires both a solemnization of the marriage before someone authorized to perform marriages and a license. There is also a ten-day waiting period between issuance of the license and the solemnization of the marriage. Harvey and Wanda decided that they wanted to marry before Harvey transferred, so they went to the minister of their church and had the ceremony performed. They did not obtain a license. Harvey returned six months later, and Harvey and Wanda have lived as husband and wife ever since. Wanda now seeks a divorce and comes to you asking whether she has a valid marriage. What do you tell Wanda?

2. Would your answer to Question 1 be different if the state law regarding licenses specifically indicated that a marriage without a license is invalid?

3. Would your answer to Question 1 be different if Harvey and Wanda had not held themselves out as being married?

In states that recognize common law marriage (see below), another curative approach to the presence of procedural irregularities is to simply regard the relationship as a common law marriage as distinct from a ceremonial marriage, which, as discussed below, is a distinction without a real difference. Other jurisdictions have adopted a variety of saving or curative devices that permit formal recognition of a marriage in the absence of a valid ceremony.

One such device is the presumption in favor of marriage according to which purported marriages are assumed valid and will be treated as such unless the party challenging the marriage can prove its nonexistence. At a minimum, that party must prove that a ceremony was not held anywhere — a difficult matter to accomplish. Another saving device is marriage by estoppel or ratification whereby a party who has held him- or herself out as married will be precluded from then denying the existence of the marriage even in the absence of a valid ceremony. The putative spouse doctrine also functions as a saving device. According to this doctrine, when a marriage is celebrated and one or both of the parties is ignorant about an existing impediment to the formation of a valid marriage, the marriage becomes valid upon removal of the impediment. There may also be an additional requirement of a good faith belief in the validity of the marriage on the part of at least one spouse at the time the impediment is removed.

4. Common Law Marriage

A common law marriage is one that is created by the conduct of the parties in the absence of a formal ceremony. This was a well-established English practice, and most American colonies accepted common law marriage as a practical reality in a new country whose scattered populace made access to religious and civil officials difficult. However, by the close of the nineteenth century, common law marriage had come under increasing attack by an organized marriage law reform movement. Convinced that the modern American family had lost its moral footing, activists argued that overly relaxed marriage and divorce laws were contributing to social decay and promiscuity. Reformers feared that by treating these "irregular" relationships like true marriages, the law was condoning immoral conduct, especially on the part of women, as it was mostly economically dependent wives who sought to establish the existence of a common law marriage following the death of their spouses. *See* Michael Grossberg, Governing the Hearth 83-95 (1985).

As a result of these challenges coupled with the increasingly urban nature of the country, which made it easier for most couples to find an approved officiant to preside over their wedding, common law marriage began to lose favor. Accordingly, by 1900, only about half the states permitted common law marriage. These numbers continued to dwindle over the course of the twentieth century, and today only a small number of states and the District of Columbia allow common law marriages. Joanna L. Grossman and Lawrence M. Friedman, Inside the Castle: Law and the Family in Twentieth Century America 80-81 (2011).

Where still permitted, establishment of a valid common law marriage generally requires proof of three elements:

- a mutual agreement to become husband and wife (or, as discussed below, possibly now husband and husband or wife and wife);
- cohabitation, and
- reputation in the community as husband and wife. (In some states, this third element is expressed as a requirement that the parties hold themselves out as husband and wife.)

Because it can be difficult to prove that the parties agreed to become husband and wife, especially since many disputes over whether a valid common law marriage existed arise after the death of one partner, some courts will infer agreement from the fact of cohabitation and reputation, thus obviating the need for direct proof.

Given that common law marriage pre-dates the marriage equality movement, most statutes as well as cases not surprisingly speak in terms of the formation of a common law marriage between persons who hold themselves out as and/or establish a reputation in the community as a *husband* and *wife*. So the question has recently presented itself as to whether a same-sex couple can establish a common law marriage in a state that recognizes both, such as Iowa, New Hampshire, or Rhode Island, as well as the District of Columbia. Although to date there do not appear to be any decisions on this issue, the answer may turn on whether the state marriage laws now employ gender-neutral language, as is the case in Rhode Island, whose marriage codification law reads as follows:

> Marriage is the legally recognized union of two (2) people. Terms relating to the marital relationship or familial relationships shall be construed consistently with this section for all purposes throughout the law, whether in the context of statute, administrative or court rule, policy, common law, or any other source of civil law.[5]

Once a common law marriage is established, the parties are considered married for all intents and purposes. They are entitled to all the benefits afforded to spouses, and dissolution of the relationship requires the filing of a divorce action. Once created, the status cannot be informally terminated. Accordingly, it is very important to distinguish common law marriage from "mere" cohabiting relationships; cohabitation may give rise to certain entitlements, but it does not lead to the creation of a spousal relationship.

When a couple establishes a valid common law marriage in a state that allows them, their marriage will be recognized elsewhere so long as the parties met the requirements of their home state. This conforms to the general rule that a validly contracted marriage will be recognized in all states, including a state that it could not have been entered into in the first place, unless it is in contravention of that state's public policy. The question of recognition becomes more complex when a couple from a state that does not allow common law marriage spends time in a second state that does allow it, satisfies the requirements for establishing a common law marriage there, and then returns to their home state. Some states will not recognize the marriage unless the parties had actually established a new domicile in the second state. Other states take a looser view and will extend recognition simply based on visits made to a jurisdiction that allows common law marriage. Still others take a middle position and will accept the marriage if the parties had sufficient contact with the second state to give rise to evidence of their relationship and reputation in that community.

---

[5]R.I. Gen. Laws, Chapter 15-1-1. *See* Peter Nicolas, Common Law Same-Sex Marriage, 43 Conn. L. Rev. 931 (2011), and Same-Sex Common Law Marriage and Social Security Dependents & Survivor Benefits, www.nolo.com/legal-encyclopedia (accessed June 8, 2016).

Case Preview

Jennings v. Hurt

Jennings v. Hurt is an example of the problems courts encounter in trying to determine whether a valid common law marriage exists. The plaintiff, Sandra Jennings, brought an action against the actor William Hurt claiming she was his common law wife. In order to prove that a common law marriage existed, the court was required to look at the evidence that the parties presented to prove the parties held themselves out as husband and wife.

As you read *Jennings v. Hurt*, consider the following:

1. What evidence does Jennings present to show she was Hurt's common law wife?
2. What evidence does Hurt present to show that he was not her common law husband?
3. What evidence does the court find to be most persuasive?

Jennings v. Hurt

N.Y. L.J., Oct. 4, 1989, at 24 (Sup. Ct. N.Y. County),
***aff'd*, 554 N.Y.S.2d 220 (App. Div. 1990),**
***appeal denied*, 568 N.Y.S.2d 347 (N.Y. 1991)**

South Carolina is one of the thirteen states (including the District of Columbia) that recognize common-law marriages. South Carolina became a common law state early in the eighteenth century when it adopted the law of common-law marriage which was recognized in the Ecclesiastic Courts in England. . . .

South Carolina law is aptly stated in the case of *Fryer v. Fryer*, S.C. Eq. 85 (S.C. App. 1832):

> Marriage, with us, so far as the law is concerned has ever been regarded as a mere civil contract. Our law prescribes no ceremony. It required nothing but the agreement of the parties, with an intention that the agreement shall, per se, constitute the marriage. They may express the agreement by parol, they may signify it by whatever ceremony their whim, or their taste, or their religious belief, may select: it is the agreement itself, and not the form in which it is couched, which constitutes the contract. The words used, or the ceremony performed, are mere evidence of a present intention and agreement of the parties. . . .

Although common-law marriages were abolished in New York as of April 29, 1933, New York does give effect to common-law marriages if they are recognized as valid under the law of the state in which it was supposedly contracted.

The sole question to be decided by this court is whether Sandra Jennings is the common-law wife of William Hurt? Since it is conceded that the parties never had a ceremonial marriage, the answer to that question rests upon certain events that allegedly transpired during the parties' stay in South Carolina and the law of South Carolina. . . .

Jennings and Hurt met in Saratoga, New York in the summer of 1981 while each of them was working there. Shortly thereafter, upon their return to New York City, the parties began living together. [They ceased living together in 1984.] At the time their relationship began, Jennings knew Hurt was still married. The parties had many discussions in which Hurt explained to Jennings his disappointment at his own failure in marriage and his family's history in terms of failed marriages. Hurt frequently discussed his belief that marriage was a promise or a commitment to "God" and that he was experiencing "dismay about having broken that promise." Because of his feelings and pain relating to this subject, Hurt explained that marriage was "not in the cards" for him. This is corroborated by Hurt's conversation with Mary Beth Hurt when he asked for a divorce. Jennings herself stated "he wanted me to know that he did not necessarily mean a marital commitment. . . ."

In the Spring of 1982 Jennings became pregnant. Hurt's counsel began drafting an agreement governing the parties' financial arrangements of living together and for the support of the expected child. The earliest of these agreements is dated May 1982. The pregnancy prompted Hurt to commence divorce proceedings to his marriage to Mary Beth Hurt. In September 1982, Hurt went to see his former wife to tell her he wanted to finalize the divorce since "Sandy is having a baby."

On October 31, 192, Jennings joined Hurt in South Carolina where he was already engaged in the filming of the "Big Chill." During their stay in South Carolina from October 31, 1982 to January 10, 1983, the parties lived in the same house and shared a bed. Their social circle consisted of the cast and others connected with the film project. During this period as well as earlier and later times, their relationship was volatile and permeated by arguments.

On December 3, 1982, Hurt's divorce became final. He learned this sometime later from counsel. Jennings testified that she learned of his divorce on December 27, 1982 when he approached her with another version of the "prenuptial agreement" that had been the subject of negotiations between the parties and their counsel. That on that date he said they should sign the agreement, have blood tests and get married. Parenthetically, it is noted that South Carolina does not require blood tests in order to obtain a marriage license. She testified that they then went to a Notary Public to get the agreement signed and returned home. Hurt then spoke to his attorney and after that conversation a fight ensued in which he stated Jennings had tricked him, that the agreement was not valid because she did not have legal counsel. Jennings then allegedly went into the bedroom and started packing to go home to her mother, whereupon Hurt, according to Jennings, . . . "threw my suitcase on the ground and we had a huge fight and he ended up telling me that it didn't matter because as far as he was concerned we were married in the eyes of God and we had a spiritual marriage and this didn't matter. We were more married than married people."

Jennings' claim to be Hurt's common-law wife is based inter alia, on these events. . . .

Documents admitted in evidence indicate [that] on December 27, 1982, Hurt's signature was notarized on the document entitled "Paternity Acknowledgment"; that on December 28, 1982, Jennings' signature was notarized on a sublease for her New York apartment, and that on December 28, 1982, Jennings spoke with someone at her attorneys' telephone number for 17 minutes. [T]he undisputed fact that Hurt signed a paternity acknowledgment on [December 27, 1982] is inconsistent with any immediate intention to marry, but is consistent with Hurt's testimony that though his commitment to his child was unequivocal, he had deep reservations about his relationship with Jennings.

The only evidence introduced of a holding forth as husband and wife while the parties were in South Carolina was a conversation with [lessors] in connection with the parties' renting of accommodations for their stay in South Carolina in which Hurt allegedly referred to Jennings as his wife and a telephone call by Hurt to Jennings' obstetrician, Dr. Credle's office, in which he asked about his "wife." The conversation with the [lessors] occurred on October 31, 1982 and thus is irrelevant because it pre-dates the removal of the impediment to marriage. The date of the conversation with Mrs. Credle is unknown but in any event is of little significance.

[The friends with] whom the parties socialized knew Jennings and Hurt were not married. [There is also not a] preponderance of credible evidence that the parties held themselves out as husband and wife after December 27, 1982. There is no evidence that Jennings filed tax returns or other forms as married. Significantly, the one document on which Jennings is alleged to have her name "Sandra Cronsberg Hurt" is clearly an altered xerox copy of the original with "Hurt" added afterwards and the document re-xeroxed. Indeed, documents signed by Hurt prior to the commencement of a lawsuit, i.e., will, pension, jury form — all indicated he considered himself single. Hurt's accountant testified that but for one tax return, where by error, the box "married" was checked, all taxes have been filed by Hurt as "single."

The testimony of persons who worked for Jennings for several months, years ago, and who each remember one isolated incident of Hurt referring to Jennings as his "wife" is unbelievable and even if true is barely relevant to prove a holding forth as husband and wife. . . . Hurt's employee's testimony is rejected as totally unworthy of belief. She appears as a disgruntled former employee attempting to get even as well as protect her own interests in a lawsuit. . . .

The courts of South Carolina [are] reluctant to declare a common-law marriage unless the proof of such marriage is shown by strong and competent testimony. . . . Jennings's claim that a common-law marriage existed stems, to a large extent, from her present recollection of Hurt's alleged utterance after an argument on December 27, 198[2], about seven years ago, that as far as he was concerned they were married in the eyes of God and had a spiritual marriage. To which utterance Jennings says she agreed. Even were this court to find this testimony credible, the event described by Jennings and the words allegedly spoken do not evince an "intent" to solemnize a marriage but rather the kind of words used by one desiring to continue the parties' present state of living together, i.e., in a relationship short of marriage. . . .

Moreover, where as in this case, the relationship began while one of them was already married, a subsequent divorce does not per se transform this illicit relationship into a common-law marriage. Instead the prior relationship is presumed to continue and the party claiming a common-law marriage must show by a preponderance of the evidence that the relationship underwent some fundamental change following the removal of the impediment. . . . Accordingly, it would be incumbent on Jennings to show an agreement to enter a common-law marriage after the impediment was removed. . . . The evidence shows a paucity of any "declaration or acknowledgement of the parties" of a marital state. Not one friend of either of the parties testified that the parties held themselves out as married.

Indeed, [a cast member] testified that at his wedding Jennings "wished us luck and that we have a good marriage and expressed the hope that she would be next." This statement belies any change in the relationship of the parties having taken place on December 27 or 28, 1982. It indicates that the prior illicit relationship continued although a hope, at least by one of the parties, to one day marry existed. . . .

. . . For all the foregoing reasons the court finds that Sandra Jennings is not the common-law wife of William Hurt.

Post-Case Follow-Up

After the court denied the claim by Jennings that she was the common law wife of Hurt, she sought to amend her complaint to allege three other causes of action in an attempt to obtain some remedy. The Appellate Division of the Supreme Court of the State of New York rejected the claims, stating:

We further find that the Supreme Court properly denied plaintiff's motion for leave to amend her complaint to allege three new causes of action since these causes of action were insufficient as a matter of law (see, *East Asiatic Co. v. Corash*, 34 AD2d 432). The first proposed cause of action, to impose a constructive trust on an apartment owned by defendant, cannot stand since plaintiff failed to establish that she had a property interest in the apartment. Nor did she establish all of the necessary elements for a constructive trust (see, *Onorato v. Lupoli*, 135 AD2d 693).

The second proposed cause of action, relating to defendant's alleged breach of a promise to support plaintiff in the future, is too vague to sufficiently state a cause of action (see, *Dombrowski v. Somers*, 41 N.Y.2d 858). Moreover, while plaintiff claims that this cause of action sounds in fraud, it arose directly from the breach of contract and is therefore a contract claim instead of a cause of action in fraud (*Marks v. Nassau County Assn. for Help of Retarded Children*, 135 AD2d 512). The third proposed cause of action, that defendant falsely promised to support plaintiff if she would have his child and give up her career, is void as against public policy (see, *McCall v. Frampton*, 81 AD2d 607). The law does not recognize a cause of action for sacrificing career opportunities in order to act as a "wife" (see, *Baron v. Jeffer*, 98 AD2d 810).

The court was very harsh in denying any remedies for Jennings in light of her failure to establish a valid marriage. We will see in the next section of this chapter that other courts have been more lenient in recognizing potential claims for parties who live in a marital-like relationship.

Jennings v. Hurt: Real Life Applications

1. Utilizing the *Jennings* case, what would you advise a client couple to do if they want to ensure their common law marriage is recognized?

2. Kesha and Julius are college students who are not married and do not live together. They go to school in Washington, which does not recognize common law marriages. However, over their winter break they go on a ski trip to Montana with a group of their friends. While there they learn that Montana is a common law marriage state. As a joke, they decide to profess their love to each other and pronounce themselves husband and wife. They return to Washington and tell people they were married in Montana, and jokingly refer to each other as husband and wife. Kesha meets and is now engaged to Harry. Julius objects to the engagement claiming that he and Kesha are married. What do you tell Julius?

C. LEGAL RECOGNITION OF NONMARITAL COUPLES

As noted in the chapter introduction, states traditionally have drawn a bright line between marriage and other forms of intimate association. This fixed demarcation has long been considered necessary in order to safeguard the state's interest in marriage as a vital social institution. Placed outside the realm of sanctioned family life, unwed couples have thus been excluded from the rights and privileges of marriage.

However, starting in the 1970s, the law began moving away from a strict reliance on marriage as the exclusive marker for determining family status and the corresponding entitlement to benefits. To some extent, this shift responds to the marriage equality movement. Although unwilling to grant formal legal equality to same-sex couples, some states were instead willing to extend partial rights based on a growing awareness of the hardships caused by a nonrecognition policy, such as, for example, where a life partner is denied hospital visitation rights because he or she is not considered family. However, as exemplified by the case of *Marvin v. Marvin*, discussed below, it also responds to concerns of fairness raised by heterosexual couples who, for a variety of reasons, have chosen to live together rather than marry.

In this section, we consider three approaches that courts and lawmakers have taken with respect to the extension of rights and obligations to unmarried couples, namely, permitting cohabitants to sue for property and support rights upon the dissolution of their relationship, the recognition of domestic partnerships and civil unions, and the formal protection of "relational interests." Although each approach is distinct, a critical commonality is the partiality of recognition. Unlike marriage, with the possible exception of some civil union laws, none of these approaches provides an unmarried couple with an across-the-board family status; rather, rights and recognition are limited and contextual.

Although certainly not as controversial as the issue of same-sex marriage has been, the extension of legal rights to unmarried couples has nonetheless triggered considerable debate. Some commentators worry that this trend will result in a culture that takes marriage less seriously. They argue that clear boundaries are needed to preserve marriage as a privileged and unique relationship. In contrast, others welcome this increased flexibility, arguing that the law must evolve in response to reality so that outmoded concepts of what constitutes a "proper" or morally sanctioned family unit are not used to deny rights to couples who either cannot or choose not to marry.

1. Cohabitation

Before 1976, courts generally refused to get involved in dissolution disputes between cohabiting partners over money and the allocation of accumulated property. Judges did not want to appear to be sanctioning nonmarital sexual relationships, and they worried that recognizing rights between cohabiting partners would diminish the importance of marriage. However, in 1976, in the California case of *Marvin v. Marvin*, 557 P.2d 106 (Cal. 1976), the door to the courthouse was opened for the first time to cohabiting partners seeking to sort out their affairs upon the dissolution of a relationship.

Presently, few, if any, states continue to bar suits between cohabitating partners who are seeking to resolve support and property disputes at the dissolution of their relationship. However, these actions are filed in civil court, as opposed to the family courts. In resolving disputes between cohabiting parties, courts typically look to see if they had entered into an agreement (whether verbal, express, or implied) about property and support rights, although courts in some states have not limited themselves to a contractual remedy. For example, trust theories have been used to distribute property from one partner to the other, based on a showing that the titled partner was either actually holding it for the benefit of his or her partner or had engaged in some kind of fraud or overreaching.

Most couples do not sit down and negotiate a contract regarding the support and property rights they will have if they break up; courts therefore often infer agreements based on the conduct of the parties during their relationship, much as a court might infer an agreement to pay based on the acceptance of a paper that is delivered to one's door on a daily basis. In contract parlance, an agreement that is inferred from conduct is referred to as an implied-in-fact contract. In the context of cohabitation, a court might find an implied agreement to share accumulated assets because a couple made purchases from a shared account or commingled their possessions. Some courts might also consider a partner's nonfinancial contribution (e.g., homemaking services) that preserves and enhances the value of the couple's property as evidence of an intent to share in the accumulation.

Case Preview

Marvin v. Marvin

Actor Lee Marvin and Michelle Triola lived together for more than seven years, accumulating assets worth more than $1 million in the name of Marvin alone. Following their breakup, Triola sued for support and share of the accumulated assets based on what she said was an express agreement between the parties that she would give up her musical career and provide domestic services to Marvin in exchange for his financial support and shared interest in accumulated assets. Marvin, on the other hand, argued that any agreement between the parties was void because it was inextricably bound up with the sexual aspect of their relationship — a traditional barrier to enforcement of these claims.

As you read *Marvin v. Marvin*, look for the following:

1. What theories does the plaintiff indicate should be used to give her half the property acquired while living together and support payments?
2. What theories does the defendant offer to contend that the plaintiff is not entitled to recover any of the property or support payments?
3. What principles does the court indicate should govern distribution of property acquired in a nonmarital relationship?

Marvin v. Marvin
557 P.2d 106 (Cal. 1976)

During the past 15 years, there has been a substantial increase in the number of couples living together without marrying. Such nonmarital relationships lead to legal controversy when one partner dies or the couple separates. . . .

. . . Plaintiff avers that in October of 1964 she and defendant "entered into an oral agreement" that while "the parties lived together they would combine their efforts and earnings and would share equally any and all property accumulated as a result of their efforts whether individual or combined." Furthermore, they agreed to "hold themselves out to the general public as husband and wife" and that "plaintiff would further render her services as a companion, homemaker, housekeeper and cook to . . . defendant."

Shortly thereafter plaintiff agreed to "give up her lucrative career as an entertainer [and] singer" in order to "devote her full time to defendant . . . as a companion, homemaker, housekeeper and cook"; in return defendant agreed to "provide for all of plaintiff's financial support and needs for the rest of her life."

Plaintiff alleges that she lived with defendant from October of 1964 through May of 1970 and fulfilled her obligations under the agreement. During this period the parties as a result of their efforts and earnings acquired in defendant's name substantial real and personal property, including motion picture rights worth over $1 million. In May of 1970, however, defendant compelled plaintiff to leave his household. He continued to support plaintiff until November of 1971, but thereafter refused to provide further support.

In the case before us plaintiff, basing her cause of action in contract . . . maintains that the trial court erred in denying her a trial on the merits of her contention. [The] court did not specify the ground for its conclusion that plaintiff's contractual allegations [did not state a] cause of action. . . . Defendant first and principally relies on the contention that the alleged contract is so closely related to the supposed "immoral" character of the relationship between plaintiff and himself that the enforcement of the contract would violate public policy. He points to cases asserting that a contract between nonmarital partners is unenforceable if it is "involved in" an illicit relationship. . . . A review of the numerous California decisions concerning contracts between nonmarital partners, however, reveals that the courts have not employed such broad and uncertain standards to strike down contracts. The decisions instead disclose a narrower and more precise standard: a contract between nonmarital partners is unenforceable only to the extent that it explicitly rests upon the immoral and illicit consideration of meretricious sexual services. . . .

Although the past decisions hover over the issue in the somewhat wispy form of the figures of a Chagall painting, we can abstract from those decisions a clear and simple rule. The fact that a man and woman live together without marriage, and engage in a sexual relationship, does not in itself invalidate agreements between them relating to their earnings, property, or expenses. Neither is such an agreement invalid merely because the parties may have contemplated the creation or continuation of a nonmarital relationship when they entered into it. Agreements between nonmarital partners fail only to the extent that they rest upon a consideration of meretricious sexual services. Thus the rule asserted by defendant, that a contract fails if it is "involved in" or made "in contemplation" of a nonmarital relationship, cannot be reconciled with the decisions. . . .

The principle that a contract between nonmarital partners will be enforced unless expressly and inseparably based upon an illicit consideration of sexual services not only represents the distillation of the decisional law, but also offers a far more precise and workable standard than that advocated by defendant. . . .

In summary, we base our opinion on the principle that adults who voluntarily live together and engage in sexual relations are nonetheless as competent as any other persons to contract respecting their earnings and property rights. Of course, they cannot lawfully contract to pay for the performance of sexual services, for such a contract is, in essence, an agreement for prostitution and unlawful for that reason. But they may agree to pool their earnings and to hold all property acquired during the relationship in accord with the law governing community property; conversely they may agree that each partner's earnings and the property acquired from those earnings remains the separate property of the earning partner. So long as the agreement does not rest upon illicit meretricious consideration, the parties may order their economic affairs as they choose, and no policy precludes the courts from enforcing such agreements.

In the present instance, plaintiff alleges that the parties agreed to pool their earnings, that they contracted to share equally in all property acquired, and that defendant agreed to support plaintiff. The terms of the contract as alleged do not rest upon any unlawful consideration. We therefore conclude that the complaint furnishes a suitable basis upon which the trial court can render declaratory relief. . . . The trial court consequently erred in granting defendant's motion for judgment on the pleadings. . . .

As we have noted, both causes of action in plaintiff's complaint allege an express contract; neither assert any basis for relief independent from the contract. In *In re Marriage of Cary, supra,* 34 Cal. App. 3d 345, however, the Court of Appeal held that, in view of the policy of the Family Law Act, property accumulated by nonmarital partners in an actual family relationship should be divided equally. Upon examining the *Cary* opinion, the parties to the present case realized that plaintiff's alleged relationship with defendant might arguably support a cause of action independent of any express contract between the parties. . . .

Reviewing the prior decisions which had denied relief to the homemaking partner, the Court of Appeal reasoned that those decisions rested upon a policy of punishing persons guilty of cohabitation without marriage. The Family Law Act, the court observed, aimed to eliminate fault or guilt as a basis for dividing marital property. But once fault or guilt is excluded, the court reasoned, nothing distinguishes the property rights of a nonmarital "spouse" from those of a putative spouse. Since the latter is entitled to half the " 'quasi marital property' " . . . , the Court of Appeal concluded that, giving effect to the policy of the Family Law Act, a nonmarital cohabitator should also be entitled to half the property accumulated during an "actual family relationship." (34 Cal. App. 3d at p. 353.)

Cary met with a mixed reception in other appellate districts. In *Estate of Atherley, supra,* 44 Cal. App. 3d 758, the Fourth District agreed with *Cary* that under the Family Law Act a nonmarital partner in an actual family relationship enjoys the same right to an equal division of property as a putative spouse. In *Beckman v. Mayhew, supra,* 49 Cal. App. 3d 529, however, the Third District rejected *Cary* on the ground that the Family Law Act was not intended to change California law dealing with nonmarital relationships. If *Cary* is interpreted as holding that the Family Law Act requires an equal division of property accumulated in nonmarital "actual family relationships," then we agree with *Beckman v. Mayhew* that *Cary* distends the act. . . .

But although we reject the reasoning of *Cary* and *Atherley,* we share the perception of the *Cary* and *Atherley* courts that the application of former precedent in the factual setting of those cases would work an unfair distribution of the property accumulated by the couple. . . .

The principal reason why the pre-*Cary* decisions result in an unfair distribution of property inheres in the court's refusal to permit a nonmarital partner to assert rights based upon accepted principles of implied contract or equity. We have examined the reasons advanced to justify this denial of relief, and find that none have merit. . . .

First, we note that the cases denying relief do not rest their refusal upon any theory of "punishing" a "guilty" partner. Indeed, to the extent that denial of relief "punishes" one partner, it necessarily rewards the other by permitting him to retain a disproportionate amount of the property. Concepts of "guilt" thus cannot justify an unequal division of property between two equally "guilty" persons.

Other reasons advanced in the decisions fare no better. The principal argument seems to be that "[equitable] considerations arising from the reasonable expectation of ... benefits attending the status of marriage ... are not present [in a nonmarital relationship]." (*Vallera v. Vallera, supra,* 21 Cal. 2d at p. 685.) But, although parties to a nonmarital relationship obviously cannot have based any expectations upon the belief that they were married, other expectations and equitable considerations remain. The parties may well expect that property will be divided in accord with the parties' own tacit understanding and that in the absence of such understanding the courts will fairly apportion property accumulated through mutual effort. We need not treat nonmarital partners as putatively married persons in order to apply principles of implied contract, or extend equitable remedies; we need to treat them only as we do any other unmarried persons. . . .

. . . The argument that granting remedies to the nonmarital partners would discourage marriage must fail; as *Cary* pointed out, "with equal or greater force the point might be made that the pre-1970 rule was calculated to cause the income-producing partner to avoid marriage and thus retain the benefit of all of his or her accumulated earnings." 34 Cal. App. 3d at p.353. Although we recognize the well-established public policy to foster and promote the institution of marriage . . . perpetuation of judicial rules which result in an inequitable distribution of property accumulated during a nonmarital relationship is neither a just nor an effective way of carrying out that policy.

In summary, we believe that the prevalence of nonmarital relationships in modern society and the social acceptance of them, marks this as a time when our courts should by no means apply the doctrine of the unlawfulness of the so-called meretricious relationship to the instant case. As we have explained, the nonenforceability of agreements expressly providing for meretricious conduct rested upon the fact that such conduct, as the word suggests, pertained to and encompassed prostitution. To equate the nonmarital relationship of today to such a subject matter is to do violence to an accepted and wholly different practice.

We are aware that many young couples live together without the solemnization of marriage, in order to make sure that they can successfully later undertake marriage. This trial period, preliminary to marriage, serves as some assurance that the marriage will not subsequently end in dissolution to the harm of both parties. We are aware, as we have stated, of the pervasiveness of nonmarital relationships in other situations.

The mores of the society have indeed changed so radically in regard to cohabitation that we cannot impose a standard based on alleged moral considerations that have apparently been so widely abandoned by so many. Lest we be misunderstood, however, we take this occasion to point out that the structure of society itself largely depends upon the institution of marriage, and nothing we have said in this opinion should be taken to derogate from that institution. The joining of the man and woman in marriage is at once the most socially productive and individually fulfilling relationship that one can enjoy in the course of a lifetime.

We conclude that the judicial barriers that may stand in the way of a policy based upon the fulfillment of the reasonable expectations of the parties to a nonmarital relationship should be removed. As we have explained, the courts now hold that express agreements will be enforced unless they rest on an unlawful meretricious consideration. We add that in the absence of an express agreement, the courts may look to a variety of other remedies in order to protect the parties' lawful expectations.

The courts may inquire into the conduct of the parties to determine whether that conduct demonstrates an implied contract or implied agreement of partnership or joint venture . . . or some other tacit understanding between the parties. The courts may, when appropriate, employ principles of constructive trust . . . or resulting trust. . . . Finally, a nonmarital partner may recover in quantum meruit for the reasonable value of household services rendered less the reasonable value of support received if he can show that he rendered services with the expectation of monetary reward. Since we have determined that plaintiff's complaint states a cause of action for breach of an express contract, and, as we have explained, can be amended to state a cause of action independent of allegations of express contract, we must conclude that the trial court erred in granting defendant a judgment on the pleadings. The judgment is reversed and the cause remanded for further proceedings consistent with the views expressed herein.

Post-Case Follow-Up

In *Marvin*, Triola based her claim to support and a division of assets on the fact that the parties had entered into an express contract, which is an actual, articulated agreement. In holding that these agreements should be honored, the *Marvin* court recognized that most cohabiting couples do not formalize their relational expectations, and it urged other courts to consider a variety of contractual and equitable approaches when seeking to resolve claims stemming from a failed cohabiting relationship.

Courts have been more reluctant to find implied support agreements based on two traditional barriers. First, it has long been assumed that household services have no real monetary worth. Second, there is a longstanding legal presumption that household services are provided gratuitously or as a gift without expectation of compensation. These barriers, however, are breaking down. Based in part on the work of economists who have estimated what it would cost to purchase the services of a homemaker in the marketplace, courts have begun to recognize that household services have economic value and that they usually are not provided as a gift but rather, as acknowledged by the *Marvin* court, with the expectation that the parties intended a fair exchange.

Marvin v. Marvin: Real-Life Applications

1. A client has come to your office to discuss the rights she might have against her live-in boyfriend concerning the property they have acquired during their

15-year relationship. Based upon the *Marvin v. Marvin* case, identify the legal theories you will want to explore in advance of meeting with the client.

2. Tia has lived with Jun for six years. Jun promised that he would always take care of Tia if she would agree to stay home and help him raise his daughter Samantha (now age 12) from a previous marriage. Tia gave up her career as a young associate attorney in a large firm to stay home and help raise Samantha. Her relationship with Jun ended when Jun moved out saying he was in love with someone else. Tia has been trying to find work as an attorney but unfortunately has not been able to find immediate employment because of the gap in her career. She asks you whether she has a claim for support against Jun. What do you tell her?

3. Assume Tia had come to your office six years earlier and advised you that she was planning on giving up her career as a lawyer and moving in with Jun to help him raise his six-year-old daughter. She tells you Jun promises to take care of her not only while they are living together, but that if they ever break up he will continue to pay all her expenses for the same number of years as they live together. Tia wants to know what steps she can take to protect herself and to enforce the agreement if she and Jun should ever break up. What do you tell her?

The "Marital-Status" Approach

In resolving disputes between cohabiting couples, most courts have been reluctant to treat cohabitation as a status relationship. Accordingly, in contrast to a divorce case where the post-dissolution rights and obligations flow from the existence of the relationship itself, in most states, a cohabitant who seeks support or a share of accumulated assets must establish that his or her claim is grounded in a prior agreement (either express or implied) of the parties. In short, rather than creating a formal legal status for cohabitants, what courts have done is to have removed "a relationship-based impediment to their contractual freedom." However, a distinct minority of jurisdictions have taken the extra step and now treat cohabitation as a status relationship. Accordingly, parties may be found to have post-dissolution obligations to one another based on the existence of the relationship itself.

Although the majority of states continue to use contract theories as the main way to provide claims of relief between domestic partners, in 2002 the American Law Institute (ALI) recommended, in its influential *Principles of the Law of Family Dissolution* ("Principles"), that status replace contract as the dominant paradigm.

Accordingly, upon dissolution, cohabitants who have shared a "primary residence and a life together as a couple" for a significant period of time would be treated like a married couple with respect to post-relationship rights and obligations." American Law Institute, *Principles of the Law of Family Dissolution: Analysis and Recommendations* §6.03(1) (2002). It should be noted that the Principles make no distinction between same-sex and heterosexual couples.

The ALI recommendations are not without controversy. Supporters argue that a status approach is a fairer way to resolve disputes because most couples simply do not think about their relationship in contractual terms. As a consequence, if there is no agreement to enforce, the economically more vulnerable partner may end up with nothing—a particularly harsh result in the context of a long-term relationship structured along traditional gender lines. Supporters also argue that this approach advances the goal of equality by honoring a broader range of relationship choices in accordance with how people are actually living their lives, rather than simply privileging marriage above all other forms of intimate associations.

Others, however, worry that recognizing cohabitation as a formal status will weaken the institution of marriage. One fear is that recognition will blur the distinction between cohabitation and marriage, thus detracting from the unique nature of the marital bond and making it more likely that couples will simply choose to live together because marriage will no longer seem so special. Another concern is that the imposition of post-relationship obligations may contravene the actual intentions of the parties, who, in choosing cohabitation over marriage, may have purposefully been seeking to avoid the legal consequences of marriage.

2. Domestic Partnerships and Civil Unions

Starting in the mid-1980s, a small but growing number of towns and cities across the country responded to the changing reality of family life by enacting domestic partnership ordinances. The ordinances allowed qualified unmarried couples to register their relationship with the city clerk, regardless of sexual orientation. Around the same time, many employers also began offering domestic partnership benefits to their employees. Subsequently, a number of states also enacted domestic partnership laws. These laws and, in many cases employment benefits, still exist today and are gender neutral.

To register as domestic partners, a couple files an affidavit with a city or town clerk's office, which typically must attest to the following:

- that they are over the age of 18 and competent to enter into such a relationship;
- that they are cohabiting;
- that their relationship is exclusive and that neither person is married or has another domestic partner;
- that they are responsible for one another's welfare and share basic living expenses;
- that they are not related such that a marriage between them would violate state incest provisions;
- that neither has, within the preceding six months, filed a statement of domestic partnership with anyone else; and
- that if they end the relationship, they will file a certificate of dissolution.

In addition to these requirements, some localities require that one of the partners be a municipal, or in the case of statewide registries, a state employee. Additionally, reflecting their historic origins as a means of allowing same-sex couples to obtain a degree of formal recognition of their relationships at a time when marriage was an impossibility, some registries, although not all, were limited to same-sex partners.

Once registered, partners become eligible for designated benefits. In the municipal context, benefits are notably limited because municipalities have narrow legislative authority, and, for example, a city or town cannot require private employers to extend benefits to domestic partners, nor can it compel a state to extend state-conferred benefits, such as inheritance rights if a partner dies without a will. Consequently, unless one partner is a municipal employee, the only benefit of registration may be that it provides some degree of formal relationship recognition, although in some locales, limited benefits, such as jail and hospital visitation rights, may be available. Where, however, one partner is a municipal employee, registration typically offers some tangible benefits, such as health insurance coverage for his or her domestic partner, and the right to take time off to care for a domestic partner (or a member of his or her family) on the same basis that a married employee would be allowed to take time off to do the same.

The picture is quite different in the context of *state* domestic partnership registries. Here, given the far greater regulatory power of the state as compared to the authority of a town or municipality, the benefits tend to be far more extensive, with some states, such as Oregon and Hawaii (which uses the term "reciprocal beneficiaries" rather than domestic partners), offering registered couples virtually all of the rights and benefits of marriage that accrue under state law. However, as in the municipal context, some states may limit all or some of the available benefits to public employees.

In addition to domestic partner registries, a few states allow couples to enter into what is known as a "**civil union**." Civil unions were a creation of the Vermont state legislature after the state high court in *Baker v. Vermont*, 744 A.2d 865 (Vt. 1999), ordered it to rectify the disparity in the tangible treatment of same-sex and heterosexual couples by providing them with equal access to the statutory benefits and protections of marriage. However, it made clear that so long as this mandate was satisfied, the extension of marital rights to same-sex couples was not a constitutional requirement. In response, the legislature elected to create a parallel legal relationship, known as a civil union, thus preserving the status of marriage itself for heterosexual couples. The breakthrough significance of this decision was soon eclipsed by *Goodridge*'s equal marriage rights mandate, and of course now by the constitutional recognition of same-sex marriage as a fundamental right as stated in *Obergefell*.

Subsequently, approximately ten states, either through court decisions or legislative enactments, adopted this parallel relationship for same-sex couples as a way of extending the tangible benefits of marriage while preserving marriage as an exclusively heterosexual union. While the recognition of civil unions in order to advance recognition of rights of same-sex couples is no longer needed, civil unions now are potentially an opportunity for all couples who prefer to forgo the formality of a marriage to enter into civil unions as an alternative to marriage.

While it may seem that all the benefits of a marriage can be derived by a civil union, as we will see in subsequent chapters regarding children and support, the same benefits are not applicable to both relationship forms. In addition, it is also important to recognize that couples who have entered into domestic partnerships or civil unions are not eligible for federal benefits or certain other state benefits that are provided to spouses.

3. Protecting Relational Interests

Another approach that some courts have used to extend rights to cohabitants is to look beyond the lack of a formal status and instead focus on the relational interests that exist between committed cohabiting partners in order to protect the integrity of a committed union. The first case to exemplify this approach is the New York case of *Braschi v. Stahl Associates Co.*, 543 N.E.2d 49 (N.Y. 1989). In *Braschi*, New York's highest court held that the term "family" could be defined to include life partners, even though the partners were not validly married. While arising in the context of a same-sex couple, the decision reaches beyond just same-sex partners who, at the time, could not legally marry.

Case Preview

Braschi v. Stahl Associates Co.

In *Braschi*, a landlord sought to evict a tenant following the death of his life partner who had been the named tenant on the lease. The surviving partner sought protection under the noneviction provisions of New York's rent control law that prevent a landlord from evicting the "surviving spouse of the deceased tenant or some other member of the deceased tenant's *family* who has been living with the tenant." The court rejected the landlord's argument that the term "family" should be limited to persons related by blood, marriage, or adoption. Instead, the court said that in defining family for purposes of the rent control statute, one must look beyond "fictitious legal distinctions or genetic history" to the "reality of family life." Accordingly, where an unmarried couple's relationship partakes of the qualities that have made the traditional family a valued and protected social unit, the couple should be recognized as a family.

As you read *Braschi v. Stahl Associates Co.*, look for the following:

1. What regulation was involved in this decision? What rights did it grant and to whom?
2. How did the defendant think the term "family," as used in the ordinance, should be defined?
3. Why did the court reject the defendant's argument?

Braschi v. Stahl Associates Co.
543 N.E.2d 49 (N.Y. 1989)

In this dispute over occupancy rights to a rent-controlled apartment, the central question to be resolved on this request for preliminary injunctive relief ... is whether appellant has demonstrated a likelihood of success on the merits ... by showing that, as a matter of law, he is entitled to seek protection from eviction under New York

City Rent and Eviction Regulations 9 NYCRR 2204.6(d). . . . That regulation provides that upon the death of a rent-control tenant, the landlord may not dispossess "either the surviving spouse of the deceased tenant or some other member of the deceased tenant's *family* who has been living with the tenant" (emphasis supplied). Resolution of this question requires this court to determine the meaning of the term "family" as it is used in this context.

I.

Appellant, Miguel Braschi, was living with Leslie Blanchard in a rent-controlled apartment located at 405 East 54th Street from the summer of 1975 until Blanchard's death in September of 1986. In November of 1986, respondent, Stahl Associates Company, the owner of the apartment building, served a notice to cure on appellant contending that he was a mere licensee with no right to occupy the apartment since only Blanchard was the tenant of record. In December of 1986 respondent served appellant with a notice to terminate informing appellant that he had one month to vacate the apartment and that, if the apartment was not vacated, respondent would commence summary proceedings to evict him. . . .

. . . The present dispute arises because the term "family" is not defined in the rent-control code. . . .

Rent control was enacted to address a "serious public emergency" created by "an acute shortage in dwellings," which resulted in "speculative, unwarranted and abnormal increases in rents" (L 1946 ch 274, codified, as amended, at McKinney's Uncons Laws of NY §§8581 et seq.). . . .

To accomplish its goals, the Legislature recognized that not only would rents have to be controlled, but that evictions would have to be regulated and controlled as well (id.). Hence, section 2204.6 of the New York City Rent and Eviction Regulations (9 NYCRR 2204.6) . . . provides . . . noneviction protection to those occupants who are either the "surviving spouse of the deceased tenant or some other member of the deceased tenant's family who has been living with the tenant [of record]" (emphasis supplied). The manifest intent of this section is to restrict the landowners' ability to evict a narrow class of occupants other than the tenant of record. . . . Juxtaposed against this intent favoring the protection of tenants, is the over-all objective of a gradual "transition from regulation to a normal market of free bargaining between landlord and tenant." . . . One way in which this goal is to be achieved is "vacancy decontrol," which automatically makes rent-control units subject to the less rigorous provisions of rent stabilization upon the termination of the rent-control tenancy. . . .

Emphasizing the latter objective, respondent argues that the term "family member" . . . should be construed, consistent with this State's intestacy laws, to mean relationships of blood, consanguinity and adoption in order to effectuate the over-all goal of orderly succession to real property. Under this interpretation, only those entitled to inherit under the laws of intestacy would be afforded noneviction. . . . Further, as did the Appellate Division, respondent relies on our decision in *Matter of Robert Paul P.* (63 NY2d 233), arguing that since the relationship between appellant and Blanchard has not been accorded legal status by the Legislature, it is not entitled to the protections of section 2204.6(d), which, according to the Appellate Division, applies only to "family members within traditional, legally recognized familial relationships" (143 AD2d 44, 45). . . .

Contrary to all of these arguments, we conclude that the term family, as used in 9 NYCRR 2204.6(d), should not be rigidly restricted to those people who have formalized their relationship by obtaining, for instance, a marriage certificate or an adoption order. The intended protection against sudden eviction should not rest on fictitious legal distinctions or genetic history, but instead should find its foundation in the reality of family life. In the context of eviction, a more realistic, and certainly equally valid, view of a family includes two adult lifetime partners whose relationship is long term and characterized by an emotional and financial commitment and interdependence. This view comports both with our society's traditional concept of "family" and with the expectations of individuals who live in such nuclear units. . . . Hence, it is reasonable to conclude that, in using the term "family," the Legislature intended to extend protection to those who reside in households having all of the normal familial characteristics. Appellant Braschi should therefore be afforded the opportunity to prove that he and Blanchard had such a household.

This definition of "family" is consistent with both of the competing purposes of the rent-control laws: the protection of individuals from sudden dislocation and the gradual transition to a free market system. Family members, whether or not related by blood, or law who have always treated the apartment as their family home will be protected against the hardship of eviction following the death of the named tenant, thereby furthering the Legislature's goals of preventing dislocation and preserving family units which might otherwise be broken apart upon eviction. This approach will foster the transition from rent control to rent stabilization by drawing a distinction between those individuals who are, in fact, genuine family members, and those who are mere roommates . . . or newly discovered relatives hoping to inherit the rent-controlled apartment after the existing tenant's death.

The determination as to whether an individual is entitled to noneviction protection should be based upon an objective examination of the relationship of the parties. In making this assessment, the lower courts of this State have looked to a number of factors, including the exclusivity and longevity of the relationship, the level of emotional and financial commitment, the manner in which the parties have conducted their everyday lives and held themselves out to society, and the reliance placed upon one another for daily family services. . . . These factors are most helpful, although it should be emphasized that the presence or absence of one or more of them is not dispositive since it is the totality of the relationship as evidenced by the dedication, caring and self-sacrifice of the parties which should, in the final analysis, control. Appellant's situation provides an example of how the rule should be applied.

Appellant and Blanchard lived together as permanent life partners for more than 10 years. They regarded one another, and were regarded by friends and family, as spouses. The two men's families were aware of the nature of the relationship, and they regularly visited each other's families and attended family functions together, as a couple. Even today, appellant continues to maintain a relationship with Blanchard's niece, who considers him an uncle. In addition to their interwoven social lives, appellant clearly considered the apartment his home. He lists the apartment as his address on his driver's license and passport, and receives all his mail at the apartment address. Moreover, appellant's tenancy was known to the building's superintendent and doormen, who viewed the two men as a couple. Financially, the two men shared all obligations including a household budget. The two were authorized signatories of three safe-deposit boxes, they maintained joint checking and savings accounts, and joint credit cards. In fact, rent was often paid with a check from their joint checking account. Additionally, Blanchard executed a power of attorney in appellant's favor so that appellant could make necessary decisions — financial, medical and personal — for him during his illness. Finally, appellant was the named beneficiary of Blanchard's life insurance policy, as well as the primary legatee and coexecutor of Blanchard's estate. Hence, a court examining these facts could reasonably conclude that these men were much more than mere roommates.

In as much as this case is before us on a certified question, we conclude only that appellant has demonstrated a likelihood of success on the merits, in that he is not excluded, as a matter of law, from seeking noneviction protection. . . .

Post-Case Follow-Up   As seen by the opinion, the court rejected the landlord's argument that the term "family" should be limited to persons related by blood, marriage, or adoption. Instead, the court said that in defining family for purposes of the rent control statute, one must look beyond "fictitious legal distinctions or genetic history" to the "reality of family life." Accordingly, where an unmarried couple's relationship partakes of the qualities that have made the traditional family a valued and protected social unit, the couple should be recognized as a family.

Braschi v. Stahl Associates Co.: Real Life Applications

1. You are a city attorney and have been asked if there is a way you can revise the rent control statute to define family in a permissible way so as to avoid the result in *Braschi*. Based on the factors the court relied upon in *Braschi* for deciding that the plaintiff and his partner qualified as a family, how would you suggest rewriting the statute?

2. Katy and Greg are not married, but have decided to live together. They each have a child by a former marriage that lives with them as well. Assume the law is the same as in *Braschi*. The landlord has now brought an action to evict them because he has learned that they are not legally married and therefore are not a family. What will the result be?

3. Amada and John are married and live in a single-family residence. Several years ago, John's mother Marguerite came to live with them. John has recently passed away and Amada worries that she can no longer stay in the residence because she was related to Marguerite only by marriage. What do you tell Amada?

Since *Braschi*, courts have been particularly receptive to the "relational interest" approach in tort cases where one partner has suffered a financial or emotional loss (or both) following the injury or death of his or her partner. In the influential case of *Dunphy v. Gregor*, 136 N.J. 99, 642 A.2d 372 (N.J. 1994), the New Jersey Supreme Court allowed a woman to recover damages for the emotional distress she suffered after witnessing the man she was living with and engaged to marry die after being struck by a car while helping a friend to change a tire. Rejecting the defendant's argument that only family members who are related by marriage or blood should be allowed to recover for "bystander" injuries, the court focused on the nature of the relationship: "Central to a claim under bystander liability is the existence of an intimate familial relationship and the strength of the emotional bonds that surround that relationship. The harm . . . must be so severe that it destroys the emotional security derived from a relationship that is deep, enduring, and intimate. The quality of the relationship creates the severity of the loss." *Id.* at 378-379. So viewed, it is the quality and nature of the relationship, rather than simply the existence of a formal legal bond, that is important when determining if an individual is entitled to recover for bystander injuries.

With respect to expanding the rights of nonmarital partners, the relational interest approach has two inherent limitations. First, to qualify for family status, a couple must offer up the inner workings of their private life to a court for review. This disclosure can be expensive, time-consuming, and highly intrusive. Second, unmarried couples may be held to a higher standard of family life than married couples. Married couples automatically qualify for status and benefits, regardless of how they treat one another or the degree to which their relationship conforms to a domestic norm, whereas a nonmarital couple must show that their relationship satisfies specific criteria in order to be recognized as a family unit.

Damages for Loss of Consortium

Relying in part on *Dunphy*, New Mexico subsequently became the first state to allow a cohabiting partner to sue for loss of consortium (which generally encompasses the loss of material services, love, companionship, and sexual relations) occasioned by an injury to her life partner, stating that "a person brings this claim to recover for damage to a relational interest, not a legal interest. . . . The use of legal status necessarily excludes many persons whose loss of a significant relational interest may be just as devastating as the loss of a legal spouse." *Lozoya v. Sanchez*, 133 N.M. 579, 66 P.3d 948, 956 (2003). In keeping with *Dunphy*, the court concluded that where a cohabiting couple has a "close familial relationship" based on factors such as "the degree of mutual dependence, the extent of common contributions to a life together . . . [and] their emotional [support of] each other," it is as deserving of protection as a relationship between married partners.

Chapter Summary

▧ States have actively sought to shape and preserve marriage as a vital social institution, even though marriage is thought of as a private matter. Although laws no longer mandate prescribed roles based on highly gendered notions of proper marital conduct, states still regulate who can marry and the formalities that must be complied with to establish a valid marriage.

▨ Marriage is recognized as a fundamental right, and laws that burden an individual's right to marry will be subjected to careful judicial review.

▨ Cases such as *Loving v. Virginia* and *Zablock v. Redhail* paved the way for recognition of the right to marry by individuals who traditionally had been denied such right. Since the 1970s, same-sex couples have actively fought for the right to marry. In 2003, in a historic first, the Massachusetts Supreme Judicial Court ruled that it was unconstitutional to bar same-sex couples from marrying. Other jurisdictions, whether by judicial decision, voter-approved ballot measures, or legislative actions, over time followed Massachusetts's lead.

▨ In 2013, the United States Supreme Court, in *United States v. Windsor*, held that it was unconstitutional to deny federal benefits to same-sex partners who were legally married. By the time the Court took up the issue again in 2015, 37 states authorized same-sex partners to marry. The issue was finally resolved in 2015 in *Obergefell v. Hodges*, which held that the right of same-sex partners to marry is a fundamental right guaranteed under the United States Constitution.

▨ In resolving disputes between cohabiting parties, courts typically look to see if they had entered into an agreement (whether verbal, express, or implied) about property and support rights.

▨ Under the traditional functional family approach, the focus is on the reality of a couple's life rather than on its legal form.

Applying the Rules

1. Anthony and Jennifer recently moved to Arizona, which does not recognize common law marriages. Anthony comes to your office and tells you he wants a divorce from his common law wife Jennifer. You inquire about the date of marriage, and Anthony indicates he is not sure when it first began. He tells you that for five years prior to coming to Arizona he and Jennifer resided Colorado, which recognizes common law marriages. They never had a formal marriage, but Anthony bought Jennifer a ring, and they referred to each other as husband and wife. They also had a joint bank account in Colorado. When they came to Arizona, they told everyone they were married and no one has ever questioned whether they were husband and wife. Anthony asks you what additional information you need to show that the parties are married. Develop a list of questions you want to ask Anthony to determine the evidence that supports, or does not support, that a marriage exists.

2. Joseph marries Judith in 1995. They have four children. Unbeknownst to Judith, Joseph, a traveling salesman, meets Molly in 2004 in a state that recognizes common law marriages. Joseph tells Molly how much he loves her, and that although

he does not want to go through the formalities of a marriage, they will be considered husband and wife. They buy a house together in the common law marriage state. They have a bank account together, and they represent themselves as husband and wife. Joseph is able to live a dual life, one with Judith and one with Molly, with neither Judith nor Molly knowing about the existence of the other — until this past month when Molly learns about Joseph's other wife. She is devastated and comes to your office for assistance. Does Molly have a valid common law marriage? What remedies does Molly have, if any?

3. Your firm has been asked to draft a city ordinance that defines family in a way that is consistent with the holding of the court in *Braschi*. Draft a definition that would satisfy the relation test stated in *Braschi*.

4. Harry and Wilma come to your office asking for legal advice. The parties were married six months ago in your state. The law in your state provides the following:

> A valid marriage is one that is solemnized by a person authorized to perform marriages and a license is obtained and issued within one year prior to the solemnization of the marriage. Before obtaining a license, if a party has been convicted of a crime, regardless of whether the conviction results in a fine, jail time or imprisonment, the parties must attend a marriage counseling program before a marriage license will issue.

Harry had been convicted of marijuana possession many years ago in a neighboring state at a time when marijuana was not legal in that state. Harry admitted to the charge, paid a fine, and did community service. However, when they applied for the marriage license approximately two months prior to being married, Harry and Wilma did not disclose Harry's criminal conviction on their marriage license application. They tell you they did not disclose this information because the parties would have had to go to a class, and they were afraid that it might affect Harry's current employment if anyone found out he had a conviction. The clerk of the court issued a marriage license to Harry and Wilma after they filled out the application, and the marriage was solemnized by a person authorized to perform marriages in your state. Harry and Wilma ask you if they have a valid marriage. What do you tell them?

5. Lana and Chin have been living together for the past six years. Chin gave up his career as a teacher in order to stay home to take care of the parties' two dogs and a cat, as well as take care of the house and yard so that Lana could continue working as an emergency room physician. Lana promised that if Chin stayed home and took care of the house so that she could continue to work, she would pay for the house and all the expenses, but that everything they acquired together would be considered theirs equally. The title to the house that was purchased during their relationship, as well as all bank accounts, are in Lana's name alone. Recently, Lana has asked Chin to move out. Chin is concerned that Lana

will not honor their agreement. Assume a common law marriage is not available to Chin. What remedies does Chin potentially have to claim that he is entitled to the assets that were acquired during the relationship?

6. Adele and Denis live in a senior assisted living facility that defines family members as those related by blood, adoption, or marriage. Anyone meeting this definition may live in the same residence together; however, unrelated parties must pay for separate residences. Adele and Denis would like to share a residence. They do not want to get married because they are afraid it will affect the Social Security benefits that they each receive. They would like to argue, however, that they are a functional family. What challenges might Adele and Denis face in making this argument?

Family Law in Practice

1. You have been asked to examine a statute that provides that a person who can afford child support but refuses to pay the support owed will be denied a marriage license. Research the full case of *Zablocki v. Redhail*, 434 U.S. 374 (1977) and read the concurring opinions of Justice Stewart and dissent opinion of Justice Powell. Would the statute pass constitutional muster under Justice Stewart's reasoning? Would this have been an easier case for Justice Powell to convince the other Justices of his reasoning? Why or why not?

2. Research the law of marriage in your state. What steps must a couple follow to create a formal marriage? Determine the effect of a technical failure to comply with these requirements.

3. Research whether common law marriages are valid in your state? What elements are necessary to establish a common law marriage? Even if your state does not permit common law marriages, will it recognize a common law marriage validly entered into in another state?

4. You have been asked to draft a memo for the senior partner for a client of the firm. The client is in the process of ending a long-term cohabiting relationship. Research the law in your state regarding the rights of cohabiting partners and then write up your results in a short in-house memorandum.

5. Determine what the law is in your state with respect to bigamy. Are there civil and criminal penalties? Are there any cases on polygamous relationships in your state? Write a memorandum explaining your findings.

Premarital and Postmarital Agreements

In Chapter 2, we saw that the trend has been away from state regulation of marriage toward a legal model that emphasizes individual choice. With this increased emphasis on private ordering, premarital agreements (also known as prenuptial agreements), which are entered into before marriage, have gained in both legal and social acceptance. More recently, postmarital (or postnuptial) agreements have also become more common. These arrangements allow couples to control at least some of the terms of dissolution in the event their marriage ends in divorce. While these agreements were at one time considered important only for wealthy individuals who were entering into a marriage with substantial income and assets, now these agreements are attractive to individuals regardless of financial status. They allow individuals who have children from a previous relationship to protect assets intended for his or her children from claims of the new spouse in the event of a divorce, and offer couples a way to determine their rights and obligations in advance of a divorce, which can then avoid lengthy and expensive litigation.

Although both premarital and postmarital agreements have become an increasingly important dimension of the private ordering of marriage, they have not been accepted without controversy and judicial scrutiny. Accordingly, as discussed in this chapter, in many states these marital contracts are reviewed more carefully than ordinary contracts. The standard of review may be higher, and certain types of provisions, particularly those involving children, are likely to be unenforceable even if the parties knowingly and voluntarily agreed to the terms, although the trend is clearly in favor of treating them like other agreements.

Key Concepts

- Purpose of premarital agreements
- Legal requirements for premarital agreements
- Enforcement of premarital agreements
- Purpose of postmarital agreements
- Enforcement of postmarital agreements

A. THE TRADITIONAL APPROACH TO PREMARITAL AGREEMENTS

Prior to the early 1970s, premarital agreements were considered a way to protect property acquired prior to marriage at the time of death of the spouse that held the property. Thus, in the event of death of the spouse with the property, rather than have all the property automatically go to the living spouse, the property would be distributed in accordance with the terms of the premarital agreement. This was a particularly important way for wealthy individuals to ensure that their assets stayed within the family and not be at risk of going to a spouse who might later remarry and divest the family lineage of significant assets. Gradually, individuals who held a substantial amount of assets also saw it as a way of controlling division of assets in the event of a possible divorce.

Until the early 1970s, premarital agreements made in contemplation of a possible divorce were generally considered void as against public policy. The attempt to take control away from the courts in equitably distributing assets or awarding support was seen as a form of overreaching by the wealthy spouse that potentially left the other spouse, most commonly the wife, at risk of impoverishment. Although courts no longer disfavor such agreements, the public policy concerns that historically led states to withhold recognition from premarital agreements continue to retain some force today, and those concerns inform the debate over whether the agreements should be treated like "ordinary" contracts or whether, because of their unique nature, they should occupy a special place in the law. These concerns have also shaped the development of the rules and standards governing the enforceability of premarital agreements. Historically, the most significant fear was that premarital agreements would encourage divorce because the party who stood to benefit from the agreement would have less incentive to remain in the marriage when things got rocky. According to this way of thinking, a wealthy man whose wife had waived her right to support would be more inclined to walk away from a troubled marriage than a man who knew he would be burdened with alimony payments, thus undermining the state's interest in preserving marriage as a fundamental social unit.

A related fear was that the enforcement of premarital agreements would lead to the post-divorce impoverishment of women. In opinion after opinion, judges expressed the concern that women would be pushed into signing agreements by financially secure and sophisticated men, and they would give up future rights they did not even know they possessed. As discussed below, this protective impulse has shaped much of the present law regarding enforceability.

Refusing recognition of premarital agreements was also a logical extension of the principle that spouses lacked the authority to alter the terms of the marital relationship because defining the rights and obligations of spouses was a public, rather than a private, matter. Accordingly, since a husband could not legally shed his duty of support during the marriage, it was considered unfair to allow him to contract out of this obligation in the event of divorce.

Another powerful apprehension was that if couples entering into a marriage were allowed to contract with one another, marriage would be reduced to a commercial enterprise. The vision of couples participating in protracted financial negotiations in contemplation of a possible divorce was an uncomfortable one that suggested the world of family was no different from the world of commerce and that spouses were more like business associates than intimate companions.

B. THE GROWING ACCEPTANCE OF PREMARITAL AGREEMENTS

In 1970, the Florida Supreme Court, in the historically significant case of *Posner v. Posner*, 233 So. 2d 381 (Fla. 1970), held that premarital agreements made in contemplation of divorce are not per se invalid, and other states soon followed suit. This trend corresponded with changing notions about marriage and divorce. As individuals acquired greater legal freedom to structure the terms of their marriage, it was a logical development that they be permitted to structure the terms of marital dissolution. The acceptance of no-fault divorce, which eliminated many of the traditional barriers to marital dissolution, also contributed to the acceptance of premarital agreements. With the increased acceptability and availability of divorce, the argument that premarital agreements would facilitate marital dissolution no longer carried the same weight that it had when divorces were more difficult to obtain. (See Chapter 4 for more detail on "no-fault" divorce reform.) In fact, some argue that premarital agreements actually encourage marriage because they allow individuals who might otherwise be wary of getting married, based on a fear of what they might lose upon dissolution, to control the terms of any future divorce.

Another key factor underlying the acceptance of premarital agreements was the changing status of women. Today, courts no longer assume, as they once did, that women are so financially unsophisticated that they will not be able to comprehend the significance of these agreements and will be taken advantage of by prospective husbands. In a related vein, the financial dependence of married women is no longer presumed. Thus, the protective impulse behind nonrecognition is now seen as outdated — a relic of the time when women were regarded as lacking legal capacity and in need of the paternalistic protection of the law.

This shift in thinking is exemplified by the Pennsylvania Supreme Court's approach in *Simeone v. Simeone*, 581 A.2d 162 (Pa. 1990), in which it repudiated this paternalism as an outmoded relic.

Case Preview

Simeone v. Simeone

In *Simeone v. Simeone*, the Supreme Court of Pennsylvania takes a "hardline" approach to prenuptial agreements. In treating them more like ordinary contracts, the court moves away from the dominant view that prenuptial agreements should be reviewed under a stricter standard than those applicable to contracts entered into in the business realm.

As you read *Simeone v. Simeone*, look for the following:

1. According to the lower court's reading of the precedent case of *Estate of Geyer*, when will a premarital agreement be upheld?
2. What does the Pennsylvania Supreme Court see as the underlying presumption of the *Geyer* decision and why does the court believe the presumption is no longer valid?
3. What is the type of full and fair disclosure that is required in order to uphold a premarital agreement?

Simeone v. Simeone
581 A.2d 162 (Pa. 1990)

At issue in this appeal is the validity of a prenuptial agreement executed between the appellant, Catherine E. Walsh Simeone, and the appellee, Frederick A. Simeone. At the time of their marriage, in 1975, appellant was a twenty-three year old nurse and appellee was a thirty-nine year old neurosurgeon. Appellee had an income of approximately $90,000 per year, and appellant was unemployed. Appellee also had assets worth approximately $300,000. On the eve of the parties' wedding, appellee's attorney presented appellant with a prenuptial agreement to be signed. Appellant, without the benefit of counsel, signed the agreement. Appellee's attorney had not advised appellant regarding any legal rights that the agreement surrendered. The parties are in disagreement as to whether appellant knew in advance of that date that such an agreement would be presented for signature. Appellant denies having had such knowledge and claims to have signed under adverse circumstances, which, she contends, provide a basis for declaring it void.

The agreement limited appellant to support payments of $200 per week in the event of separation or divorce, subject to a maximum total payment of $25,000. The parties separated in 1982, and, in 1984, divorce proceedings were commenced. Between 1982 and 1984 appellee made payments which satisfied the $25,000 limit. In 1985, appellant filed a claim for alimony pendente lite. A master's report upheld the validity of the prenuptial agreement and denied this claim. . . .

We granted allowance of appeal because uncertainty was expressed by the Superior Court regarding the meaning of our plurality decision in *Estate of Geyer*, 516 Pa. 492, 533 A.2d 423 (1987) (Opinion Announcing Judgment of the Court). The Superior Court viewed *Geyer* as permitting a prenuptial agreement to be upheld if it either made a reasonable provision for the spouse or was entered after a full and fair disclosure of the general financial positions of the parties and the statutory rights being relinquished. Appellant contends that this interpretation of *Geyer* is in error insofar as it requires disclosure of statutory rights only in cases where there has not been made a reasonable provision for the spouse. . . .

There is no longer validity in the implicit presumption that supplied the basis for *Geyer* and similar earlier decisions. Such decisions rested upon a belief that spouses are of unequal status and that women are not knowledgeable enough to understand the nature of contracts that they enter. Society has advanced, however, to the point where women are no longer regarded as the "weaker" party in marriage, or in society generally. Indeed, the stereotype that women serve as homemakers while men work as breadwinners is no longer viable. Quite often today both spouses are income earners. Nor is there viability in the presumption that women are uninformed, uneducated, and readily subjected to unfair advantage in marital agreements. Indeed, women nowadays quite often have substantial education, financial awareness, income, and assets.

Accordingly, the law has advanced to recognize the equal status of men and women in our society. . . . Paternalistic presumptions and protections that arose to shelter women from the inferiorities and incapacities which they were perceived as having in earlier times have, appropriately, been discarded. . . . It would be inconsistent, therefore, to perpetuate the standards governing prenuptial agreements that were described in *Geyer* and similar decisions, as these reflected a paternalistic approach that is now insupportable.

Further, *Geyer* and its predecessors embodied substantial departures from traditional rules of contract law, to the extent that they allowed consideration of the knowledge of the contracting parties and reasonableness of their bargain as factors governing whether to uphold an agreement. Traditional principles of contract law provide perfectly adequate remedies where contracts are procured through fraud, misrepresentation, or duress.

. . . Prenuptial agreements are contracts, and, as such, should be evaluated under the same criteria as are applicable to other types of contracts. . . . Absent fraud, misrepresentation, or duress, spouses should be bound by the terms of their agreements.

Contracting parties are normally bound by their agreements, without regard to whether the terms thereof were read and fully understood and irrespective of whether the agreements embodied reasonable or good bargains. . . . Based upon these principles, the terms of the present prenuptial agreement must be regarded as binding, without regard to whether the terms were fully understood by appellant. Ignorantia non excusat.

Accordingly, we find no merit in a contention raised by appellant that the agreement should be declared void on the ground that she did not consult with independent legal counsel. To impose a per se requirement that parties entering a prenuptial agreement must obtain independent legal counsel would be contrary to traditional principles of contract law, and would constitute a paternalistic and unwarranted interference with the parties' freedom to enter contracts.

Further, the reasonableness of a prenuptial bargain is not a proper subject for judicial review. . . .

By invoking inquiries into reasonableness, however, the functioning and reliability of prenuptial agreements is severely undermined. Parties would not have entered such agreements, and, indeed, might not have entered their marriages, if they did not expect their agreements to be strictly enforced. If parties viewed an agreement as reasonable at the time of its inception, as evidenced by their having signed the agreement, they should be foreclosed from later trying to evade its terms by asserting that it was not in fact reasonable. . . .

Further, everyone who enters a long-term agreement knows that circumstances can change during its term, so that what initially appeared desirable might prove to be an unfavorable bargain. Such are the risks that contracting parties routinely assume. Certainly, the possibilities of illness, birth of children, reliance upon a spouse, career change, financial gain or loss, and numerous other events that can occur in the course of a marriage cannot be regarded as unforeseeable. If parties choose not to address such matters in their prenuptial agreements, they must be regarded as having contracted to bear the risk of events that alter the value of their bargains.

We are reluctant to interfere with the power of persons contemplating marriage to agree upon, and to act in reliance upon, what they regard as an acceptable distribution scheme for their property. A court should not ignore the parties' expressed intent by proceeding to determine whether a prenuptial agreement was, in the court's view, reasonable at the time of its inception or the time of divorce. . . .

In discarding the approach of *Geyer* that permitted examination of the reasonableness of prenuptial agreements and allowed inquiries into whether parties had attained informed understandings of the rights they were surrendering, we do not depart from the longstanding principle that a full and fair disclosure of the financial positions of the parties is required. Absent this disclosure, a material misrepresentation in the inducement for entering a prenuptial agreement may be asserted. *Hillegass*, 431 Pa. at 152-53, 244 A.2d at 676-77. Parties to these agreements do not quite deal at arm's length, but rather at the time the contract is entered into stand in a relation of mutual confidence and trust that calls for disclosure of their financial resources. *Id.*, 431 Pa. at 149, 244 A.2d at 675. . . .

McDERMOTT, Justice, dissenting.

I dissent. . . . I am in full agreement with the majority's observation that "women nowadays quite often have substantial education, financial awareness, income, and assets." . . . However, the plurality decision I authored in *Estate of Geyer*, 516 Pa. 492, 533 A.2d 423 (1987), as well as the Dissenting Opinion I offer today, have little to do with the equality of the sexes, but everything to do with the solemnity of the matrimonial union. I am not willing to believe that our society views marriage as a mere contract for hire. . . . In this Commonwealth, we have long declared our interest in the stability of marriage and in the stability of the family unit. Our courts must seek to protect, and not to undermine, those institutions and interests which are vital to our society. . . .

. . . Thus, while I acknowledge the longstanding rule of law that pre-nuptial agreements are presumptively valid and binding upon the parties, I am unwilling to go as far as the majority to protect the right to contract at the expense of the institution of marriage. Were a contract of marriage, the most intimate relationship between two people, not the surrender of freedom, an offering of self in love, sacrifice, hope for better or for worse, the begetting of children and the offer of effort, labor, precious time and care for the safety and prosperity of their union, then the majority would find me among them.

In my view, one seeking to avoid the operation of an executed pre-nuptial agreement must first establish, by clear and convincing evidence, that a full and fair disclosure of the worth of the intended spouse was not made at the time of the execution of the agreement. . . . In addition to a full and fair disclosure of the general financial pictures of the parties, I would find a pre-nuptial agreement voidable where it is established that the parties were not aware, at the time of contracting, of existing statutory rights which they were relinquishing upon the signing of the agreement. . . . It is here, with a finding of full and fair disclosure, that the majority would end its analysis of the validity of a pre-nuptial agreement. I would not. An analysis of the fairness and equity of a pre-nuptial agreement has long been an important part of the law of this state. . . . I am not willing to depart from this history, which would continue to serve our public policy.

At the time of dissolution of the marriage, a spouse should be able to avoid the operation of a pre-nuptial agreement upon clear and convincing proof that, despite the existence of full and fair disclosure at the time of the execution of the agreement, the agreement is nevertheless so inequitable and unfair that it should not be enforced in a court of this state. . . .

It is also apparent that, although a pre-nuptial agreement is quite valid when drafted, the passage of time accompanied by the intervening events of a marriage may render the terms of the agreement completely unfair and inequitable. While parties to a pre-nuptial agreement may indeed foresee, generally, the events which may come to pass during their marriage, one spouse should not be made to suffer for failing to foresee all of the surrounding circumstances which may attend the dissolution of the marriage. Although it should not be the role of the courts to void pre-nuptial agreements merely because one spouse may receive a better result in an action under the Divorce Code to recover alimony or equitable distribution, it should be the role of the courts to guard against the enforcement of pre-nuptial agreements where such enforcement will bring about only inequity and hardship. It borders on cruelty to accept that after years of living together, yielding their separate opportunities in life to each other, that two individuals emerge the same as the day they began their marriage.

At the time of the dissolution of marriage, what are the circumstances which would serve to invalidate a pre-nuptial agreement? This is a question that should only be answered on a case-by-case basis. However, it is not unrealistic to imagine that in a given situation, one spouse, although trained in the workforce at the time of marriage, may, over many years, have become economically dependent upon the other spouse. In reliance upon the permanence of marriage and in order to provide a stable home for a family, a spouse may choose, even at the suggestion of the other spouse, not to work during the marriage. As a result, at the point of dissolution of the marriage, the spouse's employability has diminished to such an extent that to enforce the support provisions of the pre-nuptial agreement will cause the spouse to become a public charge, or will provide a standard of living far below that which was enjoyed before and during marriage. In such a situation, a court may properly decide to render void all or some of the provisions of the pre-nuptial agreement. . . .

The majority is concerned that parties will routinely challenge the validity of their pre-nuptial agreements. Given the paramount importance of marriage and family in our society, and the serious consequences that may accompany the dissolution of a marriage, we should not choose to close the doors of our courts merely to gain a measure of judicial economy. . . .

Post-Case Follow-Up

The dissent in *Simeone* has no trouble finding that the historical underpinnings of the past that frowned upon premarital agreements because of unequal bargaining positions of the sexes is no longer valid. However, the dissent is concerned about the fairness in the context of a marriage. There are two elements of fairness that the dissent finds troubling. The first is whether at the time of execution there has been adequate disclosure of the finances of the parties. This element appears to be equivalent to the issue of whether it is fair to enter into a contract that waives certain rights if there has not been adequate disclosure. The second is whether the agreement is fair at the time it is enforced. The passage of time may change circumstances so that what seemed fair at the time of execution may not be fair several years or even decades later. The dissent would leave it to the court to make a determination of what is fair at the time of enforcement instead of enforcing a contractual waiver of rights that occurs before marriage but may not be fair to one of the parties due to a change in circumstances that occurred during the marriage.

The majority does not appear to have the same concerns. Rather, so long as the parties voluntarily entered into the agreement and it was not unconscionable, the premarital agreement will be enforced. As we will see, courts have interpreted these provisions to allow for enforcement of the agreements so long as these requirements are met at the time of signing regardless of the change in circumstances that occur after marriage.

Simeone v. Simeone: Real Life Applications

1. Alice is a very successful medical doctor prior to the time she meets Fred, a school teacher. Alice has acquired prior to the marriage a home she owns free and clear, two automobiles, and investment accounts worth over $500,000. Three days prior to the marriage, Alice presents Fred with a premarital agreement that states that regardless of any contributions the parties make after marriage to the improvements of the home, or repair of the automobiles, the property will all be considered Alice's separate property. The agreement also provides that in the event of divorce, and regardless of the length of the marriage, neither party will owe the other party any alimony. Alice insists that although she loves Fred very much she will not go forward with the marriage unless Fred agrees to sign the premarital agreement. Fred has no concerns about the agreement because he knows their love will last forever and there is no possibility of a divorce. Eight year later, all is not well in the marital relationship of Fred and Alice. Alice has continued to earn

a substantial income. Fred, however, has been out of a teaching job for the last three years due to cutbacks in the school system. Fred has now sought your legal advice. How might a court decide Fred's request for alimony from Alice under *Simeone v. Simeone*? Are there any arguments that Fred has that might strengthen his claim for alimony? What arguments do you anticipate from Alice?

2. Assume the same facts as above, but the agreement was entered into three weeks prior to the marriage. Prior to signing the agreement, Fred had sought your legal advice and your notes in the case file show that you explained to Fred the legal consequences of entering into the agreement. However, despite your legal advice that Fred would be giving up an interest in certain assets and the right to alimony from Alice in the event of the divorce, Fred decided to sign the agreement. Would a court view Fred's claim that the agreement is unenforceable differently?

   Assume the same facts as in Question 1 above, but the agreement provides that in the event of a divorce Fred will be entitled to $1,000 a month in alimony from Alice for as many years as the length of the marriage. Would your arguments for Fred change? Would Alice's arguments change? What would a court probably decide if Fred filed an action in court to increase his amount of alimony due to the fact that circumstances changed during the marriage?

C. LEGAL REQUIREMENTS

Premarital agreements are contracts. Accordingly, to be enforceable they must, at a minimum, satisfy certain threshold requirements generally applicable to all contracts. However, as discussed below, unlike with most other contracts, satisfying these requirements may not be enough. To meet these threshold requirements:

1. There must be an offer and an acceptance of the offer.
2. The contract must be supported by **consideration**. Consideration is the bargained-for exchange of something of value — here, the mutual promise of marriage, and ultimately a marriage. However, the consideration must not be something that is a violation of public policy.
3. The parties must have the capacity to enter into a contract.
4. The subject matter of the agreement cannot be illegal.

Prenuptial agreement
Shutterstock.com

Additionally, in most jurisdictions, premarital contracts come within the **statute of frauds**, and thus must be in writing in order to be enforceable. The agreement will also need to be signed by both parties, and most likely the signatures may need to be both witnessed and notarized.

THE UNIFORM PREMARITAL AGREEMENT ACT

In 1983, the National Conference of Commissioners on Uniform State Laws promulgated the Uniform Premarital Agreement Act (UPAA). The UPAA, or some form of it, has been adopted in over half of the states. The Act has undergone changes over the years, but two key provisions merit attention: (1) the content of premarital agreements; and (2) the circumstances under which a premarital agreement will be enforceable. These provisions are set forth below.

§3 Content

(a) Parties to a premarital agreement may contract with respect to:

(1) the rights and obligations of each of the parties in any of the property of either or both of them whenever and wherever acquired or located;

(2) the right to buy, sell, use, transfer, exchange, abandon, lease, consume, expend, assign, create a security interest in, mortgage, encumber, dispose of, or otherwise manage and control property;

(3) the disposition of property upon separation, marital dissolution, death or the occurrence or nonoccurrence of any other event;

(4) the modification or elimination of spousal support;

(5) the making of a will, trust, or other arrangement to carry out the provisions of the agreement;

(6) the ownership rights in and disposition of the death benefit from a life insurance policy;

(7) the choice of law governing the construction of the agreement; and

(8) any other matter, including their personal rights and obligations, not in violation of public policy or a statute imposing a criminal penalty.

(b) The right of a child to support may not be adversely affected by a premarital agreement.

§6 Enforcement

(a) A premarital agreement is not enforceable if the party against whom enforcement is sought proves that:

(1) the party did not enter the agreement voluntarily; or

(2) the agreement was unconscionable when it was executed and, before execution of the agreement, that party:

(i) was not provided a fair and reasonable disclosure of the property or financial obligations of the other party;

(ii) did not voluntarily and expressly waive, in writing, any right of disclosure of the property or financial obligations of the other party beyond the disclosure provided; and

(iii) did not have, or reasonably could not have had, an adequate knowledge of the property or financial obligations of the other party.

(b) If a provision of a premarital agreement modifies or eliminates spousal support and that modification or elimination causes one party to the agreement to be eligible for support under a program of public assistance at the time of separation or marital dissolution, a court, notwithstanding the terms of the agreement, may require the other party to provide support to the extent necessary to avoid eligibility.

(c) An issue of unconscionability of a premarital agreement shall be decided by the court as a matter of law.

1. The Fairness Requirement

As a general rule, our legal system emphasizes **freedom of contract** — the right of each individual to freely structure his or her affairs. A corollary of this principle is that once parties have entered into a contract, they are entitled to rely upon it, and courts will protect the expectancies that arise from the terms of the agreement. Without proof of conduct that rises to the level of fraud, misrepresentation, duress, or the like, courts typically will not refuse to enforce a contract because it is more favorable to one party. Unless these more serious kinds of concerns can be established, considerations of fairness with respect to either the process by which the contract was negotiated, such as where a party felt rushed into signing it, or the resulting terms, such as where a person agrees to pay more for a painting than it is worth, are essentially irrelevant. Thus, as a general rule, adherence to the freedom-of-contract principle means that an individual cannot avoid contractual obligations because he or she subsequently realizes that the deal is unfair or more favorable to the other side. The primary exception to this rule is the doctrine of **unconscionability**, which allows a court to inquire into issues of fairness in outrageous situations; for this doctrine to apply, there usually must be gross overreaching by a party who is in a vastly superior bargaining position.

However, when a dispute involves a premarital contract, courts typically review the agreement for evidence of unfairness in either the process of negotiating the agreement, referred to as **procedural fairness**, or in the resulting terms, referred to as **substantive fairness**. This hands-on approach, as distinct from the traditional hands-off approach to contract review, flows from a number of considerations. First, by entering into a premarital contract, parties are substituting their own terms for state laws that determine rights of support and property distribution between divorcing spouses. In effect, these agreements create private law in an area long considered to be under the exclusive authority of the state because of its special interest in the marriage. Thus, the subject matter of premarital agreements is quite different from that of more ordinary contracts, such as those governing the purchase and sale of real estate.

Second, parties to a typical contract stand at "arm's-length" distance from one another — they are generally not intimately connected and each party can be assumed to be acting in his or her own self-interest. In contrast, parties to a premarital agreement are in an intimate relationship, or what the courts refer to as a "confidential relationship," and are thought to be more vulnerable to being unduly influenced by the other. This risk is compounded by the fact that the parties often are negotiating from positions of unequal bargaining power. Premarital agreements are usually proposed by the prospective spouse with greater wealth who stands to gain more from avoiding state divorce laws, and the other party may feel that she or he has no choice but to sign or face the cancellation of the wedding. Closely related, at least in the early days of recognition, were lingering concerns about the inability of a prospective bride to comprehend the details of the financial terms being proposed by her future husband, particularly where differences in wealth were pronounced.

Third, the performance of contractual obligations usually begins within a reasonably short and clearly defined time period after the contract is executed. In contrast, with premarital contracts, the time of performance is uncertain or may never come to be since the triggering event is divorce. Performance of the terms could thus come several years or even several decades after execution of the contract. With the passage of time, unforeseen events may intervene that would make performance of the original terms unfair.

Finally, perhaps this heightened standard of review reflects a continued uneasiness about the contracting of obligations of family life, rooted in a sense that the domestic realm should remain distinct from the commercial realm. Courts may be reluctant to fully import legal standards developed in the realm of impersonal dealings into the realm of intimate relationships.

2. Requirements of Procedural Fairness

Although the clear trend is in favor of treating premarital contracts more like ordinary agreements with a corresponding emphasis upon individual autonomy and choice, most courts still look to see if the parties treated each other fairly when negotiating the terms of the agreement. If a court determines that in the course of negotiating the agreement one party did not treat the other fairly, such as by not fully disclosing assets, it may invalidate the agreement.

The requirement of full and fair disclosure is usually the most important consideration, and the general rule is that both parties have an affirmative duty to make full disclosure even where this information is not requested by the other. Although the standard for determining what constitutes adequate disclosure varies from state to state, more than a mere recitation of numbers is necessary. Thus, for example, a party may be required to determine the value of his or her property and to disclose assets that he or she is entitled to receive in the future. If disclosure is not adequate, entry into the agreement is not considered voluntary, as a party cannot freely relinquish assets or income that he or she did not know of or know the correct value of.

In some states, a limited exception to the disclosure requirement may be made where one party has actual and specific knowledge of the other potential spouse's assets. However, a general familiarity with the other's financial reputation is unlikely to justify the failure to disclose.

In preparing premarital agreements, even if not specifically required by state law, most attorneys will prepare a full schedule of their client's income and assets, which is attached to the agreement as an exhibit (see Exhibit 3.1). Great care must be taken to obtain complete and accurate information, as this may determine the subsequent enforceability of the agreement.

EXHIBIT 3.1 **Schedule of Assets for Sandra Lope**

	Fair Market Value	Encumbrance	Net Values
Real Estate			
Location: 16 Armand Rd.			
Recorded at: Norfolk County,			
Registry of Deeds;			
Book No. 814, Page No. 9	$240,000	$170,000	$70,000
Personal Property			
Household Furnishings:			
Complete set of bedroom, living room, dining room, and kitchen furniture	$3,800	$0	$3,800
Other Household Items (list all worth more than $100):			
Tiffany lamp	$600	$0	$600
Indoor gym equipment	$1,500	$0	$1,500
Computer	$2,500	$0	$2,500
Kitchen appliances (including refrigerator and microwave)	$1,100	$0	$1,100
Antique phonograph	$1,200	$0	$1,200
Collections:			
Rare jazz records	$3,500	$0	$3,500
Jewelry (list all worth more than $100):			
Antique diamond ring	$1,200	$0	$1,200
Rolex watch	$1,400	$0	$1,400
Automobiles:			
2001 VW Bug	$16,000	$4,000	$12,000
Bank Accounts:			
Savings account, Union Federal Bank, account no. 1743	$4,000	—	—
Individual Retirement Account, Union Federal Bank, account no. 97363	$12,000	—	—
Stocks and Bonds:			
80 shares of General Utility Stock	$800	—	—

Note: This sample Schedule of Assets is for one party only. In actuality, both parties would complete one.

Often a client is given a written questionnaire to complete regarding his or her income and assets. Exhibit 3.2 shows a sample list of the information a client might be asked to provide.

EXHIBIT 3.2   **Sample Questions for Compiling Schedule of Assets**

1. Do you own any real estate or have an interest in any realty? If yes, please provide a detailed list, including location of the real estate, nature of your interest, purchase date, purchase amount and amount of your down payment, current fair market value, and the amount of your equity in the real estate.
2. Please provide an itemized list of all household furnishings and effects owned by you, including the fair market value of each item.
3. Please provide an itemized list of all artwork owned by you, including the fair market value of each item.
4. Please provide an itemized list of all collections owned by you, including but not limited to collection items such as stamps, coins, cards, antiques, rare books, guns, and records. Include the fair market value of each collection.
5. Please provide an itemized list of all jewelry owned by you, including the fair market value of each item.
6. Please provide a detailed list of all stocks, bonds, retirement accounts, pension plans, and profit-sharing plans, including the nature of your interest, identifying information for each item, and the current value of your interest in each.

In evaluating procedural fairness, some courts also consider factors such as whether the party challenging the agreement understood its provisions at the time of signing, whether she or he was made aware of the legal rights being waived (such as, for example, a right to spousal support) by entry into the agreement, and whether she or he had the opportunity to review the agreement with an independent attorney. Most jurisdictions require only that a party have the opportunity to review the agreement with an attorney; actual consultation is not required. The primary objective is to prevent one partner from presenting the other with an agreement for the first time at the rehearsal dinner and telling him or her that it must be signed if the wedding is to proceed as planned. As with the requirement of financial disclosure, these elements also relate to whether entry into the agreement was free and voluntary.

In jurisdictions where freedom of contract is emphasized over considerations of procedural fairness, courts may not be particularly concerned with the above considerations. In contrast, a court that gives high priority to freedom of contract principles will interpret the fairness requirement very narrowly in seeking to uphold the contract.

Some courts use a somewhat flexible approach to evaluating formation fairness. They may be stricter if the parties do not stand on equal footing, such as where one partner is much wealthier or better educated than the other. However, if they stand on relatively equal footing with respect to income, assets, and education, the court may be less concerned with procedural irregularities. Also, as discussed below, if the outcome is fair, courts may be less concerned with procedural irregularities.

3. Requirements of Substantive Fairness

In addition to reviewing whether the process of contract formation was fair, courts in many jurisdictions will also review the actual terms of the agreement to see if they are fair. Fairness can be measured as it existed at the time the contract was executed, or as it exists at the time of performance, or both. Again, this kind of review is a substantial departure from the usual contract law approach that gives individuals "freedom" to make bad deals. Subject to the limited unconscionability exception, a person cannot avoid an ordinary contract because he or she subsequently realizes that it is unfair or one-sided.

At Formation

In jurisdictions where the terms of a premarital agreement are reviewed for fairness, a court would first evaluate them in light of the circumstances as they existed at the time the contract was executed. For example, looking back to the time of contract formation, the waiver of alimony by a two-career couple not intending to have children appears equitable, whereas a waiver by a spouse planning to stay home and raise a large family would not. At this phase of the review, events taking place after execution are not considered.

States differ in the standards they use to determine if the terms were fair at the time of execution. Some will not enforce provisions that are "unreasonable," such as a waiver of support by a spouse with a good job but with a much lower earning potential than his or her partner, although something more than a mere inequality of result is generally required. Other states will strike only clauses that are unconscionable or so unfair that they "shock the conscience." In a few jurisdictions, alimony waivers are considered per se unfair and will not be enforced, although this is a minority approach.

At Performance

In addition to determining if the terms were fair at the time the contract was executed, some courts will also review them to see if they are fair at the time of divorce. This is sometimes referred to as the "second glance doctrine." Here, traditional freedom of contract principles are clearly subordinated in favor of protecting an economically vulnerable spouse. Many courts, however, consider this too great an interference with rights of contractual freedom, adhering to the view that once parties have made an agreement that is fair at the time of execution, they are entitled to rely on it. Accordingly, the only proper role of the court is to protect legitimate expectations arising from the agreement. By way of example, let us return to our two-career couple who did not plan to have children and included an alimony waiver in their prenuptial agreement. Assuming this was fair at the time of execution, if they then changed their minds and decided to have children, the waiver might be deemed unfair at the time of performance if one parent had cut back on employment to care for them. At second glance, terms that appeared fair at the time of contract formation would now work a hardship because of changed circumstances.

Courts will usually take a second glance only at support-related clauses, and they tend to employ a very high standard of review in order to strike a balance between avoiding hardship and honoring contractual expectations. At this stage, many courts will invalidate only a term waiving or limiting support rights where enforcement would leave a party unable to meet basic needs or would force him or her onto public assistance. Other courts are less strict and will invalidate a clause if enforcement would result in a substantial reduction in a party's standard of living, even if poverty is not threatened.

4. The Interdependence of Procedural and Substantive Fairness

Although the above discussion treated the requirements of procedural and substantive fairness as independent variables, many courts regard them as interdependent. Accordingly, where the substantive terms are fair, a court may choose to overlook procedural deficiencies; for example, financial disclosure will not be insisted on as a pure formality. Likewise, if the result is clearly unfair, a court may presume that the procedure was inherently flawed and proceed to review the agreement with particular care.

5. The Growing Emphasis on Freedom of Contract Principles over Substantive Fairness

Although many courts still review premarital contracts to determine if the terms are fair to both parties, it should come as no surprise that the trend is away from such review in favor of strict enforcement in order to protect the reliance interests of the parties. Accordingly, assuming that a party can show that the agreement was entered into voluntarily, and was not unconscionable when executed, even if circumstances change during the marriage, the agreement will be enforced. *In re Marriage of Bonds* provides an example of where the financial circumstances of husband changed dramatically during the marriage. However, despite these changes, the court indicated that absent a finding the agreement was not entered into voluntarily or it was unconscionable when executed, it would be upheld.

Case Preview

In re Marriage of Bonds

In re Marriage of Bonds examined the issue of whether a premarital agreement entered into shortly before marriage was valid and should be upheld. California had enacted a statute similar to the Uniform Premarital Act that provided, in part, that an agreement will not be enforced if either of the following is true: (1) the party did not execute the agreement voluntarily; and (2) the agreement was unconscionable when it was executed.

The premarital agreement was entered into when Sun and Barry were 23 years old and just one day before the wedding. Because the agreement waived earnings and acquisitions during the marriage, if the agreement were to be upheld, Sun would lose significant assets acquired during the marriage upon dissolution of the marriage. Sun argued that, based upon a number of factors, the agreement was not entered into voluntarily. Barry, on the other hand, dismissed these arguments claiming that, despite the fact she did not have independent counsel, she voluntarily entered into the agreement. The trial court upheld the agreement and Sun appealed. The Court of Appeal reversed the decision and remanded it back to the trial court on the issue of voluntariness. Barry petitioned to the California Supreme Court, which agreed to hear the case.

Barry Bonds
s_bukley / Shutterstock.com

As you read *In re Marriage of Bonds,* look for the following:

1. What were the arguments that Sun raised as to why the agreement was not entered into voluntarily and how did the court address each argument?
2. Why is unconscionability not an issue in this case?
3. Why did the court reject the idea that the presence of independent counsel for Sun was not necessary to make the agreement enforceable?

In re Marriage of Bonds
24 Cal. 4th 1 (Cal. 2000)

In this case we consider whether appellant Susann (known as Sun) Margreth Bonds voluntarily entered into a premarital agreement with respondent Barry Lamar Bonds. . . . [A]s we shall explain, we conclude that substantial evidence supports the determination of the trial court that the agreement in the present case was entered into voluntarily.

I

. . .

On February 5, 1988, in Phoenix, the parties entered into a written premarital agreement in which each party waived any interest in the earnings and acquisitions of the other party during the marriage. That same day, they flew to Las Vegas, and were married the following day.

Each of the parties then was 23 years of age. Barry, who had attended college for three years and who had begun his career in professional baseball in 1985, had a contract to play for the Pittsburgh Pirates. His annual salary at the time of the marriage ceremony was approximately $106,000. Sun had emigrated to Canada from Sweden in 1985, had worked as a waitress and bartender, and had undertaken some training as a cosmetologist. . . . Although her native language was Swedish, she had used both French and English in her employment, education, and personal relationships when she lived in Canada. She was unemployed at the time she entered into the premarital agreement.

[Barry filed a petition for legal separation on May 27, 1994, which was later amended to a divorce. Barry sought to enforce the premarital agreement. Sun sought to invalidate the agreement. Both parties testified as to the facts surrounding execution of the agreement.]

Barry testified that he was aware of teammates and other persons who had undergone bitter marital dissolution proceedings involving the division of property, and recalled that from the beginning of his relationship with Sun he told her that he believed his earnings and acquisitions during marriage should be his own. He informed her he would not marry without a premarital agreement, and she had no objection. He also recalled that from the beginning of the relationship, Sun agreed that their earnings and acquisitions should be separate, saying "what's mine is mine, what's yours is yours." Indeed, she informed him that this was the practice with respect to marital property in Sweden. She stated that she planned to pursue a career and wished to be financially independent. Sun knew that Barry did not anticipate that she would shoulder her living expenses while she was not employed. She was not, in fact, employed during the marriage. Barry testified that he and Sun had no difficulty communicating.

. . .

Sun's testimony at trial differed from Barry's in material respects. She testified that her English language skills in 1987 and 1988 were limited. Out of pride, she did not disclose to Barry that she often did not understand him. She testified that she and Barry never discussed money or property during the relationship that preceded their marriage. She agreed that she had expressed interest in a career as a cosmetologist and had said she wished to be financially independent. She had very few assets when she took up residence with Barry, and he paid for all their needs. Their wedding arrangements were very informal, with no written invitations or caterer, and only Barry's parents and a couple of friends, including Barry's godfather Willie Mays, were invited to attend. No marriage license or venue had been arranged in advance of their arrival in Las Vegas.

. . .

Sun testified that on the evening before the premarital agreement was signed, Barry first informed her that they needed to go the following day to the offices of his lawyers. . . . She was uncertain, however, whether Barry made any reference to a premarital agreement. She testified that only at the parking lot of the law office where the agreement was to be entered into did she learn, from Barry's financial adviser, Mel Wilcox, that Barry would not marry her unless she signed a premarital agreement. She was not upset. She was surprised, however, because Barry never had said that signing the agreement was a precondition to marriage. She did not question Barry or anyone else on this point. She was under the impression that Barry wished to retain separate ownership of property he owned before the marriage, and that this was the sole object of the premarital agreement. She was unaware the agreement would affect her future and was not concerned about the matter, because she was nervous and excited about getting married and trusted Barry. . . .

Sun recalled having to hurry to arrive at the lawyers' office in time both to accomplish their business there and make the scheduled departure of the airplane to Las Vegas so that she and Barry could marry the next day. Sun recalled that once they arrived at the lawyers' office on February 5, 1988, she, her friend Margareta Forsberg, Barry, and Barry's financial adviser Mel Wilcox were present in a conference room. She did not recall asking questions or her friend asking questions, nor did she recall that any changes were made to the agreement. She declared that her English language skills were limited at the time and she did not understand the agreement, but she did not ask questions of anyone other than Margareta Forsberg or ask for more time, because she did not want to miss her flight and she was focused on the forthcoming marriage ceremony. She did not believe that Barry understood the agreement either. . . .

Barry and other witnesses offered a different picture of the circumstances leading to the signing. . . . Barry and his attorney . . . recalled that approximately two weeks before the parties signed the formal agreement, they discussed with Sun the drafting of an agreement to keep earnings and acquisitions separate . . . and that at the meeting the attorneys informed Sun of her right to independent counsel. Additionally, [they] read the agreement to her paragraph by paragraph and explained it as they went through it, also informing her of a spouse's basic community property rights in earnings and acquisitions and that Sun would be waiving these rights. . . . Furthermore, Barry and the two attorneys each confirmed that Sun and Forsberg asked questions during the meeting and were left alone on several occasions to discuss its terms, that Sun did not exhibit any confusion, and that Sun indicated she understood the agreement. They also testified that changes were made to the agreement at Sun's behest. . . .

The trial court observed that the case turned upon the credibility of the witnesses. In support of its determination that Sun entered into the agreement voluntarily, "free from the taint of fraud, coercion and undue influence . . . with full knowledge of the property involved and her rights therein," the trial court made the following findings of fact: "Respondent [Sun] knew Petitioner [Barry] wished to protect his present property and future earnings. Respondent knew . . . that the Agreement provided that . . . Petitioner's present and future earnings would remain his separate property. . . . Respondent is an intelligent woman and though English is not her native language, she was capable of understanding the discussion by Attorney Brown and Attorney Megwa regarding the terms of the agreement and the effect of the Agreement on each [party's] rights. [The trial court also determined that Sun] had sufficient knowledge and understanding of her rights regarding the property affected by the Agreement, and how the Agreement adversely affected those rights. [Sun] had the opportunity to read the Agreement prior to executing it. . . . [Sun] also had an adequate and reasonable opportunity to obtain independent counsel prior to execution of the Agreement. The court also determined that Barry and Sun were not in a confidential relationship at the time the agreement was executed.

The Court of Appeal in a split decision reversed the judgment rendered by the trial court and directed a retrial on the issue of voluntariness. The majority stressed that Sun lacked independent counsel, determined that she had not waived counsel effectively, and concluded that under such circumstances the evidence must be subjected to strict judicial scrutiny to determine whether the agreement was voluntary.

We granted Barry's petition for review.

Pursuant to Family Code section 1615, a premarital agreement will be enforced unless the party resisting enforcement of the agreement can demonstrate either (1) that he or she did not enter into the contract voluntarily, or (2) that the contract was unconscionable when entered into and that he or she did not have actual or constructive knowledge of the assets and obligations of the other party and did not voluntarily waive knowledge of such assets and obligations. In the present case, the trial court found no lack of knowledge regarding the nature of the parties' assets, a necessary predicate to considering the issue of unconscionability, and the Court of Appeal accepted the trial court's determination on this point. We do not reconsider this factual determination, and thus the question of unconscionability is not before us. . . . [T]he only issue we face concerns the trial court's determination that Sun entered into the agreement voluntarily.

Neither the article of the Family Code in which section 1615 is located, nor the Uniform [Premarital Agreement] Act [as adopted by California] defines the term "voluntary." . . . To the extent it is unclear on the face of the statute what was intended by the Legislature in employing the term "voluntary," we consult the history of the statute and consider its general intent.

. . .

[The court reviewed the history and cases and found that courts should consider whether the evidence indicates coercion or lack of knowledge, and that coercion may arise from the proximity of execution of the agreement to the wedding or from surprise in the presentation of the agreement; the presence or absence of independent counsel or of an opportunity to consult independent counsel; inequality of bargaining power, including relative age and sophistication of the parties; whether there was full disclosure of assets; and from the parties' understanding of the right being waived under the agreement or at least the intent of the agreement.]

We have considered the range of factors that may be relevant to establish the involuntariness of a premarital agreement in order to consider whether the Court of Appeal erred in according such great weight to one factor [—] the presence or absence of independent counsel for each party. . . .

It is clear from the history of the Uniform Act that the commissioners rejected the view that independent counsel was essential to the enforceability of premarital agreements. Although the proposed Uniform Act initially contained a proviso stating that premarital agreements were presumptively valid unless the party against whom enforcement was sought was not represented by independent legal counsel or there was not full disclosure, the commissioners eventually removed any reference to independent counsel. . . .

Finally, and perhaps most significantly, the rule created by the Court of Appeal would have the effect of shifting the burden of proof on the question of voluntariness to the party seeking enforcement of the premarital agreement, even though the statute expressly places the burden upon the party challenging the voluntariness of the agreement. . . .

We conclude that although the ability of the party challenging the agreement to obtain independent counsel is an important factor in determining whether that party entered into the agreement voluntarily, the Court of Appeal majority erred in directing trial courts to subject premarital agreements to strict scrutiny where the less sophisticated party does not have independent counsel and has not waived counsel according to exacting waiver requirements.

. . .

[W]e believe that both the Court of Appeal majority and Sun err to the extent they suggest that the Uniform Act or its California analog established that persons who enter into premarital agreements must be presumed to be in a confidential relationship, a status that would give rise to the fiduciary duties between spouses. . . .

The primary consequences of designating a relationship as fiduciary in nature are that the parties owe a duty of full disclosure, and that a presumption arises that a party who owes a fiduciary duty, and who secures a benefit through an agreement, has done so through undue influence.

. . .

Finally, we conclude that the trial court's determination that Sun voluntarily entered into the premarital agreement in the present case is supported by substantial evidence.

. . .

The trial court determined that there had been no coercion. It declared that Sun had not been subjected to any threats, that she had not been forced to sign the agreement, and that she never expressed any reluctance to sign the agreement. It found that the temporal proximity of the wedding to the signing of the agreement was not coercive, because under the particular circumstances of the case, including the small number of guests and the informality of the wedding arrangements, little embarrassment would have followed from postponement of the wedding. It found that the presentation of the agreement did not come as a surprise to Sun, noting that she was aware of Barry's desire to "protect his present property and future earnings," and that she had been aware for at least a week before the parties signed the formal premarital agreement that one was planned.

. . .

With respect to the presence of independent counsel, although Sun lacked legal counsel, the trial court determined that she had a reasonable opportunity to obtain counsel. . . .

. . .

With respect to the question of inequality of bargaining power, the trial court determined that Sun was intelligent and, evidently not crediting her claim that limited English made her unable to understand the import of the agreement or the explanations offered by Barry's counsel, found that she was capable of understanding the agreement and the explanations proffered by Barry's attorneys. . . .

The judgment of the Court of Appeal is reversed to the extent that it reversed the judgment of the trial court on the issue of the voluntariness of the premarital agreement.

Post-Case Follow-Up

The court in *Bonds* finds no trouble in holding that, despite the fact that the premarital agreement was entered into just a day before the wedding and Sun did not have independent counsel, the premarital agreement is valid. While neither the Uniform Act nor the California Family Code section that to a large extent mirrored the Uniform Act defined voluntariness, the court found there to be substantial evidence that the agreement was entered into voluntarily and that there was not duress or coercion to enter into the agreement. Accordingly, findings by the trial court such as the meeting Barry's attorneys had with Sun the week before the wedding to explain the premarital agreement, the simplicity of the concept that both would hold their earnings during the marriage as separate property, and Sun's ability to understand the concepts helped establish that Sun entered into the agreement voluntarily.

It is clear from the decision in *Bonds* that whether a contract is entered into voluntarily is highly dependent on the facts surrounding the execution. Yet it is also clear that the agreement will be presumed valid unless the person challenging the agreement can show it was not entered into voluntarily or is unconscionable. Thus, under the Uniform Premarital Agreement Act a party against whom enforcement of the agreement is sought has the burden to prove the agreement was not executed voluntarily or was unconscionable when executed.

In re Marriage of Bonds: Real Life Applications

1. In *Bonds*, the wedding was not a formal affair and more of an impromptu ceremony. Assume instead that Barry and Sun had sent out invitations for a wedding to over 300 of their family and friends for an elaborate affair on a remote island off the coast of Florida. The wedding guests all started to arrive two to three days before. Although Barry and Sun had talked about the possibility of having a premarital agreement, the matter was never formally discussed, and never discussed after the invitations were sent out, which was approximately two months before the wedding. The night before the wedding, Barry's attorneys approached Sun with the premarital agreement and asked her to sign it. Although she was advised she could have independent counsel, she did not know any lawyers and did not know where she could find anyone at this late date. Sun was also afraid

if she did not sign it and the wedding was canceled she would experience social embarrassment and humiliation in front of their friends and families. Accordingly, she signed the agreement. Assume all other facts are as stated in the case. Would the outcome of the case be different under those circumstances? What factors would Barry argue to justify upholding the agreement even in light of these circumstances?

2. Assume that the facts are as set forth in the case, but that Sun is three months pregnant. Would that change the outcome of the case? Why might that change in facts change the result? What are the arguments for still upholding the agreement?

3. The court does not find that the parties were in a confidential relationship with each other. What factors would have to exist to find the parties were in a confidential relationship with each other and therefore owed each other a fiduciary duty? Why is the premarital agreement treated more like a commercial contract than an agreement entered into after marriage?

D. COMMON TYPES OF PROVISIONS

In light of the above history, it is not surprising that even in more liberal jurisdictions, courts may be reluctant to accept certain types of provisions. Moreover, as discussed below, with respect to clauses involving children, traditional family law principles also factor into the general rule of nonenforceability. Although the discussion is far from exhaustive, we now consider kinds of provisions that many couples include in their premarital agreements.

1. Property

Perhaps the most common and generally least controversial type of premarital provisions are those that address how the property that the parties accumulated over the marriage is to be allocated in the event of divorce. In effect, these provisions allow a couple to opt out of the legal rules that would otherwise control the disposition of their property (see Chapter 8).

Most significant here is a determination of what assets will be regarded as separate, and thus unreachable by the other spouse in the event of a divorce, and what is to be considered marital property that is subject to distribution under applicable state rules. The ability to insulate property from the potential divorce claims of a spouse can be particularly important to an individual who already has children, as it enables him or her to preserve and eventually bequeath the intended assets to them.

Many patterns are possible here. Parties might simply seek to ensure that assets they come into the marriage with will continue to be defined as their sole and separate property, regardless of how they might otherwise be classified at the time of divorce under state law. Parties might also seek to classify all assets purchased during the marriage as the separate property of the acquiring spouse, free from any claims of the other, or they might set out a schema for determining which assets are to be considered separate and which are to be considered marital that differs from the classification pattern under state law.

2. Spousal Support

Courts have typically been more wary of provisions in which one or both spouses waive their right to spousal support. Of particular concern is that a spouse might not be able to make ends meet and thus end up on public assistance. Accordingly, some courts will not enforce alimony waivers, often based on the view that they are "void as against public policy," although this traditional approach is now a distinctly minority position.

In the majority of states that now permit parties to waive spousal support rights, many have addressed concerns about potential post-divorce impoverishment through rules governing the review process. Thus, as discussed above, many require that the terms of the waiver be closely examined to ensure that they are fair, even if such a substantive review is not required for the property provisions. Some also mandate a second glance (as discussed earlier) to ensure that even if fair at the time of enactment, the waiver is still fair at the time of divorce. In addition to or in lieu of substantive fairness requirements, some states also employ heightened procedural fairness requirements to ensure that a support waiver is truly free and voluntary.

3. Child Custody and Support

Despite the clear trend in favor of allowing spouses to structure in advance the consequences of divorce, this trend stops when it comes to provisions regarding children. Reflecting longstanding family law principles, that it is the duty of the court to ensure that the best interest of the children is protected, this general prohibition on the enforceability of child-related provisions is unlikely to change.

With respect to premarital efforts to determine custodial arrangements in the event of divorce, courts are in accord that spouses cannot determine in advance what would be in the "best interest" of their future offspring were they to eventually divorce. Consider for example an agreement that provides that in the event of a divorce, both parents will have joint custody of any minor children. Assume that one parent is an alcoholic, abusive, or otherwise unfit as a parent. It would not be appropriate for the court to simply accept the terms of the prenuptial agreement regarding custody without making an independent determination of the best interest of the minor children. (See Chapter 5.) Although, as we have been discussing, parties can modify the application of other rules, such as those governing the distribution of assets, through private ordering, the state retains a duty to ensure that custodial arrangements are carefully tailored to promote the well-being of children at the time of divorce.

Similarly, courts will not enforce provisions intended to modify or eliminate either party's child support obligations. Mandated by state law, the right to support runs to the child, not to the custodial parent, and thus cannot be waived or limited by a "third party."

E. POSTMARITAL CONTRACTS

Although still less common than premarital agreements, a growing number of couples are now entering into postmarital contracts in order to determine the financial aspects of dissolution in the event their marriage ends in divorce. A couple might also choose to enter into a postmarital agreement in order to modify the terms of an agreement they entered into prior to their marriage based on a change in circumstances arising during the course of their marriage.

Many states now recognize the validity of these agreements, although for some of the reasons discussed below, their enforceability may be governed by stricter standards than those governing premarital agreements. A few states have determined either by statute or judicial decision that they are not enforceable, while others have not yet addressed the issue.

Some commentators have suggested two primary reasons that might make postmarital contracts a more attractive option than contracts of the prenuptial variety. First, because the parties are already married, the dreaded last minute situation where one party presents the other with an agreement at the rehearsal dinner and says "sign or the wedding is off" is avoided, thus potentially making them less coercive. Second, and perhaps more important, the actual circumstances of a couple's life together may be clearer as their life together enfolds, thus enabling them to more carefully tailor an agreement to their actual, as distinct from their projected, needs. For example, if it turns out that "a couple's first child has autism, the wife may choose to forgo a career opportunity to care for her child. A postnuptial contract would allow her to tailor her rights upon divorce to ensure that her sacrifice is borne equally by both parents," in a way that would not have been possible prior to the marriage on account of this unforeseen circumstance. Sean Hannon Williams, Postnuptial Agreements, 2007 Wis. L. Rev. 827, 828.

However, many courts that have considered the issue have instead concluded that postmarital contracts should be held to a higher standard of review than premarital agreements. Of particular concern is that potential for coercion may be greater in the context of an ongoing marriage than it is prior to the wedding, as one spouse may threaten divorce if the other refuses to sign an agreement that is presented unilaterally at a rocky moment in the relationship. (*See id.* at 838-845 for a discussion of some of these cases.) For example, in a 2010 case of first impression, the Massachusetts high court, although rejecting the wife's claim that "marital agreements . . . should be declared void against public policy because they are 'innately coercive,'" concluded that "a marital agreement stands on a different footing from a premarital agreement" because "parties have greater freedom to reject an unsatisfactory . . . contract" before they have embarked on married life. *Ansin v. Craven-Ansin*, 457 Mass. 283, 929 N.E.2d 955, 962 (2010). However, once married, a party may feel coerced into signing an agreement in order to save "a long, existing family relationship to which she [or he] has committed her [or his] best years.'" *Id.* at 962, quoting C.P. Kindregan Jr. & M.L. Inker, Family Law and Practice §50:15 (3d ed. 2002). The party may know that the failure to give in to a spouse's unilateral demand would result in "'the destruction of a family and the stigma of a failed marriage.'" *Id.* at 962-963, quoting *Pacelli v. Pacelli*, 319 N.J. Super. 185, 190, 725 A.2d 56 (App. Div. 1999).

Chapter Summary

- Premarital and postmarital agreements are contracts that allow married couples to control the terms of their dissolution in the event the marriage ends in divorce.
- Couples choose to enter premarital and postmarital agreements to alter how properties and assets accumulated before and during the marriage are allocated in the event of divorce, and the amount and length of spousal support, if any.
- Until the 1970s, premarital agreements made in contemplation of divorce were generally considered void as against public policy in large part because they were thought to encourage divorce.
- As contracts, premarital agreements must meet threshold requirements in order to be enforceable, and in addition, adhere to procedural and substantive fairness requirements.
- Although less common, and harder to enforce, many states now also recognize postmarital agreements.
- Postmarital agreements must be fair and equitable at the time of execution and must not be unconscionable when enforced.

Applying the Rules

1. Henry and Sylvia were married in 1993. Sylvia had just completed medical school, and Henry was a nurse. At the time, neither of them had substantial assets. However, it was anticipated that Sylvia's income would increase substantially during the marriage. The parties entered into a premarital agreement that provided that in the event of a divorce, regardless of their economic circumstances at the time, neither party would be entitled to alimony. Sylvia now seeks a divorce. She wants to meet with you to discuss the following facts: She continues to earn a substantial salary as a medical doctor, but she is concerned because Henry was recently in an accident and can no longer work. His only income is through disability insurance that the parties had purchased during

the marriage. Sylvia says she will want to know whether the premarital agreement is enforceable. What questions do you want to ask Sylvia to determine whether the agreement can be enforced?

2. Assume the same facts as Question 1, but the agreement was not signed prior to marriage. Instead the parties set the agreement aside and did not sign the agreement until three years after they were married but before Henry's accident. Would your questions for Sylvia differ if this agreement had been entered into after the parties were married and before Henry's disability?

3. Sheila and Alberto were married ten years ago, and at the time they entered into a premarital agreement. The agreement has a number of provisions, including a waiver of alimony in the event of a divorce and a provision that should the parties have children Sheila will be the party with sole custody of the children in the event of a divorce. The parties agreed that neither party would seek child support from the other. Alberto comes to you and tells you he would like to file for divorce. However, he is concerned because the parties have two little girls, ages 4 and 6, and he is afraid if he files for divorce Sheila will try to enforce the premarital agreement. He would like to know if he can enforce the waiver of alimony (since he is the income-earning spouse and Sheila is a stay-at-home mom), but he does not want to give up custody of his children. What do you tell Alberto?

4. Ted and Tom entered into a cohabitation agreement at a time when they could not legally marry. The cohabitation agreement provided that neither of them owed a duty of support to the other and that all assets acquired were the asset of the party acquiring the property. Subsequently, after same-sex marriage became legal, Ted and Tom married. Tom would like to file for divorce. Tom wants to know whether the cohabitation agreement that he entered into with Ted can be treated like a premarital agreement and enforced. What questions would you want to ask Tom to determine if the cohabitation agreement can be considered a premarital agreement? What factors do you think would influence a court to treat the agreement as a premarital agreement? What arguments can be made against treating it as a premarital agreement?

5. Emily is a graduate student at a local university and is engaged to Todd, also a graduate student. Neither Emily nor Todd has substantial assets. However, Emily's parents have substantial assets and have set up trust funds for Emily and their other children. The trust funds provide that Emily will start receiving $100,000 a year after she marries, and then the balance of the trust when both parents are deceased. The law in your state provides that all gifts and inheritances are the separate property of the party receiving them, but Emily would still like to have a premarital agreement written up. Emily wants to make sure that she takes all the steps necessary to make sure the premarital agreement is enforceable should she and Todd ever divorce. What steps do you recommend that Emily take?

Family Law in Practice

1. Review your state statutes and court cases in your state concerning premarital agreements. Are premarital agreements recognized in your state? If they are, determine the following:

   a. What is required for premarital agreements to be enforceable? For example, what kind of disclosure is required?

   b. What is the applicable standard of review for premarital agreements? Are they treated like ordinary contracts?

   c. Do the courts in your state consider procedural fairness? Substantive fairness?

   d. Will courts in your state take a "second glance" at any of the terms to see if they are fair at the time of execution? How is the concept of fairness defined?

   (Note: If premarital agreements are not recognized in your jurisdiction, find a recent case that sets out the rationale for nonrecognition and explain the reasoning of the court.)

2. Is there a statute in your state governing postmarital agreements? If there is no statute, are there cases in your state? What is the law in your state regarding postmarital agreements?

3. You are a new associate working in a small law firm. A new, wealthy client has come to the office because he wants a premarital agreement drafted. His prospective wife, although not wealthy, has a job that pays well. He is 36, and she is 35. It is the first marriage for both of them. They do not plan to have children. The partner you work for has asked you to draft a letter to the client. In the letter you are to explain how the law in your jurisdiction treats premarital agreements, and what steps need to be taken to best ensure that the agreement will be enforced. You should also inform the client about the kinds of provisions that he should consider including in the agreement. (Note: If you are in a nonrecognizing jurisdiction, then assume you are in a state that is very concerned about fairness and follows the second glance approach.)

4. Assume you are a clerk working for a justice in your state's highest court. The court will soon be reviewing a case involving a dispute in which a wife is seeking to set aside a premarital agreement on the following two grounds. First, when she signed the agreement, she did not understand that she was giving up her right to alimony. Second, she believes that the alimony waiver is unfair given that her husband is extremely wealthy, and she has become disabled over the course of the marriage. She says the waiver was unfair at the time of execution and is even more so now at the time of performance. The justice you work for knows the trend is to treat premarital agreements more like ordinary contracts, and she wonders if it is time for your state to join this trend. She would like you

to write her a short memo in which you set out some of the pros and cons of adopting this approach.

5. Jake and Jan have lived in your state for the past five years. They have no plans to divorce. However, Jake has been offered an opportunity to transfer to another state to take a better position with his employer, which will mean the possibility of more money for Jake in the future. Jan has an excellent job in your state that pays well, and she has an opportunity for advancement and a transfer to the other state with her same employer if she can continue working in your state for the next two years. The parties have decided that Jake should take the job in the other state and Jan will stay in your state until she can transfer. However, Jan is afraid that this move will put a strain on their relationship, and she is worried that the parties will eventually divorce. Jan would like some protection of her finances in the event the marriage does not survive the move by Jake. She has asked you whether a postmarital agreement is possible, and if so, what should be included in the agreement. Prepare an outline of the information you want to convey to Jan when you meet with her based upon the law in your state. If your state does not recognize postmarital agreements, use the readings to draft your outline.

The Law of Divorce, Annulment, and Legal Separation

Divorce is the legal unwinding of a marital relationship. Marriage creates a legal bond; divorce severs it. As law students and future lawyers, your immediate focus is naturally on learning about the legal rules that govern marital dissolution; however, the law does not exist in a vacuum. For divorcing couples, the process is multidimensional, with profound emotional, spiritual, economic, and legal consequences. Lives are profoundly reshaped — often in unanticipated ways. For some, divorce brings tremendous relief and a welcome opportunity to build a new life; for others, it brings loneliness, emotional turmoil, and financial distress. Capturing some of these complexities, Joshua Ehrlich, a clinical psychologist who specializes in working with divorcing couples, explains:

> When a marriage falls apart, it has a cascading effect: Old traumas bubble to the surface, mixing and mingling inextricably with devastation at the current loss and, potentially, generating overwhelming emotional suffering. The partnership, instead of providing a longed-for buffer from life's harshness, has itself become harsh. . . . [A]dults who have delighted in being on the inside of an intimate couple are, catastrophically, on the outside again.

Joshua Ehrlich, Divorce and Loss 6 (2014).

This chapter focuses on the substantive law of divorce. As you read the chapter and as you work with people going through a divorce, it is very important

Key Concepts

- State regulations regarding who can marry
- History of divorce laws
- Fault divorce grounds and defenses
- History and impact of no-fault divorce
- Grounds of no-fault divorce
- The divorce "counterrevolution"
- The law of annulment
- Legal separation

that you remain aware that applicable legal principles are not mere abstractions but touch the core of people's lives. Accordingly, divorce law should not be thought of in isolation from its human context, a theme that is discussed more in Chapter 6.

A. HISTORICAL ROOTS OF OUR DIVORCE LAWS

During the latter part of the twentieth century, the nation underwent a sweeping "no-fault divorce" revolution. Starting with California in 1970, eventually all states adopted some form of no-fault divorce, as it is often called. Now an integral part of our legal landscape, many people today take the availability of no-fault divorce for granted, which can also be framed as an assumption that if one is in an unhappy or unfulfilling marriage he or she has a *right* to divorce his or her spouse. However, this is a relatively new way of understanding the process of marital exits. To understand the significance of this change, we begin with a historical overview of divorce law starting in premodern England, as our present system is rooted in this tradition.

1. Religious Underpinnings

Throughout history, many societies practiced divorce by mutual consent of the parties. This was true in what was to become England and much of Western Europe until sometime into the tenth or eleventh century, when marriage came under the authority of the Catholic Church. As the church gained in influence, a cohesive theology emerged, and a systematic body of canon law, including laws regulating marriage, was developed. *See* Mary E. O'Connell, Alimony After No-Fault: A Practice in Search of a Theory, 23 New Eng. L. Rev. 437, 444-447 (1988).

According to the teachings of the Catholic Church, marriage was a sacrament. It conferred grace on a couple and was a spiritual instrument of salvation. The relationship between a husband and a wife was thought to mirror the loving bond between Christ and his Church. Like the bond between Christ and his Church, the marital bond between a husband and wife was considered to be **indissoluble**.

The Vatican
Andrei Rybachuk / Shutterstock.com

Since it was a sacrament, marriage was placed under the exclusive authority of the church. Divorce was strictly prohibited, but an individual could petition the ecclesiastical courts for an **annulment** or a legal separation (also known as a *divorce a mensa et thoro* — a divorce from board and bed). Neither of these procedures ran afoul of the doctrine of indissolubility. As discussed later in this chapter, an annulment is a statement that due to existing impediments no valid marriage was ever created, and a divorce from board and bed allowed an innocent spouse to live apart from her or his sinful spouse without dissolving the marital bond.

    In the early 1500s, the Protestant Reformation challenged many of the Catholic Church's teachings, including those related to marriage. According to Reformation thinkers, marriage was not a sacrament — it was of this world and carried no promise of spiritual redemption. Having divested marriage of its holy and redemptive status, the Protestants accepted the necessity of divorce in cases involving grievous marital sins committed in violation of Christian principles. *See* John Witte, Jr., The Reformation of Marriage Law in Martin Luther's Germany: Its Significance Then and Now, 4 J.L. & Religion 295 (Summer 1986).

2. The English Experience

Influenced by the Reformation, many Western European nations became Protestant. Divorce was permitted, and both marriage and divorce came under the control of civil rather than religious authorities. However, in England, the pattern was different. Although King Henry VIII broke with the Catholic Church in 1534 and established the Church of England, the Catholic view of marriage as a sacrament was retained. As a result, divorce was not permitted, and marriage remained under Church control until 1857 — far later than the rest of Western Europe. By way of historical interest, it should be noted that King Henry's decision to break from the Church was at least in part motivated by the fact that the Pope refused to annul his marriage to Catherine of Aragon when she failed to provide him with a son.

King Henry VIII
Shutterstock.com

3. The American Experience: Divorce in the Colonies

Divorce generally was accepted much earlier in this country than it was in England due mainly to the influence of Protestantism. During the colonial period, the availability of divorce varied from region to region. In the New England colonies, divorce was available from the start, although in some areas, only the legislature had the authority to dissolve a marriage. Here, the colonists, mainly Pilgrims and Puritans, although profoundly religious, believed that marriage was a civil concern. For them, the family unit was the foundation on which their pious commonwealth was based. Because these two domains were so closely intertwined, family instability was thought to threaten the stability of the community. Accordingly, if a spouse maltreated his or her partner, and reconciliation was impossible, the New England colonists believed it was important for the innocent spouse to be released from the marriage so he or she could move on to form a new functional family unit. The guilty spouse was usually prohibited from remarrying and creating another dysfunctional family that would again threaten the well-being of the community. *See* Glenda Riley, Divorce: An American Tradition 9-15 (1991).

    In contrast, divorce was unheard of in most of the Southern colonies. Here, the teachings of the Church of England held sway, and marriage was regarded as indissoluble, although, as in England, both annulments and divorces from board and bed were permitted. The middle colonies appear to have occupied a middle position between New England, where divorce was well established, and the South, where it was prohibited.

The Rising Tide

Following the colonies' independence from England, two trends became apparent. The divorce rate began to rise rapidly, and many states, including the once-recalcitrant Southern states, amended their laws to add new divorce grounds, making divorce somewhat easier to obtain.

A number of factors contributed to this loosening of laws and attitudes. For one, revolutionary ferment found its way into the domestic sphere. Leaders such as Thomas Jefferson transposed arguments about individual rights to liberty and happiness from the struggle against England to the marital context. Divorce was needed to oust spousal tyrants and ensure that women were not trapped in domestic regimes that denied them their humanity. Thus, themes that fueled the revolution contributed to an acceptance of divorce. Norma Basch, Framing American Divorce: From the Revolutionary Generation to the Victorians 19-30 (1999). This connection between divorce and the emancipation of women would be picked up by women's rights reformers in the next century.

Changing expectations about the marital relationship also contributed to a greater acceptance of divorce. With industrialization, production moved out of the home, and the family no longer stood at the center of economic activity. The significance of marriage as an economic arrangement diminished, and spouses increasingly looked to each other for love and companionship. As spouses came to expect more from one another, the risk of disappointment also increased, as marriage did not always provide the parties with what they were looking for. As a result, there was an increased acceptance of divorce as a necessary safety valve for spouses who were trapped in failed marriages. Riley, *supra*, at 53-84.

Despite these changes, divorce was still understood in very narrow terms. Rooted in the Puritan belief of marital wrong as sinful conduct, divorce required serious **marital fault**, and only an **innocent spouse** was entitled to a divorce. Divorce was understood as a remedy for the innocent spouse and a punishment for the guilty one. It was not regarded as a right, but as an evil made necessary by the realities of human existence. O'Connell, *supra*, at 454-455.

Nonetheless, the rising divorce rates and the expansion of divorce grounds, which in a few states went as far as permitting divorce whenever "just and

Regulation of Marriage for Slaves

In no region of the country did slaves have formal access to divorce, mainly because the colonists refused to honor the validity of marriages between enslaved persons. However, although their practices were not formally recognized, slaves created their own marriage rituals, and historians have located records indicating that some African-American churches granted divorces to married slaves. Additionally, although again outside the formal bounds of the law, some plantation owners may have recognized and regulated marriage and divorce among their slaves.

In the modern era, the lack of access to formal means of dissolving a relationship had been an issue for same-sex couples due to their lack of marriage rights. As we saw in Chapter 2, even if permitted to marry in one state, divorce was not necessarily recognized in a state prohibiting same-sex marriages.

reasonable," evoked a storm of outrage by those who feared that these trends sig-naled the moral disintegration of both family and society. The debate raged, and in 1885, the National Divorce Reform League, later renamed the National League for the Protection of the Family, was established to limit the spread of divorce and restore moral order.

By the turn of the century, anti-divorce activists could claim some success. They helped slow the move toward more expansive divorce grounds and secured the repeal of some liberalized divorce laws. Riley, *supra*, at 108-112. For the most part, until the no-fault divorce reform movement of the 1970s, divorce remained firmly linked — at least officially — to grievous marital wrongdoing (but see the discussion of collusive divorce below). By retaining the link to fault, divorce law supported the permanency of marriage through limiting the permissible grounds for marital exits while also acknowledging the reality of spousal cruelty and marital failure.

B. FAULT DIVORCE: COMMON GROUNDS AND DEFENSES

In the wake of no-fault divorce reform, fault divorce tumbled from its place of pre-eminence. Some states abolished fault-based divorce altogether and now have only no-fault grounds; in other states, no-fault grounds were added to existing fault grounds, and fault divorce remains an option. The following discussion focuses on three of the most commonly available fault grounds and the primary defenses to charges of marital misconduct. As always, you need to check the specifics of your state's laws because other statutory options may be available.

1. Fault Divorce Grounds

There are three common fault grounds for divorce — adultery, desertion, and cru-elty. (See Chapters 7 and 8 for a discussion of the role that fault plays in determin-ing the division of property and spousal awards.)

Historically, adultery has been regarded as the most serious marital wrong and has been the most widely accepted ground for divorce. **Adultery** is generally defined as an act of sexual intercourse by a married person with someone other than his or her spouse. In the past, the law did not treat a husband's extramarital relations as seriously as a wife's transgressions. In many states, a woman could not obtain a divorce for adultery unless she could also establish aggravating circum-stances, such as cruelty, or that her husband had engaged in a course of adulterous conduct, whereas a man had to show only that his wife had committed a single adulterous act. Although no longer legally true today, some experts believe that social attitudes have not necessarily changed, and that many people continue to regard adultery by a woman, especially if she is a mother, as a greater wrong than when committed by a man.

Because there are usually no eyewitnesses, a claim of adultery, when disputed, is generally established by circumstantial evidence. A party must show that his or her spouse had both the opportunity and the disposition or inclination to commit adultery. Relevant evidence might include love letters, public displays of affection, and frequent visits to a home or hotel, or the introduction of venereal disease into the marriage.

Recently, several courts have addressed the question of whether "adultery" is limited to acts of sexual intercourse between a man and a woman, or whether it can be defined to include sexual relations between a married person and someone of the same sex. Most courts that have considered this issue have concluded that adultery is not limited to heterosexual intercourse. As one court explained: "We view appellant's definition of adultery as unduly narrow and overly dependent upon the term sexual intercourse. . . . [E]xplicit extra-marital sexual activity constitutes adultery regardless of whether it is of a homosexual or heterosexual character." *RGM v. DGM*, 410 S.E.2d 564, 566-567 (S.C. 1991).

However, in 2003, the New Hampshire Supreme Court in *In re Blanchflower* reached the opposite conclusion. Relying on both the dictionary meaning of *adultery* and nineteenth-century case law, the court held that the "concept of adultery was premised upon a specific act. To include in that concept other acts of a sexual nature, whether between heterosexuals or homosexuals, would change beyond recognition this well established ground for divorce." *In re Blanchflower*, 150 N.H. 226, 230, 834 A.2d 1010, 1013 (2003).

Desertion (or abandonment) has long been accepted as an appropriate ground for divorce. Prior to no-fault divorce, desertion was particularly important in states that did not recognize cruelty or construed it narrowly (see below). As a general rule, desertion requires a departure from the marital residence. Some courts have held that the refusal to have a sexual relationship with one's spouse satisfies the separation requirement even if the parties remain in the marital home; however, withdrawal from other aspects of the marital relationship is unlikely to be considered desertion.

In most jurisdictions, a spouse must prove the following elements to establish desertion:

1. there has been a voluntary separation;
2. for the statutory period;
3. with the intent not to return;
4. without consent; and
5. without justification.

For the separation to qualify, the departing spouse must leave of his or her own will. An involuntary departure, such as where a person is drafted, jailed, or committed to a mental hospital, is not desertion. The separation must exist continuously for the statutory time period. Interruptions by, for example, a good faith offer of reconciliation or even a single act of sexual intercourse may stop the time from running. As a general rule, the calculation of time begins again if there is a second departure — the time periods cannot be added together.

It is not desertion if the "stay-at-home" spouse consents to the departure because desertion by its very nature is a nonconsensual act. If the departure is justified, such as where a spouse flees physical abuse, it is also not classified as desertion.

In fact, the spouse who has caused the departure through his or her misconduct may be considered as the deserting spouse based on the doctrine of **constructive desertion**, which imputes the act of desertion to the spouse responsible for the other's departure.

Case Preview

Flanagan v. Flanagan

In *Flanagan*, the Maryland Court of Special Appeals examined whether the trial court erred in granting the divorce based on the ground of mutual and voluntary separation, and in not granting the divorce based on Mrs. Flanagan's (wife/appellee) claim of constructive desertion or Mr. Flanagan's (husband/appellant) claim for divorce based on the ground of desertion. The facts indicated that the wife had physically left the residence because the husband had engaged in conduct that could have been considered a constructive divorce, such as drinking, soliciting extramarital relationships, and verbal abuse.

As you read *Flanagan v. Flanagan*, look for following:

1. What was the basis of the wife's claim that she was entitled to a divorce on the grounds of constructive desertion?
2. Why did the appeals court state that the "Chancellor's analysis of the mutual and voluntary separation" might well have been flawed?
3. Why did the court conclude that this did not matter with regard to the ultimate disposition of the case?
4. What influence did the fact that neither party wanted to reconcile have on the court's decision?

Flanagan v. Flanagan
956 A.2d 829 (Md. Ct. Spec. App. 2008)

The parties were married on November 23, 1984. It was a second marriage for each, and they have no children together. Ms. Flanagan left the family home on February 2, 2005.

On April 11, 2006, appellee [Wife] filed a Complaint for Absolute Divorce on the ground of constructive desertion. Appellant [Husband] filed an Answer and a Counter-Complaint for Absolute Divorce on May 17, 2006, on the ground of actual desertion. Among other things, each party sought a monetary award and attorneys' fees. At the time of trial on September 19, 2006, appellant was 68 years old and appellee was 64 years of age.

. . .

Appellee recounted that she moved out of the marital home on February 2, 2005, leaving appellant a letter explaining her decision. She and appellant had lived separate and apart since that date, with no hope of reconciliation.

The letter was admitted into evidence. [Wife cited her reasons for leaving, including Husband's drinking and Internet sexual contacts, not honoring the agreements made during joint counseling of not engaging in certain behavior, and the fact that she felt she had to walk on eggshells when Husband would drink because he would "erupt and spew forth confrontational, threatening and accusatory verbal bile enumerating my real and imagined slights, transgressions and shortcomings covering the last twenty plus years."]

Ms. Flanagan added: "I have resolved not to live my life under these conditions any longer. I want peace."

. . .

In addition, appellee suggested [in her testimony] that appellant was "threatening in his manner." But, she described only one incident of physical force, which occurred in January 2003, when appellant "threw a wallet" at appellee after a session of joint counseling.

[Husband/appellant] stated that on the afternoon of February 2, 2005, [he called Wife and she advised him she was moving out.]

Appellant admitted to "prowling" for women on the internet in order to "add a little spice to [his] sex life." He explained that in 2002 he had a "severe prostatitis attack," which rendered him "dysfunctional." This condition prevented the parties from engaging in a physical relationship, and "stupidly" prompted him to visit online chat rooms. . . .

In addition, appellant categorically denied ever striking appellee at any time during their marriage. He explained [that one incident] was a result of appellee rummaging through his things, and he "threw [his wallet] at her [saying] here, take the whole wallet and, and be done with it."

With regard to his alcohol consumption, appellant insisted that his drinking at home was limited to "a couple of cocktails" before or with dinner every other day or so, but that "after dinner I didn't drink anything at all." As for social drinking outside the home, he explained:

> [Appellee] had a very serious problem with her husband before me, we made some agreements that if I were to have drink number three, if I was out at any social engagement, if I had drink number three . . . I would hand her voluntarily the car keys. There would be no fighting over who was going to drive home because she had had some pretty wild rides in the past with her [first] husband.

. . .

On February 27, 2007, the [lower] court issued a "Memorandum Opinion," in which it found voluntary separation as the grounds for divorce. However, neither party had advanced the ground of voluntary separation.

. . .

Appellant [Husband] contends that the chancellor erred in granting a divorce on the ground of voluntary separation, arguing [the conclusion was not supported by the evidence]. He also contends that appellee was not entitled to a divorce on the grounds of constructive desertion, because appellee was not "fearful of physical violence," nor had there ever been any such violence. . . .

Appellee [Wife] responds that appellant's "argument on the grounds of divorce alleges mistakes in both fact and law." She maintains that "there was ample evidence in the record to support the Chancellor's findings," because it was "undisputed that at the time of the hearing, the parties had been physically separated for more than twelve (12) months, and there was no reasonable expectation of reconciliation. At some point after the initial separation, the separation became mutual and voluntary." She insists that "[t]he element[s] of mutuality and separation need not coincide at the inception of the separation." . . .

Alternatively, appellee asserts: "Assuming arguendo that the Chancellor's analysis of the mutual and voluntary separation was flawed, there was ample evidence in the record for the Chancellor to award Mrs. Flanagan a divorce on the grounds of constructive desertion." Moreover, she argues that any error is "harmless." . . .

While the Wife physically deserted the marital home, the Husband allegedly constructively deserted her prior to her leaving. The undisputed testimony was that in February of 2005, [appellee] decided to leave the marital home. She did so after years of her husband's soliciting extramarital sexual relationships on the internet, his heavy drinking, and verbal abuse. . . . Neither party has attempted reconciliation. Insofar as the separation became mutual and voluntary and both parties indicate there is no reasonable expectation of reconciliation in their Complaint and Counterclaim, the Court grants an absolute divorce. . . .

Assuming arguendo that the Court made an error in granting the divorce on the grounds of mutual and voluntary separation, what difference does it make? It doesn't. Both of these parties want a divorce. The only aspect of this case that is affected by the circumstances that contributed to the estrangement of the parties is the marital award. The statutory factor that requires the Chancellor to consider the circumstances that contributed to the estrangement of the parties does not require a finding of constructive desertion as a prerequisite to ordering a marital award, it only requires the Chancellor to consider the circumstances of the separation. For the reasons set forth in Part II of this Argument, the Chancellor's findings of fact with respect to the circumstances that contributed to the estrangement of the parties was not clearly erroneous. . . .

In Maryland, the permissible grounds for divorce are governed by statute . . . which include the following:

(2) desertion, if:
  (i) the desertion has continued for 12 months without interruption before the filing of the application for divorce;
  (ii) the desertion is deliberate and final; and
  (iii) there is no reasonable expectation of reconciliation;

(3) voluntary separation, if:
  (i) the parties voluntarily have lived separate and apart without cohabitation for 12 months without interruption before the filing of the application for divorce; and
  (ii) there is no reasonable expectation of reconciliation;

As noted, appellee's complaint alleged constructive desertion, while appellant alleged actual desertion in his counterclaim. . . .

In regard to a voluntary separation, the evidence must establish that the parties were separated voluntarily for the requisite period. . . .

In order to establish the existence of the twelve month voluntary separation ground for divorce a vinculo . . . three elements must be shown: (i) an express or implied agreement to separate, accompanied by a mutual intent not to resume the marriage relationship; (ii) voluntarily living separate and apart without cohabitation for twelve months prior to the filing of the bill of complaint; and (iii) that the separation is beyond any reasonable hope of reconciliation.

In contrast, "[a]cquiescence in or assent to what one cannot prevent does not amount to a voluntary agreement to separate." . . . Nevertheless, the elements of mutuality and separation need not coincide at the inception of the separation. Indeed, an involuntary separation may later be transformed into a voluntary separation. Thus, a separation that begins as a desertion may later achieve "voluntary" status.

. . .

In sum, the cases teach that a voluntary separation must be accompanied by a mutual intent to terminate the marriage; mutuality of intent is a component of voluntariness. Voluntary, "'when used in reference to a common act of two or more persons affecting their common relationship . . . means that they acted in willing concert in the doing of the act.'"

In order to be awarded a decree of divorce for voluntary separation, the plaintiff must establish that the parties entered into a mutual and voluntary agreement to separate and not to resume the marital relationship. The separation for the purposes of the statute commences on the date that this agreement occurs even if the parties have separated prior to reaching this agreement. . . .

Accordingly, we agree with appellant that the court erred in granting a divorce on the ground of voluntary separation. Nevertheless, we are equally convinced that any error was harmless.

. . .

The findings of the court below were tantamount to a finding of constructive desertion, and were supported by the record. Notably, the court below found that appellee "decided to leave the marital home . . . after years of her husband's soliciting extramarital sexual relationships on the internet, his heavy drinking and verbal abuse." Moreover, as appellee points out, "only slight corroboration is required," and it may "come from the other spouse." Among other things, appellant admitted to having prowled on the internet to "jazz up [his] sex life."

In sum, because the court made findings to support the award of divorce based on constructive desertion, which findings were not clearly erroneous, we regard as harmless the court's error in its Memorandum Opinion, in which it found a voluntary separation.

Post-Case Follow-Up

The court agreed that this was not a situation of voluntary separation because there was no evidence that when Mrs. Flanagan left the marital residence "the parties had a mutual agreement to separate with the intent to end the marriage." However, it concluded that the granting of a divorce on this basis was a harmless error because the court had made findings to "support an award of divorce based on constructive desertion."

Flanagan v. Flanagan: Real Life Applications

1. Tom and Ashley have been married for 20 years. Tom comes to your office and tells you that for the past five years Ashley has been going out with friends on the weekend and coming home drunk. When she does this, she becomes verbally abusive to him. They have not had a vacation together for years, but she takes long trips with her friends and sometimes does not return for two to three weeks at a time. He has asked her if she wants a divorce or if she will agree that they should live separate and apart. She refuses. Tom believes that Ashley does not want to be married to him any longer, but likes the lifestyle he is able to provide for them and does not want to give that up. Tom wants to know if under these circumstances he can leave Ashley and file for divorce. Based on the *Flanagan* case, does Tom have grounds for constructive desertion?

2. Assume the same facts in Question 1, except that Ashley leaves the house and then files for divorce. Tom tells you although Ashley is difficult, he still loves her and does not want a divorce. Are there grounds for a divorce under *Flanagan*?

3. Heidi and Enrique have been married for five years. They have now realized that they are not destined to be married long term. Heidi comes to you and asks if it is possible for her to just voluntarily separate from Enrique. What do you tell Heidi?

In most states, **cruelty** was not initially included as a ground for divorce, but by the late 1800s, most divorce statutes had been amended to add it as a ground. It soon became the most commonly used ground. Statutes employ a variety of terms such as "extreme cruelty," "cruel and inhuman treatment," and "indignities," but the meaning is generally the same. Initially, borrowing from ecclesiastical law, cruelty was narrowly defined to include only repeated acts of severe physical abuse that inflicted bodily harm. The concept has gradually expanded and in most states it now includes acts of mental as well as physical cruelty, although some jurisdictions require that the mental cruelty result in some kind of physical symptoms. Proof that the symptoms abated or improved after the parties separated may also be required. The thinking here is that by requiring "objective" evidence of physical impairment, trivial or false claims of cruelty will be weeded out. However, many courts accept fairly general and unsubstantiated statements about loss of sleep, changes in appetite, and increased anxiety as proof of physical impairment.

2. Fault Divorce Defenses

When marital fault is alleged, the defendant-spouse can raise legal defenses to absolve him- or herself of marital wrongdoing. If successful, the divorce cannot be granted on the basis of the alleged fault. However, because most divorce actions are ultimately settled, these defenses are of little practical significance. Moreover, because of the availability of no-fault divorce, when cases are contested, the dispute almost always involves matters of custody, support, and the like, rather than the grounds for the divorce itself. Nonetheless, some familiarity with the major defenses is important, as a defendant-spouse may need to raise a defense in responding to a fault complaint. (See Chapter 6 on the divorce process.)

The essence of the defense of **connivance** is consent. This defense has primarily been used in adultery cases in which the defendant-spouse seeks to prove the party seeking the divorce consented to the adultery, such as by helping to arrange the liaison. In some states, a more passive course of action, such as a spouse's not actively seeking to prevent a known affair, constitutes connivance.

The essence of the defense of **condonation** is forgiveness. If a spouse forgives his or her partner's marital misconduct, this misconduct can no longer be the basis of a divorce action; condonation restores the marital innocence of the erring spouse. In some states, if a spouse reengages in wrongful activity, the condonation may be canceled and the original divorce grounds revived.

States differ as to what constitutes forgiveness. In some states, engaging in sexual relations after the plaintiff has learned of the misconduct is by itself condonation; here, the plaintiff's state of mind is irrelevant. In other states, the plaintiff's state of mind is key; the plaintiff must actually forgive the defendant — forgiveness will not be inferred from resumed intimacy.

Case Preview

Lawrence v. Lawrence

Lawrence v. Lawrence looks at the issue of whether there has been condonation. In this case, Husband had an affair, which Wife knew about. After Wife learned of the affair, she filed for divorced based upon adultery or alternatively upon irreconcilable differences. The parties continued to reside together for a period of time, although the divorce complaint was never dismissed. Husband asked for summary judgment on the claim of adultery because Wife had forgiven him. The lower court granted his motion for summary judgment on the issue of adultery.

As you read *Lawrence v. Lawrence*, look for the following:

1. Why does the court say "condonation places the offending spouse on a form of temporary probation"?
2. What is the court's reasoning for reversing the chancellor's grant of partial summary judgment and remanding the case?
3. What arguments by the wife did the court find persuasive?

Lawrence v. Lawrence
956 So. 2d 251 (Miss. Ct. App. 2006)

April and Andy were married on May 16, 1998. They had two children. Noah Andrew was born on July 19, 1999. Emma Katherine was born on July 30, 2000. . . .

In the spring of 2003, April and Andy separated for approximately a week. When Andy returned to the marital home, April confronted him about rumors of an affair. At first, Andy denied the affair, but later admitted the affair and begged forgiveness. On April 17, 2003, April filed her initial complaint for divorce on the grounds of adultery or, in the alternative, irreconcilable differences. April and Andy, even though the complaint for divorce was filed, continued to reside together and were not legally separated. Affidavits from April and Andy indicate that Andy admitted his affair, which occurred in 2002. They attempted to reconcile, but April's complaint for divorce was never dismissed.

In the fall of 2003, April began to ask Andy to leave the marital residence, and the divorce proceedings were resumed. They continued to reside in the same household.

In December of 2003, April met Brian Sellers. The following May, April moved from the marital home into a rental home in Caledonia.

In June of 2004, the chancellor entered a temporary order that granted April custody of the two minor children and ordered Andy to pay child support. For several months prior to the temporary order, Andy did not deposit his paycheck into the couple's joint bank account and did not provide any financial support for the children.

On August 4, 2004, Andy filed a motion for summary judgment. He claimed that he was entitled to judgment on the claim of adultery because April condoned his affair. The result was that Andy's adultery could no longer support the grounds for divorce pled in April's complaint for divorce.

ANALYSIS

April argued that condonation was conditional on Andy's continued good behavior. In *Wood v. Wood,* 495 So. 2d 503, 505 (Miss. 1986), the supreme court held:

> The defense of condonation is recognized in our law. *Stribling v. Stribling,* 215 So. 2d 869, 870 (Miss. 1968); *Starr v. Starr,* 206 Miss. 1, 39 So. 2d 520, 523 (1949). Condonation is the forgiveness of a marital wrong on the part of the wronged party. Condonation may be expressed or implied. . . . The mere resumption of residence does not constitute a condonation of past marital sins and does not act as a bar . . . to a divorce being granted. Compare Miss. Code Ann. §93-5-4 (1972). Condonation, even if a true condonation exists, is conditioned on the offending spouse's continued good behavior. If the offending party does not mend his or her ways and resumes the prior course of conduct, there is a revival of the grounds for divorce. *Manning v. Manning,* 160 Miss. 318, 321, 133 So. 673, 674 (1931).
>
> In practical effect, condonation places the offending spouse on a form of temporary probation. Any subsequent conduct within a reasonable time after resumption of cohabitation which evidences an intent not to perform the conditions of the condonation in good faith, may be sufficient to avoid the defense of condonation. . . .

In her response to the motion for partial summary judgment, April offered her affidavit where she testified about her belief that Andy resumed the marital relationship "merely as a ploy to defeat the grounds of adultery" and that he "has continued to have an affair."

We conclude that April's affidavit presented a genuine issue of material fact and Andy was not entitled to a judgment as a matter of law. In *Wood,* the supreme court held that:

> [a]ny subsequent conduct within a reasonable time after resumption of cohabitation which evidences an intent not to perform the conditions of the condonation in good faith, may be sufficient to avoid the defense of condonation, even though the conduct so complained of in and of itself may not be grounds for divorce.

Wood, 495 So. 2d at 505. Based on this language, Andy's intent in the resumption of the marital relationship is indeed an issue to be determined by the chancellor. Simply engaging in the act of sex does not seal the defense of condonation. Thus, April's personal belief that Andy resumed the marital relationship "merely as a ploy to defeat the grounds of adultery" presents a genuine issue of material fact in dispute that does not entitle Andy to a judgment as a matter of law on his defense of condonation.

Accordingly, we reverse the chancellor's entry of a partial summary judgment, and we remand for further proceedings consistent therewith. . . .

Post-Case Follow-Up

If a spouse alleges adultery as a ground for divorce, a valid defense is condonation. However, as the court makes clear, to have a valid defense of condonation there must be forgiveness by the wronged party. Simply residing together, or even having a sexual relationship, does not necessarily constitute a forgiveness, particularly if there is not an intent by the wronged party to avoid the wrongful conduct in the future. These are factual issues that the court finds cannot be decided on summary judgment. Accordingly, once the case is remanded to the lower court, the chancellor will need to take evidence on the issue of condonation to see if there truly has been a forgiveness of the wrongful behavior.

Lawrence v. Lawrence: Real Life Applications

1. Assume you are an attorney in the firm that represents Mr. Lawrence. On remand, you now have to develop a case to show the defense of condonation. Prepare a list of questions you want to ask Mr. Lawrence to find out more about the evidence that exists to show that Mrs. Lawrence had forgiven him for his adultery.

2. Assume you are an attorney in the firm that represents Mrs. Lawrence. On remand, you know that Mr. Lawrence is going to allege the defense of condonation. What questions do you want to ask Mrs. Lawrence to find out more

about the evidence that exists to show that she did not forgive Mr. Lawrence for
adultery?

3. You clerk for the judge who has now had the case of *Lawrence v. Lawrence*
remanded to your court. Mr. Lawrence presents the same evidence as set forth
in the case on the issue of condonation. Mrs. Lawrence presents the same evidence to show that she never forgiven Mr. Lawrence. The judge has asked you
to write a brief memorandum on whether a valid defense of condonation exists.
Write the memorandum and give your opinion on how the judge should rule.

The defense of **recrimination** has been subject to much criticism and has been
abolished in many jurisdictions. Here, a defendant-spouse, rather than seeking to
defeat a divorce by minimizing the wrongfulness of his or her conduct, seeks to
defeat it by showing that the plaintiff-spouse, rather than being an innocent victim, is also guilty of marital wrongdoing. When mutual wrongdoing is established,
neither spouse is entitled to a divorce, and the couple must remain married even
though each has treated the other badly. Although seemingly illogical, this defense
is rooted in the view of divorce as a remedy for the innocent; accordingly, when
both spouses are guilty of marital transgressions, neither qualifies as the innocent
victim entitled to relief. In some states, the harshness of this result has been modified by the doctrine of **comparative rectitude**, which allows a court to grant a
divorce if the plaintiff-spouse's wrongdoing is adjudged to be less serious than the
defendant's.

Collusion involves an agreement by a couple to obtain a divorce and the deliberate crafting of a case for presentation to the court. Collusion can occur in several
ways. The parties could agree that one spouse would actually commit a marital
wrong, such as adultery, in order to provide grounds for divorce (this would also be
considered connivance). More likely, the parties would agree to fabricate a marital
wrong, exaggerate the extent of their discontent with one another, or fail to present
a valid defense. This ground runs counter to the basic assumptions of the fault
system, which conceptualizes divorce as an adversarial process. The reality is that
although collusion is generally classified as a defense, it is unlikely to be raised by
either party because it would prevent the granting of the divorce that the parties
were attempting to set up.

C. NO-FAULT DIVORCE

During the 1960s, fault divorce came under increasing attack, and in 1970, California became the first state to enact a no-fault divorce law. By 1985, no-fault divorce
was available in most states; however, it would not be until 2010, when New York
became the last state to enact a no-fault statute, that this option would be available to divorcing couples in all states. As part of this effort to move away from

the adversarial model of the past, many states also began to use the word *dissolution* instead of divorce, thus signaling a new emphasis on the state of the marriage rather than the conduct of the parties.

1. The Underpinnings of Reform

During the 1960s, there was a groundswell of support for divorce reform. Critics of the fault system argued that it was outmoded and ineffectual and that the time had come to give couples the option of divorcing without having to prove marital wrongdoing. The following discussion sets out some of their major criticisms.

Reformers pointed to the practice of collusion as an indication that something was not working with the fault model. In a collusive divorce, spouses who wanted out of their marriage would agree to divorce and then carefully stage the process. In most cases, the defendant would simply fail to appear at the divorce hearing, and the trial court would accept the plaintiff's pro forma recitation about fault. In other cases, fault evidence was manufactured; most commonly, acts of adultery were staged. Some lawyers even helped in the process by providing the paramour, most often the office secretary, to pose for the adulterous photographs. It has been suggested that judges may have been aware of the collusive nature of many divorce actions, but chose to ignore it.

According to historians, the practice of collusion began at the end of World War I and became increasingly frequent over the course of the following decades. It thus appears that although the law on the books was strict in terms of fault requirements, for much of the twentieth century the reality was quite different, as couples were successfully exiting marriages in the absence of proven fault. *See* Lawrence M. Friedman, Rights of Passage: Divorce Laws in Historical Perspective, 63 Or. L. Rev. 649 (1984).

Reformers hoped that the introduction of no-fault divorce would bring the law into conformity with actual practice and end the hypocrisy of collusive divorce.

Another powerful criticism was that in noncollusive cases, the focus on fault increased the anger and hostility between the parties, especially since financial awards were often influenced by considerations of fault. The legal system was blamed for heightening antagonism by forcing couples into an adversarial posture, thus destroying any hope of reconciliation and making reasoned custody negotiations impossible. Reformers hoped that by eliminating fault, the process would become less adversarial and thus less destructive to the parties and their children.

Fault divorce was further criticized as being out of keeping with the contemporary understanding of marital relationships. Reformers argued that the messy reality of people's marriages did not conform to the fault model, which naively assumed that all marital breakups involved a good spouse and a bad spouse and that this determination could be made simply by identifying who had committed the marital wrong. To reformers, it had become apparent that the named ground was often a symptom of marital distress rather than the actual cause of the breakup. For example, an affair, rather than being the singular "bad" act that brought a marriage to an end, might instead be a response to a complete withdrawal of affection on the part of the other spouse, thus making it unfair to characterize the affair as the only marital transgression.

In light of rising divorce rates, it was also clear to reformers that strict divorce laws were not forcing couples to resolve their difficulties and remain together in furtherance of the state's interest in marital permanency. Moreover, in keeping with the trend toward greater individual autonomy and privacy within the domestic realm, reformers argued that the right of an unhappy spouse to leave a marriage should not be subordinated to the state's interest in family preservation. Rather than being forced into legal pigeonholes in accordance with the state's view of what kinds of wrongs justified marital departures, reformers believed that an unhappy spouse should have greater control over when and why to leave a marriage. In effect, divorce began to be seen as more of a right than a strictly controlled remedy for a spouse aggrieved by marital wrongdoing.

In seeking to shift the balance from the historic interest of the state in family preservation toward the right of an unhappy spouse to leave a failed marriage, some reformers were influenced by the women's rights movement, which insisted that women be seen as autonomous, self-defining individuals, rather than primarily as dependent members of family units. Claiming greater educational and employment rights for women, activists encouraged women not to remain trapped in marriages that threatened their physical and emotional well-being. As with no-fault reform, here too we see a greater emphasis on the needs and aspirations of individual spouses within a marriage, rather than upon the enduring social importance of the marital unit.

2. No-Fault Laws

Beginning with California in 1970, no-fault reform swept the country. Within 15 years, the legal landscape had been radically altered. When California reformed its law, it essentially opted to abolish all fault grounds and replace them with a single no-fault standard. A significant number of states followed California's lead and now have only no-fault grounds. A majority of states, however, chose to maintain their existing fault grounds and add no-fault provisions, thus creating a dual system of divorce.

In those states that have retained fault grounds, a party usually has a choice between whether to file a fault or a no-fault divorce. A number of considerations may affect this decision. For example, as discussed in Chapter 7, although the role of fault is no longer a critical consideration in spousal support awards, in some states it may have some bearing on the determination. States may also have different time frames or filing procedures for the different categories of divorce that might influence the path that a party chooses. There may also be "intangible" considerations, such as where a victim of intimate partner abuse may feel that it is important to clearly label and identify the harm done during the marriage that lead to the dissolution of the marriage.

No-Fault Grounds

There are two primary no-fault grounds: marital breakdown and living separate and apart, with the former being the most common. A few states have combined these grounds and require proof of both a marital breakdown and a separation. Although both grounds will be discussed below in greater detail, keep in mind that many states have unique requirements, making familiarity with the laws of your jurisdiction essential.

Marital Breakdown

Marital breakdown is the principal no-fault ground. Statutes use a variety of terms to express this essential concept — such as "**irreconcilable differences**" or the "irretrievable" or "irremediable breakdown" of the marriage. Whichever term is used, the emphasis is on the failed state of the marital relationship rather than on the conduct of the spouses.

At least in theory, the judge at the divorce hearing is supposed to conduct a searching inquiry into whether the marriage is in fact broken and beyond hope of repair. (See Chapter 6 on the divorce process.) Factors relevant to this determination include the following:

- the degree to which the parties are unable to relate to one another;
- the extent of any differences between them;
- prior efforts to resolve their marital difficulties; and
- whether there is any hope of reconciliation.

Many states specifically bar evidence of fault; in other states such evidence is not considered relevant, except perhaps to help establish the extent of the breakdown.

No-fault hearings were not intended to be mere rubber stamps of the parties' decision, and judges in most states have considerable discretion to decide whether or not a marriage is truly over. In fact, some reformers hoped to give judges more freedom to deny a divorce if they believed there was any hope of reconciliation than they had under the fault system, where proof of fault mandated the granting of the divorce. Accordingly, in some states, a judge can stay the proceedings until the parties have sought counseling if the judge is not convinced that the marriage is over.

In reality, however, it appears that searching inquiries into whether a marriage is really over are rare. Couples are generally taken at their word that the marriage is beyond repair, and a few states have eliminated the requirement of a hearing if there are no collateral issues to resolve.

Many states do not require both parties to agree that the marriage is over before a no-fault divorce can be granted. This raises the possibility that a spouse could seek to block the divorce by expressing his or her continued love and belief that the marriage was still intact or not beyond repair; but most judges will grant a divorce in this situation on the basis that a viable partnership does not exist where each spouse has such a radically different view of the relationship. When faced with this situation, a judge, where allowed to do so, might stay the proceedings and order the couple into counseling.

Living Separate and Apart

The other major no-fault ground is that the parties have lived separate and apart for a statutory period of time. Time periods range from about 18 months to three years, with most falling somewhere in between. The underlying assumption is that the separation itself is proof of marital breakdown, and judicial inquiry into the relationship's demise is not required. The term "separate and apart" has generally been construed to require separate residences, but some courts have granted a divorce when a couple remained under the same roof but had essentially ceased all interaction for the requisite time period.

Some courts impose an intent requirement and will not qualify the separation even if it lasts for the statutory period unless the parties intended for it to be a permanent one. Thus, if a separation begins as a temporary one, the statutory period will not start to run unless and until the parties decide to make the separation permanent. Some states also require that the separation be voluntary on the part of both parties. Accordingly, if the parties are living apart because of desertion, flight from abuse, or over the objection of one spouse, the separation is not voluntary and will not qualify the parties for a divorce. Similarly, a separation caused by involuntary circumstances such as deployment, hospitalization, or incarceration would not be a valid ground for divorce. Also, when one spouse is mentally incompetent, a separation initiated by the other spouse will not generally be regarded as voluntary if the non-initiating spouse lacks the ability to comprehend what is going on and to give his or her consent. In a few states, the separation need be voluntary only on the part of one spouse.

Where voluntariness is required, a separation that begins involuntarily can be converted into a voluntary one if the parties agree they wish to live apart. The running of the statutory period is calculated from the time the parties reached this agreement rather than from the time of the initial separation. Many jurisdictions, however, do not impose a voluntariness requirement; accordingly, virtually any separation for the statutory time period can ripen into a divorce action.

3. The Divorce Counterrevolution

From very early on, no-fault divorce was subject to harsh criticism from those who believe that the removal of fault facilitated easy exits from marriage, thus undermining the stability of family life. Proclaiming that "[d]isposable marriage cheapens the commitment and degrades our vows of fidelity and lifelong love,"[1] on Valentine's Day in 1996, State Representative Jesse Dahlman of Michigan introduced one of the nation's first comprehensive divorce reform bills, which, among other measures, proposed eliminating "unilateral" no-fault divorce by requiring proof of fault if one spouse objected to the divorce.

Since then a number of "pro-family" groups, such as Marriage Savers and Defending Our Fathers House, have promoted a variety of divorce-reform measures to make a no-fault divorce more difficult to obtain. This goal is opposed by many who fear that a return to a stricter divorce regime is out of step with today's families, and will also create many of the hardships of the past, including making it more difficult for spouses to leave an abusive marriage. After looking at some of the key arguments on both sides of this debate, we consider some of the legislative

---

[1]Jesse Dalman and Susan Agar, Abolish No-Fault Divorce?, http://divorceonline.com (accessed June 8, 2016).

proposals that reformers have introduced, with varying degrees of success, in order to tighten the borders of divorce.

The Debate

Some critics believe that no-fault divorce has contributed to a "divorce culture" that emphasizes individual happiness and fulfillment over commitment to one's spouse and children. According to this view, rather than accepting that all marriages have their ebbs and flows and that it takes communication and efforts to sustain a marriage, no-fault divorce encourages spouses to walk out the door in pursuit of their own individual goals. No-fault divorce is sometimes blamed for lessening the meaning of connection and permanence with its seductive promise of an easy way out.

Critics further contend that children are the primary victims of this trend toward loosened marital ties. They point to both the economic and psychological dislocation that often follows divorce, and criticize parents for placing their own needs over the needs of their children. Although generally not opposed to divorce that is truly fault based, they criticize adults whom they see as placing their own need for fulfillment over their children's need for stability and sustained connections.

Many others, however, challenge the view that no-fault divorce is responsible for altering our understanding of marital commitment. Pointing to the widespread practice of collusive divorce during the fault era, they argue that no-fault divorce responded to rather than initiated changes that had already taken place in society's understanding of marriage. Supporting this view, no-fault supporters point out that divorce rates began to rise before no-fault reform owing to a number of factors, including increased social acceptance of divorce, the Vietnam War (studies consistently show that divorce rates increase during times of war), the women's rights movement, and changing economic conditions.[2] Accordingly, supporters argue that eliminating no-fault divorce is a misguided strategy that will not accomplish its intended goal of significantly reducing the rate of divorce.

Another concern of no-fault supporters is that eliminating no-fault divorce will recreate many of the problems of the past such as the practice of collusive divorce, trapping women in abusive marriages. Focusing on domestic violence victims, one study concluded that no-fault divorce has led to a "striking decline" in female domestic violence rates and "a decline in females murdered by their intimates."[3] The authors suggest that this is due both to the increased availability of divorce and to the fact that "the switch to a unilateral divorce regime redistributes power

---

[2]Donna S. Hershkowitz and Drew R. Liebert, The Direction of Divorce Reform in California: From Fault to No-Fault . . . and Back Again?, http://ajud.assembly.ca.gov/sites/ajud.assembly.ca.gov/files/reports/1197%20divorcere-form97.pdf. *See also* Stephen Bahr, Social Science Research on Family Dissolution: What It Shows and How It Might Be of Interest to Family Law Reformers, 4 J.L. Fam. Stud. 5, 8 (2002).

[3]Justin Wolfers and Betsey Stevenson, Bargaining in the Shadow of the Law: Divorce Laws and Family Distress 19 (Stanford Law and Economics Olin Working Paper No. 273; Stanford Law School, Public Law Working Paper No. 73, December 2003).

in a marriage, giving power to the person who wants out, and reducing the power previously held by the partner interested in preserving the marriage."[4]

Interestingly, Barbara Defoe Whitehead, a self-described critic of contemporary divorce practices, also raises concerns about the impact that the elimination of no-fault divorce would have on battered women.[5] She explains:

> Some marriages will be preserved that probably should end, including those that involve physical abuse and violence. Unfortunately, fault is likely to be most successful in deterring socially isolated and timorous women, often battered wives, from seeking divorce. It would be a cruel irony indeed if a pro-marriage policy unintentionally became a pro-bad-marriage policy.

Id. at 5. Whitehead also points to another possible unintended consequence of reform — that restricting the availability of no-fault divorce may deter people from marrying in the first place. She argues that based on life experience and cultural messages about the high rates of marital failure, young adults are already apprehensive about marital commitments. If they then hear how hard it is to get divorced, they may "interpret legal restrictions on divorce as yet another reason to avoid marriage." *Id.* at 6. Thus, Whitehead argues that the current reform effort may backfire and may "further undermine and weaken the commitment to marriage, the very institution it intends to save. Worse, it sends a glum and dispiriting message to a generation already deeply pessimistic about the chances for a lasting marriage." *Id.*

Supporters of no-fault divorce are also concerned about the well-being of children. They recognize the impact that divorce can have on children but focus on the harms of growing up in a household that is rife with conflict. Again challenging the critics' understanding of causality, they point out that many of the emotional and psychological harms that are attributed to divorce may be due to longstanding problems in the family. Accordingly, efforts to compel parents to remain together may exacerbate rather than alleviate childhood distress. Moreover, no-fault supporters point out that the impact of divorce can be mitigated by carefully structured custody and visitation plans to account for the needs of the children and by support awards that are sufficient to offset the potential economic disruption of divorce.

Legal Reforms

Based on concerns about no-fault divorce, reform measures that aim to make marital dissolution more difficult have been introduced in many states. By increasing the barriers to divorce, it is hoped that spouses will be more inclined to work out their differences, rather than opting for no-fault's promise of an "easy" escape from commitment. These measures have met with some success, but they have also been resisted based on the kinds of concerns discussed above, such as that they will entrap spouses in destructive marriages and discourage people from marrying in the first place. Another important concern is the potential intrusiveness of these

---

[4]*Id.* at 2.
[5]Maggie Gallagher and Barbara Defoe Whitehead, End No-Fault Divorce? First-Things: The Journal of Religion and Public Life, August/September (1997) http://www.firstthings.com/article/1997/08/001-end-no-fault-divorce (accessed June 22, 2016).

measures, as they limit the ability of individuals to decide when a marriage is in fact over. Framed slightly differently, the concern is that these proposals seek to limit choice in furtherance of an idealized notion of marital life that may bear little connection to a couple's daily reality.

Not surprisingly, many of these reforms target no-fault divorce. Some measures propose eliminating no-fault as a ground for divorce altogether; others seek to limit its availability to couples who do not have minor children, and still others seek to impose waiting periods on couples between when they file for divorce and the dissolution action. Another approach is to require **mutual consent**, thus eliminating the option of "unilateral" no-fault divorce. Accordingly, absent fault, both parties must agree to the divorce — one spouse cannot terminate the marriage over the objection of the other. Based on the view that the state has a legitimate interest in keeping spouses together for the benefit of their offspring, mutual consent provisions are often tied to the presence of minor children. Of concern to opponents is that if one spouse refuses to consent, a divorce cannot be granted until a couple's youngest child turns 18, thus keeping embattled spouses locked together in an unhappy union.

A more recent idea that has been proposed in a few states is to designate the party who is opposed to the divorce the "responsible spouse," and then provide him or her with leverage in the fight to save the marriage by way of a disproportionate share of the marital assets and parenting time (unless the party opposing the marriage is guilty of marital fault). Under this model, "[a]n unhappy mate could [still] file for divorce, but he/she would pay a price of less child custody and fewer assets."[6]

Rather than focusing on making it more burdensome to obtain a divorce as a way to encourage couples to stick it out, other reform measures instead focus on strengthening marriage as the key to lowering the divorce rate. Two important measures include premarital counseling requirements and the controversial concept of covenant marriage, which, as discussed below, is currently available as an option in three states.

Premarital Counseling

Seeking to prevent divorce by strengthening marriage at the front end, a handful of states have passed laws to encourage couples to participate in **premarital counseling**. By way of an incentive, participants are typically offered a discount on the marriage license fee. Another possible approach is to set a longer waiting period for the issuance of a marriage license, which can then be waived for couples who have gone through the premarital counseling process.

Although research on the effectiveness of this approach is limited, some studies suggest that participation in premarital counseling may help to weed out poorly matched couples before they actually tie the knot, and it may also improve the communication skills of those who do marry, although the impact on the actual divorce

---

[6]Marriage Savers, http://www.marriagesavers.org (accessed June 8, 2016).

rate is, as of yet, unclear.[7] Moreover, because premarital counseling laws are far less restrictive of individual autonomy and choice than other divorce reform measures, they have generated less opposition from those who do not believe the state should seek to compel unhappy couples to remain together for the benefit of their children or for the good of society.

Covenant Marriage

Designed to counter what some regard as the destructive effects of no-fault divorce, covenant marriage seeks to educate potential married couples about the seriousness of the vow of marriage and equip them with information about the difficulties often encountered in marriage. In 1997, the state of Louisiana passed the nation's first **covenant marriage** law, which emphasizes the permanency of marriage and limits the availability of divorce.

Since then, although covenant marriage bills have been considered in a majority of states, only Arizona and Arkansas have followed Louisiana's lead and enacted such a measure into law. To some, the failure of covenant marriage to take hold points to the inherent limitations of a two-tiered approach to marriage, while others argue that it reflects the corrosive effect of our anti-marriage culture.[8] Over the years, commentators have raised the concern that the term "covenant marriage" suggests the use of state law to infuse biblical values into a civil relationship. As an article by Katherine Shaw Spaht, who drafted the original Louisiana law, makes clear, this association is no accident. Rather, as she explains, the appropriation of the term "covenant" in "covenant marriage" was chosen to communicate the understanding that "legal marriage represents a serious commitment and mutual faithfulness, albeit an imperfect reflection of God's love and eternal faithfulness," and that entry into this more exalted union "is closer to the Christian conception of marriage than a 'standard' marriage." Katherine Shaw Spaht, Mulieris Dignitatem: The Vocation of Wife and Mother in a Legal Covenant Marriage, 8 Ave Maria L. Rev. 365, 367 (2010).

Unique to the Louisiana law are provisions that "communicate" to married couples the kind of behavior that is expected of them, including the imposition of greater familial obligations upon "the covenant wife who becomes a mother" — an identity that "finds fuller expression in the law of covenant marriage." *Id.* at 395.

The following language from Louisiana's statute captures the essence of what covenant marriage entails:

> A covenant marriage is a marriage entered into by one male and one female who understand and agree that the marriage between them is a lifelong relationship. Parties to a covenant marriage have received counseling emphasizing the nature and purposes of marriage and the responsibilities thereto. Only when there has been a complete and

---

[7] For a discussion of this research, see Alan J. Hawkins, Will Legislation to Encourage Premarital Education Strengthen Marriage and Reduce Divorce?, 9 J.L. Fam. Stud. 79 (2007).

[8] *See, e.g.*, Nathan Bracken, Foundational Marriage: A Counteroffer to Covenant Marriage in Utah, 7 J.L. Fam. Stud. 427 (2005); and Katherine Shaw Spaht, Covenant Marriage Seven Years Later: Its as Yet Unfilled Promise, 65 La. L. Rev. 605, 628 (2005).

total breach of the marital covenant commitment may the non-breaching party seek a declaration that the marriage is no longer recognized.

La. Rev. Stat. §9:272 (2004). There are defining features that distinguish covenant marriage from a "non-covenant" marriage.

First, prospective spouses must take some initial steps in order to enter into a covenant marriage. They must undergo premarital counseling and then sign a declaration of intent attesting that they have satisfied the counseling requirement, they understand that marriage is a lifelong commitment, and they will take all reasonable steps to preserve their marriage, including further counseling as needed. They also must disclose to one another any information that could negatively affect their ability to enter into the marriage and must attest to the fact of full disclosure. Perhaps the key distinguishing factor is that the prospective spouses in a covenant marriage agree in advance that they will not seek a no-fault divorce. By eliminating this option, they commit themselves to divorcing only if there has been a complete breach of the marital commitment, which occurs as essentially defined along traditional fault lines or if the spouses have lived separate and apart for two years.

Proponents hope that entering into a covenant marriage will cause couples to take their marital commitments more seriously. They hope that the counseling requirements and the limits on divorce will reinvigorate marriage by requiring spouses to work hard at their relationships, thus counteracting the seductiveness of easy divorce and restoring the primacy of marital commitment.

Many serious concerns, however, have been raised about covenant marriage. As noted above, one concern is that it infuses a biblical conception of marriage into state law. This potentially acts as a breach of the required boundary between church and state. In a related vein, critics worry that this subordination ideal will reinvigorate a tradition of female subordination within marriage, thus disrupting the modern trend toward greater spousal equality.

Also of concern is that it is impossible to predict the future, and committing oneself in advance to a particular course of action may work to a spouse's detriment. Thus, for example, if a husband turns out to be abusive, by entering into a covenant marriage, a woman has committed herself to participating in counseling with him, when the best and safest course of action may be for her to disengage from the relationship as quickly as possible. Moreover, once having committed to what some have dubbed "super-marriage," the psychological consequences of disentanglement are likely to be greater, thus making it more difficult for an at-risk spouse to extricate herself from this "lifelong" commitment.

D. ANNULMENTS

Marriages can also be "terminated" by the granting of an annulment. Although annulments are rare, it is nonetheless important to have a basic understanding of the law in this area. A client who comes to your office may want an annulment for religious reasons, or a client may be confused about the law, believing, for example, that an annulment is the only way to end a short-term or unconsummated marriage.

As you read this section, keep in mind that we are speaking only about the civil annulment process. A number of religious bodies also grant annulments in accordance with their own internal principles and procedures.

1. Distinguished from Divorce

An **annulment** is a retroactive declaration that no valid marriage ever existed between the parties. The modern annulment action emerged out of ecclesiastical practice. Unlike divorce, the procedure was consistent with the religious belief in the indissolubility of the marital relationship because an annulment establishes that the parties were never validly married.

Divorce is premised on the existence of a valid marriage. It operates to dissolve the legal bond between spouses based on problems that arose during the course of the marriage. It operates prospectively to terminate the bond from the date of the divorce forward. In contrast, an annulment works retrospectively to invalidate the marital bond based on a defect that existed at the time the marriage was celebrated — it is a statement that because of this defect, the marriage was flawed from its inception. Accordingly, an annulment cannot be granted for a problem that arises after a marriage is celebrated because a valid marriage would have been established, and annulment speaks to marital invalidity. Thus, although common, it is technically incorrect to speak of an annulment as terminating a marriage because it is a declaration that the parties were never in fact married.

2. Annulment Grounds

Grounds for annulment vary from state to state. Most of the grounds can be grouped into two categories: those involving breaches of state marital restriction laws and those involving a lack of capacity or intent. This distinction has important practical significance as the first category of marriages are generally void while the second are voidable.

Void Marriages

An annulment can be granted if a marriage is contracted in violation of a marital restriction law. Specific grounds include bigamy, incest, and being under the age of capacity (see Chapter 2, Section A.2). Incestuous and bigamous marriages are void from their inception and cannot be ratified by cohabitation or consent. In contrast, a marriage that is contracted when one or both parties were under age is generally voidable, and continued cohabitation beyond the age of consent will ratify the marriage.

A decree of annulment is not actually required to invalidate a marriage that is **void** from its inception as it is regarded as having never taken place. However, a party may prefer to obtain a decree of annulment in order to eliminate any confusion about his or her marital status.

Voidable Marriages

An annulment may also be granted if one party lacked the capacity or the intent to contract a real marriage due to fraud, duress, mental incapacity, insanity, and, possibly, incurable impotence. Of these, considerations of fraud probably come up the most. To warrant an annulment, the fraud must go to the "essentials" of the marriage. This concept has traditionally been limited to the sexual and procreative aspects of marriage, such as concealing a pregnancy by another man, misrepresenting an intent to consummate the marriage, or misrepresenting an intent to have children where no such intent exists. Some jurisdictions have expanded the concept of fraud to include other critical aspects of the marital relationship, such as religious beliefs — for example, where one party pretends to be deeply religious in order to entice the other into marriage.

In contrast to a marriage contracted in violation of a state restriction law, a marriage premised on the lack of capacity or intent is generally considered voidable rather than void. A **voidable** marriage is considered valid until and unless it is invalidated by a decree of annulment. As a general rule, the annulment petition can be filed only by the "innocent" spouse — the one not responsible for the defect. The annulment may be denied if the spouse seeking the annulment knew about the defect at the time of celebration or ratified the marriage by cohabitation after learning of it (prior knowledge and ratification are not defenses if the marriage is void). For instance, using the example of religious misrepresentation, if the deceived partner remains in the marriage after learning about the deception, she or he will probably be deemed to have ratified the marriage and would not be entitled to an annulment. Similarly, a court might find that the passage of years has mitigated the impact of the defect because the parties would have had the time to establish an independent relationship.

3. Consequences of an Annulment Decree

As a matter of logic, if an annulment decree undoes a marriage back to the date of celebration, then any children born to the couple would be "illegitimate"; additionally, no marital rights to support or property would accrue. Although this was the common law approach, this is no longer the case in most states.

Children

In keeping with the modern legal approach to children of unmarried parents (see Chapter 12), children of an annulled marriage are no longer considered "illegitimate." Accordingly, the law treats these children similarly to children of divorcing parents when it comes to custody, visitation, and support determinations.

Spousal Support and the Division of Property

Because alleviating financial hardship is considered important enough to outweigh the risk that a party will have been required to support someone eventually determined not to be his or her spouse, many courts will award temporary support during the pendency of an annulment action. However, regardless of need, support will not usually be awarded to a spouse who is denying the validity of the marriage because these are regarded as mutually inconsistent claims. A number of states have enacted statutes allowing an award of permanent alimony in cases of need following an annulment, but some permit an award only if this spouse entered into the marriage with a good faith belief in its validity. In authorizing support, these statutes eschew reliance on legal formalities and recognize that the declaration of invalidity does not mitigate the financial needs of an economically dependent partner. In the absence of express statutory authorization, a court might make an alimony-like award, such as it might do in a cohabitation case. With respect to property, many statutes expressly authorize the court to make a distribution of accumulated assets much as it would do in a divorce case (see Chapter 11).

Revival

Following an annulment, difficult questions may arise regarding the nature of third-party obligations when such obligations turn on the recipient's marital status. Using a hypothetical, two situations will be briefly discussed.

Let's assume that the marriage of Juan and Maria ended in divorce and that Juan was to pay support until such time as Maria remarried. Now assume that Maria remarries and Juan stops paying alimony based on the fact of her remarriage. What happens if Maria's second marriage is subsequently annulled? Because annulment effectively cancels out the second marriage, Maria could logically argue that there was no remarriage and that Juan's support obligation is subject to **revival**. Moreover, she could claim that he owes her money back to the date he stopped paying. Most courts would reject Maria's claim for support on the basis that Juan had a right to rely on the marriage as it appeared, as distinct from its technical, legal status, and his support obligation would not be revived.

However, when benefits such as Social Security are involved, courts are much more likely to revive payments upon an annulment. For example, if before her second marriage, Juan had died, and Maria was receiving Social Security benefits, these payments would cease upon her remarriage, but if this second marriage were annulled, most courts would revive the payments because the payor does not rely on the remarriage in the same way as a former spouse would when planning for the future.

E. LEGAL SEPARATION

The third remedy for an unhappy marriage is a legal separation — also known as a "judicial separation," a "limited divorce," and, historically speaking, a *divorce a mensa et thoro* (a divorce from board and bed). A **legal separation** is a judicial decree formally permitting or, perhaps more accurately, requiring, spouses to live apart. In some states, a separation can be granted for an unlimited period of time; in others, there are durational limits. Grounds are generally similar to those found in fault-based divorce laws, although some statutes simply give a judge the discretion to decide if sufficient cause for a separation exists. The no-fault concept has not permeated this action, perhaps because, unlike with a divorce, a couple can always agree to separate without a court decree.

A legal separation does not terminate the marital relationship. Accordingly, it does not free the parties to remarry. As part of its decree, a court can determine custody and award both child and spousal support. In some states, a division of property also may be ordered; in others, the distribution of property is prohibited unless and until the parties actually divorce. One might wonder why an unhappy spouse would file for a legal separation rather than for a divorce. One reason might be religious beliefs that do not permit divorce because the marital bond is considered indissoluble, but would allow a separation because this does not dissolve the marriage. A variety of personal and emotional reasons also might influence the decision to seek a separation rather than a divorce. An individual wishing to live apart from his or her spouse may not be ready to file for divorce but might need the protection of court orders — if, for example, he or she fears the other spouse might disappear with the children — or the financial support that the court could award. A spouse also might hope to send a wake-up call to his or her partner.

Religious Divorces

In addition to a civil divorce, there may also be a need to obtain a religious divorce. For example, under Jewish law, in order for a wife to have a recognized divorce her husband must give her a "get." A get is a document where the husband expressly acknowledges his intention to divorce his wife and sever all bonds with her. Similarly, if a party who has been married under the Catholic faith is later divorced, in order to have the divorce recognized by the Catholic Church the party must have his or her previous marriage annulled under the canons of Catholicism. The grounds for annulment under canon law differ from the grounds for a civil divorce.

A number of states provide for the conversion of a separation into a divorce after the passage of a specified period of time. Where conversion is not allowed, filing for a separation and then filing for divorce (should a divorce eventually be desired) entails a significant duplication of efforts; therefore, a client's reasons for wanting to start with a legal separation rather than initiating divorce proceedings should be carefully explored. For instance, if the client knows that the marriage is over but isn't quite ready emotionally to implement the decision, it is worth exploring whether it makes sense to wait to initiate legal proceedings until he or she is ready to proceed with the divorce.

A complaint for a legal separation should be distinguished from an action for separate maintenance. Although similar, the essence of a complaint for separate maintenance is a claim for support. Thus, the focus is on the plaintiff's need for support, rather than on the reason for the parties' separation. The decree usually does not involve findings on the reason for separation nor does it specifically authorize the parties to live apart, although reconciliation generally terminates the support obligation. Also, in most states the court cannot order a division of property or determine custody as part of a separate maintenance action.

Chapter Summary

- Divorce is a legal action that dissolves the marital bond.
- Historically, divorce law was premised on marital fault, and a divorce could be granted only to an innocent spouse based on marital wrongdoing.
- Beginning in the 1960s, concerns about collusion and the adversarial nature of the fault system, among other considerations, led to no-fault reform. Some states eliminated fault grounds altogether and enacted pure no-fault systems. Others added no-fault grounds as an option. The principal no-fault grounds are marital breakdown and living separate and apart for a statutorily prescribed time period.
- Some now believe divorce has become easy, and a tightening up of the rules, through counter-reforms, such as covenant marriage options and mandatory waiting periods, have been adopted in some states.
- An annulment is a declaration that no valid marriage ever existed between the parties due to an impediment that was present at the time of celebration. Annulments are usually based on a lack of capacity or intent, or a violation of a marital restriction law.
- A legal separation is a decree that the parties have good cause for living apart. It does not terminate the marital relationship, and the parties cannot remarry. It is distinguishable from an action for separate maintenance, which focuses on support rather than on the reason for the underlying separation.

Applying the Rules

1. Eliza and Ricardo had been married for ten years before Eliza filed for divorce. Eliza and Ricardo live in a state that provides that the court must make a finding of irretrievable breakdown of the marriage, and it must be supported by substantial evidence. You represented Ricardo at trial. At trial Eliza testified that Ricardo behaved in such a way that she could not reasonably be expected to live with him. She said that they often argued over how money should be spent, that Ricardo was controlling over what television shows they would watch at night, and that he often left his dirty clothes around the house. Ricardo testified that he did not believe the marriage was irretrievably broken and that these were all things that could be fixed if Eliza would just agree to go to counseling. The trial judge found that the marriage was irretrievably broken. What are your strongest arguments for asking the trial judge to reconsider the ruling?

2. A state statute provides that if any party opposes the granting of a divorce, the court must make a finding that there are irreconcilable differences. In order

to find irreconcilable differences that court must make one of three findings: (1) the party opposing the finding has committed adultery; (2) the party opposing the finding has behaved in such a way that the party filing for divorce should not be expected to live with the other party; or (3) the parties have lived separate and apart for at least 12 months preceding the filing of the petition for dissolution of marriage. Kia advises you that she wants to file for divorce. She says that she knows her husband Diego will oppose the petition. She says that the reason she wants a divorce is that she just does not love Diego anymore and wants to move on with her life. What do you tell Kia?

3. Pam marries John, her long-time boyfriend, in Las Vegas, Nevada. Two weeks later she comes to your office and says she wants to annul her marriage to John. She says that while she loves John she never intended to marry him at that time. She tells you that while they were in Las Vegas they thought it would be fun to just have a "pretend" wedding at one of the local wedding chapels. She had no idea it was a "real" wedding with someone authorized to perform the ceremony. She says that she never realized before the ceremony that John believed it was real and that they were actually getting married. She tells you John will not just agree to an annulment. Does Pam have grounds for an annulment? What grounds should Pam state? What defenses might John be able to allege?

4. Delia has sought your legal advice regarding a divorce based on the grounds of adultery. She advises you that her husband is having an affair and she intends to file for divorce, but she wants to make sure the divorce is not barred by her inadvertently engaging in any contact that might constitute a defense to the grounds of adultery. What would you tell Delia she should do (or not do) in order to avoid giving her husband a defense to the grounds of adultery?

Family Law in Practice

1. Locate your state's divorce law and determine the following:
   - Are fault grounds still used, or is your state a "pure" no-fault jurisdiction?
   - If yes, what grounds are available? What defenses are available?
   - What no-fault ground(s) is (or are) available in your state?
   - What must a party show to qualify for a no-fault divorce?

   Having reviewed the statute, identify and describe any recent changes that are designed to slow down the divorce process (such as waiting periods or counseling requirements) or limit divorce options (such as limiting no-fault divorce to couples without children).

2. A client has come to your office. She is unhappy in her marriage but does not know what she wants to do. You, as her attorney, need to draft a letter explaining her legal options. At this point, you do not have all the facts, but, based on a brief interview, you know the following:

- She thinks that her husband never loved her and that he married her solely to make his family happy.
- They have been married for three years, during which time, based on his wishes, they have lived totally separate lives, although they have had sexual intercourse on occasion.

In your letter you should explain the general differences as to divorce, annulment, and legal separation and discuss the specific requirements of the laws in your state.

3. Assume you are a legislative aide in a state that is considering enacting a covenant marriage law along the lines of Louisiana's law. The state senator you work for has asked you to prepare a "briefing" memo in which you explain the basic requirements of covenant marriage and set out the arguments in favor of and against such a law.

4. Assume you are a law clerk for a family court judge who has recently taken a divorce case under advisement because it raises a new issue of law. The wife filed for divorce on the grounds of adultery because her husband has engaged in an intimate relationship with another man. The husband denies this is adultery, asserting that the concept only covers heterosexual intercourse. The judge has asked you to locate cases from other jurisdictions that have addressed this issue, and write an interoffice memorandum in which you first analyze the case law and then set out your thoughts as to how she should rule in this matter.

Child Custody

In cases involving **child custody** where a determination must be made as to which parent has primary control over the decisions about and care for the child, disputes between divorcing parents and allocating rights and responsibilities between two parents is often a daunting task. The parents are likely to have very different perceptions of the arrangement that would be best for their children. Judges often have to make agonizingly difficult choices that have profound and lasting consequences for the parents and their children. Increasingly, judges are also being called on to resolve custody and/or visitation disputes between a child's legal parent and a "third party," most commonly a co-parent (as discussed, the term "third party" is highly contested when applied to a co-parent), stepparent, or grandparent. These cases raise complex questions about how we define parent-hood and the weight and meaning of the associated relational interests.

Attorneys often have to address the emotional issues surrounding their client's wishes within the context of the legal framework that must be presented to the court. In making these determinations, courts generally rely on the "**best interest of the child**" standard to resolve the conflict. This standard is gender neutral and enables a judge to tailor a decision to meet the specific needs of the children in any given family. On the flip side, the flexibility of the standard means that outcomes can be unpredictable and possibly subjective, thus infusing the determination process with a sense of indeterminacy. When the dispute involves a "third party," there is far less certainty about the appropriate standard, as the best interest approach assumes that both parties stand in equal legal relationship to the children in question, which, as we will see, is not the case in the third-party context. Before considering the contemporary legal framework for resolving custody disputes, we begin with a historical overview.

Key Concepts

- The best interest standard
- Alternative custody standards
- Types of custody arrangements
- Visitation options
- Parenting support programs
- Post-divorce disputes
- Nonparent custody and visitation arrangements

A. THE BEST INTEREST STANDARD

As discussed in Chapter 1, our early custody laws were infused with normative assumptions about gender. Until well into the eighteenth century, a father had complete command over the education, training, and discipline of his children, and owned their labor. In turn, a father was charged with the responsibility of supporting his children and preparing them, particularly his sons, for passage into the world. In sharp contrast, mothers were simply entitled to "reverence and respect." As a corollary of their status as the ultimate domestic authority, the paternal preference rule gave fathers a near-absolute right to custody in the event of divorce. Understood as a proprietary right, this preference was not calibrated to take the actual needs and certainly not the preferences of children into account.

In the late eighteenth century, the patriarchal family structure began to break down in the wake of industrialization. As home became reconceptualized as a sanctuary of rest and repose in which women's gentle influence could flourish, the favored legal status of fathers yielded to the emerging **tender years presumption** based on new normative understandings of the importance of the mother-child bond. Whether adopted by statute or judicial decision, this presumption embodied the belief that the best interest of children was synonymous with maternal custody at least until adolescence, at which point some jurisdictions retained a paternal preference, particularly for boys, based on the assumption that fathers could best prepare children for life away from the hearth.

1. The Modern Best Interest Test

By the 1970s, as fixed notions about proper roles for men and women began to break down, the tender years presumption lost favor, and by the turn of the century, states had eliminated the explicit use of the tender years presumption in favor of a gender-neutral best interest standard. Formally uncoupled from gender determinants, the best interest of the child standard is supposed to ensure that each case is resolved on its own merits, with neither parent being given an advantage based on assumptions about gender.

If parents reach an agreement regarding custody and visitation, a judge will review the terms at the divorce hearing (see Chapter 9) to determine whether they promote the best interest of the children. In most states, the judge conducting this review is not required to defer to the wishes of the parents as embodied in their agreement; rather, the agreement is simply viewed as expressive of their preferences and is only one of many factors in the assessment of best interest. Based, however, on the belief that parents are in a better position than the court to know what is best for their children, some states have begun to give more weight to their custodial preferences, by, for example, adopting a presumption that, without clear evidence to the contrary, the agreed-upon terms are in the best interest of the children.

Where custody is contested, the focus of the contest is supposed to be on the needs of the child rather than on the right of either parent to custody. However, an important question to consider is whether embattled parents are truly able to place the actual needs of their children at the front and center of the custody determination, or whether their positions are shaped more by their own needs and desire to emerge victorious over their spouse.

The frequently criticized indeterminacy of the best interest standard can make it very difficult for a court to sort out what really is at stake in a contested custody case. Similarly, many argue that the rule's pliability gives judges virtually unfettered, and hence as a practical matter nearly unreviewable, discretion to decide what is the best arrangement for children based on these competing narratives. Accordingly, as discussed below, despite the potential benefits of flexibility and adaptability of the best interest standard, some experts have argued that children would be better served by custody rules that lead to more predictable and consistent outcomes, such as the American Law Institute's (ALI) innovative approximation standard.

BEST INTEREST OF THE CHILD STANDARD

Although state statutes vary in terms of the factors that a judge must consider when determining best interest, Arizona law is a good example of the kinds of considerations that frequently are included in the best interest litmus. As is the case in most jurisdictions, it also requires the judge to make specific findings on the record regarding the child's best interest. An interesting point to note with the Arizona statute is that it does not use the term "custody" but instead refers to "legal decision-making" and parenting time — terms that more aptly describes what "custody" means on a practical level.

§25-403. Legal Decision-Making; Best Interests of Child

A. The court shall determine legal decision-making and parenting time, either originally or on petition for modification, in accordance with the best interests of the child. The court shall consider all factors that are relevant to the child's physical and emotional well-being, including:

1. The past, present and potential future relationship between the parent and the child.

2. The interaction and interrelationship of the child with the child's parent or parents, the child's siblings and any other person who may significantly affect the child's best interest.

3. The child's adjustment to home, school and community.

4. If the child is of suitable age and maturity, the wishes of the child as to legal decision-making and parenting time.

5. The mental and physical health of all individuals involved.

6. Which parent is more likely to allow the child frequent, meaningful and continuing contact with the other parent. This paragraph does not apply if the court determines that a parent is acting in good faith to protect the child from witnessing an act of domestic violence or being a victim of domestic violence or child abuse.

7. Whether one parent intentionally misled the court to cause an unnecessary delay, to increase the cost of litigation or to persuade the court to give a legal decision-making or a parenting time preference to that parent.

8. Whether there has been domestic violence or child abuse pursuant to section 25-403.03.

9. The nature and extent of coercion or duress used by a parent in obtaining an agreement regarding legal decision-making or parenting time.

10. Whether a parent has complied with chapter 3, article 5 of this title.

11. Whether either parent was convicted of an act of false reporting of child abuse or neglect under section 13-2907.02.

B. In a contested legal decision-making or parenting time case, the court shall make specific findings on the record about all relevant factors and the reasons for which the decision is in the best interests of the child.

Formulating a Child-Centered Approach to Determining Custody

The best interest test requires an analysis of a child's needs and an assessment of which parent can best meet those needs. It is intended to be a flexible, child-centered approach that takes a child's individual circumstances into account when making a custody determination. The inherent flexibility of this approach allows for an individualized consideration of all relevant factors. Its child-centered nature means that parents do not have claims to a particular custodial arrangement based upon their own needs or interests.

On the flip side, the best interest standard has been criticized for being vague and indeterminate, which gives judges room to import their personal views into their determinations, thus making results unpredictable and possibly idiosyncratic, and severely limiting the scope of meaningful appellate review. As articulated by Robert Mnookin in his classic work on the subject:

> The determination of what is "best" . . . for a particular child is usually indeterminate and speculative. For most custody case, psychological theories simply do not yield confident predictions of the effects of alternative custody dispositions. Moreover, even if accurate predictions were possible in more cases, our society today lacks any clear-cut consensus about the value to be used in determining what is "best. . . ."[1]

Some states have attempted to address the indeterminacy concern by adopting statutory guidelines enumerating specific factors that a judge must take into account when making a custody decision. The Arizona statute excerpted above is a typical example of this multifaceted approach. As an attorney assisting a parent with a custody dispute, it is incumbent to go through the factors that a judge will use to determine the best interest of the child in order to provide evidence on each element.

Although statutes with enumerated factors require consideration of each enumerated factor, there is usually no requirement to prioritize the factors or to give the individual factors equal weight. Accordingly, a judge generally has the discretion to

---

[1]Robert Mnookin, Child-Custody Adjudication: Judicial Functions in the Face of Indeterminacy, 39 Law & Contemp. Probs. 226, 229 (1976). *See also* Robert Mnookin, Child Custody Revisited, 77 Law & Contemp. Probs. 249 (2014).

assign the weight to each factor that he or she believes it merits based on either the circumstances of the case or individual beliefs about what considerations are most important. In turn, parents will often choose the factors that favor their position and minimize the other factors in presenting a disputed custody issue to the court. For example, one judge might regard the preference of the child as the primary consideration, while another might attach little weight to it.

Moreover, the factors do not lend themselves to precise definitions. For example, in the Arizona statute, what does the term "adjustment to home, school, and environment" mean? One judge might emphasize the emotional environment of a parent's home, while another might consider more tangible qualities, such as whether a child must share a room or have his or her own room. In short, although these statutes set out the framework within which custody determinations are to be made, the attorney retains a considerable amount of leeway to argue the importance of each factor, and the judges retain considerable decisional discretion based on the weight and meaning they assign to the individual statutory factors.

Having said this, some factors tend to be given more weight than others in the best interest litmus, although again there are no fixed rules about this. These include the parent-child bond, past caretaking, time availability, stability of environment, preference of the child, and domestic violence.

The Parent-Child Bond

Important to any custody determination is the attempt to evaluate the strength and integrity of the bond that each parent has with his or her children. In some cases, such as where one parent is abusive or disengaged from the family, this task is easy. However, given that most parents have a deep attachment to their children, this assessment can be difficult and may require a multifaceted approach in which a judge weighs a variety of considerations, such as (1) the amount of time each parent spends with the children; (2) the quality and the appropriateness of the interactions; (3) the degree of emotional engagement; and (4) whom the child relies on for emotional and other kinds of essential support. Perhaps more than with any other factor, it is here that the report of a psychologist, a court-appointed advisor, or a guardian ad litem who has been appointed to conduct a custody evaluation may be particularly useful to the parties in helping them come to a resolution regarding custody even before it is taken to a judge for a decision.

Past Caretaking

Past caretaking has always been an important consideration in custody determinations. More recently, in response to growing criticism of the indeterminacy of the best interest standard, some states now give greater weight to considerations of the caretaking role of each parent during the marriage, and favor the primary caretaker. Some states have accomplished this by statute, while others leave it to judicial discretion.

A number of distinct, mutually supportive rationales promote reliance on past caretaking as a critical factor in the decisional matrix. First, there is general agreement among experts that a child usually develops the strongest psychological bond with the parent who has been most involved with his or her daily care (i.e., the primary caretaker) and that the preservation of this relationship is essential to a child's healthy development. This attachment theory "suggests that a strong, caring parent-child dyad leads to a strong secure attachment [and an emotionally secure child]. This same theory posits that if the care provided is unsupportive or unpredictable, then insecurity is manifested."[2]

Predictability is another major reason that past caretaking has become an increasingly important consideration in custody determinations. Predictability is important for two distinct reasons. First is the belief that reliance on past caretaking will reduce some of the inherent uncertainty about how a child will be cared for following a divorce. A parent's prior commitment to providing primary care is seen as a reasonably reliable predictor of how he or she will respond to the child's needs in the future, whereas determining how a parent who has not been intimately involved with caretaking will respond is far more speculative. Accordingly, reliance on past caretaking patterns provides a protective buffer for children, carrying forward familiar rhythms and interactions.

Second, this predictability enables couples to enter into custody negotiations with a clearer sense of what they would be likely to gain or lose by going to court. This is particularly important for women because studies have shown that mothers are likely to give up some economic benefits in order to secure custody of their children. If results were more predictable, going to court would be less of a risk, and there would be less need to sacrifice financial entitlements for custodial security.[3] (See the discussion of the primary caretaker presumption below.)

Lastly, reliance on past caretaking accords with the overall trend in favor of the private ordering of family relationships. By looking to the arrangements that the parties agreed on for the care of their children, greater weight is being given to what they believe (or, perhaps, more accurately, believed) makes sense for their family rather than to what a judge believes is best.

Weaving together these themes, Katherine T. Bartlett eloquently explains what she regards as the virtues of reliance upon past caretaking as a determinative factor:

> Past caretaking has both adjudicative and substantive virtues as a determinant of a child's best interests. In terms of adjudication, it requires the determination of past facts, which courts are accustomed to doing, rather than speculations about the future, which they are not. Because a past-caretaking factor is more determinate than factors relating to the quality of parenting styles or abilities it reduces the opportunity for judges to rely on their own biases about childrearing . . . and it reduces the incentives for parents to engage experts to criticize and undermine the other. . . .[4]

---

[2]Robert F. Kelly and Shawn L. Ward, Allocating Custodial Responsibilities at Divorce: Social Science Research and the American Law Institute's Approximation Rule, 40 Fam. Ct. Rev. 350, 356, 358 (2002).

[3]*See* Margaret F. Bring, Feminism and Child Custody Under Chapter Two of the American Law Institute's Principles of the Law of Family Dissolution, 8 Duke J.L. & Poly. 301, 308-309 (2001).

[4]Katherine T. Bartlett, Prioritizing Past Caretaking in Child-Custody Decisionmaking, 77 Law & Contemp. Probs. 29, 32 (2014). *See also* Elizabeth S. Scott, Gender Politics and Child Custody: The Puzzling Persistence of the Best-Interests Standard, 77 Law & Contemp. Probs. 69 (2014).

However, as we will see when we return to the topic of past caretaking when we review the American Law Institute's approximation rule as an alternative standard later in this chapter, among other concerns, many argue that reliance on this factor is a thinly veiled attempt to reinstate the tender years presumption to the decided detriment of fathers.

Time Availability

The time that a parent has available to devote to his or her children is another important consideration. This is a sensible concern that tends to favor the parent with a less demanding work schedule who accordingly has more flexibility to respond to the needs — both routine and unanticipated — of the children. This factor frequently overlaps with the consideration of both the parent-child bond and past caretaking, as the parent with the greater time availability is likely to be the one who has been most closely involved with the children and is thus likely to be the one that the children are most attached to and reliant upon for their nurture. Of course, it is also possible that this parent is nonetheless disengaged from the children or abusive, thus clearly making it dangerous to simply rely upon this constellation of factors without an inquiry into the actual dynamics and quality of the parent-child relationships.

Stability of Environment

Children generally have a need for stability and continuity in the wake of divorce's dislocation. Accordingly, judges often give considerable weight to a parent's ability to maintain a stable home environment. The emphasis on stability may lead a judge to look with disfavor on a parent who has moved around a lot. This can be problematic where the frequency of moves is attributable to the economic strain occasioned by the marital breakup. In order to avoid penalizing a parent in this situation, it is important for judges to consider a number of factors, including intangible ones such as continuity of care, when assessing the stability of a child's environment.

Preference of the Child

Given that the undisputed focus of a best interest inquiry is the child, an important consideration is how much weight should be given to a child's stated preference. This is a difficult question that has generated considerable controversy.

Historically, the custodial preferences of children carried little, if any, weight. This disregard of their views reflected the traditional understanding of children as lacking an independent legal identity. As we have seen, children traditionally were defined by their dependent and subordinate status within the family unit, and they were not thought to have a separate voice with which to express a preference. However, now that children, especially as they reach their teen years, are regarded as distinct legal persons with some degree of autonomy and say about their lives, all states allow for consideration of their custodial preferences.

As a general rule, states do not have a fixed minimum age at which they will take the views of children into account. Rather, like the Arizona statute excerpted above, the children's wishes will be taken into account only if they are of "suitable age and maturity." Thus, the older a child is, the more seriously his or her choice will be taken into consideration. However, a child under 11 is rarely considered of suitable age and maturity to have his or her wishes taken into consideration. Although a child may not have an absolute right to choose which parent he or she wishes to reside with, many lawyers believe there is little point in litigating a case where a child over the age of 14 has a clear preference as the court will almost always respect his or her wishes given the reality that it is very hard to compel a reluctant teenager to comply with an arrangement that she or he is unhappy with.

While chronological age is an important factor in determining whether a child's views will be elicited, and if elicited, what weight they will be given, it is not the only consideration. It is important to also look to the child's maturity, including his or her decision-making ability, and the articulated reasons for any expressed preference. Family circumstances, such as whether there is a history of violence or whether a child blames one parent for ending the marriage, may also be taken into account in assessing the reliability of the child's views.

There are conflicting views about whether children should participate in custody disputes between their parents.[5] The discussion is often framed as if there were only two possible options — that a child either participates in the custody decision or does not do so at all. However, in reading this debate, keep in mind that there are different ways in which the views of children can be heard without requiring them to actually choose which parent they wish to live with.

Some experts believe that it is too stressful for children to be brought into a custody dispute. Children often have complex, shifting views regarding the nature of their relationship with each parent and, by being drawn into the conflict, may feel as if the weight of the world has been placed on their shoulders. Given that children often blame themselves for their parents' divorce, the concern is that participation will intensify their distress.

Another concern is that a child's stated preference may be shaped by considerations unrelated to best interest, such as fear of reprisal or worry about upsetting a parent perceived as sensitive. A child may also be subject to the undue influence of a parent or may choose a distant, disapproving parent as a way of winning that parent's love. A child may also identify with the parent that she or he perceives as being more powerful in order to avoid feeling powerless or like a "loser." This is of particular concern in cases involving domestic violence because a child may seek to avoid identification with the victim, who is perceived as weak and vulnerable, in order to enhance his or her own sense of security. This tendency may be more pronounced in boys, especially as they approach adolescence. A child also may be angry at the parent who initiated the divorce and may blame that parent for

---

[5]*See generally* Jonathan W. Gould and David A. Martindale, Children's Interests: Article: Including Children in Decision Making About Custodial Placement, 22 J. Am. Acad. Matrim. Law. 303 (2009); Mark Henaghan, What Does a Child's Right to Be Heard in Legal Proceedings Really Mean? ABA Custody Standards Do Not Go Far Enough, 42 Fam. L.Q. 117 (2008); Barbara A. Atwood, Hearing Children's Voices in Custody Litigation: An Empirical Survey and Suggestions of Reform, 45 Ariz. L. Rev. 629 (2003); Robert E. Emery, Children's Voices: Listening — and Deciding — Is an Adult Responsibility, 45 Ariz. L. Rev. 621 (2003).

destroying the family. This anger, which may not be articulated, may influence the child to choose the "innocent" parent in order to get back at the other.

A further consideration is that since attorneys and judges are generally not experts in child psychology, they will not be able to unearth these complex and often deeply buried motivations and may thus give too much weight to "surface" explanations. Although the use of experts can be helpful, their presence does not necessarily solve the problem. The complexity of a situation may not be fully revealed within the necessary time frame for making a decision, and experts often reach conflicting conclusions, thus still leaving to the court the job of sorting through competing understandings of a situation.

On the other hand, experts who believe the child's preference should be seriously considered argue that children are entitled to a say in a proceeding with such significant implications for their lives and that to do otherwise is paternalistic and demonstrates a lack of respect for the ability of children to participate in important decisions. They fear that if a child is not listened to, his or her true needs might never surface, since parents, although professing concern for the child, are often seeking to vindicate their own rights and fulfill their own needs. Custody battles may become a fight for supremacy between the parents, with the child as a shadow player. Parents may thus distort, deliberately or not, the wishes of the child to suit their own position.

Although recognizing the difficulties inherent in sorting through the motivational factors, those who favor eliciting the views of children believe that judges are capable of sifting through layers of meaning. They suggest that understanding the views of a child is no more challenging than sorting through other kinds of conflicting evidence, and that making sense of the entangled strands of a family's situation is the essence of the judicial function in a custody case.

Drawing on social science research, some experts have shifted the focus away from casting children as *decision makers* to focus on the importance of incorporating them as *participants* in the decisional process. According to these studies, children who are excluded from the process "complain about feeling isolated and lonely during the divorce process, and many older youngsters express anger and frustration about being left out."[6] Providing children with a structured mechanism for giving voice to both their feelings and possible arrangements can counteract these feelings, but inclusion must be more than a symbolic gesture. Children are entitled to expect that "both their parents and the professionals involved will listen with respect to their comments. When parents indicate that they do not value and respect their children's thinking, feelings, worries, and needs, it is unlikely to be helpful, and may create cynicism and anger." Kelly, *supra* note 6, at 154.

The views of children can be elicited by a guardian ad litem (GAL) who is appointed by the court to evaluate the needs and wishes of children in contested custody cases and make recommendations to the court regarding their best interest. Typically, a GAL will interview the children, the parents, and other persons

---

[6]Joan B. Kelly, Psychological and Legal Interventions for Parents and Children in Custody and Access Disputes: Current Research and Practice, 10 Va. J. Soc. Poly. & L. 129, 150 (2003). *See also* Barbara A. Atwood, Hearing Children's Voices in Custody Litigation: An Empirical Survey and Suggestions of Reform, 45 Ariz. L. Rev. 629 (2003).

such as teachers, doctors, and possibly neighbors who might have valuable information to contribute to the best interest assessment and recommendation. In some states, the GAL is required to make any expressed wishes of the child regarding preferred custodial arrangements known to the court, even if the GAL does not believe the wishes of the child would be in the child's best interest. In other states, the GAL may be replaced with a court-appointed advisor who is able to interview the child and report the child's preference to the attorneys and the judge. In some cases, a judge may decide not to appoint a GAL or advisor and instead interview the minor child in chambers to elicit the child's preferences.

There has been a growing interest in the idea of providing children with independent legal representation in contested custody cases (as well as in other proceedings that directly impact their lives), and a number of states now provide for the appointment of independent counsel for children in some contested custody cases. Typically, these laws allow for the appointment of what is known as a **"best interest" attorney** who, in contrast to the usual "client-directed" attorney, is required to review the situation and make an independent determination of what the best interest attorney believes is in the child's best interest. The best interest attorney will then advocate a position that will serve the child's best interests even if this position is contrary to the expressed wishes of the child as to custodial arrangements. However, some statutes do allow for the appointment of a client-directed attorney "for children over a certain age, for children who have clearly expressed an objective that is different from the position taken by an assigned representative, or for children who are capable of having an attorney and directing counsel." Accordingly, in these circumstances a **child's attorney** expresses the child's preferences rather than making an independent determination of what is in the minor child's best interest.

ABA STANDARDS AND DEFINITIONS

In 2003, the American Bar Association presented Standards for the appointment and performance of lawyers serving as advocates for children. The Standards applied in cases where "temporary or permanent legal custody, physical custody, parenting plans, parenting time, access, or visitation are adjudicated, including but not limited to divorce, parentage, domestic violence, contested adoptions, and contested private guardianship cases. Lawyers representing children in abuse and neglect cases should follow the ABA Standards of Practice for Representing a Child in Abuse and Neglect Cases (1996)." The Standards set forth the definition of a Best Interests Attorney and Child's Attorney, which clearly defines their differences:

1. "Child's Attorney": A lawyer who provides independent legal counsel for a child and who owes the same duties of undivided loyalty, confidentiality, and competent representation as are due an adult client.
2. "Best Interests Attorney": A lawyer who provides independent legal services for the purpose of protecting a child's best interests, without being bound by the child's directives or objectives.

As to the representation when an attorney is appointed as a child's attorney or best interest attorney, the Standards provide, in part, the following:

D. Initial Tasks

Immediately after being appointed, the lawyer should review the file. The lawyer should inform other parties or counsel of the appointment, and that as counsel of record he or she should receive copies of pleadings and discovery exchanges, and reasonable notification of hearings and of major changes of circumstances affecting the child.

E. Meeting with the Child

The lawyer should meet with the child, adapting all communications to the child's age, level of education, cognitive development, cultural background and degree of language acquisition, using an interpreter if necessary. The lawyer should inform the child about the court system, the proceedings, and the lawyer's responsibilities. The lawyer should elicit and assess the child's views.

As to the child's attorney: "The Child's Attorney should abide by the client's decisions about the objectives of the representation with respect to each issue on which the child is competent to direct the lawyer, and does so. The Child's Attorney should pursue the child's expressed objectives, unless the child requests otherwise, and follow the child's direction, throughout the case."

Supporting the trend to have children's preferences heard, in 2006 the National Conference of Commissioners on Uniform State Laws (NCCUSL) promulgated the Uniform Representation of Children in Abuse, Neglect, and Custody Proceedings Act in order to try to bring clarity and uniformity to what is meant by child representation in these types of proceedings. Unlike the law in most jurisdictions, the Act clearly provides for two kinds of lawyers — the "best interest lawyer" for children who lack the capacity to direct a lawyer and the "child's attorney" for those who are capable of entering into the "usual client-directed relationship" with an attorney.[7] Although the best interest lawyer is not "bound by the child's directives or objectives," the Act requires that he or she consider them and "give them due weight according to the underlying reasons and the child's developmental level."[8]

Domestic Violence

Traditionally, courts did not consider interspousal violence — as distinct from physical abuse of the child — relevant to the determination of best interest. Spousal abuse was seen as connected to the marital relationship, with little or no spillover effect into the parent-child arena. However, new understandings of the dynamics of abuse have led to important changes in the law, and whether through judicial decision or legislative enactment, courts in most states are now required to take spousal violence into account when making custody determinations. This shift reflects the reality that, even if not themselves direct targets of abuse, many children are exposed to acts of parental violence, and that the exposure itself may have

---

[7]Uniform Representation of Children in Abuse, Neglect, and Custody Proceedings Act § 9 (Unif. Law Comm'n 2007)..

[8]*See id.* §§ 6 and 11.

enduring negative consequences. Accordingly, in contrast to the historic disassociation of spousal abuse from the well-being of children, the contemporary approach embodies the view that "the perpetrator of violence against any family member engages in unacceptable behavior that violates his . . . obligations as a parent."[9]

According to the research, somewhere between 70 and 87 percent of children in homes where domestic abuse is present have witnessed violence against their mothers,[10] with many of these children witnessing up to half of the incidents that take place.[11] This exposure can have a significant adverse impact on children. According to one early study, "[c]hildren who witness violence between their parents . . . are no less victimized than children who are direct victims of abuse. All our findings show that children from violent homes retain searing memories of violence between their parents."[12] Victimization has serious emotional and developmental implications. First, children exposed to domestic violence may be at a greater risk of engaging in aggressive and destructive behaviors directed at others such as bullying and assaultive conduct. Second, children of domestic violence may also suffer internal problems such as depression and anxiety.

Other negative outcomes include cognitive and behavioral delays, which can affect a child's functioning in school and ability to develop friendships. These consequences may vary with age. Younger children may express negative feelings, play aggressively, or withdraw from others. School-age children may have more academic difficulties.

There is also always the concern that children who are exposed to violence are at greater risk of both becoming abusers and being abused themselves in intimate relationships. According to one study, about one-half of the children who had witnessed violence between their parents experienced violence in their own adult intimate relationships, the boys as abusers and the girls generally as victims.[13]

In addition to directly impacting the well-being of children, partner abuse has other important implications for child custody determinations. First, men who abuse their partners are more likely to abuse their children. According to two observational studies, "fathers who were violent with their partners were also more physically and emotionally aggressive in interactions with their children."[14] There is also a positive correlation between the severity of the partner abuse and the severity of the child abuse.[15] Of additional concern is a potentially heightened risk of sexual abuse, particularly if substance abuse is involved.

---

[9]Elizabeth Scott, Parental Autonomy and Children's Welfare, 11 Wm. & Mary Bill Rts. J. 1071, 1093 (2003). *See also generally* Peter Jaffe, A Presumption Against Shared Parenting for Family Court Litigants, 52 Fam. Ct. Rev. 187 (2014).

[10]N. Zoe Hilton, Battered Women's Concerns About Their Children Witnessing Wife Assault, 7 J. Interspousal Violence 1 (1990); Leigh Goodmark, From Property to Personhood: What the Legal System Should Do for Children in Family Violence Cases, 102 W. Va. L. Rev. 237 (1999). *See also* Amy Levin and Linda G. Mills, Fighting for Child Custody When Domestic Violence Is at Issue: Survey of State Laws, 48 Social Work 463 (2003).

[11]Goodmark, *supra* note 10, at 245.

[12]Judith S. Wallerstein and Sandra Blakeslee, Second Chances — Men, Women, and Children a Decade After Divorce 113-121 (1989).

[13]*Id.* at 110-121.

[14]*Id.* at 38.

[15]Cynthia Grover Hastings, Letting Down Their Guard: What Guardians Ad Litem Should Know About Domestic Violence in Child Custody Disputes, 24 B.C. Third World L.J. 283, 314 (2004).

Also highly relevant is the fact that spousal abuse does not necessarily end upon separation and divorce; in fact, "it is well documented that separation can serve as a catalyst for increased violence" and that "escalated abuse by the batterer as a response to actual or perceived separation is so common that experts have coined the phrase 'separation assault' to describe it."[16] Accordingly, an abusive parent's right of access to the children may need to be limited in order to safeguard the well-being of the abused parent. In turn, paying attention to the safety of the custodial parent has multiple implications for the well-being of children. Not only will this vigilance shield children from continuing exposure to violence and the associated risk of harm, the reduced threat of violence may well enhance the ability of a caretaker parent to focus on the needs of her children.

Custody statutes generally take one of two approaches with respect to domestic violence. The majority of statutes direct judges to take domestic violence into account as one of the factors that must be weighed when determining custody, with a few statutes directing judges to weigh it more heavily than other considerations. The other approach is to create a rebuttable presumption against awarding sole or joint custody to a parent who has been the perpetrator of domestic violence. To rebut the presumption, a spouse might, for example, seek to show that he has successfully completed a batterer's treatment program and no longer engages in violent behavior. We will return to domestic violence in Chapter 11.

2. Factoring Parental Characteristics and Lifestyle Choice into the Best Interest Test

In determining best interest, it is not uncommon for a parent to argue that some aspect of the other parent's life will have a detrimental impact on the children, and/ or to claim that conversely he or she is better positioned to meet the needs of the children based on his or her own life circumstances. These kinds of arguments raise the question as to what weight, if any, should be given to parental characteristics or lifestyle choices when determining best interest. Are these matters of morality relevant? Is it appropriate for a judge to base decisions on his or her own views about what constitutes a proper environment for a child? Should a judge be allowed to reflect popular community views — for example, that children are better off being raised by heterosexual parents?

Judges are not supposed to make custody decisions based on their own subjective sense of what is right for a child, or on their assessment of community standards, as these kinds of individualized determinations would embody a judge's own personal view of the world, resulting in highly idiosyncratic and unpredictable outcomes. To prevent this kind of subjective decision making, the basic rule in custody decision making is that there must be a direct nexus (or connection) between the parental attribute in question and the well-being of the child. This approach is intended to limit judicial discretion and keep the child's needs at the center of the decision-making process.

---

[16]*Id.* at 283, 301-302.

However, it is worth considering whether it is realistic to think that judges can completely disregard their own views when deciding the cases that come before them. For example, what if a judge believes that interracial or same-sex relationships are inherently immoral and disruptive of the social order — how likely is it that he or she will be truly able to set aside these views and dispassionately consider whether an award of custody to a parent in such a relationship advances the child's best interest?

Considerations of Race and Culture

In *Palmore v. Sidoti*, 466 U.S. 429 (1984), the United States Supreme Court reversed a Florida trial court decision transferring custody of a young girl from her mother to her father because after the divorce the mother, who was white, married a black man. In transferring custody, the trial court had focused on the possibility that the child would suffer from the stigma of living in a racially mixed household, especially once she began school.

Case Preview

Palmore v. Sidoti

The United States Supreme Court addressed the issue of whether race could be taken into consideration in determining a change of custody. Linda Sidoti Palmore ("Mother") and Anthony Sidoti ("Father"), both Caucasians, were divorced in 1980 in Florida. At the time, Mother was awarded custody of their three-year-old daughter. A year later, Father moved to modify custody based upon a change in circumstances, claiming that Mother's cohabitation with Clarence Palmore, who was African-American, was detrimental to the child. Mother married Mr. Palmore shortly after the action was filed by Father.

As you read *Palmore v. Sidoti*, look for the following:

1. What was the trial court's rationale for changing custody from Mother to Father?
2. What constitutional issue was raised by the trial court's decision?
3. What role did race play in the trial court's custody determination? What role did it play in the Supreme Court's determination?

Palmore v. Sidoti
466 U.S. 429 (1984)

Chief Justice BURGER delivered the opinion of the Court.

We granted certiorari to review a judgment of a state court divesting a natural mother of the custody of her infant child because of her remarriage to a person of a different race.

I

When petitioner Linda Sidoti Palmore and respondent Anthony J. Sidoti, both Caucasians, were divorced in May 1980 in Florida, the mother was awarded custody of their 3-year-old daughter.

In September 1981 the father sought custody of the child by filing a petition to modify the prior judgment because of changed conditions. The change was that the child's mother was then cohabiting with a Negro, Clarence Palmore, Jr., whom she married two months later. Additionally, the father made several allegations of instances in which the mother had not properly cared for the child.

After hearing testimony from both parties and considering a court counselor's investigative report, the court noted that the father had made allegations about the child's care, but the court made no findings with respect to these allegations. On the contrary, the court made a finding that "there is no issue as to either party's devotion to the child, adequacy of housing facilities, or respectability of the new spouse of either parent." App. to Pet. for Cert. 24.

The court then addressed the recommendations of the court counselor, who had made an earlier report "in [another] case coming out of this circuit also involving the social consequences of an interracial marriage. *Niles v. Niles*, 299 So. 2d 162." Id., at 25. From this vague reference to that earlier case, the court turned to the present case and noted the counselor's recommendation for a change in custody because "[t]he wife [petitioner] has chosen for herself and for her child, a life-style unacceptable to the father and to society. . . . The child . . . is, or at school age will be, subject to environmental pressures not of choice." Record 84 (emphasis added).

The court then concluded that the best interests of the child would be served by awarding custody to the father. . . .

The Second District Court of Appeal affirmed without opinion, 426 So. 2d 34 (1982), thus denying the Florida Supreme Court jurisdiction to review the case. See Fla. Const., Art. V, §3(b)(3); *Jenkins v. State*, 385 So. 2d 1356 (Fla. 1980). We granted certiorari, 464 U.S. 913, 104 S. Ct. 271, 78 L. Ed. 2d 253 (1983), and we reverse.

II

The judgment of a state court determining or reviewing a child custody decision is not ordinarily a likely candidate for review by this Court. However, the court's opinion, after stating that the "father's evident resentment of the mother's choice of a black partner is not sufficient" to deprive her of custody, then turns to what it regarded as the damaging impact on the child from remaining in a racially mixed household. App. to Pet. for Cert. 26. This raises important federal concerns arising from the Constitution's commitment to eradicating discrimination based on race.

The Florida court did not focus directly on the parental qualifications of the natural mother or her present husband, or indeed on the father's qualifications to have custody of the child. The court found that "there is no issue as to either party's devotion to the child, adequacy of housing facilities, or respectability of the new spouse of either parent." Id., at 24. This, taken with the absence of any negative finding as to the quality of the care provided by the mother, constitutes a rejection of any claim of petitioner's unfitness to continue the custody of her child.

The court correctly stated that the child's welfare was the controlling factor. But that court was entirely candid and made no effort to place its holding on any ground other than race. Taking the court's findings and rationale at face value, it is clear that the outcome would have been different had petitioner married a Caucasian male of similar respectability.

A core purpose of the Fourteenth Amendment was to do away with all governmentally imposed discrimination based on race. See *Strauder v. West Virginia*, 100 U.S. 303, 307-308, 310, 25 L. Ed. 664 (1880). Classifying persons according to their race is more likely to reflect racial prejudice than legitimate public concerns; the race, not the person, dictates the category. See *Personnel Administrator of Mass. v. Feeney*, 442 U.S. 256, 272, 99 S. Ct. 2282, 2292, 60 L. Ed. 2d 870 (1979). Such classifications are subject to the most exacting scrutiny; to pass constitutional muster, they must be justified by a compelling governmental interest and must be "necessary . . . to the accomplishment" of their legitimate purpose, *McLaughlin v. Florida*, 379 U.S. 184, 196, 85 S. Ct. 283, 290, 13 L. Ed. 2d 222 (1964). See *Loving v. Virginia*, 388 U.S. 1, 11, 87 S. Ct. 1817, 1823, 18 L. Ed. 2d 1010 (1967).

The State, of course, has a duty of the highest order to protect the interests of minor children, particularly those of tender years. In common with most states, Florida law mandates that custody determinations be made in the best interests of the children involved. Fla. Stat. §61.13(2)(b)(1) (1983). The goal of granting custody based on the best interests of the child is indisputably a substantial governmental interest for purposes of the Equal Protection Clause.

It would ignore reality to suggest that racial and ethnic prejudices do not exist or that all manifestations of those prejudices have been eliminated. There is a risk that a child living with a stepparent of a different race may be subject to a variety of pressures and stresses not present if the child were living with parents of the same racial or ethnic origin.

The question, however, is whether the reality of private biases and the possible injury they might inflict are permissible considerations for removal of an infant child from the custody of its natural mother. We have little difficulty concluding that they are not. The Constitution cannot control such prejudices but neither can it tolerate them. Private biases may be outside the reach of the law, but the law cannot, directly or indirectly, give them effect. "Public officials sworn to uphold the Constitution may not avoid a constitutional duty by bowing to the hypothetical effects of private racial prejudice that they assume to be both widely and deeply held." *Palmer v. Thompson*, 403 U.S. 217, 260-261, 91 S. Ct. 1940, 1962-1963, 29 L. Ed. 2d 438 (1971) (White, J., dissenting).

This is by no means the first time that acknowledged racial prejudice has been invoked to justify racial classifications. In *Buchanan v. Warley*, 245 U.S. 60, 38 S. Ct. 16, 62 L. Ed. 149 (1917), for example, this Court invalidated a Kentucky law forbidding Negroes to buy homes in white neighborhoods.

"It is urged that this proposed segregation will promote the public peace by preventing race conflicts. Desirable as this is, and important as is the preservation of the public peace, this aim cannot be accomplished by laws or ordinances which deny rights created or protected by the Federal Constitution." Id., at 81, 38 S. Ct., at 20.

Whatever problems racially mixed households may pose for children in 1984 can no more support a denial of constitutional rights than could the stresses that residential integration was thought to entail in 1917. The effects of racial prejudice, however real, cannot justify a racial classification removing an infant child from the custody of its natural mother found to be an appropriate person to have such custody.

The judgment of the District Court of Appeal is reversed.

It is so ordered.

Post-Case Follow-Up

In reversing the decision, the Supreme Court made clear that social prejudice should not determine custody outcomes and that the Equal Protection Clause prohibits giving effect to personal bias through the medium of custody adjudications. Moreover, the Court made clear that harm to a child cannot be assumed even though racial prejudice may subject him or her to "a variety of pressures and stresses not present if the child were living with parents of the same racial or ethnic origin." *Id.* at 433.

Although unambivalent in condemning custody decisions premised on racial prejudice, the *Palmore* decision has not been interpreted to mean that race is *never* a permissible consideration in custody determinations. For example, in the case of *Gambla v. Woodson*, an Illinois appeals court held in a custody dispute involving a biracial child that although it would have been inappropriate for the trial court to have awarded custody to the mother "solely because she is African-American," it was not in error for having taken into account the fact that she could provide Kira with a "breadth of cultural knowledge and experience" that the father could not offer her, and was therefore in a better position to prepare her daughter for existing "as a biracial woman in a society that is sometimes hostile to such individuals." *Gambla v. Woodson*, 367 Ill. App. 3d 441, 853 N.E.2d 847, 863, 869-871 (2006), *appeal denied by Gambla v. Woodson*, 222 Ill. 2d 571, 861 N.E.2d 654 (2006), *cert. denied*, 2007 U.S. LEXIS 10286 (U.S. Oct. 1, 2007).

Palmore v. Sidoti: Real Life Applications

1. The trial court in *Palmore* focused on the damaging effect on the child living in a racially mixed household. How could the trial court have rewritten its opinion to avoid raising a federal issue?

2. Assume that you represent a client, Jeremy Smith. Jeremy tells you that he and his ex-wife, Dorothy, were divorced two years ago. Dorothy has custody of their three children. However, he recently found out that she is living with someone

who is of a different race. At first he had no concerns, but he now tells you that the children are being ridiculed at school, and he fears the children will be stigmatized for living in a biracial household. Based upon your reading of *Palmore v. Sidoti*, what would you tell Jeremy?

3. Assume the same facts as Question 2, but Jeremy tells you that Dorothy is planning on marrying her partner, who is a woman, and Jeremy feels this will cause the children to be ridiculed and stigmatized.

4. Assume the same facts as Question 2, but Jeremy tells you that the individual is Christian and Jeremy and Dorothy had decided to raise the children Jewish. Jeremy believes it will be confusing for the children to live in an interfaith household.

Cultural Background as a Factor to Consider

Custody statutes in a few states expressly identify a child's cultural background as one of the factors that is to be taken into account when assessing which parent is in a better position to meet the child's needs. In addition, in states where culture is not included as an express statutory factor, some courts have woven a consideration of a child's cultural needs into other statutory criteria for assessing best interest. Thus, for example, in evaluating the importance of maintaining a child's ongoing connection with the community in which he or she lives, a court might include a consideration of the extent to which that community offers the child an opportunity to "interact with others who share his or her heritage." *See* Cynthia R. Mabry, The Browning of America — Multicultural and Bicultural Families in Conflict — Making Culture a Customary Factor in Child Custody Disputes, 16 Wash. & Lee J. Civ. Rts. & Soc. Just. 413, 422 (2010).

Sexual Activity: Heterosexual

Another important question is what weight, if any, should be given to the sexual behavior of a parent seeking custody of a minor child. Although this once was fairly contested terrain, the unquestioned majority view is that sexual behavior by itself or the fact that a parent is living with a partner she or he is not married to is not relevant unless a detrimental effect on the child or the parent-child relationship is clearly established. In requiring proof of a nexus between the behavior of the parent and the well-being of the child, harm to the child is not to be presumed from the fact that the parent is engaged in a nonmarital relationship, as this would be tantamount to a moral pronouncement embodying the judge's subjective views rather than an assessment of the parent's actual ability to care for the child. Rather, such conduct is relevant only where detriment can be shown — for example, where sexual activity occurs in front of the children or where the parent leaves the children on their own in order to pursue a relationship.

Sexual Orientation: Gay and Lesbian Parents

Although the unquestioned majority approach is that a parent's involvement in a heterosexual dating or cohabiting relationship will not impact his or her ability to obtain or maintain custody absent a clear showing that this involvement somehow harms the child, the law's approach is somewhat more varied when it comes to gay and lesbian parents. For years, the dominant approach was to presume, without requiring proof of harm, that it was bad for a child to be raised by such a parent. This is frequently referred to as the **per se approach**, in which harm is assumed to flow from the parent's conduct without requiring proof of actual detriment.

However, most states have rejected the per se approach in favor of the nexus standard. Requiring a "sexual orientation-neutral" lens, judges may no longer treat gay and lesbian parents differently from parents who are in a heterosexual dating or cohabiting relationship. Accordingly, a parent cannot be denied custody based on a presumption of harm; rather, as when a parent seeking custody is in a heterosexual relationship, actual detriment to the child from the relationship must be proved before it can be factored into the custody outcome. In adopting the nexus approach, states have been influenced by the weight of social science studies that have concluded "that the family environments provided by lesbian and gay parents are as likely as those provided by heterosexual parents to foster and promote children's psychological well-being."[17]

Religion

The issue of religion usually comes up in custody disputes in one of two ways. A parent may claim that he or she can best meet the religious needs of the child and should therefore be awarded custody. Alternatively, a parent may claim that the religion of the other parent is detrimental to the child or is in conflict with the child's established identity, and should therefore disqualify that parent from custodial consideration. In the first situation, religion is presented as a positive, qualifying factor; in the second, it is presented as a negative, disqualifying one.[18]

In evaluating these claims, a court becomes involved in a delicate and sensitive task, as it must respect the First Amendment rights of both parents. This amendment (which is applied to the states through the Due Process Clause of the Fourteenth Amendment) prevents state interference with an individual's freedom of religion and undue state involvement with religion (e.g., expressing a preference for one religion over another). Absent a compelling interest, a state must remain neutral and uninvolved where religion is concerned.

Where a parent raises religion as a qualifying factor, it cannot be the sole custodial determinant because the judge would be expressing a preference for the religion of one parent over the religion of the other or over the lack of religious involvement. Moreover, the court would be giving preferential weight to religion, saying, in effect, that it is the most important aspect of a child's upbringing.

Must a court then disregard what a parent has to offer by way of religious education and guidance? The generally accepted view is that although a court may not

---

[17]Serena Lambert, Gay and Lesbian Families: What We Know and Where to Go from Here, 13 The Family Journal: Counseling and Therapy for Couples and Families, 43, 49 (2005). For a comprehensive discussion of these studies, see Abie Goldberg, Lesbian and Gay Parents and Their Children: Research on the Family Life Cycle (APA 2009). For an alternative perspective on the research, see Lynn D. Wardle, Considering the Impacts on Children and Society of "Lesbigay" Parenting, 23 Quinnipiac L. Rev. 541 (2004).

[18]*See generally* Cynthia M. Mabry, Blending Cultures and Religions: Effects That the Changing Makeup of Families in Our Nation Have on Child Custody Determinations, 21 J. Am. Acad. Matrim. Law. 31 (2013); Carol Wah, Restrictions on Religious Training and Exposure in Child Custody and Visitation Orders: Do They Protect or Harm the Child?, 45 J. Church & St. 14 (2003).

make a value judgment about religion (or the lack thereof) and cannot presume that one parent is better equipped to meet a child's religious needs, it may consider a child's actual religious needs and determine which parent can best meet them. Accordingly, where religion is an established part of a child's life, matching parent to child in this regard is one aspect of determining who can best provide stability and continuity of care. Thus, for example, if a child regularly attends religious services and educational classes, the court might look at which parent has been actively involved with these activities, much as it would evaluate parental involvement in other areas of the child's life. The essential concern is determining which parent will best be able to meet the ongoing needs of the child, without making a value judgment about the kind of religious upbringing a child should have.

Where religion is raised as a disqualifying factor, the parent often belongs to a religion that is considered outside of the mainstream by the parent seeking custody. Typically, the nonmember parent argues that the other's religious beliefs or practices pose a threat of harm to the child's emotional, physical, or psychological well-being. For example, a common concern is that a child will be isolated from his or her peers by restrictions that prohibit certain activities, such as participation in school celebrations, watching television, or associating with nonmembers. The parent seeking custody may also fear that the child will be alienated from him or her if the religion of the other parent espouses that, as a nonbeliever, he or she is evil and will suffer eternal consequences.

Most courts employ a **nexus approach** in these cases. With this approach, a parent must show actual harm before the other parent's actions, in this case religious practices, are considered relevant. At least in theory, this avoids the risk that a court will make value judgments about a parent's religion. Other courts employ a somewhat less exacting standard and may disqualify a parent if his or her religious beliefs and practices are shown to pose a substantial or reasonable likelihood of harm. Even under this lower standard, however, general assertions about potential isolation or confusion from being raised in a "different" environment should not be given legal effect.

Under the risk of harm standard, a number of cases have dealt with the difficult question of how to evaluate the potential risk when the parent seeking custody belongs to a religion that prohibits certain medical practices, such as blood transfusions. Some courts have held that where there is no evidence of medical need, the risk is too speculative to justify a denial of custody on that ground alone. For example, in the 1995 case of *Garrett v. Garrett*, the Nebraska Court of Appeals stated with respect to the award of custody to a mother who was a practicing Jehovah's Witness:

> . . . in order for Jeanne's religion to constitute a ground for awarding custody to Larry, we must be able to determine from the record that the Jehovah's Witness religion as practiced by Jeanne constitutes an immediate and substantial threat to the minor children's temporal well-being. . . .
>
> As evidence of an immediate and substantial threat to the minor children, Larry makes reference to the fact that even in the case of a medical emergency, Jeanne would refuse to consent to any of the children's receiving a blood transfusion. . . .

No evidence was presented showing that any of the minor children were prone to accidents or plagued with any sort of an affliction that might necessitate a blood transfusion in the near future. We cannot decide this case based on some hypothetical future accident or illness which might necessitate such treatment.

Garrett v. Garrett, 527 N.W.2d 213, 221-222 (Neb. Ct. App. 1995). On the other hand, some courts have found that such a belief in and of itself poses a substantial risk of harm and do not require specific proof that a child is actually in need of a religiously prohibited medical procedure.

Case Preview

Leppert v. Leppert

Leppert involves the issue of whether the court can consider religion as a basis for changing custody of the children. In this case, the parties had five children when they divorced. Custody of the two older children alternated between the mother and the father on a bimonthly basis, but custody of the three younger children was awarded to the mother. Father appealed the divorce judgment claiming that the religion practiced by Mother was harmful to the children.

As you read *Leppert v. Leppert*, look for the following:

1. What impact did Mother's religion have on the children?
2. What were Father's concerns regarding Mother's upbringing of the children?
3. What was the standard the court indicated should be considered in determining the adverse impact Mother's beliefs were likely to have on the children?
4. What objective evidence did the court have before it regarding the adverse impact on the children?

Leppert v. Leppert
519 N.W.2d 287 (N.D. 1994)

Joel Leppert appeals from a divorce judgment awarding physical custody of his three youngest children to their mother, Quinta Leppert. We reverse and remand to the district court.

Joel and Quinta were married June 18, 1984. Five children were born of this marriage. . . . On November 6, 1991, Judge Gordon Hoberg issued an interim order granting temporary physical custody of the five children to Joel. On January 14, 1992, Judge Mikal Simonson issued an amended order granting temporary physical custody of the three youngest children to Quinta, with the physical custody of the two older children alternating between the parents on a bimonthly basis.

The divorce trial was held on January 25, 26, and 27, 1993, and March 11 and 12, 1993. A variety of witnesses testified during the trial, including: both parents, Joel and Quinta Leppert; both paternal grandparents; Quinta's father, Gordon Winrod; [plus teachers and other relatives] and the court appointed guardian ad litem, Dr. Robert Packard.

The guardian recommended custody of all five of the children should be with Joel, allowing for limited periods of visitation with Quinta. Concluding his report, the guardian stated "Quinta, despite her many admirable traits, is likely to provide parenting that is in several crucial respects, extremely dangerous to the children's psychological and emotional health, personality and characterological development, their physical well being and even their life."

One of the guardian's primary concerns was the harmful impact of Quinta's beliefs and resulting actions. Specifically, Quinta is a devout follower of the teachings of her father, Gordon Winrod (Winrod). Her father is the supreme leader of his own religious sect known as Our Savior's Church. In all, Gordon Winrod has about 100 followers. His church is not affiliated with any religious denomination, but purports to follow the teachings of the Bible.

Winrod and his followers believe there are only two types of people in the world: God's enemies, and those who are obedient to God. Those who do not follow Winrod's teachings are not obedient to God, and they are consequently evil, and are to be hated as God's enemies. Testimony at trial stated Winrod teaches lying to God's enemies, stealing from God's enemies, and violent behavior toward God's enemies. He also rejects the authority of governments. . . . Quinta believes she has a duty to raise her children to follow Winrod. She insists that her children adopt all of his teachings and beliefs.

Joel was at one time a follower of Winrod, but has since stopped following his teachings. Since the marital separation, Quinta has moved to live with her father and several of his followers in a commune-like residence in Gainsville, Missouri. Joel has continued to live and work on the Leppert family farm in Dickey, North Dakota.

Prior to the separation, Quinta home-schooled the two oldest children. Since the separation, Joel enrolled the two oldest children in public school. . . . When the children enrolled in classes, evaluation assessments showed . . . reading and writing skills were significantly below the norm. . . . The children's social skills lagged far behind those of their classmates.

Testimony was introduced at trial that supported Joel's contention that Quinta was attempting to poison the children's relationship with Joel and his family. Tape recorded telephone conversations between Quinta and the two oldest children . . . include statements by Quinta, such as:

> ". . . [Y]our daddy's such a pin head . . . , birds of a feather flock together so do pigs and swine, that's the way your father is, he's a pig and he's a swine. . . ."

Joel also testified that the younger children started to exhibit behavior that suggests Quinta is poisoning them against Joel as well.

Home studies were conducted both in Quinta's home in Missouri, and Joel's home in North Dakota. The results of the studies were that both households would be adequate for raising the five children.

Upon completion of the trial . . . Quinta was granted custody of the three youngest children, and Joel was granted custody of the two oldest. . . . This timely appeal followed.

Two issues are raised on appeal: first, whether the district court's decision to grant custody of the three youngest children to Quinta was clearly erroneous, and second, whether the district court's decision regarding visitation was clearly erroneous. Since we hold the custody award was clearly erroneous, we remand for the district court to redetermine child support and visitation.

SCOPE OF REVIEW

Child custody determinations are findings of fact. On appeal, findings of fact are not disturbed unless clearly erroneous. "A finding of fact is clearly erroneous if the reviewing court is left with a definite and firm conviction that a mistake has been made, or if the finding was induced by an erroneous view of the law." *Reede v. Steen*, 461 N.W.2d 438, 440 (N.D. 1990) (citing *Mertz v. Mertz*, 439 N.W.2d 94, 96 (N.D. 1989).

BEST INTERESTS

Joel argues that the trial court clearly made a mistake when it awarded custody of the three youngest children to Quinta. Specifically, he argues the court erred when it refused to consider the harmful impact of Quinta's beliefs when determining the best interests of the children. We agree.

In its memorandum opinion, the trial court clearly addressed each of the enumerated factors of our best interests statute. NDCC 14-09-06.2. Subsection (f) of the best interests statute is entitled "moral fitness of the parents." See 14-09-06.2(f). Addressing this subsection, quoting *Hanson v. Hanson*, 404 N.W.2d 460 (N.D. 1987), the district court stated "that physical and [sic] emotional harm must be clearly shown, before religious beliefs may become a determining factor" in the best interests of the child analysis, but went on to find that there was not a clear showing of physical and emotional harm to the children from Quinta's practices and beliefs. We cannot agree. The guardian's report unequivocally stated that Quinta's parenting, because of her beliefs, constituted an extreme danger to the children, both physically and emotionally. Based upon such a record, the district court's finding is clearly erroneous.

Although we agree with the district court that Quinta must not be discounted from consideration as a custodial parent simply because of her religious beliefs, this does not mean her religiously motivated actions, which are emotionally and physically harmful to the children, should be ignored when determining the children's best interests. Such a holding would immunize from consideration all religiously motivated acts, no matter what their impact on the children. Almost all of the behavior of members of "other-worldly" sects would be excluded from consideration. Not only would we be ignoring the best interests of the child but the "worldly" parent would be comparatively disadvantaged.

Consideration of the harmful impact of a parent's beliefs when determining the best interests of the child is in no way intended to punish parents. "A punishment is intended as a judgment of someone who has done something wrong. It seeks to condemn behavior, to prevent its repetition, and to deter others from emulating it." To the contrary, the goal in custody determinations is to foster the health and well-being of the child, not to punish either of the parents.

The only reason for any consideration of religious beliefs when determining the best interests of the child is to take into account any harmful impact the belief system may have on the child. The best interests factors enumerated in 14-09-06.2 are secular in nature, and the courts' functions do not include determining the road to salvation. Although secular courts have no place deciding one religion is better than another, . . . they do have the duty of objectively determining whether a belief system's secular effects are likely to cause physical or emotional harm to children. We acknowledge that, ultimately, secular courts may not fully accommodate the desires of those who wholly reject secular standards. . . . Remedying a conflict such as that, however, is beyond the scope of this appeal.

There are factors the trial court appeared to ignore in the best interests analysis because they were religiously motivated. Applying the correct standard for considering the adverse impact that Quinta's beliefs are likely to have on the children, it is in the best interests of all five children that their physical custody be with Joel.

Post-Case Follow-Up

Leppert demonstrates how the only appropriate reason for considering a parent's religious beliefs is the impact they have on the children. Accordingly, while the trial court would not review the impact of certain teachings on the children on the grounds that it would be an improper interference with mother's religious beliefs, the North Dakota Supreme Court had little trouble justifying the reversal of custody because of their adverse impact.

Leppert v. Leppert: Real Life Applications

1. Kelly has come to your office advising you that she would like to appeal a decision from her divorce decree because the trial judge prohibited her from taking her three children to religious services "contrary to the Catholic faith" during periods of her visitation. Kelly asks if she has grounds to appeal. Based upon your reading of *Leppert* and the text, what would you tell Kelly?

2. Assume Kelly had agreed to settle the case and included in their agreement the following provision:

   > Mother recognizes that the children are in the process of going through confirmation classes and agrees to take the children to their confirmation classes on Saturday mornings during her visitation time.

   Kelly took the children to their confirmation class for several weeks during her visitation time, but has now decided that she no longer wishes to take the children to the classes during her time with them. She tells you that if the children miss confirmation classes, they will not be able to be confirmed as full members of the Catholic Church. She asks you whether she is required to continue to bring the children to classes because she now believes that children should be able to choose their own religion and the children have expressed to her that they do not want to continue going to the classes. What do you tell Kelly?

3. Assuming the facts in Question 1, what arguments might Kelly face if she decides to appeal the decision?

B. ALTERNATIVE CUSTODY STANDARDS

The inherent flexibility of the best interest standard enables a court to take the particular circumstances of a family into account when determining custodial arrangement. Given the complexity and variability of family relationships, there is a decided advantage of this approach. However, as discussed above, this very quality means that results may be unpredictable and idiosyncratic as the standard's indeterminacy gives judges considerable maneuvering room within which to import their own subjective views (or biases) into the best interest calculus. *See generally* Bartlett and Scott, *supra* note 4.

In particular, although the best interest standard is gender neutral on its face, there has been an ongoing and at times very heated debate over whether gender bias shapes judicial decision making. Of particular concern is that a judge can easily bury any bias in a gender-neutral recitation of the best interest factors that weigh in favor or one parent or the other.

In this regard, fathers' rights groups argue that fathers are often less valued as parents than mothers and that many judges simply assume men cannot be primary caretakers. They claim that despite the express gender neutrality of the best interest standard, for many judges it is infused with their personal beliefs about the natural superiority of maternal nurturing and caretaking abilities. Thus, for example, running silently beneath a judge's determination that a mother has the stronger bond with the child may be an unstated belief regarding the benefits of maternal care.

On the other hand, many women's groups argue that when fathers seek custody, some judges assume they are especially devoted and nurturing since primary caretaking is still not expected of men. Thus, men are likely to get "extra credit" for child caring activities that are regarded as ordinary when done by women, such as staying home with a sick child. Exacerbating this problem, some judges may regard an employed mother as being unsatisfied with her maternal role, and time away from her children is held against her. In short, there is a double standard that penalizes mothers for time spent away from their children while unduly rewarding fathers for time spent with them. Thus, for example, a biased calculus may run silently beneath a judge's conclusion that the time availability factor favors the father.

1. The Primary Caretaker Presumption

Emerging out of dissatisfaction with the vagaries of the best interest standard, a number of states have considered adopting a custodial presumption in favor of the parent who has been the primary caretaker. Under this standard, primary caretaking would be the sole determinant of best interest (absent unfitness).

In 1981, in the case of *Garska v. McCoy*, 167 W. Va. 59, 278 S.E.2d 357 (1981), the state of West Virginia became the first state to adopt the primary caretaker standard (although it has since moved to the ALI approximation rule). In adopting this standard, the *Garska* court focused on the harm caused to the primary care parent by the unpredictability of the best interest test:

> The loss of children is a terrifying specter to concerned and loving parents; however, it is particularly terrifying to the primary caretaker parent, who, by virtue of the caretaking function, was closest to the child before the divorce. . . . Our experience instructs us that uncertainty about the outcome of custody disputes leads to the irresistible temptation to trade the custody of the child in return for lower alimony and child support payment.

Id. In anchoring custody outcomes to a fixed standard, the court was seeking to prevent custody from being used as a bargaining weapon to extract economic concessions from the primary caretaker parent in order to ensure a favorable custody result.

This presumption has been praised for its recognition of the undervalued job of parenting and the importance of the bond between children and their primary caregivers. It has also been praised for introducing certainty into the process and protecting the often vulnerable economic status of primary caretaking parents from feeling that they must give up economic rights in order to ensure that they remain the primary caretaking parent.

The presumption has also been subject to considerable criticism. One significant concern is that the presumption is overly mechanistic and fails to account for the complexity of parent-child relationships. Fathers' rights groups have attacked the presumption for being gender biased, asserting that it is a thinly disguised effort to reintroduce the tender years presumption to the detriment of fathers. *See* Ronald K. Henry, "Primary Caretaker": Is It a Ruse?, 17 Fam. Advoc. 53 (1994). Others strongly dispute this claim of disguised gender bias. First, it is noted that if a father is the primary caregiver, the presumption will favor him, and second, that if more mothers than fathers are awarded custody under this standard, this simply reflects the actuality of how families allocate caretaking responsibilities rather than generalized assumptions about gender-appropriate roles.

It has also been argued that the presumption can work against women as well. Although a stay-at-home mom, or one who is employed on a part-time basis, would certainly be identified as the primary caretaker, the concern is that a judge may not recognize that a woman who works full time may nonetheless still be the primary caregiver. Based on an assumption that the worlds of work and home are incompatible, her continued domestic and caretaking responsibilities may be rendered invisible.

Despite the considerable interest and discussion that the primary caretaker presumption has generated, only two states have adopted it, and neither now employ it.

Nonetheless, its novel approach to resolving disputed custody cases is worth considering as it sheds further light on the ongoing debate over whether the needs of children are best served by rules that promote flexibility or those which yield more predictable and consistent results. Moreover, it played a role in shaping the ALI approximation rule to which we now turn our attention.

2. The American Law Institute's Approximation Rule

In 2002, after more than a decade of research, the American Law Institute published the *Principles of the Law of Family Dissolution: Analysis and Recommendations* in order to bring "conceptual clarification and improved adaptation to social needs to the dissolution process."[19] With respect to custody, the Principles recommend shifting from the best interest standard to a more objective "approximation" standard that would allocate custodial responsibilities between divorcing parents in rough proportion to the amount of time each parent spent engaged in caretaking responsibilities during the marriage. In short, the post-divorce parenting arrangement would *approximate* their pre-divorce arrangement.

To date, West Virginia (previously the only state to formally adopt a primary caretaker presumption) is the only state to have formally adopted this approach. Accordingly, if parents have been unable to reach an agreement, the court is required to "allocate custodial responsibility so that the proportion of custodial time the child spends with each parent approximates the proportion of time each parent spent performing caretaking functions for the child prior to the parents' separation," unless such an arrangement would be "manifestly harmful to the child." W. Va. Code §48-9-206 (2012). However, at least a few courts are beginning to rely on the approximation rule in resolving disputed custody cases. For example, in a 2007 case, the Iowa Supreme Court, although making clear that the "wholesale adoption of the approximation rule would require legislative action," nonetheless determined that the "approximation principle" was an appropriate factor to take into account in "determining whether to grant joint custody" since "by focusing on historic patterns of caregiving [it] provides a relatively objective factor for the courts to consider." *In re Marriage of Hansen v. Hansen*, 733 N.W.2d 683, 697 (Iowa 2007).

According to proponents, the predictability of the approximation approach is one of its primary benefits. By limiting judicial discretion, parties are better able to anticipate what the outcome is likely to be if the case were to go to trial, which in turn provides them with a clearer framework within which to negotiate custody arrangements. With the result more predictable, proponents argue that primary caretakers will be less likely to bargain away economic rights in order to secure custody, thus promoting outcomes that are related to the needs of children, rather than to the bargaining positions of the parties. Another primary benefit of this approach according to its proponents is that it provides children with greater stability and continuity of care because, to the extent it is possible, their parents would continue

---

[19]ALI Press Release, May 15, 2002, http://www.ali.org.

to play the same role in their lives that they did prior to the divorce. In short, children would be buffered from some of the radical reconfiguring of the parent-child relationship that so often accompanies a divorce.

However, some important concerns have also been raised about the approximation rule. First, some commentators worry that it is too deferential to parents and not sufficiently child-centered. What if, for example, past caretaking arrangements were adopted to meet the need of the parents rather than to provide optimal care for the children? What if other ways of allocating custodial responsibilities would be better for the children? However, reflecting what is believed to be the rule's overly mechanistic approach to determining custody, these kinds of considerations would not be relevant. Another important question is whether it is overly optimistic to assume that arrangements that worked when the parents presumably got along with one another will continue to work in the aftermath of dissolution when parental cooperation and goodwill is apt to be at a minimum. (Note: This concern also applies to the more familiar joint custody context and will be developed further in that section.)

Additionally, as with the primary caretaker presumption, the argument is made that this approach is simply an effort to sneak the tender years presumption back into custody determinations. However, once again, proponents argue that if mothers end up with more custodial time as a result of the approximation rule, this outcome reflects the reality of existing caretaking arrangements that the parties themselves decided upon, rather than suggesting a built-in gender bias in favor of women.

C. CUSTODY ARRANGEMENTS

Resolution of a custody case becomes even more complex when one takes the variety of custodial and visitation arrangements that are available into account. Traditionally, custody was essentially a unitary concept — one parent, usually the mother, was responsible for raising the young child and making all significant decisions affecting the child's life, and the other parent simply visited. In fact, up until the 1970s, many courts actually refused to order shared custody instead opting to give custody to one parent over the other.

However, beginning in the 1970s, as discussed below, the wisdom of this approach was challenged, and joint custody emerged as an approach that would enable children to maintain an ongoing relationship with both parents following a divorce. As of today, joint custody is a readily available option and in many states is the preferred custody arrangement.

1. Distinguishing Physical and Legal Custody

For the sake of clarity, the terms "physical custody" and "legal custody" will initially be defined in reference to one parent, but as will become apparent, either can be shared. (This is often referred to as joint custody.) Also, in light of the current emphasis on cooperative post-divorce parenting (see Section E, below), there has been a growing move away from this traditional terminology, which often promotes a "winner take all" mentality, with the winner emerging as the custodial parent and the loser relegated to the status of visiting parent. Thus, for example, the ALI Principles use the term "custodial responsibility" instead of physical custody to refer to the time that each parent has with his or her children regardless of the actual time allocation between them. In addition, the Arizona statute excerpted earlier in this chapter uses "parenting time" and "legal decision-making." However, for the sake of clarity, this book will use the traditional nomenclature that was briefly identified earlier.

Physical custody refers to where a child lives. A parent with physical custody maintains a primary residence for the child and is generally responsible for the child's daily care. With physical custody comes the authority to make all of the day-to-day decisions that arise in the course of caring for a child.

Legal custody refers to decision-making authority. Whereas physical custody incorporates the right to make routine decisions, legal custody gives a parent the right to make major decisions affecting the health, welfare, and education of a child, such as whether a child should go to private school or begin mental health counseling. As a general rule, major decisions are distinguished from day-to-day decisions by their importance and their nonrepetitive nature, although, as discussed in the following section, this distinction is often easier to state than to apply.

2. Distinguishing Sole and Joint Custody

The term **sole custody** refers to the vesting of custodial rights in one parent; either legal or physical custody can be sole. With an award of *sole physical custody*, the child lives with one parent and that parent has primary caretaking responsibility. With an award of *sole legal custody*, one parent has the authority to make all of the major decisions affecting the child. Where both custodies are vested in one parent, the other parent will generally have visitation rights without significant parenting responsibilities.

Joint custody refers to the sharing of rights and responsibilities; both legal and physical custody can be allocated on a joint basis. *Joint legal custody* denotes the sharing of decision-making authority, and *joint physical custody* denotes the sharing of the day-to-day responsibility for raising a child.

Taking a Closer Look at Joint Custody Arrangements

Two joint custody arrangements are most likely: A couple may share both physical and legal custody, or one party may have sole physical custody and share legal custody with the other parent. It is also theoretically possible for a couple to share physical custody, with sole legal custody assigned to one parent. This arrangement occurs in situations where the parties are able to manage the logistics of a shared parenting schedule, but are in constant conflict, and cannot communicate to be able to have joint legal custody.

Where parents share legal custody, neither one is supposed to make a major decision affecting the child without the participation and consent of the other parent, absent emergency circumstances. Where parents disagree, no action can be taken until a resolution is reached. This can have serious implications for the well-being of a child, where, for example, parents disagree about whether the child needs to be evaluated by a therapist. Ultimately, these disputes may have to be submitted to a court for resolution.

In situations where one parent has sole physical custody with joint legal custody, the distinction between major and day-to-day decisions can become critical. Some decisions are easy to characterize: enrollment in a private school, elective surgery, or mental health counseling are clearly major issues. The choice between blue socks or green or whether to attend a friend's birthday party are clearly of the daily variety. But what about ear piercing? Or violin versus tuba lessons? Or a significant change in hairstyle? These decisions are harder to characterize and can lead to tremendous conflict over who has the right to make such decisions.

Where parents have joint physical custody, both are responsible, though not always equally, for the day-to-day care of the child. Here, many arrangements are possible. A child could spend roughly equal amounts of time with each parent, rotating between the households according to a fixed schedule that allocates time on a daily, weekly, monthly, or even yearly basis. Each parent would maintain a home for the child, who would in effect have two principal places of residence. It is also possible for the sharing to be less equal. A child might have one primary residence but spend a significant amount of time with the other parent, who would remain much more directly and consistently involved in the child's life than the traditional visiting parent.

The Joint Custody Controversy

The growing trend in favor of joint custody awards began sometime in the 1970s based on a number of considerations. First, a number of studies indicated that fathers tended to drift out of their children's lives following a divorce, causing children to feel a sense of abandonment and rejection. Rather than blaming fathers for not caring about their children, joint custody proponents regarded this disengagement as a result of the awkwardness and insignificance of being cast in a visitor's role and they hoped that by being given a more meaningful post-divorce role in their children's lives, fathers would remain more connected to them. Second, an emerging fathers' rights movement was seeking to combat what they perceived as anti-male bias in the family courts, and joint custody became a central demand as a way of wresting custodial control from women. Third, corresponding to the no-fault goal of making divorce a less adversarial process, it was hoped that joint custody would encourage parents to stop fighting over their children and to work out a cooperative arrangement where neither emerged the victor. *See generally* Richard Warshak, The Custody Revolution (1992).

Although it has become more commonplace, joint custody remains a contentious issue. Most experts agree that where parents freely choose joint custody and are committed to making it work, it can be a positive arrangement because it gives a child meaningful contact with both parents. However, making it work can be extremely difficult. Parents need to be able to set aside their anger and disappointment in the other as a spouse and respect him or her as a parent. In short, they must have the ability to distinguish between their spousal and their parenting roles, which can be extremely difficult to do. In short, as succinctly stated by the New York Court of Appeals, "joint custody is encouraged primarily as a voluntary alternative for relatively stable, amicable parents behaving in mature civilized fashion." *Braiman v. Braiman*, 379 N.E.2d 1019, 1021 (N.Y. 1978).

Even where parents are able to work things out between them, concerns have been raised that joint custody may overburden children, as it requires them to negotiate life in two different households. This can be particularly difficult for some children either because of their temperament or because of their developmental stage. For example, when parents do not live in the same community, adolescents may resent having to be away from their friends and social network on a regular basis. *See* Judith S. Wallerstein and Sandra Blakeslee, Second Chances — Men, Women, and Children a Decade After Divorce 256-273 (1989).

The far more contentious issue is whether courts should be able to impose joint custody where one parent objects to it. According to fathers' rights proponents, it is essential for courts to have this authority in order to counteract the bias they believe exists against fathers in the divorce courts. They argue that if joint custody were allowed only where it was agreed upon, mothers could routinely defeat the claims of fathers by objecting to it. Fathers' rights groups thus have lobbied for laws that create a presumption in favor of joint custody. They have also have brought class action lawsuits asserting that state laws that do not ensure each parent an equal share of parenting time violate their fundamental right to the care and custody of their children. This argument has generally not been successful as courts have typically concluded that the best interest of children trumps a parent's asserted right to equal custodial time.

Serious doubts by scholars and judges have emerged about the wisdom of allowing courts to compel joint custody over the objection of a parent, particularly in high-conflict families. As the Iowa Supreme Court explained in reversing the trial court's award of joint custody to embattled parents:

> The degree of conflict between parents is an important factor in determining whether joint physical custody is appropriate. Joint physical care requires substantial and regular interaction between divorced parents on a myriad of issues. Where the parties' marriage is stormy and has a history of charges and countercharges, the likelihood that joint physical care will provide a workable arrangement diminishes. It is, of course possible that spouses may be able to put aside their past strong differences in the interest of the children. Reality suggests, however, that this may not be the case. In short, a stormy marriage and divorce presents a significant risk factor that must be considered. . . . [T]he prospect for successful joint custody is reduced when there is a bitter parental relationship and one party objects to the shared arrangement.

In re Marriage of Hansen, 733 N.W.2d 683, 698 (Iowa 2007). Another critical concern is that the frequent interaction that joint custody demands may keep spousal animosity alive, with a detrimental spillover effect on the children, who may experience serious mental health problems as a result of continuing exposure to parental anger and arguments.

A related concern is that in states that permit the imposition of joint custody over the objection of one party, a party who opposes such an arrangement may be seen as hostile to the idea of shared parenting. This may result in award of primary custody to the parent who was agreeable to joint custody based on the view (which may be encoded in the custody statute) that he or she is the "friendly parent," who is more likely to permit regular access to the other parent. Of concern in this regard is that a "friendly parent" approach may divest a primary caretaker parent of custody based on his or her appropriate concerns about the ability of the parties to share custody. Of course, the equities are different if the concerns are baseless or grounded in an improper motive, such as revenge, rather than in a genuine concern for the well-being of the children.

Concerns about joint custody presumptions or preferences are particularly salient in cases in which there is a history of domestic violence. As many commentators have pointed out, successful shared parenting arrangements require the ability to cooperate and communicate effectively, and these characteristics are likely to be absent in a relationship that was marked by violence. Moreover, the frequency of the interaction demanded by joint custody may keep the victim at risk of continued harm, with a deleterious spillover effect on the children. Recognizing the seriousness of these concerns, most statutes expressly recognize that where there is a history of violence, joint custody is not likely to be in a child's best interest, and these cases are therefore exempt from any statutory preference in favor of joint custody.

D. VISITATION

At the opposite end of the custodial spectrum from a shared physical and legal custody arrangement is one in which both custodies are vested in a single parent, and the other is a noncustodial parent. The general assumption is that it is in a child's best interest to have continued contact with this parent; in virtually all cases, a noncustodial parent (referring here to a parent without physical custody) will be granted visitation rights. Because this parent plays a less significant role in the life of a child than the custodial parent does, courts generally use a lower standard for deciding about visitation than they do for deciding about custody. Accordingly, a parent who may not be capable of providing the day-to-day care and nurture that a child needs will, in most cases, be considered capable of spending some meaningful time with the child on a regular basis, unless it is determined that continued contact poses a risk of emotional or physical harm to a child, in which case visitation rights will be denied or subject to limitations.

However, before we take a closer look at the visitation rights of noncustodial parents, it is important to understand the legal status of this parent. Of critical importance is the fact that the loss of custody in the context of a divorce action does not sever the parent-child relationship; a mother or father who does not have either legal or physical custody of a child is still that child's parent. (The termination of parental rights is covered in Chapter 13.) The retention of one's legal status as a parent has important ramifications, including the following:

1. Because custodial determinations are not permanent, a noncustodial parent may always seek to modify the existing arrangement and thus may acquire custodial rights at some point in the future; in contrast, a termination of parental rights results in a permanent severance of the parent-child relationship.
2. Noncustodial parents retain a number of important rights. These include visitation rights; the right of access to school, medical, and other records; and the right to make medical decisions in the event of an emergency or the unavailability of the custodial parent.
3. In addition to these rights, a noncustodial parent remains subject to a support obligation.
4. With the legal relationship intact, benefits and statutory rights that depend on the existence of a parent-child relationship will most likely not be lost. For example, if a noncustodial parent dies without a will, the child will be entitled to a share of the estate under a state's intestacy laws. However, entitlements that depend on proof of actual dependency may be denied.

Thus, although loss of custody may be a devastating event in a mother or father's life, she or he is still a parent. This may seem like a legal abstraction to a noncustodial parent, who may no longer feel like a parent; however, the legal relationship carries with it a bundle of rights and an ongoing support obligation.

1. The Visitation Schedule

Setting aside for the moment those cases in which visitation may pose a threat to a child's physical or emotional well-being, the traditional model of the "zoo daddy" who shows up on Sundays to take the kids to the zoo and out for dinner has given way to the ideal of a visiting parent who remains closely involved in his or her children's lives. Accordingly, although there is so much variability in visitation arrangements that it is hard to state with any certainty how much time the "average" visiting parent spends with his or her children, the unquestioned trend is to increase visitation time and frequency well beyond the traditional four hours on Sunday afternoon in order to foster a meaningful parent-child relationship.

When the parents live close to one another, the noncustodial parent may be able to see the child on a regular basis, which can provide this ongoing sense of continuity and familiarity. The schedule may well include some overnight time and some extended time during school and summer vacations. When the parents do not live near each other, visitation will, of course, be less frequent, and it will be harder for the noncustodial parent to remain connected to the rhythms of a child's daily life. This may be offset somewhat by extended visitation time over the summer and school vacations.

Visitation arrangements, as set out in a court order, separation agreement, or parenting plan (see below), can be open-ended, spelled out in elaborate detail, or somewhere in between. An open-ended arrangement generally provides for a right of reasonable or liberal visitation and leaves the details up to the parties. This kind of arrangement usually works best if the parties have been separated for a while and have informally worked out and implemented a mutually satisfactory schedule. Because an open-ended agreement requires frequent communication, it is not likely to succeed if the parties are angry and hostile, or have not been successful at working out an informal arrangement. The constant negotiations necessitated by an open-ended schedule may serve to keep the anger between the parties alive longer and prevent them from settling into a reasonably calm visitation pattern, to the clear detriment of the children.

In contrast, a visitation arrangement can be spelled out with great specificity, detailing precisely when each and every visit is to occur and who is responsible for transporting the children to and from the visits. The allocation of times during summer and school vacations and holidays may similarly be spelled out with precision. The agreement may also include specific guidelines for when a parent may deviate from the schedule.

A middle-ground approach is to provide a fairly set schedule, with a proviso that this does not represent the full extent of the visiting parent's rights and that he or she may also visit at mutually agreed upon times. This minimizes the negotiations inherent in a completely open-ended arrangement but also builds in a degree of flexibility that may benefit both parents — especially if it is written to accommodate both of their needs.

Parents often do not anticipate how emotionally difficult the visitation process can be for both them and the child, especially around holidays and when a former partner begins to date. Accordingly, at least in the initial period following a divorce, a good argument can be made that most parents do better with a specific visitation plan that minimizes the need for constant negotiations. Frequently, after the initial emotional intensity has dissipated, parents are better able to be more flexible in responding to the needs of the other parent.

2. The Distinction Between Joint Physical Custody and Sole Custody with Visitation Rights

The formal boundary between sole custody with visitation rights and joint physical custody cannot always be fixed with precision, although some states have set a minimum amount of time that a parent must spend with a child for the arrangement to qualify as joint custody. For example, the following arrangement could, absent specific statutory criteria, be characterized either way: A child lives with his mother during the week and spends every weekend — from Friday at 6:00 P.M. until Sunday evening — with his father. He also has dinner with his father every Wednesday night.

As noted above, there has been a move away from the use of these terms, and many attorneys try to avoid them when negotiating an agreement because they carry a lot of emotional baggage and can exacerbate parental conflict. For example, if parents have negotiated an arrangement in which the children are to be with the mother 70 percent of the time and with the father 30 percent, the mother may object to calling this joint physical custody because it obscures the fact that she has the children most of the time. On the other hand, the father might object to his time being identified as visitation as this term carries the implication of minimal involvement. Accordingly, alternative language such as "primary care parent" and "secondary care parent" or just plain "parenting time" and defining the amount of time with both parents can be substituted. In addition, the agreement may refer to shared parenting responsibilities with each parent having custody when the children are with him or her, regardless of how the total time is allocated.

3. When Unrestricted Visitation Is Not in a Child's Best Interest

Despite the priority that the law gives to preserving the relationship between a child and the noncustodial parent, there are situations in which continued contact is considered not to be in a child's best interest, such as where it would place a child at risk of emotional or physical harm, and a court may prohibit post-divorce contact. Another possibility is that visitation would be allowed subject to restrictions, such as having them supervised by a third party. The parent might also be required to be in therapy and/or attend some kind of parenting class as a condition of a possible future lifting of the prohibition or restriction on contact.

Restrictions on visitation may also be imposed where a history of domestic violence places the custodial parent at risk even if the child has not been a direct victim of the abuse. Here, restrictions are generally aimed at limiting contact between the parents, such as that the child is dropped off and picked up at a neutral location (for instance, an agency that provides custody exchange services) at a timed interval so there is no contact between the parents. However, of course, if there is a direct risk to the child, visitation may be cut off or required to be supervised.

Frequently, a parent who has been denied or has restricted visitation rights will return to court at some point after the divorce seeking to change the arrangement. Judges vary in their approach to these cases — some lean toward giving parents a second chance, while others take a more cautious view based on the concern that the potential risk of harm outweighs the potential benefits of preserving the parent-child relationship. In any case, an important consideration is likely to be whether the parent has complied with any requirements that were imposed for the purpose of minimizing the risk of harm, such as that he or she attend therapy or parenting education courses.

E. PARENTING PLANS, PARENTING COORDINATORS, AND PARENT EDUCATION PROGRAMS

Although, as discussed above, the trend has shifted away from joint custody presumptions, the preferred approach today is to create a structure that enables both parents to maintain meaningful post-divorce connections with their children, whether through the actual sharing of custodial rights or a generous visitation schedule that fosters regular and sustained contact. In short, although the presumptive approach may be waning in popularity, this does not signal a return to the traditional "zoo daddy" model, which held out no expectation that the visiting parent would have a sustained and meaningful role in his children's lives.

Although studies indicate that children usually fare better when they sustain a quality post-dissolution relationship with both parents, the research also makes clear that continued parental conflict and hostility, which can be exacerbated by frequent contact, has a deleterious impact on children. To minimize post-divorce animosity and enhance the ability of parents to coordinate caring for their children, parenting plans, parenting coordinators, and parenting education programs have become increasingly popular legal options. *See* Joan Kelly, Psychological and Legal Interventions for Parents and Children in Custody and Access Disputes: Current Research and Practice, 10 Va. J. Soc. Poly. & L. 129 (2002).

However, the availability of these interventions does not necessarily mean that the cooperative post-divorce parenting model is appropriate in all cases. Where there is a high degree of parental conflict or a history of domestic violence, caution should be used because, regardless of the supports provided, these parents will probably not be able to safely and effectively navigate the degree of coordination and communication required by a post-divorce cooperative parenting arrangement.

1. Parenting Plans

A growing number of states now require parents to develop and submit a parenting plan to the court for approval if custody is to be shared, and a few states require the submission of a plan in all cases involving minor children. In other states, judges have the option of requiring the submission of a plan in any case where they deem it appropriate to do so. A **parenting plan** is a written agreement in which the parents detail how they intend to care for their children following a divorce. Designed to minimize hostility and foster cooperative parenting, parenting plans generally must cover all aspects of child rearing, including how time between the two households is to be divided, how responsibilities are to be allocated, and how decisions are to be made and disputes resolved. Depending on the state, other matters, such as parental relocation and child support, may also be addressed. In some states, parents may be required to participate in mediation if they cannot agree upon the terms of a plan.

Parenting plans appear to make a good deal of sense where parties are committed to post-divorce cooperative parenting. If carefully crafted, they provide parents with a detailed blueprint for how to manage their post-dissolution parenting roles, including how to handle disputes over child-related decisions, and the allocation of time and responsibilities. Exhibit 5.1 shows a sample schedule for allocating holiday time between parents. However, paralleling the criticisms of joint custody with which these plans are often, but not exclusively, associated, serious concerns have been raised about the appropriateness of requiring parenting plans in cases involving domestic violence or a high degree of conflict. Accordingly, exemptions or special protections have been incorporated into many of these laws to cover situations where the kind of cooperative arrangements envisioned by parenting plans is either not safe or not feasible.

EXHIBIT 5.1   Sample Holiday Parenting Time

The parents acknowledge that holiday parenting time shall take priority over regular parenting time and summer parenting time. Unless otherwise agreed to in writing the parents mutually agree that holiday parenting time shall be exercised as follows:

Thanksgiving Day: (Thursday at 12 noon until Monday morning drop off at school). Mother will have the Children for Thanksgiving in all even numbered years; Father will have the Children for Thanksgiving in all odd numbered years.

Christmas Eve/Christmas Day: (Christmas Eve is defined as December 24th at 12:00 noon until December 25th at 12:00 noon; Christmas Day is defined as December 25th at 10:00 A.M. until December 26th at 10:00 A.M.). Christmas Eve: Mother in all odd numbered years and Father in all even numbered years. Christmas Day: Mother in all even numbered years and Father in all odd numbered years.

Easter Sunday: (Saturday evening preceding at 5:00 P.M. until Monday morning drop off at school (or 9:00 A.M. if no school)). With Mother in all odd numbered years, Father in all even numbered years.

Mother's Day: (Saturday preceding at 5:00 P.M. until Monday morning drop off at school (or 9:00 A.M. if no school)). With Mother each year.

Father's Day: (Saturday preceding at 5:00 P.M. until Monday morning at 9:00 A.M.). With Father each year.

July 4th: Commencing July 4th at 12:00 noon until July 5th at 12:00 noon. With Father in all odd numbered years; with Mother in all even numbered years.

Three Day Holiday Weekends (i.e., Memorial Day, Labor Day, Martin Luther King, Jr. Day): The parent who is scheduled to have the children for their regular scheduled weekend on a Three Day Holiday Weekend will extend his or her parenting time to Tuesday drop off at school (or 9:00 A.M. if no school).

School vacations: Fall break shall be with Father in all even numbered years and Mother in all odd numbered years. Spring break shall be with Father in all even numbered years and Mother in all odd numbered years.

Parents' Birthdays: Will follow the regular schedule.

Children's Birthdays: The regular parenting schedule shall be followed. However, the Parent who is not scheduled to have the birthday child in his or her care shall be entitled to up to two (2) hours of access with the birthday child (and his/her sibling if desired) if on a school day or up to four (4) hours of access with the birthday child (and his/her sibling if desired) if on a non-school day. The exact times for the access periods shall be determined by the Parent who has physical custody of the birthday child if the Parents cannot otherwise agree on the times.

Halloween: (5:00 P.M. until drop off at school the following morning or 9:00 A.M. if no school). Mother will have the Children for Halloween in all even numbered years; Father will have the Children for Halloween in all odd numbered years.

2. Parenting Coordinators

In some states, **parenting coordinators** are appointed who are tasked with the responsibility of helping parties to successfully implement their parenting plan. A number of states have specific provisions permitting the appointment of parenting coordinators, while others rely upon "existing statutes that allow for 'mediators' or 'special masters' as a basis for appointing parenting coordinators." In the absence of any such statutory authority, it is arguable that "the discretion given to judges to fashion orders in the best interest of . . . children, could be extended . . . to order [parents] to cooperate with a parenting coordinator." Marlene Eskind Moses with Beth A. Townsend, Parenting Coordinators: The Good, The Bad and the Ugly, 48 Tenn. B.J. 24, 25 (2012).

Although the scope of their authority varies from state to state, parenting coordinators typically focus on helping parents to develop strategies for resolving conflicts that arise around custody. However, as a general rule, they do not have the authority to alter the parameters of the parenting plan or to change the allocation of custodial rights and responsibilities between the parents. In some states, parenting coordinators are able to make certain decisions when the parents are unable to resolve a conflict that arises over a day-to-day parenting issue, or such issues as choice of school, which extra-curricular activities a child should participate in, or whether sleepovers with friends are permitted. However, parenting coordinators generally just make recommendations, which are typically subject to court review. Parenting coordinators may also have the authority to made recommendations to the court.

3. Parenting Education Programs

A related trend is the enactment of laws setting up parenting education programs for divorcing parents. Depending on the state or the circumstances of the family, these programs may be mandatory or offered on a voluntary basis, and, like parenting plans, they are intended to facilitate the transition to post-divorce parenting. These programs are designed to educate parents about their behaviors that potentially could impact their children. The hope is that, once they gain such awareness, parents will modulate negative behaviors so that they can respond more effectively to the needs of their children.

Most court-affiliated parent education programs are of very short duration, lasting somewhere between a total of two and four hours. Based on concerns that have been raised about their limited effectiveness, some experts in the field have begun to suggest that the adoption of a more time-intensive model would better equip parties with the skills and knowledge needed in order to parent more effectively following a divorce.[20] Online programs are becoming an increasingly popular way for parents to fulfill court-mandated education requirements, and these programs are often somewhat longer than the typical classroom option. At the end of the online

---

[20]*See* Amanda Sigal, Irwin Sandler, Sharlene Wolchik, and Sanford Braver, Do Parent Education Programs Promote Healthy Postdivorce Parenting? Critical Distinctions and a Review of the Evidence, 49 Fam. Ct. Rev. 120 (2011).

program a test is given to ensure the parent has completed all the exercises and listened to each segment in the online program.

Again, important concerns have been raised about parent education programs where there has been a history of domestic violence; in states where participation is mandatory, judges are usually allowed to waive the attendance requirement for good cause, such as where necessary to protect a party from the risk of abuse. Other options have also been suggested that would enable a victim of domestic violence to attend a

Online education website
Courtesy of The Center for Divorce Education

parent education class while also protecting her safety, such as by having the parents attend class on different nights or in different locations. Jill R. Bowers, Elissa Thomann Mitchell, Jennifer L. Hardesty, and Robert Hughes, Jr., A Review of Online Divorce Education Programs, 49 Fam. Ct. Rev. 776 (2011).

A more recent innovation is for courts to offer educational programs for the children of divorcing parents to help them understand and cope with the changes in their lives. Children are usually grouped according to age, and the curriculum is adapted to the development needs of the targeted age. Although these programs are usually offered on a voluntary basis, they may be required in some jurisdictions. For instance, under local court rules in Kentucky, children in many parts of the state are required to attend the children's component of the state's Divorce Education program. That portion of the overall program is designed to "provide a sense of security, awareness and understanding as a beginning point for children learning to cope with dual parenting in separate households." Children in grades 1 through 5 attend Kids' Time, and those in grades 6 through 8 attend Tweens' Time. For a description of Kentucky's Divorce Education programs, see http://courts.ky.gov/courtprograms/divorceeducation/Pages/default.aspx (accessed June 8, 2016).

F. POST-DIVORCE DISPUTES

Following a divorce, disputes often arise regarding custody or visitation arrangements — or both — and a parent may return to court seeking to either enforce or change existing arrangements. A custodial parent may also return to court seeking judicial permission to relocate to another state if his or her spouse objects to the move.

1. Complaints for Modification and Contempt

Following a divorce, parents often express concern about the custodial arrangements and wish to change them. Because the primary concern is always the best interest of the children, courts have continuing jurisdiction to modify custody and visitation arrangements until such time as the children reach the age of majority and are no longer subject to the custodial authority of their parents.

Grounded, however, in the principles of **res judicata**, which prevents a court from reexamining an issue that already has been litigated, modifications of the custody arrangements are not intended to offer dissatisfied parents a second bite at the apple. In order to obtain a modification a parent must establish that there has been a change in circumstances, with many jurisdictions expressly requiring proof that the change was unforeseeable, such that the existing arrangement is no longer in the best interest of the children. Thus, for example, in a situation of joint legal custody, it may turn out that the parents cannot make decisions without a protracted struggle, and the parent with physical custody feels this is interfering with his or her ability to meet the needs of the child. Or a parent may realize that the other parent, who had been sober for an extended time period at the time of the parties' divorce, has relapsed and is again abusing alcohol and is thus not able to care for the child properly.

In situations where a parent may relapse, it is important that courts retain the power to review existing arrangements to ensure that the needs of the children are still being met. Because courts have a duty to ensure that custodial arrangements do not pose a risk of harm to a child, a court must assess the situation, even where it appears that in bringing the action, the parent was motivated by hostility rather than a genuine concern for the child.

In contrast, sometimes a post-divorce dispute centers around a parent's failure to comply with the terms of the existing custodial and visitation arrangements, such as where someone claims that the custodial parent refuses to let him or her visit with the children, or a custodial parent is upset that his or her former spouse consistently fails to show up to see the children at the agreed-upon times.

In cases where a child is being withheld from a parent, , a party can bring a contempt action against the other seeking enforcement of the existing arrangement, or an action for custodial interference. If there is good reason for not permitting visitation with the other parent, such as a parent shows up intoxicated to the visitation, then there may be good grounds for not allowing the visit, It may be appropriate to seek a modification in such cases. Unfortunately, however, there is no real remedy for a custodial parent who is seeking to compel the other parent to comply with taking the visitation set forth in the parenting plan. As a general rule, a court lacks the power to force a parent to see her or his children if the parent chooses not to.

2. Relocation Disputes

Following a divorce, most jurisdictions do not permit a custodial parent to move out of state with the child without first obtaining the consent of the other parent or the court. As might be expected, relocation disputes are fraught with bitterness. A custodial parent is likely to resent the potential limitation on the ability to seek a better life, especially in light of the fact that a visiting parent can move about freely without having to secure anyone's consent, and the noncustodial parent is likely to resent the potential loss of regular access to the child. Similar dynamics are likewise common in cases of shared custody.

States take a variety of approaches to relocation cases. Until the latter decades of the twentieth century, most states held the custodial parent who wished to move to a fairly high standard of justification for the intended move, and typically required proof that the move was due to "exceptional circumstances" and/ or that it provided a "real advantage" to the children. However, as exemplified by the influential New Jersey case of *D'Onofrio v. D'Onofrio*,[21] which focused on the interconnected well-being of the children and the custodial parent as a primary family unit, many jurisdictions began looking more favorably at these relocation requests. Accordingly, so long as the custodial parent is able to establish that the move is motivated by good faith—such as by a job opportunity or the desire to move closer to extended family, rather than by a desire to interfere with the rights of the noncustodial parent, permission is likely to be granted.[22]

Case Preview

D'Onofrio v. D'Onofrio

Phyllis D'Onofrio (Mother) and Dominick D'Onofrio (Father) divorced in December 1973 in New Jersey. Mother was given custody of the two children, with Father having reasonable but unspecified visitation. Thereafter Mother brought an application for permission to relocate to South Carolina with her children, a boy age 6 and a girl age 4. Although Father objected, the application was granted. The court did include provisions for visitation in both New Jersey and South Carolina.

As you read *D'Onofrio v. D'Onofrio*, look for the following:

1. What was the purpose of the anti-removal statute that was enacted by the New Jersey legislature?
2. What are the factors that must be shown by a parent in order to obtain permission to relocate out of the state with children after a divorce?
3. Why does the court say Mother met her burden to overcome the anti-removal statute?

---

[21]365 A.2d 27, 29-30 (N.J. Super. Ct. Ch. Div. 1976), *aff'd*, 365 A.2d 716 (N.J. Super. Ct. App. Div. 1976).
[22]*See generally* Samara Nazir, The Changing Path to Relocation: An Update on Post-Divorce Relocation Issues, 22 J. Am. Acad. Matrim. Law. 483 (2009); Lucy S. McGough, Starting Over: The Heuristics of Family Relocation Decision Making, 77 St. John's L. Rev. 291 (2003); Charles P. Kindregan, Family Interests in Competition: Relocation and Visitation, 36 Suffolk U. L. Rev. 31 (2002).

D'Onofrio v. D'Onofrio

365 A.2d 27 (N.J. Super Ct. App. Div. 1976)

PRESSLER, J.C.C., Temporarily Assigned.

. . .

The court is keenly aware that of all adjudicatory proceedings, none requires greater judicial thoughtfulness nor imposes graver judicial responsibility than the delicate and sensitive litigation which involves the status of young children or which may affect to any substantial degree existing parental relationships. The resolution of the issue here presented, essentially one of visitation, concededly does not implicate the same degree of wrenching emotional content and permanency of consequence inevitably involved in contested adoption and custody actions. It is nevertheless of critical significance to the lives of both of these parents and their children. The issue is also one of sufficient importance to have invoked a clear and long-standing statement of legislative policy, namely, that children of divorced parents not be removed from this jurisdiction without the consent of the non-custodial parent "unless the court, upon cause shown, shall otherwise order." N.J.S.A. 9:2-2. The questions to be here determined then, in view of this anti-removal policy and its evident purpose, are first, the factors and considerations which constitute an adequate showing of cause for relieving the custodial parent of the obligation to remain with the children in this jurisdiction, and second, whether such a showing was here made by the mother.

. . . N.J.S.A. 9:2-4 declares that the custodial rights and obligations of both parents are equal and that it is the "happiness and welfare" of the children which shall be determinative of the custodial question. N.J.S.A. 9:2-4 also enjoins, without qualification or exception, the removal of the children from this jurisdiction "where the mother or father resides in this State and is the suitable person who should have the custody of such child for its best welfare." . . . The main thrust of the anti-removal provision of N.J.S.A. 9:2-4 was clearly to prevent the defeat of an award of custody either already made or pending. The thrust of the anti-removal provision of N.J.S.A. 9:2-2, however, is addressed not primarily to the basic custodial question but rather to the preservation of the mutual right of the children and the noncustodial parent to develop and maintain their parental relationship after custody has already been awarded to the other parent, a relationship based upon that institution which has come to be known as "visitation." Unlike its N.J.S.A. 9:2-4 counterpart, the anti-removal provision of N.J.S.A. 9:2-2 is subject to the exercise of judicial discretion and this, patently, because of the legislative recognition of the obvious fact that visitation by the non-custodial parent is not inherently incompatible with the residency of the children in another state. Thus, when our courts speak of the "cause shown" criterion of N.J.S.A. 9:2-2 in terms of the best interests and welfare of the child, they speak, as a matter of content, not to the whole range of considerations which must be taken into account in deciding which of the parents shall have custody. They speak rather to one aspect of the child's welfare, namely his interest in continuing, by appropriate visitation, as reasonable, healthy and affectionate a relationship as possible with the parent with whom he does not reside. . . .

Even under the best of circumstances and where the custodial parent is support-ive of a continuing relationship between the child and the noncustodial parent, the nature of a parental relationship sustainable by way of visitation is necessarily and inevitably of a different character than that which is possible where the parents and children reside together as a single-family unit. The fact remains that ordinarily the day-to-day routine of the children, especially young ones, and the quality of their environment and their general style of life are that which are provided by the custo-dial parent and which are, indeed, the custodial parent's obligation to provide. The children, after the parents' divorce or separation, belong to a different family unit than they did when the parents lived together. The new family unit consists only of the children and the custodial parent, and what is advantageous to that unit as a whole, to each of its members individually and to the way they relate to each other and function together is obviously in the best interests of the children. It is in the context of what is best for that family unit that the precise nature and terms of visita-tion and changes in visitation by the noncustodial parent must be considered.

Where the residence of the new family unit and that of the noncustodial parent are geographically close, some variation of visitation on a weekly basis is tradition-ally viewed as being most consistent with maintaining the parental relationship, and where, as here, that has been the visitation pattern, a court should be loathe to interfere with it by permitting removal of the children for frivolous or unper-suasive or inadequate reasons. See *Grove v. Grove*, 26 N.J. Super. 154, 97 A.2d 505 (App. Div. 1953). Where, however, the custodial parent can demonstrate that a real advantage to herself and the children will result from their removing their residence to a place so geographically distant as to render weekly visitation impossible, then the court must weigh a number of determinative factors in order to accommodate the compelling interests of all of the family members. It should consider the pro-spective advantages of the move in terms of its likely capacity for improving the general quality of life for both the custodial parent and the children. It must evalu-ate the integrity of the motives of the custodial parent in seeking the move in order to determine whether the removal is inspired primarily by the desire to defeat or frustrate visitation by the noncustodial parent, and whether the custodial parent is likely to comply with substitute visitation orders when she is no longer subject to the jurisdiction of the courts of this State. It must likewise take into account the integ-rity of the noncustodial parent's motives in resisting the removal and consider the extent to which, if at all, the opposition is intended to secure a financial advantage in respect of continuing support obligations. Finally, the court must be satisfied that there will be a realistic opportunity for visitation in lieu of the weekly pattern which can provide an adequate basis for preserving and fostering the parental rela-tionship with the noncustodial parent if removal is allowed. The court should not insist that the advantages of the move be sacrificed and the opportunity for a better and more comfortable life style for the mother and children be forfeited solely to maintain weekly visitation by the father where reasonable alternative visitation is available and where the advantages of the move are substantial. It is at least arguable . . . that the alternative of uninterrupted visits of a week or more in duration several times a year, where the father is in constant and exclusive parental contact with the children and has to plan and provide for them on a daily basis, may well serve the paternal relationship better than the typical weekly visit which involves little if any exercise of real paternal responsibility.

It is further clear that a noncustodial parent is perfectly free to remove himself from this jurisdiction despite the continued residency here of his children in order to seek opportunities for a better or different life style for himself. And if he does choose to do so, the custodial parent could hardly hope to restrain him from leaving this State on the ground that his removal will either deprive the children of the paternal relationship or depreciate its quality. The custodial parent, who bears the essential burden and responsibility for the children, is clearly entitled to the same option to seek a better life for herself and the children, particularly where the exercise of that option appears to be truly advantageous to their interests and provided that the paternal interest can continue to be accommodated, even if by a different visitation arrangement than theretofore. Relating these observations to the facts here as found and hereafter recited, the court is satisfied that the move here contemplated should be allowed.

[The court also explained that Mother and the children live in an apartment in New Jersey located on a busy street with no convenient play area. The rent that Mother had to pay and the lack of job opportunities were also issues. Comparatively, mother would have family close by if she were to move to Rock Hill, South Carolina, and the children, having frequently visited Rock Hill, South Carolina] are confident and happy there and, to the limited extent that they understand what is involved, look forward to the move.

Mrs. D'Onofrio finds her situation difficult, and with obvious justification. She is employed, taking care of the children essentially on a 24 hour a day basis, has barely enough income to meet the family's needs, and is receiving from her former husband not only minimal financial support but also very little support and assistance in the burdens of raising the children. Although she has genuinely attempted to maintain herself and her children in New Jersey, she has now concluded that they would manage better by returning permanently to Rock Hill. She has found employment there as a bookkeeper for a chemical company at a starting net salary of $147 a week. She has located a desirable apartment in a garden-type complex bordering a wooded area and providing superior recreational facilities for the children at a monthly rental of $155. She will be near her family, including not only her parents and siblings but also cousins, aunts, uncles, nieces and nephews, some of whom will be available to help with child care. Not only will the standard of living and physical environment of the mother and the children be considerably improved but they will also enjoy the benefits of being surrounded by a large and helpful extended family.

Now as to the paternal considerations. The father, since the divorce, has been seeing the children every Friday, on birthdays and holidays. He sometimes picks them up at their home, but more often Mrs. D'Onofrio takes them to his parents' home, which appears to be the visitation headquarters. Although he spends time with them there, he frequently leaves them for part of the day with their grandmother, with whom Mrs. D'Onofrio enjoys a cordial relationship. Mrs. D'Onofrio, who candidly admits that the children love their father, has repeatedly asked him to keep them with him overnight, but he has never yet done so, claiming both that the fact of his employment is inconsistent with such an arrangement and that, having remarried, he doesn't have room for them. His claimed net income from his municipal employment after payment of taxes, alimony and support is in excess of $8,000. There are no children of the present marriage. His second wife works, but her income was not indicated. Mrs. D'Onofrio suggested, but he denied, that he earns additional income by moonlighting. As to his attitude toward the proposed move, the court accepts Mrs. D'Onofrio's testimony, despite her former husband's variant version, that when she first discussed it with him, he had no objection provided she would agree to forego the weekly child support and would arrange to transport the children to New Jersey for visitation at Christmas, Easter and during the summer.

The court found Mrs. D'Onofrio to be an impressive and credible witness and a concerned, sensitive and effective parent. It is true that the visitation problems which typically come before the courts are those of the noncustodial parent seeking to enforce his visitation rights which the custodial parent is trying to subvert. As one court was compelled to observe, "Experience has shown that only too often, unless the court exercises its power to protect the welfare of the children, a separated wife is not likely to provide reasonable visitation privileges voluntarily. The children may well be used as weapons to inflict punishment upon the other parent for real or imagined wrongs." *Smith v. Smith*, supra, 85 N.J. Super. at 469, 205 A.2d at 87. Without detracting from the force of that observation, it must nevertheless be kept in mind that that is the situation the courts see. They are not confronted, because there is no legal basis therein for relief, with the converse situation of the custodial parent who genuinely seeks to encourage a greater degree of participation and responsibility by a noncustodial parent who assumes either no role or, as here, a minimal role with the children. The court is obliged to conclude that had the father here extended himself further on behalf of the children, both financially and otherwise, the mother would not have felt compelled to make this move.

In view of all of the foregoing, this court is satisfied that the mother has shown the required cause. She has expressed her desire, not merely her willingness, to transport the children to New Jersey so that they can spend two weeks with their father during the summer, one week at Christmas and one week in the spring. The court has ordered her to do so and is confident of her intent to comply with that order. Hopefully, the father will be able to make arrangements to accommodate them even though those visits will make greater demands of him than the weekly visits he now shares with his mother. The order also accords him liberal visitation in South Carolina and further permits him to withhold $15 a week of his support payments to create a source of funds to pay for the children's transportation to New Jersey. That visitation being practical and realistic, this court could not in good conscience, and simply because weekly visitation may be more convenient for the father, require this mother and her children to endure indefinitely their separation from family, their present subsistence level and their continuing financial struggle when happier prospects are already within their grasp.

Post-Case Follow-Up

The court in *D'Onofrio* recognized that maintaining the relationship between the child and the noncustodial parent is important in considering permitting the children to relocate out of state with the custodial parent. However, the importance of continuity of care within the custodial household and the needs of the family are also important considerations. Accordingly, courts will review the impact the relocation, or lack of relocation, will have on the children. Assuming that a practical and realistic schedule can be developed to allow the noncustodial parent reasonable visitation, it is more likely a relocation will be permitted.

D'Onofrio v. D'Onofrio: Real Life Applications

1. Assume that you represent Sheila Barnes in a state that has the same statute as in the *D'Onofrio* case. Sheila advises you that she was divorced two years ago and was awarded primary physical custody of her twin girls who are seven years old. She has recently been offered a job in another state approximately 400 miles away from her current residence. The new job offers her almost double her current salary, with hours that would allow her the ability to also occasionally work from home so she could be with the girls; taking this job eventually could lead to even further advancement.

    a. Under *D'Onofrio*, what do you tell Sheila the likely result will be if she moves to remove the children from the state?
    b. What arguments can she anticipate from the children's father?
    c. What factors will it be important for her to show the court in order to be granted the ability to relocate?

2. Assume you represent the father in the *D'Onofrio* case. What arguments do you believe should have been made by Father in order to prohibit the relocation?

3. In *D'Onofrio*, assume the parties had joint physical custody and Father indicated he was willing to keep the children in New Jersey with him and Mother could have visitation. Would those additional facts change the court's decision? Why?

The relationship between the child and the noncustodial parent is certainly not an irrelevant consideration in jurisdictions favoring the custodial parents in relocation disputes. However, given that the primary focus is on the importance of continuity of care within the custodial household and what is needed to make that family function effectively, the fact that visitation will occur on a less regular basis is generally not enough to prevent a move. It may be enough to defeat the move, however, when considered with other relevant factors, such as where the move is not prompted by reasons calculated to benefit the custodial household in a meaningful way. This calculus is likely to be more complex and fine-grained in jurisdictions that, even if favoring the custodial parent, have adopted multifactorial tests for evaluating relocation requests.

States that favor the custodial parent generally approach the issue differently where the parents share physical custody. In this situation, the child has two distinct post-divorce households, and his or her best interest is not so clearly identified with one parent as it is when one parent has sole custody. In this situation, a court may be more likely to decide that preserving the status quo is in the child's best interest and deny the relocation request — or more precisely, since a court cannot prevent a parent from moving, but only from relocating with a child, the court may frame the result as a "contingent custody transfer" in which it orders a transfer of sole custody to the other parent if the party who wishes to relocate proceeds with his or her plans to do so.

Other jurisdictions give more weight to the interests of the noncustodial parent in preserving his or her relationship with the child. In these jurisdictions, courts generally do not take an expanded view of best interest and thus do not assume that changes for the better in the custodial parent's life naturally benefit the child. Accordingly, although states employ a range of different standards, with some using a multifactored approach, at a minimum, the parent may need to prove that the move is motivated by something more than a good faith desire to improve his or her life and that it will provide a demonstrable advantage to the child, which is not available in the state.

Recently, however, it appears that the trend in favor of custodial parents may be slowly moving in the other direction as commentators have questioned the validity of the assumption that the well-being of the child is so enmeshed with that of the custodial parent that disruption of the bond with the other parent is of little consequence. Thus, for example, one recent study suggests that children might be adversely impacted when they move more than an hour's drive from the noncustodial parent, while others suggest that relocation outcomes might vary based upon a complex array of factors, such as the age of the children, how soon the move follows the time of separation, and the nature and frequency of contact the children and the noncustodial parent have before the move. Accordingly, some courts have begun to apply a more individualized assessment of relocation requests that are less reliant on the expanded concept of best interest, which ties the welfare of the child to the well-being of the custodial parent within the context of this newly constituted domestic unit.

3. Virtual Visitation

In 2001, in *McCoy v. McCoy*, after finding that the custodial mother had a good faith reason for relocating to California, a New Jersey court concluded that in assessing whether the existing visitation arrangement could be restructured to "accommodate and preserve the relationship that the child had with her father," the trial court had failed to give adequate weight to the mother's "suggested use of the Internet to enhance visitation." *McCoy v. McCoy*, 764 A.2d 449, 454 (2001).

Characterizing her proposal as "both creative and innovative," the appeals court concluded that if the "actual" proposed visitation arrangement was inadequate, the judge should have considered this supplemental means of communication. In what is generally considered to be a groundbreaking approach, the court stressed that technology could be used to ensure "continued development" of the child's relationship with her father, while also preserving the mother's right to move. *Id.*

Today, the concept of virtual visitation, which refers to the use of "email, instant messaging, webcams, and other internet tools to provide regular contact between a noncustodial parent and his or her child," is no longer regarded as groundbreaking, and many courts routinely consider the availability of virtual means of communication when deciding relocation cases. David Welsh, Virtual Parents: How Virtual Visitation Legislation Is Shaping the Future of Custody Law, 11 J.L. Fam. Stud. 215 (2008).

Taking this trend a step further, in an effort to enhance the post-divorce relationship between a child and the noncustodial parent, some judges now include virtual visitation provisions in cases that do not involve an out-of-state move.

When fashioning virtual visitation orders, the growing tendency is for courts to be quite specific about what kind of technology is to be used, who is to pay for it, and when and under what conditions it is to take place. In this regard, the most valuable communications tools are generally considered to be those, such as webcams and Skype, that make "real" time communication possible, thus enabling a parent to be present, albeit virtually rather than physically, in his or her child's life. However, as some commentators have noted, not all judges are fully versed in the wide range of available technologies, and their orders may thus not take full advantage of cutting-edge modalities.

In general, courts do not appear to be factoring the possibility of virtual communication into the relocation decision itself as a threshold matter; custodial parents are thus still expected to establish a legally sufficient reason for the proposed move. Accordingly, in *McCoy*, for example, it was only after the mother had shown, to the court's satisfaction, that the move was prompted by the prospect of a better job and a better climate for her daughter who suffered from asthma, that it considered the possibility of using virtual visitation to supplement the father's actual time with his daughter. In short, it does not appear that courts are relying on the availability of virtual visitation to short-circuit the relocation decision itself.

Concerns, however, have been raised that judges may begin to rely on the availability of this technology in making the underlying relocation decision itself. Here, it would not simply be a way to supplement other avenues of communication once an independent decision had been made, but it would be a factor in the decisional matrix, to be weighed along with other considerations, such as the reason for the move and the best interests of the child. This raises profound questions about the nature of human interaction and how meaningful relationships are maintained with people who are not in physical proximity. Must connection occur in person for it to count as meaningful contact? Can one really "interact" virtually? What is lost when technological connections replace physical contact? What does it mean for human relationships when spatial proximity is no longer needed for "real time" communication? These and other related questions will only become more pressing in the coming years as the distance between virtual and actual reality continues to diminish.

Finally, some states have enacted virtual visitation statutes, and a number of other states are considering such measures. Generally speaking, these legislative enactments are aimed at ensuring greater uniformity and consistency within any given jurisdiction with respect to the circumstances under which virtual visitation can be ordered and how such orders are to be structured. Thus, for example, a statute may spell out that virtual visitation orders are meant to supplement in-person contact and not to serve as a substitute for it. In addition, these laws may also be able to address the growing concern of some commentators that in cases involving a history of domestic violence, the use of "electronic communication may give the abusive ex-spouse the ability to invade the privacy of his or her former spouse."[23] Particularly worrisome is that it may be used to ferret out that parent's whereabouts in situations where safety needs dictate the non-disclosure of location.

G. THE CUSTODIAL AND VISITATION RIGHTS OF "NONPARENTS"

Until this point, the focus of this chapter has been on custody and visitation disputes between divorcing parents. In these disputes, the rights of each party, at least in a formal legal sense, are deemed to be equal. Each is entitled to try to establish that an award of custody to him or her would further the best interest of the child.

In this section, we turn to a consideration of custody and visitation disputes between parents and "nonparents"—namely, grandparents, stepparents, and co-parents, although, as we will see, the term "nonparent" is problematic in the co-parent context, as it assumes the lack of a parental status, which is often the issue in controversy. In reading this section, you should bear in mind that, as discussed in Chapter 1, parents have a fundamental right to direct the upbringing of their children, including deciding who will have access to them, which gives them an automatic preference in cases where a "nonparent" seeks some kind of visitation (or custodial) rights.

1. Grandparents

At common law, grandparents had no legal right of access to their grandchildren. Rather, parents were said to have a moral but not a legal obligation to permit grandparents to spend time with their grandchildren. In essence, a grandparent's right of access to his or her grandchildren was derivative rather than direct as it was dependent upon the will of the child's parent. Grounded in the legal rule that parents have the right to control the upbringing of their children, this approach was also intended to protect children from the potentially devastating impact of a legal

---

[23]*See* Jim McKay, Virtual Parenting, Government Technology (2006), http://www.govtech.com/featured/Virtual-Parenting.html?page=2 (accessed June 8, 2016). *See also* David Welsh, Virtual Parents: How Virtual Visitation Legislation Is Shaping the Future of Custody Law, 11 J.L. & Fam. Stud. 215 (2008).

battle between their parents and grandparents over whether a relationship could be developed or maintained.

This approach began to change in the 1960s, and today all states have statutes that, to varying degrees, modify the common law rule of no access. Some states have enacted specific grandparent visitation laws, while others include grandparents within a broader third-party visitation statute. The enhanced legal status of grandparents reflected several developments. First, with the graying of the population, the organizational and political clout of senior citizens, an important force behind these laws, has increased. Second, as the divorce rate rose, increased attention was focused on the importance of providing children with continued access to essential relationships in order to help buffer the dislocation of divorce. Most notably in this regard was a heightened awareness of how important and stabilizing the relationship between a grandparent and child can be, including the recognition that in some families, grandparents may fill the role of additional or substitute caretaker. *See* Patricia S. Fernandez, Grandparent Access: A Model Statute, 6 Yale L. & Poly. Rev. 109 (1988).

In looking at grandparent visitation statutes, it is helpful to ask two questions. First, under what circumstances does a grandparent have standing to seek visitation rights? Second, what substantive standards are to be used to resolve the dispute? With regard to standing, most statutes require that there be some kind of family disruption, such as divorce or parental death, in order for a grandparent to have the right to maintain a legal action. In other states, the statutes give grandparents a more general right to seek visitation without specifying the circumstances under which a petition can be filed. However, based on considerations of family privacy, many courts will not allow a petition to go forward where the family is "intact" and require some kind of disruption or proof of parental unfitness as a prerequisite to the maintenance of an action.

Turning to the substantive standards that are used to resolve the dispute in cases where a grandparent has established that she or he does have standing to maintain an action, some states use the best interest of the child, although judges generally require proof of something more than simply that the child would enjoy a continued relationship with the grandparent. Moreover, the Supreme Court's decision in the 2000 case of *Troxel v. Granville*, 530 U.S. 57 (2000), although far from definitive, has limited the ability of judges to disregard the views of a fit parent regarding what is best for his or her child. Other states have adopted a higher burden of proof, most frequently by requiring the grandparent(s) to establish that the denial of visitation rights would harm the child.

As grandparents began turning to the courts to gain access to their grandchildren after contact had been denied or limited by a son or daughter (or by a daughter- or son-in-law), some parents responded by challenging the constitutionality of the grandparent visitation laws, arguing that such laws were an unwarranted intrusion into the realm of family privacy. Initially, courts tended to uphold the validity of the statutes, finding that any intrusion into a fit parent's right to direct the upbringing of his or her children was offset by the benefit to the child of a continued relationship with his or her grandparent. As expressed by the Kentucky Supreme Court in the case of *King v. King*, these early decisions tended to sentimentalize the grandparent-grandchild relationship:

> While the Constitution . . . does recognize the right to rear children without undue governmental interference, that right is not inviolate. . . .
>
> In an era in which society has seen a general disintegration of the family, it is not unreasonable for the General Assembly to attempt to strengthen familial bonds. . . . There is no reason that a petty dispute between a father and son should be allowed to deprive a grandparent and grandchild of the unique relationship that ordinarily exists between those individuals. . . .
>
> If a grandparent is physically, mentally and morally fit, then a grandchild will ordinarily benefit from contact with the grandparent. . . . Each benefits from contact with the other. The child can learn respect, a sense of responsibility and love. The grandparent can be invigorated by exposure to youth, can gain an insight into our changing society, and can avoid the loneliness which is so often a part of an aging parent's life. These considerations by the state do not go too far in intruding into the fundamental rights of the parents.

828 S.W.2d 630, 632-633 (Ky. 1992). In 1993, however, starting with the decision of Tennessee Supreme Court, in the case of *Hawk v. Hawk*, courts began to give greater consideration to the rights of parents to decide who should have access to their children:

> . . . Bill and Sue Hawk argue that grandparent visitation is a "compelling state interest" that warrants use of the state's parens patriae power to impose visitation in "best interests of the children." . . . We find, however, that without a substantial danger of harm to the child, a court may not constitutionally impose its own subjective notions of the "best interests of the child" when an intact, nuclear family with fit, married parents is involved.
>
> The requirement of harm is the sole protection that parents have against pervasive state interference in the parenting process.
>
> . . . [I]t is not within the power of a court, . . . to make significant decisions concerning the custody of children, merely because it could make a better decision or disposition. The State is parens patriae and always has been, but it has not displaced the parent in right or responsibility. . . .

855 S.W.2d 573, 580-583 (Tenn. 1993) (internal citations omitted). The court goes on to critique the Kentucky Supreme Court's *King* decision:

> . . . the *King* majority engaged in a sentimental reflection on the "special bond" between grandparent and grandchild. . . . In his dissent, however, Justice Lambert disputed the constitutionality of a statute "which has as its only standard the subjective requirement of 'best interest of the child'" adding that "mere improvement in quality of life is not a compelling state interest and is insufficient to justify invasion of constitutional rights."

Id. at 583.

Case Preview

Troxel v. Granville

This case involved an unmarried couple with two children. After the relationship ended, the father moved in with his parents. He saw his children on a regular basis, with the visits often taking place at his parents' home. About two years after the separation, the father committed suicide. The grandparents continued to visit with the children. The mother then decided to limit the visits, and the grandparents sued for increased access to their granddaughters.

As you read *Troxel v. Granville*, look for the following:

1. Why did the Washington Supreme Court believe the visitation statute was unconstitutional under the federal Constitution?
2. What are the fundamental rights of parents that the U.S. Supreme Court addresses?
3. What role did the burden of proof play in the Court's ruling?

Troxel v. Granville
530 U.S. 57 (2000)

Justice O'CONNOR announced the judgment of the Court and delivered an opinion, in which THE CHIEF JUSTICE, Justice GINSBURG, and Justice BREYER join.

Section 26.10.160(3) of the Revised Code of Washington permits "[a]ny person" to petition a superior court for visitation rights "at any time," and authorizes that court to grant such visitation rights whenever "visitation may serve the best interest of the child." Petitioners Jenifer and Gary Troxel petitioned a Washington Superior Court for the right to visit their grandchildren, Isabelle and Natalie Troxel. Respondent Tommie Granville, the mother of Isabelle and Natalie, opposed the petition. The case ultimately reached the Washington Supreme Court, which held that §26.10.160(3) unconstitutionally interferes with the fundamental right of parents to rear their children.

Tommie Granville and Brad Troxel shared a relationship that ended in June 1991. The two never married, but they had two daughters, Isabelle and Natalie. Jenifer and Gary Troxel are Brad's parents, and thus the paternal grandparents of Isabelle and Natalie. After Tommie and Brad separated in 1991, Brad lived with his parents and regularly brought his daughters to his parents' home for weekend visitation. Brad committed suicide in May 1993. Although the Troxels at first continued to see Isabelle and Natalie on a regular basis after their son's death, Tommie Granville informed the Troxels in October 1993 that she wished to limit their visitation with her daughters to one short visit per month.

In December 1993, the Troxels commenced the present action by filing . . . a petition to obtain visitation rights with Isabelle and Natalie. . . . At trial, the Troxels requested two weekends of overnight visitation per month and two weeks of visitation each summer. Granville did not oppose visitation altogether, but instead asked the court to order one day of visitation per month with no overnight stay. In 1995, the Superior Court issued an oral ruling and entered a visitation decree ordering visitation one weekend per month, one week during the summer, and four hours on both of the petitioning grandparents' birthdays.

Granville appealed, during which time she married Kelly Wynn. Before addressing the merits of Granville's appeal, the Washington Court of Appeals remanded the case to the Superior Court for entry of written findings of fact and conclusions of law. On remand, the Superior Court found that visitation was in Isabelle and Natalie's best interests:

> "The Petitioners [the Troxels] are part of a large, central, loving family, all located in this area, and the Petitioners can provide opportunities for the children in the areas of cousins and music.
>
> ". . . The court took into consideration all factors regarding the best interest of the children and considered all the testimony before it. The children would be benefitted from spending quality time with the Petitioners, provided that that time is balanced with time with the childrens' [sic] nuclear family. The court finds that the childrens' [sic] best interests are served by spending time with their mother and stepfather's other six children."

Approximately nine months after the Superior Court entered its order on remand, Granville's husband formally adopted Isabelle and Natalie.

The Washington Court of Appeals reversed the lower court's visitation order and dismissed the Troxels' petition for visitation, holding that nonparents lack standing to seek visitation under §26.10.160(3) unless a custody action is pending. In the Court of Appeals' view, that limitation on nonparental visitation actions was "consistent with the constitutional restrictions on state interference with parents' fundamental liberty interest in the care, custody, and management of their children." Having resolved the case on the statutory ground, however, the Court of Appeals did not expressly pass on Granville's constitutional challenge to the visitation statute. Id.

The Washington Supreme Court granted the Troxels' petition for review and, after consolidating their case with two other visitation cases, affirmed. The court disagreed with the Court of Appeals' decision on the statutory issue and found that the plain language of §26.10.160(3) gave the Troxels standing to seek visitation, irrespective of whether a custody action was pending. 137 Wash. 2d, at 12, 969 P. 2d, at 26-27. The Washington Supreme Court nevertheless agreed with the Court of Appeals' ultimate conclusion that the Troxels could not obtain visitation of Isabelle and Natalie pursuant to §26.10.160(3). The court rested its decision on the Federal Constitution, holding that §26.10.160(3) unconstitutionally infringes on the fundamental right of parents to rear their children. In the court's view, there were at least two problems with the nonparental visitation statute. First, according to the Washington Supreme Court, the Constitution permits a State to interfere with the right of parents to rear their children only to prevent harm or potential harm to a child. Section 26.10.160(3) fails that standard because it requires no threshold showing of harm. Id., at 15-20, 969 P. 2d, at 28-30. Second, by allowing "'any person' to petition for forced visitation of a child at 'any time' with the only requirement being that the visitation serve the best interest of the child," the Washington visitation statute sweeps too broadly. Id., at 20, 969 P. 2d, at 30. "It is not within the province of the state to make significant decisions concerning the custody of children merely because it could make a 'better' decision." The Washington Supreme Court held that "[p]arents have a right to limit visitation of their children with third persons," and that between parents and judges, "the parents should be the ones to choose whether to expose their children to certain people or ideas."

We granted certiorari, 527 U. S. 1069 (1999), and now affirm the judgment.

The demographic changes of the past century make it difficult to speak of an average American family. The composition of families varies greatly from household to household. While many children may have two married parents and grandparents who visit regularly, many other children are raised in single-parent households. In 1996, children living with only one parent accounted for 28 percent of all children under age 18 in the United States. Understandably, in these single-parent households, persons outside the nuclear family are called upon with increasing frequency to assist in the everyday tasks of child rearing. In many cases, grandparents play an important role. For example, in 1998, approximately 4 million children — or 5.6 percent of all children under age 18 — lived in the household of their grandparents.

The nationwide enactment of nonparental visitation statutes is assuredly due, in some part, to the States' recognition of these changing realities of the American family. Because grandparents and other relatives undertake duties of a parental nature in many households, States have sought to ensure the welfare of the children therein by protecting the relationships those children form with such third parties. The States' nonparental visitation statutes are further supported by a recognition, which varies from State to State, that children should have the opportunity to benefit from relationships with statutorily specified persons — for example, their grandparents. The extension of statutory rights in this area to persons other than a child's parents, however, comes with an obvious cost. For example, the State's recognition of an independent third-party interest in a child can place a substantial burden on the traditional parent-child relationship. . . .

The Fourteenth Amendment provides that no State shall "deprive any person of life, liberty, or property, without due process of law." We have long recognized that the Amendment's Due Process Clause, like its Fifth Amendment counterpart, "guarantees more than fair process." . . . The Clause also includes a substantive component that "provides heightened protection against government interference with certain fundamental rights and liberty interests."

The liberty interest at issue in this case — the interest of parents in the care, custody, and control of their children — is perhaps the oldest of the fundamental liberty interests recognized by this Court. More than 75 years ago, in *Meyer v. Nebraska*, 262 U.S. 390, 399, 401 (1923), we held that the "liberty" protected by the Due Process Clause includes the right of parents to "establish a home and bring up children" and "to control the education of their own." Two years later, in *Pierce v. Society of Sisters*, 268 U.S. 510, 534-535 (1925), we again held that the "liberty of parents and guardians" includes the right "to direct the upbringing and education of children under their control." We explained in *Pierce* that "[t]he child is not the mere creature of the State; those who nurture him and direct his destiny have the right, coupled with the high duty, to recognize and prepare him for additional obligations." Id., at 535. We returned to the subject in *Prince v. Massachusetts*, 321 U.S. 158 (1944), and again confirmed that there is a constitutional dimension to the right of parents to direct the upbringing of their children. "It is cardinal with us that the custody, care and nurture of the child reside first in the parents, whose primary function and freedom include preparation for obligations the state can neither supply nor hinder." Id., at 166.

In subsequent cases also, we have recognized the fundamental right of parents to make decisions concerning the care, custody, and control of their children. See, e.g., *Stanley v. Illinois*, 405 U.S. 645, 651 (1972) ("It is plain that the interest of a parent in the companionship, care, custody, and management of his or her children 'come[s] to this Court with a momentum for respect lacking when appeal is made to liberties which derive merely from shifting economic arrangements'" (citation omitted)); *Wisconsin v. Yoder*, 406 U.S. 205, 232 (1972) ("The history and culture of Western civilization reflect a strong tradition of parental concern for the nurture and upbringing of their children. This primary role of the parents in the upbringing of their children is now established beyond debate as an enduring American tradition"); *Quilloin v. Walcott*, 434 U.S. 246, 255 (1978) ("We have recognized on numerous occasions that the relationship between parent and child is constitutionally protected"); *Parham v. J.R.*, 442 U.S. 584, 602 (1979) ("Our jurisprudence historically has reflected Western civilization concepts of the family as a unit with broad parental authority over minor children. Our cases have consistently followed that course"); *Santosky v. Kramer*, 455 U.S. 745, 753 (1982) (discussing "[t]he fundamental liberty interest of natural parents in the care, custody, and management of their child"); *Glucksberg*, supra, at 720 ("In a long line of cases, we have held that, in addition to the specific freedoms protected by the Bill of Rights, the 'liberty' specially protected by the Due Process Clause includes the righ[t] . . . to direct the education and upbringing of one's children" (citing *Meyer* and *Pierce*)). In light of this extensive precedent, it cannot now be doubted that the Due Process Clause of the Fourteenth Amendment protects the fundamental right of parents to make decisions concerning the care, custody, and control of their children.

Section 26.10.160(3), as applied to Granville and her family in this case, unconstitutionally infringes on that fundamental parental right. The Washington nonparental visitation statute is breathtakingly broad. According to the statute's text, "*[a]ny person* may petition the court for visitation rights *at any time*," and the court may grant such visitation rights whenever "visitation may *serve the best interest of the child*." §26.10.160(3) (emphases added). That language effectively permits any third party seeking visitation to subject any decision by a parent concerning visitation of the parent's children to state-court review. Once the visitation petition has been filed in court and the matter is placed before a judge, a parent's decision that visitation would not be in the child's best interest is accorded no deference. Section 26.10.160(3) contains no requirement that a court accord the parent's decision any presumption of validity or any weight whatsoever. Instead, the Washington statute places the best-interest determination solely in the hands of the judge. Should the judge disagree with the parent's estimation of the child's best interests, the judge's view necessarily prevails. Thus, in practical effect, in the State of Washington a court can disregard and overturn any decision by a fit custodial parent concerning visitation whenever a third party affected by the decision files a visitation petition, based solely on the judge's determination of the child's best interests.

. . .

Turning to the facts of this case, the record reveals that the Superior Court's order was based on precisely the type of mere disagreement we have just described and nothing more. . . .

First, the Troxels did not allege, and no court has found, that Granville was an unfit parent. That aspect of the case is important, for there is a presumption that fit parents act in the best interests of their children. As this Court explained in *Parham*:

> "[O]ur constitutional system long ago rejected any notion that a child is the mere creature of the State and, on the contrary, asserted that parents generally have the right, coupled with the high duty, to recognize and prepare [their children] for additional obligations. . . . The law's concept of the family rests on a presumption that parents possess what a child lacks in maturity, experience, and capacity for judgment required for making life's difficult decisions. More important, historically it has recognized that natural bonds of affection lead parents to act in the best interests of their children." 442 U.S., at 602.

Accordingly, so long as a parent adequately cares for his or her children (i.e., is fit), there will normally be no reason for the State to inject itself into the private realm of the family to further question the ability of that parent to make the best decisions concerning the rearing of that parent's children.

The problem here is not that the Washington Superior Court intervened, but that when it did so, it gave no special weight at all to Granville's determination of her daughters' best interests. More importantly, it appears that the Superior Court applied exactly the opposite presumption. . . .

The judge's comments suggest that he presumed the grandparents' request should be granted unless the children would be "impact[ed] adversely." In effect, the judge placed on Granville, the fit custodial parent, the burden of disproving that visitation would be in the best interest of her daughters. The judge reiterated moments later: "I think [visitation with the Troxels] would be in the best interest of the children and I haven't been shown it is not in [the] best interest of the children." Id., at 214.

The decisional framework employed by the Superior Court directly contravened the traditional presumption that a fit parent will act in the best interest of his or her child. . . . In an ideal world, parents might always seek to cultivate the bonds between grandparents and their grandchildren. Needless to say, however, our world is far from perfect, and in it the decision whether such an intergenerational relationship would be beneficial in any specific case is for the parent to make in the first instance. And, if a fit parent's decision of the kind at issue here becomes subject to judicial review, the court must accord at least some special weight to the parent's own determination.

Finally, we note that there is no allegation that Granville ever sought to cut off visitation entirely. Rather, the present dispute originated when Granville informed the Troxels that she would prefer to restrict their visitation with Isabelle and Natalie to one short visit per month and special holidays. In the Superior Court proceedings Granville did not oppose visitation but instead asked that the duration of any visitation order be shorter than that requested by the Troxels. While the Troxels requested two weekends per month and two full weeks in the summer, Granville asked the Superior Court to order only one day of visitation per month (with no overnight stay) and participation in the Granville family's holiday celebrations. . . . The Superior Court gave no weight to Granville's having assented to visitation even before the filing of any visitation petition or subsequent court intervention. The court instead rejected Granville's proposal and settled on a middle ground, ordering one weekend of visitation per month, one week in the summer, and time on both of the petitioning grandparents' birthdays.

Considered together with the Superior Court's reasons for awarding visitation to the Troxels, the combination of these factors demonstrates that the visitation order in this case was an unconstitutional infringement on Granville's fundamental right to make decisions concerning the care, custody, and control of her two daughters. Accordingly, we hold that §26.10.160(3), as applied in this case, is unconstitutional.

Post-Case Follow-Up

In deciding this case, the Court made clear that it was not declaring as a matter of constitutional principle that all third-party visitation laws are an impermissible encroachment on the rights of parents, or that harm must be established before allowing visitation over the wishes of a parent. Instead, the Court held only that, at a minimum, some "special weight" must be given to the stated preference of a fit parent. This result is far from definitive; as the current state of the law shows, the standard is subject to multiple interpretations. *Troxel* can be read broadly to require almost complete deference to parents, so long as they are fit; it also can be read more narrowly to, for example, place a burden on grandparents to show that something more than the child's best interest is needed in order to override the wishes of a fit parent.[24]

After *Troxel*, the Washington legislature amended its grandparent visitation statute in an attempt to try to make it constitutional. The statute was amended as set forth in Wash. Rev. Code §26.09.240 and as detailed below.

Troxel v. Granville: Real Life Applications

1. Assume you represent the maternal grandparents who wish to be awarded sole legal and physical custody of their five-year-old grandson. There is no dispute that the mother is unfit and does not have visitation with the children. The grandparents tell you that while the father is not unfit he does travel a lot for

---

[24]For a discussion of post-*Troxel* decisions, see Joan Catherine Bohl, That "Thorny" Issue, California Grandparent Visitation Law in the Wake of *Troxel v. Granville*, 36 Golden Gate U. L. Rev. 121 (2006); Kristine L. Roberts, *Troxel v. Granville* and the Courts' Reluctance to Declare Grandparent Visitation Statutes Unconstitutional, 41 Fam. Ct. Rev. 14 (2003).

his employment and therefore they do not believe he can provide a stable home environment for their grandson. What is a court likely to do?

2. The Washington statute was held unconstitutional as applied. Assume Washington's statute read instead as follows: "In deciding whether grandparents should be given visitation rights, the court shall give special weight to the legal parents' opinion of what serves their child's best interests and consider all relevant factors including the historical relationship, if any, between the child and the person seeking visitation." Would such a change in the statute pass constitutional muster?

3. The lower court in *Troxel* seemed to have presumed that the visitation request should be granted, thus placing "on Granville, the fit custodial parent, the burden of *disproving* that visitation would be in the best interest of her daughters." Assume the statute required the grandparents to show that the visitation was in their granddaughters' best interest. Assume you are a law clerk for a lower court judge in a case with the same facts as in *Troxel*, but the burden of proof is on the grandparents. The judge has asked your thoughts on the result. What would you tell the judge?

GRANDPARENTS' VISITATION RIGHTS

After *Troxel*, the Washington legislature amended its grandparent visitation statute in an attempt to try to make it constitutional. The statute was amended as follows:

Wash. Rev. Code §26.09.240. Visitation rights — Person other than parent — Grandparents' visitation rights.

(1) A person other than a parent may petition the court for visitation with a child at any time or may intervene in a pending dissolution, legal separation, or modification of parenting plan proceeding. A person other than a parent may not petition for visitation under this section unless the child's parent or parents have commenced an action under this chapter.

(2) A petition for visitation with a child by a person other than a parent must be filed in the county in which the child resides.

(3) A petition for visitation or a motion to intervene pursuant to this section shall be dismissed unless the petitioner or intervenor can demonstrate by clear and convincing evidence that a significant relationship exists with the child with whom visitation is sought. If the petition or motion is dismissed for failure to establish the existence of a significant relationship, the petitioner or intervenor shall be ordered to pay reasonable attorney's fees and costs to the parent, parents, other custodian, or representative of the child who responds to this petition or motion.

(4) The court may order visitation between the petitioner or intervenor and the child between whom a significant relationship exists upon a finding supported by the evidence that the visitation is in the child's best interests.

(5)(a) Visitation with a grandparent shall be presumed to be in the child's best interests when a significant relationship has been shown to exist. This presumption may be rebutted by a preponderance of evidence showing that visitation would endanger the child's physical, mental, or emotional health.

(b) If the court finds that reasonable visitation by a grandparent would be in the child's best interest except for hostilities that exist between the grandparent and one or both of the parents or person with whom the child lives, the court may set the matter for mediation under RCW 26.09.015.

(6) The court may consider the following factors when making a determination of the child's best interests:

(a) The strength of the relationship between the child and the petitioner;

(b) The relationship between each of the child's parents or the person with whom the child is residing and the petitioner;

(c) The nature and reason for either parent's objection to granting the petitioner visitation;

(d) The effect that granting visitation will have on the relationship between the child and the child's parents or the person with whom the child is residing;

(e) The residential time sharing arrangements between the parents;

(f) The good faith of the petitioner;

(g) Any criminal history or history of physical, emotional, or sexual abuse or neglect by the petitioner; and

(h) Any other factor relevant to the child's best interest.

(7) The restrictions of RCW 26.09.191 that apply to parents shall be applied to a petitioner or intervenor who is not a parent. The nature and extent of visitation, subject to these restrictions, is in the discretion of the court.

(8) The court may order an investigation and report concerning the proposed visitation or may appoint a guardian ad litem as provided in RCW 26.09.220.

(9) Visitation granted pursuant to this section shall be incorporated into the parenting plan for the child.

(10) The court may modify or terminate visitation rights granted pursuant to this section in any subsequent modification action upon a showing that the visitation is no longer in the best interest of the child.

However, this section was declared unconstitutional and invalid in 2005 by the Washington Supreme Court in *In re Parentage of C.A.M.A.*

2. Stepparents

Traditionally, if a second marriage ends in divorce, a stepparent has not been entitled to visitation rights or custody on the theory that his or her status derives from the marriage and thus lasts only as long as the marriage does. This result would, of course, be different if the stepparent had adopted the child because adoption creates a permanent parent-child relationship that is not dependent on the continued existence of the marriage. However, compelled by the awareness that stepparents often play a critical role in the lives of children, particularly when the noncustodial parent is uninvolved, the law has gradually begun to give stepparents greater rights upon marital dissolution in the absence of an adoptive relationship.

Some states have statutes that specifically allow a stepparent to seek visitation, and possibly also custodial, rights following a divorce. In other states, in the absence of a statute, courts have used a number of theories to extend parental-like rights to stepparents at the time of marital dissolution. For instance, a Michigan court extended parental status based on the concept of equitable parenthood and permitted a stepparent to be treated as a parent where

> (1) the husband and child mutually acknowledge a relationship as father and child, or the mother of the child has cooperated in the development of such a relationship over a time prior to the filing of the complaint for divorce, (2) the husband desires to have the rights afforded to a parent, and (3) the husband is willing to take on the responsibility of paying child support.

Atkinson v. Atkinson, 160 Mich. App. 601, 608-609, 408 N.W.2d 516, 519 (1987).

Other courts have extended rights to stepparents based on the doctrine of *in loco parentis*, which literally means standing in the place of the parent. Here, parental rights (and obligations, such as the duty to pay child support) may be extended to someone who has assumed the role of a parent over an extended period of time through the provision of sustained nurturance and support. To be *in loco parentis*, a stepparent must intend to participate in a child's life as a parent — a casual relationship will not give rise to this status. Although this doctrine has been used to extend a stepparent-child relationship beyond the end of a marriage of the stepparent to the child's parent, a limitation is that the relationship can be terminated at will by the stepparent (or the child), thus bringing the legal bond with its corresponding rights and duties to an end. (See the discussion below of the *in loco parentis* doctrine in the context of co-parent custody/visitation cases.)

In jurisdictions where stepparents can pursue post-dissolution claims, the approach tends to be more liberal where visitation, as distinct from custody, is at issue. Where there is a meaningful connection between a stepparent and child, a court may recognize the importance of continuing this bond beyond the marriage and allow visitation based on a best interest standard. However, in the wake of *Troxel*, some courts have been inclined to require more than proof of best interest, while others see a clear distinction between a grandparent and someone who has been in an actual parental role. Where custody is at issue, the traditional preference in favor of biological parents means that considerably more weight will be given to the expressed views of the legal parent. To prevail, a stepparent may need to establish unfitness or the presence of "extraordinary circumstances" that would merit depriving the biological parent of custody.

3. Co-Parents

Like heterosexual couples, many same-sex couples decide that they wish to share in the joys of raising a child together (for the purpose of our discussion, we will assume a lesbian couple, as the major reported cases to date have involved co-mothers, but the general legal principles would likely be applicable to gay male couples as well).[25] Accordingly, based on their mutual intent to share in the raising of a child, they agree that one partner will be inseminated and give birth to a child that they will then raise together.[26]

Although both women may regard themselves as the parents of their child, and the child may likewise regard both women as his or her mother, the law has not generally seen it this way. Despite the intent of the parties and their actual parenting arrangements, only the parent with the actual biological or adoptive connection to the child has traditionally been regarded as a legal parent, thus relegating the co-parent to the status of "legal stranger" to the child.

However, the law has begun to change in response to cases brought by co-parents who have sought to establish their right to maintain an ongoing relationship with the child they helped to raise when their relationship with the legal parent ends. Seeking to be recognized as legal parents, co-parents have used a number of legal theories, such as those discussed above in relationship to stepparents, to advance their claims. Regardless of which approach is used, at the heart of these cases is the desire to be recognized as a parent based on shared intent and the reality of her parental relationship with the child. Although, as discussed below, a growing number of jurisdictions have responded favorably to these claims, others have not been sympathetic and continue to regard a co-mother as a legal stranger based on her lack of a biological or adoptive connection to the child. Here, great weight is given to traditional understandings of parenthood and the right of exclusivity that this status confers.

Where denied parental status, a co-mother is then essentially treated as a third party. In jurisdictions where third-party standing is limited to a defined class of persons, such as grandparents and stepparents, she most likely will not be able to assert the right to an ongoing relationship with the child, regardless of the weight and nature of the bond between them. Typically relying on the constitutional principle in *Troxel* that legal parents have a fundamental interest in the "care, custody, and protection" of their child, which encompasses the right to determine who has access to him or her based upon the presumption that a fit parent will make decisions that promote his or her child's best interest, the court in these cases never even reaches the question of what impact the severing of the bond with the co-parent will have on the child.

---

[25]However, this may not always be the case. For example, different legal theories and principles might be applicable if a surrogate mother is also asserting parenting rights, or a dispute turned on the interpretation of a parenting statutes that distinguishes between the establishment of paternity and maternity, or only addresses the former.
[26]As discussed in Chapter 14, adoption is another option. Also, although an analysis of this situation is beyond the scope of this text, it is possible that one partner could provide the egg while the other carries the baby, thus giving both women a biological connection to the child.

In jurisdictions where standing is conferred on a broader group of persons — such as all persons with a significant relationship with a child — a co-parent may be able to assert her claim, although it is also possible that a court would refuse to recognize the relationship as significant. If able to meet this jurisdictional threshold, the dispute would still be characterized as one between a parent and a nonparent, and the parental preference would be triggered. Accordingly, unlike a divorcing mother and father, the parties would not begin on equal footing, and the co-parent would need to show something more than best interest to overcome the preference, such as that the child would suffer actual harm from the severing of the relationship, which is clearly a more difficult standard to meet.

However, courts in number of states have moved beyond this formalistic conception of what it means to be a family and have extended parental status and rights to co-parents. Additionally, although not our primary focus, it should be noted that once a co-parent is found to be a legal parent with the right to maintain a relationship with the child of her union following its dissolution, it is most likely that a court would also conclude that, like any separated parent, she is liable to pay child support. We now examine some of these approaches. Moreover, as discussed in Chapter 11, parenting presumptions based either upon state parentage laws or marriage are becoming increasingly available to same-sex couples.

De Facto Parent Status

In 1996, in the landmark case of *Holzman v. Knott*, the Supreme Court of Wisconsin became the first court to expressly extend de facto parent status to a same-sex co-parent. 193 Wis. 2d 649, 533 N.W.2d 419, *cert. denied*, 516 U.S. 976 (1995). Since then, a number of other states have followed suit. In *Holzman*, a same-sex couple decided to have and rear a child together. Following the termination of the relationship, Holzman sought visitation rights when her former partner, the child's biological mother, refused to allow her to see the child. Rejecting the assertion that a biological parent has a constitutionally protected right "to determine who shall visit her child," the court concluded that a party with a "parent-like" relationship with a child that has been disrupted by the termination of that relationship has standing to seek visitation (note that this case did not involve custody). To determine if there is a parent-like relationship, a party must be able to establish the following elements:

1. The legal parent consented to and fostered the relationship.
2. She resided with the child in the same household.
3. She assumed the responsibilities of parenthood.
4. She was in the parental role long enough to establish meaningful connection with the child.

Id. at 436-437. Since *Holzman*, courts adopting this approach have stressed the importance of a couple's mutual decision to have and raise a child together. Thus, for example, in a subsequent case from Massachusetts, the parties sent out joint birth announcements; embodied their parenting intent in a range of legal documents, including a co-parenting agreement; gave the child both of their last names; and fully shared parenting responsibilities. *E.N.O. v. L.M.M.*, 429 Mass. 824, 711 N.E.2d 886, *cert. denied*, 528 U.S. 1005 (1999). Similarly, in a case from Rhode Island in which the co-parent was granted visitation rights, the child was given a hyphenated name; the names of both parties appeared on the baptismal certificate and the birth announcements; and both parties fully participated in the raising of the child. *Rubano v. DiCenzo*, 759 A.2d 959 (R.I. 2000).

This element of mutual consent ensures that this status is not one that a court can impose on a legal parent; rather, recognition of a co-parent honors a reality that would not have existed but for the consent and active cooperation of that parent. It also means that a court cannot be said to be encroaching upon the exclusive domain of the legal parent. As explained by the New Jersey Supreme Court:

> This opinion should not be viewed as an incursion on the general right of a fit legal parent to raise his or her child without outside interference. What we have addressed here is . . . the volitional choice of a legal parent to cede a measure of a parental authority to a third party. . . . In such circumstances the legal parent has created a family with the third party and the child, and has invited the third party into the otherwise inviolable realm of family privacy.

V.C. v. M.J.B., 163 N.J. 200, 748 A.2d 539, 553 (2000). This requirement also responds to the concern raised by some that a nanny or babysitter could somehow end up as a de facto parent simply by participating in the life of a child. Further responding to this concern, some courts have stressed that the caretaking functions must be performed "for reasons primarily other than financial compensation. *E.N.O.*, 711 N.E.2d at 891, n.6.

Once recognized as a de facto parent, a party is no longer a "legal stranger." However, the question still remains as to whether a de facto parent stands on equal footing with her former partner, much as a divorcing husband and wife would. For instance, the New Jersey Supreme Court stated that "[o]nce a third party has been determined to be a psychological parent to a child, under the previously described standards, he or she stands in *parity* with the legal parent." *V.C.*, 748 A.2d at 554-555. The court went on to emphasize, however, that "parity" does not require equality of treatment, and that because ". . . in the search for self-knowledge, the child's interest in his or her roots will emerge," if "the evidence concerning the child's best interests (as between a legal parent and psychological parent) is in equipoise," custody should be awarded to the legal parent.

In contrast, in a more recent co-parent custody case, the Supreme Court of Washington, in rejecting the biological mother's claim that such a determination interfered with her fundamental rights as a parent, concluded that once a parent is determined to be a de facto parent she stands in "legal parity" with the biological parent. In light of its conclusion that the two parents occupy "equivalent parental positions," the court thus concluded that a de facto parent likewise has a "fundamental liberty interest" in the "care, custody, and control" of the parties' child. *Carvin v. Britain (In re Parentage of L.B.)*, 155 Wash. 2d 679, 122 P.3d 151, 178 (2005), *cert. denied*, 12 S. Ct. 2021 (2006). UPA, Article 7, §703 (2000) (amended 2002).

Chapter Summary

- Historically, fathers had an absolute right to the custody of their children. With industrialization, the rights of fathers yielded to the tender years presumption, which assumed that mothers were the best caretakers of young children.
- Currently, most state statutes use a best interest of the child standard. At least in principle, this is a child-centered, gender-neutral approach to resolving custody disputes.
- Where parental conduct or lifestyle is at issue, most jurisdictions employ the nexus approach and require proof of harm. However, this standard has been criticized for its lack of predictability and objective criteria.
- Custody has both a legal and a physical component; either may be awarded on a sole or a joint basis. Although there has been an increased focus on shared custody, this approach has been subject to criticism, especially in cases involving a history of domestic violence.
- A noncustodial parent is presumptively entitled to visitation unless there is a risk of harm to the child. To facilitate post-divorce parenting, there has been an increased focus on parenting plans and parenting education.
- Custody and visitation disputes have increasingly involved claims by "third parties," most notably grandparents, stepparents, and co-parents.

Applying the Rules

1. Max Murphy seeks your legal advice concerning a request to change custody of his minor children. He informs you that he and his ex-wife divorced four years ago. The children are now 12 and 8. He is concerned because the mother has recently started cohabiting with a man she is not married to and who he believes regularly smokes cigarettes in the house and around the children. He would like to know if he has grounds to modify custody based upon this information. What do you tell Mr. Murphy?

2. Alice and Steve Mayes are in the process of getting a divorce. During the marriage they adopted a child, Ana, from Russia, which is where Alice's parents are from. Steve is not of Russian descent. Alice has sought your legal advice because she would like to be the primary physical custodian of Ana because she believes it is more important for Ana to spend extended time with her so she can teach Ana about her Russian heritage. Alice would like to know what role the child's cultural/racial heritage should play in what Alice is sure to be a custody dispute. What are the benefits of giving weight to this factor? What are the potential risks?

3. Assume you are an appeals court judge in Florida and that the *Palmore* case is back before the court. This time, assume that the father returned to court and

won custody of his daughter, whom we'll call Carrie, based on the following facts. Carrie is now school-aged and has been subjected to taunting and harassment. This has been very upsetting to Carrie. She has been experiencing difficulty eating and sleeping and cries every morning about having to go to school. The mother has filed an appeal with your court. As a judge, decide whether the trial court decision should be affirmed or reversed, and write an opinion explaining your decision.

4. Janis Blakely has come to your office. She informs you that three years ago she filed a petition for dissolution of marriage and requested sole physical custody of her two young boys who at that time were 4 and 2. Father objected and requested joint legal custody and physical custody. The court ultimately awarded joint legal custody but gave Mother primary physical custody with Father having visitation one day a week for dinner and every other weekend from Friday evening until return to Mother's home or school on Monday morning. The parties equally divide the holidays. A year ago Janis remarried. Father also has remarried. She would like to relocate with the children out of state where she has family and her new husband has received an offer for a more lucrative job. The statute in your state provides that the primary consideration for relocation of the children out of state is whether the relocation will be in the children's best interest.

   a. Under such a standard, what do you tell Janis about her ability to relocate?
   b. Assume you file the petition to relocate for Janis and the judge appoints a custody evaluator to determine whether the move is in the children's best interest. The custody evaluator recommended that Mother not be permitted to move the boys to the other state because it will put a further strain on the boys' tenuous relationship with their father and that there is no evidence that Mother will be supportive of continuing a relationship with father. What would you recommend that Janis do after receiving the report from the custody evaluator?
   c. Assume that the court, after receiving the report, orders that primary physical custody be granted to Father in the event Mother moves. Do you have grounds for an appeal? If so, what are they? If not, explain why.
   d. Would it make a difference if Mother was relocating out of state 200 miles away versus 2,000 miles away? What about whether Mother is relocating close to an airport in a major metropolitan area versus a rural area?

5. You are an associate in a law firm. One of the senior partners has just advised you that she is preparing a presentation on the myriad of ways in which the law has responded to the parenting claims of same-sex co-parents. Starting with the traditional approach, explain what you see as the strengths and weaknesses of each approach.

Family Law in Practice

1. Locate the custody provisions of your state's divorce statute and answer the following questions:
   - Have any specific guidelines for determining best interest been adopted by statute or judicial decision?
   - Based on the guidelines or key court decisions, what factors are to be considered when determining custody?
   - Is domestic violence a factor to be considered? If so, how?
   - Is joint custody a permissible option? If yes, is there a presumption in favor of joint custody? Can it be ordered over the objection of a parent?

2. Assume you are working in a law firm, and the supervising partner has asked for your assistance in a custody relocation dispute in which your firm is representing the father. The father is seeking to prevent his former wife, who is the custodial parent, and children from moving out of state to another state that is about 350 miles away. Assume that the children are ages 5 and 7, that the father visits with them regularly and has a good relationship with both children, and that money is not a significant concern. The attorney has asked you to prepare an in-house legal memorandum in which you analyze the relevant statutory section, if any, and controlling case law in your state on this issue.

3. You need to prepare the first draft of a parenting plan for a divorce case you are working on. You represent the wife and are concerned that the parties will not be able to effectively carry out the joint custody arrangement that they want. You need a very detailed plan that at a minimum covers the allocation of time and responsibilities, how decisions are to be made, and a process for resolving any disputes that come up. The plan needs to be drafted with particular care so that it facilitates the intended custodial arrangement. Following are the relevant facts:
   - The parties have agreed to share physical and legal custody of their daughter, Melinda, age 4.
   - Both parents work full time, although the mother's schedule is more flexible, and she tends to work shorter hours than the father; however, she travels about once a month.
   - The parties want to try to make this arrangement work, but communication is tense and has gotten worse since the father has begun living with his new girlfriend.
   - The parties live in the same town.
   - The mother worries that the father is too strict and rigid in relationship to Melinda, and the father worries that the mother is too permissive and sets no rules.

   (Note: If the courts in your state have a standard parenting plan form, you should use this form for the assignment. If there is no standard form, be sure

to research your state statutes to determine what provisions must be included in the parenting plan.)

4. Assume you are a clerk for a trial judge who is facing a case that raises a new issue in your jurisdiction. He will be deciding a lesbian co-parenting case next week, and would like to know what the law from other jurisdictions says about this issue. For now, he would like you to concentrate on the various arguments on the merits and ignore the procedural issues. In short, focus on the arguments in favor of and against recognizing the co-parent as a legal parent and not on issues such as standing, jurisdiction, and the like.

5. Assume you are representing a mother who would like to argue at trial that she should have primary physical custody of her three children. Develop a list of interview questions to ask the client to determine that she has been the primary caretaker of the three children.

6. Determine if there is a required parenting program in your state. What is the requirement? When must it be taken? Can it be taken online or must it be taken in person?

7. Research your state law to determine if parenting coordinators may be appointed to help parents resolve parenting disputes. If you have a state law, identify the state law and the scope of a parenting coordinator's authority. If your state does not have a law that permits parenting coordinators, is there another mechanism the courts use to help parties resolve parenting disputes that arise after a parenting plan is in place?

Child Support

Child support is the recognition that both parents are responsible for the expenses incurred in raising a child. Generally, the support is based upon a number of factors, including the time spent with each parent, the income of each parent, and the extraordinary expenses that are required for the child. Determining the basis and amount of support is the subject of this chapter.

In the 1970s, the issue of child support came under intense public scrutiny. Studies documented that in almost half of the families with an absent parent, no child support was awarded, and where awarded, amounts were generally inadequate.[1] Moreover, where orders *were* entered, there was a high rate of non-compliance. Census data consistently showed that slightly less than 50 percent of custodial parents received the full amount of child support they were entitled to, while almost 30 percent received nothing. Joseph I. Lieberman, Child Support in America: Practical Advice for Negotiating and Collecting a Fair Settlement 11 (1988).

In 1974, hoping to force absent parents to become financially responsible and thereby reduce federal welfare expenditures, Congress passed the Child Support Enforcement and Establishment of Paternity Act of 1974, which added **Title IV-D** to the Social Security Act. Since 1974, Congress has amended Title IV-D multiple times and passed other child support legislation intended to strengthen the ability of both states and Tribes and Tribal organizations to establish and collect child support awards in a timely and efficient manner.

Key Concepts

- Federal and state agencies for establishing and enforcing child support systems
- Child support guidelines
- Enforcement of child support obligations
- Modifications of support awards
- Tax implications relating to child support

---

[1] Highlighting the problem in a dramatic way, one study showed that two-thirds of noncustodial fathers in Denver paid more in monthly car payments than in child support payments. *See* Lucy Yee, What Really Happens in Child Support Cases: An Empirical Study of Establishment and Enforcement of Child Support Orders in the Denver District Court, 57 Denv. L.J. 21 (1979).

A. HISTORICAL OVERVIEW

According to English common law, fathers had a moral but not a legal duty to support their children; mothers had neither. In contrast, in this country, most states adopted the view that even in the absence of a specific statute, fathers owed their children a legal duty of support, and mothers had a support duty to the extent that fathers were unable to fulfill theirs. A father's obligation was enforceable through the common law doctrine of necessaries, which allowed wives and children to pledge a husband's/father's credit to purchase necessaries that he had failed to provide.

Eventually, this paternal duty was embodied in a variety of statutes. Civil liability was imposed through family responsibility or family expense statutes. Family responsibility statutes essentially required fathers (or other relatives) to support their children so they did not become a public burden; family expense statutes permitted the taking of parental property to satisfy debts incurred in meeting the family's needs. Nonsupport was also made a crime in all states.

B. THE ADMINISTRATIVE FRAMEWORK FOR THE ESTABLISHMENT AND ENFORCEMENT OF CHILD SUPPORT ORDERS

The Child Support Enforcement and Establishment of Paternity Act of 1974 ("Child Support Enforcement Act") established the federal Office of Child Support Enforcement (OCSE). The OCSE is located within the Administration for Children and Families (ACF) in the United States Department of Health and Human Services (HHS). OCSE is the national oversight agency with responsibility for helping states to develop, manage, and run their child support programs effectively and in accordance with federal law. A state that does not comply with federal law risks losing a percentage of its federal funding for the administration of its child support program. More recently, the OCSE inaugurated a Tribal IV-D Program, which provides direct funding to Indian Tribes and Tribal organizations for the administration of comprehensive Tribal IV-D child support programs.

In addition, the OCSE is responsible for operating the Federal Parent Locator Service (FPLS). The FPLS "is an assembly of systems operated by OCSE to assist states in locating noncustodial parents, putative fathers, and custodial parties for the establishment of paternity and child support obligations, as well as the enforcement and modification of orders for child support, custody, and visitation. It also identifies support orders or support cases involving the same parties in different States."[2]

---

[2]Federal Parent Locator Service, http://www.acf.hhs.gov/programs/css/resource/federal-parent-locator-service-information-for-families (accessed June 8, 2016).

1. At the State Level: The IV-D Agency

The Child Support Enforcement Act required each state to develop a comprehensive child support program and to designate a single state agency — often referred to as a **IV-D agency** — to administer the program. IV-D agencies must provide the following five basic services to custodial parents:

- assistance in locating absent parents;
- establishment of child support awards;
- periodic review of awards;
- enforcement of support awards; and
- where necessary, the establishment of paternity

Before looking at these components of the child support system, it is important to look at how custodial parents access the services of a IV-D agency. As will become clear, the process differs depending on whether or not the parent is a recipient of public assistance through TANF (Temporary Aid to Needy Families), the federal block grant program that provides time-limited support to low-income families.

2. Eligibility for IV-D Services

A custodial parent who applies for TANF benefits is automatically referred to a IV-D agency for child support services. In order to receive benefits, the parent must agree to assign his or her right to child support to the state, and must also agree to cooperate with the state in its effort to establish paternity, where necessary, and obtain support, unless he or she can establish good cause for noncooperation, such as the fear of abuse.[3] With the assignment, the noncustodial parent's support obligation runs to the state rather than to the custodial parent because the state will be paying support and essentially seeking reimbursement from the noncustodial parent.

Once support is collected on behalf of a family receiving public assistance, federal law provides the state with several distribution options. A state can keep all of the collected funds in order to reimburse itself (and the federal government) for assistance

Temporary Aid for Needy Families

Aid to Families with Dependent Children
SSA History Museum & Archives

At the federal level, there was a growing awareness that many women and children were being forced to turn to public assistance, namely, Aid to Families with Dependent Children (AFDC, more commonly referred to as "welfare"), because they were not receiving the child support they were entitled to. The AFDC program was begun in 1935 through an amendment to the Social Security Act to provide financial assistance to widows with minor children to enable them to keep their children with them. However, by the 1970s, the vast majority of families on AFDC required

---

[3]Regarding the good cause exception, see generally Aviva Nusbaum, The High Cost of Child Support in Rape Cases: Finding an Evidentiary Standard to Protect Mother and Child from Welfare's Cooperation Requirement, 82 Fordham L. Rev. 1131 (2013); Susan Notar and Vicki Turetsky, Models for Safe Child Support Enforcement, 8 Am. U. J. Gender Soc. Poly. & L. 657 (2000).

assistance because of paternal nonsupport rather than paternal death. In 1996, as part of a sweeping welfare reform act known as the Personal Responsibility and Work Opportunity Reconciliation Act (PRWORA), Congress abolished AFDC and replaced it with Transitional Assistance to Needy Families (TANF). Pub. L. No. 104-193 (1996).

payments made to the family. However, in some cases the agency may choose to "pass through" all of the collected funds to the family, or it can pass through a portion of the funds and retain the balance for reimbursement purposes. Although advocates for low-income families have encouraged states to adopt a "family-first" approach and pass through all of the collected support in order to help lift children out of poverty, few states have adopted this approach. Most either retain all of the collected funds, or pass through a limited amount, typically 50 or 100 dollars to the family.[4] If a state does pass through collected funds, it typically disregards this amount when determining the family's continued eligibility for public assistance.

IV-D agencies also must provide child support assistance to families who are not applying for or receiving public assistance. Today, in contrast to the early years of the IV-D program, most of the families who receive child support services are not on public assistance, although many are former welfare recipients. This represents a shift "from an emphasis on recouping federal funds to the current mission of ensuring the support and care of America's children, without regard to receipt of government assistance." Office of Child Support Enforcement, for Attorneys in Child Support Enforcement, ch. 3 (3d ed. 2002), http://www.acf.hhs.gov/sites/default/files/ocse/ncjfcj20bench20cards1.pdf. A parent in this category must complete an application requesting IV-D services and may be charged a nominal fee. Because public funds are not involved, the use of a IV-D agency is optional; there is no assignment of support rights or a cooperation requirement, and all collected support payments go directly to the custodial parent. (Private child support agencies are discussed below.)

3. Locating Absent Parents

A major barrier to obtaining and enforcing child support orders is that many noncustodial parents cannot be located, and some try to conceal their identity to avoid paying child support. To address this problem, the Child Support Enforcement Act established the **Federal Parent Locator Service** (FPLS), which is operated by the OCSE, and required each state IV-D agency to establish its own parent locator service.

If a custodial parent does not know where the other parent is, he or she can request assistance from the state parent locator service. The locator service will check the records of other state agencies, such as the registry of motor vehicles or department of revenue, to see if it can locate the absent parent; credit-reporting agencies are also an important source of information. The locator service must

---

[4] *See* Paul Legler and Vicki Turetsky, More Child Support Dollars to Kids: Using New State Flexibility in Child Support Pass-Through and Distribution Rules to Benefit Government and Families (2006), Center for Law and Social Policy, www.clasp.org/admin/site/publications/files/0305.pdf (accessed June 8, 2016).

also search the State Case Registry, a database with information regarding all state support cases, and the State Directory of New Hires, a database containing information submitted by employers containing information about all new hires, to determine if there is a match. If the parent cannot be located within the state, and there is cause to believe the parent is in another state, the parent locator service in the second state must initiate a search as described here.

If the parent still cannot be located, the state locator service can ask the FPLS to assist in the search. Requests for federal assistance must come from a IV-D agency; individuals cannot file a direct request for federal assistance. Information needed to track down a parent can be obtained from both internal and external data sources. Internal to the FPLS is the Federal Case Registry of Child Support Orders (FCR), a comprehensive database containing information on all U.S. child support cases, and the National Directory of New Hires, a database including information about all new hires nationwide and persons who have applied for unemployment. Additionally, the FPLS can conduct an external search through the databases of other federal agencies, such as the Internal Revenue Service or the Social Security Administration. (See Section D, on enforcement, below for more information on these databases.)

Although the increased focus on the centralization and exchange of information facilitates the child support collection process, it also raises concerns about the privacy rights of individual family members. Of particular concern is the need to "ensure that the databases are secure enough so that abusers are unable to penetrate their safeguards to locate abused women and children." Notar and Turetsky, *supra* note 3, at 698. Accordingly, federal law contains multiple safeguards to protect against the unauthorized use or disclosure of confidential information gathered by IV-D agencies. Additional layers of protection are required in cases involving domestic violence, such as the inclusion of a domestic violence indicator or flag on an at-risk individual's file to restrict disclosure of any information that might jeopardize that person's safety.

C. CHILD SUPPORT GUIDELINES

To address the problem of inadequate and inconsistent awards, federal law requires each state to adopt child support guidelines. The guidelines must provide specific numeric criteria for the computation of support awards, and calculations must result in a presumptively correct support amount. Deviations from the guideline amount are permitted, but only where justifiable based on the circumstances of the case. Some states have opted for a guideline approach that enumerates specific factors that a decision must consider when determining if a deviation is warranted, while others have opted for a more general approach.

Guidelines are controlling with respect to both temporary and "permanent" child support awards. In this regard, it should be noted that the term "permanent" does not mean forever, but rather serves to distinguish awards that are entered at the time of divorce from those that are entered during the pendency of the case and are thus interim in nature. The guidelines also control in cases in which the parents reach agreement on the support amount. To guard against the risk that a parent might bargain away support rights in exchange for something else of value, most commonly custody, any deviation from the presumptive amount must be justified to the court or reviewing agency.

1. Guideline Formulas

Although federal law requires states to adopt child support guidelines, it left the job of developing the actual guidelines up to the states. In developing their guidelines, most states have adopted the percentage-of-income model, while a minority of states employ an income-shares model. However, even within these two models, "there are variants . . . used by different states." Sanford L. Braver, Ira Mark Ellman, and Robert J. MacCoun, Public Intuitions About Fair Child Support Allocations: Converging Evidence for a "Fair Shares" Rule, 20 Psychol. Pub. Poly. & L. 146, 147 (2014). Accordingly:

> Some states in each group base the support amount on gross parental income, and other use net (after-tax) parental income. States within each group differ in whether, and how, they adjust the base support amount to account for things like health care expenses, child care costs, or the allocation of parenting time between the parents.

Id. However, despite these differences, the essential approach to determining the basic support amount is stable within each system, thus permitting a discussion of how this amount is typically calculated. After considering these approaches, we also take a look at a hybrid approach that a handful of states employ, which is often referred to as the "Melson formula" after Judge Elwood F. Melson, Jr., of the Delaware Family Court.

The Percentage of Income Model

The **percentage of income approach** (or fixed percentage approach) sets the support amount as a fixed percentage of the noncustodial parent's income. Usually, the only relevant variable is the number of children in the household, although some states permit consideration of other factors, such as shared custody arrangements. Thus, for example, the support percentage might be set at 25 percent of the noncustodial parent's income for one child; at 30 percent for two children; and at 34 percent for three children. See Exhibit 6.1 for a sample worksheet for calculating percentage of income.

The advantage of this model is its simplicity. However, by not building in consideration of multiple factors, the results may be inequitable. For example, a custodial parent who is employed part time or at home with young children would get the same amount of support as a custodial parent who is employed at a well-paying job. On the other hand, this problem may be mitigated by way of permissible deviations from the basic amount or the ability to adjust for extraordinary expenses (both are discussed below).

EXHIBIT 6.1 **Child Support Worksheet (Percentage of Income Model)**

Effective as of 7/22/2008   State of Tennessee - Department of Human Services   3/14/2016 - 9:34 AM
Child Support Worksheet

Part I. Identification

		PRP	ARP	SPLIT

Indicate the status
of each parent or
caretaker by placing
an "X" in the
appropriate column

Name of Mother:
Name of Father:
Name of non-parent Caretaker:
TCSES case #:
Docket #:
Court name:

Name(s) of Child(ren)	Date of Birth	Days with Mother	Days with Father	Days with Caretaker

Part II. Adjusted Gross Income

			Mother \ Column A	Father \ Column B	Nonparent Caretaker \ Column C
	1	Monthly Gross Income	$	$	
	1a	Federal benefit for child	+	+	
Use Credit Worksheet	1b	Self-employment tax paid	-	-	
to calculate line items	1c	Subtotal	0.00	0.00	
1d - 1e	1d	Credit for in-home children	- 0.00	- 0.00	
	1e	Credit for not-in-home children	- 0.00	- 0.00	
	2	Adjusted Gross Income (AGI)	$ 0.00	$ 0.00	
	2a	Combined Adjusted Gross Income	$0.00		
	3	Percentage Share of Income (PI)	0%	0%	

Part III. Parents' Share of BCSO

			Mother \ Column A	Father \ Column B	Nonparent Caretaker \ Column C
	4	BCSO allotted to primary parent's household	$ 0.00	$ 0.00	$ 0.00
	4a	Share of BCSO owed to primary parent	$ 0.00	$ 0.00	
	5	Each parent's average parenting time	N/A	N/A	
	6	Parenting time adjustment	$ N/A	$ N/A	
	7	Adjusted BCSO	$ 0.00	$ 0.00	

EXHIBIT 6.1   **(continued)**

Effective as of 7/22/2008   **State of Tennessee - Department of Human Services**   3/14/2016 - 9:34 AM
                                          Child Support Worksheet

Part IV. Additional Expenses

		Mother \ Column A	Father \ Column B	Nonparent Caretaker \ Column C
8a	Children's portion of health insurance premium	$	$	$
8b	Recurring uninsured medical expenses	$	$	$
8c	Work-related childcare	$	$	$
9	Total additional expenses	$ 0.00	$ 0.00	$ 0.00
10	Share of additional expenses owed	$ 0.00	$ 0.00	
11	Adjusted Support Obligation (ASO)	$ 0.00	$ 0.00	

Part V. Presumptive Child Support Order

		OBLIGATION	
12	Presumptive Child Support Order (PCSO)	$ 0.00	$ 0.00

* Enter the difference between the greater and smaller numbers from Line 11 except in non-parent caretaker situations

Low Income?   N   (N=15% Y=7.5%)
Current Order Flat %?   N   (N / Y)

Modification of Current Child Support Order

13a	Current child support order amount for the obligor parent	$	$
13b	Amount required for significant variance to exist	$ 0.00	$ 0.00
13c	Actual variance between current and presumptive child support orders	$ 0.00	$ 0.00

Part VI. Deviations and FCSO

Deviations must be substantiated by written findings in the Child Support Order

14	Deviations (Specify):	$	$
15	Final Child Support Order (FCSO)	$ 0.00	$ 0.00
16	FCSO adjusted for Federal benefit, Line 1a, Obligor's column.	$ 0.00	$ 0.00

Comments, Calculations, or Rebuttals to Schedule

Preparer's Use Only

Name: _____   Date: 3/14/2016
Title: _____

The Income Shares Model

The income shares approach is premised on the assumption that children are entitled to receive the same share of parental income that they would have had the family stayed together. To arrive at the support amount, the income of both parents is combined and a basic support obligation computed. See Exhibit 6.2. This obligation is then allocated between the parents in proportion to income, with the noncustodial parent paying his or her share in support payments and the custodial parent assumed to be paying his or her share in direct expenditures on the children.

Critics of this approach argue that it falls short in two ways that are particularly applicable in sole custody cases. First, it ignores the fact that following a divorce, the expenses of the custodial parent generally increase because he or she now must pay for services — such as baby-sitting, household cleaning, and repairs — to compensate for losing the contribution the other parent would have made to the household. Second, it discounts the large non-economic contribution the custodial parent makes to the well-being of the children. Another criticism is that "there are formidable conceptual and empirical difficulties in identifying what parents in intact families in fact spend on their children." Braver, Ellman, and MacCoun, *supra*, at 147-148.

The Melson Formula

Under the hybrid Melson approach, a noncustodial parent is first permitted to keep a minimum level of income for his or her essential needs. This is referred to as a self-support reserve. Then, until the basic needs of the children are met, the parent cannot retain income above this minimum level; it must be allocated to child support. Once these needs are provided for, a percentage of the remaining parental income is allocated to increasing the basic support amount, thus enabling the children to benefit from a higher standard of living.

Defining Income

Most guidelines define "income" broadly. All states include earned employment income in their definition,

The Melson Formula

The Melson formula was named after Judge Elwood F. Melson of the Delaware Family Court. It was explained in the Delaware case of *Dalton v. Clanton*, 559 A.2d 1197 (Del. 1989). These are the basic procedures performed in an application of the Melson formula:

Step 1: Determine Available Income of Each Parent. The Melson Formula starts with net income. After determining net income for each parent, a self-support reserve ("primary support allowance") is subtracted from each parent's income. This reserve represents the minimum amount.

Step 2: Determine Children's Primary Support Needs. The next step in applying the formula is to compute the primary support amount for each dependent. Like the self-support reserve, the primary support amount represents the minimum amount required to maintain a child at a subsistence level. . . . Work-related child care expenses are added to primary support as are extraordinary medical expenses. The child's primary support needs are pro-rated between the parents based upon available net income as determined in Step 1. . . .

Step 3: Determine Standard of Living Allowance (SOLA). After primary support obligations of each parent are calculated in Step 2, including obligations for child care expenses and extraordinary medical expenses, a percentage of remaining income is also allocated to support of the child. The standard of living allowance enables the child to benefit from the higher living standard of a parent. . . . If a parent has dependents other than the child for whom support is being sought, and such other dependents are not covered by a court order, primary support amounts for such dependents are deducted from obligor income available for the Standard of Living Allowance.

EXHIBIT 6.2 **Child Support Worksheet (Shared Income Model)**

NO. _____

Child Support Worksheet

_____)
Petitioner)
and)
_____)
Respondent)

	DOB:					
	Age:					
Youngest Grade Estimated:				Actual Grade:		
Presumptive Termination Date:			Calculate			
Number of Minor Children:			Children 12 or Over:			

Primary Residential Parent Is (X): ☐ Father ☐ Mother ☐ Equal

Father **Mother**

	Monthly	Annually	Hourly
Gross Monthly Income: Father:			
Mother:			

Court Ordered Spousal Maintenance (Paid) / Received: [Mandatory]

Court Ordered Child Support of Other Relationships (Paid) [Mandatory]

Custodian of F: ☐ M: ☐ Other Child(ren) Subject of Order [Mandatory]

Support of Other Natural or Adopted Children **Not** Ordered: [Discretionary]

Father's ☐ Other Child[ren] Deduction Of:

Mother's ☐ Other Child[ren] Deduction Of:

Adjusted Gross Income

Combined Adjusted Gross Income

Basic Child Support Obligation For Children:

Additions To Child Support Obligation:

Adjustment For _____ Children Over Age 12 at _10_ % [Discretionary]

Medical, Dental and Vision Insurance Paid By: [Mandatory]

Monthly Childcare Costs For _____ Child(ren) Paid By: [Discretionary]
Less: Federal Tax Credit Allowed To Custodian of 25%:

Extra Education Expenses Paid By: [Discretionary]

Extraordinary (Gifted or Handicapped) Child Expenses Paid By: [Discretionary]

Total Child Support Obligation

Each Parent's Proportionate Percentage of Combined Income

Each Parent's Proportionate Share of Total Support Obligation

Parenting Time Costs Adjustment [Mandatory]

Parenting Time Table _A_ For _____ Days At _____

Total Additions To Child Support Obligation From Above Paid By Each Parent

Preliminary Child Support Obligation

Adjustment For Essentially Equal Time With Each Parent

Self Support Reserve Test: Obligor's Adjusted Gross Income: $_____ [Discretionary]
Less Paid Arrearages Allowed: $ [Discretionary]
Less Self Support Reserve Amount: (903.00) 903.00
Self Support Reserve Test **Not** Applied (**X**): ☐ Max. C.S.

Final Child Support Obligation Payable By Obligor:

although treatment of sporadic income, such as that earned from occasional odd jobs or overtime, varies. In some states, sporadic income is excluded. In other states, it is averaged over time and added to regular earnings.

Most guidelines also recognize the concept of **imputed** (or **attributed**) **income**. Here, a parent who is voluntarily unemployed or underemployed may be treated as if he or she has income commensurate with his or her earning capacity, and support calculated based on this amount rather than on actual earnings. By attributing income to a parent and setting the support amount accordingly, a parent must find suitable employment or face sanctions for not meeting the support obligation. In some states, if a noncustodial parent remarries or cohabits and voluntarily stops working in reliance on the new partner's income, a portion of the household income will be attributed to that parent. In states where the income of the custodial parent is factored into the support equation, income may also be attributed to this parent where he or she is voluntarily under- or unemployed. However, most courts will not impute income if a parent has reduced his or her earnings due to child-related responsibilities, at least not until the child reaches a certain age — commonly age 6.

The ability to attribute income is important in situations where a parent deliberately reduces earnings in order to avoid a support obligation. However, what if a parent has reasons other than the avoidance of support for reducing his or her income? For example, take the situation of an attorney who after years of working in a major firm decides she is burned out and wants to open a small practice with a resulting loss of income. Should she be permitted to drastically reduce support payments? Is this fair to the children? On the other hand, is it fair to force a parent to remain in a particular career track by maintaining a support obligation based on earning potential? Another consideration that some courts take into account is whether the income reduction actually promotes the best interest of the child, such as where a parent cuts back on his or her work hours in order to spend more time with the child. *See generally* David W. Griffin, Earning Capacity and Imputing Income for Child Support Calculations: A Survey of Law and Outline of Practice Tips, 26 J. Am. Acad. Matrim. Law. 365 (2014).

Some states, either through guidelines or judicial decision, also permit income to be imputed to assets a party owns, such as jewelry or antiques, even if they are not income earning. The rationale for such a policy "is to discourage spouses from placing all of their assets into non-income yielding forms and thus shielding all of their assets from consideration in support." Laura W. Morgan, Imputing Income to Non-Income and Low-Income Earning Assets, 17 Am. J. Fam. L. 191 (2004).

The definition of *income* almost always includes investment earnings, rents, profit shares, dividends, annuities, and governmental benefits, such as Social Security retirement and unemployment benefits. Some states also include the value of non-income-producing assets — such as jewelry, antiques, and undeveloped real estate — within the meaning of the term "income."

Sherman v. Sherman

The parties were married on April 28, 1983, in Kansas City, Missouri. The parties had two children: Nicole Sherman, born on May 20, 1984; and Alicia Sherman, born on August 4, 1987. In August 2000, Husband filed a petition for dissolution of marriage, and Wife filed an answer and counter-petition for legal separation. Although the parties submitted worksheets on the correct amount of child support, the trial court rejected the worksheets and entered its own child support number based upon what the trial court believed was the correct amount.

As you read *Sherman v. Sherman*, look for the following:

1. What were the two points that Husband raised to object to the amount of child support ordered by the trial court?
2. Why did Wife claim that income should be imputed to Husband?
3. What factors did the court look to in determining whether income should be imputed to the husband?
4. Why does the court find that it is not able at this time to determine whether the trial court's decision that the child support pursuant to the worksheet is unjust and inappropriate for not being "sufficient to cover the reasonable needs of the children"?

Sherman v. Sherman
160 S.W.3d 381 (Mo. Ct. App. 2004)

Francis E. Sherman (Husband) appeals the judgment of the Circuit Court of Jackson County dissolving his marriage to the respondent, Janet A. Sherman (Wife), with respect to the court's award of child support and division of property.

Husband raises [two points on appeal related to child support]. In Point I, he claims that the trial court erred in awarding Wife child support, as calculated pursuant to the court's Form 14 worksheets, based, in part, on imputing gross monthly income to Husband of $1,000 for earnings from the family business, FNJ Maintenance Company (FNJ), because the imputation of income to Husband was not supported by substantial evidence. In Point II, Husband claims that the trial court erred in rebutting its presumed child support amounts (PCSAs) as being unjust and inappropriate for not being "sufficient to cover the reasonable needs of the children" and ordering him to pay $1,500 per month in child support because in doing so, the court failed to consider all relevant factors, as required by Rule 88.01.1.

. . .

During the marriage, Husband was employed by Carondelet Health Center and its predecessors (Carondelet). At the time of trial his annual gross income was $76,646.38. Wife was also employed at Carondelet during the marriage as a labor and delivery room nurse. However, after being diagnosed with multiple sclerosis in April of 1997, she was forced to resign in September of that same year. At the time of trial, as a result of her condition, she was receiving Social Security disability benefits of $940 per month and social security benefits for the children of $480 per month.

During the marriage, the parties started a family business, FNJ, which provided contract maintenance services for businesses. There was considerable testimony at trial concerning the amount of income, if any, that was still being generated by FNJ. Husband testified that, although FNJ had been profitable in the past, it was no longer a viable concern, having lost its last maintenance contract. Wife contended that Husband, using his best efforts, was capable of earning income from FNJ of $769 per month and requested that the court impute this amount.

The trial court entered its judgment of dissolution on February 22, 2002, dissolving the parties' marriage and awarding them joint legal and physical custody of the children. The trial court ordered Husband to pay Wife $1,500 per month in child support. In addition, Husband was ordered to pay 78% of all medical and dental expenses not reimbursed by insurance; to tithe a sufficient amount to cover Alicia's tuition expense at St. Thomas More Grade School; and to pay 78% of all costs, including tuition, associated with Nicole's attending Notre Dame de Sion High School.

. . .

With respect to child support, both parties submitted Form 14 [child support] worksheets as required, which the trial court rejected. The court prepared two Form 14s, using different maintenance credits for Husband, $935 and $185, based on the automatic reduction in maintenance that was ordered. In its Form 14s, the trial court imputed $1,000 in gross monthly income to Husband, which it found he was capable of earning from FNJ, which was awarded to him as marital property. Using the $935 maintenance credit, the trial court calculated the PCSA as being $1,003 per month, and using the $185 maintenance credit, it calculated the PCSA as being $1,102. The court then rebutted both amounts as being unjust and inappropriate, finding the correct amount of child support to be $1,500 per month. This appeal follows.

In Point I, Husband claims that the trial court erred in awarding Wife child support, as calculated pursuant to the court's own Form 14 worksheets, based, in part, on imputed gross monthly income to Husband of $1,000 for earnings from the family business, FNJ, because the imputation of income was not supported by substantial evidence. Specifically, he claims that the record did not support the imputation of income to him in that there was insufficient evidence from which the court could find that FNJ was, at the time of the hearing, a viable and profitable business from which Husband, exercising his best efforts, was capable of realizing income of, at least, $1,000 per month.

In calculating the PCSA, the trial court was required to determine each party's gross monthly income. In that regard, the trial court found that Husband's gross monthly income was $7,615 in both of its Form 14 worksheets, including $1,000 for the income the court found he was capable of earning from FNJ. However, as noted in the facts, Husband testified at trial that FNJ was defunct and had no income. He testified further that the company's sole remaining service contract had been terminated as of June 30, 2001; that he had not sought any other contracts; and that he had no intention of continuing the business in that it was no longer viable as a profitable enterprise due to increased labor costs and competition, and because he was tired of the business. Although Wife only requested an imputation of income to Husband of $769 per month, which according to Wife's testimony was based on Husband's income from FNJ in 2000, the trial court, in calculating the PCSA, imputed income to him from FNJ of $1,000 per month. Husband claims that the evidence was insufficient to support this imputation of income.

It has long been recognized in the law that a parent will not be permitted to escape the responsibility to support the parent's children by deliberately limiting his or her work to reduce income. *Williams v. Williams*, 55 S.W.3d 405, 414 (Mo. App. W.D. 2001). To avoid such a situation, the trial court may impute income to the parent in determining the court's child support award, based on what the parent could earn by using his or her best efforts.

. . .

To impute income to a parent in determining an award of child support, there must be evidence in the record to support a finding that the parent has the capacity and opportunity to earn the income that is imputed. *Monnig v. Monnig*, 53 S.W.3d 241, 245 (Mo. App. W.D. 2001). Thus, Civil Procedure Form No. 14, Directions, Comments for Use and Examples for Completion of Form No. 14, Line 1: Gross Income, Comment H, provides:

> When determining whether to include imputed income and, if so, the amount to include in a parent's "gross income," a court or administrative agency shall consider all relevant factors, including:
>
> (1) The parent's probable earnings based on the parent's work history during the three years, or such time period as may be appropriate, immediately before the beginning of the proceeding and during any other relevant time periods;
> (2) The parent's occupational qualifications;
> (3) The parent's employment potential;
> (4) The available job opportunities in the community; and
> (5) Whether the parent is custodian of a child whose condition or circumstances make it appropriate that the parent not be required to seek employment outside the home.

These factors are not all-inclusive or exhaustive, they are simply factors to be considered along with any other relevant factors in determining if and what amount to impute. The question then, in determining whether to impute income to a parent in calculating the Form 14 PCSA, is whether, applying all relevant factors, including those factors found in Comment H that are relevant, there is evidence to support a finding that the parent is deliberately limiting his or her work to reduce income to avoid paying child support. *Davis v. Dep't of Soc. Servs., Div. of Child Support Enforcement*, 21 S.W.3d 140, 141 (Mo. App. W.D. 2000).

Husband was employed and working full time for Carondelet Health Systems, earning an annual salary of $76,647. However, Wife contended at trial that Husband was underemployed in that although he claimed that FNJ was no longer in operation, based on past history, Husband, using his best efforts, was capable of earning

$769 per month from the business, which Wife requested the trial court impute to Husband for purposes of child support. Wife also claimed FNJ was in fact still operating and earning money contrary to Husband's denial. It is not possible to know whether the trial court imputed income to Husband because he voluntarily limited his income by causing the termination of the Carondelet contract, because he did not pursue other contracts, or merely because FNJ was an ongoing business that was generating income. The court simply found that "[h]e also runs a business, FNJ. He is capable of earning at least $1,000 per month in this business." Hence, our analysis involves determining whether the evidence was sufficient to support the trial court's finding that Husband, using his best efforts, could earn, at least, $1,000 per month from operating FNJ. We must do so in light of all relevant factors, including the factors of Comment H.

The record establishes that for several years prior to the filing of the dissolution proceeding, FNJ's profitability was steadily declining. In that regard, FNJ's tax returns for the five preceding years reflect that FNJ had taxable income of:

$52,127 in 1995;
$43,552 in 1996;
$30,731 in 1997;
$26,425 in 1998;
$9,206 in 1999; and,
$9,238 in 2000.

Wife's request for imputation of income of $769 per month was based on FNJ's income in 2000, while the trial court's imputation of $1,000 per month was perhaps based on averaging FNJ's income for three years prior to the dissolution proceeding commencing—1998, 1999, and 2000 ($1,246.36 per month). Although the Form 14 imputation factors permit past earnings to be considered in determining whether the imputation of income is appropriate and in what amount, it is well settled that "[p]roof that a parent has previously made more money . . . is not alone a sufficient basis upon which to impute income at those levels." *Haden v. Riou,* 37 S.W.3d 854, 861 (Mo. App. W.D. 2001). There must also be evidence of available employment in the community for which the parent is not only qualified, but from which he could earn the amount sought to be imputed. *Silverstein v. Silverstein,* 943 S.W.2d 300, 302 (Mo. App. E.D. 1997).

For several years prior to the parties' dissolution proceeding, FNJ only had one contract—a contract to clean the Carondelet Health Campus, which consisted of the Carondelet Medical Building, St. Joseph Medical Mall, and St. Joseph Medical Building. The Carondelet service agreement was terminated effective June 30, 2001. . . .

The reason for the termination of the contract was not fully developed at trial but there was evidence that Husband did not re-bid the contract in 2001. . . .

Although there was considerable evidence to the contrary, "[t]he trial court is free to believe or disbelieve all, part or none of the testimony of any witness." *T.B.G. v. C.A.G.,* 772 S.W.2d 653, 654 (Mo. banc 1989). . . .

Husband also stated that he did not try to find other work for FNJ after the Carondelet contract was terminated. He testified that his reasons for not doing so were ". . . the market, the competition, and the headache. I'm tired of it." No evidence was presented to indicate there were other opportunities for FNJ or the probable income that could be earned from those opportunities. Taken together with the evidence that he did not re-bid the Carondelet contract, the trial court could have reasonably inferred that Husband voluntarily reduced his income.

Another theme played out by Wife during trial was that FNJ was still operating despite Husband's assertion to the contrary. Wife introduced documents from the company that processes FNJ's payroll to show that Husband was underreporting FNJ's income. The records indicated payroll activity between July 18, 2001, and October 31, 2001, a period after the termination of the Carondelet contract. The court could have used this evidence to support a finding that FNJ was still operating.

Again, we do not know the precise reason the court imputed income to Husband. Regardless, the evidence does not support the imputed amount of $1,000 a month. Historically, Husband has demonstrated an ability to earn income through his FNJ enterprise. But, the evidence in this somewhat unique case is insufficient to support the value imputed to his ability.

Apparently the trial court focused exclusively on FNJ's earnings for the previous three years to impute the $1,000 per month amount, perhaps, as indicated above, through some kind of averaging. However, Comment H to Form 14 makes it clear that the process to impute income is both backward looking and forward looking. In addition to a parent's work history, the court must consider future employment and income potential and the availability of earning opportunities in the community. Indeed, the first non-exclusive factor listed in Comment H directs the court to consider the parent's probable earnings based on his or her work history during the past three years — if such time period would be appropriate. In this case, it had been some three years prior to trial since FNJ had revenue anywhere near $1,000 a month. We also note that the earnings decline predates the filing of the petition for dissolution. Where income is relatively steady or historically fluctuates, averaging revenue from previous years might be a good predictor of future income. However, in this case it is not.

The most obvious conclusion we can reach from a review of FNJ's financial history is that its income was dramatically and consistently dropping, from a high of $52,127 in 1995, to $9,238 in 2000. To impute income of $12,000 per year to Husband requires an inference that the steep decline in FNJ's earnings would not only be halted but would be reversed. There is simply no evidence in the case from which to make this inference. We give great deference to a trial court's conclusions, but those conclusions still must be based upon substantial evidence. *Baker v. Baker,* 60 S.W.3d 19, 24 (Mo. App. E.D. 2001). "Although a court is permitted to impute the income to a parent that he or she earned in the past, an award of child support must always be supported by evidence of the parent's ability to pay.'" *Haden,* 37 S.W.3d at 861 (quoting *State ex rel. O.A. v. Anthony,* 947 S.W.2d 832, 835 (Mo. App. W.D. 1997)).

The purpose of imputation of income is to provide the appropriate level of support for the children. If a parent is deliberately limiting income to escape family responsibilities imputation encourages the parent to take advantage of income producing opportunities. The ultimate goal in preventing underemployment is to garner more assets for the family. However, imputing an amount that has no basis in the evidence or is beyond the capability of the parent does not legitimately achieve this goal.

Even assuming FNJ would have re-bid and secured the Carondelet contract, there is no substantial evidence from which to impute $1,000 a month in income to Husband. Although there was evidence of continued payroll activity, the amount of income, if any, generated by that activity was never established.

In summary, while there is evidence to support the conclusion that Husband voluntarily reduced his income, the record simply does not support the imputation of income in the amount of $1,000 per month as the trial court did. As the record now stands, it is impossible to determine what the appropriate amount of imputation would be, not knowing what FNJ might have realistically hoped to realize in income from available opportunities. Thus, because the imputation of income is critical to the trial court's mandatory calculation of the PCSA in the first step of the procedure for determining child support outlined in *Woolridge v. Woolridge,* 915 S.W.2d 372 (Mo. App. W.D. 1996) (the "Woolridge procedure"), we must reverse and remand the court's award for further proceedings to allow the trial court to reconsider the issue of imputation of income to Husband and compute the PCSA accordingly.

. . .

In Point II, Husband claims that the trial court erred in rebutting the PCSA as being unjust and inappropriate for not being "sufficient to cover the reasonable needs of the children" and ordering him to pay $1,500 per month in child support because in doing so, the court failed to consider all relevant factors, as required by Rule 88.01. Specifically, he claims that in rebutting the PCSA and ordering him to pay $1,500 a month in child support, the trial court was required, but failed, to consider his "financial resources and needs." Thus, the question presented concerns whether the trial court erroneously declared and applied the law with respect to the rebuttal step of the Woolridge procedure in ordering child support.

Logically, the resolution of the claim raised in this point is contingent on what the record would support as being Husband's financial resources with which to meet his child support obligation. And, of course, that cannot be determined until the imputation of income issue discussed in Point I is resolved on remand. Moreover, on remand, the resolution of the imputation issue may cause the trial court's child support award to ultimately change, which would directly bear on the issue of whether Husband has the financial means with which to satisfy the court's award, whatever it might be. Thus, the issue of whether Husband is financially able to pay the child support amount ordered is not ripe for our review.

. . .

CONCLUSION

The judgment of the trial court is affirmed in all respects except its award of child support, which is reversed, and the case is remanded for the trial court to reconsider the issue of imputation of income to Husband in calculating the PCSA and enter its child support order, all in accordance with the mandatory Woolridge procedure, Civil Procedure Form 14, Rule 88.01, §452.340, and this opinion. The court may take additional evidence on this issue.

Post-Case Follow-Up

The court in *Sherman v. Sherman* explains the general law in working with child support worksheets. While the worksheets are based on precise income amounts, a judge is free to disregard the worksheets if it can be proven that the income attributed to one party is not sufficient. Accordingly, even though Father had actual income that was used for the worksheet, the actual income may not be appropriate if a parent is working either below earning capacity or purposefully decreasing income in order to avoid paying higher child support. Courts are naturally concerned about the ability of a parent to manipulate income to the detriment of the minor children and of the custodial parent who may be receiving support.

Sherman v. Sherman: Real Life Applications

1. Keith and Mallory are in the process of getting a divorce. They have two minor children, ages 12 and 14. Since the youngest child began school, both parties have worked. However, recently Keith was laid off from his job due to budget cuts at his office. He has been searching for new employment but as of yet has not found anything. You represent Mallory. Mallory advises you that she is afraid that Keith is not searching enough for employment in order to avoid paying child support. Using the factors in the *Sherman* case, what advice would you give Mallory?

2. Assume the same facts as in Question 1 but that Keith left his employment voluntarily because he did not get along with his supervisor. Does your advice to Mallory change?

3. Debra and Du are in the process of getting a divorce. The parties have always lived a very lavish lifestyle primarily because Debra has a substantial trust fund that she uses to fund this lifestyle. A few months before she filed for divorce, Debra announced that she was no longer going to be using her trust funds to pay for expenses for the family and in fact ceased doing so. As a result, for the past few months the parties have lived solely on Du's income of $120,000 a month. Du asks you whether a court would disregard the child support worksheet since it does not seem reasonable that Debra can afford to pay more for the needs of the children but now is refusing to do so.

   a. What are the possible issues to consider in arguing that the basic child support worksheet should be disregarded?
   b. What arguments can you anticipate from Debra?
   c. Are there additional facts you would want to know before giving Du any advice?

Setting the Income Base

In addition to defining income, the relevant income base must be determined. Here, states have three basic choices: Support can be calculated based on gross income, adjusted gross income, or net income.

A considerable number of states use the **gross income** of the support obligor as the base for determining the support amount. The advantage of this approach is its simplicity and the fact that income cannot be manipulated because no deductions are taken before the support amount is calculated. On the other hand, gross income may not be an accurate measure of the income that is actually available to the support obligor.

Other states use an **adjusted gross income** base. To arrive at this amount, federal and state tax obligations, including Social Security, are deducted from gross earnings; non-voluntary payroll withholdings, such as union dues, retirement payments, as well as prior support obligations, also are usually deducted. Support is then based on this adjusted amount. Many believe this is the fairest approach, as it is a more accurate measure of the obligor's available income, although it does not permit the same kind of discretionary deductions that are allowable under the net income approach.

Still other states use a **net income** base, which allows for further deductions than the adjusted gross income base. In addition to the above-discussed kinds of adjustments, gross income is further reduced by, for example, voluntary payroll withholdings and job-related expenses before the support amount is calculated. The drawback of this approach is that it can be manipulated to show a reduced income, thus limiting the support base. On the other hand, it may be the most accurate indicator of actual available income.

2. Consideration of Specific Factors

Many child support guidelines include a number of factors that are to be taken into account when calculating the support amount. Others, most notably those employing a percentage of income approach, fix a basic amount varied only by a limited number of factors, such as the number of children, and then identify factors that will justify a deviation from the presumptive amount. Under either approach, commonly considered factors include

- income of the custodial parent;
- income of a new partner;
- income and resources of the child;
- multiple families;
- extraordinary expenses;
- health insurance; and
- custody and visitation arrangements.

Income of the Custodial Parent

With the exception of states using the percentage of income approach, most guidelines take the income of the custodial parent into account. Under the income shares approach, the income of both parents is combined to establish a basic support obligation. This amount is then allocated in proportion to income, and the noncustodial parent contributes his or her share in support payments. Another approach is to base the initial support calculation on the noncustodial parent's income and then reduce it to account for the custodial parent's income. States generally use a percentage reduction formula, rather than a dollar-for-dollar offset, as this could significantly reduce the amount of support available to the children. In some states, the custodial parent's income is disregarded until it reaches a threshold amount, and then only income above this threshold is considered.

Income of a New Partner

If either parent remarries or cohabits with a new partner, the question often arises as to how this partner income should be treated. As a general rule, this person has no direct support obligation to the children. Accordingly, few, if any, guidelines require inclusion of this income, and some specifically exclude it from consideration. However, because it may free up parental income, some states permit consideration of partner income as a basis for deviating from the presumptive guideline amount.

Income and Resources of the Child

Situations may arise where a minor child has independent resources; for example, he or she may receive governmental benefits, have income from a part-time job, or be the beneficiary of a trust or an inheritance. Most states do not build this into their support formulas or treat this as income to the custodial parent. Again, however, this income may be considered in determining if a deviation from guidelines is appropriate.

Multiple Families

A majority of people who are divorced remarry, and many then have children with their new spouses. Cases involving multiple families raise difficult questions about how (often scarce) resources can be fairly allocated between two households.[5]

A thorny question is whether a noncustodial parent should be allowed to reduce support to his or her first family upon establishing a new household, especially if he or she has additional children with this new partner. The traditional guideline approach puts "first families first" and does not permit reductions based on obligations to a subsequent family. The children from the first family are said to have a preexisting, hence superior, claim to the income, which the parent should have considered before starting a second family. However, based on the recognition that this approach may shortchange the children in the second family, who have no control over their place in the birth order, some states do permit support

---

[5]Although questions about multiple families usually arise in the course of a modification proceeding, the topic will be discussed here in keeping with the organizational format of many guidelines.

adjustments to account for obligations to subsequently born children. In some of these jurisdictions, the presence of subsequent children can also be used as a "shield" to defend against a request for an upward modification but not as a "sword" to request a downward modification.

Given the high failure rate of second marriages, another difficult issue is how support payments to a second family are to be calculated if this relationship also dissolves. If a parent is already paying child support under a court order to a prior family, most guidelines permit him or her to deduct this amount from income before the support order for the second family is calculated. This arguably favors the first family, as the income base available to them is larger; however, it is generally thought fair to protect this family's standard of living from fluctuations based on changes in the noncustodial parent's life over which the family has no control.[6]

Extraordinary Expenses

Guidelines are generally based on the assumption that the custodial parent is responsible for the ordinary costs of raising a child. A trickier question is whether she or he is also responsible for extraordinary expenses, or whether these should be dealt with separately. The term **extraordinary expense** has been defined as "any large, discrete, legitimate child-rearing expense that varies greatly from family to family or from child to child," as distinct from **ordinary expenses**, which tend to be "relatively small, predictable, and fairly consistent in families of the same size and income level." Sally F. Goldfarb, Child Support Guidelines: A Model for Fair Allocation of Child Care, Medical and Educational Expenses, 21 Fam. L.Q. 325, 331 (1987).This issue most often arises with respect to medical, child care, and educational expenses; as far as medical expenses are concerned, some guidelines specify that unreimbursed medical expenses in excess of an identified dollar amount per occurrence or calendar year are considered extraordinary expenses, while other guidelines identify the qualifying kinds of expenditures.

States use a number of approaches when dealing with extraordinary expenses, and within a particular state, the approach may vary depending on the category of expense. One common approach is to treat extraordinary expenses as an "add-on" to the basic support amount. The expense is prorated between the parents based on their income, and the noncustodial parent's share is added to the support amount. Another possibility is to permit deviations from the guideline amount to account for extraordinary expenses. For example, a judge might be permitted to increase the basic support amount if the custodial parent were faced with significant medical bills. This deviation would most likely be temporary in nature, and the guideline amount would be reinstated once the custodial parent was no longer facing these expenditures.

---

[6]*See generally* Adrienne Jennings Lockie, Multiple Families, Multiple Goals, Multiple Failures: The Need for "Limited Equalization" as a Theory of Child Support, 32 Harv. J.L. & Gender 109 (2009); Marianne Takas, U.S. Dept. of Health and Human Services, The Treatment of Multiple Family Cases Under State Child Support Guidelines (1991).

Health Insurance

Under federal law, state child support guidelines must address how parents will provide for the health care needs of their children through either health insurance coverage or cash medical support. Strengthening this mandate, all child support orders obtained through a state IV-D agency must include a medical support provision, and the agency must petition the court or administrative authority to include private health insurance coverage in the support order if it is available through one or both parents. If ordered, an employer-sponsored group health plan must provide coverage to the children named by the court (or a qualified administrative agency) in what is known as a **qualified medical child support order** (**QMCSO**).

With respect to the cost of coverage, some state guidelines allow the noncustodial parent to deduct the amount of the premium that is attributable to family coverage from gross income before calculating the support amount. Correspondingly, if the custodial parent is providing the insurance, a portion of the premium amount may be added to the basic support obligation. Another approach is to prorate the cost of the insurance between the parents based on their proportion of the total income, and then add the obligor's share to the support payments. Still other state guidelines consider the provision of health insurance as a ground for deviating from the presumptive support amount.

Custody and Visitation Arrangements

Support guidelines are generally based on the assumption that one parent has physical custody and the other has visitation rights, and visitation-related expenditures thus do not typically impact the support calculation. However, guidelines may permit adjustments to account for situations where a parent either spends a significant amount of time with a child or, conversely, hardly sees the child at all. Some guidelines spell out what time allocation will trigger a support reduction or a deviation from the presumptive amount, such as where the child spends more than a specified percentage of time or more than a certain number of overnights with the noncustodial parent, while other guidelines leave it to the decision maker to decide when a reduction is warranted. Although less frequently addressed by guidelines, non-visitation also may be the basis for an upward revision of support, as the custodial parent is assuming responsibility for visitation-associated expenses that the guidelines implicitly allocated to the noncustodial parent.

Financial Disclosure

A proper child support order cannot be calculated unless all relevant information has been disclosed. Accordingly, most, if not all, states require each party to make full financial disclosure to the other, usually by completing and filing a **financial affidavit**. Some also require the filing of supporting documents, such as tax returns and wage stubs. Additionally, to encourage attorneys to monitor and prevent the filing of fraudulent or inaccurate financial affidavits, some states require the affidavit to be signed by the lawyer as well as by the party submitting it.

Nonetheless, affidavits often do not provide a complete financial picture. The form may not call for full disclosure. Also, affidavits provide a snapshot of a party's current financial situation, but do not give a picture of his or her financial situation over time; for instance, an affidavit probably would not reveal a reduction in income or a transfer of assets or income that took place before the affidavit was completed, although subsequent changes may be revealed by updating requirements. Accordingly, a party may need to engage in other discovery to gain a more complete picture of the other side's financial situation.

Most guidelines leave the amount of the reduction to the discretion of the decision maker, although limits may be placed this discretion. Some judges take a cautious approach to these reductions based on the recognition that increased visitation does not necessarily result in substantial savings in child-related expenditures, as the custodial parent usually remains responsible for them.

Turning to custodial arrangements, it is often assumed that joint physical custody and split custody (where at least one child lives with each parent) will cancel the support obligation because both parents are providing for the children on an equal basis. This assumption, however, is not accurate.

First, although an arrangement may be identified as joint custody, the time allocation between the two households may not be equal. Second, even where it is equal, one parent, typically the primary caregiver during the marriage, often continues to assume greater parenting responsibilities, including making most of the purchases for the child. Thus, although both parents maintain a home for the child, the cost of raising the child is not borne equally. Another concern is that eliminating the support award will put the lower-income parent in a worse financial situation than that parent would have been in had he or she maintained sole custody and received the guideline amount.

Accordingly, although most guidelines permit consideration of these custodial arrangements in determining the support amount, they do not automatically trigger its elimination. One approach that is used is to compute a support obligation for each parent as if he or she had sole custody, offset the amounts, and order the parent with the greater obligation to pay the net amount to the other. Of course, support may be eliminated where parents earn close to the same amount and really share responsibility for raising the children.

D. ENFORCING THE CHILD SUPPORT OBLIGATION

In addition to addressing the problem of inadequate and inconsistent awards, federal child support laws also address the endemic problem of nonpayment by support obligors, which has resulted in a substantial national support arrearage. Seeking to rectify this problem, an elaborate network of interconnected databases has been created for the collection and exchange of child support–related information (discussed above in Locating Absent Parents).

Federal law requires states to adopt specific support enforcement methods. Going beyond these requirements, many states have adopted additional enforcement mechanisms such as lottery-winning intercepts or the use of the "Denver boot," "a steel, fifty-pound clamp that is attached to an automobile tire, effectively immobilizing the vehicle by preventing it from being driven until the offender responds to the legal system," which in this context would mean satisfaction of the support debt.[7] These are government enforcement mechanisms, often not available to private attorneys attempting to enforce child support awards on behalf of

---

[7]Drew A. Swank, Das Boot! A National Survey of Booting Programs' Impact on Child Support Compliance, 4 J.L. Fam. Stud. 265, 268 (2002).

their clients. Supplementing support collection efforts at the state level, the Federal Office of Child Support Enforcement administers a "federal offset program."

After considering key enforcement mechanisms, we turn to the enforcement process in interstate cases, followed by a discussion of the contested entry of private collection agencies into the child support arena. We conclude this section by looking at the continued availability of traditional state law remedies for the enforcement of child support orders.

1. Support Enforcement at the State Level Within the Cooperative Federal/State Framework

In this section, we consider a variety of remedies that federal law requires state government agencies to implement as part of their child support programs. These should be distinguished from the traditional enforcement remedies of criminal nonsupport and contempt actions discussed below.

Income Withholding

Under federal law, all child support orders must include a wage (or income) withholding provision that enables support payments to be directly deducted from a noncustodial parent's paycheck, in much the way taxes are withheld. Income also can be withheld from other forms of periodic payments, such as those received from a pension plan or government benefits. Where benefits are concerned, the general rule is that they must be a form of remuneration for employment, such as Social Security or unemployment benefits; needs-based benefits, such as Supplemental Security Income (SSI) payments, are not generally subject to withholding.

All child support orders must include a wage withholding provision that is to take place immediately, which means that a party does not have to wait for an arrearage to accrue before the withholding goes into effect. There are only two exceptions to the immediate withholding requirement: (1) when good cause to suspend it is established; and (2) when the parties enter into a written agreement providing for an alternative arrangement. Revised Program Instructions for Immediate Wage Withholding (1994) http://www.acf.hhs.gov/programs/css/resource/instructions-immediate-wage-withholding-orders-issued-not-being-enforced.

If the withholding is suspended, it must take effect once a federally specified arrearage has accrued. The noncustodial parent is entitled to notice that withholding is to commence. He or she may challenge the effectuation of the withholding, but may raise only mistakes of fact, such as a miscalculation of the arrearage. The validity of the underlying order cannot be challenged.

Employers are responsible for withholding the designated amount. An employer who fails to withhold child support will be responsible for the amount of support that should have been withheld. Also, fines can be levied against an employer who takes adverse action against an employee because of the withholding.

One problem has been that withholding does not keep up with a parent's job changes if the parent does not provide the information necessary to effectuate the withholding with his or her new employer. The new data-matching process addresses this problem. Information in the State or National Directory of New Hires can be matched with information in the Federal or State Case Registry, which enables the state to contact the new employer and direct it to begin withholding wages in accordance with the existing support order.

Liens

Under federal law, states must now have a law that creates a lien against the personal and real property of the noncustodial parent in the amount of unpaid support. This non-possessory interest operates as cloud against title, and prevents the noncustodial parent from selling, transferring, or borrowing against the property until the arrearage is paid.

Under federal law, the lien must arise as a matter of law, which means that it happens automatically, without any required action on the part of the custodial parent. However, under state law, the custodial parent may need to take certain steps to "perfect" the lien, such as recording a copy of the support order in the appropriate office or registry of public records, in order for it to have priority over other liens.

Credit Reporting

Under federal law, IV-D agencies must report to **credit-reporting** agencies the name of any parent whose support arrearage has reached a specific dollar amount. Before the report is made, the parent must be given notice and an opportunity to correct any inaccurate information. Although reporting does not result in an immediate transfer of income to the custodial parent, it is hoped that the threat of a negative credit report will serve as an inducement to support obligors who might otherwise be tempted to avoid paying child support.

Licenses

Federal law also requires states to adopt procedures by which they can withhold, suspend, or restrict an individual's professional or occupational license, driver's license, or recreational and sporting licenses due to the nonpayment of support. As with credit reporting, these sanctions do not directly transfer money to the custodial parent. Rather, it is hoped that the threat of losing or having restrictions placed on one's license will operate as a strong deterrent to the nonpayment of support.

2. The Federal Offset Program

The Federal Offset Program assists states to enforce child support obligations through a variety of remedies including the Federal Tax Refund Offset and the

Administrative Offsets

In addition to tax refund offsets, two other administrative offset remedies for child support enforcement exist. The first allows designated federal payments other than tax refunds to be offset. States have the option to participate in the offset program. Generally, the debt must be at least $25 that is owed and must be at least 30 days past due. This offset can be applied to federal payments that would be made to the obligor on a recurring basis or even on a nonrecurring payment. The second is the Multistate Financial Institution Data Match, which authorizes the federal OCSE to obtain and transfer the account information of delinquent parents to state child support agencies for enforcement purposes. For additional information, see the Overview of the Federal Offset Program (2014), http://www.acf.hhs.gov/programs/css/resource/overview-of-the-federal-offset-program.

Passport Denial Program. These are administered by OCSE in tandem with other federal (and state child support) agencies.

The Federal Tax Offset Program

Acting in tandem with the two federal agencies, the Internal Revenue Service (IRS) and the Financial Management Service (a bureau of the United States Department of the Treasury), as well as state child support agencies, the OCSE can intercept a federal tax refund owed to a noncustodial parent and use the funds to pay a past-due child support obligation. This remedy is available only in cases that are being handled through a state IV-D agency. In other words, a custodial parent acting on his or her own cannot request that delinquent support payments be collected through a tax intercept.

The noncustodial parent is entitled to receive a pre-offset notice that explains the process, including how to challenge the offset. Available arguments are limited. The parent can argue that no support is owed, that the arrearage calculation is incorrect, or that the refund is owed to his or her new spouse and therefore is not subject to the intercept, but the validity of the underlying order itself cannot be challenged.

The Passport Denial Program

Following certification by a state that a noncustodial parent owes at least $2,500 in back child support, the OCSE can submit that parent's name to the Department of State (DOS), which will then refuse to issue him or her a passport. If the parent already has a passport, DOS can revoke or otherwise restrict its use. A parent is not automatically released from the Passport Denial Program when the support arrearage drops below $2,500, as it is up to each state to determine the terms of release, with some requiring that the full arrearage be paid first. As with the tax intercept, this process can be initiated only by a state IV-D agency.

3. Interstate Cases

A significant number of child support cases involve parents who live in different states. The process of obtaining and enforcing support orders across state lines has been notoriously difficult due to the lack of coordination between states, the lack of access to information, and the low priority given to these cases, which has made them the bane of the child support system. To address these problems, federal law now requires the IV-D agency in each state to have a central registry that coordinates interstate cases. States are also required to give interstate cases the same priority that they give to cases involving their own residents. Moreover, as discussed here, the Uniform Interstate Family Support Act (UIFSA) and the Full Faith and Credit for Child Support Orders Act (FFCCSOA) are intended to address the ongoing enforcement problems raised by the potential for multiple and conflicting support orders in multistate cases.

The Uniform Interstate Family Support Act (UIFSA)

In 1992, the National Conference of Commissioners on Uniform State Laws (NCCUSL) adopted the Uniform Interstate Family Support Act (UIFSA) to replace earlier uniform acts that had failed to satisfactorily solve the problems of multiple and conflicting support orders. Subsequently, in 1996, the Personal Responsibility and Work Opportunity Reconciliation Act (known colloquially as the "welfare reform" law) required states to adopt and implement UIFSA by 1998 in order to remain eligible for federal child support funds. In 2000, the child support community asked the NCCUSL to review UIFSA, and in 2001, the NCCUSL approved a number of important amendments. To date, states have not been required to adopt these amendments, although many have done so. Accordingly, although UIFSA's "basic principles have remained constant,"[8] it is important to be aware that there is some variability between states depending upon whether or they have adopted the 2001 amendments or not.

EXCLUSIVE JURISDICTION PROVISION OF UIFSA

§205. Continuing, Exclusive Jurisdiction to Modify Child-Support Order

(a) A tribunal of this State that has issued a child-support order consistent with the law of this State has and shall exercise continuing, exclusive jurisdiction to modify its child-support order if the order is the controlling order and:

(1) at the time of the filing of a request for modification this State is the residence of the obligor, the individual obligee, or the child for whose benefit the support order is issued; or

(2) even if this State is not the residence of the obligor, the individual obligee, or the child for whose benefit the support order is issued, the parties consent in a record or in open court that the tribunal of this State may continue to exercise jurisdiction to modify its order.

(b) A tribunal of this State that has issued a child-support order consistent with the law of this State may not exercise its continuing, exclusive jurisdiction to modify the order if the order has been modified by a tribunal of another State pursuant to this [Act] or a law substantially similar to this [Act].

---

[8]John J. Sampson and Barry J. Brooks, Uniform Interstate Family Support Act (2001), with Prefatory Notes (with Still More Annotations), 36 Fam. L.Q. 329, 339 (2002). This discussion is based largely on the text of the Act and the Prefatory Notes.

(1) all of the parties who are individuals file consent in a record with the tribunal of this State that a tribunal of another State that has jurisdiction over at least one of the parties who is an individual or that is located in the State of residence of the child may modify the order and assume continuing, exclusive jurisdiction; or

(2) its order is not the controlling order.

(c) If a tribunal of another State which has issued a child-support order pursuant to this [the Uniform Interstate Family Support Act] or a law substantially similar to this [that Act] which modifies a child-support order of a tribunal of this State, tribunals of this State shall recognize the continuing, exclusive jurisdiction of the tribunal of the other State.

(d) A tribunal of this State that lacks continuing, exclusive jurisdiction to modify a child-support order may serve as an initiating tribunal to request a tribunal of another State to modify a support order issued in that State.

(e) A temporary support order issued ex parte or pending resolution of a jurisdictional conflict does not create continuing, exclusive jurisdiction in the issuing tribunal.

As the comments to this section state, this is probably the most crucial provision of the UIFSA because it creates the one-child-support-order-at-a-time principle that is a fundamental requirement of the UIFSA.

The primary purpose of UIFSA is to avoid the proliferation of competing orders in interstate cases with the resulting confusion regarding validity and enforceability. Accordingly, its "most revolutionary concept is its 'one-order' system," which effectively means that "once a support order is entered, that order controls the child support obligation regardless of whether the parents or child later moves to another state."[9] This then becomes the *Controlling Order* that must be honored by other states.

In order to facilitate the ability of a custodial parent to obtain support in his or her home state, URISA contains a very broad long-arm jurisdiction provision for the assertion of personal jurisdiction over the support obligor both with respect to the initial order and its modification and enforcement. This order can then be enforced directly in the state where the noncustodial parent is located. Enforcement can be done directly through the sending of the wage withholding to the employer who must then withhold wages as directed, unless it is contested by the obligor based on the narrowly permitted ground of "mistake of fact." Although these orders are frequently sent by the child support agency on behalf of the custodial parent, this is not required, and a parent or someone acting on his or her behalf, such as an attorney or private collection agency (see below), can also send the order.

The order can also be enforced by the appropriate court in the obligor's home state. This process is initiated by the registration of the order with the court.

---

[9]TEMPO, 2001 Revisions to Uniform Family Support Act (2001), http://www.acf.hhs.gov/programs/css/resource/2001-revisions-to-the-uniform-interstate-family-support-act-uifsa (accessed June 8, 2016).

Importantly, the registered order continues to be "the order of the issuing State."[10] Accordingly, the "role of the responding state is limited to enforcing that order except in the very limited circumstances where modification is permitted."[11]

Also very important to the creation and stability of a "one-order" system, the issuing state retains continuing exclusive jurisdiction to modify the order so long as either parent or the child remains in that state, or, if they have all moved, the parties consent to the continued jurisdiction of this state.[12] By vesting continuing authority in the original home state, UIFSA avoids the potential confusion of multiple orders. Only when all parties have left the issuing state, and have not consented to its continued jurisdiction, will modification jurisdiction shift to a new state. Thereafter, "the party petitioning for jurisdiction must be a nonresident of the responding State and must submit himself or herself to the forum state, which must have personal jurisdiction over the defendant."[13] The prefatory comments explain the rather puzzling "nonresident" rule as follows: "A colloquial short-hand summary of the principle is that ordinarily the movant for modification of a child support order must 'play an away game.'"[14]

The Full Faith and Credit for Child Support Orders Act

Reinforcing UIFSA's "one-order" system, the federal Full Faith and Credit for Child Support Orders Act (FFCCSOA) requires states to give "full faith and credit" to properly issued orders from other states.[15] FFCCSOA is intended to be consistent with UIFSA with regard to which order is controlling in the event of multiple orders. It also tracks UIFSA's modification rules based on the same concept of continuing exclusive jurisdiction in the home state until such time as both parties and the child have moved away, or the parties consent to continued jurisdiction.[16]

Hague Convention on Enforcement of Child Support

In 2007, the United States became a signatory of the new Hague Convention on the Enforcement of Child Support and Other Forms of Family Maintenance. As a result, UIFSA was amended in 2008 for the limited purpose of incorporating the principles of this international accord into state law. In large measure, "the amendment to the existing text was merely to add 'or a foreign country' to the directives about how a 'tribunal of this state' should deal with an order or another action of a 'state.'" John J. Sampson, Uniform Family Support Act (Last Amended or Revised in 2008), 43 Fam. L.Q. 75, 85 (2009).

In 2014, Congress approved legislation requiring all states to adopt the 2008 amendments to UIFSA as a condition of receiving continued federal support for their child support programs.

---

[10]Sampson and Brooks, *supra* note 8, at 345.
[11]*Id.*
[12]This consent exception was added by the 2001 amendments.
[13]Sampson and Brooks, *supra* note 8, at 346.
[14]*Id.*
[15]FFCCSOA can be found at 28 U.S.C. §1738B (2001).
[16]However, as discussed in Steven K. Berenson, Home Court Advantage Revisited: Interstate Modification of Child Support Orders Under UIFSA and FFCCSOA, 45 Gonz. L. Rev. 479 (2009/2010), a potential for conflict between the two Acts in light of the fact that "FFCCSOA permits a party to seek modification in their 'home court,' provided the court has personal jurisdiction over the non-moving party," while UIFSA requires this party to bring the action in the home state of the other party. *Id.* at 485.

4. Enforcement Under State Law Procedures

In addition to the remedies discussed above, a support award can also be enforced through traditional state remedies, such as a **criminal nonsupport** or a **contempt proceeding**. These remedies can be pursued by an individual or by a IV-D state agency on behalf of a custodial parent who is receiving its services.

Criminal Nonsupport

Most, if not all, states make the failure to support minor children a crime. Generally, nonsupport is classified as a misdemeanor. As in all criminal proceedings, the goal is punishment of the offender and vindication of the public interest. However, most states will suspend the sentence if the defendant agrees to pay support, which accomplishes the civil goal of providing support to the children. If the payment is not made following the suspension, the sentence will be re-imposed.

For a conviction, the failure to support must be willful. The state has the burden of proving willfulness by establishing that the defendant had the ability to provide support and deliberately failed to do so. Some states also require proof that the nonsupport left the children in "destitute or necessitous" circumstances. In these states, support from the custodial parent or a third party that keeps the children out of poverty may bar a conviction. The defendant is entitled to the procedural protections that apply in all criminal cases, including the privilege against self-incrimination. This may make proof of ability to pay difficult because the defendant cannot be forced to testify or to disclose adverse information through discovery.

For these reasons, criminal nonsupport actions generally are not the remedy of choice. However, they can be useful where the failure to pay support is flagrant or where the obligor is self-employed, thus precluding wage withholding. The willful failure to pay a past-due support obligation on behalf of a child in another state is now a federal crime. In addition, under the Deadbeat Parents Punishment Act of 1998, it is a felony to travel interstate (or internationally) in order to avoid an unpaid support order that meets specified durational and amount requirements. Child Support Recovery Act, *as amended by* "Deadbeat Parents Act," Pub. L. No. 105-187 §2, 112 Stat. 618 (1998) (codified at 118 U.S.C. §228).

Contempt

A contempt action can be brought where an obligor fails to comply with a court order of support. Contempt actions can be either civil or criminal in nature. A contempt action is usually not the remedy of choice, but it can be a useful supplemental remedy, especially where a parent is self-employed and thus not amenable to a wage withholding.

The purpose of a **civil contempt** proceeding is to secure compliance with the support order, and a jail sentence may be imposed for this purpose. In most states, the obligor must have the present ability to pay the ordered support amount in order to be found in civil contempt. If found in civil contempt, the obligor must be given the opportunity to avoid jail or, if jailed, to secure release by purging the contempt, usually by satisfying the terms of the underlying order.

The purpose of a **criminal contempt** proceeding is to punish the support obligor for violating the court order. In contrast to a civil contempt proceeding, if a jail sentence is imposed, the intended purpose is to punish the violation rather than to secure compliance with the order. Accordingly, unlike in a civil contempt, an obligor cannot purchase his or her freedom by complying with the order. In turn, this means that the present ability to pay is not a required element; rather, the state must prove ability to pay during the time of non-compliance.

5. Enforcement by Private Child Support Collection Agencies

Over the course of the past 15 years or so a new player has entered the child support enforcement field to help custodial parents collect child support that is owed to them, namely, the **for-profit child support collection agency**. These agencies promise to fill the existing gap in enforcement services that IV-D agencies seem unable to meet. Many in the child support field argue that this is an idea whose time has come — that we need to face the reality that despite considerable progress, IV-D agencies are not able to handle the high volume of existing support cases. *See* Laura W. Morgan, Private Attorney Access to Child Support Enforcement Tools: Recommendations of the Interstate Commission, 16 Am. J. Fam. L. 169 (2002).

Some have argued that if we are to solve the current support crises, these private agencies (as well as the private bar) need enhanced power and increased resources. To this end, a variety of legislative proposals have been introduced that would give these private entities access to the databases, the parent locator resources, and the enforcement tools, such as tax refund intercepts, of the IV-D agencies.

Yet many in the field are wary of these agencies and do not want to encourage their proliferation or their access to governmental databases and enforcement tools based on apprehensions that access to information may lead to breaches of privacy or to the potential misuse of highly confidential information. Concerns have also been raised about some of these agencies' business practices, particularly the fees they charge, which can be as high as 50 percent of the collected support, thus diverting funds intended for the support of children. Moreover, these fees often are demanded even if the money is ultimately collected and disbursed by the IV-D agencies. Drew A. Swank, Note from the Field: Child Support, Private Enforcement Companies, and the Law, 2002 Army Law. 57, 58.

Other criticized practices include contracts that are almost impossible to cancel, harassment of the support obligor, threats of arrest without proper authority, and the collection of fees from current, rather than past, support as required. *Id.*

E. THE MODIFICATION AND ADJUSTMENT OF SUPPORT AWARDS

Once a child support amount has been established, subsequent events may occur that warrant a change in the amount. Where this occurs, a parent may seek a modification of the support order (note that the requirements of UIFSA must be complied with in interstate cases). Additionally, states must implement a review and adjustment procedure for all support cases enforced through the IV-D agency.

1. Modification Based on Changed Circumstances

Child support orders are not generally considered final judgments and are subject to modification. However, as is the case with custody and spousal support, modification actions are not designed to give parents a second bite at the apple; that is, issues that have already been decided are not supposed to be relitigated.

Rather, consistent with principles of *res judicata*, the petitioner must show that there has been a change in circumstances that justifies an upward or downward revision of the support amount. Most, if not all, states also require that the change was not foreseeable at the time the order was entered. Support amounts agreed on by the parties in a separation agreement are also subject to modification, as the right to adequate support belongs to the child and cannot be bargained away by a parent. However, some courts give considerable weight to parties' agreements and impose a greater burden on the petitioner to prove that a modification is warranted.

Either party can seek a modification. Typically, a custodial parent who is seeking an upward revision looks to changes such as increased needs of the children, an increase in the other parent's income, remarriage of the noncustodial parent, or a decrease in his or her own income. Typically, a noncustodial parent who is seeking a downward revision looks to changes such as a decrease in his or her own income, responsibility for a second family, an increase in the custodial parent's income, remarriage of the custodial parent, or employment of the child. As with the initial determination, any modification to an existing order must comport with the applicable child support guidelines with respect to both what factors may be taken into consideration and any resulting changes in the support amount.

A particularly contentious question that can arise in a modification action is whether a noncustodial parent can seek a reduction in support payments if the custodial parent is interfering with his or her visitation rights. The absolute majority view is that visitation and support issues are independent variables and should not be linked. Exceptions to this policy of non-linkage may occur in extreme situations — for example, where a parent falsifies employment information to avoid paying support or a custodial parent hides a child to prevent visitation from taking place.

In addition to the above-mentioned types of change of circumstance grounds for a modification action, state guidelines typically include a modification provision authorizing a change in the amount of support when there is a significant difference between the current support and the presumptive guideline amount. This difference is usually expressed either as a dollar (e.g., a $50 difference) or a percentage (e.g., 15 percent difference) of the support amount.

2. The Review and Adjustment Procedure

Under federal law, states are required to implement procedures for the periodic review and, if appropriate, the adjustment of child support orders. The review must be conducted every three years if the custodial parent is receiving Transitional Aid to Needy Families. In other cases, the support agency will review the order at least every three years at the request of either parent without a parent having to show that there has been a substantial change in circumstances. A request for a review can be made at any time based on a substantial change in circumstances. Where the state's child support guidelines or changes in the cost of living justify a modification, a support order will be adjusted either upward or downward to account for the changes.

F. DURATION OF THE PARENTAL SUPPORT OBLIGATION

In general, a parent has an obligation to support his or her child until the child reaches 18 — the age of majority. In certain situations, however, the support obligation may be terminated before majority or extended beyond it. These durational issues are generally controlled by state law.

1. Termination of Support Prior to Majority

Support can be terminated prior to majority only under very limited circumstances, such as emancipation of the minor, death of the parent paying support, or the termination of parental rights. A custodial parent does not generally have the authority to agree to a termination of support because, again, the right of support belongs to the child not to the parent.

Emancipation

Emancipation extinguishes the reciprocal rights and obligations that exist between a parent and child and releases the child from the authority and control of his or her parents. The majority of states have enacted emancipation statutes. Although these laws vary quite a bit, most require proof that the minor is at least 16 years of age, living independently, and capable of managing his or her own affairs. Most also require proof that emancipation is in the minor's best interest. In some jurisdictions, an emancipation petition can be filed by either a minor or by parents. However, in order to protect minors from effectively being abandoned by their parents in cases of serious family discord, others only allow them to be filed by minors.

A minority of jurisdiction have not enacted an emancipation law. Instead, they rely on the common law doctrine of emancipation under which certain acts, most notably marriage and entry into the armed services, are regarded as creating a status that is incompatible with parental control and thus serve to emancipate the minor. In some states, a child who is living on his or her own and is self-supporting may also be considered emancipated.

As a general matter, once emancipated, a minor becomes a legal adult, with all of the legal rights and responsibilities that accompany this status. As a logical corollary, emancipation typically abrogates the duties and authority of a parent vis-à-vis the emancipated minor, including that of child support. However, some states recognize the doctrine of partial or limited emancipation according to which a minor is regarded as an adult for limited purposes only, such as medical decision making. In this context, the parent-child relationship, remains fully intact in all other contexts. Most importantly for present purposes, in situations where a minor is only emancipated for a particular purpose, the parental support obligation is likely to remain in full force and effect.

Case Preview

Diamond v. Diamond

Diamond v. Diamond arises from a New Mexico statute that provides that a minor may be emancipated from his or her parents "for one or more purposes." The issue before the New Mexico Supreme Court was whether a minor emancipated for one purpose was emancipated for all purposes or whether a parent, in this case the mother, had an obligation to continue to provide support for her minor daughter. Jhette Diamond (Daughter), then 16 years old, petitioned the district court in January 2007 for a declaration of emancipation. The daughter had left the mother Adrienne Diamond (Mother)'s home at age 13 and had been living with several different households since that time. In the emancipation order the trial court reserved for Daughter the right to receive financial support from Mother.

After additional hearings, the district court reaffirmed its prior ruling that emancipation does not necessarily cut off a minor's right to child support. Mother appealed, and the Court of Appeals agreed with Mother that Daughter cannot collect child support payments under the New Mexico law since a court issuing an emancipation order cannot pick and choose the purposes for which a child is emancipated. Daughter petitioned for review to the New Mexico Supreme Court.

As you read *Diamond v. Diamond*, look for the following:

1. What are the factors the court uses to determine emancipation?
2. Why does the court believe it is possible to be emancipated for some purposes and not others?
3. What impact did its interpretation of the law in other states have on the court?

Diamond v. Diamond
283 P.3d 260 (N.M. 2012)

. . .

The [New Mexico Emancipation] Act defines an emancipated minor as any person sixteen years of age or older who "has entered into a valid marriage, whether or not the marriage was terminated by dissolution," who "is on active duty with any of the armed forces of the United States of America," or who has received a declaration of emancipation pursuant to the Act. Section 32A-21-3. The Act sets forth three prerequisites to emancipation by judicial declaration. "Any person sixteen years of age or older may be declared an emancipated minor for one or more purposes enumerated in the [Act] if he is [1] willingly living separate and apart from his parents, guardian or custodian, [2] is managing his financial affairs and [3] the court finds it in the minor's best interest." Section 32A-21-4.

. . .

As for the legal effect of emancipation, under the Act

"[a]n emancipated minor shall be considered as being over the age of majority for one or more of the following purposes: A. consenting to medical, dental or psychiatric care without parental consent, knowledge or liability; B. his capacity to enter into a binding contract; C. his capacity to sue and be sued in his own name; D. his right to support by his parents; E. the rights of his parents to his earnings and to control him; F. establishing his own residence; G. buying or selling real property; H. ending vicarious liability of the minor's parents . . . or I. enrolling in any school or college.

III. STANDARD OF REVIEW

[¶24] "The setting of child support is within the trial court's discretion and is reviewed on appeal only for an abuse of that discretion." *Styka v. Styka*, 1999-NMCA-002, ¶8, 126 N.M. 515, 972 P.2d 16. This appeal, however, does not implicate the district court's discretion in awarding support to Daughter so much as its determination that the Act allows an emancipated minor to pursue child support. ". . . In interpreting a statute, the Court's "primary goal is to ascertain and give effect to the intent of the legislature." *Jolley v. AEGIS*, 2010-NMSC-029, ¶8, 148 N.M. 436, 237 P.3d 738 (internal quotation marks and citation omitted). In assessing intent, "we look first to the plain language of the statute, giving the words their ordinary meaning, unless the Legislature indicates a different one was intended." *Oldham v. Oldham*, 2011-NMSC-007, ¶10, 149 N.M. 215, 247 P.3d 736 (internal quotation marks and citation omitted). . . .

IV. DISCUSSION

A. *Plain Language and Legislative History of the Act*

1. *"One or More . . . Purposes"*

Emancipation confers on eligible minors some or all of "the rights and status of adults." In setting forth the nine possible legal effects of emancipation, the Act refers to "one or more of the [enumerated] purposes." Daughter interprets the Act to authorize a district court to "craft an order of emancipation to address only those purposes which meet the best interests of the child seeking emancipation," and asserts that there is nothing absurd about granting a minor many of the legal privileges of adulthood while in appropriate circumstances allowing that minor to pursue parental support. Mother in turn argues that where the Act refers to "one or more . . . purposes" of emancipation, the phrase should be interpreted to mean "all the purposes."

According to Mother, allowing a district court to decide the individual purposes for which a minor is emancipated would lead to an "absurd scenario" where the minor could be freed from parental control but prevented from, for instance, establishing his or her own residence. In Mother's view, loss of any entitlement to parental support therefore is a necessary consequence of emancipation, because "[t]here's no such thing as a limited emancipation."

The plain meaning of the phrase "one or more . . . purposes" is that a minor may be declared to be emancipated under the Act for a single enumerated purpose, for all nine enumerated purposes, or for any intermediate number of enumerated purposes. "As a rule of construction, the word 'or' should be given its normal disjunctive meaning unless the context of a statute demands otherwise," *Hale v. Basin Motor Co.*, 110 N.M. 314, 318, 795 P.2d 1006, 1010 (1990), or if "adherence to the literal use of the word leads to absurdity or contradiction," *State v. Block*, 2011-NMCA-101, ¶21, 150 N.M. 598, 263 P.3d 940. Our courts have employed this common-sense principle in a variety of statutory contexts. See generally *State v. Dunsmore*, 119 N.M. 431, 433, 891 P.2d 572, 574 (Ct. App. 1995) ("The use of the disjunctive 'or' indicates that the statute may be violated by any of the enumerated methods."); *State v. Tsosie*, 2011-NMCA-115, ¶27, 150 N.M. 754, 266 P.3d 34 (Where a statute offers a list of various alternative definitions for a particular term, "[t]he Legislature's use of the word 'or' indicates that any of the listed definitions" could apply.); *Schneider Nat'l, Inc. v. State Taxation & Revenue Dep't*, 2006-NMCA-128, ¶¶9-10, 140 N.M. 561, 144 P.3d 120 (The word "or," in a statute providing that a limitations period begins after "mailing or delivery," "indicate[s] that mailing and delivery are alternative acts."); see also *State v. Downey*, 2008-NMSC-061, ¶26, 145 N.M. 232, 195 P.3d 1244 ("The use of the disjunctive 'or' in Rule 11-702 permits a witness to be qualified under a wide variety of bases . . .").

The Act's reference to "one or more of the following purposes" for which emancipation may be granted cannot be viewed as haphazard or isolated. The Act employs this key phrase not only in enumerating the nine possible grounds for emancipation, Section 32A-21-5, but also in investing the district court with the authority to declare a minor to be emancipated, Section 32A-21-4 ("Any person sixteen years of age or older may be declared an emancipated minor for one or more of the purposes enumerated in the [Act]" if specified prerequisites are met.). The Act also directs a district court granting a minor's petition to "immediately issue a declaration of emancipation containing specific findings of fact and one or more purposes of the emancipation." Section 32A-21-7(D). This last reference to "one or more purposes" is especially significant, because there is no logical reason for requiring courts to identify the specific purposes for which emancipation is being granted if every emancipation automatically fulfills all of the enumerated purposes.

The history of the Act's passage thus provides further confirmation that the plain meaning of "one or more purposes" is consistent with the Legislature's intent. Contrary to the Court of Appeals' determination that the Act does not authorize partial emancipation, *Diamond*, 2011-NMCA-002, ¶24, 149 N.M. 133, 245 P.3d 578, we hold that the Act's directive that emancipation may be declared for "one or more purposes" expressly authorizes partial emancipation.

2. "Managing [One's] Own Financial Affairs"

The Act requires that a minor must be living independently and "managing his own financial affairs" in order to be emancipated. Section 32A-21-4. Mother argues that "in the context of [the Act], 'managing his financial affairs' is synonymous with being financially independent, self-supporting, self-sufficient . . . , it is axiomatic that to be emancipated you must be self-supporting and if you are self-supporting you are not in need of or entitled to support." Daughter responds that managing one's financial affairs is not the equivalent of total financial self-sufficiency. We agree with Daughter.

The Act does not define the phrase "managing [one's] financial affairs," but that term logically would include obtaining income and transacting for the necessities of life. Our caselaw usually employs the term in guardianship and conservatorship proceedings, where, for example, a court must find an adult "incapacitated and unable to manage an estate and financial affairs" in order to appoint a conservator for that person. *In re Conservatorship of Chisholm,* 1999-NMCA-025, ¶12, 126 N.M. 584, 973 P.2d 261. Here, the district court determined that Daughter had been living independently and that Daughter had paid for all of her expenses out of her own earnings since March 2005, with no support from Mother. Daughter sought emancipation, in part, to obtain health insurance and open a bank account, further evidence of her intent and capacity to manage her own affairs but for certain legal impediments of minority.

The Court of Appeals agreed with Mother and found the district court's interpretation of the Act "paradoxical," explaining that "a minor cannot be 'managing his own financial affairs' if he is receiving financial and other support from his parents." *Diamond,* 2011-NMCA-002, ¶23, 149 N.M. 133, 245 P.3d 578. We do not see management of one's financial affairs and entitlement to support as inherently contradictory. Certainly, in other proceedings courts routinely award support without any finding or implication that the recipient is incapable of managing his or her affairs. See generally *Mitchell v. Mitchell,* 104 N.M. 205, 214, 719 P.2d 432, 441 (Ct. App. 1986) (awarding spousal support based on circumstances of supporting spouse and recipient spouse).

The Act itself contemplates that an emancipated minor may receive public assistance: An emancipated minor "shall not be denied benefits from any public entitlement program which he may have been entitled in his own right prior to the declaration of emancipation." Section 32A-21-6. A minor entitled to public assistance is necessarily not entirely self-supporting, at least not after he or she begins to receive the assistance payments. Under the Court of Appeals' interpretation of the Act, Daughter would be managing her own financial affairs if she were receiving financial support from the State, but not if she were receiving support from Mother. . . . Finally, in the present case, the district court expressly did not emancipate Daughter with respect to her entitlement to support, so for that sole purpose she retained the status of minority. That determination explains why the district court set Daughter's eighteenth birthday or high school graduation, whichever occurred later, as the date terminating Mother's support obligation. Up until that moment, for support purposes only, Daughter remained a minor.

B. *Partial and Complete Emancipation in Other States*

Although we find ample support for our interpretation of the Act in its plain language and legislative intent, a brief review of several other states' emancipation statutes, illustrative rather than exhaustive, indicates a diversity in approach to defining the legal effects of emancipation. Some states have determined that emancipation should always entail a fixed rather than a flexible set of legal consequences. For example, in contrast to the Act's provision that emancipation may be ordered for "one or more purposes," California's emancipation statute directs that an emancipated minor "shall be considered as being an adult for the following purposes," Cal. Fam. Code Ann. §7050 (West 1992, operative Jan. 1, 1994), that is, for all of the seventeen purposes enumerated by the California statute, including "the minor's right to support by the minor's parents," id. §7050(a), the parent's rights to "the minor's earnings and to control the minor," id. §7050(b), and the minor's capacity to "establish [his or her] own residence," id. §7050(e)(15). California courts have recognized the California legislature's deliberate choice to create a form of statutory emancipation with the same set of legal consequences for each affected minor. . . .

Consistent with California's approach and in contrast to ours, Vermont law provides that an emancipation order "shall recognize the minor as an adult for *all purposes* that result from reaching the age of majority, including . . . terminating parental support and control of the minor and [parental] rights to the minor's income." Vt. Stat. Ann. tit. 12, §7156(a) (West 1995) (emphasis added), §7156(a)(6). Pennsylvania state law does not set forth a specific statutory mechanism for a minor to obtain a declaration of emancipation, but nonetheless expressly provides that "[a] court shall not order either or both parents to pay for the support of a child if the child is emancipated." 23 Pa. Cons. Stat. Ann. §4323(a) (West 1985).

Other states, while perhaps not favoring parental support for emancipated minors, do not foreclose it either. Under Nevada law, for example, an emancipation decree confers the right of majority for six enumerated purposes, including entering into contracts or incurring debts, Nev. Rev. Stat. §129.130(3)(a) (1987, as amended through 2003), obtaining medical care without parental consent, id. §129.130(3)(d), and establishing the minor's own residence, id. §129.130(3)(f), but not elimination of support from a parent. Whether to award support, however, is left to the discretion of the court considering the emancipation petition, with the default under the statute for support to cease upon emancipation: "Unless otherwise provided by the [emancipation] decree, the obligation of support otherwise owed a minor by his or her parent or guardian is terminated by the entry of the decree." Id.

On the other hand, New Mexico is far from the only state where a minor's emancipation does not presumptively extinguish a parent's support obligation. Montana's emancipation statute probably resembles New Mexico's most closely. If a Montana court grants a petition for emancipation, it must issue an order that "specifically set[s] forth the rights and responsibilities that are being conferred upon the youth[, which] may include but are not limited to one or more" of a list of six purposes. Mont. Code Ann. §41-1-503(2) (2009). Those purposes include the right to live in housing of the minor's choice, id. §41-1-503(2)(b), the right to enter into contracts and incur debts, id. §41-1-503(2)(d), the right to consent to medical care, id. §41-1-503(2)(e), and the right to "directly receive and expend money to which the youth is entitled and to conduct the youth's own financial affairs," id. §41-1-503(2)(c). The Montana statute, like ours, does not define emancipation to automatically end a parent's support obligation.

At least one state goes further than New Mexico by not merely permitting but mandating parental support for emancipated minors. Under Michigan's emancipation statute, a court may declare a minor emancipated "for the purposes of, but not limited to, all of the following [fourteen purposes]," Mich. Comp. Laws Ann. §722.4e(1) (West 1968, as amended through 1988, effective Mar. 30, 1989), a list that does not include child support. Instead, Michigan law explicitly provides that "[t]he parents of a minor emancipated by court order are jointly and severally obligated to support the minor," except that the parents are not liable for debt incurred by the minor during the period of emancipation, id. §722.4e(2).

The point of the foregoing review is to illustrate the wide variety of approaches states employ to determine what legal consequences emancipation should have, particularly with respect to the provision of child support. Our Legislature could easily have decided that emancipation ipso facto extinguishes a parent's support obligation to a child, an alternative that it initially considered and that some other states have adopted. Instead, the Legislature ultimately chose to confer authority on the district courts to determine in each particular case whether an emancipated minor is entitled to support.

C. Emancipation at Common Law

While our holding that the Act allows a district court to reserve a minor's right to financial support from a parent follows from the plain language of the Act, it is consistent with the treatment of emancipation under the common law. Historically, American courts recognized a "correlative" relationship between a parent's duty to support his or her minor child and the parent's entitlement to the child's services and earnings. 1 Homer H. Clark, Jr., The Law of Domestic Relations in the United States §9.3, at 548-49 (2d ed. 1987). Under this approach, the father [was] entitled to the services and earnings of his minor children, because he [was] bound to support and educate them. The right grows out of the obligation, and is correlative to it. When one ceases the other ceases also. The helplessness of the infant, demanding the tutelage and support of the father, in contemplation of law terminates in ordinary cases at twenty-one [then the age of majority], and the child becomes emancipated from parental control and entitled to his own earnings.

Emancipation developed largely to protect minors from claims against their wages asserted by their parents or by third parties. . . . A minor could only be emancipated through parental consent, although that consent could be implied as well as express. *Inhabitants of Lowell v. Inhabitants of Newport,* 66 Me. 78, 89 (1876). A parent's abandonment of a minor, or even oral expressions of an intent to abandon the minor, could constitute an implied consent to emancipation.

Courts have long recognized that common-law emancipation may be partial, that is, conferring some but not all of the aspects of adult status on the minor. See

Lufkin v. Harvey, 131 Minn. 238, 154 N.W. 1097, 1098 (1915) ("A minor may be emancipated for some purposes and not for others."). . . .

. . .

D. *Public Policy Considerations*

The Legislature's decision to allow district courts to determine the extent of an emancipated minor's rights and responsibilities also comports with our state's public policy. "In New Mexico, there is a strong tradition of protecting a child's best interests in a variety of circumstances." *Sanders v. Rosenberg,* 122 N.M. 692, 694, 930 P.2d 1144, 1146 (1996) (internal quotation marks and citation omitted); see also *Bustamento v. Analla,* 1 N.M. 255, 255 (N.M. Terr. 1857) (noting, in ruling on a custody dispute, that "[i]t is to the benefit and welfare of the infant to which the attention of the court ought principally to be directed"). Furthermore, "[i]t is well-settled law that when [a] case involves children, the trial court has broad authority to fashion its rulings in [the] best interests of the children." *Sanders,* 122 N.M. at 694, 930 P.2d at 1146 (internal quotation marks and citations omitted).

. . .

More specifically, the district courts are properly "invested with broad discretion and flexibility in determining an award of child support." *DeTevis v. Aragon,* 104 N.M. 793, 800, 727 P.2d 558, 565 (Ct. App. 1986) (citing *Henderson v. Lekvold,* 95 N.M. 288, 621 P.2d 505 (1980); *Spingola v. Spingola,* 91 N.M. 737, 580 P.2d 958 (1978)); see also *Fosmire v. Nicoleau,* 144 A.D.2d 8, 16, 536 N.Y.S.2d 492 (N.Y. App. Div. 1989) (In matters involving the protection of minor children, "the court must be allowed wide latitude and broad flexibility . . . because of the endless variety of human situations which can be presented in cases of this nature. There are no preordained answers and the result in any case will be totally dependent upon the unique facts involved therein.").

Giving effect to the plain meaning of the Act is consistent with our state's public policy favoring judicial determination of the best interests of the minor. A district court could, for example, where appropriate declare a minor emancipated for a single purpose, such as "consenting to medical, dental or psychiatric care without parental consent, knowledge or liability," Section 32A-21-5(A), or attending college, Section 32A-21-5(I). Similarly, a district court has the discretion to declare a minor emancipated for a greater number of purposes, or all of the purposes, set forth in the Act. The critical inquiry remains the best interests of the minor, Section 32A-21-4 and Section 32A-21-7(C), which the court determines on the basis of specific findings of fact, Section 32A-21-7(D). The mere possibility that a district court might abuse its discretion in declaring a minor emancipated for particular purposes does not provide a sufficient basis for reading words out of the Act.

V. CONCLUSION

The Act provides that emancipation may be declared for "one or more purposes," including the minor's right to support by his or her parents. . . . Because the Court of Appeals failed to give effect to that language, we reverse.

Post-Case Follow-Up

While some states view an emancipated minor as fully and completely separated from his or her parents for all purposes, the New Mexico legislature does not go that far. The court is persuaded by the fact that the plain use of the words used by the legislature "for one or more purposes" means that a minor can be emancipated for one purpose and not all purposes. Based upon this conclusion, the court could have simply stopped there. However, the court goes on to justify its decision under common law and public policy considerations, and drawing from the law of other states. Based upon these considerations, the court has no problem holding that Daughter may pursue her claim against Mother for support.

The court also explains that it is in the best interest of the minor child to permit a claim for support. The court uses the broad policy of the ability of a judge to fashion relief that is in the minor child's best interest to extend that ability to find a child emancipated for one purpose but not necessarily from support.

Diamond v. Diamond: Real Life Applications

1. Assume you represent Mother in *Diamond v. Diamond*. What might you have been able to argue to persuade the trial court in the first instance that you should not be responsible for support of Daughter once she was emancipated?

2. Assume the same facts as in *Diamond* but there was substantial evidence that Mother had provided support to Daughter up until the time she filed for emancipation and Daughter had not lived separate and apart from Mother prior to the petition for emancipation. Would these additional facts change the result?

3. You have been asked to represent Tanya, a 16-year-old who wants to be emancipated from her parents. She advises that she still wants the financial support of her parents, but she cannot live in the same household as them any longer because her parents want to move out of state and she would like to stay in state and continue at her same high school. She advises that her best friend's parents have offered for her to live at their house but she must be able to pay her own expenses. Tanya estimates that would be approximately $1,500 a month, which she does not have but wants her parents to pay for if she is emancipated. Based upon *Diamond v. Diamond*, what do you tell Tanya?

Parental Death

At common law, the death of a parent terminated the support obligation. This responsibility did not pass to the decedent's estate, although the estate was liable for arrearages that had accrued prior to death. Many states now have statutes that authorize a court to hold the parent's estate responsible for continued support payments unless the parties otherwise agreed in a separation agreement.

In the absence of a specific statute or separation agreement, many judges believe that they lack the authority to order post-death support, as this would upset the estate plan of the decedent who has a legal right to disinherit his or her children. According to this view, ordering such support would give greater rights to children of divorced parents compared to children of still-married parents. Other judges take a different view of the matter and may continue support following the death of the noncustodial parent. These judges give greater weight to providing for children than to protecting the stability of estate plans and the expectations of beneficiaries. This approach also recognizes that a noncustodial parent may be more likely to disinherit his or her children, thus creating a greater need for a remedy.

Adoption or Termination of Parental Rights

Where parental rights are extinguished through adoption or an involuntary termination proceeding, the parental support obligation is likewise extinguished. The only issue is identifying *when* the obligation ceases. The general rule is that this occurs upon the actual cessation of the parent-child relationship rather than upon the consent to the adoption.

2. The Extension of Support Beyond Majority

With the age of majority now set at 18 in most states, the question often arises as to whether an adult child has a right to continued support if he or she is still in high school or wishes to attend college. Most, if not all, states provide for the continuation of support until a child completes high school, even if he or she turns 18 prior to graduation. In short, emancipation for child support purposes is deemed to be the later of these two occurrences. However, the picture is far less clear when it comes to post-minority support for a child who wishes to attend college.

The question as to whether a parent can be required to pay child support or to contribute to the educational expenses of an adult child has become increasingly pressing given that in today's advanced economy a college degree (or other type of post-secondary education) is generally regarded as necessary to ensure some measure of financial autonomy and stability. Of particular concern in this regard is the fact that children of divorced parents are significantly less likely than children of still-married parents to receive financial help from one or both parents for college. Monica Hof Wallace, A Federal Referendum: Extending Child Support for Higher Education, 58 Kan. L. Rev. 665 (2010).

Capturing this imbalance, one commentator writes that

parents of intact families achieve extraordinary wealth transfer by providing higher education for their children. This transfer exists almost entirely outside of the traditional child support system. As a result, the equality principle on which child support is based fails to accommodate children of non-intact families in receiving higher education.

Id. at 667. To remedy this inequity, the author suggests that the federal child support laws should be amended to require "states, when establishing their guidelines, to provide for some level of post-secondary support absent any agreement between the parents." *Id.* at 686. However, this proposal raises the below-noted counter equity argument that doing so would impose a *formal* duty on divorced parents that is not likewise imposed on parents who are married.

As for the approaches that states do take, a sizable minority of jurisdictions have enacted statutory provisions that permit a judge to order the continuation of child support up to a certain post-minority age, typically 21 or 22, if the child is a full-time student or regularly attending school. In some of these states, in addition to or in lieu of child support, a parent can be ordered to pay a share of the child's educational expenses. Where both types of payments are ordered, the child support amount is typically adjusted downward to account for the parent's contribution to the costs of his or her child's education.[17] Even if not expressly authorized by statute, most states will enforce an agreement between parents that obligates one or both of them to provide child support for a post-minority child who is attending college.

In the absence of a specific statute, courts generally take one of two approaches to the award of support for post-minority students. Many judges believe it is not fair to require divorced parents to pay for their children's college education, since, had the family remained together, the parents would have been free to decide whether or not to contribute to their children's college education, and the children would have no legal claim to such support.

Other courts take the position that education is a basic parental obligation and will order support in appropriate cases. These courts often point out that had the parents remained together, it can be assumed that they would have made a reasonable effort to finance their children's education and that divorce should not work a deprivation. They are also aware that if support is not ordered, the financial burden will most likely fall on the custodial parent.

In deciding whether to order support so a child may attend college, courts generally look at a number of factors, including the reasonable expectations of the child, academic interest and ability, and the parents' financial status. Courts may also try to determine whether the family would have provided a college education had the parents remained together. Unfortunately, these factors may work against a young person who is not from a middle-class family, as a judge may decide that a college education is not necessary or within reasonable expectations.

[17]*See* Madeline Marzno-Lesnevish and Scott Adam Laterra, Child Support and College: What Is the Correct Result?, 23 J. Am. Acad. Matrim. Law. 335 (2009).

Case Preview

McLeod v. Starnes

The issue in *McLeod v. Starnes* concerned whether a father could be ordered to pay the college expenses for his adult child. The parties divorced in 1993 after five years of marriage. From the time of the divorce to this action, Father's income gradually increased until it reached the current level of $250,000 a year. In August 2006, the parties' older child, Collin, enrolled as a student at Newberry College. Collin sought all the financial opportunities he could, including scholarships, loans, and grants. Father supported Collin's decision to attend Newberry College and even wrote an e-mail in March 2006 agreeing to repay all of Collin's student loans upon graduation from college. He even co-signed a promissory note for the student loans. Father also agreed to pick up "odd expenses from [Collin]'s education" and told Collin that he could call Father whenever he needed a little bit of help. Unfortunately, Father did not pay as he had promised. In March 2007, Mother brought an action seeking an award of college expenses.

The trial court was faced with the precedent established in South Carolina two years earlier. The South Carolina Supreme Court in *Webb v. Webb* found that it was a violation of equal protection to require a divorced parent to pay for college expenses when the payment could not be required from intact households. The *Webb* case had overruled prior South Carolina law that had permitted situations when a divorced parent could be required to pay.

As you read *McLeod v. Starnes*, look for the following:

1. Why is the court willing to overlook the doctrine of *stare decisis* in this case?
2. What was the potential violation of equal protection that was at issue in this case?
3. What are the factors the court considers in deciding whether colleges expenses should be paid by the noncustodial parent?

McLeod v. Starnes
723 S.E.2d 198 (S.C. 2012)

Less than two years ago, this Court decided *Webb v. Sowell*, 387 S.C. 328, 692 S.E.2d 543 (2010), which held that ordering a non-custodial parent to pay college expenses violates equal protection, thus overruling thirty years of precedent flowing from *Risinger v. Risinger*, 273 S.C. 36, 253 S.E.2d 652 (1979). We granted permission in this case to argue against precedent. . . . Today, we hold that *Webb* was wrongly decided and remand this matter for reconsideration in light of the law as it existed prior to *Webb*.

In *Webb*, we held that requiring a parent to contribute toward an adult child's college expenses violated the Equal Protection Clause. 387 S.C. at 332-33, 692 S.E.2d at

545. We are not unmindful of the imprimatur of correctness which stare decisis lends to that decision. However, stare decisis is not an inexorable command: "There is no virtue in sinning against light or persisting in palpable error, for nothing is settled until it is settled right. . . . There should be no blind adherence to a precedent which, if it is wrong, should be corrected at the first practical moment." . . . Furthermore, [w]hen the court is asked to follow the line marked out by a single precedent case it is not at liberty to place its decision on the rule of stare decisis alone, without regard to the grounds on which the antecedent case was adjudicated. . . . Therefore, "[s]tare decisis should be used to foster stability and certainty in the law, but[] not to perpetuate error." *Fitzer v. Greater Greenville S.C. Young Men's Christian Ass'n*, 277 S.C. 1, 4, 282 S.E.2d 230, 231 (1981), superseded by statute on other grounds, S.C. Code Ann. §33-55-200, et seq. (2006). Stare decisis applies with full force with respect to questions of statutory interpretation because the legislature is free to correct us if we misinterpret its words. However, the doctrine is at its weakest with respect to constitutional questions because only the courts or a constitutional amendment can remedy any mistakes made. *Agostini v. Felton,* 521 U.S. 203, 236 (1997).

We are at the first practical moment to reexamine *Webb,* a "single precedent case" concerning a constitutional question because it is the first and only case in this State finding an equal protection violation in these circumstances. We now believe *Webb* reversed the burden imposed on parties operating under rational basis review for equal protection challenges and should therefore be overruled.

In *Webb,* we were asked to determine whether requiring a non-custodial parent to pay college expenses was a violation of equal protection. 387 S.C. at 330, 692 S.E.2d at 544. "The sine qua non of an equal protection claim is a showing that similarly situated persons received disparate treatment." *Grant v. S.C. Coastal Council,* 319 S.C. 348, 354, 461 S.E.2d 388, 391 (1995). Absent an allegation that the classification resulting in different treatment is suspect, a classification will survive an equal protection challenge so long as it rests on some rational basis. . . . Under the rational basis test, a classification is presumed reasonable and will remain valid unless and until the party challenging it proves beyond a reasonable doubt that there "is no admissible hypothesis upon which it can be justified." *Carolina Amusement Co. v. Martin*, 236 S.C. 558, 576, 115 S.E.2d 273, 282 (1960). If we can discern any rational basis to support the classification, regardless of whether that basis was the original motivation for it, the classification will withstand constitutional scrutiny. The classification also does not need to completely achieve its purpose to withstand constitutional scrutiny.

In *Webb,* the majority viewed the classification created by *Risinger* for equal protection purposes as those parents subject to a child support order at the time the child is emancipated. Without any elaboration, the majority concluded that there is no rational basis for treating parents subject to such an order different than those not subject to one with respect to the payment of college expenses. Id. Upon further reflection, we now believe that we abandoned our long-held rational basis rule that the party challenging a classification must prove there is no conceivable basis upon which it can rest and inverted the burden of proof. By not investigating whether there is any basis to support the alleged classification or refuting the bases argued, we effectively presumed *Risinger*'s reading of what is now section 63-3-530(A)(17) unconstitutional. Our treatment of this issue thus essentially reviewed *Risinger* under the lens of strict scrutiny as opposed to rational basis. . . . Our decision in *Webb* therefore rests on unsound constitutional principles, and stare decisis does not preclude our reconsideration of the issue addressed in that case.

As with any equal protection challenge, we begin by addressing the class *Risinger* created under section 63-3-530(A)(17). Mother argues that the appropriate classification is divorced parents versus non-divorced parents. In his brief, Father adheres to the class *Webb* analyzed of parents subject to a child support order at the time of emancipation versus those who are not subject to one. However, Father argued Mother's proposed classification before the family court. He therefore cannot argue *Webb*'s class on appeal. See *State v. Dunbar*, 356 S.C. 138, 142, 587 S.E.2d 691, 694 (2003) ("A party may not argue one ground at trial and an alternate ground on appeal."). We accordingly review *Risinger* through the same lens used by the family court: whether it improperly treats divorced parents differently than non-divorced parents.

This State has a strong interest in the outcome of disputes where the welfare of our young citizens is at stake. As can hardly be contested, the State also has a strong interest in ensuring that our youth are educated such that they can become more productive members of our society. It is entirely possible "that most parents who remain married to each other support their children through college years. On the other hand, even well-intentioned parents, when deprived of the custody of their children, sometimes react by refusing to support them as they would if the family unit had been preserved." *In re Marriage of Vrban*, 293 N.W.2d 198, 202 (Iowa 1980). Therefore, it may very well be that *Risinger* sought to alleviate this harm by "minimiz[ing] any economic and educational disadvantages to children of divorced parents." *Kujawinski v. Kujawinski*, 376 N.E.2d 1382, 1390 (Ill. 1978). . . . There is no absolute right to a college education, and . . . *Risinger* and its progeny, does not impose a moral obligation on all divorced parents with children. Instead, the factors identified by *Risinger* and expounded upon in later cases seek to identify those children whose parents would otherwise have paid for their college education, but for the divorce, and provide them with that benefit.

We accordingly hold that requiring a parent to pay, as an incident of child support, for post-secondary education under the appropriate and limited circumstances outlined by *Risinger* is rationally related to the State's interest. While it is certainly true that not all married couples send their children to college, that does not detract from the State's interest in having college-educated citizens and attempting to alleviate the potential disadvantages placed upon children of divorced parents. Although the decision to send a child to college may be a personal one, it is not one we wish to foreclose to a child simply because his parents are divorced. It is of no moment that not every married parent sends his children to college or that not every divorced parent refuses to do so. The tenants of rational basis review under equal protection do not require such exacting precision in the decision to create a classification and its effect.

Indeed, Father's refusal to contribute towards Collin's college expenses under the facts of this case proves the very ill which *Risinger* attempted to alleviate, for Father articulated no defensible reason for his refusal other than the shield erected by *Webb*.

What other reason could there be for a father with more than adequate means and a son who truly desires to attend college to skirt the obligation the father almost certainly would have assumed had he not divorced the child's mother? Had Father and Mother remained married, we believe Father undoubtedly would have contributed towards Collin's education. Collin has therefore fallen victim to the precise harm that prompted the courts . . . to hold that a non-custodial parent could be ordered to contribute towards a child's college education. Thus, this case amply demonstrates what we failed to recognize in *Webb*: sometimes the acrimony of marital litigation impacts a parent's normal sense of obligation towards his or her children. While this is a harsh and unfortunate reality, it is a reality nonetheless that *Risinger* sought to address.

. . .

We now hold *Risinger* does not violate the Equal Protection Clause because there is a rational basis to support any disparate treatment *Risinger* and its progeny created. In fact, the case before us particularly demonstrates the need for a rule permitting an award of college expenses in certain circumstances in order to ensure children of divorce have the benefit of the college education they would have received had their parents remained together. Accordingly, we reverse the order of the family court and remand this matter for a determination of whether and in what amount Father is required to contribute to Collin's college education under the law as it existed prior to *Webb*.

Post-Case Follow-Up

Mother argued that the family court was incorrect when it ruled that Father was not obligated to pay college expenses. This was a risky position for Mother to take given that the law as it existed at the time Mother raised the issue provided that it would be a violation of equal protection to hold a parent responsible for college expenses. However, the court allowed Mother to raise the issue and argue against *stare decisis* so that the court could overrule its prior decision.

The court seems persuaded, at least in part, by the fact that *Webb v. Webb* was a single precedent case and had overruled years of prior authority for ordering post-secondary school expenses. The court also was persuaded by the fact that Father had agreed to pay the expenses and then did not hold true to his word. In a sense, Father had created a contract with Collin by agreeing to pay. Although not at issue in this case, there may be circumstances where the adult child may be a third-party beneficiary to a contract and able to sue in his own right for payment.

McLeod v. Starnes: Real Life Applications

1. Assume the facts in *McLeod v. Starnes*, but instead of Collin being the oldest child, he is the youngest of three children. Neither parent paid for the other two children to go to college. Rather, each child took out loans or worked to be able

Expanded Post-Majority Child Support

In a recent law review article, Professor Sally F. Goldfarb calls for the creation of a new legal remedy known as "'expanded post-majority child support,'" to be modeled after "state statutes and case law that permit child support awards for adults who are in college." Sally F. Goldfarb, Who Pays for the "Boomerang Generation"? A Legal Perspective on Financial Support for Young Adults, 37 Harv. J.L. & Gender 45, 49 (2014).

This proposal is grounded in the recognition that in "stark contrast to family patterns that prevailed during the middle of the twentieth century" the transition from adolescence to adulthood is considerably more protracted, which has resulted in the greater financial dependence of young adults on their parents. *Id.* at 50, 50-68.

According to Goldfarb, expanded post-majority child support will also address what she refers to as "troubling patterns of inequality." *Id.* at 48. The first inequity that she is concerned with is that young adults whose "parents are divorced, separated or never married receive less support than those whose parents are married to each other." The second is that "divorced, separated, or never married mothers bear a heavier burden of support for adult children than divorced, separated, or never married fathers." *Id.* at 48-49.

to afford college. Would the decision in *McLeod v. Starnes* be different? What if the two older children did not attend college and Collin was the first one to want to attend college? Would that change the court's decision?

2. Assume that the Father had disagreed that Collin should attend Newberry College and expressly disavowed any financial responsibility. Would that change the court's decision?

---

3. Mental and Physical Disabilities

With a handful of exceptions, all states permit courts to continue support beyond age 18 where an adult child is mentally or physically disabled and is incapable of self-support. Effectively, whether based on the common law or a statute, the underlying rationale for this approach is that where a disability renders a child "unable to support oneself, this prevents the child from becoming emancipated; accordingly 'the presumption of emancipation upon reaching majority is inapplicable.'" Kathryn Burns, Post-Majority Child Support for Children with Disabilities, 51 Fam. Ct. Rev. 502, 504 (2013), quoting *Riggs v. Riggs*, 353 S.C. 230, 235 (2003).

However, in many jurisdictions, a significant limiting factor is that the disability must have begun while the child in question was a minor. Accordingly, if a child becomes disabled after reaching adulthood, parents cannot be required to pay child support even if their child is not able to be self-supporting.

G. TAX IMPLICATIONS OF CHILD SUPPORT AWARDS

There are two basic tax questions to consider with regard to the payment of child support:

- How are payments to be treated for tax purposes?
- What is the relationship between paying support and claiming the dependency exemption for the children?

1. Characterization of Child Support Payments

The basic rule is that child support payments are not considered income to the custodial parent and are not subject to taxation. Because payments are not includible in income to the recipient, the noncustodial parent is not entitled to deduct the amount of the payments from his or her income. In effect, payment of child support is a tax-neutral event.

This changes, however, if child support payments are lumped together with alimony payments so that a single support payment is made without designating how much is for alimony and how much for child support. This is commonly referred to as **unallocated support**. Where support is unallocated, the entire amount will be treated as alimony. Unlike child support, alimony is regarded as taxable income to the recipient and entitles the payor spouse to deduct the payments from his or her gross income.

Given this potential tax benefit, a support obligor may be tempted to characterize the entire support amount as alimony. This could also benefit the support recipient because the tax savings realized by the obligor could be passed on, in whole or in part, as additional support payments. This would, of course, increase the recipient's taxable income but, where he or she is in a lower tax bracket, could result in a net gain.

To deter parties from disguising child support payments as spousal support, the federal tax code now includes rules regarding the treatment of unallocated support payments. Where support is unallocated, reductions that are tied to a contingency relating to a child or to a time associated with such a contingency create a refutable presumption that the amount of the reduction was in fact child support, and it will be treated as such.

Child-related contingencies include reaching majority, marriage, and completing school. For example, if the wife is to receive $500 per month with no contingencies other than remarriage or death, the full amount will be considered alimony. But if the agreement calls for payments to be reduced to $200 per month at the child's eighteenth birthday, the IRS will recharacterize the amount of the reduction as child support. Moreover, if a creative attorney tries to avoid this rule and has the reduction occur two months before the child's birthday, the IRS will consider this as occurring at a time associated with a child-related contingency and will again presume that this amount is child support. The presumption can be rebutted by proof that the timing of the reduction was selected based on independent, non–child-related considerations.

2. The Dependency Exemption and Child Tax Credit

The basic rule is that the custodial parent is entitled to claim the children as dependents for federal tax purposes. However, because the noncustodial parent is usually in a higher tax bracket, the dependency exemption may be worth more to this parent. Accordingly, as part of divorce negotiations, parties often negotiate over who will take the dependency exemption. If the custodial parent agrees that the noncustodial parent can claim the children, the custodial parent must effectuate this by signing a written release. The release can be made permanent or for a temporary period. Parties may also agree to alternate years for claiming the exemption or to each claim the exemption for a different child.

Since 1997, decisions about which parent will claim the children as dependents have assumed an even greater importance because the parent who claims the child is now also entitled to a child tax credit. Unlike the dependency exemption, which permits an adjustment to gross income, the child tax credit gives a parent an actual credit against his or her tax liability.

Chapter Summary

- In 1974, Congress enacted the Child Support Enforcement and Establishment of Paternity Act, marking the entrance of the federal government into the child support arena.
- States must now have a comprehensive child support program in effect, which is administered by a single entity, known as a IV-D agency.
- Child support awards must be based on guidelines that use numeric criteria to arrive at a presumptive amount; deviations are permitted under limited circumstances.
- States must also have an array of enforcement mechanisms in place to help with the collection of child support, most significantly income withholding.
- To address the challenges of interstate cases, all states must now have a central registry for the coordination of interstate cases. Furthermore, all states have adopted UIFSA, which eliminates the problem of conflicting orders. Under FFCCSOA, all states must give full faith and credit to child support orders of other states.
- A parent's support obligation generally lasts until a child reaches the age of majority (18) but, under limited circumstances, it can be terminated earlier or extended beyond this point.
- Support orders can be modified based on a change in circumstances; they are also subject to a periodic review and adjustment process.
- Child support payments are not considered income to the recipient — nor are they deductible by the payor. If folded into an unallocated support award, the entire amount will be treated as alimony unless reductions are tied to child-related contingencies.
- Unless released, the dependency exemption belongs to the custodial parent. The parent who takes the dependency exemption is also entitled to the child tax credit.

Applying the Rules

1. Jennifer and Larry were divorced in 2012. Since that time, Larry has failed to pay all of his child support payments and now owes past due support in the amount of $8,000. What are the mechanisms Jennifer can utilize to collect on her back support? Does it matter that Jennifer has a well-paying job and is not on public assistance? Are there administrative in addition to potential court remedies that Jennifer can utilize?

2. Assume the following facts: Mother and Father divorce when their child Aria is three years old. Father seeks your legal advice and tells you that Mother has primary custody of Aria, and shortly after the divorce he moved out of state. For the first few years, he still saw Aria regularly, but now he has remarried and his visits are infrequent. He is now happy and actively participating in the raising of his two new children.

   He wishes to reduce support to his first child because he feels resentful about providing for a child he has no relationship with and money is tight in his new household. He asks your opinion on whether he can reduce child support. What do you tell him? What do you base your opinion on? Does your answer change if Mother has interfered with his visits without good reason? Does your answer change if Mother left him because he was abusive?

3. Barry and Priya have two children when they divorce. Barry has custody of the two children, ages 2 and 4. He works half-time. Priya is a corporate executive and hates her work. She earns a good salary and pays enough child support so that Dad and the children are reasonably comfortable. It is important to Dad that the children not be in full-time day care. Priya decides to leave her job and pursue her lifelong dream of being a freelance writer. Assume that Priya is acting in good faith; she is not making this job change for the purpose of avoiding child support. Will the court impute income to her based on her earning capacity and use this figure for the calculation of support? What factors will the court weigh in making the decision?

4. Mateo and Janet were married in 1990. Janet's daughter from a previous marriage, Amy, now age 27, was adopted by Mateo. The parties also had two children of their own, Nathan who is now 21 and Gabriela who is now 16. Both Amy and Nathan went to college, and the parties paid for the college tuition. Mateo filed for divorce last year, and the trial judge has just ruled that Mateo is to pay Gabriela's reasonable college expenses, including books, tuition, and housing. Reasonable expenses are considered those incurred in pursuing a four-year college degree at an in-state college. Mateo has come to you and wants to know if he has grounds for appeal. What do you tell Mateo? Assume the court had also ordered that Mateo pay for a car so that Gabriela could travel to and from school. Would there be grounds for an appeal? Is there an obligation to treat all the children the same?

5. Harvey and Claire were divorced four years ago. They have four minor children and Claire is the primary custodian. At the time of the divorce, Claire was not working as she was primarily responsible for taking care of the minor children, and Harvey was working as a clerk at a local home improvement store. Harvey comes to you and advises you that he has recently reduced his hours to part time because he is now a first-year law student. He tells you that while he has less income now, he will have more income in the future so he believes his decision to go to law school was a good one. He asks you if you believe he can modify his child support amount based upon his change in circumstances. Based upon the readings in this chapter, what will you tell Harvey?

Family Law in Practice

1. Obtain a copy of your state's child support guidelines and answer the following questions:

   a. What approach is used?
   b. How is income of the custodial parent treated?
   c. How is income of the child treated?
   d. What happens when the obligor has a prior family? A subsequent family?
   e. How are extraordinary expenses treated?
   f. What other factors influence the amount?

2. Obtain a copy of the child support worksheet that is used in your state to calculate support awards. Using the worksheet and consulting the guidelines where necessary, calculate a support award based on the following facts:

   a. Mom has custody of the two children, ages 4 and 9.
   b. Her gross income is $22,000; her adjusted gross income is $18,700.
   c. She has yearly child care expenses of $8,000.
   d. Dad's gross income is $46,000; his adjusted gross income is $39,000.
   e. He spends what would be considered a typical amount of time visiting with his children.
   f. Dad maintains a family health insurance policy that covers the children — the cost of this policy to him is $380 per month and the cost of maintaining an individual policy would be $190 per month.
   g. The nine-year-old child has severe learning disabilities, which require the hiring of special tutors — the monthly cost of this is $225.
   h. Neither parent has other children.

3. Determine whether your state has implemented any support enforcement tools that go beyond those that are required under federal law.

4. Develop a client intake questionnaire for use in cases where support is an issue. Make sure you consult the guidelines so that all relevant considerations are accounted for.

5. Assume that you have a client seeking a divorce from her husband, who left the state five years ago. Since that time, she has had no contact with him, but she does know where he is living. Locate the UIFSA as adopted by your state and determine whether your state can exercise personal jurisdiction over him for purposes of entering a child support order. Now, do the same but with the following change. Assume that the client and her husband never lived together in your state but that she moved here following their separation. However, the husband makes periodic visits to see the child. Under this set of facts, can your state obtain personal jurisdiction over him? Explain your answer.

Spousal Support

At the time of divorce, one spouse may be required to provide financial support to the other. This support, traditionally known as **alimony**, from the Latin *alimonia*, meaning nourishment or sustenance, is now also commonly referred to as spousal maintenance or spousal support. As discussed in Chapter 4, no-fault divorce reform triggered a major restructuring of the traditional support model that was closely linked to marital fault and grounded in a vision of permanent female economic dependence. However, as we will see, the law now treats spouses equally in terms of either providing or receiving support. The determination of whether a former spouse is entitled to support is based on a number of factors that are gender neutral.

A. THE LAW OF THE INTACT FAMILY

Before exploring the historical background of alimony, it is interesting to note how courts have treated support obligations in an intact marriage. Traditionally, courts have not interfered with the level of spending and support in a marriage. Recall in Chapter 1 the reluctance of courts to interfere into private matters in the home that did not rise to the level of criminal wrongdoings. Similarly, this right to privacy regarding what goes on in an intact family, absent criminal actions, is not something that the courts will traditionally regulate.

The traditional support obligation was that a husband, as the wage earner, had an obligation to support a wife for necessities, but beyond that there was no obligation to provide for luxury items. Wives had little control even over their own finances.

Key Concepts

- Support obligations in an intact marriage
- Historical implications of support and fault
- Impact of no-fault reform on spousal support
- Factors in determining spousal support
- Structuring and enforcing spousal support
- Means for modifying or terminating support
- Spousal support and taxation

Case Preview

McGuire v. McGuire

The *McGuire* case provides an example of how the court traditionally has taken a very limited interest in the level of support provided in an intact household. In this case Lydia McGuire, while still married to Charles McGuire, brought an action in equity to recover suitable maintenance and support money, and for costs and attorneys' fees.

At the trial level, the court rendered a decree in favor of Mrs. McGuire holding that she was entitled to a number of things to make her life more comfortable and to a lifestyle they could afford. This included the ability to use Mr. McGuire's credit and to obligate him to pay for certain items in the nature of improvements and repairs to the marital home, and furniture and appliances. The trial court also required Mr. McGuire to purchase a new automobile, and ordered him to pay travel expenses of Mrs. McGuire to visit her adult daughters at least once a year. She was also provided with a personal allowance in the sum of $50 a month and awarded $800 for her attorneys' fees.

As you read *McGuire v. McGuire*, look for the following:

1. What complaints did Mrs. McGuire have against Mr. McGuire?
2. What does the court say about the fact that the parties are still living under the same roof?
3. What options does Mrs. McGuire have if she wants to change the standard of living provided by Mr. McGuire?

McGuire v. McGuire
59 N.W.2d 336 (Neb. 1953)

The record shows that the plaintiff (Mrs. McGuire) and defendant (Mr. McGuire) were married in Wayne, Nebraska, on August 11, 1919. At the time of the marriage the defendant was a bachelor 46 or 47 years of age and had a reputation for more than ordinary frugality, of which the plaintiff was aware. She had visited in his home and had known him for about 3 years prior to the marriage. After the marriage the couple went to live on a farm of 160 acres located in Leslie precinct, Wayne County, owned by the defendant and upon which he had lived and farmed since 1905. The parties have lived on this place ever since. [Plaintiff's first husband died in 1914, leaving plaintiff and two daughters. When plaintiff's husband died his 80 acres of property was inherited one-third to plaintiff and one-third to each of the daughters who were then 9 and 11 years old.] Both of these daughters are [now] married and have families of their own.

On April 12, 1939, the plaintiff transferred her interest in the 80-acre farm to her two daughters. The defendant signed the deed.

At the time of trial plaintiff was 66 years of age and the defendant nearly 80 years of age. No children were born to these parties. The defendant had no dependents except the plaintiff.

The plaintiff testified that she was a dutiful and obedient wife, worked and saved, and cohabited with the defendant until the last 2 or 3 years. She worked in the fields, did outside chores, cooked, and attended to her household duties such as cleaning the house and doing the washing. For a number of years she raised as high as 300 chickens, sold poultry and eggs, and used the money to buy clothing, things she wanted, and for groceries. She further testified that the defendant was the boss of the house and his word was law; that he would not tolerate any charge accounts and would not inform her as to his finances or business; and that he was a poor companion. The defendant did not complain of her work, but left the impression to her that she had not done enough. [Plaintiff recited a number of complaints against the defendant including not providing her with any money, not buying her clothes, except a coat 4 years previous, not taking her to a motion picture show for the past 12 years, not belonging to any organizations or charitable institutions, or contributing to any charitable institutions.] The plaintiff further testified that the house is not equipped with a bathroom, bathing facilities, or inside toilet. The kitchen is not modern. She does not have a kitchen sink. Hard and soft water is obtained from a well and cistern. . . . She had requested a new furnace but the defendant believed the one they had to be satisfactory. . . . The plaintiff was privileged to use all of the rent money she wanted to from the 80-acre farm, and when she goes to see her daughters, which is not frequent, she uses part of the rent money for that purpose, the defendant providing no funds for such use. . . .

It appears that the defendant owns 398 acres of land with 2 acres deeded to a church, the land being of the value of $83,960; that he has bank deposits in the sum of $12,786.81 and government bonds in the amount of $104,500; and that his income, including interest on the bonds and rental for his real estate, is $8,000 or $9,000 a year. There are apparently some Series E United States Savings Bonds listed and registered in the names of Charles W. McGuire or Lydia M. McGuire. . . .

. . .

It becomes apparent that there are no cases cited by the plaintiff and relied upon by her from this jurisdiction or other jurisdictions that will sustain the action such as she has instituted in the instant case.

. . . [W]hile a wife [under the cases] had no right to the interference of the court for her maintenance until her abandonment or separation, there might be an abandonment or separation, within the sound construction of the statute, while the parties continued to live under the same roof, as where the husband utterly refused to have intercourse with his wife, or to make any provision for her maintenance, and thus he might seclude himself in a portion of his house, take his meals alone or board elsewhere than in his house, and so as effectively separate himself from his wife and refuse to provide for her as in case of actual abandonment, although in whatever form it might exist there must be an abandonment. . . .

There are also several cases, under statutes of various states, in which separate maintenance was refused the wife, where the husband and wife were living in the same house. These cases are to the effect that it is an indispensable requirement of a maintenance statute that the wife should be living separate and apart from her husband without her fault, and that therefore, a wife living in the same house with her husband, occupying a different room and eating at a different time, was not entitled to separate maintenance. See *Lowe v. Lowe*, 213 Ill. App. 607.

. . .

In the instant case the marital relation has continued for more than 33 years, and the wife has been supported in the same manner during this time without complaint on her part. The parties have not been separated or living apart from each other at any time. In the light of the cited cases it is clear, especially so in this jurisdiction, that to maintain an action such as the one at bar, the parties must be separated or living apart from each other.

The living standards of a family are a matter of concern to the household, and not for the courts to determine, even though the husband's attitude toward his wife, according to his wealth and circumstances, leaves little to be said in his behalf. As long as the home is maintained and the parties are living as husband and wife it may be said that the husband is legally supporting his wife and the purpose of the marriage relation is being carried out. Public policy requires such a holding. It appears that the plaintiff is not devoid of money in her own right. She has a fairsized bank account and is entitled to use the rent from the 80 acres of land left by her first husband, if she so chooses.

. . .

Reversed and remanded with directions to dismiss.

YEAGER, Justice (dissenting).

I respectfully dissent.

. . .

From the beginning of the married life of the parties the defendant supplied only the barest necessities and there was no change thereafter. He did not even buy groceries until the last 3 or 4 years before the trial, and neither did he buy clothes for the plaintiff.

. . .

There is and can be no doubt that, independent of statutes relating to divorce, alimony, and separate maintenance, if this plaintiff were living apart from the defendant she could in equity and on the facts as outlined in the record be awarded appropriate relief.

If relief is to be denied to plaintiff under this principle it must be denied because of the fact that she is not living separate and apart from the defendant and is not seeking separation.

. . .

In the light of what the decisions declare to be the basis of the right to maintain an action for support, is there any less reason for extending the right to a wife who is denied the right to maintenance in a home occupied with her husband than to one who has chosen to occupy a separate abode?

If the right is to be extended only to one who is separated from the husband equity and effective justice would be denied where a wealthy husband refused proper support and maintenance to a wife physically or mentally incapable of putting herself in a position where the rule could become available to her.

It is true that in all cases examined which uphold the right of a wife to maintain an action in equity for maintenance the parties were living apart, but no case has been cited or found which says that separation is a condition precedent to the right to maintain action in equity for maintenance. Likewise none has been cited or found which says that it is not. . . .

In primary essence the rule contemplates the enforcement of an obligation within and not without the full marriage relationship. The reasoning contained in the opinions sustaining this right declare that purpose. . . .

I conclude therefore that the conclusion of the decree that the district court had the power to entertain the action was not contrary to law.

. . .

Post-Case Follow-Up

McGuire stands for the proposition that before a court will interfere with the standard of living of the household the parties must be separated and living apart. The court may well have been persuaded by the fact that the marriage had lasted for over 33 years and Mrs. McGuire had never filed any action for support. They continued to reside together and neither had filed for separation or divorce. Thus, when the parties remain in an intact family, the court will not interfere in private matters of the household. Mrs. McGuire's remedy, should she decide she wishes to pursue a claim, is to file for a divorce.

McGuire v. McGuire: Real Life Applications

1. Tom and Jenny have been married for 20 years. Jenny constantly complains that Tom spends too much money on things for himself and not for the household. For example, he spends a lot of time bidding online at auctions for personal items that have little benefit to the household such as rare books, art items that he likes, and curios that are just cluttering up the house. She is especially concerned because he recently took some of their savings and bought a piece of art for over $10,000. She would like to bring an action to prohibit Tom from spending any money unless both parties agree to the expenses. Does Jenny have a claim against Tom? What are Tom's defenses?

2. Assuming that instead of purchasing the items in Question 1, Tom has a gambling habit and is constantly spending the parties' savings in order to fund his gambling habit. What are Jenny's remedies?

3. Jameill and Kate have been married for 30 years. Jameill comes to your office and relays the following: He and Kate have three grown children. Kate was

always the stay-at-home mom, but once their youngest child graduated from high school, two years ago, Kate decided to do volunteer work at the local hospital. Now she spends so much time volunteering that she does not have time to do any of the grocery shopping, cleaning, or cooking. Jameill says he has tried to talk to Kate about this, but she tells him that she has no desire to be a "housewife" any longer and enjoys volunteering. Jameill's job as a salesman does not make enough for them to afford to hire help, and his hours are long and he is often out of town. He is doing as much as he can in keeping the house clean and the clothes washed, but it seems the more he does the less Kate does. He says he has tried getting Kate to go to marriage counseling with him and she refuses. He asks you what his remedies are for requiring Kate to help around the house. Based on your reading of *McGuire*, what do you tell Jameill?

B. HISTORICAL OVERVIEW

American spousal support laws are rooted in the English ecclesiastical practice of awarding alimony as part of a divorce from board and bed, which, as discussed in Chapter 4, enabled a couple to live apart without severing the marital bond. Alimony was considered an extension of the husband's marital duty to support his wife, who upon marriage lost most of her property rights and control over her earnings. The amount of the support award was influenced by the degree of the husband's fault as well as by the value of the property that he had acquired from the wife during the marriage.

In continuing the practice of awarding alimony, most U.S. jurisdictions followed the rule of limiting support to innocent wives, and courts commonly spoke of it as the measure of damages paid to an injured wife to compensate her for the loss occasioned by her wrongdoing husband, much like damages in a tort or breach of contract action. Without alimony, a guilty husband would be benefiting from his wrongdoing — a result at odds with the prevailing view of divorce as a remedy for the grievously wronged.

Despite this remedial framing of divorce, some judges questioned the logic of extending the marital duty of support when the relationship giving rise to it had been dissolved. However, running underneath the marital fault explanation there seems to have been a quiet awareness that spousal support was an economic necessity without which divorced wives would be without the means to support themselves. *See* Mary O'Connell, Alimony After No-Fault: A Practice in Search of a Theory, 23 New Eng. L. Rev. 437 (1988).

1. Alimony Prior to the No-Fault Reform Era

As discussed in Chapter 4, our thinking about divorce was radically reshaped in the 1970s in the wake of no-fault reform. Because alimony was bound up with considerations of fault, this reform triggered a transformation in the nature of the spousal support obligation. Before looking at this shift, we briefly consider key characteristics of the support obligation as it existed prior to no-fault divorce reform:

1. Although alimony was still linked to determinations of fault, this link had become weaker as the fault premise undergirding our divorce system was increasingly being called into question. Accordingly, the idea of alimony as a form of damages was beginning to lose hold. *Id.* at 482-491.
2. The concept of alimony was highly gendered. In most states, alimony could not be awarded to husbands, as women had no duty to support their husbands. Alimony, by its very nature, was understood as a male responsibility.
3. Alimony awards were "permanent" and incorporated an assumption of continued female economic dependence.

As the underlying fault rationale for alimony was called into question, some courts began to speak disparagingly of women who sought support. In the words of one judge, alimony had ensured a "perpetual state of indolence" and had the potential to convert a "host of physically and mentally competent young women into an army of alimony drones who neither toil nor spin and become a drain on society and a menace to themselves." *Doyle v. Doyle*, 5 Misc. 2d 4, 158 N.Y.S.2d 909, 912 (1957). This fear appears to have been unfounded, however, as the average alimony award was modest; for instance, in 1968, the median award was $98 per month, nowhere near the amount needed to secure a life of indolence. *See* Lenore J. Weitzman, The Divorce Revolution: The Unexpected Social and Economic Consequences for Women and Children in America 145 (1985).

In reality, the average alimony award is modest.
Shutterstock.com

2. Impact of No-Fault Reform on the Support Obligation

With no-fault reform, the traditional legal framing of divorce as a necessary evil that was only justifiable in cases of grievous marital wrongdoing gave way to a greater acceptance of divorce as a solution for unhappy marriages. The elimination of fault as an essential precondition for the granting of a divorce led many in the field to reconceptualize marriage as a partnership that, as in the business world, is terminable by either party based on dissatisfaction with the relationship. In keeping with the partnership model, the desirability of allowing each partner to make a clean break from the marriage was emphasized, and, as with the dissolution of a business relationship, continuing obligations deriving from the failed marital relationship were henceforth to be kept to a minimum. As discussed in this chapter, the declining role of fault and the corresponding emergence of the partnership model of marriage prompted a reconceptualization of the traditional support model.

Property Division as the Primary Distributive Event

With no-fault reform, many states began to emphasize property division as the preferred way to adjust the post-divorce economic rights of the parties. As the division of property is a final, unmodifiable event (see Chapter 8), it was thought to more closely correspond with the emerging partnership model of marriage than did an award of spousal support. As in a business, the assets of the failed enterprise would be distributed, leaving the former partners free to pursue other endeavors unencumbered by the past. Alimony, which embodied expectations of continued obligations, was to be deemphasized and awarded only in exceptional cases. Underlying the emphasis on property division was an often unstated assumption that the divorcing spouses should be equally capable of achieving economic self-sufficiency regardless of any differences in their labor market participation during the marriage.

Shifting the Focus from Moral to Economic Considerations

As discussed, prior to no-fault reform, alimony awards were often linked to marital conduct. The court looked back into the marriage and used alimony as a way to partially compensate an innocent wife for past harms. With the uncoupling of alimony from fault, alimony awards have been re-anchored to economic considerations and, in a blame-free manner, are supposed to respond to financial needs arising out of the marital relationship. However, as discussed below, a recurring concern is the current lack of a clear conceptual framework within which support awards are to be determined, thus leading to a lack of consistency and predictability. Nonetheless, in keeping with the clean-break approach, the overall emphasis has been to move away from the idea of a continuing financial obligation in the form of support from one spouse to the other even where need or financial inequality exists .

Degendering the Support Obligation

The support obligation has also been uncoupled from its origins as a male-only responsibility. As we saw in the first chapter, the Supreme Court has held that gender-specific alimony laws are unconstitutional because they carry the "inherent risk of reinforcing stereotypes about the 'proper place' of women and their need for special protection." *Orr v. Orr*, 440 U.S. 268, 288 (1978) (citing *United Jewish Orgs. v. Carey*, 430 U.S. 144, 173-174 (1977)). Thus, in theory, spousal support is now a gender-neutral concept and is no longer premised on an assumption that married women, as a class, are financially dependent and incapable of self-support.

Shifting from an Assumption of Female Economic Dependence to an Assumption of Economic Self-Sufficiency

Following no-fault reform, the idea of permanent alimony awards fell out of favor. Seen as embodying outmoded assumptions regarding female economic dependence and requiring ongoing entanglement, a clear trend developed in favor of short-term support awards intended to help a spouse to acquire the skills needed to become self-supporting. (See Section D.3, below, for a discussion of rehabilitative alimony.) In sharp contrast to the past, this shift embodied the assumption that all married women, regardless of the role they played during the marriage, should be self-supporting either at the time of divorce or following a brief transitional period. This preference thus comported with both the changing role of women and the partnership model of marriage that minimizes the ongoing responsibility of a former spouse.

3. Critique of the "Clean Break" Approach

The **clean-break approach**, where there is no long-term duty of spousal support, has an appealing simplicity. At least in theory, as with former business partners, each spouse exits the failed enterprise with a share of the accumulated assets and is thereafter free of economic entanglements stemming from this joint undertaking. Accordingly, each spouse is now free to rebuild a new life on his or her own accord. Despite this surface appeal, the clean-break approach has been subject to significant criticism due to the fact that it fails to account for the gendered reality of family life and economically disadvantages many women.

To begin with, some critics of this approach argue that the analogy itself is flawed because it is based on a distortion of what actually occurs in the business realm; namely, that the decision to dissolve a business concern does not bring all mutual obligations between partners to a screeching halt. Rather, following the actual dissolution of a partnership, there may well be a protracted period in which the partners wind up their affairs. During this time, the partners "continue to be linked by mutual obligations and continue to share a fiduciary relationship," and no matter how "'strained' the relationships between the partners may actually be, the UPA (Uniform Partner Act) views the process of winding up as a 'cooperative'" venture. Cynthia Lee Starnes, Mothers as Suckers: Pity, Partnership, and Divorce Discourse, 90 Iowa L. Rev. 1513, 1546 (2005).

Of primary concern, critics of the clean-break approach argue that its gender-neutral approach masks the fact that many women in heterosexual marriages still do the bulk of the domestic labor, particularly where there are children. For example, according to one study, even when both spouses are employed full time, "a mother still does 40 percent more child care and about 30 percent more housework than the father."[1] Accordingly, in order to accommodate these domestic responsibilities, married women are far more likely than their spouses to "sacrifice professional goals in order to focus on the family" and to "restrict their work hours, find

---

[1]Rachel Biscardi, Dispelling Alimony Myths: The Continuing Need for Alimony and the Alimony Reform Act, 36 W. New Eng. L. Rev. 1, 7-8, quoting Division of Labor, Marriage and Family Encyclopedia, http://family.jrank. org/pages/408/Division-LaboroContemporary-Divisions-Labor.html. *See also* Julie-Anne Geraghty Stebbins, The Rehabilitation Illusion: How Alimony Reform in Massachusetts Fails to Compensate for Caregiving, 36 W. New Eng. L. Rev. 407 (2014).

work close to home, give up opportunities for advancement, and suffer decreased earnings."[2]

In turn, this marital division of labor has serious and long-lasting economic implications that endure well beyond the end of the marital relationship. In families in which wives devote considerable effort to the domestic realm, they generally leave the marriage with a diminished earning capacity due to the workplace accommodations that they made, such as passing up promotions, or working shorter hours, in order to accommodate their domestic responsibilities. In contrast, a husband who has been far less encumbered by household and child-related responsibilities is likely to exit the marriage with an enhanced earning capacity due to the fact that he has not had to juggle work and family obligations to the same extent as his spouse.[3]

Accordingly, the underlying assumption that a division of assets will permit both parties to begin life anew with an equal capacity for economic self-sufficiency often ignores the far-reaching economic consequences of this marital history. Compounding this problem, this approach mistakenly assumes that all divorcing couples have accumulated sufficient assets over the course of marriage to ensure the post-divorce economic security of both spouses — a reality that is simply not the case in many, if not all, marriages.

Closely related is the concern that the clean-break approach ignores the fact that many divorcing couples have minor children. It thus is premised upon an ideal of post-divorce disengagement that simply does not correspond to the reality of those families who have minor children. Not only is there likely to be a continued financial obligation by way of child support payments, the contemporary stress on cooperative parenting is likely to require ongoing and regular communication between former spouses regarding custodial arrangements and the needs of their children.

Some of these concerns, coupled with concerns about the lack of theoretical coherence as to the underlying purposes of spousal support and the lack of predictability in awards, have begun to influence lawmakers. A variety of support reforms are again being considered, including the use of alimony guidelines, and a number of courts have shown a renewed commitment to indefinite support awards.

C. SUPPORT DETERMINATIONS

Whether adopted by statute or by judicial decision, most states now use a multifactor test to determine if spousal support should be awarded in an individual case, and if so, the amount to be awarded, and the form that the award should take (see below for this consideration). Although, as in custody cases, judges are typically required to consider all of the enumerated factors, they likewise generally have the discretion to give each factor the weight they believe it merits in light of the

---

[2]Biscardi, *supra* note 1, at 8.
[3]*See generally* Alicia Brokars Kelly, Actualizing Intimate Partnership Theory, 50 Fam. Ct. Rev. 258 (2012); Alicia Brokars Kelly, Rehabilitating Partnership Marriage as a Theory of Wealth Distribution at Divorce: In Recognition of a Shared Life, 19 Wis. L.J. 141 (2004).

particular circumstances of the case. This gives judges the flexibility to consider the unique circumstances of a divorcing couple's situation, but as many commentators have objected it also makes outcomes highly indeterminate.

In this section, we first look at the common kinds of factors that courts weigh in deciding about spousal support. Reflecting the concerns about the unpredictability and uncertainty of this approach, we look at some of the reform proposals that are currently being considered, followed, in the next section, by a discussion of the basic ways that support awards can be structured. We then consider some of the reform proposals that are currently being considered.

1. Determining the Amount of Support

In most states, judges are required to consider a variety of factors when making a determination about the appropriateness of support in an individual case, such as

- financial need;
- earning potential;
- age;
- duration (length) of the marriage;
- physical and mental health;
- income and financial resources;
- the marital standard of living; and
- contribution to the marriage.

Below is the family code included in the 2014 edition of the Texas Statutes.

TEXAS FAMILY CODE

Tex. Fam. Code §8.052 (Texas Statutes, 2014 Edition)

A court that determines that a spouse is eligible to receive maintenance under this chapter shall determine the nature, amount, duration, and manner of periodic payments by considering all relevant factors, including:

(1) each spouse's ability to provide for that spouse's minimum reasonable needs independently, considering that spouse's financial resources on dissolution of the marriage;

(2) the education and employment skills of the spouses, the time necessary to acquire sufficient education or training to enable the spouse seeking maintenance to earn sufficient income, and the availability and feasibility of that education or training;

(3) the duration of the marriage;

(4) the age, employment history, earning ability, and physical and emotional condition of the spouse seeking maintenance;

(5) the effect on each spouse's ability to provide for that spouse's minimum reasonable needs while providing periodic child support payments or maintenance, if applicable;

(6) acts by either spouse resulting in excessive or abnormal expenditures or destruction, concealment, or fraudulent disposition of community property, joint tenancy, or other property held in common;

(7) the contribution by one spouse to the education, training, or increased earning power of the other spouse;

(8) the property brought to the marriage by either spouse;

(9) the contribution of a spouse as homemaker;

(10) marital misconduct, including adultery and cruel treatment, by either spouse during the marriage; and

(11) any history or pattern of family violence, as defined by Section 71.004.

Additionally, although greatly diminished in importance and eliminated from consideration in a number of jurisdictions, many states still include marital fault as one of the factors that must be considered, and in some jurisdictions it may operate as a bar to support under certain circumstances. Moreover, where marital fault in the traditional sense of the word is not identified as a factor, economic fault may be a permissible consideration. Thus, for example, in assessing a wife's need for support, the court might give weight to the fact that the other spouse had squandered the family fortune on a third party for a nonmarital purpose, thus placing the innocent spouse in an economically vulnerable position.

It should also be noted that "contribution to the marriage" is not limited to financial considerations but is generally intended to account for a spouse's non-monetary contributions to a marriage in the domestic realm. This allows for the recognition that a spouse may have a diminished capacity for self-support because of a primary commitment to the home and/or child rearing.

The general rule is that a judge must consider all of the enumerated factors but can assign them whatever weight he or she believes is appropriate in light of the circumstances of each case. For example, in a case involving a disabled spouse, a judge might give significant weight to considerations of health, need, and earning capacity and little weight to the fact that the spouses were only married for a short period of time (for example, less than five years). However, in another short-term marriage case, the same judge might give considerable weight to this factor and decide that the brevity of the relationship precludes a support order. In yet another short-term marriage situation where one party — let's say a husband in his early 60s — gave up a good job to move across country to join his new spouse and has been unable to find work, the same judge might again discount duration in favor of the combined weight of need, age, earning potential, and, possibly, contribution, with respect to the sacrifice he made so the couple could be together.

This being said, financial need and length of marriage are arguably the most important considerations in the calculation of support. If a marriage is of long duration, for example 20 years or more, and one spouse has been the primary wage earner while the other spouse gave up a career to take care of the household, these considerations may outweigh all others. Accordingly, a judge may well view other considerations, such as the age, health, and earning capacity of a spouse, through the prism of financial need and length of marriage, as these factors tend to build off one another in a cumulative manner.

2. Searching for Greater Certainty: Alimony Guidelines and the American Law Institute's Compensatory Principle

As indicated by the above discussion, an important advantage of the multifactor approach to alimony determinations is the flexibility that it gives judges to make individualized determinations that fit the facts of each case, rather than having to squeeze everyone into a one-size-fits-all support package. However, the flexibility of this approach has been the source of much critical commentary. At the heart of these concerns is the lack of consistency and predictability. In particular, as in the child custody context, the lack of a coherent framework makes it difficult for parties to negotiate a settlement as it is hard to assess the value of a negotiated exchange if one does not know what one is giving up or gaining in the exchange process.

Some commentators have also raised the concern that when courts weigh these factors, they do so in the absence of a clear conceptual framework regarding the purpose of support. Thus, each factor is weighed separately without a clear understanding of how it fits into a cohesive whole — a whole that is impossible to articulate with clarity because the factors point in multiple directions.[4]

Thus, for instance, the fault factor looks backward into the marriage and preserves the historical association between support and punishment, while other factors, such as need, direct a judge to look ahead into the future. Still other factors, such as contribution, suggest a compensatory purpose, and some, such as earning capacity, may reflect multiple impulses — a judge might be inclined to look to the future to determine if a spouse will be capable of self-support and/or back into the marriage to determine if there has been a diminution of earning capacity due to the assumption of domestic responsibilities. As one judge wryly put it: "Modern spousal support encompasses at least . . . five separate and distinct functions. Yet we treat them as one. In short, we are calling every animal in the zoo a cat, and in doing so, we lose our ability to apply rational criteria to decision-making." Gordon, *supra* note 4, at 301 (citing Leslie Herndon Spillane, Spousal Support: The Other Ohio Lottery, 24 Ohio N.U. L. Rev. 281, 318-331 (1998)).

This brief discussion reveals a theme that weaves through the family law field as a whole, namely, the abiding tension between the need for discretion and flexibility on the one hand, and the desirability of predictability and coherence on the other. Given, as we have seen, that the law of spousal support is clearly tilted in favor of a flexible, individualized approach, there has been a growing push to incorporate greater predictability and coherence into the support determination process. We now look briefly at two such proposals.

Spousal Support Guidelines

When it comes to child support, as was discussed in Chapter 6, the tension between flexibility and predictability has clearly been resolved in favor of the latter.

---

[4]*See* Marie Gordon, Spousal Support Guidelines and the American Experience: Moving Beyond Discretion, 19 Can. J. Fam. L. 247 (2002); June Carbone, The Futility of Coherence: The ALI's *Principles of the Law of Family Dissolution*, Compensatory Spousal Payments, 43 J.L. & Fam. Stud. 43 (2002).

Governed by a federal framework, all states have adopted child support guidelines that employ specific numeric criteria for the computation of support awards. Accordingly, whether the case is litigated or settled, parties participate in the process with a fairly stable sense of the likely support amount.

Seeking this same kind of predictability, some family law experts have recommended a similar approach to spousal support. The use of clear guidelines and numeric criteria would remove the guesswork from the process and allow parties to negotiate their differences based on a clear understanding of what a court is likely to do. To this end, a few states and a number of counties have recently adopted a guidelines approach to spousal support awards, and this appears to be a slowly growing trend.

However, even where adopted, spousal support guidelines do not necessarily provide the same degree of certainty that is typically provided by child support guidelines. Perhaps the most obvious reason for this difference is that in the child support context, the underlying obligation is assumed; accordingly, guidelines do not need to focus on the question of whether the support should be awarded in the first place. Instead, as required by federal law, they can simply be structured to provide a computational framework that yields a "presumptively correct support amount."

In contrast, there is not a parallel entitlement to spousal support; accordingly, in any given case, the issue is typically not simply *how much* support is due, but *whether* it is due at all, and if so, for how long and for what purpose is it to be paid? As a result, it is clearly more difficult to develop spousal support guidelines that readily yield a "presumptively correct support amount" as these multiple determinations often shade into one another.

In addition to this complexity, in some jurisdictions, guidelines are only used for the purpose of determining temporary spousal support awards, and they thus do not control the ultimate outcome, which remains indeterminate. Furthermore, guidelines may be developed for the purpose of providing parties with a starting point for negotiations, rather than being structured to provide a presumptively correct support amount, which once again leads to less predictability than is the case with regard to child support.

The ALI's Compensatory Principle

Another proposed approach has been to provide a clear doctrinal rationale for spousal support awards beyond simply the articulation of financial "need" in combination with other related considerations. To this end, seeking to clearly link the necessity for support to the actual economic consequences of the marital relationship, the ALI's *Principles of the Law of Family Dissolution* urges a compensatory focus that seeks to allocate the "financial losses that arise at the dissolution of a marriage according to equitable principles that are consistent and predictable in application."[5] Central to this shift is the recognition that, especially in long-term

---

[5]Geoffrey C. Hazard, Jr., Foreword to the *Principles of the Law of Family Dissolution: Analysis and Recommendations*, at §5.02 cmt. a (proposed final draft 1997), cited in Carbone, *supra* note 4, at 64-65.

marriages, there often is a "loss in living standard experienced at dissolution by the spouse who has less wealth or earning capacity."[6]

As articulated in the Principles, loss is directly related to a spouse's contribution to the marriage, and thus rather than suggesting dependency, as support so often does, this reframes support as a necessary and coherent response to the prior allocation of marital roles and responsibilities. As one commentator put it: "In the paradigm shift that this approach follows, there is an implicit recognition of 'entitlement' rather than 'charity.' Payments are made because they are earned rather than pled for. 'Need' is more clearly defined as being an outcome of loss, rather than a reason in and of itself."[7]

D. STRUCTURING THE SUPPORT AWARD

As developed in this section, support can be structured in a variety of ways to accomplish different objectives. Each approach has its own rules regarding the modification and termination of the support award.

1. Permanent Alimony

"Permanent" alimony is probably what most people think of when they think of alimony, but since no-fault reform this approach has arguably been eclipsed by rehabilitative support (discussed below). The primary purpose of **permanent alimony** is to provide financial assistance to the spouse in an economically weaker position. It is payable in regular intervals on an ongoing basis.

Permanent alimony can also serve a compensatory purpose. As previously discussed, a spouse (usually the wife) who restricts her participation in the paid labor force to care for her family experiences a loss of earning capacity over the course of the marriage. At the same time, the earning capacity of her spouse is enhanced, as he is freed up to focus on his labor market participation. Although this may be a mutually beneficial arrangement during the marriage, upon divorce the spouses stand on very different footing — in effect, there has been a transfer in earning ability from one spouse to the other. Alimony payments may be used to offset this result and compensate a spouse for the

Interview Checklist

In any case where spousal support is an issue, it is necessary to develop a picture of the ways in which each spouse has contributed to the marriage. Focus on both financial and nonfinancial contributions. To do this, obtain the kinds of information about both parties listed below. It is unlikely that you will be able to obtain all of the necessary information about your client's spouse from an interview; discovery will probably be needed to complete the picture. However, you can start with obtaining complete employment histories for each job held by both spouses during the marriage and for a reasonable time before it, including the following information:

- job titles
- promotions
- salaries
- hours worked
- general responsibilities

Also, you will want to obtain the educational histories of each spouse, including any specifics on

- career training;
- career goals, including any educational plans; and

---

[6]Carbone, *supra* note 4, at 65 (citing §5.05 of the *Principles of the Law of Family Dissolution*).
[7]Gordon, *supra* note 4, at 269.

details on any gaps in the parties' employment histories — especially those stemming from child rearing or other domestic responsibilities.

Finally, it is important to ascertain factors that may affect the parties' employment potential, such as

- earning capacity
- general market outlook for each spouse's career/job health
- considerations that may impact future employment

opportunity cost of having invested a significant portion of her time in the domestic realm to the detriment of her earning ability. Unlike that of rehabilitative support, the goal of permanent alimony is not to help a spouse achieve economic self-sufficiency, and there is no duty to use the money for this purpose. Accordingly, a defining aspect of a permanent support award is that it is not subject to a durational time limitation.

However, although permanent alimony is not subject to durational limits, *permanent* does not necessarily mean forever. Rather, the term is used to distinguish support awarded at the time of divorce from support awarded during the pendency of the divorce action — known as **alimony pendente lite**, or **temporary alimony** — which is intended to assist a spouse during this interim period. Thus, although not subject to pre-established durational limits, permanent alimony is subject to reduction or termination based on a **change in circumstances**, with the near universal rule being that remarriage of the recipient spouse or the death of either one terminates the obligation. (See Section E, below.)

2. Lump-Sum Support

Although not a frequently used option, many states authorize the award of a **lump-sum support** payment, sometimes referred to as **alimony in gross**. Unlike permanent alimony, this approach involves the payment of a sum certain, which is typically paid in a single installment, although it can also be made payable in periodic installments until the full amount of the support award is reached.

Once ordered, most states agree that the recipient acquires a vested right to the entire amount, thus making it nonmodifiable based on a change in circumstances, including remarriage of the recipient. This remains true even where the lump sum is payable in installments. If the payor dies before the full amount is paid, the balance is chargeable to his or her estate; likewise, if the recipient dies before receiving payment in full, the balance due can be collected by his or her estate. Accordingly, along the lines of the old adage "a bird in the hand is worth two in the bush," a recipient may prefer to accept a potentially smaller but definite lump-sum payment instead of running the risk that periodic payments will not always be made.

3. Rehabilitative or Transitional Support

As noted above, following no-fault reform, **rehabilitative support**, often called **transitional support**, became the preferred approach in many jurisdictions. Rehabilitative support is awarded on a time-limited basis for the purpose of enabling an economically dependent spouse to obtain the education or training necessary to become financially self-sufficient.

To establish the durational limit, a court will try to predict how long it will take for a spouse to become self-sufficient and then set this as the date for the expiration of the obligation; in some states, maximum time limits are set by statute. In some states, courts may retain jurisdiction and extend the time limit if a spouse can show that despite a good faith effort he or she has not been able to achieve the degree of self-sufficiency contemplated at the time of the award. Many jurisdictions, however, do not permit extensions even where a spouse is not yet self-sufficient despite a good faith effort. Here, rather than focusing on the economic situation of the spouse seeking to achieve self-sufficiency, the courts prioritize the expectancy interest of the payor spouse and his or her wish to plan for the future unencumbered by unexpected obligations from a previous marriage.

Although there is general agreement that the goal of rehabilitative support is self-sufficiency, there is disagreement about what this means. A few states take a bare-bones approach and consider a person self-sufficient if, at the end of the rehabilitative period, he or she is not dependent on public assistance. Other courts, particularly in situations involving a long-term marriage, define self-sufficiency by reference to the marital standard of living. Here, the goal is met when a spouse is able to obtain employment that would enable him or her to approximate the prior marital standard of living.[8]

Rehabilitative support took hold quickly during the period of no-fault reform, as it represented a break from the traditional alimony model that was associated with outmoded assumptions about fault and the economic incapacity of divorced women. Its underlying objectives were commendable and consistent with the new approach to restructuring family obligations following divorce. Rehabilitative support sets out to accomplish the following goals:

- to enable previously economically dependent spouses to develop their earning potential and realize true independence;
- to enable spouses to make a clean break and begin life anew on equal footing in keeping with the partnership view of marriage; and
- to release spouses from ongoing financial obligations derived from a failed relationship.

Beginning in the mid-1980s, however, a countertrend emerged. Appellate judges began to set aside rehabilitative awards, denouncing them as an abuse of judicial discretion. One judge went so far as to label them a "male-oriented, sexist approach."[9] These reversals have generally come in cases of long-term marriages where a woman has forgone labor market participation or has moved in and out of the workplace based on the needs of her family. According to the courts, the goal

---

[8]See, for example, Biscardi's comparative analysis of Texas's minimalist approach with Tennessee's marital standard of living approach. Biscardi, *supra* note 1, at 417-423. *See also* Alicia Brokars Kelly, The Marital Partnership Pretense and Career Assets: The Ascendancy of Self over the Marital Community, 81 B.U. L. Rev. 59, 107 (2001).
[9]*Avirett v. Avirett*, 187 N.J. Super. 380, 383, 454 A.2d 917, 919 (Ch. Div. 1982) (overruled on other grounds). For discussion of this trend, see Joan M. Krauskopf, Rehabilitative Alimony: Uses and Abuses of Limited Duration Alimony, 21 Fam. L.Q. 579 (1988).

of economic self-sufficiency is illusory in these situations because a woman who has been family-centered will not be able to recapture her lost earning potential, and a rehabilitative award would leave the spouses with a gross disparity in earning capacity — a result that undervalues her contribution to the marriage.

Accordingly, some trial courts have become a bit more circumspect, particularly in cases involving long-term marriages where responsibilities have been allocated along traditional gender lines. Rather than assuming that a rehabilitative award is appropriate, a court might instead place a burden on the party seeking to limit support to show how the other spouse will be able to achieve meaningful financial independence within the proposed time frames. This may require evidence about available educational programs and labor market conditions in the spouse's area of interest that indicate a likelihood of employment at a decent wage.

However, the tide may again be turning in the wake of the more recent movement to adopt spousal support guidelines — a movement, that at least in part, has again been fueled by a hardening of attitudes toward former spouses who collect support for extended periods of time following a divorce. Thus, for example, primary proponents of Massachusetts's sweeping 2011 alimony reform law, which, among other measures, set durational limits on virtually all support awards, included an organization of alimony paying men and the closely associated Second Wives and Partners Club who lobbied to end unreasonably long and inconsistent alimony awards.

Case Preview

Turner v. Turner

This case arose out of the dissolution of a 31-year marriage between E. Diane Turner and Donald Turner. The Turners started their marriage with very modest means, but over the course of 31 years built up a very successful business in which most of the stock was owned by the husband and the wife held a very small share. The Maryland Court of Special Appeals examined the issue of the relationship between spousal support and a division of marital assets, as well as the appropriateness of rehabilitative versus permanent support, different earning capacities, imputed income, and fault. The court also paid close attention to the statutory factors for determining spousal support.

As you read *Turner v. Turner*, look for the following:

1. What are the facts that the court found legally significant?
2. Why did the lower court reduce the original support amount?
3. Why did this court impute income to the wife?
4. What factors did the court consider when discussing the gross disparity in the parties' earning capacity?

Turner v. Turner

809 A.2d 18 (Md. Ct. Spec. App. 2002)

This appeal arises from two law suits instituted by E. Diane Turner, appellant. . . . One involves the dissolution of the marriage of appellant and Donald Turner, appellee. The other concerns Mr. Turner and the family business, Baltimore Stage Lighting, Inc. ("BSL" or the "Company"), appellee, a close corporation wholly owned by the Turners.

In a sense, the Turners epitomize the rags to riches American dream. At the outset of their lengthy marriage, the Turners were of modest means. Then, they combined their enterprising spirit with creativity and determination to create BSL, a very profitable business.

I. FACTUAL AND PROCEDURAL SUMMARY

The divorce case was filed on July 15, 1997, initially on the ground of desertion. It was later amended to allege adultery. The corporate suit . . . contains twelve counts. Ms. Turner alleged . . . that Mr. Turner misappropriated corporate funds to finance his drug habit, for which she sought various remedies in her capacities as stockholder and employee. She also claimed an equitable ownership of a 50% interest in BSL. . . .

After thirty-one years of marriage, the couple separated in June 1997. At the time of the trials, they were in their early 50's, and generally in good health.

While working full-time at another job, Mr. Turner devoted his evenings to the development of a lighting business. . . . By 1974, it had grown so much that appellee began to work for it on a full-time basis. The business evolved into BSL. . . . Although Mr. Turner became the president of BSL, it is undisputed that Ms. Turner was actively involved in BSL from its inception, and worked full-time in the business for many years. . . .

While both parties devoted considerable time and effort to BSL, appellee was paid a significantly higher salary than appellant. Moreover, Mr. Turner owned 65 shares of BSL stock, while only 10 shares were titled to appellant. Ms. Turner testified that she periodically discussed with appellee her desire to hold title to an amount of BSL stock equal to his. She claimed that appellee assured her that they had an "equal" interest in BSL, and "it didn't make any difference" how the stock was titled. . . .

Ms. Turner recalled that problems in the marriage surfaced in 1995, when she noticed that Mr. Turner was coming home less frequently. By 1996, she suspected that he was involved with drugs and other women. Ms. Turner's concerns were confirmed in January 1997, when she discovered that appellee was using cocaine and had a relationship with another woman. Appellant also learned on June 9, 1997, that appellee had been removing cash from BSL. Soon afterwards, the parties separated. . . .

Ms. Turner . . . seeks to review the amount of alimony that was awarded, contending that it is inadequate to meet her needs. . . .

Significantly, the court below substantially reduced appellant's alimony from $2000 a week to $2000 per month, expressly because it believed the marital award would generate an income stream for appellant's support; it clearly regarded the marital award as a significant component of appellant's support. . . .

II. ATTRIBUTION OF INCOME TO APPELLANT

[A]ppellant had "no intention to seek employment, and her only source of revenue has been alimony payments." Moreover, appellant believed she had "paid her dues." Nevertheless, the court imputed earned income to appellant of $35,000. In so doing, Ms. Turner . . . argues that it was grossly unfair for the court "to essentially force [her] to get employment, inevitably as a start-up employee" given the length of the parties' marriage, her age, contributions to BSL, and appellee's egregious conduct.

This contention shall not detain us long. Appellant conflates the court's finding of employability, for which it attributed income to appellant for purposes of the alimony analysis, with the view that the court has forced her to obtain employment outside the home. As we see it, the court's finding that appellant is capable of employment does not mean that she must actually obtain employment. Put another way, appellant has not been driven into the marketplace, as she seems to suggest; whether appellant actually chooses to obtain employment remains entirely up to her. Nevertheless, appellant is clearly employable, given her age, health, work experience, skills, and the absence of minor children in the home. Therefore, the court was more than justified in attributing potential earnings to appellant as a predicate to determining the appropriate amount of alimony.

III. THE ALIMONY AWARD

Appellant contends that, even if she is capable of earning $35,000 annually . . . [u]nder the circumstances attendant here, she maintains that the alimony award of $2000 a month is "grossly inadequate." Appellant advances several grounds to support her claim. In particular, she suggests that appellee earns substantially more than the court found, and therefore the court erred as to the annual income attributed to him for purposes of making its alimony determination. Further, while recognizing that she received a sizeable marital award, appellant asserts that the award merely "placed [her] long-term assets on a par with that of her husband." Appellant also complains of the inequity in being forced out of BSL, a business that she worked hard to develop, and of having to "start all over," with the attendant difficulty of finding suitable employment, while appellee is allowed to "reap the rewards" of their joint effort. Appellant is particularly disgruntled in light of appellee's conduct, which led to the dissolution of the marriage.

For his part, appellee argues that, in deciding the amount of alimony, the trial court properly considered the division of marital property and the income stream that appellant's share will inevitably generate. Appellee also relies on *Blaine v. Blaine*, 336 Md. 49, 646 A.2d 413 (1994), for the view that "the formerly dependent spouse ordinarily is not entitled to have his or her standard of living 'keep pace' with that of the other spouse after the divorce, or to share in the other spouse's future accumulations of wealth." Id. at 70. . . .

Thus, our sole focus here concerns the amount of the monthly alimony award. . . . It is well settled that "the 'policy of this State is to limit alimony, where appropriate, to a definite term in order to provide each party with an incentive to become fully self-supporting." *Digges v. Digges*, 126 Md. App. 361, 386, 730 A.2d 202 (quoting *Jensen v. Jensen*, 103 Md. App. 678, 692, 654 A.2d 914 (1995)), *cert. denied*, 356 Md. 17

(1999). . . . In the seminal case of *Tracey v. Tracey*, 328 Md. 380, 614 A.2d 590 (1992), the Court of Appeals explained:

> The purpose of alimony is not to provide a lifetime pension, but where practicable to ease the transition for the parties from the joint married state to their new status as single people living apart and independently. Expressed otherwise, alimony's purpose is to provide an opportunity for the recipient spouse to become self-supporting. The concept of alimony as life-long support enabling the dependent spouse to maintain an accustomed standard of living has largely been superseded by the view that the dependent spouse should be required to become self-supporting, even though that might result in a reduced standard of living.

Id. at 391 (citations and quotations omitted).

The party seeking indefinite alimony bears the burden of satisfying the statutory criteria. . . . Notably, "self-sufficiency per se does not bar an award of indefinite alimony. . . . If a court projects that a party will become self-supporting, subsection (2) provides that, if and when a party makes as much progress toward becoming self-supporting as can reasonably be expected, an award of indefinite alimony may still be justified if the standards of living will be unconscionably disparate. . . .

To the extent that the court found that appellant currently earns $175,000 per year, or even $200,000 a year, the finding was not supported by the evidence. Among other factors, the propriety of the annual alimony award of $24,000 must be measured against the income appellee actually earns. . . .

Significantly, in light of the divorce, appellant no longer has to divide or apportion between himself and appellant the salaries previously generated by BSL for the two corporate employees who were also the only owners of the Company. . . . Because appellant no longer draws a salary from BSL, that money is now available to appellee, minus any cost of hiring someone to do the work that appellant once performed. Therefore, Mr. Turner can undoubtedly retain for himself a large portion of the $80,000 to $85,000 that appellant, individually, had been paid while the parties were married. . . .

[T]he court's finding that appellee earns between $175,000 and $200,000 is between $60,000 and $85,000 less than appellee's actual earnings or earnings capacity over the past several years. Based on the evidence, appellee could reasonably expect to earn about $260,000 annually from BSL. Moreover, as best we can determine, the earnings that the court attributed to appellee did not include the value of the benefits provided to him by BSL, such as a car, insurance, phone, and bonuses. It follows that appellee's current salary of about $260,000 exceeds appellant's imputed income of $35,000 by about $215,000, exclusive of her investment income. . . .

Even if we agreed with the court's income calculations for appellee of $175,000 to $200,000, our conclusion as to the court's alimony award would be the same. By the court's own analysis, appellee's income is quite substantial and likely to increase. Whether appellee earns $175,000, $200,000, or $260,000 a year, we believe the court erred and/or abused its discretion with respect to its alimony award. In reaching our conclusion, we rely, in part, on many of the court's own findings. We explain.

As the circuit court found, this was a marriage of considerable length, and it was appellee's "conduct [that] gave rise to the estrangement between the parties." Moreover, the court recognized that during their thirty-one years of marriage, both parties made "significant contributions" and devoted "substantial time and effort" to "the development of BSL from a fledgling company" to a significant corporate entity. The court found that appellant "was equally involved [with appellee] in the development of the business.". . . Nevertheless, . . . Mr. Turner alone retains "the controlling ownership interest" in BSL; only he "remains enmeshed" in BSL, notwithstanding that "BSL has been as much [appellant's] career and a focal point for her interests . . . as it was for her husband." Of particular import, the court expressly found that, as a consequence of the dissolution of the marriage, appellant "lost her career path . . . ," and now has an earning capacity of $35,000 a year.

The parties' lengthy mutual involvement in the lucrative family business distinguishes this case from others that suggest that, after divorce, a dependent spouse cannot expect to "keep pace" with the economic status of the person who was the primary economic provider during the marriage. See, e.g., *Blaine*, 336 Md. at 70. Although we do not suggest that appellant was necessarily entitled to economic parity upon divorce, we recognize, as did the circuit court, that this is a case in which both parties helped to create BSL, and appellant worked for the Company for almost 25 years. . . . While recognizing the length and value of appellant's efforts, the circuit court noted that Mr. Turner's "career path is set, and will continue to prove lucrative," but appellant has been completely "derailed." In awarding appellant $24,000 a year in alimony, the court was of the view that the "significant assets" with which both parties left the marriage would yield an adequate supplement to appellant's alimony and earned income. As noted, the court awarded appellant 55% of the marital property, which included the value of BSL. Appellee maintains that the marital award is sufficient to rectify any inequity in earnings, despite the fact that he received marital property of almost equal value.

As the trial court found, appellant played a vital role in helping the parties to amass their wealth. Yet, the almost equal division of the value of the Company hardly puts appellant on an equal footing with Mr. Turner. Appellee alone retains control of BSL, not merely 55% of its value, while appellant is no longer employed by the Company. Therefore, appellee alone will continue to benefit from the opportunity to maintain lucrative employment with BSL, annually drawing about a quarter of a million dollars in salary, benefits, and bonuses. In contrast, appellant must now decide whether to confront the uncertainties of the marketplace, in the hope of obtaining new employment that will likely yield an income that is less than half of what appellant earned in her own name while at BSL, and a fraction of what the couple earned collectively. While the parties were married, it was not particularly significant as to how they apportioned their salaries, because both benefited economically from the success of the enterprise that they jointly formed. . . .

As we indicated, [Family Law] §11-106(b)(3) entitles the court to consider the standard of living that the parties established during the marriage. In order to live as appellant was accustomed during the marriage — a lifestyle that she helped the parties to achieve — the unassailable fact is that appellant must supplement her income by using money generated from investments. . . . Recent times have underscored the difficulty of predicting a yield on investments, and the challenges of relying on the stock market as a supplement to support.

Family Law §11-106(b)(9) provides that, in regard to the alimony determination, the court must consider "the ability of the party from whom alimony is sought to meet" his own needs, along with the needs of appellant. . . . In contrast to appellant, because appellee's career remains intact, and he continues at the helm of a prosperous company, with a salary that far exceeds his expenses, it is unlikely that he will have to use investment income or invade the corpus of investments to meet current expenses. Instead, it appears that Mr. Turner will be in a position to maintain the corpus and reinvest the income generated by his investments, thereby adding to his wealth and widening the disparity in the parties' economic status.

Appellant is the one who has been deprived of an opportunity to continue to enjoy the sizeable economic rewards of working for BSL, while appellee will continue to work there, earning far more than appellant can ever hope to achieve. In light of all the circumstances discussed above, including the length of the marriage, the reasons for and consequences of the parties' estrangement, the wife's contributions to BSL, the couple's respective economic positions and financial resources, the undetermined amount of investment income that appellant can reasonably expect to earn from her share of the marital assets, and the court's reliance on an incorrect amount of earned income for appellee, we conclude that the court erred and abused its discretion in its award of indefinite monthly alimony in the amount of $2000. Therefore, we shall vacate the alimony award and remand for further proceedings.

Post-Case Follow-Up

The court imputes income to Mrs. Turner of $35,000, finding that this is her earning capacity should she decide to seek employment. Accordingly, while Mrs. Turner is free to not work, she cannot then voluntarily use her desire not to work as a reason to increase her spousal support award. However, on the other hand, the court found that in considering the factors in determining the amount of support, the trial court had erred in limiting support to $2,000 a month. Rather, in considering the length of marriage, the involvement of both parties in the business, the lifestyle of the parties during the marriage, the ability of Mr. Turner to meet his own needs while also paying support to Mrs. Turner, as well as the fault of Mr. Turner in causing the dissolution of the marriage, it was appropriate to vacate the award of $2,000 a month and remand the case for further proceedings.

Turner v. Turner: Real Life Applications

1. Assume that in the *Turner* case the parties did not own a business but instead Mr. Turner worked in an office earning $200,000 a year and Mrs. Turner did not work outside the home. What factors in awarding spousal support in an amount of greater than $2,000 would still be relevant to the court's determination?

2. Sally has come to your office and advises you that she has been married to Doug for 35 years and they have decided to divorce. Doug was a medical doctor until he retired three years ago. Now he does consulting work and lectures around the country at various medical schools, earning approximately $120,000 to $150,000 a year to supplement the parties' retirement income from their various assets, which generate $5,000 a month. Sally tells you that she has built up the consulting business for Doug and she is the one who books his speaking engagements. Now that he has built up the business he tells Sally he can hire someone to do her job for $24,000 a year. Sally wants to know what factors the court will consider in awarding her spousal support. Both Sally and Doug are 60 years old. Sally says she is not aware of any fault on the part of either party; they have just grown apart and want to move on with their lives separately.

a. Assume that Sally comes to you after trial of her dissolution matter where the trial court attributed $24,000 a year in income to her, gave her half the retirement accounts so she generates $2,500 a month from the accounts, and awards her $1,000 a month in spousal support. Based on *Turner*, what grounds might you have to vacate the support award?

b. Assume instead you represent Doug. What would you argue in defense of Doug to uphold the award?

4. The Professional Degree Cases

Although the permanent, lump-sum, and rehabilitative approaches to spousal support are relatively easy to characterize, there has been considerable confusion regarding what to do in cases where one spouse supports the other through a professional degree program, thus increasing the degreed spouse's future earning capacity, but the marriage ends before these gains are realized. In this section, we consider the various options.

The Degree as Property

One option is to treat the degree as marital property and subject it to division along with the other marital assets. However, the overwhelming majority of jurisdictions have rejected this approach based on the view that a degree, or the enhanced earning capacity it represents, does not fit within the meaning of the term "property." In deciding against this approach, courts have focused on the difficulty of valuing a degree, as this would require speculation about the course someone's career will take. However, it is at least worth noting that despite the reluctance of the family courts to engage in this kind of valuation, it is done routinely in personal injury cases when deciding how much to award a plaintiff for lost future earnings. Courts have also focused on other characteristics that distinguish a degree from other forms of property such as that acquisition of a degree requires substantial personal effort and sacrifice; that it lacks an objective value in the open market; and that it is personal to the holder and cannot be sold, transferred, or left to future generations (see Chapter 8).

Spousal Support Options

Although generally declining to treat the degree or the enhanced earnings it represents as marital property, courts may consider it when determining the appropriateness and amount of support. One approach is to fashion a reimbursement alimony award; another is to consider the non-degreed spouse's contribution as a relevant factor in the support calculus.

Reimbursement Alimony

The Supreme Court of New Jersey is generally credited with developing the concept of reimbursement alimony in the 1982 case of *Mahoney v. Mahoney*, 453 A.2d 527 (N.J. 1982), in which the husband left the marriage soon after earning an advanced degree with the wife's dedicated support. Many jurisdictions have followed New Jersey's lead and will reimburse a spouse for contributions to the other spouse's education, recognizing that the supporting spouse made significant sacrifices based on the reasonable expectation that he or she would share in the future gain represented by the degree. Through reimbursement, courts can adjust this imbalance by

Supreme Court of New Jersey
Courtesy of the New Jersey Judiciary

returning the contribution to the spouse who will not participate in the anticipated benefits because of divorce.

Case Preview

Mahoney v. Mahoney

Melvin and June Mahoney were married in Indiana in 1971 and separated in 1978. At the time of the marriage, Melvin had an engineering degree and June a B.S. degree. They both contributed to the household expenses with the exception of the time between September 1975 and January 1977, when Melvin attended the Wharton School of the University of Pennsylvania and received an M.B.A. degree. During this time, June contributed about $24,000 to the household expenses and Melvin made no contributions.

June had argued that the degree was "property" to be valued and subject to equitable distribution. The lower court rejected the argument that the degree was "property" and did not award June any interest in the value of the degree. The

Supreme Court of New Jersey agreed that it was not "property" but still addressed the issue of how to compensate June, who had made financial contributions toward Melvin's professional education.

In reading *Mahoney v. Mahoney*, look for the following:

1. Why does the court believe it is inequitable for the wife in this case to not be reimbursed for her contributions?
2. What are the factors the court considers important in looking at whether reimbursement support is appropriate?
3. Why does the court consider the degree-holding spouse's earning capacity as a form of permanent alimony?

Mahoney v. Mahoney
453 A.2d 527 (N.J. 1982)

[After reviewing the case law and determining that an educational degree is not "property" to be equitably distributed, the court reviewed whether there was an ability to consider the degree for purposes of an award of alimony.]

This Court does not support reimbursement between former spouses in alimony proceedings as a general principle. Marriage is not a business arrangement in which the parties keep track of debits and credits, their accounts to be settled upon divorce. Rather, as we have said, "marriage is a shared enterprise, a joint undertaking . . . in many ways it is akin to a partnership." *Rothman v. Rothman*, 65 N.J. 219, 229, 320 A.2d 496 (1974). . . . But every joint undertaking has its bounds of fairness. Where a partner to marriage takes the benefits of his spouse's support in obtaining a professional degree or license with the understanding that future benefits will accrue and inure to both of them, and the marriage is then terminated without the supported spouse giving anything in return, an unfairness has occurred that calls for a remedy.

In this case, the supporting spouse made financial contributions towards her husband's professional education with the expectation that both parties would enjoy material benefits flowing from the professional license or degree. It is therefore patently unfair that the supporting spouse be denied the mutually anticipated benefit while the supported spouse keeps not only the degree, but also all of the financial and material rewards flowing from it.

Furthermore, it is realistic to recognize that in this case, a supporting spouse has contributed more than mere earnings to her husband with the mutual expectation that both of them — she as well as he — will realize and enjoy material improvements in their marriage as a result of his increased earning capacity. Also, the wife has presumably made personal financial sacrifices, resulting in a reduced or lowered standard of living. Additionally, her husband, by pursuing preparations for a future career, has foregone gainful employment and financial contributions to the marriage that would have been forthcoming had he been employed. He thereby has further reduced the level of support his wife might otherwise have received, as well as the standard of living both of them would have otherwise enjoyed. In effect, through her contributions, the supporting spouse has consented to live at a lower material level while her husband has prepared for another career. She has postponed, as it were, present consumption and a higher standard of living, for the future prospect of greater support and material benefits. The supporting spouse's sacrifices would have been rewarded had the marriage endured and the mutual expectations of both of them been fulfilled. The unredressed sacrifices — loss of support and reduction of the standard of living — coupled with the unfairness attendant upon the defeat of the supporting spouse's shared expectation of future advantages, further justify a remedial reward. In this sense, an award that is referable to the spouse's monetary contributions to her partner's education significantly implicates basic considerations of marital support and standard of living — factors that are clearly relevant in the determination and award of conventional alimony.

To provide a fair and effective means of compensating a supporting spouse who has suffered a loss or reduction of support, or has incurred a lower standard of living, or has been deprived of a better standard of living in the future, the Court now introduces the concept of reimbursement alimony into divorce proceedings. The concept properly accords with the Court's belief that regardless of the appropriateness of permanent alimony or the presence or absence of marital property to be equitably distributed, there will be circumstances where a supporting spouse should be reimbursed for the financial contributions he or she made to the spouse's successful professional training. Such reimbursement alimony should cover all financial contributions towards the former spouse's education, including household expenses, educational costs, school travel expenses and any other contributions used by the supported spouse in obtaining his or her degree or license.

This result is consistent with the remedial provisions of the matrimonial statute. N.J.S.A. 2A:34-23. A basic purpose of alimony relates to the quality of economic life to which one spouse is entitled and that becomes the obligation of the other. Alimony has to do with support and standard of living. See *Khalaf v. Khalaf*, 58 N.J. 63, 69, 275 A.2d 132 (1971). We have recently recognized the relevance of these concepts in accepting the notion of rehabilitative alimony, which is consonant with the basic underlying rationale that a party is entitled to continue at a customary standard of living inclusive of costs necessary for needed educational training. *Lepis v. Lepis*, 83 N.J. 139, 155 n.9, 416 A.2d 45.

The statute recognizes that alimony should be tailored to individual circumstances, particularly those relating to the financial status of the parties. Thus, in all actions for divorce (fault and no fault), when alimony is awarded, the court should consider actual need, ability to pay and duration of the marriage. In a "fault" divorce, however, the court "may consider also the proofs made in establishing such ground in determining . . . alimony . . . that is fit, reasonable and just." N.J.S.A. 2A:34-23. There is nothing in the statute to suggest that the standards for awarding alimony are mutually exclusive. Consequently, the financial contributions of the parties during the marriage can be relevant. Financial dishonesty or financial unfairness between the spouses, or overreaching also can be material. The Legislature has not precluded these considerations. Nothing in the statute precludes the court from considering marital conduct — such as one spouse contributing to the career of the other with the expectation of material benefit — in fashioning alimony awards. See *Lepis v. Lepis*, supra.

The flexible nature of relief in a matrimonial cause is also evidenced by the equitable distribution remedy that is provided in the same section of the matrimonial statute.

The Court does not hold that every spouse who contributes toward his or her partner's education or professional training is entitled to reimbursement alimony. Only monetary contributions made with the mutual and shared expectation that both parties to the marriage will derive increased income and material benefits should be a basis for such an award. For example, it is unlikely that a financially successful executive's spouse who, after many years of homemaking, returns to school would upon divorce be required to reimburse her husband for his contributions toward her degree. Reimbursement alimony should not subvert the basic goals of traditional alimony and equitable distribution.

In proper circumstances, however, courts should not hesitate to award reimbursement alimony. Marriage should not be a free ticket to professional education and training without subsequent obligations. This Court should not ignore the scenario of the young professional who after being supported through graduate school leaves his mate for supposedly greener pastures. One spouse ought not to receive a divorce complaint when the other receives a diploma. Those spouses supported through professional school should recognize that they may be called upon to reimburse the supporting spouses for the financial contributions they received in pursuit of their professional training. And they cannot deny the basic fairness of this result.

As we have stated, reimbursement alimony will not always be appropriate or necessary to compensate a spouse who has contributed financially to the partner's professional education or training. "Rehabilitative alimony" may be more appropriate in cases where a spouse who gave up or postponed her own education to support the household requires a lump sum or a short-term award to achieve economic self-sufficiency. The Court specifically approved of such limited alimony awards in *Lepis v. Lepis*, 83 N.J. 139, 155 n.9, 416 A.2d 45 (1980), stating that we did "not share the view that only unusual cases will warrant the 'rehabilitative alimony' approach." However, rehabilitative alimony would not be appropriate where the supporting spouse is unable to return to the job market, or has already attained economic self-sufficiency.

Similarly, where the parties to a divorce have accumulated substantial assets during a lengthy marriage, courts should compensate for any unfairness to one party who sacrificed for the other's education, not by reimbursement alimony but by an equitable distribution of the assets to reflect the parties' different circumstances and earning capacities. In *Rothman*, supra, the Court explicitly rejected the notion that courts should presume an equal division of marital property. 65 N.J. at 232 n.6, 320 A.2d 496. "Rejecting any simple formula, we rather believe that each case should be examined as an individual and particular entity." Id. If the degree-holding spouse has already put his professional education to use, the degree's value in enhanced earning potential will have been realized in the form of property, such as a partnership interest or other asset, that is subject to equitable distribution. See *Stern*, supra, 65 N.J. at 346-47, 331 A.2d 257.

The degree holder's earning capacity can also be considered in an award of permanent alimony. Alimony awards under N.J.S.A. 2A:34-23 must take into account the supporting spouse's ability to pay; earning capacity is certainly relevant to this determination. Our courts have recognized that a primary purpose of alimony, besides preventing either spouse from requiring public assistance, is "to permit the wife, who contributed during marriage to the accumulation of the marital assets, to share therein." *Lynn v. Lynn*, 153 N.J. Super. 377, 382, 379 A.2d 1046 (Ch. Div. 1977), rev'd on other grounds, 165 N.J. Super. 328, 398 A.2d 141 (App. Div. 1979). . . . Even though the enhanced earning potential provided by a degree or license is not "property" for purposes of N.J.S.A. 2A:34-23, it clearly should be a factor considered by the trial judge in determining a proper amount of alimony. If the degree holder's actual earnings turn out to diverge greatly from the court's estimate, making the amount of alimony unfair to either party, the alimony award can be adjusted accordingly.

III

We [have stated previously], that while earning potential should not be treated as a separate item of property, [p]otential earning capacity is doubtless a factor to be considered by a trial judge in determining what distribution will be "equitable" and it is even more obviously relevant upon the issue of alimony.

We believe that . . . presents the best approach for achieving fairness when one spouse has acquired a professional degree or license during the marriage. Courts may not make any permanent distribution of the value of professional degrees and licenses, whether based upon estimated worth or cost. However, where a spouse has received from his or her partner financial contributions used in obtaining a professional degree or license with the expectation of deriving material benefits for both marriage partners, that spouse may be called upon to reimburse the supporting spouse for the amount of contributions received.

In the present case, the defendant's financial support helped her husband to obtain his M.B.A. degree, which assistance was undertaken with the expectation of deriving material benefits for both spouses. Although the trial court awarded the defendant a sum as "equitable offset" for her contributions, the trial court's approach was not consistent with the guidelines we have announced in this opinion. Therefore, we are remanding the case so the trial court can determine whether reimbursement alimony should be awarded in this case and, if so, what amount is appropriate.

The judgment of the Appellate Division is reversed and the cause remanded for further proceedings not inconsistent with this opinion.

Post-Case Follow-Up

The court recognizes that it is not possible to divide the "degree" but that there were sacrifices Mrs. Mahoney had made in order for Mr. Mahoney to obtain the degree. In fashioning the award, the court held that the supporting spouse was entitled to be reimbursed for all financial contributions made to the training of the other spouse, including "household expenses, educational costs, school travel expenses and any other contribution used by the supported spouse in obtaining his or her degree or license." Thus, it is fair for her be able to reclaim some of the initial investment that she made in Mr. Mahoney's career path.

Mahoney v. Mahoney: Real Life Applications

1. Courtney and Lloyd have been married for five years. During this entire time, Lloyd supported Courtney while she was in medical school. After Courtney graduated from medical school, Lloyd filed for divorce and seeks reimbursement alimony for the money he contributed to the marital household while Courtney was in school. Her education was paid for by her grandfather, who had established an education trust. However, other than paying for her own education, Courtney did not contribute to any of the household expenses while she was in school. Lloyd contributed approximately $60,000 toward household expenses during this time. Lloyd asks you if he has a claim for reimbursement alimony. What do you tell him?

2. Assume the same facts as in Question 1, but during the time Courtney is in school, Lloyd has continued to advance in his career and as a result the parties have accumulated many marital assets, including a house, cars, and valuable artwork. Does the fact that the parties have substantial marital assets change your advice to Lloyd?

3. Assume the same facts as in Question 1, but that now Lloyd is earning approximately $250,000 a year in his employment as a result of the promotions and advancements he obtained during the marriage. Does that fact change your advice to Lloyd?

Consistent with their focus on dashed expectations, courts have generally disallowed reimbursement where the marriage continued for a reasonable period of time after the degree was obtained on the theory that the supporting spouse would have realized his or her expectation during the marriage. Moreover, unlike where the divorce follows on the heels of the degree, there is likely to have been an accumulation of assets that can be divided.

Some courts have broadened the concept of reimbursement alimony beyond simply providing recompense for actual expenditures to include "lost opportunity costs," such as forgone income while the degree-holding spouse was enrolled in school and possibly also for forgone educational opportunities. Alternatively, some courts have instead provided rehabilitative support so the non-degreed spouse could also obtain further education.

An important critique of the reimbursement approach is that it only repays a spouse's initial investment in the career of the other and does not provide the spouse with any return on the investment through giving him or her a share of the increased earnings attributable to the enhanced earning capacity. Simply put: "[T]his approach treats the supporting spouse as a lender, not as an investor in the asset."[10]

---

[10]*See* Kelly, *supra* note 8, at 59, 107.

The Degree as a Relevant Factor

A number of courts have declined to embrace the concept of reimbursement. Instead, they prefer to consider the degree as one of the factors that must be weighed in determining if support should be awarded. This is a flexible approach enabling courts to emphasize different considerations. Thus, one court might give greater weight to the contribution and sacrifice of the supporting spouse, while another might focus on the enhanced earning capacity of the degree-holding spouse relative to the stagnant or possibly even diminished earning capacity of the supporting spouse.

E. POST-DIVORCE MODIFICATION AND TERMINATION OF SUPPORT

As with custody or child support, following a divorce, either party may seek to revise the spousal support amount by filing a complaint for **modification**. Some states have enacted specific modification statutes that set out the basic requirements for these post-divorce actions, while in others the requirements have been established by judicial decisions. In either event, the basic principles discussed below are fairly stable; however, as always, the precise procedural and substantive details vary from state to state.

This action is usually filed in the court that entered the original support order, which has continuing jurisdiction over the matter. If a support order is not entered at the time of divorce, a court may lose jurisdiction; accordingly, some courts will order payment of a nominal support amount, such as a dollar per month, in order to preserve its jurisdiction should the need for support arise in the future. The complaint for modification must be based on a change in circumstances that makes the original order unfair. States use different yardsticks to measure unfairness. Some employ a strict unconscionability standard, while others employ a more relaxed standard. Again, the general rule is that the change must have been unforeseeable. Accordingly, a future job change that was known about at the time of the original order cannot generally be the basis for a modification, as this should have been accounted for in the original order. Similarly, most jurisdictions will not base a modification upon inflation or cost-of-living increases in the obligor's salary, as these events are foreseeable and could have been addressed.

Medical Insurance

The issue of continued medical coverage frequently arises with considerable urgency at the time of divorce because one spouse, typically the primary wage earner, may have a group policy through his or her employer that provides family coverage. Many states now have laws that authorize the court to order a spouse to continue to provide health insurance coverage for his or her former spouse, at least during the time that a support order is in effect.

Although there is no federal law comparable to state statutory provisions requiring the continued provision of health insurance, divorced spouses may be entitled to post-divorce coverage under COBRA (short for the Consolidated Omnibus Budget Reconciliation Act), which was passed by Congress in 1986. Under COBRA, employers with more than 20 employees must provide the spouse of a divorcing employee with a temporary extension of group health coverage if a timely request is made. However, the covered spouse is responsible for the entire amount of the premium since COBRA does not hold the employer or the employed spouse responsible for the cost of the continued coverage. COBRA, Pub. L. No. 99-272, 100 Stat. 82 (29 U.S.C. §§1161 et seq.) (1986).

In addition to being unforeseeable, courts may require that the change be involuntary. Accordingly, an obligor who seeks to reduce payments because she has left the corporate world to become an artist will probably not be successful. Likewise, a support recipient who relocates to a luxury apartment complex and then seeks an upward revision based on the increased rent is not likely to succeed.

1. Modifiability and Termination of "Permanent" Support

Remarriage, cohabitation, and a change in financial circumstances are the most common reasons for a modification action.

Remarriage

In most states, the statutory rule is that an award of "permanent" support automatically terminates upon the remarriage of the recipient spouse. In some of these jurisdictions, termination occurs immediately upon remarriage without the need for any kind of court action, while in others the support obligor must file a modification petition, which almost certainly will be granted. The principle underlying the termination rule is that the recipient's new spouse has a support obligation, and a person is not entitled to be supported by both a spouse and a former spouse at the same time.

The basic rule — that remarriage terminates the spousal support obligation — has also been firmly established by judicial decision in states that do not have a statutory termination provision through judicial decision. Although some of these jurisdictions follow the automatic termination approach, others are more flexible. A few treat remarriage as simply a factor to be considered in determining whether a change in circumstances justifies a modification, although the more common approach is to presume termination, absent a showing of extraordinary circumstances. The concept of "extraordinary" is typically defined narrowly, and the burden of proof is placed upon the alimony recipient, rather than, as is usually the case, on the person seeking the modification.

This termination rule raises difficult questions about what should happen if a spouse who is receiving rehabilitative support remarries during the rehabilitative period. From a recipient's perspective, the remarriage may be irrelevant, as he or she is seeking to regain economic independence. However, from the payor's perspective, it may seem unfair to have to pay support in a situation in which a former spouse now has access to another source of income. Jurisdictions tend to divide on this issue, with some giving greater weight to the recipient's interest in completing the education he or she embarked on, while others are more focused on shifting responsibility to the new spouse.

The general rule is that remarriage by the paying spouse does not entitle him or her to a downward revision of support. Courts generally focus on the voluntary aspect of the act and the inequity to the former spouse. However, remarriage combined with other circumstances, such as the birth of children, may support a downward revision (see Chapter 9). Conversely, if the payor spouse remarries someone with substantial income or assets, the question may arise as to whether the recipient spouse can rely on this as a change in circumstances warranting an upward adjustment. While it is clear that the recipient has no direct claim on the new spouse's income, some courts may be willing to consider a modification based on the fact that this money may liberate some of the former spouse's income.

Cohabitation

Whereas remarriage almost always terminates alimony, the result is less certain where a recipient cohabits with a new partner because, unlike marriage, cohabitation does not impose a legal duty of support. The majority approach is to focus on whether cohabitation has resulted in an improvement in the recipient's financial situation — and only where it has will support be reduced or terminated. Some states impose an initial threshold requirement: The party seeking to reduce or terminate support must show that the relationship is not merely fleeting but instead rises to a certain level of intensity and commitment. Only when this has been shown will the court consider the cohabiting party's financial situation. A few states employ a rebuttable presumption that cohabitation automatically improves a party's financial situation. This presumption shifts the burden of proof to the cohabiting spouse to show that his or her financial situation has not improved as a result of the relationship.

A Change in Financial Circumstances

Parties frequently seek to modify support based on a change in the financial circumstances of one or both of them. As noted above, a court will generally not grant a request for modification based upon foreseeable changes, such as an annual cost-of-living salary increase. On the other hand, an increase in salary based on an unexpected promotion by the paying spouse may warrant an upward revision of support for the spouse receiving support. However, many jurisdictions will not modify based on this type of event alone and instead also require proof of an increased financial need on the part of the recipient spouse. A mutual change in circumstances is generally required on the theory that the recipient spouse does not have an automatic right to share in this gain as it is unrelated to the marital enterprise. In response, the recipient spouse might argue that he or she is entitled to a share in this increase to compensate for the fact that the original order did not provide adequate income, but was all that the payor spouse could afford at the time. Here, the modification would serve a compensatory purpose. If the recipient spouse's financial circumstances improve, a downward revision is generally allowed.

2. Modifiability of Other Types of Support

Even where a change in circumstances can be established, spousal support awards other than permanent alimony are generally considered nonmodifiable.

With lump-sum support, the support recipient is deemed to have acquired a vested right to the full amount, even if it is payable in installments. Accordingly, the clear majority rule is that these types of awards are not modifiable as the entitlement to a set amount is fixed at the time of divorce.

The rules regarding modifiability of rehabilitative support are more complex and variable. Because this award is for a designated purpose, most courts — absent extraordinary circumstances — will not modify it for reasons unrelated to the original purpose of the award. For example, whereas a change in circumstance such as a job promotion might warrant an increase in permanent alimony, it would not warrant an increase in rehabilitative support, as this is incidental to the goal of helping the support recipient achieve economic self-sufficiency.

Some courts will not modify a rehabilitative award to extend the durational limit or increase the support amount even where the request is directly related to the goal of achieving economic self-sufficiency. Although this may be fair where the party has not taken reasonable steps to obtain education or training, it can be a harsh result where the person has made a good faith effort but the original time estimate was inadequate or where she or he has encountered unanticipated obstacles such as illness or the loss of affordable child care.

The general rule is that reimbursement alimony is not modifiable or terminable by the death of either party or the remarriage of the recipient spouse. This is a logical result because the award is not based on present financial circumstances but rather is designed to repay a spouse for past expenditures. Accordingly, post-divorce changes in circumstances are irrelevant. However, it is hard to imagine a court refusing to make some adjustment, perhaps in the nature of a temporary suspension of payments, in a case of genuine hardship such as serious illness.

3. Agreement of the Parties to Prohibit Modification

Sometimes parties include a clause in a separation agreement stating that neither will seek to modify the support award in the future. Such a clause often is insisted upon by the supporting spouse, who wants to limit his or her obligation. Although these provisions are generally enforceable, some jurisdictions may refuse to honor such a clause on public policy grounds, especially if enforcement would force a spouse into public assistance. In this regard, the support duty may be explained as having a public dimension that cannot be abrogated by a private agreement.

F. ENFORCEMENT OF SPOUSAL SUPPORT AWARDS

As is often the case with child support orders, once spousal support has been ordered, the risk of nonpayment is substantial, and the recipient may need to take action to enforce the order.

1. Contempt

In most states, the primary enforcement mechanism is an action for **contempt**, which, as with child support, can be either civil or criminal in nature. Most likely, an obligor will not be found in contempt if the inability to pay existed at the time the support payments were due. A more complicated question, which jurisdictions split on, is whether present inability to pay is a valid defense where the defendant had the ability to pay at the time payments were due.

If a defendant is found to be in civil contempt, the court will order him or her to pay the overdue amount, and a payment schedule is usually established. To compel payment, the court may impose a jail sentence, but, in keeping with the remedial purpose of a civil contempt action, the defendant must be given the opportunity to purge the contempt by paying the arrearage and thus avoid jail. The right to purge oneself of the contempt is ongoing, and the jail sentence is imposed for an indefinite time terminable upon payment of the arrearage. Where there is a present inability to pay (and this is not considered a valid defense), a jail sentence will generally not be imposed because the obligor does not have the means to purge the contempt. In contrast, a sentence in a criminal contempt case is imposed for a fixed period of time because the purpose is punitive, and the defendant cannot shorten it by purging the contempt.

2. Other Enforcement Measures

In seeking to enforce a spousal support award, a recipient who also has a child support order in place may be able to obtain enforcement assistance from the state's child support agency, and many of the same collection tools, such as wage withholding and tax refund intercepts, are available to secure spousal support payments (see Chapter 6). Additionally, some states have extended the availability of these enforcement tools to spousal support recipients who do not have a child support order in place.

Bankruptcy and the Support Obligation

Filing for **bankruptcy** provides an individual who is overwhelmed by debt with the opportunity to discharge qualified debts, thus enabling him or her to make a "fresh start." What then happens if the individual seeking to be relieved of his or her debts has existing financial obligations to a spouse or child stemming from a divorce or separation?

Until recently, the Bankruptcy Code prevented the discharge of debts that were in the nature of support payments; however, the Code allowed the discharge of debts that were in the nature of a property settlement, such as payments being made to a former spouse to effectuate the debtor's buyout of the equity in the marital home, subject to a possible hardship exception. However, the Bankruptcy Abuse Prevention and Consumer Protection Act of 2005 eliminated the distinction between debts for support and those in the nature of a property settlement with regard to personal bankruptcy filings. Accordingly, the rule of non-dischargeability has now been extended to most property settlement obligations.[11]

---

[11]This is a brief, simple introduction to the relationship between support obligations and bankruptcy law; however, this area of the law is quite complex. For further detail, see Daniel A. Austin, For Debtor or Worse: Discharge of Marital Debt Obligations Under the Federal Bankruptcy Abuse Prevention and Consumer Protection Act of 2005, 51 Wayne L. Rev. 1369 (2005).

Moreover, as with child support, spousal support awards can be enforced across state lines under the Uniform Interstate Family Support Act (UIFSA). However, it is important to note that child support collection is the primary priority of the interstate system and dominates enforcement efforts.

G. THE TAX CONSEQUENCES OF SPOUSAL SUPPORT AWARDS

As developed in this section, spousal support payments have tax implications for both the payor and the recipient spouse. As we will see in Chapter 10, the rules are quite different in the child support context.

1. The Basic Rule of Income and Deductions

The basic tax rule is that spousal support payments are considered income to the recipient and are included in his or her taxable income; correspondingly, the payor is entitled to a deduction from gross income for spousal support payments he or she has made.[12] To qualify as alimony, payments must be in cash or a cash equivalent, must cease at the death of the recipient, and must be required under a divorce or separation instrument, and the parties may not live in the same household at the time payments are made. If parties wish to avoid this rule of includibility/deductibility, they may specifically state that payments that would otherwise qualify as alimony are not includible in the income of the recipient nor deductible by the payor. In effect, this means that for tax purposes, the payments are no longer considered to be alimony.

The basic rule of includibility/deductibility is straightforward; however, under the following two circumstances, the tax consequences may be other than what the parties intended.

2. Unallocated Payments

Where both spousal support and child support are to be paid, it may be better financially for the parties if the payments are characterized as spousal support. This gives the payor a deduction for the entire amount, and the tax savings may then be used to increase the amount of support payments. Although this increases the recipient's taxable income, he or she may nonetheless realize a net gain.

If a separation agreement provides for a support amount without designating how much is for spousal support and how much is for child support, the entire amount will be treated as spousal support. However, if the agreement provides for

---

[12]The spousal support rules can be found in §71 of the Internal Revenue Service Code, 26 U.S.C. §71 (2012). Please be aware that these rules are complex and are presented here in a simplified manner. For a discussion of key concepts, see the Internal Revenue Service Publication 505 (2015), available at www.irs.gov/publications.

reductions in support based on child-related contingencies (such as reaching age 18, marriage, or establishing a separate residence) or at a time that is "clearly associated" with a child-related contingency, a rebuttable presumption arises that the amount of the reduction was in the nature of child, rather than spousal, support. Rebuttal requires proof that the reduction was in fact attributable to a valid non–child-related reason. Even if the agreement does not specifically mention the contingency, the Internal Revenue Service may treat a reduction as child-related if it finds that it occurred at a time associated with such a contingency, unless again the parties can establish a valid non–child-related explanation for the reduction.

Reclassification can have significant tax repercussions, especially for the obligor. If payments are reclassified, it means that the obligor has been taking a deduction that he or she is not entitled to, since child support, unlike alimony, is not deductible from gross income.

3. Recapture of Excess Payments

As discussed in Chapter 7, payments made from one spouse to the other as part of a property settlement are neither deductible from the income of the payor spouse nor includible in the income of the recipient spouse. For example, if an agreement calls for a husband to buy out his wife's interest in the marital residence by paying her $300 a month over three years, these payments are "tax neutral." However, over the years, divorcing couples have often attempted to disguise these payments as alimony, thus allowing the payor to deduct them from gross income.

To deter parties from doing this, the Tax Code now includes "alimony **recapture** provisions." These provisions are triggered when parties engage in what is referred to as "excess front loading" of support payments in the first three years following a divorce. These front-loaded payments serve as a red flag that the parties may be attempting to disguise payments that are in the nature of a property settlement as support payments. If uncovered, the excess or disguised payments must then be included in the gross income of the payor, as he or she is deemed to have taken an unwarranted deduction. This amount is thus "recaptured" for tax purposes. The recipient becomes entitled to a corresponding deduction.

Chapter Summary

- Prior to no-fault reform, the notion of permanent commitment and obligation to support was much more prevalent. Upon divorce, if one spouse was at fault, the other spouse had a claim to continued support.
- After no-fault reform, marriage was often analogized to a partnership, with divorce as the vehicle for making a clean break from the past.
- With the partnership model of marriage, property distribution became the preferred approach to adjusting economic rights between spouses, while the

clean-break approach is criticized for failing to account for economic disparities between spouses that frequently result from the marital division of labor.

■ In deciding whether to provide spousal support, judges usually consider multiple factors, with need as a central determinant.

■ Permanent support awards are subject to modification based on changed circumstances and are terminable upon remarriage or death of either party. Some states permit the modification of a rehabilitative award if, despite a good faith effort, the recipient has not become self-sufficient. Lump-sum payments are generally not modifiable.

■ Support payments are included as taxable income of the recipient and deductible by the payor. Parties may choose to opt out of this rule but must specifically agree to such an opt out.

Applying the Rules

1. Amit and Marcy have been married for 15 years. Amit has been the primary wage earner. While Marcy has a teaching certificate, the parties decided when their first child was born that Marcy should stay home because it would cost more for day care than Marcy could make working. The parties have two children at the time that Amit files for divorce: Gabby, who is 13 years old, and Mason, who is 7. Amit earns approximately $80,000 a year. If Marcy goes back to work full time as a teacher she will earn approximately $36,000 a year. She estimates that she needs approximately $5,000 a year to maintain the same standard of living the parties had during the marriage. What factors will the court look to in determining whether Marcy is entitled to support? If you represent Marcy, what is the range of spousal support you will argue to the court to award to her?

2. Jake and Jane have been married for six years. Jane had worked during the marriage until the last year when she was in an automobile accident. Since that time she has suffered from back pain and is unable to sit or stand for long periods of time. She also suffers from severe migraines, making it difficult to work. Jane has come to your office and wants to know if the court will attribute income to her even if she cannot work. What do you tell Jane? Is there any additional information you need to know?

3. Wes and Jeanne have been married for 18 years. The parties married right after college. Jeanne has a nursing degree and worked as a registered nurse for the first 15 years of the marriage. For the first five years of the marriage, Wes was pursuing his masters and doctoral degree in psychology. Wes is now a prominent doctor of psychology and earns approximately $300,000 a year. Jeanne stopped working approximately three years ago in order to pursue her hobby of painting. Jeanne contributed approximately $50,000 toward the marital expenses for

the first five years of the marriage when Wes was in school and not contributing financially to the marriage. Does Jeanne have a claim for reimbursement alimony?

4. Sam and Peggy were married for 22 years when Peggy petitioned for divorce. They settled all the issues except spousal support. The trial court awarded Peggy permanent spousal maintenance based upon the following facts: Peggy was a legal secretary and worked outside of the home during most of the marriage. In the early years of the marriage, she provided support for Sam while he worked on receiving his degree in engineering. The trial court also found that Peggy was the primary caretaker of the three children who are now grown. After Sam received his degree, his income rose substantially and his earnings exceed $200,000. Peggy is now trying to obtain her B.A. so she can go to law school. Weighing wife's needs in the context of her marital standard of living, the trial court gave Peggy $2,000 a month until she completes her B.A. and then $1,500 until her death, Sam's death, or her remarriage. Sam comes to you and wants to know if he has grounds for an appeal.

   a. What are Sam's best arguments for an appeal?
   b. Does Sam have the ability to modify the award after a period of time?
   c. What would be the grounds for modification?

5. Barbara and Leonard were divorced after 22 years of marriage. They settled all their issues without a court trial and agreed that Barbara was entitled to spousal support for a period of eight years in the amount of $5,000 per month. The parties also agreed in their settlement documents that the spousal support was modifiable only upon a substantial and continuing change of circumstances. The parties agreed that a change in circumstances would include if Barbara started earning in excess of $50,000 a year. Barbara now comes to you five years after the divorce and tells you that Leonard is claiming she earns in excess of $50,000 a year because even though she only earns $45,000 a year, her employer contributes to a retirement plan on her behalf in the amount of $10,000 a year. She asks you if Leonard would be successful in showing she had a substantial and continuing change in circumstances to justify the modification.

6. Assume the same facts as Question 5. How would you argue for Leonard that there has been a change in circumstances to justify a modification?

Family Law in Practice

1. Locate the statutory provisions that govern the award of spousal support for your state and determine the following:

   a. What factors, if any, are enumerated for court consideration?
   b. Can marital fault be considered? If yes, under what conditions?

c. Do any of the sections specify what kinds of support can be awarded? If so, identify the available support approaches and describe their statutory features.

2. You are preparing for a negotiation session in a pending case. Research and draft an in-house memo regarding the approach that your jurisdiction takes in spousal support cases involving professional degrees. In approaching this assignment, locate all the relevant cases and analyze them carefully. (Note: If your jurisdiction does not have any professional degree cases, rehabilitative alimony cases can be substituted.)

3. Mary Smith was married to her husband for eight years. They have two minor children, ages 6 and 8. Ms. Smith is a paralegal with an associate's degree in paralegal studies. She has worked half time since the birth of her first child. She presently earns $18,000 per year. Her husband, David Smith, is the director of personnel at a large company. He earns $140,000 per year. As your client, Mary Smith has asked you to determine if she could be awarded spousal support. You do not have all the necessary information, but she has asked you to provide her with her range of options. To do this, examine the cases in your jurisdiction and write her a letter in which you identify what additional information will be needed in order to determine how much, if anything, you client is likely to receive in spousal support. (You can assume that Ms. Smith will have primary physical custody of the children.)

4. Following a lengthy trial, a client of yours was denied spousal support. You are considering filing an appeal, but first you need to conduct some initial research assessing whether you think the judge made an error of law. You believe your client is certainly entitled to rehabilitative support and possibly to permanent support. Here are the facts: Tom (your client) and his wife Melanie were married for eight years. Melanie was a corporate executive and worked extremely long hours. The couple has no children. They agreed that because Melanie earned so much money, Tom would not work outside of the home, but would maintain their house, pursue his various interests in the arts and music, and serve as a volunteer for various charitable enterprises. In year three of their marriage, Melanie obtained her Ph.D. in Business Administration; she had begun work on this degree the year before the couple married. Tom has an associate's degree in commercial art, although he has never pursued this line of work. In year five, Tom was diagnosed with multiple sclerosis; so far, the disease has been mild with no impact on his level of functioning.

After locating the cases that you think are relevant, write an informal in-house memorandum in which you discuss whether you think the client is entitled to support and why. Be sure to discuss and cite all relevant cases.

5. Assume you are a legal counsel to a state representative who is considering introducing a bill that would adopt the ALI's compensatory approach to the award of spousal support. The legislator has asked you to read up on this proposal and to prepare a background memo for him in which you explain the ALI approach, including how it differs from your state's present approach to spousal support, and identify at least two key possible advantages and disadvantages of this new approach.

8

The Division of Marital Property

This chapter focuses on the division of **marital property**, the property acquired during the marriage, at the time of divorce. As noted in Chapter 7, since the advent of no-fault divorce, the trend has been to treat the division of property as the primary economic event between divorcing spouses. The rationale for this development is that a division of property, as distinct from an award of alimony, is more in keeping with the modern partnership view of marriage, which seeks to allow both spouses to make a clean break from the past, unencumbered by the failed relationship.

Jurisdictions divide property in primarily two different ways. In a community property jurisdiction, the property acquired during the marriage, with certain exceptions, is divided equally, and if there is a need after division of the property to provide for one spouse, the court may make up the difference in the form of spousal support. In equitable distribution jurisdictions, courts take into consideration all the marital property and may divide it in an unequal way in order to assist the spouse with the lesser earning capacity or to achieve fairness and equity between the parties. However, the growing reliance on the division of property as the primary distributive event has been criticized for failing to recognize that this approach may not account for the fact that spouses often exit from a marriage with very different earning capacities based, at least in part, on the marital allocation of work and family commitments.

Key Concepts

- The division of property in community property states
- The division of property under the equitable distribution approach
- The difference between marital property and separate property
- The four-step process for marital property distribution
- The tax implications for property transfer or disbursement in divorce

A. OVERVIEW OF THE TWO MARITAL PROPERTY SYSTEMS

Although the differences have become less pronounced over time, two marital property systems exist in this country. In this section, we compare the community property and the common law approaches to marital property.

1. The Community Property Approach

Initially, the majority of states looked to English common law when devising rules regarding marital property rights, but eight states, based on patterns of colonial influence and territorial acquisition, looked to Spanish or French civil law and adopted their community property approach. These states are Arizona, California, Idaho, Louisiana, Nevada, New Mexico, Texas, and Washington. (It should be noted that since 1986 Wisconsin has generally been regarded as a community property state based on statutory changes.)

Unlike English common law, civil law did not consider the husband and wife to be a single person (see Chapter 1). A wife's legal existence survived marriage — her identity did not merge into her husband's. Marriage was considered a partnership of two individuals, and married women retained the right to own property. However, although recognizing the legal personhood of married women, civil law did not regard the spouses as equal partners in the marital enterprise. Husbands were given the right of exclusive management and control over marital assets, and, in some jurisdictions, they also had this authority over their wives' separate property. This has changed over time, and the rights of management and control are now equal.

Based on this understanding of marriage as a partnership, the community property approach assumes that each spouse acts for the benefit of the marital unit rather than for his or her own individual gain. The contribution of each spouse to the marriage, including domestic and child-rearing contributions, is recognized, entitling each spouse to share in the financial gains of the marriage. This is accomplished by giving both parties an immediate, vested interest in one-half of the property acquired during the marriage with the exception of property acquired through gifts, inheritances, or bequests. Upon divorce, this community property is subject to division based on a theory of co-ownership without regard to financial contribution. Although most community property states initially divided property on an equal basis, many now use an equitable division standard that (as discussed further below) allows a court to make an unequal distribution based on considerations of fairness.[1]

Similarly, most debts that are incurred during the marriage are regarded as "community debts," and are likewise allocated between the spouses upon divorce

---

[1]*See generally* Scott Greene, Comparison of the Community Property Aspects of the Community Property and Common-Law Marital Property Systems and Their Relative Compatibility with the Current View of the Marriage Relationship and the Rights of Women, 13 Creighton L. Rev. 71, 88 (1979); Judith T. Younger, Marital Regimes: A Story of Compromise and Demoralization, Together with Criticism and Suggestions for Reform, 67 Cornell L. Rev. 45 (1981).

without regard for who incurred it. Thus, debts such as credit cards, taxes, and loans that were incurred during the marriage are generally divided equally. However, a debt that is incurred by one spouse for his or her own benefit rather than for the benefit of the marriage may be characterized as separate — which is not always an easy determination to make. For example, student loans that are used only for the benefit of one spouse, cosmetic surgery performed shortly before the dissolution of marriage, and behaviors including addictions and gambling, may, under appropriate circumstances, be allocated solely to the party incurring the debt since the incurring spouse acquired all the benefit or committed all the waste of community money for his or her own benefit.

In addition, property that is not acquired through the expenditure of marital efforts or funds is considered separate property and belongs to the acquiring spouse rather than to the community. For example, stocks purchased with separate funds that naturally increase over the course of the marriage with no effort made by the spouse holding the stock may be still considered separate property even though the increase in the stocks occurred during marriage.

Typically, separate property includes assets brought into the marriage, as well as gifts, inheritances, and bequests acquired by one spouse during the marriage, and property acquired in exchange for separate property. Neither spouse acquires rights in the other's separate property because it stands apart from the marital enterprise. At divorce, each spouse takes his or her separate property, although in a few states, courts may have limited authority to transfer separate property in cases of extreme hardship. The distinction between separate and community property is easy to state; however, in practice, navigating the boundaries between the two can be difficult (see Section B.2, below).

2. The Common Law Approach

As discussed in Chapter 1, the common law vision of the marital relationship assumed the loss of a wife's legal identity. The common law approach to marital property rights flowed directly from this understanding of the marital relationship. Here, there was no notion of a marital enterprise representing the cumulative efforts of both spouses — there was simply

California Community Property Law

The California Family Law Code is an example of how property acquired during marriage (except by gift, will, or inheritance) is divided equally upon divorce. The pertinent sections provide:

- Family Code Section 760. Except as otherwise provided by statute, all property, real or personal, wherever situated, acquired by a married person during the marriage while domiciled in this state is community property.

- Family Code Section 2550. Except upon the written agreement of the parties, or on oral stipulation of the parties in open court, or as otherwise provided in this division, in a proceeding for dissolution of marriage or for legal separation of the parties, the court shall, either in its judgment of dissolution of the marriage, in its judgment of legal separation of the parties, or at a later time if it expressly reserves jurisdiction to make such a property division, divide the community estate of the parties equally.

the husband who owned all of the property except for his wife's realty, which he controlled.

Even as married women gradually acquired property rights through the passage of the Married Women's Property Acts, the concept of a marital community did not take hold in the common law states. Instead, traditional common law property concepts, which extolled the virtues of individual rights, were extended to married women. *See* Younger, *supra* note 1, at 61-64. Property was his or hers depending on who supplied the purchase funds — which in reality meant that it was mostly his. In contrast to the community property states, the nonfinancial contributions of a homemaker spouse did not give rise to ownership rights.

Until fairly recently, most common law states divided property according to **title**. This meant that the spouse who owned an asset was entitled to it at divorce. Mitigating the potential harshness of this approach, a number of courts developed the **special equity rule** under which a spouse who had made a financial contribution to property titled in the name of the other could be granted an equitable interest in the asset, thus entitling him or her to a share at divorce. Some courts expanded this rule to provide rights based on the nonfinancial contributions of a homemaker spouse. Begun as an exception, this rule helped pave the way for the shift from a title-based approach to the division of marital property to the equitable distribution rules now in effect in all common law states.

3. Title to Equitable Distribution

As in the case of spousal support, no-fault divorce also helped to usher in changes in the rules of property distribution. All common law states now divide marital property according to equitable distribution principles rather than title. Influenced by the sharing doctrine long recognized in community property states, the **equitable distribution approach** acknowledges that the accumulation of marital assets derives from the efforts of both spouses. Accordingly, at divorce, a spouse's nonfinancial contributions to the well-being of a household will give rise to an enforceable property interest in accumulated assets.

Following the community property approach, the majority of equitable distribution jurisdictions classify property at divorce as either marital or separate. This is often referred to as the **dual property approach** because a formal distinction is made between the two categories of assets. The distributive authority of the courts is restricted to the marital estate, although a few states have created a limited exception to this rule and permit distribution of separate property in cases of hardship. The classifying principle is essentially the same as in the community property states. Property acquired during the marriage through the efforts of either spouse or the expenditure of marital funds is considered marital because it derives from the contribution each is credited with making to the partnership. **Separate property** is that which is unrelated to this joint undertaking and generally includes property owned prior to marriage, gifts, inheritances, and property acquired in exchange for separate property.

In contrast to the dual property approach, a minority of states have adopted what is known as an **all property approach**. Here, no formal distinction is made between separate and marital property, and courts are empowered to distribute all assets, regardless of when and how they were acquired. This is sometimes referred to as the **"hotchpot of assets" approach**. It should be noted, however, that the informal practice among attorneys in all property states when negotiating a settlement may be to disregard property that would be considered separate in a community or dual property state, or to allocate it separately from the balance of the marital estate in order to give greater weight to its nonmarital identity.

THE "ALL PROPERTY" OR "HOTCHPOT OF ASSETS" APPROACH

The Uniform Marriage and Divorce Act provides a sample of the approach, which takes all the assets of the parties and makes them available for an equitable division based upon specific factors.

§307. [Disposition of Property]

(a) In a proceeding for dissolution of a marriage, legal separation, or disposition of property following a decree of dissolution of marriage or legal separation by a court which lacked personal jurisdiction over the absent spouse or lacked jurisdiction to dispose of the property, the court, without regard to marital misconduct, shall, and in a proceeding for legal separation may, finally equitably apportion between the parties the property and assets belonging to either or both however and whenever acquired, and whether the title thereto is in the name of the husband or wife or both. In making apportionment the court shall consider the duration of the marriage, and prior marriage of either party, antenuptial agreement of the parties, the age, health, station, occupation, amount and sources of income, vocational skills, employability, estate, liabilities, and needs of each of the parties, custodial provisions, whether the apportionment is in lieu of or in addition to maintenance, and the opportunity of each for future acquisition of capital assets and income. The court shall also consider the contribution or dissipation of each party in the acquisition, preservation, depreciation, or appreciation in value of the respective estates, and the contribution of a spouse as a homemaker or to the family unit.

(b) In a proceeding, the court may protect and promote the best interests of the children by setting aside a portion of the jointly and separately held estates of the parties in a separate fund or trust for the support, maintenance, education, and general welfare of any minor, dependent, or incompetent children of the parties.

When it comes to debts, they similarly "belong" to the spouse who incurred them during the marriage. At the time of divorce, in contrast to historic practices, many common law jurisdictions now allocate responsibility for the debts between the spouses in accordance with the applicable equitable distribution principles; however, in the absence of a statute that expressly vests a court with this authority, some judges may regard this as a discretionary rather than an obligatory judicial function.

With the adoption of equitable distribution laws, the difference between common law and community property states has become less pronounced, although the all property approach is exclusively identified with common law states. Accordingly, this chapter will focus on general legal concepts and will not distinguish between the two approaches unless relevant; however, you should bear in mind that regardless of which approach is followed, each state has its own rules and standards.

Before proceeding, however, one essential difference between these property regimes should be noted. In community property states, the ownership interest of each spouse attaches at the time of property acquisition. Consequently, co-ownership rights come into being during the marriage; at the time of divorce, the court is dividing property that is already jointly owned by the spouses. In contrast, in common law states, each spouse holds the property acquired during the marriage as his or her own, and the ownership interest of the nonacquiring spouse does not attach until the time of divorce. As a result, when property is divided, a spouse may resent that something that "belongs" to him or her is being taken away and given to the other spouse as a consequence of the divorce rather than recognizing that the accumulated assets represent the cumulative efforts of both parties.

B. THE PROPERTY DISTRIBUTION PROCESS

The process of dividing property between divorcing spouses can be broken down into four steps:

1. identification of the assets as property or not;
2. the classification of assets as marital or separate;
3. the valuation of the assets; and
4. the distribution of the assets.

Before we discuss these four steps, a few general points should be considered. First, in many divorces, particularly where the parties have few assets, the division of property is relatively simple, and couples often figure this out themselves without involving their attorneys or applying formal legal principles. A couple may simply divide their belongings based on need or preference. Of course, a client's attorney should always make sure that his or her client understands that without engaging in a more formalized distribution process there is no way to make sure that the client is getting the share of assets that he or she may legally be entitled to.

Second, when couples do fight about property, the fight is often rooted in the emotional undertow of divorce. An object may be treasured for its sentimental meaning or it may have tremendous symbolic importance for one or both parties. For example, if your client is fighting fiercely for the old brown sofa, it may have become the symbolic locus of his or her anger and he or she may not really care about the sofa itself. Alternatively, the client may believe it is worth fighting for based on its sentimental worth — perhaps it was the couple's first purchase, thus standing as a reminder of happier times. If you are involved in helping to resolve a property dispute, it is important to be aware of these potential dynamics so you can help a client sort out what is going on; that way needless time, money, and emotional energy is not spent pursuing an object for the wrong reason.

Third, when property entitlements are contested, the governing rules are often quite complex and variable. For example, there are multiple approaches to valuing a closely held corporation, which differ from the multiple approaches to valuing pension plans or commodity futures. Another example is that the classification of a gift may turn on whether it was given to a spouse by a third party or by the other spouse, while the classification of an asset's appreciated value will likely depend upon whether the appreciation is active or passive or a combination of the two. This chapter will address these kinds of issues, but it is worth bearing in mind both that property disputes can be a trap for the unwary, and that in complex cases, the services of experts, such as a forensic accountant, an appraiser, and/or an actuary, may well be necessary.

Finally, a concern that often arises in divorce cases is whether or not a spouse might seek to hide, transfer, or otherwise dispose of assets during the pendency of the case. Accordingly, once a divorce has been filed, it is not uncommon for one of the parties to file a motion asking the judge to prohibit any disposition of assets pending a resolution of the case. If a party has reason to believe that the filing and subsequent service of the motion on the other spouse might trigger a sudden clearing of a bank account, or "gifting" of assets to a friend etc., the motion can be filed on an ex parte basis so that the restraining order is in effect prior to the giving of notice.

1. Is It Property?

Most cases do not involve definitional questions. During the marriage, couples accumulate items such as furniture, jewelry, cars, and household goods, which are so clearly property that this definitional step is bypassed without any thought to the matter. However, there are times when it is not clear whether a particular item, such as the goodwill of a professional practice or an unvested pension, is in fact property.

Since the enactment of equitable distribution laws and the increased emphasis on the division of property as the primary economic event between divorcing spouses, these definitional questions have assumed increasing importance, and this is an ever developing and expanding area of the law. When working on a case, you must carefully consider all possible property interests. This means there is much room for creative legal thinking. Who knows? Given the right opportunity, you may "discover" a new form of property!

As discussed below, most definitional battles focus on whether or not a particular intangible interest should be treated as property or not. The outcome can have significant consequences for the economic future of the divorcing spouses because intangibles, such as a pension or the goodwill of a business, may be very valuable. Each of these areas will be looked at more closely in the sections below, as well as how family pets are treated in a divorce.

The Tangible/Intangible Distinction

Traditionally, property was defined as a tangible item over which an individual could exercise absolute dominion and control. **Tangible property** possesses little or no definitional problems as it is what we normally think of as property — it has a physical presence and can be touched, seen, and transferred from one person to another.

Over time, however, the definition of property has expanded. Moving beyond physical presence, property is now usually described in relational terms as the "bundle of rights" a person has in something. In essence the concept has been "dephysicalized," and thus, **intangible assets** — assets that lack a physical presence and cannot be ascertained by the senses — may very well come within the concept of property. *See* Willard H. DaSilva, Property Subject to Equitable Distribution, *in* Valuation and Distribution of Marital Property (John P. McCahey ed., 1985).

Intangible assets often involve the right *to* something, such as the future right to participate in a pension plan or, as evidenced by a stock certificate, the right to participate in the management of a corporation and receive a proportional share of earnings.

Few property distribution statutes provide a definition of the term "property," so courts have had to struggle with the concept. Some jurisdictions are expansive and consider a broad array of intangibles to be property. Other jurisdictions are more restrictive and tend to exclude intangibles that lack traditional property attributes. Accordingly, if an intangible asset cannot easily be transferred to another person, is difficult to value, and cannot be owned jointly, a court in a restrictive jurisdiction is likely to determine that it is not property. Thus, for example, in comparing a professional degree with a car, one can see how such a court might refuse to consider a professional degree property. Unlike the car, the degree cannot be transferred or left to someone as an inheritance. Thus, the degree's worth is much harder to determine because it cannot be jointly owned by the marital estate. Underlying these distinctions — and potentially significant to the courts — is that many of these intangibles, such as a degree or goodwill, seem closely connected to the personal efforts of the holder.

Unvested Pensions, Accrued Leave Time, Licenses, Degrees, and Professional Goodwill: Are They Property?

In this section, we look at a few of the intangible assets that have posed definitional difficulties for the courts — unvested pensions, accrued vacation and sick leave time, licenses, degrees, and professional goodwill. Before proceeding, it should be noted that sometimes the question we are considering here — whether an intangible asset is property or not — is framed as an inquiry into whether the asset should be considered a separate rather than a marital asset because of its special characteristics, such as that it is personal to the holder and nontransferable. Regardless of how the inquiry is framed, the relevant considerations are quite similar — for example, professional goodwill (discussed below) may be not be deemed as property because it is personal to the holder, or it may be deemed separate property for the same reason.

Unvested Pensions

Pensions are an important job-related benefit. They are a form of deferred compensation: An employee earns the right to the benefit in the present, but realization of the benefit is deferred until retirement or some other future date after the employee has left his or her job. Some pension plans are funded solely by employer contributions (called a **defined benefit plan**); others are funded solely by employee contributions (called a **defined contribution plan**); and some are funded by a combination of employer and employee contributions.

An individual's interest in his or her pension is either vested or unvested. When rights are vested, an employee does not forfeit retirement benefits when he or she leaves the place of employment prior to retirement. Vesting usually occurs after an employee has worked for an employer for a specified number of years. In contrast, if an employee who is not vested leaves the job, he or she forfeits the retirement benefits. The right to retirement benefits is thus contingent on continued employment through the vesting period. In this regard, it should be noted that concept of vesting applies only to the employer's contribution; an employee is always vested with respect to his or her own contribution such as with a defined contribution plan.

Vested pensions are easily defined as a property interest, and although the clear modern trend is to also treat unvested pensions as property, this approach is far from uniform. Accordingly, rather than regarding unvested pensions as a form of property, some jurisdictions continue to regard them as a mere expectancy interest because the right to benefits is contingent upon continued employment through the vesting period, which may or may not take place. In short, the uncertain and conditional nature of the interest takes it out of the property category, which in turn means it is not subject to division upon divorce.

Other jurisdictions give greater weight to a spouse's interest in an unvested pension because, although presently uncertain, the right to benefits will become legally enforceable upon the happening of a future contingency — fulfillment of the time requirement. Here, this greater certainty serves to distinguish an interest in an unvested pension from a true expectancy, such as the hope of being named a beneficiary in a will, which is completely speculative, and accordingly supports treating unvested pensions as property rather than as a non-distributable expectancy.

In defining unvested pensions as property, many jurisdictions have been influenced by equitable considerations. A pension may be a couple's most valuable asset, and its exclusion based on a technical distinction would effectively disregard the contribution of a homemaker spouse to the marital enterprise because as only the employed spouse would enjoy the right to retirement benefits. Another fairness consideration is that although contingent, the right to at least a portion of the pension benefits would have been acquired during the marriage, thus properly making it part of the marital estate, while its exclusion would effectively treat it as a separate asset despite its integral connection to the efforts of a spouse. (See Section B.2, below, regarding the classification of assets.)

Accrued Vacation and Sick Leave Time

Many employers permit their employees to accumulate unused sick and vacation time. Upon retirement, an employee may be paid the value of this accrued time. The question has arisen in a number of cases as to whether this accrued time is a marital asset, which is capable of valuation and division upon divorce. Although the courts that have considered this issue are divided, the modern approach leans toward inclusion.

In seeking to determine whether accrued leave time is an asset, many courts have framed it as a question of whether this time is essentially an alternative form of wages and thus outside the definition of property, or whether it is more akin to deferred compensation for services rendered, such as a pension, and thus includible within the definition. Capturing the former approach, a Kentucky Court of Appeals concluded that accrued leave time was "less tangible, more difficult to value, and more personal than pension and retirement benefits" and therefore should not be classified as property, but instead regarded as a non-divisible alternative form of wages." *Bratcher v. Bratcher*, 26 S.W.3d 797, 801 (Ky. Ct. App. 2000).

In contrast, courts in a growing number of jurisdictions now regard accrued vacation and sick leave as a type of compensation earned for services already performed, and thus treat it as a property interest that is subject to division upon divorce. However, as the case below makes clear, recognition in an individual case may turn on whether the employee had "an enforceable right to be paid for accrued leave time" in accordance with "the terms of any agreement between the employee and employer," and/or on whether the employee's interest is capable of valuation. *In re Marriage of Cardona*, 2014 CO 3, 316 P.3d 626, 634-636 (2014).

Case Preview

In re Marriage of Cardona

The issue in this case was whether the husband's accrued vacation and sick leave were part of the marital estate that should be divided upon dissolution of the marriage. The trial court divided the value of the accrued vacation and sick leave. After an appeal by the husband, the Court of Appeals reversed. The wife sought relief from the Colorado Supreme Court for her share of the value of the husband's accrued vacation and sick leave.

As you read *In re Marriage of Cardona*, look for the following:

1. What holdings from other jurisdictions does the court find persuasive in coming to its conclusion in this case?
2. Why does the husband argue that accrued unused vacation and sick leave is not marital property?

In re Marriage of Cardona
316 P.3d 626 (Colo. 2014)

. . .

Marta Doris Castro ("Wife") and Felipe Cardona ("Husband") co-petitioned for dissolution of their marriage in May 2007. In its August 2009 Permanent Orders, the trial court divided Husband's accrued, unused vacation and sick leave as marital property.

. . .

Husband's accrued leave was reflected in his most recent pay stub attached to his sworn financial statement. The pay stub indicated that he had an available total of 279.76 hours of vacation time and 171.85 hours of sick time, for a total of 451.61 hours of accrued leave. The pay stub did not indicate the cash value of the accrued leave, or whether Husband was entitled to cash payment for any portion of the leave.

At the permanent orders hearing, Wife's attorney called Husband to testify to the amount of his accrued vacation and sick leave, the rate at which it accrued, and the fact that the accrued time rolled over from year to year. During this exchange, Wife's attorney asked Husband, "If your job was terminated today they would pay you that accrued leave? You'd be entitled to that?" Husband responded, "According to the law I think that's the way it works yes." This statement was the only evidence presented regarding Husband's potential entitlement to payment for the accrued leave.

Nearly a year after the hearing, Wife filed her proposed permanent orders. . . . Wife requested, among other things, that the court award her half of Husband's accrued leave, which Wife valued at $23,232.00. In its permanent orders, the trial court . . . divided the value of Husband's accrued vacation and sick leave as part of its division of the marital estate and required Husband to pay wife $11,616.00 for her "interest in this pay."

On appeal, Husband argued that accrued leave is not marital property. A divided panel of the court of appeals agreed and reversed. The majority reasoned that Husband's accrued leave was analogous to unvested stock options or an interest in a discretionary trust and "is thus not property subject to distribution on dissolution." . . .

. . .

We are asked to determine whether a spouse's accrued vacation and sick leave is marital property subject to equitable division under the UDMA (Uniform Dissolution and Marital Act). This question presents a difficult issue, and one of first impression in Colorado. As the court of appeals recognized, courts in other jurisdictions are split on the issue.

In Colorado, section 14-10-113, C.R.S. (2013), of the UDMA requires the court to make an equitable distribution of marital property after considering all relevant factors, including the contributions of each spouse, the value of property set apart to each spouse, the economic circumstances of each spouse, and any increase, decrease, or depletion in the value of any separate property during the marriage. *Balanson*, 25 P.3d at 35; *Hunt*, 909 P.2d at 529; *In re Marriage of Jones*, 812 P.2d 1152, 1154 (Colo. 1991). We require a two-step analysis to determine whether an interest is "marital property" subject to equitable division in a dissolution proceeding: "first, a court must determine whether an interest constitutes 'property'; if so, the court must then determine whether the property is marital or separate." . . . Once an interest is deemed to be marital property, the court must value the property in order to make an equitable distribution. Under section 14-10-113(5), C.R.S. (2013), property shall be valued as of the date of the decree or the date of the hearing on disposition of property if such hearing precedes the date of the decree.

This case concerns the first step of the marital property analysis: whether accrued vacation and sick leave is "property" for purposes of the UDMA. Although the UDMA does not define the term "property," we have previously noted that the legislature intended the term "property" under the UDMA to be broadly inclusive. . . . We have also held that enforceable contractual rights constitute property, but interests that are speculative are "mere expectancies" that are not property.

In resolving this issue of first impression, we consider case law from other jurisdictions, as well as relevant Colorado precedent. We conclude that where a spouse has an enforceable right to be paid for accrued vacation or sick leave, as established by an employment agreement or policy, such accrued leave earned during the marriage is marital property for purposes of the UDMA. Where the value of such leave at the time of dissolution can be reasonably ascertained, it must be equitably divided as part of the marital estate. However, where a court cannot reasonably ascertain the value of such leave at the time of dissolution, the court should consider a spouse's right to such leave as an economic circumstance of the parties when equitably dividing the marital estate. In this case, no competent evidence was presented to establish that Husband had an enforceable right to payment for his accrued leave. Thus, we conclude that the trial court erred in considering the purported cash value of such leave as part of the marital estate. We therefore affirm the judgment of court of appeals on narrower grounds.

Courts in other jurisdictions disagree on whether accrued leave constitutes marital property subject to equitable division in a dissolution proceeding. Our review of these decisions reveals that whether courts treat a spouse's accrued leave as marital property generally depends on whether the court conceives of such leave as an alternative form of wages, or instead as a form of deferred compensation for services performed.

Courts that conceive of accrued vacation and sick leave as "really only an alternative form of wages" intended to "replace[ ] wages on the days when the worker does not work" have concluded that such accrued leave is not marital property. *Thomasian v. Thomasian*, 79 Md. App. 188, 556 A.2d 675, 681 (1989). . . .

Courts that have held that accrued leave is not property also stress that the accrued leave may not be presently convertible to cash, and may be dissipated when the employee spouse uses the leave time. These courts further note that certain types of leave, such as sick leave, may be used only in the event of illness. Consequently, these courts consider such accumulated leave to have, at most, only a future value that is "indeterminate and speculative."

By contrast, courts that view accumulated leave as deferred compensation for services performed have concluded that unused leave is marital property. *Schober v. Schober*, 692 P.2d 267, 268 (Alaska 1984). . . . Under this view, where an employee spouse has a "vested right to receive payment" for accrued vacation or sick days, such accrued leave is property "because [the accrued vacation or sick days] are, in effect, a debt due to him as part of the compensation he has earned for work he has already performed." *Abrell*, 337 Ill. Dec. 940, 923 N.E.2d at 802-03 (Garman, J. dissenting). In this respect, accrued leave is akin to other types of deferred compensation, such as a pension. Id. . . .

Courts that conclude that accrued leave is property consistently require the employee spouse to have a vested or contractual right to receive payment for such leave. . . . Accordingly, we hold that where a spouse has an enforceable right to be paid for accrued vacation or sick leave, such accrued leave earned by a spouse during the marriage is marital property for purposes of the UDMA.

Post-Case Follow-Up

The *Cardona* court sided with those jurisdictions who have concluded that accrued leave time should be considered marital property where the employee spouse has an enforceable right to receive payment for that time as it is akin to a form of deferred compensation. It accordingly rejected the position that taken by some jurisdictions, namely, that accrued leave is an alternative form of wages and thus not property that is subject to division.

Marriage of Cardona confirms that when a spouse has an employment agreement or there is an employment policy that permits payment for accrued vacation or sick leave, the vacation and sick leave is considered marital property subject to equitable division. The first step, though, is to identify the enforceable right. Without identifying that a party has a right to the accrued leave, there is no right.

Once the enforceable right is ascertained, the next step is to value the property. This may be in the form of a dollar value, subject to equitable division, or if it cannot be reasonably ascertained the property right may be considered as part of the economic circumstances of the parties in considering the division of other property in the marital estate.

In re Marriage of Cardona: Real Life Applications

1. Steve and Ashley have been married for 25 years. At the trial on the dissolution of marriage, Steve testifies that he earns 40 hours of vacation time a year, plus 24 hours of paid sick leave. Steve further states that his vacation time rolls over every year, but that his sick leave does not. At the time of the filing of the dissolution, Steve has accrued 120 hours of vacation time and has 8 hours of sick leave. The value of both can be determined. Is Ashley entitled to any of the accrued time?

2. David and Alicia have been married for 13 years. At the time of filing the dissolution of marriage Alicia has 80 hours of accrued vacation. However, before

the trial, Alicia decides she needs time to prepare for trial and uses two weeks of paid vacation so that by the time of trial she has no vacation. The trial judge rules that since Alicia has no accrued vacation at the time of trial, there is no value of accrued vacation to divide with David. Does David have grounds for an appeal? What would be David's best arguments? What arguments in response does Alicia have?

3. Salvador has no accrued vacation time and 30 hours of sick time at the time he files for dissolution of marriage from Sally. The sick time does not roll over from year to year. Salvador is concerned that the trial judge may award Sally half of the sick time when it is possible that Salvador may never use his sick leave. What advice do you give to Salvador?

Licenses and Degrees

A **license** is an intangible asset that permits a person to engage in some activity. Certainly there are many licenses that do not have any particular value at the time of dissolution and are not considered marital property, such as a driver's license. However, the issue becomes more difficult when the license translates into increased earning potential, particularly in situations where it was acquired or earned during the marriage. Thus, courts struggle with the issue of whether a license to practice law or a medical license earned during the marriage is a marital asset. Similarly, college degrees, like a license, may increase a party's earning capacity.

Most jurisdictions reject the notion that a license or a degree is a marital asset that allows the increased earning potential of a spouse to be divided upon dissolution of the marriage. However, the New York Court of Appeals took a different view in the case of *O'Brien v. O'Brien*, 489 N.E.2d 712 (N.Y. 1985).

Case Preview

O'Brien v. O'Brien

The issue in this case was whether Husband's license to practice medicine was marital property subject to equitable division. At the time of the marriage, both parties were teachers. However, shortly thereafter Husband went to medical school. By the time of the divorce he had earned his medical license.

The court looked at whether the license was marital or separate property and whether his increased earning capacity was therefore subject to division.

As you read *O'Brien v. O'Brien*, look for the following:

1. Why does the court classify the license as property?
2. What was the equitable contribution that Wife made to the property?
3. Why does the court reject Husband's argument that Wife should be entitled to spousal maintenance instead of a division of property?

O'Brien v. O'Brien
489 N.E.2d 712 (N.Y. 1985)

Judge SIMONS[.]

In this divorce action, the parties' only asset of any consequence is the husband's newly acquired license to practice medicine. The principal issue presented is whether that license, acquired during their marriage, is marital property subject to equitable distribution under Domestic Relations Law §236(B)(5)....

We now hold that plaintiff's medical license constitutes "marital property" within the meaning of Domestic Relations Law §236(B)(1)(c) and that it is therefore subject to equitable distribution pursuant to subdivision 5 of that part....

I

Plaintiff and defendant married on April 3, 1971. At the time both were employed as teachers at the same private school. Defendant had a bachelor's degree and a temporary teaching certificate but required 18 months of postgraduate classes at an approximate cost of $3,000, excluding living expenses, to obtain permanent certification in New York. She claimed, and the trial court found, that she had relinquished the opportunity to obtain permanent certification while plaintiff pursued his education. At the time of the marriage, plaintiff had completed only three and one-half years of college but shortly afterward he returned to school at night to earn his bachelor's degree and to complete sufficient premedical courses to enter medical school. In September 1973 the parties moved to Guadalajara, Mexico, where plaintiff became a full-time medical student. While he pursued his studies defendant held several teaching and tutorial positions and contributed her earnings to their joint expenses. The parties returned to New York in December 1976 so that plaintiff could complete the last two semesters of medical school and internship training here. After they returned, defendant resumed her former teaching position and she remained in it at the time this action was commenced. Plaintiff was licensed to practice medicine in October 1980. He commenced this action for divorce two months later. At the time of trial, he was a resident in general surgery.

During the marriage both parties contributed to paying the living and educational expenses and they received additional help from both of their families. They disagreed on the amounts of their respective contributions but it is undisputed that in addition to performing household work and managing the family finances defendant was gainfully employed throughout the marriage, that she contributed all of her earnings to their living and educational expenses and that her financial contributions exceeded those of plaintiff. The trial court found that she had contributed 76% of the parties' income exclusive of a $10,000 student loan obtained by defendant. Finding that plaintiff's medical degree and license are marital property, the court received evidence of its value and ordered a distributive award to defendant.

Defendant presented expert testimony that the present value of plaintiff's medical license was $472,000. Her expert testified that he arrived at this figure by comparing the average income of a college graduate and that of a general surgeon between 1985, when plaintiff's residency would end, and 2012, when he would reach age 65.

After considering Federal income taxes, an inflation rate of 10% and a real interest rate of 3% he capitalized the difference in average earnings and reduced the amount to present value. He also gave his opinion that the present value of defendant's contribution to plaintiff's medical education was $103,390. Plaintiff offered no expert testimony on the subject.

The court, after considering the life-style that plaintiff would enjoy from the enhanced earning potential his medical license would bring and defendant's contributions and efforts toward attainment of it, made a distributive award to her of $188,800, representing 40% of the value of the license, and ordered it paid in 11 annual installments of various amounts beginning November 1, 1982 and ending November 1, 1992. The court also directed plaintiff to maintain a life insurance policy on his life for defendant's benefit for the unpaid balance of the award and it ordered plaintiff to pay defendant's counsel fees of $7,000 and her expert witness fee of $1,000. It did not award defendant maintenance.

A divided Appellate Division . . . concluded that a professional license acquired during marriage is not marital property subject to distribution. It therefore modified the judgment by striking the trial court's determination that it is and by striking the provision ordering payment of the expert witness for evaluating the license and remitted the case for further proceedings. . . .

II

The Equitable Distribution Law contemplates only two classes of property: marital property and separate property (Domestic Relations Law §236[B][c], [d]). The former, which is subject to equitable distribution, is defined broadly as "*all* property acquired by either or both spouses during the marriage and before the execution of a separation agreement or the commencement of a matrimonial action, *regardless of the form in which title is held*" (Domestic Relations Law §236[B][1][c] [emphasis added]; see, §236[B][5][b], [c]). Plaintiff does not contend that his license is excluded from distribution because it is separate property; rather, he claims that it is not property at all but represents a personal attainment in acquiring knowledge. He rests his argument on decisions in similar cases from other jurisdictions and on his view that a license does not satisfy common-law concepts of property. Neither contention is controlling because decisions in other States rely principally on their own statutes, and the legislative history underlying them, and because the New York Legislature deliberately went beyond traditional property concepts when it formulated the Equitable Distribution Law. . . . Instead, our statute recognizes that spouses have an equitable claim to things of value arising out of the marital relationship and classifies them as subject to distribution by focusing on the marital status of the parties at the time of acquisition. . . .

Section 236 provides that in making an equitable distribution of marital property, "the court shall consider: any equitable claim to, interest in, or direct or indirect contribution made to the acquisition of such marital property by the party not having title, including joint efforts or expenditures and contributions and services as a spouse, parent, wage earner and homemaker, and *to the career or career potential of the other party* [and] the impossibility or difficulty of evaluating any component asset or any interest in a business, corporation or *profession*" (Domestic Relations Law §236[B][5][d][6], [9] [emphasis added]). Where equitable distribution of marital property is appropriate but "the distribution of an interest in a business, corporation *or profession* would be contrary to law" the court shall make a distributive award in lieu of an actual distribution of the property (Domestic Relations Law §236[B][5][e] [emphasis added]). The words mean exactly what they say: that an interest in a profession or professional career potential is marital property which may be represented by direct or indirect contributions of the non-title-holding spouse, including financial contributions and nonfinancial contributions made by caring for the home and family. . . .

The determination that a professional license is marital property is also consistent with the conceptual base upon which the statute rests. As this case demonstrates, few undertakings during a marriage better qualify as the type of joint effort that the statute's economic partnership theory is intended to address than contributions toward one spouse's acquisition of a professional license. Working spouses are often required to contribute substantial income as wage earners, sacrifice their own educational or career goals and opportunities for child rearing, perform the bulk of household duties and responsibilities and forego the acquisition of marital assets that could have been accumulated if the professional spouse had been employed rather than occupied with the study and training necessary to acquire a professional license. In this case, nearly all of the parties' nine-year marriage was devoted to the acquisition of plaintiff's medical license and defendant played a major role in that project. She worked continuously during the marriage and contributed all of her earnings to their joint effort, she sacrificed her own educational and career opportunities, and she traveled with plaintiff to Mexico for three and one-half years while he attended medical school there. The Legislature has decided, by its explicit reference in the statute to the contributions of one spouse to the other's profession or career (see, Domestic Relations Law §236[B][5][d][6], [9]; [e]), that these contributions represent investments in the economic partnership of the marriage and that the product of the parties' joint efforts, the professional license, should be considered marital property. . . .

Plaintiff's principal argument, adopted by the majority below, is that a professional license is not marital property because it does not fit within the traditional view of property as something which has an exchange value on the open market and is capable of sale, assignment or transfer. The position does not withstand analysis for at least two reasons. First, as we have observed, it ignores the fact that whether a professional license constitutes marital property is to be judged by the language of the statute which created this new species of property previously unknown at common law or under prior statutes. Thus, whether the license fits within traditional property concepts is of no consequence. Second, it is an overstatement to assert that a professional license could not be considered property even outside the context of section 236(B). A professional license is a valuable property right, reflected in the money, effort and lost opportunity for employment expended in its acquisition, and also in the enhanced earning capacity it affords its holder, which may not be revoked without due process of law (see, *Matter of Bender v. Board of Regents*, 262 App Div 627, 631; *People ex rel. Greenberg v. Reid*, 151 App Div 324, 326). That a professional license has no market value is irrelevant. Obviously, a license may not be alienated as may other property and for that reason the working spouse's interest in it is limited. The Legislature has recognized that limitation, however, and has provided for an award in lieu of its actual distribution (see, Domestic Relations Law §236[B][5][e]).

Plaintiff also contends that alternative remedies should be employed, such as an award of rehabilitative maintenance or reimbursement for direct financial contributions (see, e.g., *Kutanovski v. Kutanovski*, 109 AD2d 822, 824; *Conner v. Conner*, 97 AD2d 88, 101, supra; *Lesman v. Lesman*, 88 AD2d 153, 158-159, supra). The statute does not expressly authorize retrospective maintenance or rehabilitative awards and we have no occasion to decide in this case whether the authority to do so may ever be implied from its provisions (but see, *Cappiello v. Cappiello*, 66 NY2d 107). It is sufficient to observe that normally a working spouse should not be restricted to that relief because to do so frustrates the purposes underlying the Equitable Distribution Law. Limiting a working spouse to a maintenance award, either general or rehabilitative, not only is contrary to the economic partnership concept underlying the statute but also retains the uncertain and inequitable economic ties of dependence that the Legislature sought to extinguish by equitable distribution. Maintenance is subject to termination upon the recipient's remarriage and a working spouse may never receive adequate consideration for his or her contribution and may even be penalized for the decision to remarry if that is the only method of compensating the contribution. . . .

Turning to the question of valuation, it has been suggested that even if a professional license is considered marital property, the working spouse is entitled only to reimbursement of his or her direct financial contributions. . . . Such a result is completely at odds with the statute's requirement that the court give full consideration to both direct and indirect contributions "made to the acquisition of such marital property by the party not having title, including joint *efforts* or expenditures *and contributions and services as a spouse, parent*, wage earner *and homemaker*" (Domestic Relations Law §236[B][5][d][6] [emphasis added]). If the license is marital property, then the working spouse is entitled to an equitable portion of it, not a return of funds advanced. Its value is the enhanced earning capacity it affords the holder. . . .

Post-Case Follow-Up

O'Brien v. O'Brien holds that a professional license acquired during marriage is marital property subject to equitable division. Thus, the spouse who did not acquire the license but who has made an equitable contribution toward acquiring the property is entitled to an equitable portion of the enhanced earning capacity afforded by the license.

New York is the only state that holds that a medical license is marital property. However, in other states the fact that a spouse may have a medical license that was earned during marriage and now has the ability to earn additional income may be used as a factor in awarding spousal support to the other party.

O'Brien v. O'Brien: Real Life Applications

1. Beatrice and Glen marry when Beatrice has only her associate degree. Glen is an accountant and makes approximately $45,000 a year. During the marriage, Beatrice goes back to school and obtains her B.A. and eventually a teaching certificate. You represent Glen in his marital dissolution action. It is estimated that the value of Glen's contribution to the marriage during the time that Beatrice was obtaining her college degree was worth approximately $80,000. In addition, as a result of Beatrice's degree she now has an earning capacity of at least $35,000 a year. Under the rationale of the *O'Brien* decision, does Glen have any claim in Beatrice's increased earning capacity by way of a distribution of property as a result of her college degree?

2. Assume the same facts as Question 1 except that Beatrice instead earned a bachelor's degree in psychology, and then went on to earn her masters and doctorate degrees in psychology. Shortly after she obtained her doctorate, she received an offer to work at a prestigious hospital in the local area earning over $120,000 a year.

   a. Does Glen have any claim that the degree is marital property subject to division?

   b. Does the fact that Beatrice earned college degrees versus a professional license make a difference?

   c. If the trial court found it was not marital property, what arguments could you make on appeal?

Goodwill of a Professional Practice

Goodwill is an intangible asset that is most commonly identified with commercial businesses. It can be defined generally as a business's good reputation in the community that generates the expectation of continued future patronage. Put another way, it is the value of a business that "exceeds the combined value of the net assets" of that business.[2] Because it can readily be valued and transferred for consideration if the business is sold, there is little question that the goodwill of a business is an intangible property interest that is subject to distribution upon divorce.

There is less agreement, however, where the goodwill of a professional practice is involved. A minority of jurisdictions do not regard the goodwill of a professional practice as property. Underlying this exclusion is the belief that the goodwill attaches to the individual professionals in the practice rather than to the practice itself. So attached, professional goodwill is thus regarded as both nontransferable and hard to value; moreover, even if a value could be assigned, it is viewed as being too tied to the vagaries of the individual's career path to have real meaning. Thus, lacking these essential attributes of property — transferability and amenability to valuation — this minority of jurisdictions regards professional

---

[2]*See* Diane Green Smith, 'Til Success Do Us Part: How Illinois Promotes Inequities in Property Distribution Pursuant to Divorce by Excluding Professional Goodwill, 26 J. Marshall L. Rev. 147 (1992).

goodwill more like future earning capacity, which can be considered fashioning support awards, rather than as a marital asset. At the other end of the spectrum, a number of jurisdictions take the view that professional goodwill attaches to the practice itself rather than to the individual partners, and thus is fully included in the marital estate.

Most states, however, take an in-between position and seek to distinguish between "enterprise" and "personal" goodwill. Here, goodwill that is attributable to the reputation of an individual is not considered property because, as noted above, it cannot be readily valued or transferred, whereas goodwill that is attributable to the reputation of the business itself is considered part of the marital estate and subject to division at the time of divorce. As with unvested pensions, some courts that treat personal professional goodwill as an intangible asset may also be influenced by the fact that the goodwill, although securing future benefits, is built up during the marriage, thus making exclusion unfair.

Divorce and the Family Pet

One area that has received considerable attention recently is how disputes over the family pet should be resolved. The debate over the family pets is not over whether family pets are tangible or intangible, but rather over whether they should be treated as an item of property (like a chair), and thus subject to equitable distribution rules, or as a member of the household (like a child), and thus subject to something akin to a "best interest of the pet" standard.

Courts have increasingly been confronted with this issue as a growing number of divorce cases involve a dispute over the future of a beloved family pet (sometimes now referred to instead as a "companion animal"). This uptick has been attributed to a number of related factors. One consideration is the developing cultural awareness of the important role that pets can play in humans' lives. This recognition is supported by research indicating the beneficial impact that a relationship with a loved animal can have on a person's well-being, for example, by helping to calm someone with an anxiety disorder, or to ease the loneliness that typically accompanies the death of a partner. Another consideration is that as more couples choose not to have children, pets are likely to play a more important role in a greater number of households, and conflicts over them may take on additional weight and meaning as a relationship ends.

However, as it presently stands, based on established legal doctrine, pets are generally considered to be the "personal property" of their "owners." Accordingly, upon divorce the determination of a pet's future is controlled by property distribution principles. Thus, for example, a court might award a dog to the spouse who came into a marriage with the pet based on the classification principle that the dog is a separate asset, rather than to the spouse who had been the pet's primary caretaker over the course of the marriage — an approach that might approximate the "best interest" standard used to resolve custody disputes involving children. In effect, this "pet as property" approach means that the fate of the family dog or cat will be resolved by reference to the same principles that govern the distribution of the household furniture or a couple's automobiles.

Over the past 15 or so years, this approach has increasingly been challenged by a number of legal scholars, animal rights activists, and litigants seeking to maintain their post-dissolution relationship with a pet, who argue that pets should be moved out of the property category and treated more as family members. Seeking to more accurately express the underlying relational dimensions of this proposed shift in legal classification, advocates also propose a linguistic shift from "owner" to "guardian," in order to connote "a greater sense of responsibility" and from "pet" to "companion animal" in order to better capture the enduring connections that exist between humans and the animals who live with them.[3] It is worth noting that this shift in nomenclature has been incorporated into some municipal ordinances.

Correspondingly, advocates of the recharacterization of pets from property to family member argue that conflicts between divorcing spouses over a pet should be treated as akin to a custody dispute rather than as a disagreement over the allocation of marital assets, and that a standard akin to the "best interest of the companion animal" should be employed to determine custody and visitation rights. This standard would recognize that unlike a chair, animals are living beings who are both loyal and loving and, like children, are dependent upon adults to provide for their basic needs. Moreover, as with a child, the loss of relationship cannot be redressed by providing a spouse with an offsetting asset to compensate him or her for the deprivation caused by award of the pet to the other spouse.[4]

However, courts and legislatures have not generally been receptive to these arguments, and pets generally continue to be treated as property in the marital dissolution context. For example, in a 1995 Florida divorce case, the appeals court concluded that the trial court had erred in awarding custody of the couple's dog to the husband with visitation rights to the wife because under Florida law a dog is personal property and "[t]here is no authority which provides for a trial court to grant custody or visitation pertaining to personal property." *Bennett v. Bennett*, 650 So. 2d 109, 111 (Fla. Dist. Ct. App. 1995).

As a policy matter, the court further stated: "Determinations as to custody and visitation lead to continuing enforcement and supervision problems (as evidenced by the proceedings in the instant case). Our courts are overwhelmed with the supervision of custody, visitation, and support matters related to the protection of our children. We cannot undertake the same responsibility as to animals." *Id.*

Taking this a step further, a Pennsylvania appeals court refused to enforce an agreement between a couple regarding the allocation of custodial and visitation rights between divorcing spouses, stating:

> In seeking "shared custody" and a "visitation" arrangement, Appellant appears to treat Barney, a dog, as a child. Despite the status owners bestow on their pets, Pennsylvania law considers dogs to be personal property. . . . Appellant, however, overlooks the fact

---

[3]Rebecca Huss, Separation, Custody and Estate Planning Issues Relating to Companion Animals, 74 U. Colo. L. Rev. 181, 198-199 (2003). *See also* Elizabeth Paek, Fido Seeks Full Membership in the Family: Dismantling the Property Classification of Companion Animals by Statute, 25 Haw. L. Rev. 481, 486-490 (2003).

[4]*See generally* Huss and Paek, *supra* note 3, and David Favre, Living Property: A New Status for Animals Within the Legal System, 93 Marq. L. Rev. 1021 (2010); Tabby T. McLain, Adapting the Child's Best Interest Model to Custody Determinations of Companion Animals, 6 J. Animal L. 151 (2010); Christopher D. Seps, Treating Pets as Persons in Tort and Custody Disputes, 2010 U. Ill. L. Rev. 1339.

that any terms set forth in the Agreement are void to the extent that they attempt to award custodial visitation with or shared custody of personal property. . . . As the trial court aptly noted, Appellant is seeking an arrangement analogous, in law, to a visitation schedule for a table or a lamp.

Desanctis v. Prichard, 803 A.2d 230, 233 (Pa. Super. Ct. 2002). Similarly, in the 2014 case of *Hamet v. Baker*, the Supreme Court of Vermont affirmed the trial court's conclusion that it lacked the authority to "impose an enforceable visitation order for the dog" on the grounds that "an order of property division is final and not subject to modification" and that in contrast to "enforcement of other kinds of property division orders, enforcement of a family companion animal would require the power of modification, since the animal's well-being . . . could be a substantial factor in the analysis." *Hamet v. Baker*, 2014 VT 39, 97 A.3d 461, 465 (2014).

Although courts have continued to resist treating disputes between divorcing spouses over a family pet as akin to a child custody dispute, animal lovers can take heart in the fact that some judges have quietly begun to pay attention to the post-dissolution needs of family pets within the "pet as property" paradigm. Accordingly, in *Hamet v. Baker*, although firm in its view that "pet animals are property" and thus subject to the rules of equitable distribution, the Vermont high court made equally clear that they are "a special category of property" due to the fact that they "are alive and form emotional attachments with their owners that run in both directions." *Id.* at 463. In light of the fact that the state's equitable distribution rules permit the consideration of relevant factors beyond those enumerated in the statute (which, it should be noted, is the case in many jurisdictions), the court concluded where pets are concerned "the welfare of the animal and the emotional connection between the animal and each spouse" can be taken into account in fashioning an award. *Id.* at 464. *See also Whitmore v. Whitmore*, 2011 Va. App. LEXIS 57 (unpublished opinion).

Clearly, these considerations would not be relevant when deciding which party was entitled to, say, a lamp or sofa, which might lead one to the conclusion that the court smuggled considerations of the dog's best interest into its equitable distribution analysis.

2. Classification of Property

The classification of property as marital or separate is a crucial step in both common law dual property and community property states because it determines the pool of assets that is subject to division at the time of divorce (although, in a few states, courts can reach separate property in cases of hardship). In theory, classification is not relevant in all property states; however, in practice, classification principles may influence how attorneys and possibly judges approach the distribution of property.

Marital and separate property are typically defined in relationship to one another: One is what the other is not. Thus, not uncommonly, a statute will define marital property as all property acquired during the marriage, except for that which is considered separate. Separate property is then specifically defined, and almost always includes property owned at the time of marriage, gifts, inheritances, and items received in exchange for separate property. Some statutes also identify specific assets, such as appreciation on separate property, unvested pensions, and professional licenses, as coming within the definition of separate property (as noted above, sometimes questions regarding whether an asset is subject to division can be alternatively framed as one of definition or as one of classification).

The rationale underlying the distinction between marital and separate property is that marital assets owe their existence to the overall contributions of both spouses to the marriage as a shared enterprise, and thus at divorce are subject to the claims of both regardless of who actually acquired which asset, while separate assets are not attributable to the efforts of either spouse, and thus "belong" to the acquiring spouse. In the event of a dispute over the characterization of an asset, most jurisdictions employ a presumption that all property owned at the time of divorce is marital; accordingly, the burden of establishing that an asset is indeed separate is up to the spouse seeking to disaggregate it from the marital estate.

Marital or Separate: The Significance of Timing

A central characteristic of marital property is that it is acquired *during* the marriage through the effort of either spouse. This means that as a general rule, property that a spouse comes into the marriage with remains his or her separate property. This distinction usually is straightforward, but a few situations require elaboration.

Determining the Time of Acquisition

If a person purchases an asset, such as a car, before getting married and then makes payments on it after the marriage, is the car a premarital or a marital acquisition? One approach known as the **inception of title rule** fixes the time of acquisition at the time of initial purchase because this is when title or the right to title is obtained. Once set, the characterization cannot be changed, and postmarital contributions have no impact on the classification. Here, property is a unitary concept and value cannot be apportioned between the marital and the separate estates, although the nonowner spouse might be entitled to some reimbursement for any payments that he or she makes.

However, most jurisdictions have rejected this approach as too formalistic and incompatible with sharing principles because it focuses on title to the exclusion of contribution. The preferred approach to determining the time of acquisition is the **source of funds rule**. Here, acquisition is seen as a dynamic process that unfolds over time as payment is made; one might say that each payment effectuates a partial acquisition. Accordingly, an asset can be both marital and separate, and its value apportioned between the two estates in proportion to contribution.

Property Acquired in Contemplation of Marriage or During Cohabitation

Usually, there is no doubt that an asset that is owned by a person at the time of marriage is his or her separate property. However, sometimes purchases may be made in contemplation of marriage. In this situation, some jurisdictions have stretched statutory categories and will treat this property as marital based on the parties' intent to use it as such. Here, intent displaces the timing of acquisition as the controlling factor.

A related question is how property acquired during a period of premarital cohabitation will be treated. Reluctant to treat cohabitation as the legal equivalent of marriage, most courts do not consider assets acquired during a period of cohabitation as marital. However, if, while cohabiting, property is purchased in contemplation of marriage, it might come within the above rule and be treated as marital based on the parties' intent rather than on the fact of cohabitation.

Fixing a Cut-Off Point for Marital Acquisitions

Timing questions that can influence classification also arise at the other end of the relationship — specifically, at what point in the dissolution process will acquired assets no longer be considered marital? Strictly speaking, a husband and wife remain legally married until a final decree of divorce is entered; thus, property that is acquired up until this moment in time is technically marital. However, motivated by practical and policy considerations, most jurisdictions use an earlier cut-off point after which time property that is acquired is no longer considered marital despite the continuation of the legal relationship.

To signal the effective end of the marital partnership, most state statutes fix the cut-off point at the date of legal separation, the initiation of a permanent separation, or the filing of a dissolution action, although a few states leave it to the discretion of the judge. Although utilizing different moments in time, each of these approaches reflects the underlying view that once spouses have gone their separate ways, the theoretical justification for pooling based on mutual contribution and effort no longer exists. It should be noted that practical problems can arise where the cut-off point is the date of permanent separation. Frequently, a separation that is intended to be permanent is followed by a series of contacts, some or all of which may rise to the level of reconciliation, which makes it difficult to fix the date of separation, particularly if the spouses disagree about the meaning and impact of these post-separation contacts.

Marital or Separate: The Challenge of Classifying Certain Types of Assets

Although the distinction between marital and separate property is easy to state, applying it can be difficult. As discussed here, certain types of assets raise unique classification issues. Although far from comprehensive in nature, this discussion will give you an overview of some of the issues that can arise. As with definitional contests, classification disputes are not mere legal abstractions, but rather determine what assets are subject to reach in the distribution process.

Gifts

A **gift** is a voluntary transfer of property made with donative intent, meaning that the gift-giver simply wishes to give the recipient something without requiring anything in exchange. For a gift to be effective, the transfer must be complete — the donor must fully relinquish all vestiges of ownership and control.

In the divorce context, a gift is generally classified as separate property, as it is not acquired through the effort of either spouse. Sometimes, however, a transfer that appears to be a gift is really not, such as when the donor, rather than being motivated by donative intent, is providing compensation for services rendered. Community property jurisdictions have long distinguished between gifts made with true donative intent and those which really are a form of compensation, and accordingly treat the latter as marital property because the acquisition is tied to the recipient's efforts. This distinction is now also made in some common law dual property jurisdictions.

For example, assume that Bob and Karen are married. One day Karen's great-aunt Ernestine gives her a beautiful oil painting that is worth a lot of money. At first glance, classification appears obvious: The painting is a gift to Karen and is thus her separate property. However, what happens if the next time Bob and Karen visit Ernestine, she mentions that she gave the painting to Karen as a way of thanking her for taking such good care of her during her last illness? Now, arguably, if the couple were to divorce, Bob could argue that the painting should be classified as marital property because it was not given to Karen as a gift but as a form of compensation and thus was acquired through the expenditure of marital efforts.

What if instead of being from a third party, the gift is from one spouse to another? Should these be treated in the same manner? What if the gift was purchased from marital funds — should the source of contribution or the nature of the exchange control the classification? In some states, interspousal gifts have been exempted from the general characterization of gifts as separate property either by statute or judicial decision, with some of these states limiting the exclusion to gifts that were purchased with marital funds. The underlying rationale here is that unlike third-party gifts, interspousal gifts derive from partnership efforts. In contrast, other jurisdictions focus on the gift aspect of the transaction, rather than on the source of funds. These courts treat completed interspousal gifts in the same manner as third-party gifts, even where purchased with marital funds.

Damage Awards

Damage awards, such as those from personal injury cases, as well as disability or workers' compensation benefits, often trigger difficult classification questions (which in some jurisdictions may instead be framed as definitional questions). By way of illustration, this discussion will focus on personal injury awards.

If an injury occurs during the marriage, a minority of jurisdiction employ what is known as the **mechanistic approach**, which classifies the entire personal injury award as marital. Conceptually, this is similar to the inception of title rule as the timing of the entitlement to the award controls its classification. Courts that follow this rule often do so because "personal injury proceeds are not included in the statutory definitions of separate property or the exceptions to marital property."[5]

---

[5]Patrick M. Erne, Personal Injury Awards and Divorce: Pennsylvania Should Adopt the Analytical Approach Through Statute to Promote Fairness and Consistency, 23 Widener L.J. 843, 854 (2014); *see also* Aloysius A. Leopold, "Loss of Earning Capacity" Benefits in the Community Property Jurisdiction — How Do You Figure?, 30 St. Mary's L.J. 367, 388-389 (1999).

In contrast, most states now employ the **analytical approach**, according to which an award is divided into component parts and allocated between the separate and marital estates in accordance with general classification principles. Accordingly, most states will classify the portion of the award attributable to lost wages and medical expenses as marital property because it compensates for economic loss incurred during the marriage. The portion of the award attributable to the pain and suffering of the injured spouse is then classified as separate property because it is so intimately connected to the injured spouse that it is deemed to exist apart from the marriage. If the award also compensates the injured person for future economic losses, this portion of the award usually would be classified as separate because the other spouse has no recognized interest in these future rights.[6]

Appreciation of Separate Property

Difficult classification issues can arise in situations where separate property has increased in value over the course of the marriage. One approach is to tie the classification of the appreciation to the classification of the underlying asset. This means that if the asset is characterized as separate, any appreciation in value — even if it occurred during the marriage — will also be classified as separate. This approach is similar to the previously discussed inception of title rule that fixes ownership at the time of acquisition.

As with the inception of title rule, most jurisdictions have rejected this approach as too rigid and not in keeping with contemporary sharing principles. The preferred approach is to classify appreciation based on the reason for the increase. If the increase is unrelated to spousal efforts and is due to causes such as inflation or market conditions, it is usually considered the separate property of the spouse who owns the asset. This kind of increase is often referred to as **passive appreciation**. If instead the gain is due to the investment of marital funds or efforts, it is usually considered marital. This kind of increase is often referred to as **active appreciation**. If the gain is attributable to both passive and active forces, it can be apportioned between the separate and marital estates.[7]

---

[6]A third method, which is of little practical relevance today, is to treat the entire award as the separate property of the injured spouse. This is referred to as the "unitary" approach.
[7]*See generally* Joan M. Krauskopf, Classifying Marital and Separate Property: Combinations and Increase in Value of Separate Property, 89 W. Va. L. Rev. 996, 997 (1987). For discussion of specialized rules developed by some states regarding appreciation, see Suzanne Reynolds, Increases in Separate Property and the Evolving Marital Partnership, 24 Wake Forest L. Rev. 239, 291-299 (1989).

Case Preview

Innerbichler v. Innerbichler

This case arose out of a dissolution of a 14-year marriage. Shortly before the marriage, Husband started a business. The business, over time, grew as a result of a number of circumstances that occurred after the marriage. One of the issues on appeal was whether the appreciation in the value of Husband's 51 percent ownership interest was marital property. The trial court determined that it was and awarded Wife her half share of the appreciation.

The wife had a number of experts testifying on her behalf who had to look at both the value of the business at the time of the marriage and how the value of the business increased over time. Husband argued that the value of the business was a result of work done prior to the marriage. Wife argued that the value was a direct result of actions that occurred after marriage.

As you read *Innerbichler v. Innerbichler*, look for the following:

1. What was the position of each party regarding how the appreciation of the business should be classified?
2. What role did the valuation experts have in the trial court?
3. What arguments were raised by Husband to show that the appreciation of the business was not marital property subject to division?
4. What arguments were raised by Wife to show that the appreciation was marital property subject to division?
5. Why were Husband's arguments not persuasive to the court?

Innerbichler v. Innerbichler

752 A.2d 291 (Md. Ct. Spec. App. 2000)

. . .

The parties were married on January 21, 1984, when Mr. Innerbichler (the "Husband") was 41 years old and appellee (the "Wife") was 33. . . . [More than year prior to marriage, Husband had co-founded TAMSCO with his friend William Bilawa. At trial a number of experts testified for both parties.] The primary disputes centered on the fair market value of TAMSCO, whether the appreciation in value of TAMSCO constituted marital property, and, if so, the value of the marital interest.

. . .

When TAMSCO was founded, appellant was married to Barbara Innerbichler ("Barbara"). In 1983, as part of his divorce settlement with Barbara, appellant claimed that he waived his interest in the home that they occupied, allegedly worth about $300,000.00, in exchange for Barbara's agreement to waive her claim to TAMSCO, which appellant contends was worth at least as much as the home.

In June 1983, about six months before appellant's marriage to appellee, appellant submitted an application on behalf of TAMSCO to the United States Small Business

Administration ("SBA") to obtain "8(a) certification." According to appellant, who is an Hispanic American, the "8(a) program" was established during the Nixon years to assist small businesses owned and controlled by socially and economically disadvantaged persons. . . .

[Wife] insists that TAMSCO was in its "embryonic stages" when the parties were first married. Ample evidence was presented at trial showing that TAMSCO was in its fledgling stage of development at the time of the marriage.

According to the 8(a) application, submitted in June 1983, TAMSCO was "a new business" with only two employees, and its operating equipment consisted of two electric typewriters, a bookcase, a file cabinet, a conference table, and chairs, having a total value of less than $2,000.00. Although appellant maintains . . . that, at the time of TAMSCO's 8(a) application, TAMSCO "had already completed contracts of significant value and had other contracts pending, all of which established its viability to the SBA," the SBA application listed only two contracts that TAMSCO had completed in the preceding three years: a $13,000.00 contract commenced in February 1983 and a $6,000.00 contract completed in May 1983. . . .

On April 14, 1984, some 83 days after the parties' marriage, TAMSCO obtained the desired 8(a) certification. It is undisputed that the 8(a) program enabled TAMSCO to obtain lucrative sole source government contracts, the first of which was awarded to TAMSCO in September 1984. TAMSCO grew rapidly after the award of the 8(a) certification. For fiscal year 1983, the company reported approximately $52,000.00 in revenues, and $188,000.00 in revenues for fiscal year 1984. By the end of fiscal year 1992, TAMSCO had been awarded contracts totaling $356,439,719. For 1995, TAMSCO generated revenues of $46 million and employed over 500 people. In 1996, TAMSCO earned $47,000,000.00 in revenues, followed by $51,000,000.00 for fiscal year 1997.

. . .

Although [Husband/]appellant concedes that most of TAMSCO's lucrative contracts were obtained and performed after his marriage to [Wife/]appellee, he maintains that neither TAMSCO nor the post-marriage appreciation in the company's value constituted marital property. He argues that the company was created before the marriage and its success was directly linked to an Army contract awarded prior to the marriage. . . .

At trial, [Husband] also maintained that he was not solely responsible for TAMSCO's success. To the contrary, he asserted that both he and Bilawa were responsible for making many of the important corporate decisions. [Husband] also contends here, as he did below, that TAMSCO "flourished" as a result of many "external factors" unrelated to [Husband], including the "dramatic increase in defense spending" and "the expanding defense industry during the Reagan Administration," as well as the company's 8(a) status.

. . .

[The trial] court awarded . . . a monetary award to the Wife in the amount of $2,880,000.00.

The monetary award was based largely on the court's determination as to TAMSCO's value. The court expressly indicated that it found the testimony of the Wife's expert as to TAMSCO's value "more persuasive" than appellant's expert. Based on the opinion of the Wife's expert, the court concluded that TAMSCO had a fair market value of $8.3 million. The court also determined that appellant's 51% ownership interest in TAMSCO was worth $4,233,000.00, and that appellant's pre-marital interest in TAMSCO was worth $153,000.00.

Additionally, the court found that the post-marriage "increase in value of TAMSCO is marital," and that "the Husband's share (51%) of the increased value of TAMSCO stock is marital," because TAMSCO's "success is attributable to a large degree to the work efforts of the Husband throughout the marriage." . . .

DISCUSSION

A.

As we noted, the court determined that TAMSCO had a value of $8,300,000.00, and appellant's 51% ownership interest amounted to $4,233,000.00. After deducting appellant's pre-marital interest in TAMSCO of $153,000.00, the court arrived at the sum of $4,080,000.00 as the post-marital value of appellant's 51% interest. In effect, the trial court attributed all of the appreciation to appellant's efforts; 51% of that appreciation, corresponding to appellant's ownership interest, represented marital property for purposes of the monetary award. The court then concluded that appellee was entitled to half of the marital property; her share amounted to $2,788,140.25. After deducting $104,804.50 for the pension transfer, and $74,653.00 for the marital property titled in appellee's name, the court granted the Wife a monetary award of $2,581,864.75.

Title 8 of the Family Law Article of the Maryland Code provides for the equitable distribution of marital property. "'Marital Property' means the property, however titled, acquired by 1 or both parties during the marriage." F.L. §8-201(e)(1). Pursuant to F.L. §8-201(e)(3), marital property does not include property that is:

(i) acquired before the marriage;
(ii) acquired by inheritance or gift from a third party;
(iii) excluded by valid agreement; or
(iv) directly traceable to any of these sources.

Property that is initially non-marital can become marital, however. See *Brodak v. Brodak*, 294 Md. 10, 26-27, 447 A.2d 847 (1982). Moreover, the party who asserts a marital interest in property bears the burden of producing evidence as to the identity of the property. *Noffsinger v. Noffsinger*, 95 Md. App. 265, 281, 620 A.2d 415, cert. denied, 331 Md. 197, 627 A.2d 539 (1993). Conversely, "[t]he party seeking to demonstrate that particular property acquired during the marriage is nonmarital must trace the property to a nonmarital source." Id. at 283, 620 A.2d 415; see *Golden v. Golden*, 116 Md. App. 190, 205, 695 A.2d 1231, cert. denied, 347 Md. 681, 702 A.2d 290 (1997) (recognizing that the increased value of property acquired during the marriage is marital property, unless it can be directly traced to a non-marital source). See also *Harper v. Harper*, 294 Md. 54, 69-70, 448 A.2d 916 (1982). If a property interest cannot be traced to a nonmarital source, it is considered marital property. *Noffsinger*, 95 Md. App. at 281, 620 A.2d 415; see *Melrod v. Melrod*, 83 Md. App. 180, 187, 574 A.2d 1, cert. denied, 321 Md. 67, 580 A.2d 1077 (1990).

. . .

As we noted earlier, the trial court made several critical findings as to TAMSCO, including that the appreciation of TAMSCO constituted marital property because the company's dramatic success was "attributable to a large degree to the work efforts" of appellant. For purposes of calculating the monetary award, the court also concluded that 51% of that appreciation, corresponding to appellant's ownership interest in the company, was marital property.

As we previously observed, appellant contends that the court erred in finding that TAMSCO constituted marital property. He argues that "TAMSCO was brought into the marriage as an established, flourishing non-marital asset. By the time the parties married, the ground work had already been laid to make TAMSCO a success." In addition, the Husband quarrels with the court's decision to attribute the appreciation of TAMSCO solely to his efforts. He maintains that TAMSCO's growth was the result of the efforts of many people as well as several other factors, such as the thriving defense industry. In his view, "[t]his is a classic case of being in the right place at the right time." Moreover, appellant complains that the court should not have treated 51% of the appreciation as marital property, merely because he owned 51% of the company. Appellant asserts that the court was required to ascertain the precise portion of TAMSCO's increase in value for which appellant was responsible, and that only the portion attributable to his work efforts could qualify as marital property.

The court was not clearly erroneous in rejecting appellant's claim that TAMSCO was entirely non-marital property. Although it is undisputed that TAMSCO was created before the marriage, the evidence that we summarized earlier supported the court's conclusion that TAMSCO's value soared after the marriage. For example, when TAMSCO submitted its application for SBA 8(a) certification in June 1983, it had only completed a $13,000.00 contract and a $6,000.00 contract, and a $131,000.00 contract was in progress. Moreover, TAMSCO owned little in the way of tangible property. At the time of the marriage, the business had only two full-time employees and operated from Bilawa's kitchen. TAMSCO received its 8(a) certification after the marriage, and all of the 8(a) contracts were performed during the marriage. By the time TAMSCO graduated from the SBA Section 8(a) program in 1993, it had received over $356,000,000.00 in Section 8(a) revenue, placing it among the top 10 such firms nationally.

Appellant also challenges the court's decision to treat all of the appreciation as marital property. He relies on the court's own acknowledgment that appellant was merely responsible, "to a large degree" (and thus not entirely), for the increased value. On the other hand, appellant also seems to suggest that the court miscalculated the monetary award, because it did not find that all of the appreciation was marital property.

We are of the view that the court found that all of TAMSCO's appreciation constituted marital property, and it attributed all of the appreciation to appellant's work efforts. After comparing the financial status of TAMSCO before and after the marriage, the court focused on the extent of appellant's role in the corporation and his work efforts on behalf of TAMSCO, concluding that "the increase in value of TAMSCO is marital. . . ."

Moreover, notwithstanding the court's statement that appellant was responsible "to a large degree" for TAMSCO's success, we are satisfied that the court did not err, on the record before it, when it attributed all of the appreciation to appellant's efforts for purposes of calculating the monetary award. It follows that the court did not err by failing to assign a specific percentage of responsibility to appellant in achieving that corporate growth.

. . .

In determining the marital or non-marital character of disputed property that has its origins as non-marital property, the cases distinguish between passive ownership and increases in value resulting from the active efforts of the owner-spouse. See *Wilen v. Wilen*, 61 Md. App. 337, 354-55, 486 A.2d 775 (1985). In *Mount v. Mount*, 59 Md. App. 538, 549-50, 476 A.2d 1175 (1984), we recognized that there are various ways in which property that increases in value may become marital. We said:

> Property can produce other property in many different ways. In some instances, it may require active intervention and management by the owner or some assistance by the owner's spouse; in other instances, non-marital property can accrete or produce income without any effort at all on the part of the owner or the owner's spouse. In either case, all, some, or none of the income or accretion generated by or from the initial property may be used for family purposes. . . .

. . .

Although the trial court attributed the entire appreciation to appellant's efforts, appellant only owned 51% of TAMSCO. Therefore, the court properly concluded that only 51% of that appreciation, corresponding to appellant's ownership interest, constituted marital property for purposes of a monetary award. After subtracting the premarital value of TAMSCO ($153,000.00), the court multiplied the value of TAMSCO by 51% to determine the value of appellant's ownership interest in the company. The court then allocated half of that value (i.e., ½ of 51% of the appreciation) to the Wife's monetary award. . . .

. . .

Post-Case Follow-Up

Innerbichler v. Innerbichler is an example of how a spouse may be entitled to a percentage of the increased value of separate property. There was no question that TAMSCO was the separate property of the husband, having been acquired prior to marriage. As discussed earlier, property obtains its character at the time of acquisition. However, the issue then becomes how to compensate the non-owner spouse for the increase in value that occurred during the marriage. As the court discusses, the labor that caused the increase in value was done during the marriage and thus was directly connected to the marital enterprise as a whole. Accordingly, the court has no problem finding that this increase in value should be considered property subject to division.

Innerbichler v. Innerbichler: Real Life Applications

1. Pam and Joe have been married for 18 years. Prior to the marriage, Pam purchased 400 shares of KCD stock at a value of $1,000 dollars. At the time of dissolution, the stock is now worth $20,000. Pam has not taken any active role in buying or selling the stock. Is Joe entitled to an equitable share of the increase in value?

2. Jim owns a home acquired prior to marriage worth $85,000. After his marriage to Jane, the two decide to rent the home out and purchase another home as their marital home. Jim has a full-time job so Jane takes over the management of the home, seeking tenants whenever a tenant moves out, collecting rent, and taking care of all maintenance. Jane has done this for over ten years when Jim files for divorce. At the time of divorce, the home is now worth $220,000. Is Jane entitled to any increase in the value of the property? How would you argue for Jane?

3. Patrick owned a printing business, People Printers, that he acquired shortly before his marriage to Peggy. At the time of the marriage, the business was just getting started and had only $50,000 in annual sales. Subsequent to the marriage, Patrick worked in the business full time. Fifteen years later, Peggy filed for divorce. The business now has annual sales of over $500,000 primarily due to its change from being a walk-in printing business to being a web-based business where customers can e-mail their work orders and People Printers will design, format, copy, and deliver the finished product in less than a few hours. In order to obtain additional capital, Patrick took on a partner several years ago but still owns 51 percent of the company. Does Peggy have any claim to the increased revenue?

Property Received in Exchange for Separate Property

What happens if a spouse exchanges or sells separate property during the marriage? Most jurisdictions treat property that is received in exchange for separate property as separate: The exchange is regarded as an alteration in the form of the asset, which leaves its underlying separate nature intact.

Generally, based on the presumption that all property owned at the time of divorce is marital, the party seeking to segregate an asset from the marital estate has the burden of proving its separate identity. Where exchanged property is involved, segregation requires tracing the asset directly back to a separate source. Tracing can be simple, such as where one painting has been exchanged for another, or it can be complex, such as where there have been successive exchanges or where funds from an account containing separate and marital funds have been used. If the tracing fails, and the separate identity of the asset cannot be established, it will be treated as marital. As discussed below, this result is transmutation by commingling.

Transmutation

Our final classification topic is transmutation. **Transmutation** refers to a post-acquisition change in an asset's classification from separate to marital or from marital to separate, although almost all transmutation cases involve the reclassification of separate assets. Transmutation can occur in four ways: (1) by agreement, (2) by joint titling, (3) by commingling, and (4) by use.

Transmutation by Agreement

The simplest way that transmutation can occur is where the parties agree to recharacterize property. Statutes in many community property states and a few common law jurisdictions specifically authorize this result, although the term "transmutation" is usually not used. In the absence of express authority, most courts will uphold an agreement between spouses to recharacterize property. The agreement may need to be in writing and conform to whatever requirements the particular jurisdiction imposes on marital agreements.

Transmutation by Joint Titling

Property may be transmuted if a spouse places separate property or property purchased with separate funds in joint name—for example, where one spouse purchases a car with inherited funds and then takes title in both names. In most jurisdictions, joint titling triggers a rebuttable presumption that the separate asset has transmuted into a marital one because the titling demonstrates an intent to bestow a benefit on the marital estate. To rebut the presumption, a spouse may be able to show that the intent of joint titling was not to confer a benefit upon the marital estate but instead was done for estate planning purposes or to satisfy the requirements of a lender or because of pressure from his or her spouse. If the presumption is rebutted, the property will not transmute but rather will retain its original characterization as separate property.

Transmutation by Commingling

The most common way for property to transmute is by commingling. When separate property has been mixed with marital property, it will be treated as marital unless the party wishing to segregate the asset can establish its separate identity. Here the failure of a party to keep assets separate may be regarded as evidence of an intent to benefit the marital estate. The party wishing to claim an asset as separate must be able to "uncommingle" the mass of property. As with exchanged property, this is done by tracing. If the separate identity of the asset cannot be established with sufficient certainty, the tracing fails and the property is deemed to have transmuted by commingling.

Transmutation by Use

A few jurisdictions allow transmutation by use. For example, if a spouse permits the other to use his or her separately owned car on a regular basis, this use could transmute the car into a marital asset. This approach has been both praised for promoting sharing principles and criticized as an encroachment on individual property rights that effectively punishes a spouse for his or her generosity.[8] Depending

---

[8]*See* Krauskopf, *supra* note 7, at 1008. For a discussion of some of this and other related considerations in relationship to the marital home, see Brett R. Turner, Unlikely Partners: The Marital Home and the Concept of Separate Property, 20 J. Am. Acad. Matrim. Law. 69 (2006).

on the situation, the same result might also be accomplished by reference to the commingling doctrine.

3. Valuation

Before they can be divided between spouses, marital assets need to be valued. **Valuation** involves determining the worth of the assets so that an appropriate distribution can be effectuated. Where an equitable as distinct from an equal distribution standard is used, separate assets also may need to be valued, as the value and nature of this estate may influence the allocation of marital property. For example, if one spouse has considerable separate assets, it may be fair to give the other spouse a greater share of the marital estate (see Section B.4, below).

However, as a practical matter where property issues are resolved by agreement rather than at trial, parties often divide up their belongings without having them valued, as valuation can be both expensive and time consuming. Of course, this means that there is no real way of knowing whether the settlement is fair, especially if potentially valuable assets are involved. In this situation, attorneys usually include a provision in the separation agreement in which the parties acknowledge that they have knowingly and willingly dispensed with a valuation and have divided their property without full knowledge of its worth.

When property issues are resolved at trial, it can be a reversible error for the court to divide property without first determining value. Although valuation may be framed as the court's responsibility, in many jurisdictions, a party who fails to present evidence of value is deemed to have waived his or her right of appeal on this issue.

Valuation Methods

Few statutes specify how assets should be valued, and a wide range of approaches are generally acceptable. When a trial court is presented with competing valuation methods, it has relative freedom to select among the approaches or to combine them to arrive at its own value.

A common valuation approach is to determine an asset's fair market value. **Fair market value** is generally described as the price a willing buyer would pay to a willing seller where neither party is under any compulsion to buy or sell. Establishing this price requires detailed knowledge of the asset as well as the specific market conditions that would influence transferability. Although common, the fair market value approach is far from universal and would not be appropriate where, for example, a closely held corporation or a pension is involved, as neither has a readily determinable market value.[9]

Other valuation methods include the **income approach**. Here, a determination is made of the amount of income that an asset may produce over a certain period of time, which is then capitalized over the life expectancy of the asset and discounted

---

[9]For detail on valuation approaches, see The Handbook for Divorce Valuations (Robert E. Kleeman, Jr., R. James Alerding, and Benjamin D. Miller eds., 1999).

to present day value. Another approach is the **cost approach**, which entails an assessment of what it would cost to replace the asset if necessary.

The Role of Experts

The valuation of assets is generally outside the expertise of lawyers and requires the use of experts. As a general rule, there is no such thing as an all-purpose valuation expert. Instead, an expert must be carefully selected based on his or her specialized knowledge. For example, an accountant may be the most appropriate person to value a professional corporation but would not be the best choice where a rare stamp collection is involved; this would require the services of a rare stamp appraiser. Where real estate is involved, a real estate broker or appraiser would be appropriate, but if the present value of a pension needs to be determined, the services of an actuary would be required as this entails an assessment of how future risks impact the value of the employee spouse's interest.

Clearly, in any single case, the valuation process may require more than one expert. This can greatly increase the time and expense of a divorce proceeding and can significantly disadvantage the spouse with less income, who may lose the battle of the experts. To address this problem, some courts, upon request, may order one spouse to pay the costs of the other's experts or may appoint its own expert and order one party to pay all or most of the costs. The expense and time involved in hiring experts may encourage couples to settle rather than litigate; alternatively, it may encourage the financially more secure spouse to litigate vigorously in order to outdo the other.

Time of Valuation

An important valuation issue is when value should be determined. Possible dates include time of (1) separation, (2) trial, or (3) entry of the decree of dissolution. Traditionally, most jurisdictions selected a single valuation time and used that date in all cases. However, the trend is toward greater flexibility, with a preference for determining value as close to the date of distribution as possible. That being said, most courts will readily depart from this approach where required by considerations of fairness. For example, if after separation one party dissipates assets, the court may use the date of separation for valuation purposes. This date might also be used if an asset has appreciated in value based on the post-separation efforts of one spouse.

4. Distribution

After property has been classified as marital or separate and valued, the actual distribution must be effectuated. The majority of states use an **equitable distribution** standard, which directs courts to divide the property in a manner that is described as fair, just, or equitable. A minority of states, made up mainly of community property jurisdictions, use an **equal distribution** standard. These courts must divide marital property equally between the spouses — although a few states permit deviations based on equitable considerations, such as where one spouse has no other resources and is otherwise likely to end up on public assistance. A few states use a hybrid approach. Here, property is to be divided equitably, but there is a rebuttable presumption that equitable is in fact equal. Accordingly, a party seeking a greater share of the assets would have the burden of proving why this is fair under the particular circumstances.

With the exception of the hybrid states, appellate courts in jurisdictions using an equitable distribution standard have generally made clear that it is inappropriate for trial courts to rely on fixed formulas or presumptions. However, it is generally acceptable for a court to use a 50-50 split as its starting point, as long as this does not result in an overly mechanistic approach to the allocation of assets. Nonetheless, as a practical matter, some judges and lawyers seem to assume that equitable means equal, thus implicitly placing a burden on the party seeking a greater share of the assets to justify why this division is appropriate.

A frequent concern raised by commentators who have examined the economic impact of divorce on women is that a division that appears equal or equitable on its face may have a very different value to each spouse based on differences in earning capacity, as the spouse with higher earnings can more readily replace items that were lost in the distribution. This problem may be exacerbated if the low-earning spouse also has custody of the children, as the custodial parent often has increased household needs. Moreover, as we have seen, these considerations are often linked, because a spouse with greater domestic responsibilities frequently has a diminished earning capacity. One solution that some have suggested is for courts to look beyond ensuring that the distribution appears equitable or equal solely at the time of divorce, and assess the relative impact of the distribution on each spouse over time in light of earning potential and domestic arrangements as well. When this suggests a diverging value, the allocation could be adjusted to ensure greater fairness over time. *See generally* Joan Williams, Do Wives Own Half? Winning for Wives After *Wendt*, 32 Conn. L. Rev. 249 (2000).

Consideration of Enumerated Factors

Most states with an equitable distribution standard have a statute that enumerates the factors that must be considered in determining how property is to be allocated. Some statutes are general in their approach, while others are detailed. Frequently, the factors that must be considered are the same as those that must be considered in making a spousal support award.

The following section from the New Jersey statute is a good example of a fairly detailed approach to what must be taken into account when determining the distribution of property:

> In making an equitable distribution of property, the court shall consider, but not be limited to, the following factors:

> a. The duration of the marriage or civil union;
> b. The age and physical and emotional health of the parties;
> c. The income or property brought to the marriage or civil union by each party;
> d. The standard of living established during the marriage or civil union;
> e. Any written agreement made by the parties before or during the marriage or civil union concerning an arrangement of property distribution;

f. The economic circumstances of each party at the time the division of property becomes effective;

g. The income and earning capacity of each party, including educational background, training, employment skills, work experience, length of absence from the job market, custodial responsibilities for children, and the time and expense necessary to acquire sufficient education or training to enable the party to become self-supporting at a standard of living reasonably comparable to that enjoyed during the marriage or civil union;

h. The contribution by each party to the education, training or earning power of the other;

i. The contribution of each party to the acquisition, dissipation, preservation, depreciation or appreciation in the amount or value of the marital property, or the property acquired during the civil union as well as the contribution of a party as a homemaker;

j. The tax consequences of the proposed distribution to each party;

k. The present value of the property;

l. The need of a parent who has physical custody of a child to own or occupy the marital residence or residence shared by the partners in a civil union couple and to use or own the household effects;

m. The debts and liabilities of the parties;

n. The need for creation, now or in the future, of a trust fund to secure reasonably foreseeable medical or educational costs for a spouse, partner in a civil union couple or children;

o. The extent to which a party deferred achieving their career goals; and

p. Any other factors which the court may deem relevant.

N.J. Stat. Ann. §2A:34-23.1 (amended 2004).

As we have seen in other contexts, most statutes set out the factors that must be considered in dividing property, but do not require that equal weight be given to each one. Accordingly, judges are free to weigh the factors as deemed appropriate in light of the circumstances of the individual case. This approach maximizes the flexibility and discretion of the court and is generally considered to be consistent with the goal of achieving a fair result, but, as we have seen, the potential downside of this flexibility is that it can lead to inconsistent results.

In some jurisdictions, judges must make detailed findings of fact showing the consideration given each statutory factor. In others, a more general statement in support of the result is acceptable. In states using an equal distribution standard or presumption, findings of fact are usually required only when the judge departs from the norm and makes an unequal distribution.

Effectuating the Distribution

There are many ways that property can be divided between the parties. The simplest and most common way to distribute property is for each spouse to take possession of a designated portion of the assets. For example, the wife might get the living room furniture and the husband the dining room furniture; the wife the computer and the husband the stereo; each might get one-half of the linens, the towels, the kitchen items, and so on until everything is distributed.

If a couple has a significant asset — such as a business, a valuable collection, or (as discussed in greater detail below) a house or pension — with no other comparable assets, a number of options are possible. Probably the simplest alternative is to award one spouse the major asset and give the other a greater share of the remaining assets. However, this may not always be feasible because the remaining property is often not of sufficient offsetting value. Another option is for the asset to be sold and the proceeds divided. Or one spouse could retain the asset and buy out the other's marital interest in it. Where a buyout occurs, a lump-sum payment (where feasible) is generally preferable to installment payments because it provides a clean break and minimizes the risk of nonperformance.

The Marital Residence

Many property disputes center on the marital residence, most likely due to the convergence of financial, emotional, and practical considerations. In the event of a dispute, a court may consider the desirability of enabling the children to remain in their home because this provides them with some stability at a time of tremendous change. In fact, some property distribution statutes expressly include this as a factor for judicial consideration.

Dispositional options for the marital residence include the following:

1. Sell the house and divide the proceeds.
2. One spouse keeps the house, buying out the other spouse or exchanging offsetting assets.
3. Keep the house in joint name, with one spouse having the right of exclusive use and occupancy until a future dispositional date.

If neither spouse wishes to retain the house, it can be sold and the proceeds divided equally or in accordance with the overall distribution formula. In some cases, a sale may be the ultimate result because no other option is feasible.

If the parties agree in principle that one spouse can retain the house, the question becomes how this can be accomplished. Often the simplest solution is to give the other spouse an asset or assets of roughly equal value; sometimes a pension will be used as the offsetting asset. Frequently, however, there will not be enough resources to do this, since a house is often the most valuable asset a couple owns. Another option is for the acquiring spouse to buy out the interest of the other spouse. To do this, the acquiring spouse usually takes out a home equity loan or refinances the existing loan. Again, this may not be feasible because he or she may not qualify for the loan or have the ability to make the loan payments.

If neither of the above options is feasible, another possibility is to keep the property in joint name and give one spouse the right of exclusive use and occupancy until a designated time in the future, such as the emancipation of the youngest child or the remarriage of the occupying spouse. Upon the earliest of these to occur, the occupying spouse would be required to effectuate a buyout of the other spouse's interest or to sell the house and allocate the proceeds according to a preexisting formula. The non-occupying spouse is often given the right of first refusal.

The advantage of this approach is that it enables a spouse to remain in the home, which may be particularly important where children are involved, without having to either give up a share of other assets or go into debt. But there is also a significant drawback: The property continues to be owned by two people with enough relational difficulties that they cannot live together. For this arrangement to have any hope of working, it is best that all necessary details be spelled out in the court's order or in the parties' separation agreement. It may also be advisable for the court to retain jurisdiction in case problems arise after the divorce. Some of the issues that need to be addressed are the following: Who pays for repairs? Who pays for improvements that increase the value of the house? How are these expenses accounted for upon sale? What if the occupying spouse neglects the house and its value declines? How are sale proceeds to be allocated? How is appreciation accounted for? Even when these details are worked out with care, the emotional risk factor involved in this approach remains a wild card.

Pensions

This section provides a very basic introduction to the two principal ways that pensions can be divided between divorcing spouses: the present value approach and the "if, as, and when" approach. You should be aware that this discussion does not address a variety of important and relevant considerations that may affect this process, such as the type of pension being distributed, and whether it is private or public. This is another complex area of practice that contains many traps for the unwary.

The **present value approach** determines the present value of the pension and then assigns the non-employee spouse an offsetting share of property. The primary advantage of this approach is that the matter is resolved at the time of divorce and is not left hanging until some future date. However, it also presents some potential disadvantages. First, it is often difficult and costly to determine the present value of a pension plan because it is not payable until some time in the future and a number of contingencies — such as the salary of the employee spouse — can influence its value or affect whether it is payable at all. Second, there may not be enough offsetting property; even where there is, the non-employee spouse gets the offsetting property immediately, while the employee spouse must wait until a future date to enjoy his or her share of the distribution. Additionally, if the plan is not vested, the employee spouse bears the risk of not receiving a full share of the distribution; however, she or he has some control over this, as a voluntary job change can be postponed until after the pension has vested. Accordingly, this approach is not generally used if a plan is unvested or the employee spouse is years away from retirement.

The other general approach, known as the **"if, as, and when" approach**, is to award the non-employee spouse a share of pension funds "if, as, and when" the employee spouse receives them. Typically, at the time of divorce, the court uses a formula for allocating the future payments between the spouses; however, it is also possible that a court might instead opt to reserve jurisdiction over the matter and defer the determination of the non-employee's share until the pension actually matures and is thus payable. In determining the percentage amount, most states use a "marital fraction" formula that calculates the non-employee's share based on the ratio that the years of the marriage bear to the total number of years of employment at the time of distribution.

The primary advantages of this distribution method are that it avoids the need to determine the present value of the plan; an offsetting award is not required; and the risk of nonreceipt is not borne solely by the employee spouse because the non-employee spouse receives his or her share "if, as, and when" the employee spouse does. If the employee leaves before his or her pension vests, neither spouse gains or loses in a differential fashion. However, a potential disadvantage to the non-employee spouse is the fact that the other spouse has control over this eventuality and thus has the ability to defeat the interest of the non-employee spouse. This could give the employee spouse the upper hand in the event of postmarital disagreements, as he or she could threaten to quit work if the other spouse does not capitulate to his or her demands.

Where the pension funds are actually reached, distribution is usually made pursuant to a **Qualified Domestic Relations Order** (**QDRO**), which is served on the administrator of the pension. A QDRO is a judgment or decree of a state court that enables the non-employee spouse to receive all or part of the benefits that are payable to the employee spouse. A QDRO must be carefully drafted so it satisfies the legal requirements of the Employee Retirement Income Security Act (ERISA), as modified by the Retirement Equity Act of 1984 (REA).

Prior to REA, pension funds could not be reached in a divorce because of ERISA's general anti-assignment rule prohibiting the transfer of an employee's pension funds to a third party. This anti-assignment provision was included in ERISA in order to further the Act's goal of protecting "employees by barring pension benefits from being used to satisfy judgments." Margaret R. Cooper, A Family Practitioner's Guide to Overcoming QDRO Phobia, 8 Del. L. Rev. 213, 2014 (2006). However, this anti-assignment provision conflicted with state divorce laws, which, as we have seen, regard pensions as divisible marital assets. REA resolves this conflict by "allowing assignment of pension benefits pursuant to court orders that meet the statutory requirements of a qualified domestic relations order." *Id.*

In order to be effective, a QDRO must be drafted with extreme care, and contain all necessary statutory requirements, including, but far from limited to the formulas used to determine the amounts of payment, how payments are to be made, and when payments will begin and end.[10] As one commentator cautions, this requires far more than "uncritically filling in the blanks of a QDRO obtained from a form book or an individual's retirement-plan administrator," in order to avoid the growing number of attorneys who "have been exposed to malpractice liability due to their failure to handle QDROs appropriately."[11]

---

[10]*See generally* The Handbook for Divorce Valuations, *supra* note 9. *See also* Terrence Cain, A Primer on the History and Proper Drafting of Qualified Domestic-Relations Orders, 25 T.M. Cooley L. Rev. 417 (2011); Margaret R. Cooper, A Family Practitioner's Guide to Overcoming QDRO Phobia, 8 Del. L. Rev. 213 (2006).
[11]Cain, *supra* note 10, at 422.

<u>**Sample QDRO for the Collection of "Past-Due Child Support"**</u>
<u>**(For use with Defined Contribution Plans)**</u>

CENTRAL LEGAL SERVICES, INC.
By: _____, Esq.
   200 State Street
   Boston, MA 02021
   (617) 333-3333
   Attorneys for Plaintiff

_____

_____,	:	**SUPERIOR COURT OF MASSACHUSETTS**
	:	**CHANCERY DIVISION/FAMILY PART**
	:	**SUFFOLK COUNTY**
Plaintiff	:	**DOCKET NO.: FM-12-345-67**
	:	
v.	:	Civil Action
	:	
_____,	:	**QUALIFIED DOMESTIC**
	:	**RELATIONS ORDER**
Defendant	:	**(for collection of**
	:	**child support arrears)**

This matter having been brought before the Court by Central Legal Services, Inc., John Doe, Esq., representing the Plaintiff, _____, and _____, Esq., representing the Defendant, _____, and it appearing that a Judgment of Divorce was entered by the Court on _____, and it further appearing that the Defendant owes child support arrears to the Plaintiff for the minor children of the marriage under a prior order of this Court in the amount of $_____ as of _____, and for other good cause shown:

It is on this _____ day of _____, 2017

ORDERED as follows:

C. TAX CONSEQUENCES OF PROPERTY TRANSFERS INCIDENT TO A DIVORCE

For federal tax purposes, property transfers between spouses either during a marriage or after a marriage ends if it is incident to a divorce are not taxable events.[12] To understand the significance of this rule, it is helpful to step outside the divorce context for a moment. Assume that *A* purchases a painting for $10,000 and five years later sells it to *B* for $20,000. Upon the sale, *A* has realized a gain of $10,000, which is subject to taxation. However, if *A* were married to *B*, and this transfer were made during the marriage or incident to a divorce, *A* would not realize any taxable gain even if *A* receives an asset worth $20,000 in exchange for the painting.

Let us now analyze the transfer from *B*'s perspective. Where *A* and *B* are strangers, and *B* purchases the painting for $20,000, *B* acquires what is referred to as a cost basis in the painting of $20,000. If *B* subsequently transfers the property, his or her gain will be computed using this basis as the starting point. Accordingly, if he or she sells the painting for $35,000, he or she will realize a gain of $15,000 ($35,000 – $20,000). However, if *A* and *B* are spouses, and the transfer is incidental to a divorce, the tax consequences for *B* are quite different. Here, *B* acquires *A*'s basis of $10,000 — it is literally carried over from *A* to *B* (as it would be in the case of a gift). Now, if *B* sells the painting for $35,000, he or she will realize a gain of $25,000 ($35,000 – $10,000).

Clearly, this rule impacts the actual value of a property transfer because the recipient of appreciated property may eventually be accountable for a significant gain. These potential tax consequences must be taken into account when effectuating a division; otherwise, parties may not actually receive the value that they believe they have agreed to.

Chapter Summary

■ Historically, courts in common law states had limited distributive authority — property followed title. Courts in community property states had much greater authority; marriage was viewed as a partnership, and all property acquired through the expenditure of marital efforts or funds was divisible.

■ Now, most states, including all community property states, distinguish between separate and marital property, although some permit distribution of all property owned by a couple at the time of divorce. Most of these states employ a rebuttable presumption that all property owned by a couple at the time of divorce is marital.

---

[12]I.R.C. §1041. *See generally* Craig D. Bell, Need-to-Know Divorce Tax Law for Legal Assistance Officers, 177 Mil. L. Rev. 213 (2003).

▓ A division of property entails (1) a determination whether the asset in question is in fact "property"; (2) the classification of property as either marital or separate (this step is not required in all property states because the courts in these jurisdictions can reach both separate and marital property); (3) the value of each asset must be determined; and (4) the assets must be allocated in accordance with the applicable legal standard, with states employing either an equitable or an equal division rule.

▓ The transfer of property incident to a divorce does not result in a taxable gain or loss to the transferring spouse; however, the recipient acquires a carry-over basis in the transferred asset that may result in a significant gain at the time of a future transfer.

Applying the Rules

1. Manuel and Christina were married in an equitable distribution state in January 2005. The couple's child, John, was born in December 2005 and Christina was his primary caregiver during the marriage. Manuel is a certified public accountant and a partner in the firm of Smith & Black. Manuel owns a 50 percent interest in Smith & Black. Manuel also owns a 12½ percent share in Golden's Men's Store. He purchased his share in 2010 with proceeds from a tort settlement resulting from a car accident. The parties also have two bank accounts: a checking account and a savings account. The money from Manuel's accounting business is deposited into the accounts. Manuel and Christina separated in August 2015. How should the assets be divided?

2. Will and Ann were married for 20 years. During the last five years of the marriage, Will was self-employed as an independent consultant working in the information technology field and had a number of clients who continually utilized his services. Four months after Ann filed for divorce, Will started a new company with his sister-in-law, Georgia, called InfoWorks. InfoWorks provides consulting services for a number of businesses. Virtually all of Will's previous clients became clients of InfoWorks. What remedies, if any, does Ann have to obtain an equitable distribution of the revenue from InfoWorks that is attributable to Will's former clients?

3. Mr. Jones worked hard at a small company to provide for his family. He never particularly enjoyed his work but took his financial obligations to his family seriously. His wife, Ms. Jones, happily stayed home and raised the children and took care of the house.

   The Joneses are getting divorced after 15 years of marriage. During this time, Mr. Jones contributed to his pension plan at work, and he is fully vested. Mrs. Jones asks you whether the pension plan is subject to division. What do you tell her? What arguments can you expect to receive from Mr. Jones? Does it make a difference if the dissolution of marriage takes place in an equitable distribution versus a community property state?

4. Al and Stacey have been married for ten years. Al has been very depressed for more than eight years during the marriage. As a result, Al has bounced from job to job with frequent periods of unemployment and has contributed little by way of caring for the house and the children. Stacey has held down a steady job and has done most of the home care and child care.

   There is no question that their contributions are grossly unequal. Upon dissolution of the marriage, the court must divide the marital home with equity in the amount of $50,000, Stacey's 401(k) that she earned from her employment that has a value of $30,000, two vehicles that have a combined value of $10,000, and a savings account with approximately $22,000. Assume you are in an equitable distribution state. How should Al's depression impact the property division? Does it make any difference to the issue if Stacey knew about Al's depression before the marriage? Does it make any difference if, instead of being depressed, Al was an alcoholic? Drug dependent? Physically ill? Lazy?

5. Tony is a partner in a major law firm. When he married Amy 20 years ago, they were both associates at the firm. Shortly after getting married, Amy left the practice of law to stay home and raise their four children and maintain the parties' home. Tony became a very high powered and sought after litigator, and over the past few years, he has won some major lawsuits. At the divorce trial, the business valuator that Amy hired estimated that the average partner with the same number of years of practice as Tony makes $300,000. However, Tony makes $750,000. Amy claims that the increased professional goodwill that Tony enjoys was all developed during the marriage and that she should be entitled to a percentage of it.

   a. What are Amy's best arguments for prevailing on this theory?
   b. What arguments will Tony make in response?
   c. Assume you are the trial judge making the decision. What would you decide?

Family Law in Practice

1. Locate the property distribution statute for your state and try to answer the following questions based on the statutory language. Note that all questions will not be relevant in all jurisdictions.

   a. Are you in a community property or an equitable jurisdiction state?
   b. Does your state use a dual property or an all property approach?
   c. How is marital/community property defined? How is separate property defined?
   d. Are there any statutory presumptions?

    e. Is there a cut-off date for the acquisition of marital property?

    f. What factors must a court consider when making a distribution?

2. Review the relevant cases in your jurisdiction to determine what factors the courts seem to think are the most important when allocating property. Write a memo analyzing your findings.

3. Interview an attorney who works in the family law field. Ask him or her about the following:

    ▨ In what proportion is property usually divided between the spouses?

    ▨ Under what circumstances does this vary?

    ▨ What factors do lawyers and judges seem to think are the most important?

    ▨ How are the nonfinancial contributions of spouses with regard to domestic responsibilities viewed? Are they respected as much as financial contributions?

4. Consider the following hypothetical. Your client, Ms. Perez, is getting divorced from Mr. Rivera. The parties have two small children, and Ms. Perez will have physical custody. The couple owns a small house. Ms. Perez wishes to remain there while the children are young. In theory, Mr. Rivera has no problem with this, but he's not going to let her do this without receiving what he is entitled to. The house is worth about $150,000, and there is an outstanding mortgage of $120,000. Mr. Rivera has a vested pension plan, but its value has not yet been determined.

    What are all of the possible ways that a settlement could be structured? Set out the advantages and disadvantages of each possible option.

5. Draft a comprehensive checklist that can be used when working on cases to ensure that all property has been considered.

6. Consider the following hypothetical and consider how appreciation of premarital property is handled in your state. Your client, Rita Small, came into the marriage with a summer home and a rare stamp collection. Both assets appreciated in value during the course of the marriage. Although she does not yet have accurate or complete information about the increases in value, you can assume that the increase in the value of the stamp collection is attributable to market forces and the increase in the value of the house is attributable to market forces as well as to improvements that were made by the husband. Write a memo explaining how the appreciation will be classified. Be sure to consider whether your jurisdiction treats passive and active appreciation differently.

7. The judge you work for has asked you to do some research in preparation for a divorce case that includes a dispute over a much-loved family dog. She wants you to do the following:

    a. Determine if there are any statutes in your state that are relevant to determining the legal status of pets.

   b. Determine if there are any cases in your state that would have bearing on this matter — do not limit yourself to divorce cases.
   c. Locate and read at least three articles on the topic, and provide the judge with a summary of the different arguments that are presented in terms of how pets should be treated in a divorce case.

9

The Divorce Process

The first eight chapters of this book focused on the substantive law relating to marriage and divorce. However, to truly understand how the substantive law fits together it is important to consider how the law works in practice.

Accordingly, this chapter will focus on the divorce process. More specifically, it will focus on a range of practices and procedures that are either unique to divorce actions or take on different contours. These differences are due mainly to the intense emotional backdrop against which many of these cases unfold as well as the greater laxity of many procedural rules in the family law context.

This chapter takes you through each stage of the divorce process from the initial client interview to the final divorce hearing. As you read the chapter and go through the exercises, you will note how the concepts previously discussed are put into practice. Although ethical issues are not discussed in this chapter, as they are covered elsewhere in your law school curriculum, it is imperative that you remain aware at all times that your interactions with clients are strictly governed by the applicable professional conduct rules. Accordingly, from the initial client interview be aware of ethical considerations relating to, among others, the scope of representation and the duty of due diligence and promptness; requirements of confidentiality; and the avoidance of any conflict of interest.

A. THE INITIAL CLIENT INTERVIEW

Unfortunately, outside of the clinical context, most law school classes and texts do not cover client interviewing skills, perhaps because they do not appear to

Key Concepts

- The structure of a client interview
- Process for filing a divorce petition
- The discovery phase
- Common divorce motions
- Avoiding trial with negotiation, mediation, or arbitration
- Elements of the separation agreement
- The divorce trial

require specialized legal skills and knowledge. However, a poorly conducted interview can have long-term repercussions. A client who leaves a law office feeling disrespected or unheard may not develop the trust and confidence essential to a good working relationship in the family law context. Good interviews do not just happen; they require sensitivity and skill.

1. Cultural Awareness

It is important to be attuned to the role that culture can play in the communication process, as the failure to do so may lead to misunderstandings with potentially serious consequences. At the same time, of course, one also needs to avoid the pitfall of stereotyping individuals based on assumptions about group characteristics. That being said, sociolinguist Diana Eades provides us with a powerful example of how differences in cultural approaches to seeking information played a major role in the conviction of an Australian Aboriginal woman for killing her abusive husband.

As recounted by Eades, during the trial phase, using standard interviewing techniques, which are based on the assumption that direct questions are the best

Sociolinguist Diana Eades, who specializes in language in the legal process, and intercultural communication, particularly involving Australian Aboriginal people who speak varieties of English
Courtesy of Diana Eades

way to elicit information, the woman's appointed attorneys did not learn from their client that she had been the victim of horrific spousal abuse. Eades was called in as an expert in the appeal, and concluded that it would have been very difficult for them to have elicited this information during the course of a standard client interview.[1] As she explained: When "Aboriginal people want to find out what they consider to be significant or . . . personal information, they do not use direct questions. . . . People volunteer some of their own information, hinting about what they are trying to find out. Information is sought out as part of a two-way exchange."[2] Moreover, as Eades further explained, personal information is not generally shared in the absence of a developed, trusting relationship.[3] This is a dramatic example of the failure of cultural sensitivity, but it is an important reminder of how cultural differences (as well as other differences, including class and

---

[1]Diana Eades, Lawyer-Client Communication: "I Don't Think the Lawyers Were Communicating with Me": Misunderstanding Cultural Differences in Communicative Style, 52 Emory L.J. 1109, 1118 (2003). The defendant's conviction was reversed on appeal, at least in part due to Ms. Eades's testimony. The article also provides a description of how the appeal came about.
[2]*Id.* at 1118.
[3]*Id.* at 1120

educational backgrounds) can lead to communication difficulties between clients and legal professionals.

2. The Emotional Context

Another important consideration in conducting effective interviews in the context of a marital dissolution is understanding the emotional impact of divorce. Clients going through a divorce have rarely been to a legal office and they generally are unfamiliar with the legal process. Clients enter a law office with intense feelings and emotional needs that cannot be ignored. The breakup of a marriage can wreak emotional havoc in a person's life. Profound feelings of jealousy, anger, hopelessness, and despair are often unleashed. As one clinician who works with divorcing couples explains: "The loss of self-esteem is often excruciating. Feelings of inadequacy, worthlessness, and unattractiveness predominate. Rage, often kept in check by marriage . . . comes pouring out," which may in turn serve to block out "feelings of anguish at loss and a diminished sense of self."[4]

The intensity of these feelings have led some to describe the experience of divorce as the mirror opposite of falling in love.[5] As with the process of relationship formation, a divorcing party is also likely to go through many emotional stages: "Divorce is best conceptualized as a series of transitional life experiences rather than a single discrete event. Therefore, . . . the impact of divorce on family members will vary with the point in the transition process."[6]

Many of the clients you interview are likely to be experiencing overwhelming and constantly shifting emotions. This can make your task difficult, but if you are going to gain the full trust of your clients, they need to feel that their well-being matters to you. However, as important as providing support may be, you also need to be aware of the limitations of your role. You are not the client's friend or therapist, and you should be careful not to take on these roles, although, in some circumstances, it may be appropriate to provide a referral to a mental health professional.

Developing Good Listening Skills

The manner in which you listen to clients is vital because it signals whether you are simply going through the motions or are really paying attention to what is being said. If a client senses that you are engaged, he or she is likely to open up more

---

[4]Joshua Ehrlich, Divorce and Loss, Helping Adults and Children Mourn When a Marriage Comes Apart 7 (2015).
[5]*See* Judith S. Wallerstein and Sandra Blakeslee, Second Chances — Men, Women, and Children a Decade After Divorce: Who Wins, Who Loses — and Why 6 (1990).
[6]Mavis E. Hetherington and Kathleen A. Camara, Families in Transition: The Process of Dissolution and Reconstitution, *in* The Review of Child Development Research 406 (Ross Park ed., 1984).

because people are generally more comfortable when they sense their listener is responsive to what they are saying.[7]

Nonverbal Communication

In thinking about how you listen to someone, it is important to recognize that much is communicated nonverbally. Direct eye contact signals that you are present and engaged. It also enables you to pick up nonverbal clues from the client that might otherwise be missed.

Likewise, your body position is important. Leaning forward toward the client indicates involvement. A somewhat relaxed posture tends to reduce the distance between the interviewer and interviewee. In contrast, leaning back in a chair with legs up on a desk can signal a lack of focused attention and involvement. This position also can be intimidating to a client because it tends to enhance the status of the interviewer.[8]

Active Listening

Through a technique known as **active listening**, you can let a client know that you are really hearing what is being said. Active listening involves the use of verbal responses that reflect back to the client the informational or emotional content of what has been said.

With respect to the reflection of informational content, you should occasionally repeat back to the client some of the key information he or she has given you. This makes it clear that you have heard what has been said and have not been daydreaming about the upcoming weekend. It also helps ensure the accuracy of your information gathering because it gives the client the opportunity to correct any misunderstandings.

This should not become a mechanical process, and you should not break the flow of the story. A good time to reflect back is when the client has come to a logical break in the narrative. Be careful, however, that you do not begin to sound like a parrot, mindlessly repeating back what it has heard.

With respect to the reflection of emotional content, you should occasionally respond to what the client says she or he is going through on an emotional level. This acknowledges that you are aware of the client's emotional needs and that it is acceptable for him or her to express them. Although it may be tempting to share your personal experiences as a way of showing the client that you can understand what he or she is going through, these kinds of disclosures should be avoided. Although it is important to be supportive, you should never lose track of the fact that this is a professional relationship.

To illustrate the technique of active listening, let's assume that you are interviewing a client named Carl Johnson and that you are beginning the narrative phase of the interview. (See Section A.3, below, for a discussion on the narrative

---

[7]*See generally* Robert Dinerstein, Stephen Ellmann, Isabelle Gunning, and Ann Shalleck, Connection, Capacity and Morality in Lawyer-Client Relationships: Dialogues and Commentary, 10 Clinical L. Rev. 755 (2004).
[8]*See* Robert M. Bastress and Joseph D. Harbaugh, Interviewing, Counseling, and Negotiating: Skills for Effective Representation (1990).

phase.) You have asked him, "Why don't you tell me something about your marriage?" and he has responded as follows:

> Well, my wife and I have been married for 15 years. We met in college — she was my first true love, and has remained my only love during all these years. We have had a few rocky patches. My mother died right after our daughter was born. I became depressed. I had been very close to both my parents and had already lost my dad.
>
> My wife felt I withdrew from her and the baby. I denied it at the time, but in retrospect, I realize she was right. In any event, I thought we had a loving marriage.
>
> Well, a few years ago, my wife seemed more remote. She lost interest in sex and, well, things just seemed different. At first I attributed it to the pressure we were under. My business had gone under, I was looking for work, we had our daughter, my wife was working full-time, and I was still struggling with depression.
>
> We were also threatened with foreclosure proceedings, although we were able to save the house by borrowing money from her parents. Since then, they haven't let me forget that if I had been a proper husband, able to hold down a decent job, my family would not have been in that predicament. I also think they blame me for the fact that their daughter works so hard, but they don't understand that she loves her job.
>
> Anyway, I gradually began to get suspicious that something else was going on. My wife began to have more night meetings, a few times when I answered the phone the person at the other end hung up — all the classic signs. For a while she denied that anything was going on, but finally, about a month ago she admitted that she had been seeing someone in her office. I asked her to break it off, but she said she couldn't promise to do that and needed some time to work things out. Well, that was it. I was and still am totally destroyed. It's embarrassing to admit, but she is the only woman I have ever had sex with. As far as I am concerned the marriage is over.

This is probably a logical point to interject briefly. To reflect the emotional content, you might simply say something like: "I can see why you are devastated. This must be a very difficult time for you." You want to avoid statements like, "I know what you are going through, I remember what it was like when my husband walked out on me." This may seem obvious, but, in the intensity of the moment, the temptation to support a client in this manner can be hard to resist.

To reflect the informational content, you might say something like:

> I'd like to take a minute to make sure I understand what you have just told me; please let me know if anything I say is inaccurate.
>
> You and your wife have been married for 15 years, and despite a few rough times, you would characterize your relationship as solid. You have one child.
>
> You've struggled with depression, particularly after the death of your mother. Recently, your wife has acknowledged she is having an affair, and is not sure what she wants to do. As a result, you have decided your marriage is over.

3. A Three-Stage Approach to the Client Interview

It is useful to think of the interview as having the following three distinct stages:

1. The **opening stage** establishes the parameters of the interview and creates an atmosphere of trust.

2. The **information-gathering stage** elicits the client's basic story (narrative phase) and fills in the key details with questions (focused phase).
3. The **wrapping up or disengaging phase** concludes the interview.

This three-stage approach should not be followed mechanically. Each person you interview is unique, and you need to accommodate a range of expressive styles. Some clients may respond only to focused questions; while others, at least initially, will be so overwhelmed that they will not respond to focused questions. They may need to tell you their story over and over in their own manner and sequence. This human dimension is the great challenge that no book can fully prepare you for.

In the following sections, we will look at each stage of the interview process, using the interview with Mr. Johnson to demonstrate various points. The model presented here assumes that a preprinted form is not being used for anything more than obtaining the basic factual information needed to complete a divorce complaint — such as the place and date of the marriage, the date last lived together, and the names and birthdates of the marital children — although some offices do use forms to obtain comprehensive client information.

Stage 1: Establishing the Parameters and Creating an Atmosphere of Trust

When a client first comes to a law office, it is important to realize that he or she is probably nervous. Engaging in some preliminary chit-chat can help put a client at ease. For example, you might inquire whether he or she found the office without difficulty, whether it is still snowing, or the like. It is also a nice gesture to offer a cup of coffee or glass of water.

At the outset, in addition to introducing yourself, you should also let the client know if anyone will be working with you on the case should the client decide to retain you, such as your legal assistant or paralegal. You should then inform the client that what he or she tells you will be held in strict confidence and explain what will take place during the interview. Also, your fees and a retainer agreement need to be discussed before any work is performed. Some attorneys prefer to do this right up front at the beginning of the initial consultation. Others prefer to save the "business" side of things until the wrapping up stage. Regardless of which approach is used, it is important that before leaving your office the client fully understands your office's fee structure and billing practices.

Stage 2: Obtaining Information

Where possible, it is best to gather information in two phases. In the first phase, the client should be encouraged to tell his or her story. This can be referred to as the client narrative. In the second phase, the interviewer can complete the inquiry by asking focused questions. This is sometimes referred to as a "funneling" process because the questions begin broadly and then gradually become narrower.

Eliciting the Client Narrative

In the first phase of information gathering, the emphasis is on having the client tell his or her story. This is done by asking open-ended questions that elicit a narrative rather than a focused response. In using open-ended questions, the interviewer loses some control over the process because the client shapes the telling of the story. However, this approach respects the fact that it is the client's problem and acknowledges that "the client is an important, essential resource in the information gathering process."[9] Open-ended questions can be either general or topic-specific. By asking topic-specific questions, the interviewer focuses the field of inquiry while still calling for a narrative response.

By way of example, let's return to Mr. Johnson. As set out above, the initial question to him was, "Why don't you tell me something about your marriage?" and in answering, he mentioned he has a child. A logical follow-up question might be, "Why don't you tell me about your child?" This question is topic-specific but is still open-ended because it asks for a narrative response. Let's assume that he gives the following answer:

> Well, Sara is our only child. She's seven and is in the second grade. She's a terrific kid, I know all parents say that, but she really is special. She does real well in school, has a lot of friends, and loves sports.
>
> Lately, though, she seems to be having a bit of a hard time. I've tried to talk to her about it, but sometimes she just doesn't seem to want to talk much to me. My wife says it's because I didn't bond with her as a baby, but I think she's going through something now, maybe with all this marriage stuff. I'm sure it's nothing serious.
>
> Her last report card was very good, but her teacher says that Sara has been kind of withdrawn at school. I am very worried about how she'll react to the divorce. I guess she's kind of a sensitive kid.

As he completes talking about his daughter, you could direct him to other topic areas by asking similar questions, such as, "You mentioned earlier that a few years ago your wife started seeming remote. Why don't you describe this period to me?"

It is during this narrative phase that the technique of active listening is particularly important. If possible, it is best to take a minimum of notes during this phase because note taking can interfere with your ability to remain focused and engaged.

Funneling Process: Focused Closed-Inquiry Questions

After the narrative phase, you should proceed with more focused questions to elicit more complete information. At this point, you will probably want to take detailed notes. In this phase, you can gain greater control over the process; however, where possible, your inquiry should be informed by and responsive to what the client tells you.

To begin this phase, you might say something like this to the client:

> Mr. Johnson, you've given me a good picture of your situation. Now, what I would like to do is go back over what you have told me and ask you some specific questions so I

---

[9] *See* Don Peters, You Can't Always Get What You Want: Organizing Matrimonial Interviews to Get What You Need, 26 Cal. W. L. Rev. 256, 268 (1990).

am sure my information is complete. Also, I will now be taking notes so I have a good record of what you tell me.

You can then go back over the information in a focused manner. Here is what some follow-up questions to Mr. Johnson about his daughter might sound like:

Q: You used the word "special" in describing your daughter; why don't you tell me what you mean by that?

A: Well like I said, she does well in school, has a lot of friends, and loves sports. But, I guess beyond that, she is just a very kind and thoughtful child. She seems to have a sensitivity beyond her years. She understands a lot about the world, and really wants to help people.

Q: Does she understand what is happening at home?

A: To some extent. We've told her that Mommy and Daddy don't love each other anymore and that Daddy will be moving to a new home, but that I still love her very much. I don't think she really understands why I've been sleeping in the guest room or why Mommy and Daddy aren't speaking to each other much.

Q: Why don't you tell me more about your relationship with Sara?

A: As I said, I was somewhat depressed when she was first born, and maybe I wasn't really that involved with her care, but I think I've made up for that in the past five or so years. During this time, I've been very involved in her care.

Q: Can you describe your caretaking role?

A: Well, sometimes I bring her to school in the morning, but I usually have to be at the office pretty early and I try to pick her up from her after-school program a few times a week. I share putting her to bed at night, and on weekends I try to do a special activity with her — just the two of us.

Q: How would you characterize the division of child-care responsibilities between you and your wife?

A: Well, I think it's pretty equal. I'm a pretty involved dad — I mean maybe it's not fifty-fifty, but I'm not one of those dads who doesn't even know the names of his child's friends.

Q: At some point, I'll probably want to get more detail on the caretaking arrangements, but let me ask you a few other things first. You mentioned that your daughter has been having a hard time, and hasn't wanted to speak with you about what's going on. Can you elaborate on this?

A: Let me start with our relationship. We've been pretty close. I don't spend as much time with her as I would like, but when we're together we have a lot of fun. Sometimes I get impatient with her and then I feel badly. I guess she usually confides more in her mother; I try not to get jealous, but sometimes I feel left out. I can't express my feelings as well as my wife can — we didn't do any of that in my family, and maybe it's a male thing also — so maybe Sara feels somewhat closer with her mom. But I love my daughter and would do anything for her.

Q: Who does your daughter turn to for comfort when she is sick or doesn't feel well?

A: Both of us, but my wife is usually the one to stay home with her when she is sick. Her job is more flexible than mine is, and when I was self-employed, I couldn't afford to take the time off. Also, sometimes, I think my wife overindulges her, and keeps her home if she just has a sniffle. I don't think it's good to treat kids like babies. . . . With respect to what Sara has been going through, she's been kind of moody and withdrawn. I don't know if it's in response to what has been going on at home, or if it's just one of those things that kids go through.

> Q: Have you consulted anyone about this?
> A: No — it hasn't seemed like that big a deal. But, maybe with the divorce we should have her talk to someone. I don't really know.

Here, the interviewer is clearly trying to elicit specific information, but the questions flow from the client's answers, and there is a nice sense of give and take. This is not always possible. Where the client is less focused, the interviewer cannot be as responsive and will need to impose more of a structure in order to obtain the necessary information. Also, in reviewing these questions, you should note the constant pattern of moving from broader to narrower questions; this funneling process is also valuable within this closed-inquiry phase.

Stage 3: Wrapping Up the Interview

Once you have obtained the necessary information, it is time to wrap up the interview. At this point, you need to tell the client what will happen next and explain what he or she needs to do, if anything. For example, you may wish to give a brief overview of the process, such as the timing for filing of any initial papers, whether there is a waiting period before any decree can be entered, how many times the client is likely to be in court, and the best way to communicate questions the client may have to you.

To the extent you are able to do so, it is important to give the client some advice as to how judges typically look at their particular issues. Knowing how the courts in your jurisdiction view alimony, custody, and division of property (even just explaining the differences between community property and equitable distribution states) can be very helpful to the client who has no information and likely only knows what he or she has been told by friends or found on the Internet.

Also give the client an opportunity to ask you any questions. The client is probably feeling very overwhelmed by the amount of information provided. Accordingly, giving the client an opportunity to ask questions or seek clarification is important.

B. INITIATING A DIVORCE

Most states have specialized rules of domestic procedures that cover most family court proceedings, including, of course, divorce actions. Of course, the specific rules vary from state to state, and no attempt will be made here to catalogue the various approaches that states take. Rather, our primary focus is to look more generally at some of the typical procedural differences between divorce cases and other types of civil actions.

1. The Divorce Petition

In contrast to most types of cases, when it comes to divorce, most jurisdictions use standardized **complaint** forms, which are now often referred to as **petitions**. As you can see from the sample petition on the next page (Exhibit 9.1), the approach tends to be true notice pleading, without much detail beyond the mere essentials.

EXHIBIT 9.1   **Divorce Complaint**

DIVORCE COMPLAINT **(DISSOLUTION OF MARRIAGE)** JD-FM-159 Rev. 5-15 C.G.S. §§ 46b-40, 46b-56c, 46b-84, P.B. § 25-2, et seq.	**STATE OF CONNECTICUT** **SUPERIOR COURT** *www.jud.ct.gov*	CROSS COMPLAINT CODE ONLY **CRSCMP**

☐   **Complaint:** Complete this form. Attach a completed Summons (JD-FM-3) and Notice of Automatic Court Orders (JD-FM-158).

☐   **Amended Complaint.**

☐   **Cross Complaint:** Complete this form and attach to the Answer (JD-FM-160) unless it is already filed.

ADA NOTICE
The Judicial Branch of the State of Connecticut complies with the Americans with Disabilities Act (ADA). If you need a reasonable accommodation in accordance with the ADA, contact a court clerk or an ADA contact person listed at *www.jud.ct.gov/ADA.*

Judicial District of	At *(Town)*	Return date *(Month, day, year)*	Docket number

Plaintiff's name *(Last, First, Middle Initial)*	Defendant's name *(Last, First, Middle Initial)*

1. Plaintiff's birth name *(If different from above)*	2. Defendant's birth name *(If different from above)*

3. a. Date of marriage	3. b. Date of civil union that merged into marriage by subsequent ceremony or by operation of law	4. Town and State, or Country where marriage took place

5. *("X" all that apply)*

☐ The *("X" one)* ☐ plaintiff ☐ defendant   has lived in Connecticut for at least 12 months immediately before the filing of this divorce complaint or before the divorce will become final.

☐ The *("X" one)* ☐ plaintiff ☐ defendant   lived in Connecticut at the time of the marriage, moved away, and then returned to Connecticut, planning to live here permanently.

☐ The marriage broke down after the *("X" one)* ☐ plaintiff ☐ defendant   moved to Connecticut.

6. A divorce is being sought because: *("X" all that apply)*

☐ This marriage has broken down irretrievably.

☐ Other *(must be reason(s) listed in section 46b-40(c) of the Connecticut General Statutes):*

_____

_____

"X" and complete all that apply for items 6-13. Attach additional sheets if needed.

7. ☐   No children were born to either the plaintiff or defendant after the date of this marriage.

8. ☐   There are no children of this marriage under the age of 23.

9. ☐   The following children are either: (a) the biological and/or adoptive children of both of the parties, or (b) have been born to one of the parties on or after the date of the marriage and are claimed to be children of the marriage.
(List only children who have not yet reached the age of 23.)

Name of child *(First, Middle Initial, Last)*	Date of birth *(Month, day, year)*

10. ☐   The following children were born on or after the date of the marriage to the *("X" all that apply)*
☐ plaintiff ☐ defendant and are not children of the other party to this marriage.
(List only children who have not yet reached the age of 23.)

Name of child *(First, Middle Initial, Last)*	Date of birth *(Month, day, year)*

EXHIBIT 9.1   **(continued)**

11. If there is a court order regarding custody or support for any child listed above, name the child(ren) below and specify the person or agency awarded custody or ordered to pay support:

Child's name	Name of person or agency awarded custody	Name of person ordered to pay support
Child's name	Name of person or agency awarded custody	Name of person ordered to pay support
Child's name	Name of person or agency awarded custody	Name of person ordered to pay support

12. The *("X" all that apply)* ☐ plaintiff ☐ defendant   or any of the child(ren) listed above have received from the State of Connecticut:
    ☐ financial support *("X" one)*   ☐ Yes   ☐ No   ☐ Do not know
    ☐ HUSKY Health Insurance *("X" one)*   ☐ Yes   ☐ No   ☐ Do not know

    If yes, **you must** send a copy of the Summons, Complaint, Notice of Automatic Court Orders and any other documents filed with this Complaint to the Assistant Attorney General, 55 Elm Street, Hartford, CT 06106, and file the Certification of Notice *(JD-FM-175)* with the court clerk.

13. ☐ The *("X" all that apply)*   ☐ plaintiff   ☐ defendant is pregnant with a child due to be born on _____ .
    The other parent of this unborn child is the   ☐ plaintiff or   ☐ defendant   ☐ unknown
                                                      ☐ not the plaintiff   ☐ not the defendant.   *(date)*

14. The *("X" all that apply)*   ☐ plaintiff   ☐ defendant or any of the child(ren) listed above has received financial support from a city or town in Connecticut. *("X" one)* ☐ Yes *(State city or town:* _____ *)*
    ☐ No   ☐ Do not know. If yes, send a copy of the Summons, Complaint, Notice of Automatic Court Orders and any other documents filed with this Complaint to the City Clerk of the town providing assistance and file the Certification of Notice *(JD-FM-175)* with the court clerk.

The Court is asked to order: *("X" all that apply)*

☐ A divorce (dissolution of marriage).

☐ A fair division of property and debts.

☐ Alimony.

☐ Child Support.

☐ An order regarding the post-majority educational support of the child(ren).

☐ Name change to: _____
   _____

Regarding Parental Decision-making Responsibility:
☐ Sole custody.
☐ Joint legal custody.
☐ A parenting responsibility plan which includes a plan for the parental decision-making regarding the minor child(ren).
   AND

Regarding Physical Custody:
☐ Primary residence with: _____
☐ Visitation.
☐ A parenting responsibility plan which includes a plan for the schedule of physical care of the minor child(ren).

And anything else the Court deems fair.

Signature	Print name of person signing	Date signed
Address	Juris number *(If applicable)*	Telephone *(Area code first)*

• If this is a Complaint, attach a copy of the Automatic Court Orders before serving a copy on the Defendant.

• If this is an Amended Complaint or a Cross Complaint, you must mail or deliver a copy to anyone who has filed an appearance and you must complete the certification below.

Certification

I certify that a copy of this document was mailed or delivered electronically or non-electronically on *(date)* _____ to all attorneys and self-represented parties of record and that written consent for electronic delivery was received from all attorneys and self-represented parties receiving electronic delivery.

Name and address of each party and attorney that copy was mailed or delivered to*

*If necessary, attach additional sheet or sheets with name and address which the copy was mailed or delivered to.

Signed *(Signature of filer)* ▶	Print or type name of person signing	Date signed
Mailing address *(Number, street, town, state and zip code)*		Telephone number

Other documents may need to be filed with the petition. The requirements vary from state to state and may vary within a state depending on the nature of the divorce. The most common requirement is that the petition be accompanied by a certified copy of the parties' marriage certificate; if the marriage took place in a foreign country, a qualified translation of the certificate may also need to be filed. Also, if there are minor children, an affidavit, or similar document, may need to be filed disclosing any prior or pending custody actions involving the children.

In some states, spouses have the option of filing for a no-fault divorce jointly as co-petitioners, which effectively means there is no plaintiff or defendant. These **joint petitions** may entail special procedures or requirements. For example, in Massachusetts, parties who file a joint petition also must file an affidavit of irretrievable breakdown of the marriage, attesting to the fact that the marriage is over. See Exhibit 9.2. A signed separation agreement also must be filed at this time or shortly thereafter. In California, couples without children who have been married a short time and have few assets may be eligible to file a Joint Petition for Summary Dissolution of Marriage, which then actually enables them to get divorced without a court hearing.

2. Indigency and Access to the Courts

As in other types of civil actions, plaintiffs typically must pay a filing fee in order to initiate a divorce action. Additionally, dependent upon the local rule, if an official process server is needed to make service on the respondent, another fee will also be incurred as an essential element of the divorce initiation process. These fees can impose a serious financial hardship on low-income petitioners, which potentially could operate as barrier to court access.

However, in 1971, in response to a lawsuit filed by welfare recipients who could not afford the requisite filing fee and costs of service, the Supreme Court, in the case of *Boddie v. Connecticut*, held that because a court is the "only forum effectively empowered" to dissolve a marriage, the exclusion from this forum on account of indigency deprived the petitioners of their right to be heard in violation of the Due Process Clause. 401 U.S. 371, 376, 380-384 (1971). Consequently, divorce petitioners must be permitted to request a fee waiver in cases of financial hardship. This is typically done through the filing of a request for a **declaration of indigency**. In addition to requesting a waiver of the filing fee, a low-income plaintiff may also be able to request that the state pay for the service of process and possibly also for any costs related to discovery, such as the hiring of a stenographer for a deposition.

Efforts to extend the holding of *Boddie* to include the right to counsel in divorce cases have generally not been successful. For example, distinguishing a divorce action from criminal proceedings in which a right to counsel is constitutionally required due to the fact that "the State or Government proceeds against the individual with risk of loss of liberty or grievous forfeiture," the high court of New York held that "however desirable or necessary" the services of a lawyer may be in a divorce case, they are not "a legal condition to access," which is all that is constitutionally protected under *Boddie*. *In re Smiley*, 330 N.E.2d 53, 55, 57 (N.Y. 1975).

| EXHIBIT 9.2 | **Joint Petition and Affidavit** |

Commonwealth of Massachusetts
The Trial Court

_____ **Division**   **Probate and Family Court Department**   **Docket No.** _____

JOINT PETITION FOR DIVORCE PURSUANT TO G.L. c. 208, § 1 A

_____ and _____
Petitioner A   Petitioner B

_____   _____
(Street address)   (Street address)

_____   _____
(City/Town)   (State)   (Zip)   (City/Town)   (State)   (Zip)

1. Petitioners were lawfully married at _____

on _____ and last lived together at _____

on _____

2. The minor or dependent child(ren) of this marriage is/are:

_____   _____
(Name of child and date of birth)   (Name of child and date of birth)

_____   _____
(Name of child and date of birth)   (Name of child and date of birth)

3. Petitioners certify that no previous action for divorce, annulment or affirmation of marriage, separate support, desertion, living apart for justifiable cause, or custody of child(ren) has been brought by either against the other except: _____
_____
_____

4. On or about _____ , an irretrievable breakdown of the marriage under G.L. c. 208, § 1A occurred and continues to exist.

5. Wherefore, the petitioners request that the Court:

☐ grant a divorce on the ground of irretrievable breakdown

☐ approve the notarized separation agreement executed by the parties

☐ incorporate and merge the agreement executed by the parties

☐ incorporate but not merge said agreement, which shall survive and remain as an independent contract

☐ allow petitioner A to resume the former name of _____

☐ allow petitioner B to resume the former name of _____

☐   _____

Date _____

_____   _____
(Signature of attorney or petitioner A, if pro se)   (Signature of attorney or petitioner B, if pro se)

_____   _____
(Print name)   (Print name)

_____   _____
(Street address)   (Street address)

_____   _____
(City/Town)   (State)   (Zip)   (City/Town)   (State)   (Zip)

Tel. No. _____   Tel. No. _____

B.B.O. # _____   B.B.O. # _____

CJ-D 101A (9/07)   C.G.F

3. The Failure to File an Answer

In most civil proceedings, if the defendant fails to file an answer in a timely manner, the plaintiff may be relieved of the obligation to provide him or her with notice about subsequent case proceedings. He or she may seek to have a default judgment entered in his or her favor, which obviates the need for a hearing on the merits.

However, because of the importance of the rights at stake in a divorce case, the practice tends to be more flexible in most jurisdictions. Accordingly, even if a defendant has not filed an answer in a timely manner as required under the applicable rules of procedure, most judges will not relieve the plaintiff of the obligation to provide the defendant with notice of all related case proceedings. Moreover, most judges are reluctant to enter a default judgment, even if permitted under the rules of domestic procedure, particularly if the defendant has made any effort to preserve his or her rights.

As a result of the more relaxed rules about defaults in the divorce context, the local practice custom may be to forgo the filing of an answer. However, this failure may serve to preclude the defendant from contesting matters raised by the plaintiff or from seeking certain kinds of relief. Accordingly, given the unpredictable nature of divorce litigation, the better practice is to file an answer in all cases to ensure that a client's rights are fully protected.

C. DISCOVERY

Although the rules of discovery are covered in Civil Procedure courses, and thus will not be addressed in any detail here, it nonetheless is important to take a brief look at the role that discovery can play in divorce cases. In so doing, it is helpful to keep some of the key functions of discovery in mind, namely, that the process is intended to

1. facilitate trial preparation because both parties can use the obtained information to help develop their respective cases;
2. reduce the possibility of surprise during trial, since information is obtained in advance; and
3. enable both sides to assess the relative strengths and weaknesses of the case, which can facilitate the settlement process.

1. The Quest for Information

Particularly in complex or highly contested cases, spouses are likely to utilize the discovery process to seek a wide range of information from the other side. In turn, this information typically plays a critical role in the settlement process that is a crucial stage in most divorce cases as parties seek to control the terms of their separation, rather than risking the uncertainty of a trial over such critical dimensions of their lives (these issues are discussed in the following sections of this chapter).

Accordingly, a tremendous range of information is likely to be sought by each spouse. Although, as discussed in Chapter 7, parties in a divorce action are typically required to file an affidavit with the court that discloses their current financial status, where property or support is at issue, parties are likely to utilize the discovery process in order to obtain far more detailed information about income, expenditures, assets, and liabilities, particularly in order to establish a developed financial history that is supported by documentary evidence. They accordingly often make very liberal use of the production process to obtain an extensive array of documentation including, for example, all of the other spouse's pay stubs, canceled checks, credit card and bank statements, receipts for purchases over a specified amount, and loan payments over a specific time period, which could well be the length of the marriage. If a spouse suspects that his or her spouse may have been engaged in an affair, he or she may also engage in particularly deep discovery in order to determine if this relationship resulted in the dissipation of marital assets or funds.

Where custody is at issue, a party may be asked to provide detailed information about his or her relationship with the children, including all caretaking functions performed during the course of the marriage. Discovery can also be used to explore potential areas of concern. A party may be asked about whether he or she has ever struck the child or used drugs or alcohol in the child's presence. He or she may also be asked to provide detailed information about his or her own mental health status — a request that may well become contested on the grounds that it is beyond the permissible scope of inquiry. However, given that the rules of procedure in most states track the federal rule's broad permissible scope of inquiry and thus allow the discovery of any unprivileged matter that is *relevant* to the case, the mental stability of a parent who is seeking custody is most likely to be considered relevant. Pertinent information can also be discovered from other persons with knowledge about the children, such as neighbors, teachers, and therapists.

Although there are clearly many benefits to allowing each party to seek all relevant information from the other side, the openness of the discovery process also raises some concerns. Although a particularly sweeping scope of inquiry may well be motivated by a spouse's good faith interest in obtaining all pertinent information, it may also be motivated by anger or a desire for revenge and thus go well beyond what is really needed in order to make matters more onerous for the other side. This is especially true in the no-fault context where the relevance of obtaining information about, by way of an example, a person's extramarital affairs is questionable. Closely related, the spouse with greater financial resources may seek to "out -discover" the other side in order to push the spouse with fewer resources into a premature and potentially disadvantageous settlement. Although courts can impose some limitations, and ultimately award fees to the spouse with less resources, they generally will not interfere with discovery absent egregious behavior.

2. Discovery of Electronically Stored Information

Discovery can now be had of **electronically stored information** (ESI), which includes "emails, voicemails, instant messages, text messages, documents and spreadsheets, file fragments, digital images and video."[10] Although **e-discovery** has become increasingly important in the digital era, the process requires a certain amount of technological sophistication and may present certain stumbling blocks for the unwary practitioner. Accordingly, we briefly consider some of these complexities, before looking at how they may play out in the divorce context.

One critical issue is that documents frequently contain "invisible" information known as "**metadata**," which is generally defined as "data hidden in documents that is generated during the course of creating and editing such documents. It may include fragments of data from files that were previously deleted, overwritten or worked on simultaneously."[11] Although hidden, this "data about data" is, in fact, retrievable. Accordingly, when an attorney produces electronic files pursuant to a discovery request, he or she may inadvertently be providing the other attorney with confidential or privileged information that he or she is unaware is embedded in the produced materials in potential breach of the duty to maintain client confidentiality.

To address this problem, a number of states have concluded that the "receiving attorney has an ethical duty not to review the information" in accordance with a "strong public policy . . . against an attorney engaging in conduct that would amount to an unjustified intrusion into the opposing counsel's attorney-client relationship."[12] However, the law is clearly evolving in this arena, and as one commentator suggests, to avoid potential ethical breaches "an attorney should be charged with an active duty to stay current on technological advances in document transmission to best understand the potential risks and best methods of transmitting information to opposing parties."[13]

In a similar vein, the fact that one has deleted a document does not actually mean that it has been erased from the hard drive; accordingly, "the chances are good that unless the user has used software to erase or wipe the hard drive, significant amounts of deleted data or bits and pieces of deleted data will remain," that can be retrieved by forensic software.[14] Accordingly, if access is given to the actual computer, which may be necessary for the purpose of authenticating the requested electronic data, as with metadata, an attorney may likewise inadvertently be providing the opposing counsel with far more information than he or she realizes if unaware that deleted files are not necessarily vanquished from the computer's memory, thus again potentially compromising client confidentiality.

Although the e-discovery process is clearly not without its difficulties, a spouse who seeks to gain access to the other party's electronically stored information outside of the formal discovery process during the course of a divorce may well find out the evidence is inadmissible at trial. Additionally, he or she may well have

---

[10]Gaetano Ferro, Marcus Lawson, and Sarah Murray, Electronically Stored Information: What Matrimonial Lawyers and Computer Forensics Need to Know, 23 J. Am. Acad. Matrim. Law. 1, 2 (2010). *See also* Rachel K. Alexander, E-Discovery Practice, Theory and Precedent: Finding the Right Pond, Lure, and Lines Without Going on a Fishing Expedition, 56 S.D. L. Rev. 25 (2011).

[11]Mathew Robertson, Why Invisible Electronic Data Is Relevant in Today's Legal Arena, 23 J. Am. Acad. Matrim. Law. 199, 202 (2011), quoting NYSBA, Formal Op. 782.

[12]*Id.* at 208.

[13]*Id.* at 209.

[14]Ferro et al., *supra* note 10, at 32-35.

committed a crime under federal and state laws that are designed to protect an individual's right of privacy in the digital realm by prohibiting both the interception of electronic communications and unauthorized access to such communications. However, as illustrated by the following case, the question of what constitutes "unauthorized" use can be particularly murky in the divorce context given that spouses may both use the same computer.

| Case Preview | *Byrne v. Byrne* |

In *Byrne*, the court addressed the issue of computer access in a divorce action. The wife had taken the husband's computer and provided it to her attorney. The wife claimed the computer had information stored on it that related to the parties' finances. The defendant objected to anyone having access to the memory contents of the computer. What made the issue more complicated is that the husband's employer, Citibank, claimed that the computer actually belonged to Citibank and that it should accordingly be turned over to the corporation. This case occurred at a time when questions relating to the storing of data on computers were just beginning to enter the legal arena. Accordingly, little case law existed for the judge to rely upon in making a decision regarding whether the stored contents were subject to discovery or not.

As you read *Byrne v. Byrne*, look for the following:

1. Why does the husband claim the computer is not subject to discovery?
2. What effect did the fact that the children had access to the computer have on the court's decision?
3. How does the court analyze the computer in relationship to other types of property?

Byrne v. Byrne
650 N.Y.S.2d 499 (N.Y. Sup. Ct. 1996)

WILLIAM RIGLER, Justice.

In this matrimonial action, the parties are hotly contesting the issue of who should be permitted access to information contained in a notebook computer. It is undisputed that the computer was used by defendant as part of his employment but it is disputed as to whether the computer was also used for his own personal purposes. Plaintiff removed the computer from the marital residence and gave it to her attorney. Plaintiff believes important information concerning the finances of the parties or at least the finances of defendant is stored in the computer memory. Defendant asserts that there is nothing of use to plaintiff in the computer and that it was improper for plaintiff to take the machine to her attorney's office. The only way to determine if plaintiff is correct is for the contents of the computer memory to be opened up or "dumped" and analyzed. Defendant's employer, Citibank, has also entered the matter by asserting that the notebook computer belongs to the corporation and not defendant and thus should be turned over to it.

ANALYSIS

The Court is presently in control of the laptop computer removed from the marital residence by plaintiff. Defendant contends that the computer is personal property (allegedly not owned by him) and thus not subject to discovery.

The facts are undisputed that the laptop computer was used and controlled by defendant and was not limited in use by his employer. In fact, defendant permitted his children to use the computer for their homework. Thus, it cannot be said that plaintiff acted illegally by removing the "family" computer from the marital residence and presenting it to her attorney.

The real issue is not who possesses the computer but rather who has access to the computer's memory. The computer memory is akin to a file cabinet. Clearly, plaintiff could have access to the contents of a file cabinet left in the marital residence. In the same fashion she should have access to the contents of the computer. Plaintiff seeks access to the computer memory on the grounds that defendant stored information concerning his finances and personal business records in it. Such material is obviously subject to discovery. Therefore, it is determined that plaintiff did nothing wrong by obtaining the physical custody of the notebook computer.

Accordingly, it is ordered that:

1) At a mutually agreeable time, the parties shall appear with their computer experts at the courthouse, or mutually agreeable location, for the purpose of downloading all the memory files contained in the computer. Obviously, if defendant furnishes his passwords the process will be expedited. (The Court notes that this process is very similar to the commonly undertaken inventory of a safe deposit box.)

2) Once the material is downloaded the originals shall be deposited with the Court. A list will be generated as to the nature of the documents. The list shall be given to both counsel. Defendant's counsel may review copies of the resulting downloaded documents to determine if defendant wants to make a claim that any of the materials are subject to the attorney-client privilege. If he wants to make such a claim it must be done by motion within 10 days of the completion of the downloading process.

3) If a motion for a protective order is not made within the time limit, then all the material shall be turned over to plaintiff's counsel. Obviously, as to those documents on which there are no claims of privilege, they shall be immediately turned over to plaintiff's counsel.

4) Once the downloading process is completed, the computer, itself, may be returned to Citibank.

In all other aspects the applications are denied.

Post-Case Follow-Up

The court in *Byrne* had no trouble finding that the wife should have access to the memory content of the computer given that it was used as a family computer. It thus found that it was akin to a filing cabinet at the house that the wife could readily access.

However, the result may well have been different if, for example, the computer had not been characterized by the court as a family computer, or if the wife had gained access to password-protected information. It is important to keep in mind that this is a rapidly evolving area of the law, and the legal standards for what constitutes unauthorized access to electronically stored information tends to be both highly fact-sensitive and variable from state to state.

Byrne v. Byrne: Real Life Applications

1. Jennifer and William are in the process of getting a divorce. William owns his own construction company and has a computer he uses for work. Several months ago, William's personal laptop was damaged. Neither party disputes the fact that, as a result, William has used his work computer for his own personal use over the past few months. Jennifer seeks an order to have William turn over the computer for review claiming that the computer's hard drive may have information on it relevant to the marriage dissolution action. William objects claiming that he is the only one who has used the computer and no one else has access to the computer. How should a court rule?

2. In the marriage dissolution action of Brendan and Kathy, Brendan seeks a court order that Kathy must turn over her laptop computer for inspection. Brendan claims that while he was living in the marital residence he always had access to the computer. However, since moving out, Kathy has refused to give him access and claims that the computer is hers because Brendan abandoned it once he left the residence. How should a court rule?

3. Robert seeks discovery of Allison's computer in his divorce action. He admits that the computer is Allison's and he has never had the passwords for the computer. However, he believes that access to the e-mails will show that Allison has been having an affair and he believes that information is relevant to whether Allison has dissipated marital assets. How should a court rule?

4. Margie, a lawyer, has a laptop computer that is provided to her by her firm. However, Margie occasionally brings the laptop home and admits to you that she has used it at times for personal matters. She tells you that there is nothing on it that relates to the divorce, but she is worried about disclosing the contents of the hard drive because it has information on it regarding clients that she has an ethical duty to keep confidential. She asks you what steps can be taken to protect the information and ensure that her husband does not receive this information in the pending divorce matter. What do you tell Margie?

D. MOTION PRACTICE

Motion practice is frequently a very important aspect of divorce cases, as many important issues, such as custodial and visitation arrangements and a party's need for support, cannot wait until the final resolution of the case. Of course, any order entered in response to such a motion is temporary in nature, and will eventually be superseded by the divorce judgment. However, the fact that the relief is temporary does not lessen its importance as significant rights are often at stake. Moreover, temporary orders frequently shape the final result. This is particularly true in the case of custody and visitation arrangements, as courts are generally reluctant to disrupt arrangements if they are working well for the children. Of course, it is a different matter if the temporary arrangements prove not to be in their best interest.

Again, this section assumes your basic familiarity with the nature of motion practice. Accordingly, the discussion selectively focuses on issues that are particularly relevant in the divorce context, as well as on the kinds of motions that the divorce attorney is likely to encounter.

1. *Ex Parte* Relief: The Emergency Exception to the Notice Requirement

As you know, the general rule is that motions must be served on the other side together with notice as to when and where the motion is to be heard. Although certainly not unique to divorce cases, the nature of the issues at stake coupled with the emotionally charged context of these cases means that parties frequently fear that serious harm will occur if advance notice of a motion is given to the other side. For example, let's say that a father is threatening to take the children out of the country and the mother wants to get a court order prohibiting him from doing this. If she gives him advance notice of her intended request to the court, the father might disappear before the hearing takes place. In this situation, the court could hear her motion on an *ex parte* basis, meaning without notice; enter an order; and then provide the father with the opportunity to come to court and present his side of the story. Other examples of when *ex parte* relief may be appropriate include situations where a party is seeking protection from abuse or seeking to prevent a spouse from dissipating marital assets, as again, advance notice could trigger the very result the party is trying to avoid.

Grounded in considerations of procedural fairness, as required by the Due Process Clause, most courts will grant *ex parte* relief only if the moving party can show that giving notice poses a substantial risk of harm. In deciding whether to allow the requested relief, a court must balance the right of an individual to be heard before his or her interests are affected with the need to protect the moving party from the risk of injury or loss. Only where the risk is substantial will it outweigh the procedural rights of the other side. If an order is entered, notice will be provided and the other side will have an opportunity to be heard within a short period of time following the *ex parte* hearing.

2. Diversion to Court Conciliation or Mediation Services

In some states, the parties must sit down with staff members at the court to see if they can resolve matters before a motion can be heard by the judge. Depending on the jurisdiction, diversion may occur in all contested cases, or, may be limited to those involving disputes about custody and visitation. The majority of states have carved out an exception to mandated diversion in cases where there is a history of domestic violence based on the recognition that it can be unfair and potentially unsafe to require a victim of violence to mediate with an abusive spouse.

If an agreement is reached through this process, it is reduced to writing and presented to the judge for approval. If approved, it becomes the temporary order of the court. If agreement is not reached, the motion is then argued before the judge. In many states, the court worker participates in this court hearing. He or she may report back to the judge on what took place during their session and make recommendations. In other states, the meeting with the court worker is considered confidential, and he or she accordingly does not participate in the motion session.

While diversion to a court-based mediation or conciliation program can help couples reach mutually satisfactory agreements, an important concern that some commentators have raised, particularly with regard to pro-se litigants, is that in jurisdictions that do not privilege the conciliation discussions, a party may not realize that what they tell the court worker is not confidential and may be reported back to the judge. A related concern is that there may be tremendous pressure on the parties to settle the case, and the failure of a spouse to agree to a settlement proposal may in result in an unfavorable report or recommendation to the court.

3. Specific Divorce Motions

Motion practice in the divorce context is extremely varied. Many motions, such as those for temporary custody or support, are fairly standard, but attorneys often deploy considerable creativity in fashioning motions to address the myriad of unique disputes that often arise in the divorce context. By way of example, let's assume that a couple has temporary joint legal custody of their daughter, and the mother has physical custody. The mother gives the daughter a haircut that substantially alters the length and style of her hair. The father objects to her having done this without his consent and seeks to prevent it from recurring. He could design a motion to address this situation with a caption such as: "Motion to Prevent Wife from Altering Daughter's Hair Without the Husband's Prior Consent." Many attorneys enjoy this creative aspect of family law practice, while it drives others to distraction, particularly when they are on the receiving end of a highly original motion.

Following is a brief description of some of the common types of motions, followed by a sample motion and supporting affidavit.

Motion for Temporary Custody and Visitation

After a divorce is filed, many couples work out an informal, temporary arrangement regarding the children. Where this is not possible, one party will usually file a motion asking the court to award him or her temporary custody. After a hearing, the court will enter an order for custody and visitation, which will then be in effect until the divorce judgment is entered unless problems arise and a change is sought via another motion.

The importance of a temporary arrangement — whether through agreement or by a court order — should not be underestimated. Because courts are reluctant to disrupt children once they are settled into a satisfactory routine, temporary arrangements often ripen into permanent ones. The longer the interim stage, the more likely it is that the parent with temporary custody will end up as the custodial parent.

Temporary custody orders are also important where there is any risk that one parent might flee with the children. If an order is in place, a parent who interferes with the custodial or visitation rights of the other parent can be held in contempt of court. Moreover, a temporary custody order may be a necessary prerequisite to the initiation of criminal kidnapping charges in the event a parent disappears with the children. Accordingly, even where parties are able to work things out informally, it may be prudent to have the agreement approved by the court as a temporary custody order.

Case Preview

Lester v. Lennane

In this case, the father appealed the temporary custody and visitation orders that granted him limited time with his newborn daughter. Although discussed in the context of a paternity case, the primary issue presented in the case — namely, whether temporary custody orders are appealable — is also applicable in the divorce context.

As you read *Lester v. Lennane*, look for the following:

1. What evidence did the trial judge find persuasive in making its temporary orders?
2. What arguments does the father raise regarding his appeal of the temporary orders?
3. Why does the court dismiss the father's appeal?
4. According to the court, what alternative action should the father have taken?

Lester v. Lennane

101 Cal. Rptr. 2d 86 (Cal. Ct. App. 2000)

SIMS, J.

In this child custody case, appellant James Lennane appeals from a series of orders made in the family court. . . . Lennane appeals from a pretrial order made on July 22, 1998, limiting him to one hour a day of visitation with the newborn child of Lennane and respondent Judith Lester. . . . Lennane [also] appeals from a pretrial order made on November 13, 1998, also on the subject of temporary custody and visitation. . . . We granted Lennane's motion to consolidate the appeals.

. . .

Lennane, a former Sacramento resident living in Florida with his second wife and their eight-year-old daughter, but retaining business and family ties to Sacramento, met Lester in Sacramento in October 1997. . . .

After Lennane left Sacramento, Lester learned that she was pregnant. On December 23, 1997, she called him to tell him that she believed he was the father. . . . At his insistence, she underwent DNA testing, which confirmed his paternity.

Pretrial Proceedings

On March 24, 1998, Lester filed a Uniform Parentage Act paternity complaint and a motion for custody, child support, and health and dental costs as to the parents' yet-unborn daughter; the motion also sought attorney fees and costs. She requested primary physical custody and joint legal custody to begin after the child's birth, expected to occur on or around June 15, 1998. . . .

Lennane responded on May 13, 1998, by conceding his paternity and requesting an immediate custody evaluation and a long cause hearing to take place on June 18 or 19, 1998, on custody and support issues. . . .

Lester opposed Lennane's request for an immediate custody evaluation. She now demanded sole legal and physical custody of the child. . . .

[After hearing argument, the trial court refused to make any order on a custody ruling or to order a custody evaluation, ruling that any such evaluation was premature. However, after the birth of the minor child, Ava, the trial judge adopted on a temporary basis the recommendation of the court-appointed mediator that gave Lennane one hour of parenting time per day pending further mediation. After a custody evaluation, the evaluator recommended Lennane receive sole physical custody and that the mediator develop a short-term transitional plan to shift primary care away from Lester based on the possibility that Lennane would receive physical custody of Ava after trial. The trial judge thereafter adopted an order that increased Lennane's parenting time and also provided overnights from Saturday at 1:00 P.M. to Sunday at 1:00 P.M. Lennane appeals from this order as well as the final orders of the court.]

DISCUSSION

The Temporary Custody Orders Are Nonappealable

We must first consider whether the temporary custody orders from which Lennane purports to appeal . . . are appealable. We shall conclude they are not.

. . .

The parties have cited no statute expressly making temporary custody orders appealable, and we have found none. If the right to appeal in California is purely a creature of statute, as the overwhelming weight of authority indicates, the lack of any statute giving a litigant the right to appeal from a temporary custody order forecloses the claim that such orders are appealable.

. . .

A temporary custody order is interlocutory by definition, since it is made pendente lite with the intent that it will be superseded by an award of custody after trial. (Fam. Code, 3022, 3040, 3060-3062.) Code of Civil Procedure section 904.1 bars appeal from interlocutory judgments or orders "other than as provided in paragraphs (8), (9), and (11). . . ." (Code Civ. Proc., 904.1, subd. (a)(1)(A).) Temporary custody orders are not listed in any of those paragraphs. Therefore this statute precludes the appealability of such orders.

This result is in accord with the general rule that, under the "one final judgment" rule, appeal lies only from final judgments in actions or proceedings, or from orders after judgment that affect the judgment or its enforcement; it does not lie from interlocutory judgments or orders unless specifically made appealable by statute. . . .

. . .

One exception to the "one final judgment" rule codified in Code of Civil Procedure section 904.1 is the so-called collateral order doctrine. Where the trial court's ruling on a collateral issue "is substantially the same as a final judgment in an independent proceeding" (*In re Marriage of Skelley* (1976) 18 Cal. 3d 365, 368), in that it leaves the court no further action to take on "a matter which . . . is severable from the general subject of the litigation" (*In re Marriage of Van Sickle* (1977) 68 Cal. App. 3d 728, 735), an appeal will lie from that collateral order even though other matters in the case remain to be determined. . . . Lennane relies on this exception to the "one final judgment" rule, but his reliance is misplaced.

In determining whether an order is collateral, "the test is whether an order is 'important and essential to the correct determination of the main issue.' If the order is 'a necessary step to that end,' it is not collateral. [Citations.]" (*Steen v. Fremont Cemetery Corp.* (1992) 9 Cal. App. 4th 1221, 1227.)

. . .

[T]he temporary custody orders here are simply not "collateral." Custody is the only disputed issue in this case (aside from related attorney fees and costs). Furthermore, according to Lennane the temporary orders essentially rigged the final outcome against him: they created a status quo favoring Lester which the trial court used as the tie-breaker, under the rubric of "stability," in awarding her custody after trial. Thus neither temporary order finally resolved any matter "severable from the general subject of the litigation." (*In re Marriage of Van Sickle*, supra, 63 Cal. App. 3d at p. 735.)

. . .

But if the law left any room for doubt whether temporary custody orders are appealable, policy considerations would resolve the doubt. The very nature of such orders compels the swiftest possible review of any challenge. The writ process, not the appeal process, is the way to get that review.

In most custody dispute cases, young children bond with their primary custodial parents. The trial court must place the child's best interest first in any long-term custody decision. (Fam. Code, 3011, 3040, subd. (b).) Thus, the child's bond with the primary custodial parent will often weigh heavily in the court's mind. Once the bond is established, the court is likely to find that the child's best interest requires preserving that bond to maintain stability in the child's life.

A noncustodial parent who seeks to obtain custody will often be at a disadvantage by the time of trial if the child has bonded with the custodial parent. The noncustodial parent's only effective recourse is to obtain immediate review of any objectionable temporary custody order. This can be done by filing a petition for writ, a procedure Lennane failed to use in this case. It cannot be done by filing an appeal which will sit in abeyance while the case works its way to trial and decision — and while the bond between child and custodial parent strengthens and deepens.

For all of the above reasons, Lennane's purported appeals in cases [involving temporary orders] are dismissed.

Post-Case Follow-Up

Lester v. Lennane involved multiple appeals that were consolidated. Father had appealed both the temporary orders and the final judgment. Father argued that because the trial judge had denied him sole custody on a temporary basis it affected the final decision. The court went into great detail explaining why temporary orders, sometimes called pendente lite orders, are not appealable As expressed by the court, orders as to custody are temporary, and circumstances will change. Thus, while temporary orders are meant to provide some immediate relief as to parenting time, the test is always the best interest of the minor child. Thus, a court must look at the best interest standard both on a temporary basis and for final orders. However, as we have seen, even final orders in the custody area are never permanent. As circumstances change, a parent always has the ability to seek a modification of the parenting time orders.

Lester v. Lennane: Real Life Applications

1. Madeline and Layton are the parents of twin boys who are three years old. Layton has recently filed for divorce and filed a motion for temporary orders giving him sole legal and physical custody on a temporary basis and asked for a custody evaluation. Madeline objected, and asked that she be awarded sole legal and physical custody. The trial judge ordered a custody evaluation, but denied both parties' request for sole custody and instead ordered that the parties would share custody and have equal parenting time pending a final hearing. Can Layton appeal the temporary order denying his request for sole custody?

2. Jerry had just filed for divorce when his wife of three years, Anna, called to tell him she was pregnant. Anna, upset about the divorce, claims that she will fight

Jerry over custody and intends to seek sole legal and physical custody of the child she is pregnant with. Jerry asks whether he can file for temporary orders now before the baby is born so that he has equal parenting time. Does Jerry have a claim for temporary orders prior to the birth of the baby?

3. Assume the same facts as Question 2 above, but now assume that shortly before the baby was born Jerry brought a motion for temporary custody orders and the trial judge ruled that once the child is born, Jerry should be entitled to equal parenting time.

   a. Does Anna have a basis to appeal the temporary orders?
   b. What arguments can Anna make?
   c. What remedy does Anna have if she decides not to appeal?

Motion for the Appointment of a Guardian Ad Litem

Where custody is contested, a party may ask to have someone appointed to perform a custody evaluation or investigation. A custody evaluation is done by a mental health professional. An investigation is usually done by a **guardian ad litem** (**GAL**), sometimes referred to as a court-appointed advisor. Typically, a guardian ad litem interviews the parents and other involved adults, such as teachers and neighbors, and spends time with the children. He or she may also visit the homes of both parents. The guardian ad litem then files a written report with the court containing his or her recommendations about custodial and visitation arrangements.

In some cases, such as where there are concerns about the mental or emotional well-being of a parent or child, it may make more sense to have a custody evaluation done by a mental health professional. Here, the evaluation most likely would consist of a series of interviews and observations. Typically, each parent and each child is interviewed separately, and the children are observed alone and with each parent. Again, a written report and recommendations are filed with the court.

In either situation, the parties are entitled to a copy of the report and to an opportunity to question the guardian ad litem or the evaluator in court. This right is important because these reports tend to carry a lot of weight with judges, and parties must be given the chance to question the findings where they disagree with them.

Motion for Temporary Support

During the pendency of a divorce, a party may be in immediate need of child or spousal support and unable to wait until a finalized financial arrangement is in place. Accordingly, all states permit an interim award of child support and most permit an interim award of spousal support. Again, because this interim order may ripen into the permanent one, it is vital that all supporting financial documentation be carefully prepared and presented to the court.

Motion for Payment of Fees and Cost

As a general rule, each party is responsible for paying his or her own attorneys' fees. However, in most states, a spouse who lacks the resources to secure ongoing representation can ask the court to order the other spouse to pay his or her fees. This request can be made at trial or during the pendency of the action.

In evaluating the request, the court will compare the financial status of both parties. Where there is a significant disparity, the court may award fees. However, there is no right to a fee award, and the decision is generally within the sound discretion of the trial judge. In many states, judges tend to award fees only in cases of extreme hardship.

Motions Relating to the Protection of Assets

A common concern during the pendency of a divorce is that a party will dissipate marital assets. To protect against this, the other spouse can seek a variety of protective court orders.

A party can ask the court to issue a restraining order enjoining the other spouse from disposing of or encumbering the asset in question. He or she can also ask the court to attach property, which serves to put the world on notice that the asset is subject to an unresolved claim and makes the asset difficult to sell. The court can also freeze assets that belong to a spouse but are under the control of a third party, such as a bank. Here, the order would command the bank not to allow the spouse to withdraw or transfer funds. These motions need to be drafted with particular care, as they may need to satisfy the technical requirements of statutes outside of the scope of divorce laws that govern interests in property.

As mentioned above, if a party has a well-grounded fear that upon receiving notice of a motion to protect assets, his or her spouse is likely to dispose of the assets in question, he or she can appear before the court on an *ex parte* basis. If the court agrees that the danger is real, it will secure the asset first and then provide the other side with notice and the opportunity to be heard on the issue.

Motion for Protection from Abuse

During the pendency of the divorce, most states allow either party to seek protection from abuse by way of a motion within the divorce proceeding itself. Most commonly, a spouse can ask that the other party be ordered to leave him or her alone and, if they are still living together, that the abusive spouse be vacated from the marital premises.

In most states, this approach is not exclusive, which means that a spouse has the option of bringing a protective motion within the framework of the divorce action, filing a separate petition under the state's abuse protection act, or both. It is important to recognize that these approaches may yield different results. In particular, an order entered in response to a motion brought as part of a divorce case may have less clout than one entered pursuant to the state's abuse prevention law as it is less likely to be criminally enforceable or to enhance the arrest powers of the police (see Chapter 11).

EXHIBIT 9.3   **Sample Motion for Temporary Custody**

Although the format may vary from state to state, some elements are universal for motions for temporary orders. The sample motion for temporary custody is typical of one that may be filed in court.

PLAINTIFF'S MOTION FOR TEMPORARY CUSTODY

JERRY FREEMAN, Plaintiff

v.

CARRIE GREEN, Defendant

NOW COMES the plaintiff in the above-captioned action and asks that this Honorable Court award him temporary physical and legal custody of the party's minor daughter, Melissa, age seven years old.

In support of his Motion, Plaintiff states as follows, and also incorporates by reference, the attached Affidavit, which more fully sets out the facts in support of his request:

1. That the plaintiff has been the primary caretaker of Melissa for the past three years. Before this time, the parties shared child-care responsibilities on a more or less equal basis.

2. That over the past three years, as a result of depression and increased alcohol consumption, the wife has provided little attention or care to Melissa, and has been emotionally abusive toward her.

3. That the wife moved out of the family home approximately six months ago, and since then has had infrequent and irregular contact with Melissa.

4. That the best interest of Melissa would be served by awarding temporary legal and physical custody to the father so that continuity of care and nurturing is maintained.

WHEREFORE, the Plaintiff requests that this Honorable Court grant this Motion and award him temporary custody of Melissa.

Respectfully Submitted,

_____

Jerry Freeman
By his Attorney
Ellen Jones
Jones & Hernandez
11 Court Street
Freeport, Any State 02167

CERTIFICATE OF SERVICE

I, Ellen Jones, certify that a copy of this motion was served on the attorney of record for the defendant by mailing a copy of the same to her office address of _____ by first class mail, postage prepaid together with notice that said motion is to be heard by the Middlesex County Probate and Family Court on March 15, 2015 at 9:00 A.M.

E. AVOIDING TRIAL: NEGOTIATION AND ALTERNATIVE APPROACHES TO DISPUTE RESOLUTION

Ultimately, the overwhelming majority of divorce cases are settled before trial, most commonly through the process of negotiation. However, divorcing couples increasingly make use of two alternative approaches to resolving their differences — mediation and, although far less common, arbitration. In this section, we compare these three dispute resolution approaches. Please note that the discussion is general in nature and does not address the more formal principles and theories of each approach. We also consider two newer approaches to the resolution of disputes — the provision of "unbundled" legal services and the collaborative law model.

1. Negotiation

Through negotiation, each attorney acts on behalf of his or her client to determine if a settlement can be reached. Importantly, in contrast to mediation and arbitration, no neutral third party is involved.

Negotiations can take place on the telephone, but it is also common for one side to contact the other at some point in the divorce process to see if a settlement conference can be arranged. This conference can be either two way, involving just the attorneys, or four way, involving the attorneys as well as the clients. A four-way conference is generally more productive because the clients can play an active role in initiating and responding to settlement proposals. However, in some situations, such as where there is tremendous animosity between the parties or there is a history of abuse, it may make more sense to have the attorneys meet, at least initially, without the clients present.

Ideally, each attorney will have met with his or her client before the conference to explore what the client wants and where he or she is willing to compromise. The attorney should also help the client to anticipate what the other side is likely to request so he or she can think about possible responses. If this advance work is done, both attorneys will begin the negotiations with a good understanding of their clients' positions.

At the conference, ground rules are usually established. An important consideration is whether each issue will be negotiated separately until there is an impasse or an agreement reached or whether everything will be placed on the table at the same time. The advantage of the former approach is that it minimizes the possibility of inappropriate linkage of issues; for example, the husband offering to give the wife sole custody if she drops her request for spousal support. If the parties decide to negotiate each issue separately, any agreement reached on a single issue is usually not considered final until all other issues have been resolved. By conditioning finality of each issue on reaching a comprehensive settlement, the parties do not risk the loss of potential bargaining chips. For example, if the parties agree on a division of property, a spouse could reopen this matter if unable to get what he or she wants with respect to spousal support. Thus, a husband might back away from his agreement to allow a wife to remain in the home if, later in the negotiations, she insists on spousal support.

Once the basic framework is established, one side will open with its offer. This offer rarely represents the party's bottom line because this would leave no room for the give-and-take that characterizes the negotiation process. However, if the proposal is too outrageous, the party may not appear to be negotiating in good faith, which can jeopardize the integrity of the process. When the other side responds, they too will leave room for concessions but again should avoid unreasonable counterproposals.

As the negotiations proceed, it is common for each party to confer privately with his or her attorney. At this time, responses and new proposals can be formulated. These meetings can also serve as valuable cooling-off periods because these conferences tend to get heated.

The negotiating session can conclude in a number of ways. One party may unilaterally declare it over and may even storm out, perhaps because of frustration with the process or as a deliberate "bullying" tactic designed to exact concessions. The parties may also mutually recognize that they can go no further. At this point, they may decide that the case should be marked for trial or that they should reconvene at a future date and give settlement another chance.

If the negotiations end in agreement, one side usually offers to prepare an initial draft of a separation agreement and then send it to the other side for review. This is possible even where the parties have not ironed out all of the details; here, one side offers to see if they can work out the missing details in a mutually satisfactory manner. Although drafting the agreement is time-consuming and potentially more expensive for the client, it is usually advantageous to be the drafter because once something is in writing, it seems to acquire a presumptive validity, and suggesting changes has a bit of an uphill quality to it.

2. Mediation

Mediation is a nonadversarial approach to dispute resolution. It has become a popular option for divorcing couples who wish to resolve their differences without going to trial. Here, a neutral third party — the mediator — helps couples reach their own agreement. The mediator is not an advocate for either side but rather guides the parties through the process of reaching agreement by helping them to identify important issues, consider options, and structure a realistic settlement.

Divorce mediators come from a range of professional backgrounds, although most are either mental health professionals or attorneys. Mediators may work in interdisciplinary teams. Thus, for example, a social worker and an attorney might work together, as each brings a distinct but complementary body of knowledge and set of skills to the process. At present most states do not have formal training and licensing requirements for mediators, although a number of professional organizations have developed practice standards.

The Problem-Solving and the Transformative Approaches to Mediation

Although there has been a marked increase in the use of mediation as an alternative dispute resolution method, some experts in the field have raised the concern that the field lacks an "articulated theoretical framework" to guide practitioners, and there is therefore a lack of awareness that "very different goals and values among mediators . . . could shape competent performance in fundamentally different ways."[15] In an effort to bring a coherent theoretical framework to the field, some scholars have identified two primary mediation models: the problem-solving model and the transformative model.

According to the **problem-solving model**, the goal of mediation is to arrive at a solution that "solves tangible problems on fair and realistic terms, and good mediator practice is a matter of issue identification, option creation, and effective persuasion to 'close the deal.'"[16] This model is rooted in an "individualist ideology" that presumes that each individual acts in a contained, self-directed way in "pursuit of satisfaction of his or her own separate self interests."[17]

In contrast, the **transformative model** sees the conflict as "first and foremost a crisis in some human interaction," as a result of which "the interaction between the parties quickly degenerates and assumes a mutually destructive, alienating, and dehumanizing character."[18] Here, the primary goal of mediation is not problem solving, but changing the interactional patterns between the parties:

> [S]uccess is measured not by settlement per se but by party shifts toward personal strength, interpersonal responsiveness and constructive interaction. . . . The transformative framework is based on and reflects relational ideology, in which human beings are assumed to be fundamentally social — formed in and through their relations with other human beings, essentially connected to others, and motivated by a desire for both personal autonomy and constructive social interaction.[19]

Significantly, the role of the mediator is quite different in each model. In the problem-solving model, the mediator structures the process to help the parties reach a settlement. In the transformative model, the mediator's role is less outcome-oriented and geared more toward empowering the parties to transform their interactional patterns so that they can re-engage in a more positive way.[20]

The Mediation Process

Although different models abound, mediation is usually conceptualized as occurring in distinct stages. It is useful to keep in mind that regardless of whether

---

[15]Dorothy J. Della Noce, Robert A. Baruch Bush, and Joseph P. Folger, Clarifying the Theoretical Underpinnings of Mediation: Implications for Practice and Policy, 3 Pepp. Disp. Resol. L.J. 39, 41, 47 (2002). It should be noted that this article draws from and builds on the following work: Robert A. Baruch Bush and Joseph P. Folger, The Promise of Mediation: Responding to Conflict Through Empowerment and Recognition (1994).
[16]*Id.* at 47.
[17]*Id.* at 50.
[18]*Id.* at 51.
[19]*Id.* at 52.
[20]*Id.* at 50-52.

mediation is conceptualized as a four-stage process, as presented below, or as a seven- or eight-stage process, progression from stage to stage is rarely linear, and couples typically move back and forth between stages as new issues, conflicts, and emotions surface. There is no single fixed or correct model, and each mediator works within a framework that best suits his or her own approach to dispute resolution.[21]

Stage One: Building Trust and Establishing Parameters

During the initial session, parties are encouraged to articulate why they have come to mediation and what their expectations, concerns, and goals are. The mediator explains the process, including the nature of his or her role, the responsibilities of the participants, and the applicable ground rules, such as those relating to confidentiality. By the end of this meeting, the parties should have a clear understanding of the process and be able to make an informed decision as to whether they wish to proceed. If the mediation is to continue, a contract to mediate, which sets out the operative framework, is usually signed by the couple and the mediator.

For many mediators, this initial session also serves a screening purpose. As discussed below, some mediators do not believe mediation is appropriate where there has been a history of domestic violence. At this initial meeting, the mediator might ask about abuse or look for clues suggesting a history of abuse. If reasonably certain that abuse has taken place, the mediator might not accept the case. Other mediators, while acknowledging the importance of screening for abuse, would not reject a couple for this reason but instead would set specific ground rules, such as that physical safety is nonnegotiable.

Stage Two: Fact-Finding

To be effective, mediation requires the voluntary disclosure of all relevant information. Generally, as part of the mediation agreement, parties commit to complete disclosure and to provide copies of documents that would ordinarily be requested in the course of discovery, such as tax returns, bank statements, and asset inventories. Formal discovery is not available in mediation, and the mediator has no authority to compel disclosure. To some, this raises troubling questions about the potential fairness of the process. Of primary concern is the risk that a spouse who has less knowledge of and control over economic resources might unknowingly give up rights to income or assets. Where the mediator knows or suspects that a party is concealing assets, he or she can break off mediation and refuse to resume unless the parties confer with counsel. However, some mediators believe this would

---

[21]This discussion of the mediation process is consistent with the "problem-solving" model; it is based in part on the approach set out in the following early influential essay: Alison Taylor, A General Theory of Divorce Mediation, *in* Divorce Mediation, Theory and Practice (Ann L. Milne and Jay Folberg eds., 1988). For further detail, see also Jay Folberg, Ann L. Milne, and Peter Salem, Divorce and Family Mediation, Models, Techniques, and Applications (2004); Alison Taylor, Family Dispute Resolution: Mediation Theory and Practice (2002).

be overstepping their bounds, reasoning that the parties assumed this risk when they entered mediation.[22]

Stage Three: Identification/Creation of Options and Alternatives

After everyone is satisfied that all relevant information has been provided, the mediator helps the parties identify what they see as the various options and assists them in expanding the range of acceptable alternatives. The mediator also seeks to prevent the parties from getting locked into fixed positions before all options have been considered. Thus, a mediator is likely to take an active role in this stage of the process.

Stage Four: Negotiating and Drafting the Agreement

Once the acceptable options have been identified, the parties are faced with the task of sorting through the possibilities. At this point, the mediator generally steps back so that the parties themselves can reach the agreement, although he or she may play a critical facilitative role.

As the parties seek to reach an agreement, it is not uncommon for one or both of them to ask the mediator whether he or she thinks a certain provision is fair. This raises interesting questions about the mediator's role. Some mediators hold the view that answering such a question would compromise their stance as a neutral third party. Rather than responding, the mediator might direct the party to think about how that option would play out in his or her life and might also suggest that he or she confer with counsel. Other mediators take a more activist stance and will provide the parties with an assessment of what the likely outcome would be if the matter went to court, thus providing them a framework within which to make their decision.

A further potential complication is where the mediator realizes that the agreement is unfair and that one spouse would fare considerably better in court. Here, some mediators simply encourage each party to review the final agreement with an attorney before signing it, reasoning that when the parties agreed to the process they assumed the risk of operating outside formal legal rules. Other mediators take a more active role, especially where the unfavorable result stems from an underlying power imbalance. They might raise pointed questions to push the parties to confront the unfairness of the bargain or strongly urge consultation with counsel during the process rather than waiting until the end.

Once a settlement is reached, the mediator usually drafts an agreement embodying the parties' understanding. Most, if not all, mediators will strongly encourage each person to review the agreement with his or her lawyer before signing it, although some argue that this review really comes too late in the process to be very useful. The mediated agreement may be redrafted into a formal separation

---

[22]Conversation with Professor David Matz, Professor in the Conflict Resolution, Global Governance and Human Security Department at the University of Massachusetts, Boston. For a critical look at some of the complexities posed by mediation, see Marsha B. Freeman, Divorce Mediation: Sweeping Conflicts Under the Rug, Time to Clean House, 780 U. Det. Mercy L. Rev. 67 (2000).

agreement, which includes the standard separation agreement provisions, or it may serve as the document presented to the court for approval at the divorce hearing.

The Debate over the Appropriateness of Mediation in Cases Involving Domestic Violence

Professionals working in the family law field have responded to the increased use of divorce mediation with both enthusiasm and trepidation. According to enthusiasts, a primary advantage of mediation is that it stresses cooperation and encourages parties to work out long-term solutions that make sense for them. As a client-centered process, it stresses individual responsibility for decision making, and by not abdicating responsibility to judges or lawyers, participants gain a sense of control over their future. Moreover, it is hoped that by stressing cooperation and communication, mediation will give couples the tools they will need to resolve future disputes, thus promoting greater post-divorce stability and satisfaction.

Despite these potential benefits, many who work with battered women, including some mediators, have raised serious concerns about the appropriateness of mediation where violence is a factor. Of primary concern is that mediation emphasizes conciliation and cooperation, which assumes some degree of mutual respect and equality of status within the relationship. Where violence is present, however, there is no equality or mutuality; goals are not achieved through cooperation but rather through coercion and fear. Accordingly, a battered woman may respond based on fear and the overriding desire to remain safe. A further concern is that even a highly skilled mediator will not be able to redress this imbalance of power because it is so deeply embedded in the relationship. The requirement of neutrality, while facilitative in other contexts, will be insufficient to overcome a legacy of fear and lack of mutuality.[23]

Countering this, others point to studies that indicate that "women who feel they are being pressured into agreements usually terminate the mediation rather than submit to agreements they believe are unfair" and that domestic violence victims "who do not terminate actually are able to negotiate effectively in mediation."[24] Moreover, in contradistinction to the view that mediation silences domestic violence victims, women may instead find the process "empowering, and believe that it 'enhances their ability to stand up for themselves, solve problems, assume responsibility for themselves, and express their views.'"[25]

In any event, some mediators now attempt to screen out cases with a history of domestic violence as inappropriate for mediation. Others have adopted specific protocols, such as separate interviews, in an effort to ensure a safe process and fair results. However, those who argue against the use of mediation fear that

---

[23]*See generally* Lydia Belzer, Domestic Abuse and Divorce Mediation: Suggestions for a Safer Process, 5 Loy. J. Pub. Int. L. 37 (2002); Sarah Krieger, The Dangers of Mediation in Domestic Violence Cases, 8 Cardozo Women's L.J. 235 (2002); Penelope E. Bryan, Killing Us Softly: Divorce Mediation and the Politics of Power, 40 Buff. L. Rev. 441 (1992).

[24]Mary Adkins, Moving Out of the 1990's: An Argument for Updating Protocol on Divorce Mediation in Domestic Abuse Cases, 22 Yale J.L. & Feminism 97, 115 (2010).

[25]*Id.* at 116, quoting Nancy Ver Steegh, Yes, No, and Maybe: Informed Decision Making About Divorce Mediation in the Presence of Domestic Violence, 9 Wm. & Mary J. Women & L. 145, 183 (2003).

these protections may not be sufficient as cases may not be screened out because violence victims often downplay the seriousness of the abuse, and that although well-intentioned, "violence-sensitive" procedures are simply not enough to redress the enduring impact of violence such that a victim can participate in mediation without a profound sense of fear and disempowerment that may well result in a skewed agreement.[26]

Another option that at least one commentator has proposed is the use of e-mediation, which is an integral component of the growing field of **Online Dispute Resolution (ODR)**.[27] By way of introduction to the concept, **e-mediation** was initially used to provide "solutions to disputes that arose on the Internet" but has been increasingly used to resolve "disputes that did not originate in virtual space."[28] Arguably, a principal advantage of this virtual approach to mediation is that the physical separation of the parties can serve to "eliminate intrusions that may arise because of the body language and nonverbal hints by the abusive party, which serve as a means of intimidation and control of the victim," and may not be readily detectable by the mediator.[29] In short, the process arguably may serve to neutralize the power advantage that an abuser typically has over his victim.

3. Arbitration

Long identified with labor, commercial, and international disputes, arbitration has not traditionally been used by divorcing couples to reach a settlement agreement. Where utilized in the divorce context, it has typically been pursuant to a clause in a separation agreement in which the parties agree to submit certain post-divorce disputes to arbitration. However, there has been a notable increase in the use of pre-divorce arbitration as an alternative to litigation over the past few decades. Reflecting this trend, a number of states now have specific statutes that govern the use of arbitration in family law cases and address the details of the process.

Arbitration is similar to the judicial process in that the parties present their case to a neutral, third-party decision maker (or panel of decision makers), but the process is considerably more flexible, and the parties retain a greater degree of control than they have in court. A dispute can be submitted to arbitration only if the parties so agree; one side cannot force the other to arbitrate unless specifically required by prior agreement. The authority of the arbitrator derives from the parties' agreement — the arbitrator cannot make decisions about matters not directly entrusted to him or her by the parties. Although, as discussed below, an arbitrator's decision is usually entitled to great deference, some courts will not enforce an agreement to submit custody and visitation disputes to arbitration. Other courts

---

[26]For a discussion of some of these issues, see Dafna Lavi, Till Death Do Us Part?!: Online Mediation as an Answer to Divorce Cases Involving Domestic Violence, 16 N.C. J.L. & Tech. 253 (2015).
[27]*Id.*
[28]*Id.* at 255.
[29]*Id.* at 282-285.

have been willing to enforce these agreements, with "the caveat that any decision rendered by the arbitrator is subject to de novo judicial review."[30]

The arbitrator is typically selected by the parties. Where this is contentious, the attorneys will usually assist in the selection process. In a post-divorce dispute, a selection mechanism may be provided for in the separation agreement. The arbitrator may be a professional working under the auspices of the American Arbitration Association or any other mutually acceptable individual, such as a clergyperson, accountant, therapist, or lawyer. The choice of arbitrator often turns on the nature of the dispute and whether a particular expertise is required.

Arbitration hearings are fairly informal. They are held in a private setting and generally take less time to complete than a trial. In most instances, the arbitrator's decision is binding, subject to very limited rights of court review. As a general rule, there is a presumption in favor of the validity of the arbitral award, and a court will modify or vacate an award only under limited circumstances, such as where there has been fraud or bias, or where the arbitrator exceeded the scope of his or her authority. However, many courts review arbitral decisions more carefully when they are made in the family law context, especially when the rights of children are at stake, and some courts will not enforce provisions relating to custody and visitation. Succinctly capturing this perspective, the Supreme Court of Ohio explained: "The process of arbitration, useful when the mundane matter of the amount of support is in issue, is less so when the delicate balancing of the factors composing the best interests of a child is at issue," thus concluding that these decisions must remain with the court. *Kelm v. Kelm*, 623 N.E.2d 39, 42 (Ohio 1993).

4. The Collaborative Law Model

In addition to these three established dispute resolution alternatives, the "collaborative" law model has also surged in popularity in the divorce context, and a number of states have enacted collaborative law statutes to guide the practice. Recently determined by the ABA to be an ethical model for the practice of law, a formal opinion of the ABA's Committee on Ethics and Professional Practice provides the following description of the collaborative law process:

> **Collaborative law** is a type of alternative dispute resolution in which the parties and their lawyers commit to work cooperatively to reach settlement. . . . Participants focus on the interests of both clients, gather sufficient information to insure that decisions are made with full knowledge, develop a full range of options, and then choose options that best meet the needs of the parties. The parties structure a mutually acceptable written resolution of all issues without court involvement. The product of the process

---

[30]Andre R. Imbrogno, Arbitration as an Alternative to Divorce Litigation: Redefining the Judicial Role, 31 Cap. U. L. Rev. 413, 417 (2003). *See also* George K. Walker, Family Law Arbitration: Legislation and Trends, 21 J. Am. Acad. Matrim. Law. 521 (2008).

is then submitted to the court as a final decree. The structure creates a problem-solving atmosphere with a focus on interest-based negotiation and client empowerment.[31]

As indicated by the above passage, the hallmark of this approach is that the parties and their lawyers commit in advance to settling the case. Reinforcing the centrality of this commitment, the attorneys in a collaborative divorce agree in advance to disqualify themselves from representing their clients in court should the process break down before all issues are fully resolved. Accordingly, if a trial becomes necessary, each party will have to hire a new attorney, which some concerned commentators have noted is likely to add both time and cost as the new attorney will need to be brought up to speed on the details of the case.

The collaborative divorce process bears some resemblance to both mediation and negotiation. Like mediation, the focus is on helping the parties work through their differences in a non-confrontational manner. The parties also are encouraged to speak directly to one another in the course of the settlement process. However, in contrast to mediation, no neutral third party guides the process; rather, each spouse is represented by his or her own attorney. Individual representation aligns the collaborative law with the negotiation process that typically accompanies a divorce; however, in contrast, in addition to the emphasis on cooperation, the threat that a party will break off negotiations in favor of litigation if they do not get what they want is considerably less, as the party would have to hire a new lawyer to represent him or her in court. Thus, there is a built-in incentive to settle the case. Collaborative divorce also can be characterized as a type of unbundled legal services (see below), as an attorney is hired for the bounded purpose of settling the case, agreeing in advance not to take the matter to court should the settlement process break down.

Proponents of this approach stress that the four-way commitment to settlement fosters a creative and engaged problem-solving ethos as distinct from the typically bitter winner-take-all approach of the traditional adversarial model of lawyering. They also stress the benefit to clients of being at the center of the process. As one commentator explains, in contrast to the "traditional practice of law, where the client's voice is practically not heard and decisions . . . are for the most part those of the attorney," by "actively engag[ing] the parties throughout the process," the collaborative law model makes client "autonomy and self-definition its central motif."[32]

Not surprisingly, however, the practice also has its detractors. Of particular concern is that the disqualification requirement may potentially put an attorney in breach of the ethical requirement that he or she zealously represent the interests of his or her client, as those interests may well necessitate taking the case to court in

---

[31]ABA Committee on Ethics and Professional Responsibility, Formal Opinion 07-447 (2007). Regarding some of the ethical issues presented by the collaborative model, see Christopher M. Fairman, Growing Pains: Changes in Collaborative Law and the Challenge of Legal Ethics, 30 Campbell L. Rev. 237 (2008); Larry R. Spain, Collaborative Law: A Critical Reflection on Whether a Collaborative Orientation Can Be Ethically Incorporated into the Practice of Law, 56 Baylor L. Rev. 141 (2004).

[32]Dafna Lavi, Can the Leopard Change His Spots?!: Reflections on the "Collaborative Law" Revolution and Collaborative Advocacy, 13 Cardozo J. Conflict Resol. 61, 107-108 (2011).

the event the settlement process breaks down. Another concern is that rather than being empowering, clients may experience the emphasis on settlement as coercive, since they know that if the process fails, they will need to retain new counsel. Not only is this potentially burdensome in terms of time and money, it can also be daunting to face the prospect of having to develop trust in and rapport with a new lawyer at a time of rupture in the divorce process.[33]

5. Unbundled Legal Services

Although technically not quite an alternative mode of dispute resolution, this seems the best place to discuss an innovative approach to the practice of law that has been gaining popularity in the family law arena. In what is referred to as **"unbundled" legal services**, or **limited task representation**, an attorney agrees to provide a client with limited assistance from a menu of options instead of providing him or her with comprehensive representation. Unbundled services can include the giving of legal advice, coaching on how to handle a case, assistance with drafting pleadings (a practice that is also referred to as **ghostwriting**), and perhaps, less typically, representation in court.[34]

Clearly cost-effective, this approach has emerged as a way to provide legal assistance to low- and middle-income litigants who lack the resources to retain a lawyer for full-service representation — and who therefore would otherwise try to navigate the legal system on their own. Of particular note, an increasing number of publicly funded legal services offices that provide representation in civil matters to low-income clients have responded to funding cuts by moving to an unbundled approach as a way to "stretch the scarce attorney resources provided by federal and local governments to improve access to justice."[35] In addition to providing clients who might otherwise be completely on their own with at least some legal assistance, as one commentator remarks, this approach has also been commended for giving individuals greater choice and flexibility by "dissolv[ing] the all-or-nothing model of lawyering and creat[ing] an opportunity to access the expertise of a lawyer only when the client determines that one is needed most."[36] However, as she goes on to observe, it is important to recognize that "choice" is essentially illusory as far as low-income clients are concerned, as they are not likely to have a range of options to pick from.[37]

---

[33]For a discussion of some of the concerns that have been raised about the practice of collaborative law, in addition to Lavi, *supra* note 26, see Alexandria Zylstra, A Call to Action: A Client-Centered Evaluation of Collaborative Law, 11 Pepp. Disp. Resol. L.J. 547 (2011); Christopher M. Fairman, Growing Pains: Changes in Collaborative Law and the Challenge of Legal Ethics, 30 Campbell L. Rev. 237 (2008).

[34]For further detail, see The Changing Face of Legal Practice: Twenty-Six Recommendations for the Baltimore Conference: A National Conference on "Unbundled" Legal Services, 40 Fam. Ct. Rev. 26 (2002); *see also* the American Bar Association's Pro Se/Unbundling Resource Center, http://apps.americanbar.org/legalservices/delivery/delunbund.html (accessed June 8, 2016).

[35]Jessica K. Steinberg, In Pursuit of Justice? Case Outcomes and the Delivery of Unbundled Legal Services, 18 Geo. J. Poverty L. & Poly. 453, 463 (2011).

[36]*Id.* at 464.

[37]*Id.*

Although this practice model has been praised as an innovative response to the shortage of lawyers for middle class and low-income clients, and for building greater flexibility into the traditional lawyer-client relationship, some concerns have also been raised about this novel approach to the practice of law. One apprehension is that a client may not fully understand the allocation of responsibilities between him- or herself and the lawyer, particularly if the case turns out to be more complex or contested than originally anticipated, which is not uncommon in the divorce arena. Supporters of the unbundled approach stress that potential confusion can be avoided through the drafting of clear contracts for services; nonetheless, others worry that a party who is confronting the emotional strain of divorce may not have a clear understanding of an agreement for limited assistance, and may therefore come to expect more from the attorney, especially if the case become more involved or hotly contested than originally anticipated.[38]

Another thought-provoking concern that one commentator has recently raised is that when it comes to improving outcomes for underserved populations, rather than offering more people less, at least in the absence of clear data showing that clients with limited legal assistance actually fare better in court than those who represent themselves, might we not be better off under the traditional model that offers full representation to fewer people — a model that she argues has been shown to result in better outcomes in some contexts.[39]

F. REACHING RESOLUTION: THE SEPARATION AGREEMENT

As discussed in the section above, divorce cases may proceed along many different pathways, but the vast majority of cases are ultimately settled before trial. Where the parties are able to resolve all outstanding issues, their understanding is embodied in a separation agreement. Technically, a **separation agreement** is a contract in which the parties structure their post-divorce rights and responsibilities. However, because of the state's interest in the marital relationship, separation agreements are not treated like ordinary contracts. In most states, they are subject to careful review at the divorce hearing, and a judge can set aside an agreement or any provisions that he or she determines to be unfair or to have been agreed on without adequate disclosure.

Separation agreements are unique to each situation, but there are some standard components typically included in all separation agreements that appear after the initial recital of background, which includes items such as the names of the parties, the date of marriage, and the date the action was filed. The following sections describe each of these.

---

[38]Regarding some of the concerns about this approach to the provision of legal services, see Jessica K. Steinberg, Demand Side Reform in the Poor People's Court, 47 Conn. L. Rev. 741 (2015).

[39]Steinberg, *supra* note 35.

1. Spousal Support

In the section on spousal support in a separation agreement, each spouse might waive the right to seek support from the other. Sometimes, based on the assumption that only the wife might seek support, attorneys fail to make these waiver provisions reciprocal, but if the true intent is that neither party shall have a claim, reciprocal waivers are appropriate.

It is important to be aware that some judges will not accept a clause calling for a permanent waiver of support rights. Even where such a waiver is accepted, a court might later override it on public policy grounds if support becomes necessary to prevent a former spouse from going on public assistance.

If spousal support is to be paid, the precise nature and extent of the obligation should be spelled out. For example, if the husband is to make rehabilitative alimony payments, the agreement should define the circumstances under which the obligation can be extended, such as where the wife has been unable to complete her course of training due to no fault of her own.

Also, as discussed in Chapter 7, alimony payments are normally deductible by the payor spouse and includible in the income of the payee spouse. If the parties wish to alter this so that the payments are neither deductible nor includible, they can do so, but the agreement must specifically set out their intent.

It is common to require a support obligor to maintain life insurance for the duration of the support obligation. In the event of death, the insurance would serve as a support replacement. If the custodial parent is also employed, it makes sense to have him or her maintain insurance as well.

In this type of agreement, the other spouse is named as the beneficiary. This is the simplest way to set things up, but it requires a degree of trust that many parties do not have in one another. Another option is to name the children as direct beneficiaries, but if they are young, this is impractical. Also, where proceeds are left to minors, many states require that management of the funds be placed under court control, which can be inconvenient. Alternatively, the money could be left to the children in trust, with the surviving spouse or a third party named as trustee. This would place the spouse under a formal legal obligation to spend the money on behalf of the children; there is thus greater accountability than if he or she is simply named as the beneficiary with a contractual obligation to use the money for the children.

Last, in this case, each party is employed and has health insurance. If one spouse has been covered on the other's plan, language regarding continued coverage should be included, unless other arrangements for coverage have been made.

2. Custody

Custody involves both legal decision making and parenting time. Many agreements also include a section that spells out the visitation arrangements. Some simply provide for the right of reasonable visitation, and other agreements specify very detailed terms for visitation. Unless the parties get along well, detail can be crucial to the success of visitation arrangements. Parents often underestimate how painful the coordination of custody and visitation arrangements can be, and how easily things can fall apart. A set schedule reduces the amount of negotiation that must take place, and thus reduces the potential for conflict, although, parties can certainly include language that permits schedule changes based on mutual agreement.

Moreover, even where parents are reasonably friendly, holidays can trigger strong emotional reactions. Without a structure in place, parents may be unable to work out arrangements that permit both of them to spend holiday time with the children. As any family law attorney can attest to, the holiday season is likely to be one of their busiest and most stressful times of year.

Another matter that suggests caution when contemplating an unstructured visitation clause is the new relationship factor. Parents often fail to anticipate how painful it can be when their former spouse begins dating, especially if a relationship becomes serious. At this juncture, even parents who have been flexible and accommodating may find themselves caught up in conflict about arrangements. Mom might be less willing to let the children go to Dad's house when she suspects his new romantic interest is present, and Dad might seek increased time with the children to keep them away from Mom's new romantic interest. In short, parental jealousy and hurt may result in a distortion of previous arrangements.

3. Parental Rights Clauses

Parental rights clauses refer to a wide array of topics that might be important to the parent — for example, clauses that indicate that neither parent may disparage the other parent, neither parent may post derogatory comments about the other parent on social media sites, and even under what circumstances a parent must advise the other parent before they introduce the minor children to a new relationship. Although it is fairly standard to include a parental rights clause, these clauses are difficult to enforce because of how hard it is to prove when one parent has crossed the line.

4. Medical and School Information

Language granting both parents the rights to full medical and school information is pretty standard in most separation agreements. However, when abuse is an issue, access may need to be restricted in order to protect the safety of a spouse or child. Where a right of access to records is provided by statute, a parent may need some kind of court order in order to limit the rights of the other parent.

5. Child Support Term

Child support terms are typically a significant element in a separation agreement. In addition to establishing the support amount, it is useful to build in a review process tied to the guidelines. Some agreements also contain language defining what constitutes a change in circumstances that would warrant a modification. This can eliminate an area of possible contention, although again, it is virtually impossible to cover all possible contingencies.

Note that with respect to college education, an agreement does not have to bind the parents to a specific dollar amount. Instead, it might provide for proportional contributions and establishes a minimal level of commitment. Often parents are reluctant to commit themselves to paying for college in an agreement. However, without such a commitment, it can be difficult to get the noncustodial parent to contribute, especially if over the years he or she has become less involved with the children, and in many states, the court has no statutory authority to order contribution in the absence of an agreement. Where parents have sufficient income, the option of setting up an educational trust whereby parents are obligated to set aside money on a yearly basis should be explored.

6. Personal and Real Property Terms

It is generally advisable for the parties to divide their assets before the agreement is executed, as this avoids potential enforcement problems. If this is not feasible, the details of any post-execution transfer should be spelled out.

As discussed in Chapter 8, there are many ways to dispose of real estate in a divorce. Oftentimes, the sale option is most likely selected because neither spouse is able to buy out the interest of the other and there are no significant offsetting assets that could be used to lower the buyout price. Another option is to give the custodial parent the right of use and occupancy until some future date, but, as discussed in Chapter 8, the downside of this arrangement is that it keeps the parties enmeshed and frequently leads to unanticipated problems. With the first option, the parties must continue to interact, but only until the house is sold. If the parties are uncooperative, additional safeguards might be included relative to this time period, such as specifying what happens if the occupying party does not maintain the property or if a party fails to make a required payment.

7. Division of Debt Terms

It is important to recognize that although parties may spell out who is responsible for payment of joint debts, their arrangement is not binding on creditors, as they are not parties to the agreement. Accordingly, notwithstanding the agreement, each party remains obligated to joint creditors. It is extremely important that this be pointed out to clients; otherwise, they may not be getting what they think they agreed to.

Additionally, an indemnification clause should always be included whereby each spouse agrees to reimburse the other if called upon to pay a debt allocated to the other. However, this clause may be of limited utility because the nonpayment probably stems from a lack of funds.

8. General Provision Terms

In all states, boilerplate provisions such as those discussed in this section are routinely included in agreements. However, they should not be included without review because adjustments may need to be made in individual circumstances.

Separation Clause

A typical separation clause reads:

> The husband and wife shall continue to live apart. Each shall be free from interference, molestation, or restraint by the other. Neither shall seek to force the other to live with him or her, or to otherwise interfere with the other's personal liberty.

Despite the language in this clause establishing that neither party shall molest or restrain the other, this clause does not take the place of a protective order and should not be relied on as a substitute for one. In most states, it is not placed on record with the police and is not criminally enforceable.

General Release Clause

> A general release clause reads:

> Each party releases and forever discharges the other from all causes of action, claims, rights, or demands whatsoever, at law or in equity, he or she ever had or now has or can hereafter have against the other, by reason of any matter, cause, or thing from the beginning of the world to the date of this Agreement, except any causes of action for divorce and except further that nothing contained in this Article shall release or discharge either party from such party's covenants, promises, agreements, representations, warranties, or other undertakings or obligations as contained in this Agreement.

As drafted, this boilerplate clause is a very broad release. Each spouse is giving up all rights against the other except for filing for divorce and securing rights pursuant to the agreement. This should be carefully explained to the client, as there may be situations where such a broad waiver is not appropriate.

Waiver of Estate Claim Clause

A waiver of estate claim clause is boilerplate in separation agreements and would read as follows:

> Except as otherwise provided in this Agreement, each party waives, releases, and relinquishes any and all rights that he or she may now have in the property of the other (such as the right of election, dower, courtesy, and inheritance) and all rights he or she may now have or hereafter acquire under the laws of this state or any other jurisdiction:

a. To share, as a result of the marital relationship, in the other party's property or estate upon the latter's death; or

b. To act as executor or administrator of the other's estate, or to participate in the administration thereof.

> This Agreement shall and does constitute a mutual waiver by the parties of their respective rights of election to take against each other's last will and testament now or hereafter in force under the laws of any jurisdiction.
>
> It is the intention of the parties that their respective estates shall be administered and distributed in all respects as though no marriage had been solemnized between them. The consideration for each party's waiver and release is the other party's reciprocal waiver and release.[40]

The primary importance of this clause is to protect each spouse's estate in the event of death before divorce. It serves to shift the statutory consequences of divorce, which is a divestiture of estate rights based on marital status, to the time the agreement is executed.

Entire Understanding Clause

An important clause to include is the following entire understanding clause:

> The husband and wife have incorporated into this Agreement their entire understanding. No oral statement or prior written matter, extrinsic to this Agreement, shall have any force or effect.

This relatively simple clause is important because it prevents either party from enforcing any side agreements. For example, let's say that the wife promises the husband that he can have a certain painting in her possession, but this promise is not reflected in the agreement. After execution, the husband cannot enforce this promise because it is not included in this agreement.

Voluntary Execution Clause

It is also standard to include a clause in the general provisions section of a separation agreement that verifies the parties are entering the agreement at their own free will. Standard language for a voluntary execution clause reads:

> The husband and wife acknowledge that they are entering into this Agreement freely and voluntarily and that they have each obtained independent legal advice; that they have ascertained all the relevant facts and circumstances; that they understand their legal rights; that each is satisfied that he or she has received full disclosure as to the other's finances, assets, income, expectancies, and other economic matters; and that they clearly understand and assent to all of the provisions of this Agreement.

---

[40]This provision is taken from Stephen W. Schlissel, Separation Agreements and Marital Contracts 617-618 (1986).

Modification and Waiver Clauses

The general provisions should also include language requiring that all modifications be in writing, which precludes either party's establishing new rights based on oral representations. An example of a modification and waiver clause is:

> Any modification of this Agreement shall be in writing and shall be duly signed and acknowledged by each party in the same manner as this Agreement. No oral representation or statement shall constitute an amendment, waiver, or modification of the terms of this agreement.

Similarly, language in conjunction with the modification clause addresses rules regarding waivers to the agreement:

> A waiver by either party of any provision of this Agreement shall not prevent or stop such party from enforcing such provision in the future. The failure of either party to insist upon the strict performance of any of the terms and provisions of this Agreement by the other party shall not be a waiver or relinquishment of such term or provision; the same shall continue in full force and effect.

With this language, it is made clear that failure to insist on performance of any term will not modify the agreement and is not a waiver of that party's right to subsequently insist on strict performance. For example, if the wife agreed to take a reduced amount of child support for a few weeks because the husband was having financial difficulties, this would not modify the original agreement and at any point she could again insist on full payment.

Consent to Jurisdiction Clause

A justification clause in general provisions of the agreement typically reads:

> The parties acknowledge that this Agreement is to be construed and governed by the laws of State X. Both parties consent to the continuing jurisdiction of this State in any subsequent action to modify or enforce this Agreement.

Generally, the term "continuing jurisdiction" as used here is understood to refer to jurisdiction over the persons of both parties and is not intended to deal with jurisdiction over subsequent custody disputes.

Severability Clause

A severability clause is included in separation agreements in order to protect the validity of the agreement in the event any provision is found to be invalid or illegal. A clause found to be invalid or illegal would thus be dropped from the agreement without affecting any other clause.

Sample language for this clause would be:

> If any provision of this Agreement shall be held invalid or unlawful by any court of competent jurisdiction, the remainder of this Agreement shall nevertheless remain valid and enforceable according to its terms.

Incorporation and Merger with Spousal Support Exception Clause

At the divorce hearing, the parties' separation agreement is presented to the court for approval. If it is approved, the court incorporates the agreement into the divorce judgment. In effect, through the process of incorporation, the agreement becomes an enforceable order of the court.

Beyond this, the agreement either merges with the court decree and loses any significance as an independent contract, or it survives the incorporation and retains its significance as an independent contract. Whether the agreement merges or survives has important future consequences. If the agreement merges, it ceases to exist as a separate document and is fully modifiable and enforceable as the court's own judgment would be. If the agreement survives, it continues to exist as a contract. This makes modification more difficult because choosing survival over merger usually indicates that the parties intended for the agreement to be permanent. Moreover, if the agreement survives, it is, at least in theory, an independent contract, which may still be enforceable as such.

Consider this standard language:

> At any hearing on the Divorce Complaint, a copy of this Agreement shall be submitted to the court and shall be incorporated and, subject to the below exception, merged into the judgment of divorce and shall not retain any independent legal significance. However, Article Three shall not be merged into the judgment of divorce, but instead shall survive and retain its independent legal significance.

Frequently, as in the sample language agreement, some provisions merge and others survive the incorporation. Here, as is commonly done, the spousal support provisions survive, making modification much more difficult.

MacMillan v. Schwartz

MacMillan v. Schwartz addresses the issue that can arise when parties use incorporation versus merger language in a divorce decree. In this case, the parties entered into a settlement agreement that addressed the circumstances under which Husband would be able to modify the spousal maintenance that he had agreed to pay to Wife. The parties indicated that the settlement agreement was incorporated, but not merged, into the final decree.

As you read *MacMillan v. Schwartz*, look for the following:

1. Why does the court find it necessary to distinguish between merger and incorporation?
2. What language did the parties use in their decree with respect to merger and incorporation?
3. What effect did the fact that the agreement was incorporated, but not merged, have on the court's analysis?

MacMillan v. Schwartz
250 P.3d 1213 (Ariz. Ct. App. 2011)

Gail E. MacMillan ("Wife") appeals from the trial court's order modifying spousal maintenance. Wife argues that the trial court erred in finding her earnings from employment triggered the modification clause of the parties' spousal maintenance agreement and in determining the amount of the modified award. For the reasons that follow, we affirm.

In March 2005, Wife and William C. Schwartz ("Husband") were divorced by consent decree, incorporating into the decree a property settlement agreement ("PSA"). The PSA contained a spousal maintenance clause, which states in pertinent part: Husband shall pay spousal maintenance to Wife in the amount of $6,666.67 per month directly to Wife for a period of eight (8) years commencing April 1, 2005. . . . [F]or purposes of the modification of spousal maintenance the parties agree that in the event that Wife earns income from employment or other active business endeavors of less than $50,000.00 per year the Court shall not consider Wife's earning of said income as a change of circumstances which shall give rise to grounds for modification of said spousal maintenance. Notwithstanding the aforementioned condition, any other condition or conditions associated with change of circumstance, including but not limited to Wife's earnings from employment or from her working in another active business endeavors [sic] of $50,000 per year or greater, may be considered as grounds for modification of said spousal maintenance. The trial court found that this "fairly and equitably provide[d] for the payment of spousal maintenance." Accordingly, it awarded Wife $6666.67 per month in spousal maintenance for a period of eight years beginning April 2005.

. . . In April 2006, Wife began working full-time as a customer service representative at Company Nurse. Wife initially requested a $60,000 salary, but accepted an offer to start at $48,000 on the promise that she be promoted in January 2007 to Client Services manager with a salary of $60,000, full health benefits and matching 401(k) contributions.

. . . In January 2007, Wife became a "senior account manager" at Company Nurse with a $60,000 salary. Wife was paid this salary until August 15, 2007, but later attributed the salary increase to an accounting error and denied that she was promoted. In a letter to Company Nurse dated August 23, 2007, however, Wife stated:

> Effective January 1, 2007, my position and responsibilities here at Company Nurse changed considerably. In an effort to keep the stress to a minimum and protect my health, I have determined that it is in my best interests to return to the original terms

of my employment under which I was hired. Per our discussion, please make the necessary changes to adjust for this agreed upon change. Thank you.

From August 31 through the remainder of the year, Wife received only half her $60,000 salary, resulting in a net salary of $48,000 for 2007. Wife continued to receive full health benefits and matching 401(k) contributions.

In January 2008, Company Nurse began depositing $1000 per month into a deferred compensation plan in which Wife has been the sole participant. Company Nurse set up this plan through Wife's broker. In July 2008, Company Nurse deposited a $12,000 bonus into the plan to compensate Wife for the amount of her "reduced" salary in 2007. Company Nurse knew that Wife's salary could affect her spousal maintenance, but it denied trying to circumvent the "legal requirements of the spousal maintenance agreement between the parties." Company Nurse explained that the plan was an incentive to keep Wife from leaving employment. Combining Wife's salary with the deferred compensation plan, Wife earned an average of $60,000 in 2007, 2008 and 2009.

On May 22, 2009, Husband filed a petition to reduce spousal maintenance to $2500 per month, claiming that Wife's reasonable expenses had decreased because she had been living with her fiancé, that she delayed marrying her fiancé to prevent termination of spousal maintenance, and that her chronic fatigue syndrome had improved to the point where she can continue to be gainfully employed. Wife's fiancé moved out the next month.

In December 2009, Wife filed her own petition to modify spousal maintenance. She argued Husband's income had increased by thirty percent; he has not contributed to the living, medical, or educational expenses of their twenty-three-year-old son; Wife's illnesses might worsen to the point she cannot work; and her earning ability is impaired by age, employment history and physical condition. Wife sought to increase the amount of spousal maintenance to $10,000 per month and to extend the duration until she turns sixty-five (ten additional years).

. . .

After a consolidated hearing on the petitions, the trial court found that Wife's monthly expenses were $6245. It found that Wife earned $4000 per month in salary, another $1000 from the deferred compensation plan, and about $1667 ($20,000 annually) from interest and dividends on capital investments. The trial court then reduced Husband's spousal maintenance obligation to $4250 per month. . . .

Wife timely appeals.

. . .

Under the PSA, the parties agreed that spousal maintenance is modifiable pursuant to A.R.S. §25-327, but if "Wife earns income from employment or other active business endeavors of less than $50,000.00," it would not be considered for modification purposes. Once Wife earned $50,000 or more, however, they agreed that her "earnings from employment or from her working in another active business endeavors [sic] of $50,000 per year or greater" could be considered.

1. Income from Deferred Compensation Plan

The parties dispute whether Wife's earnings from employment trigger the modification clause of the PSA. Specifically, Wife contends that the deferred compensation plan does not fit the technical definition of "income" because she lacked exclusive control over the funds when they were deposited. Therefore, she argues the only applicable "income from employment" is her $48,000 salary, which is insufficient to trigger the modification clause. We disagree.

The consent decree expressly stated that the PSA "is incorporated, but not merged" into the decree. Had merger occurred, the PSA would have become part of the decree, and spousal maintenance would have been modifiable based only on changed circumstances under A.R.S. §25-327(A). See *LaPrader* 189 Ariz. at 247, 941 P.2d at 1272. "Incorporation" of an agreement into a decree has a different purpose than merger. Id. Incorporation is done solely "to identify the agreement so as to render its validity res judicata in any subsequent action based upon it." Id. (citing *Ruhsam v. Ruhsam*, 110 Ariz. 426, 426, 520 P.2d 298, 298 (Ariz. 1974)). In such cases, the agreement retains its independent contractual status and is subject to the rights and limitations of contract law. Id. Because the PSA was incorporated, but not merged, into the decree of dissolution, we must determine the contractual intent of the parties.

We begin by looking to the text of the agreement itself. The PSA states, in pertinent part: "Wife's *earnings* from employment or from her working in another active business endeavors [sic] of $50,000 per year or greater, may be considered as grounds for modification of said spousal maintenance." (Emphasis added.) The plain language of this clause supports Husband's position that the parties intended to consider all of Wife's "earnings" of $50,000 or more.

Husband's position is buttressed by evidence in the record of the parties' intended meaning of Wife's "earnings from income." In Wife's petition for dissolution, she sought spousal maintenance because she "is unable to support herself through appropriate employment," and "lacks *earning ability* in the labor market to support herself." (Emphasis added.) At the modification hearing, Husband testified that he agreed to provide full spousal maintenance because he believed that Wife would be unable to find full-time employment after the divorce. Wife admitted that she had these same concerns about her earning capacity.

In context, the record shows that the parties believed that Wife would have no substantial earning capacity after divorce, but that if she could earn $50,000 or more, it would be sufficient to establish that her earning capacity had changed for the purposes of modifying spousal maintenance. There is no support for Wife's contention that the parties intended to distinguish between "earnings" and "income."

We also disagree with Wife's contention that the deferred compensation plan was merely "anticipated future income" not attributable to present income. See *Richards*, 137 Ariz. at 226, 669 P.2d at 1003 (holding termination of spousal maintenance cannot be based on the anticipation that a party will earn income in the future); *Lopez v. Lopez*, 125 Ariz. 309, 311, 609 P.2d 579, 581 (App. 1980) (social security benefits actually received may be considered income, but wife's social security benefits could not be attributed to husband's income because he neither received them nor had a right to). Courts will not typically look very far into the future to address a probable change in income that may affect spousal maintenance, but will instead delay consideration of the issue until it actually occurs. *Chaney v. Chaney*, 145 Ariz. 23, 26-27, 699 P.2d 398, 401-02 (App. 1985).

Here, the earnings from the deferred compensation plan were neither anticipatory nor speculative. The evidence shows that Company Nurse set up the deferred compensation as an alternative means of paying Wife an equivalent of the $60,000 salary they promised her after January 2007. Company Nurse then deposited $1000 per month into the plan and paid an additional $12,000 bonus for "previous months['] work." Company Nurse believed that Wife was "vested" in the plan and stated that she could withdraw money from the plan after she turned fifty-five in 2010. Wife argues that the account is not in her name, but she is the only participant in the plan. While Wife speculates that she may never collect from the plan due to Company Nurse's financial difficulties, Company Nurse never told her it was in financial trouble, and it continues to deposit $1000 per month into the plan. Even though Company Nurse borrowed $26,000 from the plan, it stated, and Wife admits, it intends to repay that loan in the near future.

We thus conclude that the trial court did not abuse its discretion in determining that the deferred compensation plan combined with Wife's salary to exceed the $50,000 trigger for modification. Once that threshold was crossed, the trial court properly considered those earnings to determine whether Wife has sufficient income to meet her reasonable needs.

. . .

CONCLUSION

For the reasons stated, we affirm the modification of spousal maintenance.

Post-Case Follow-Up

Because the settlement agreement was incorporated, but not merged, into the final decree of dissolution of marriage, the agreement retained its character as an independent contract. Thus, rather than interpreting the ability to modify under the legal standards governing modification of support, the court was free to look at the intent of the parties in determining whether modification was appropriate in this case. The court determined that the intent of the parties was that modification would be triggered in the event that Wife earns at least $50,000 a year and that this included all of Wife's earnings. Had the settlement been merged, the court would have looked strictly to the statutory law for what constituted a change of circumstances.

MacMillan v. Schwartz: Real Life Applications

1. Assume Gail and William included language in their dissolution agreement stating that the agreement would be merged into the final decree. Two years after their divorce, William remarried and seeks to reduce support payments to Gail on the grounds that he is now responsible for supporting his new wife who recently has had to quit her job due to chronic illness that has worsened over the past few

months. Does Gail have a claim that her spousal maintenance should not be modified? What arguments might she be able to make on behalf of her position?

2. The property settlement agreement in *MacMillan v. Schwartz* had a provision that indicated that if Wife earns income from employment of less than $50,000 it would not be considered a change in circumstances. Assume that Gail did not have deferred compensation benefits of $1,000 per month, but just a straight salary of $48,000. Assume also that Gail was offered a promotion that earned $60,000 but turned the promotion down. Would William have a claim for modification of support based upon the fact that Gail could earn more income?

3. Meredith has asked you to write a clause for her settlement agreement that will ensure that her spousal maintenance is not modified unless she earns in excess of $60,000 and that such earned income does not include deferred compensation or other benefits. How would you write the clause in order to protect Meredith from the fate suffered by Gail in the *MacMillan* case?

G. THE DIVORCE HEARING

Once the parties have worked out their differences and reduced their agreement to writing, or it has become clear that a settlement is not possible, either an uncontested hearing or divorce trial is scheduled. We will focus on attention on the former, as it has some unique attributes. As far as divorce trials are concerned, it should, however, be noted that although rules may be applied less rigidly along the way as compared to other types of cases, once a divorce goes to trial, it proceeds with the formality of any other case.

1. The Uncontested Case

In most jurisdictions, the uncontested hearing is a relatively simple matter and may last only for five or ten minutes. The typical hearing occurs in two phases: First is the dissolution phase and second is the separation agreement review phase. Our focus is on cases that are uncontested because the parties have reached an agreement, but a case can also be uncontested because the defendant fails to appear. In the latter situation, the plaintiff must comply with the requirements of the Soldiers and Sailors Relief Act of 1940, which protects members of the military from default judgments. 50 U.S.C. §520. The plaintiff must attest to the fact that the defendant's nonappearance is not because he or she is serving in the military. If uncertain, the plaintiff may need to determine this before the divorce can proceed.

Dissolving the Marriage

During the marital dissolution phase, the plaintiff must establish that the parties have a validly contracted marriage and that the divorce grounds set forth in the complaint actually exist. Where a joint petition has been filed, either or both of the parties would testify to these matters. Establishing grounds is usually little more than a formality, but the court must be satisfied that the requisite elements are present. Also, keep in mind that "uncontested" is not synonymous with "no-fault." Parties can reach agreement regardless of the underlying grounds; thus, one could have an uncontested divorce that is premised on cruel and abusive treatment. However, once agreement is reached, the plaintiff frequently amends the complaint from fault to no-fault grounds.

Approving the Separation Agreement

In the second phase of the typical no-fault hearing, the judge reviews the separation agreement. If it is accepted, the judge will approve it for incorporation into the divorce judgment, and the agreement will either survive or merge in accordance with its terms, as discussed above.

In some states, the primary focus of the review is on procedural fairness. The judge will inquire into whether the parties entered into the agreement freely and voluntarily and whether they understand it. Even where the focus is on procedural rather than substantive fairness, the judge will usually check to see if the child support amount conforms to the guidelines, and if not, will evaluate whether the deviation is justifiable; some judges will also review spousal support arrangements. In other states, there is an additional focus on substantive fairness, and a judge will scrutinize the agreement in its entirety. In some states, judges will reject a term only if it is unconscionable; in others, judges may reject a term that is unfair or significantly favors one side over the other.

Where the judge believes the agreement is unfair, he or she will usually give the parties a chance to correct the problems and resubmit it for approval. If the necessary changes are minor, they can usually be made on the spot, and the hearing can proceed to completion. However, if the unfairness permeates the agreement, such as where one spouse was forced into signing it, the hearing will most likely be suspended until the agreement is reworked or the case recast as a contested one.

Assuming the separation agreement is approved, the judge will enter the divorce judgment. The judgment both dissolves the marriage and incorporates the separation agreement, making it an enforceable order of the court. The timing of the entry of judgment varies from state to state. In some states, the judgment enters at the conclusion of the hearing; in others, it does not enter until a certain amount of time has elapsed. In some states, the initial judgment is in the form of a decree *nisi*. This is an interim judgment, which automatically ripens into a final one unless the parties seek to revoke it. This interim judgment gives the parties a chance to be absolutely certain that they do not wish to reconcile.

Of course, the precise nature of this process varies from jurisdiction to jurisdiction. For example, it may be that rather than filing what is referred to as a joint petition with a separate agreement, the parties in an uncontested case will instead file a request for the court to enter a stipulated judgment reflecting their agreement regarding both the end of the marriage and the terms of dissolution. This request is then submitted to the court for approval, thus making it an enforceable divorce judgment.

2. The Contested Case

Needless to say, when parties are unable to resolve their differences, a divorce case proceeds to trial. In this regard, it should be noted that cases almost never remain contested because the parties are fighting over the divorce grounds; rather, it is because they are unable to reach agreement on one or more of the collateral issues, such as support or custody.

As has been noted previously, procedural rules tend to be applied in a more relaxed fashion in the divorce context. However, once a case is at the trial stage, this is no longer true, and a divorce trial proceeds much like other civil matters, which also means that the parties typically must attend a pretrial conference. If a settlement is not worked out at the pretrial stage, and the case does actually go to trial (note that divorces are bench rather than jury trials), the rules of evidence and civil procedure are in effect. In this regard, some states have specialized rules of domestic procedure that govern divorce trials, while others rely on their general rules of civil procedure, and others still use a combination of the two.

Following the trial, the judge enters the divorce decree that both dissolves the marriage and contains the court's order regarding the issues before it. As in uncontested cases, the judgment may enter as a decree *nisi*. In many jurisdictions, the order must contain detailed findings of fact and conclusions of law. These details can be crucial because much like a separation agreement, this order structures the postmarital relationship between the parties.

As in other civil proceedings, either party may file post-trial motions, with the most common being a motion for a new trial and a motion for relief from judgment. Likewise, the losing party can appeal from the court's final judgment, or from that portion of the judgment that is adverse to him or her. For purposes of appeal, a decree *nisi* is considered the final judgment — and if a party waits until the *nisi* decree ripens into a final decree, the appeal is likely to be untimely.

It is also worth taking a moment to distinguish the above-mentioned post-trial motions, which are brought to challenge the underlying divorce proceeding, from two other actions that have been mentioned elsewhere in the text, which are likewise brought subsequent to a divorce, namely, a motion/complaint for modification and a motion/complaint for contempt (the form of proceeding depends on the jurisdiction). Turning first to modifications, here the basis for the action is that circumstances have changed since the entry of the divorce, making enforcement of a particular provision unfair. It thus does not challenge the validity of the divorce decree as originally entered; rather, it focuses on subsequent events that have since made it unworkable. Accordingly, a modification action can be filed in a case that was initially settled by the parties. In similar fashion, in light of the fact that it is seeking enforcement of the underlying decree, a contempt action likewise presumes the validity of the decree, and thus can likewise be brought in a case that was settled by the parties.

Chapter Summary

■ Good case preparation begins with a well-organized client interview. At this interview, essential information is obtained and a foundation of trust is established. Active listening and respect for the client's emotional concerns are important in establishing an effective relationship.

■ The first formal step in a divorce case is the filing of the complaint (or a joint petition). The complaint and summons are then served on the defendant, who must answer within a certain period of time.

■ Once the case has been initiated, both sides usually engage in the process of discovery, which is used to acquire information about the other side in order to help prepare for trial and/or structure the settlement.

■ Frequently, during the period between filing and the final hearing, motions for temporary orders will be filed asking the court to provide interim relief. The general rule is that advance notice must be given to the other side; however, *ex parte* relief may be allowed where such notice poses a substantial risk of harm.

■ Common motions include those for support, custody, the protection of assets, and protection from abuse.

■ The most common approaches to avoiding trial using dispute resolution are negotiation, where each attorney acts in a representational capacity and seeks to obtain the best possible settlement for his or her client; mediation, where a neutral third party assists the parties to reach agreement on their own; and arbitration, the least common method, in which the dispute is presented to a decision maker who renders a binding decision.

■ A separation agreement occurs when the parties reduce their understanding to a written comprehensive separation agreement. This agreement is comprehensive and must be drafted carefully because it governs the post-divorce relationship between the parties. With the execution of the agreement, the case becomes uncontested, and a relatively simple hearing can be scheduled at which the marriage is dissolved and the agreement reviewed and approved by the court.

■ When an agreement or resolution is not reached, a trial on the merits is scheduled during which a judge resolves the dispute and enters an order reflecting his or her decision.

Applying the Rules

1. Roy comes to your office and advises you that he and his wife Crystal are contemplating a divorce. He has moved out of the house, but has recently learned that Crystal has installed spyware on his computer. He tells you the spyware intercepts his incoming e-mail, and wonders how a court will view this. What questions do you want to ask Roy to determine whether he had ever given Crystal consent to put the spyware on the computer? Assume you take Crystal's

deposition and she advises that she had consent to put eBlaster on the computer because Roy agreed that they needed to put spyware on the computer to prevent their minor children from looking at pornography. Does this affect your advice to Roy?

2. You represent Beverly Ramirez in her current divorce action against her husband Ray Ramirez. You have just completed a round of settlement negotiations. You need to draft the custody and visitation provisions of the separation agreement. Here are the facts to consider as you draft these provisions.

   a. The parties have one child, a daughter named Lucinda, age 8.
   b. Both parents work outside the home, with the mother working about 35 hours per week and the father working about 50.
   c. Both parents have a good relationship with Lucinda, although Mom is clearly the primary parent.
   d. Beverly and Ray cannot stand each other, although they think they can handle joint legal custody.
   e. The real issue is physical custody. The parties have more or less reached agreement as to when each parent will spend time with Lucinda, but they are stuck with how to define the arrangement. Dad is adamant that he not be called the visiting parent, and Mom is adamant that the arrangement not be called joint physical custody. Create a solution for the regular weekly schedule considering the agreed-on time allocations: (1) Lucinda will stay at Mom's house during the school week, with the exception of Wednesday nights, when Dad will pick her up and she will stay with him. (2) Every other week, Lucinda will stay with Dad from 10:00 A.M. on Saturday until schooltime on Monday, and he will take her to school. On the other weekends, he will spend Saturdays from 10:00 A.M. until 8:00 P.M. with her.

3. Assume that you are conducting an initial client interview with a client who is involved in a custody dispute with her husband, and that you become fairly certain the client is lying to you. What do you think you should do at this stage of the process? Do you confront the client? Do you ignore your concerns? Are there any techniques you might use for eliciting the truth? Is it your responsibility to elicit the truth?

4. Assume that you continue working with this client and, despite your concern, have established a good relationship with her. One day she comes into your office and tells you that she has been lying to you and that she is a drug addict and is frequently high when she is with her children. What do you do at this point?

5. You are representing the husband in a divorce case. The parties have three children and are involved in a bitter custody dispute. The husband strongly suspects that the wife has begun dating a local drug dealer and may have begun using drugs herself. He also worries that she is neglecting the children. The children

live with their mom but see their dad fairly regularly. Their ages are 2, 4, and 5. The mom is not employed outside the home. You need to draft a set of interrogatories relevant to custody and that will also reveal the wife's financial situation as child and spousal support are likely to become contested. Draft these interrogatories in a way that will glean useful information but avoid questions that will escalate tensions in a potentially highly volatile situation.

Family Law in Practice

1. Some states have specific laws governing the discovery process in family law cases. Research the procedural rules in your state to determine whether any specific rules exist for discovery in family law cases. If there are no specific rules, do the general civil procedure rules apply in your state?

2. Some state statutes provide that if there is a disparity in income, the party that has the greater financial resources may be required to pay the other side's attorneys' fees. Is there any such statute in your state? What are the requirements and applicable procedures? Research any applicable case law to determine how the statute has been interpreted.

3. Mediation is an effective tool for purposes of resolving family law disputes. Contact a local family law mediator about observing a family law mediation. If your local trial court has a mediation program, it may be possible to observe a mediation program offered through the courts.

4. This assignment requires you to go to your local family court. Observe at least two different types of court procedures, such as a motion session and part of a trial, and then write a paper detailing what you have observed. In your paper you should do the following:

   a. identify all participants in the proceeding, including court personnel, making sure that you use the correct titles;
   b. identify the nature of the proceeding, such as a motion for temporary support;
   c. identify what each side was trying to accomplish and how they were seeking to do this; and
   d. discuss what was most effective, and discuss any weaknesses you identified in either side's presentation of their case.

5. With respect to motion practice in your area, determine the following:

   a. how motions are served;
   b. what the time requirements for service are;
   c. how motions are marked up;

d. when, if ever, accompanying affidavits are required; and

e. whether parties are ever diverted to some kind of settlement process, and if so, under what circumstances.

6. Assume one of your divorce clients has just frantically called to inform you that her husband has just threatened to take the kids out of the country so she will never receive custody of them. Draft an *ex parte* motion with a supporting affidavit seeking to prevent the father from doing this. Draft these documents in accordance with the governing standards in your jurisdiction.

7. Recently, your firm has been receiving more requests for the production of electronically stored information. Some of the more senior attorneys in the firm are not very computer savvy, and they recognize that there are potential pitfalls they should be aware of. Prepare an interoffice memo that explains some of the complexities of this process so no member of the firm inadvertently compromises client confidentiality or makes other mistakes. You should use the information in this chapter as your starting point, but you should also find two law journal articles that go into greater depth regarding some of the potential pitfalls of responding to requests for ESI, and incorporate this information into your memo.

Jurisdiction

This chapter focuses on jurisdiction. As a general rule, a court must have both subject matter and personal jurisdiction over the defendant in order to render a binding judgment. With respect to divorce and custody actions, jurisdictional concepts are best understood if examined in relationship to specific aspects of the proceeding, as different considerations come into play at different points in the process. Specifically, we will look at the jurisdictional standards that govern the dissolution of the marital relationship, the award of support, the distribution of property, and the determination of custody.

It is important to be attuned to jurisdictional considerations and any relevant time periods within which jurisdiction must be asserted. When you are interviewing clients, inquire into where each party resides, how long each party has resided in that particular location, and the location of any marital property. There may be several choices for jurisdiction based upon the answer to these questions. Depending on the law in each state that can obtain jurisdiction, it may be important for your client to consider whether he or she would benefit from filing for a dissolution of marriage in a particular state.

A. SUBJECT MATTER AND PERSONAL JURISDICTION

To briefly review, **subject matter jurisdiction** refers to the authority of a court to hear a particular type of dispute, and is almost always established by statute. In contrast to personal jurisdiction, under which a party can voluntarily assent to jurisdiction, parties cannot confer subject matter jurisdiction on a court, and a judgment that is rendered by a court that lacks

Key Concepts

- Jurisdiction of a court to dissolve a marriage
- Jurisdiction to make, enforce, and modify child and spousal support awards
- Jurisdiction to divide property
- Jurisdiction to make, enforce, and modify custody determinations

423

subject matter jurisdiction is void. In most states, exclusive subject matter jurisdiction over divorce actions—including all collateral issues such as support, property, and custody—is vested in a specialized court, which is commonly known as the **family court** or the **family and probate court**.

Personal jurisdiction refers to a court's ability to exercise authority over a defendant. The exercise of jurisdiction must conform to the requirements of the Due Process Clause of the Fourteenth Amendment, which has been interpreted to mean that a state may not exercise authority over a defendant who lacks a sufficient relationship with that state. Accordingly, questions regarding a defendant's relationship with the forum state are often quite important to resolve in cases involving parties who live in different states. Of course, a plaintiff can always file an action in the defendant's home state, but this is typically more expensive, time-consuming, and inconvenient.

Consistent with the Due Process Clause, states can acquire personal jurisdiction over a defendant based on domicile, minimum contacts, consent, or presence.

1. *Domicile.* States have personal jurisdiction over all persons who are domiciled within its borders. A **domicile** is the place that a person considers to be his or her permanent home—the place the person leaves from and returns to. It is important to be aware of the distinction between "domicile" and "residence." A person may have several places of residence, such as a college dorm or one's family home, but may only have one domicile.
2. *Minimum contacts.* A state may exercise personal jurisdiction over a nonresident defendant who has sufficient **minimum contacts** with the state such that it is not unfair to require him or her to return to the state and respond to a lawsuit there.

    To implement this minimum contacts rule, all states have enacted **long-arm statutes**, which specify the kinds of contacts that will give rise to personal jurisdiction. Contacts typically include the following: transacting business within the state, owning property within the state, or committing a tortious act within the state. A few states have elected not to enumerate the qualifying contacts but instead employ statutory language to the effect that the state will permit the exercise of jurisdiction to the fullest extent possible under the Due Process Clause. As touched on below, many states have also enacted special long-arm provisions for use in family law cases, including, as discussed in Chapter 6, the Uniform Interstate Family Support Act (UIFSA), which contains a broad, long-arm provision for the assertion of jurisdiction over nonresident defendants in support matters.
3. *Consent.* A nonresident may consent to jurisdiction and thereby agree to submit him- or herself to the authority of the court.
4. *Presence.* A state can exercise personal jurisdiction over a nonresident who is physically present and personally served with a summons within that state.

B. DOES THE COURT HAVE JURISDICTION TO DISSOLVE THE MARRIAGE?

Having just set out the importance of personal jurisdiction, we immediately bump up against the well-worn maxim that for every rule, there is an exception. In this instance, divorce provides the exception to that requirement, as states have the power to dissolve a marriage based upon the domiciliary status of the plaintiff even if it does not have personal jurisdiction over the defendant. This does not mean, however, that it may have jurisdiction over the marital property if the property is located in another state.

1. The Importance of Domicile

When it comes to divorce, the plaintiff's relationship with the forum state, assuming other requirements are met, may be sufficient to give the state jurisdiction to dissolve the marriage despite the defendant having no relationship to the state. The classic rationale for this domicile rule comes from the Supreme Court's decision in the 1942 case of *Williams v. North Carolina* (*Williams I*), 317 U.S. 287 (1942). This case involved two individuals from North Carolina who each independently moved to Las Vegas (which had a very short residency requirement) and subsequently divorced their North Carolina spouses and then married each other. Most likely they were engaged in the practice of what was commonly referred to as a "migratory" divorce by which an unhappy spouse in the pre–no-fault era moved to another state in order to take advantage of its more relaxed divorce rules.

Las Vegas Wedding Chapel
Carol M. Highsmith, Library of Congress, Washington, D.C.

The newlyweds were then convicted of bigamous cohabitation by a North Carolina court. This presented the Supreme Court with the question of whether North Carolina was required to honor the Nevada divorce decrees under the Full Faith and Credit Clause based on the fact that the plaintiffs were legally domiciled there. Answering this question in the affirmative, the *Williams* Court explained:

> Each state as a sovereign has a rightful and legitimate concern in the marital status of persons domiciled within its borders. The marriage relation creates problems of large social importance. Protection of offspring, property interests, and the enforcement of

marital responsibilities are but a few of the commanding problems in the field of domestic relations with which the state must deal. Thus it is plain that each state . . . can alter within its own borders the marriage status of the spouse domiciled there, even though the other spouse is absent.

Id. at 298-299. In this regard, it is important to note that the holding in *Williams I* was premised on the assumption that the plaintiffs were in fact properly domiciled in Nevada.

Limiting the full reach of this decision, when the case reached the Supreme Court a second time, the Court, in the *Williams II* decision, held that although the "fact that the Nevada court found that they were domiciled there is entitled to respect and more" this finding did not preclude the North Carolina court from reexamining the question of whether the plaintiffs were properly domiciled in Nevada or not. *Williams v. North Carolina*, 325 U.S. 226, 233-234 (1945). The result in this case thus means that the in-state spouse who does not consent to the divorce may collaterally attack a divorce judgment rendered in another state based on the fact that the plaintiff was not actually domiciled there, but had instead gone there for the purpose of obtaining a divorce. If successful, the ensuing divorce judgment would not be entitled to full faith and credit.

In this regard, the Supreme Court subsequently ruled in *Sherrer v. Sherrer* that where a spouse actually participates in the out-of-state divorce and thus has had *the opportunity* to be heard on the issue of the plaintiff's domiciliary status, the doctrine of *res judicata* bars him or her from collaterally attacking the divorce judgment. 33 U.S. 343 (1948).

According to the Court, what matters here is that the defendant *had the opportunity* to contest the bona fides of the plaintiff's domiciliary status, not that he or she actually availed him- or herself of the chance to do so.

Many commentators have suggested that this domicile rule is out of keeping with the modern jurisdictional emphasis on the relationship of the defendant to the adjudicating state and recommend that a minimum contacts standard be used in divorce cases, as it is in other civil actions.[1] However, an important concern is that such a shift could prevent domestic violence victims from being able to file for divorce in a state that they have fled to escape abuse because the minimum contacts requirement would not be satisfied unless the defendant happened to have a qualifying relationship with that state. Accordingly, the victim would be forced to return to her prior home state (or if the defendant had moved, to his new home state) in order to file a divorce. Thus, so long as the plaintiff is domiciled in the state, the plaintiff may seek a divorce from a spouse who is absent from the state.

---

[1]*See* Courtney Joslin, Modernizing Divorce Jurisdiction: Same-Sex Couples and Minimum Contacts, 91 B.U. L. Rev. 1669 (2012); Rhonda Wasserman, Divorce and Domicile: Time to Sever the Note, 39 Wm. & Mary L. Rev. 1 (1997).

Case Preview

In re Marriage of Kimura

This matter involved the dissolution of marriage between Ken and Fumi, two Japanese citizens. Ken had come to the United States several years earlier to work. At the time of filing the action for dissolution of marriage, he worked and lived in Iowa and had permanent residency status. However, his wife Fumi lived in Japan and had never been to Iowa and had no contact with Iowa. Fumi filed a pre-answer motion to challenge the district court's jurisdiction to dissolve the marriage. She alleged the court did not have subject matter over the action or personal jurisdiction over her and therefore could not dissolve the marriage.

As you read *In re Marriage of Kimura*, look for the following:

1. Why did the court deny the wife's motion asserting that the court lacked subject matter jurisdiction over the divorce?
2. How does the court justify dissolving the marriage in the absence of personal jurisdiction over the wife?
3. What is the divisible divorce doctrine and how is it applied in this case?

In re Marriage of Kimura
471 N.W.2d 869 (Iowa 1991)

LAVORATO, Justice.

[Ken and Fumi were married in Japan in 1965. They had two adult children. The parties had lived apart since 1973 when Ken came to the United States. At the time of filing a petition for dissolution in December 1988 he was employed as a pediatric surgeon at the University of Iowa, in Iowa City. He alleged he had resided in Iowa for more than one year and he further alleged that there was a breakdown of the marital relationship.]

In February 1989 Fumi filed a preanswer motion in which she contested the district court's subject matter and personal jurisdiction. She asked that the Iowa proceedings be dismissed or abated.

[The district court denied Fumi's motion concluding that it had subject matter jurisdiction to grant a divorce even if it could not decide any issues requiring personal jurisdiction. Fumi thereafter filed an answer to Ken's petition denying, among other things, that Ken was a resident of Iowa for more than one year, denying the petition was filed in good faith, and denying that Ken's residency in Iowa was in good faith. Fumi did not personally appear at the final hearing, but appeared through her attorney. After the court heard evidence of Ken's residency status and the breakdown of the marriage, it dissolved the marriage of Ken and Fumi. Fumi appealed.]

II. THE DUE PROCESS CHALLENGE

Fumi poses the issue this way: "Iowa's assertion of jurisdiction over respondent (who has no contacts with Iowa) or her marriage based solely on petitioner's alleged residence in Iowa violates the due process clauses of the United States and Iowa Constitutions."

The federal fourteenth amendment prohibits a state from "depriv[ing] any person of life, liberty, or property, without due process of law. . . ." U.S. Const. amend. XIV, §1. Its counterpart is found in article I, section 9 of the Iowa Constitution and is virtually the same: "[N]o person shall be deprived of life, liberty, or property, without due process of law." When state and federal constitutional provisions contain a similar guarantee, we usually deem them to be identical in scope, import, and purpose. *State v. Scott*, 409 N.W.2d 465, 467 (Iowa 1987).

Early on, due process required the personal presence of the defendant in the forum state as a condition for rendering a binding personal or in personam judgment against the defendant. *Pennoyer v. Neff*, 95 U.S. 714, 733, 24 L. Ed. 565, 572 (1878). The rule was expanded in *International Shoe Co. v. Washington*, 326 U.S. 310, 66 S. Ct. 154, 90 L. Ed. 95 (1945). Now due process does not require such personal presence. Due process only requires that the defendant have certain minimum contacts with the forum state.

. . .

In *Williams v. North Carolina*, 317 U.S. 287, 63 S. Ct. 207, 87 L. Ed. 279 (1942) [hereinafter *Williams I*], the question was whether full faith and credit had to be given to a foreign divorce decree where only one spouse was domiciled in the foreign state and the other spouse had never been there. *Williams I*, 317 U.S. at 298-99, 63 S. Ct. at 213, 87 L. Ed. at 286. The Supreme Court held that the foreign state's high interest in the marital status of its domiciliaries required that full faith and credit be given such a decree. Id. The Court did require, however, that substituted service on the absent spouse meet due process standards, that is, reasonably calculated to give the absent spouse actual notice and an opportunity to be heard. Id.

In *Williams I* the Court had difficulty classifying dissolution proceedings. Though it did not view such proceedings as in rem actions neither did it view them as mere in personam actions. Id. at 297, 63 S. Ct. at 212-13, 87 L. Ed. at 285. According to the Court, domicile of one spouse within the forum state gave that state the power to dissolve the marriage regardless of where the marriage occurred. Id. at 298, 63 S. Ct. at 213, 87 L. Ed. at 286. This court too has deemed domicile as essential to dissolution of marriage jurisdiction.

The cases generally adopt the following explanation of the components for a dissolution of marriage proceeding:

> It is commonly held that an essential element of the judicial power to grant a divorce, or jurisdiction, is domicil. A court must have jurisdiction of the res, or the marriage status, in order that it may grant a divorce. The res or status follows the domicils of the spouses; and therefore, in order that the res may be found within the state so that the courts of the state may have jurisdiction of it, one of the spouses must have a domicil within the state.

Williams v. North Carolina reached the Supreme Court a second time. The Court held that while the finding of domicile by the state that granted the decree is entitled to prima facie weight, it is not conclusive in a sister state but might be relitigated there. *Williams v. North Carolina*, 325 U.S. 226, 238-39, 65 S. Ct. 1092, 1099, 89 L. Ed. 1577, 1586 (1945) [*Williams II*].

The divisible divorce doctrine emerged in *Estin v. Estin*, 334 U.S. 541, 549, 68 S. Ct. 1213, 1218, 92 L. Ed. 1561, 1568-69 (1948). In *Estin* the Court held that Nevada in an ex parte divorce proceeding could change the marital status of those domiciled within its boundaries. . . . But Nevada could not wipe out the absent spouse's claim for alimony under a New York judgment in a prior separation proceeding because Nevada had no personal jurisdiction over the absent spouse. Id. at 548-49, 68 S. Ct. at 1218, 92 L. Ed. at 1568. . . .

The divisible divorce doctrine simply recognizes the court's limited power where the court has no personal jurisdiction over the absent spouse. In these circumstances the court has jurisdiction to grant a divorce to one domiciled in the state but no jurisdiction to adjudicate the incidents of the marriage, for example, alimony and property division. In short, the divisible divorce doctrine recognizes both the in rem and in personam nature of claims usually raised in dissolution of marriage proceedings.

. . .

We conclude that . . . jurisdiction to grant . . . a dissolution is not to be tested by the minimum contacts standard of *International Shoe*.

We further conclude that domicile continues to be the basis for a court's jurisdiction to grant a dissolution of marriage decree. So the courts of this state have the power to grant dissolution of marriage decrees provided the petitioner is domiciled in this state. Such power exists even though the petitioner's spouse is absent from this state, has never been here, and was constructively rather than personally served.

. . .

No claim is made that the service of process here did not meet the requirements of due process. So we are left with the question whether Ken established his domicile or residency in this state.

[After deciding Ken had established residency in the state the court found that] [t]he district court did not violate Fumi's rights under either the federal or state constitutions when it dissolved the marriage even though the court had no personal jurisdiction over her."

AFFIRMED.

Post-Case Follow-Up

The court affirms the district court's granting of a divorce even though the court acknowledges it has no personal jurisdiction over wife. The court reasons that while it may not have jurisdiction over issues of alimony or division of property, it has the jurisdictional authority to dissolve the marriage based on the domiciliary status of the husband. Correspondingly, had the husband not met the domicile requirements, the court would have lacked subject matter jurisdiction over the divorce.

The case provides an example of the interplay between subject matter jurisdiction and personal jurisdiction. A state may have subject matter to dissolve the marriage because the state has an interest in the marital status of its residents, but it cannot adjudicate interest in the property that is part of the marriage absent having personal jurisdiction over the respondent.

In re Marriage of Kimura: Real Life Applications

1. Dan and Darla have lived apart for the past three years. Dan resides in California and Darla resides in Iowa where she has a teaching job. Darla comes to your office and informs you that she would like a divorce in Iowa. Darla meets the residency requirements. She asks you whether she can file for divorce in Iowa.

   a. Based upon your reading of *In re Marriage of Kimura*, what do you tell her?
   b. What questions would you like to ask Darla to determine whether California might also have jurisdiction to grant a divorce?
   c. What factors would be important to consider in helping Darla decide between filing in California or Iowa?

2. Karen and Gary lived in Arizona until Karen moved from Arizona to Arkansas with the parties' two minor children, moving into Karen's mother's home. Karen claims she moved to Arkansas for employment and as part of that employment, she was required to obtain off-site job training at a place of her employer's choosing. Her employer chose to send her to a training center in Minnesota. She left with the children to go to Minnesota. She returned to Arkansas for two weeks around Christmas, but returned to Minnesota in order to complete the required training. She then returned to Arkansas. Within two weeks of returning to Arkansas, she filed for divorce. Assume the law in Arkansas requires that a party reside in the state for more than 60 days prior to the filing of a divorce action.

   a. Does Arkansas have subject matter jurisdiction to dissolve the marriage?
   b. Does Arkansas have personal jurisdiction to dissolve the marriage?

2. Durational Residency Requirements

As discussed above, a state's authority to dissolve a marriage rests upon the domiciliary status of the plaintiff. In turn, domicile requires residency in the forum state, although by itself this is not enough — domicile also requires an intent to make that state one's permanent home. Zeroing in on the issue of residency itself, most states have implemented durational requirements that a party must satisfy before he or she can file a divorce in that jurisdiction. These requirements typically range in length from two months to a year. Although satisfaction of the durational requirement may be evidence of domiciliary intent, it is not usually dispositive of the matter.

In this regard, it should also be noted that the terms "residence" and "domicile" are often used interchangeably, which can be quite confusing. Adding to this potential confusion is the fact that some states may actually allow a divorce to be filed based upon the satisfaction of a mere residency requirement, although the judgment would then be vulnerable to attack in a collateral proceeding by the spouse residing in the non-forum state.

Durational residency requirements clearly have an impact on the ability of a party who has recently moved to a new state to file a divorce there. Although an individual can certainly return to his or her originating state to initiate the action, this can be quite burdensome. Perhaps most significantly, this is not a viable option for a victim of domestic violence who fled her home state in order to escape abuse. However, as the next case makes clear, these requirements have been found to be constitutional.

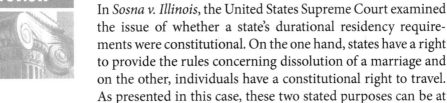

Case Preview

Sosna v. Illinois

In *Sosna v. Illinois*, the United States Supreme Court examined the issue of whether a state's durational residency requirements were constitutional. On the one hand, states have a right to provide the rules concerning dissolution of a marriage and on the other, individuals have a constitutional right to travel. As presented in this case, these two stated purposes can be at odds with one another when a party moves to a state, seeks a divorce, but does not meet the durational residency requirements.

As you read *Sosna v. Illinois*, look for the following:

1. What arguments does Carol Sosna raise in response to the claim that she does not meet Iowa's durational requirements?
2. What are the state interests in imposing durational requirements?
3. How does the Court distinguish previous durational residency laws that were found invalidated on the ground that they created two classes of persons and thus interfered with the constitutional right to travel?

Sosna v. Illinois
419 U.S. 393 (1975)

Mr. Justice Rehnquist delivered the opinion of the Court.

Appellant Carol Sosna married Michael Sosna on September 5, 1964, in Michigan. They lived together in New York between October 1967 and August 1971, after which date they separated but continued to live in New York. In August 1972, appellant moved to Iowa with her three children, and the following month she petitioned the District Court of Jackson County, Iowa, for a dissolution of her marriage. Michael Sosna, who had been personally served with notice of the action when he came to Iowa to visit his children, made a special appearance to contest the jurisdiction of the Iowa court. The Iowa court dismissed the petition for lack of jurisdiction, finding that Michael Sosna was not a resident of Iowa and appellant had not been a resident of the State of Iowa for one year preceding the filing of her petition.

. . .

The durational residency requirement under attack in this case is a part of Iowa's comprehensive statutory regulation of domestic relations, an area that has long been regarded as a virtually exclusive province of the States. . . .

The statutory scheme in Iowa, like those in other States, sets forth in considerable detail the grounds upon which a marriage may be dissolved and the circumstances in which a divorce may be obtained. . . .

The imposition of a durational residency requirement for divorce is scarcely unique to Iowa, since 48 States impose such a requirement as a condition for maintaining an action for divorce. As might be expected, the periods vary among the States and range from six weeks to two years. The one-year period selected by Iowa is the most common length of time prescribed.

Appellant contends that the Iowa requirement of one year's residence is unconstitutional for two separate reasons: first, because it establishes two classes of persons and discriminates against those who have recently exercised their right to travel to Iowa, thereby contravening the Court's holdings in *Shapiro v. Thompson, Dunn v. Blumstein*, and *Memorial Hospital v. Maricopa County*; and, second, because it denies a litigant the opportunity to make an individualized showing of bona fide residence and therefore denies such residents access to the only method of legally dissolving their marriage.

State statutes imposing durational residency requirements were, of course, invalidated when imposed by States as a qualification for welfare payments, *Shapiro*; for voting, *Dunn*; and for medical care, *Maricopa County*. But none of those cases intimated that the States might never impose durational residency requirements, and such a proposition was in fact expressly disclaimed. What those cases had in common was that the durational residency requirements they struck down were justified on the basis of budgetary or recordkeeping considerations which were held insufficient to outweigh the constitutional claims of the individuals. But Iowa's divorce residency requirement is of a different stripe. Appellant was not irretrievably foreclosed from obtaining some part of what she sought, as was the case with the welfare recipients in *Shapiro*, the voters in *Dunn*, or the indigent patient in *Maricopa County*. She would eventually qualify for the same sort of adjudication which she demanded virtually upon her arrival in the State. Iowa's requirement delayed her access to the courts, but, by fulfilling it, she could ultimately have obtained the same opportunity for adjudication which she asserts ought to have been hers at an earlier point in time.

. . .

Iowa's residency requirement may reasonably be justified on grounds other than purely budgetary considerations or administrative convenience. A decree of divorce is not a matter in which the only interested parties are the State as a sort of "grantor," and a divorce petitioner such as appellant in the role of "grantee." Both spouses are obviously interested in the proceedings, since it will affect their marital status and very likely their property rights. Where a married couple has minor children, a decree of divorce would usually include provisions for their custody and support. With consequences of such moment riding on a divorce decree issued by its courts, Iowa may insist that one seeking to initiate such a proceeding have the modicum of attachment to the State required here.

Such a requirement additionally furthers the State's parallel interests both in avoiding officious intermeddling in matters in which another State has a paramount interest, and in minimizing the susceptibility of its own divorce decrees to collateral attack. A State such as Iowa may quite reasonably decide that it does not wish to become a divorce mill for unhappy spouses who have lived there as short a time as appellant had when she commenced her action in the state court after having long resided elsewhere. Until such time as Iowa is convinced that appellant intends to remain in the State, it lacks the "nexus between person and place of such permanence as to control the creation of legal relations and responsibilities of the utmost significance." *Williams v. North Carolina*, 325 U.S. 226, 229, 65 S. Ct. 1092 1095, 89 L. Ed. 1577 (1945). Perhaps even more important, Iowa's interests extend beyond its borders and include the recognition of its divorce decrees by other States under the Full Faith and Credit Clause of the Constitution, Art. IV, §1. For that purpose, this Court has often stated that "judicial power to grant a divorce—jurisdiction, strictly speaking—is founded on domicil." *Williams*, supra. . . .

We therefore hold that the state interest in requiring that those who seek a divorce from its courts be genuinely attached to the State, as well as a desire to insulate divorce decrees from the likelihood of collateral attack, requires a different resolution of the constitutional issue presented than was the case in *Shapiro*, supra, *Dunn*, supra, and *Maricopa County*, supra.

. . .

Affirmed.

Mr. Justice MARSHALL, with whom Mr. Justice BRENNAN joins, dissenting.

The Court today departs sharply from the course we have followed in analyzing durational residency requirements since *Shapiro v. Thompson*, 394 U.S. 618, 89 S. Ct. 1322, 22 L. Ed. 2d 600 (1969). Because I think the principles set out in that case and its progeny compel reversal here, I respectfully dissent.

As we have made clear in *Shapiro* and subsequent cases, any classification that penalizes exercise of the constitutional right to travel is invalid unless it is justified by a compelling governmental interest. . . .

The Court omits altogether what should be the first inquiry: whether the right to obtain a divorce is of sufficient importance that its denial to recent immigrants constitutes a penalty on interstate travel. In my view, it clearly meets that standard. The previous decisions of this Court make it plain that the right of marital association is one of the most basic rights conferred on the individual by the State. . . .

Having determined that the interest in obtaining a divorce is of substantial social importance, I would scrutinize Iowa's durational residency requirement to determine whether it constitutes a reasonable means of furthering important interests asserted by the State. . . .

I conclude that the course Iowa has chosen in restricting access to its divorce courts unduly interferes with the right to "migrate, resettle, find a new job, and start a new life." *Shapiro v. Thompson*, 394 U.S., at 629, 89 S. Ct., at 1328. I would reverse the judgment of the District Court and remand for entry of an order granting relief if the court finds that there is a continuing controversy in this case.

Post-Case Follow-Up   In rejecting the plaintiff's challenge to Iowa's durational residency requirement, the Court stressed that in the divorce context, states have a right to insist that an individual be genuinely attached to that state as a prerequisite to filing for divorce. By doing so, the Court also finds it will insulate the ultimate divorce decree from collateral attack in another court. Unlike the situation where a party may be barred from obtaining services or benefits as the result of a durational residency requirement, in the case of a divorce, a party does not irretrievably lose a part of what she was seeking on account of the delay. Thus, durational requirements for purposes of divorce are constitutionally permissible.

Sosna v. Illinois: Real Life Applications

1. Alba and Sam have resided in North Dakota for the past five years. Alba has recently moved to South Carolina where the durational requirement to obtain a divorce is one year. Alba files for a divorce in South Carolina shortly after moving there. After Alba files for divorce, Sam files for divorce in North Dakota, and specially appears in South Carolina to dismiss the divorce action. What should be the result?

2. Jenny and Scott have been married for 40 years, residing for most of that time in Arizona. They have two adult daughters. One lives in Arizona and the other lives in California. After selling their home in Arizona, they move in with their adult daughter in California while looking for a rental home. They find a home and sign a lease on it, but shortly thereafter, Scott becomes despondent about the move and tries to convince Jenny to move back to Arizona. Jenny refuses and Scott moves back to Arizona to live with their other daughter. The residency requirement for a divorce in Arizona is 90 days. Scott files for divorce after being back in Arizona for 60 days. Jenny cannot yet file for divorce in California because California requires a party be domiciled for six months before he or she can file for divorce.

   a. What arguments can Jenny make that Arizona does not have jurisdiction?
   b. What arguments can Scott make that Arizona should exercise jurisdiction?
   c. What ruling should the court make if Jenny contests jurisdiction?
   d. Would it make a difference if Jenny appears in court and submits to the court's jurisdiction?

3. The Domestic Relations Exception to Federal Diversity Jurisdiction

Although neither Article III (the relevant constitutional provision) nor the federal diversity statute "mandate the exclusion of domestic relations cases from federal court jurisdiction," the Supreme Court made clear in its 1992 decision in *Akenbrandt v. Richards* that this is a time-honored exclusion. 504 U.S. 689, 693 (1992). As it explained, in addition to being grounded in the Court's longstanding interpretation of the federal Judiciary Act of 1789,[2] it also reflects the fact that state courts are "more eminently suited" than their federal counterparts to exercise the continued jurisdiction that is often required in domestic relations cases on account of their "close association with state and local government organizations dedicated to handling issues that arise out of conflicts over divorce, alimony, and child custody decrees."[3] In reaching this result, the *Akenbrandt* Court made clear that the domestic relations exception to diversity jurisdiction "encompasses only cases involving the issuance of a divorce, alimony, or child custody decree."[4]

C. DOES THE COURT HAVE JURISDICTION TO AWARD SUPPORT?

As discussed above, jurisdiction to dissolve a marriage is based on domicile — personal jurisdiction over the defendant is not required. However, as discussed in this section, when it comes to support, a state must have personal jurisdiction over a defendant in order for its decree to be entitled to full faith and credit in sister states.

Domicile Requirements

Several states do not have a durational residency requirement for domicile for the filing of a divorce. For example, in Alaska, South Dakota, and Washington, it is sufficient that you are a resident at the time the divorce is filed. However, there may be a waiting period after the filing before the court will grant a divorce. In South Dakota, the waiting period is 60 days and in Washington it is 90 days. Thus, it would appear that unless the residency requirement is met during these waiting periods, a court may find that there is no jurisdiction to grant a divorce.

In addition, if a spouse moves to one of these states and files an action for divorce, it is still possible for the other spouse who resides outside the state to attack the jurisdiction of the court on the residency grounds. If the spouse does not have a bona fide home in the state, or has no intent to remain, it is possible to allege that the residency requirement is not met. Thus, showing a lack of change of address, failing to register to vote in the state, failure to obtain a driver's license in the state, or not paying taxes in the state may be evidence that the spouse has no good faith intention of remaining in the state and is merely using the courts to obtain a divorce.

1. The Divisible Divorce

Given the different jurisdictional standards, it is possible that a state could have the authority to dissolve a marriage based on the domiciliary status of the plaintiff, but

---

[2]However, as the *Akenbrandt* Court itself acknowledges, the majority opinion in the referenced precedent case of *Barber v. Barber*, 62 U.S. 582 (1859), is a bit murky with respect to whether it actually reached this conclusion. *Akenbrandt*, 504 U.S. at 699 n.7.
[3]504 U.S. at 703.
[4]*Id.* at 704.

lack the personal jurisdiction necessary to enter either a child or spousal support award. This may result in what is often referred to as a "divisible divorce."

The Supreme Court first addressed this issue in its 1948 *Estin v. Estin* decision, 334 U.S. 541 (1948). In this case, the parties resided together as husband and wife in New York, until the husband left his wife. She filed a separation action in New York, which the court allowed based on his desertion, and also awarded her monthly support. The husband subsequently was granted a divorce in Nevada, which he claimed nullified the existing support order. Rejecting the husband's position, the Court explained that although the Nevada decree dissolving the marriage was entitled to full faith and credit, that court did not have the authority to effectuate a change in the wife's support rights in the absence of personal jurisdiction over her. *Id.* at 548-549. As the Court specifically stated: "The result in this situation is to make the divorce divisible — to give effect to the Nevada decree insofar as it affects marital status and to make it ineffective on the issue of alimony." *Id.* at 549.

A decade later, in the case of *Vanderbilt v. Vanderbilt*, the Court made clear that the divisible divorce doctrine was equally applicable in cases in which there was no prior order of support. 354 U.S. 416 (1957). In this case, the parties separated while living together in California. The husband moved to Nevada where he obtained a divorce and the wife moved to New York. The husband asserted that the Nevada divorce extinguished any duty of support that he owed his wife. The Court again rejected this argument, and instead concluded that the Nevada divorce court, which did not have personal jurisdiction over the wife, lacked the "power to extinguish a right that she had under the law of New York to financial support from her husband." *Id.* at 418. Accordingly, Nevada decree was deemed to be null and void to the extent that it "purported to affect the wife's right to support . . . and the Full Faith and Credit clause did not obligate New York to give it recognition." *Id.* at 419.

Personal Jurisdiction Under UIFSA

Personal jurisdiction under Section 201 of the Uniform Interstate Family Support Act exists to establish or enforce a support order in the forum state under any of the following circumstances:

1. The individual is personally served in the state.
2. The individual submits to jurisdiction by consent.
3. The individual resides with the child in the state.
4. The individual resided in the state and provided prenatal expenses or support for the child.
5. The child resides in the state as a result of the acts or directives of the individual.
6. The individual engaged in sexual intercourse in the state and the child may have been conceived by that act of intercourse.
7. The individual asserted parentage on a birth certificate filed in this state.
8. There is any other basis consistent with the constitutions of the tribunal state or the United States for the exercise of personal jurisdiction.

2. Long-Arm Jurisdiction

As the above discussion makes clear, long-arm statutes can play a particularly important role in the divorce context as they may enable a state to assert personal jurisdiction over a nonresident based on his or her contacts, thus obviating the necessity of a divisible divorce (or of the plaintiff having to initiate the action in the other spouse's home state). In addition to having a general all-purpose long-arm statute, many states have enacted specific domestic relations long-arm laws.

These may authorize the assertion of long-arm jurisdiction over a nonresident when that state had been the marital domicile of the parties. This is often a time-limited option, and personal jurisdiction will continue for only a fixed period of time, perhaps for a year or two, after the individual has left the state. Once this time period has run, the state loses its ability to assert personal jurisdiction over the defendant unless there are other independent qualifying bases. Of course, time is of the essence in these situations. Additionally, as discussed in Chapter 6, all states have enacted the Uniform Interstate Family Support Act (UIFSA), which contains a fairly sweeping long-arm provision that a state can use to acquire personal jurisdiction over a nonresident defendant to establish a spousal or child support order. However, as the classic case of *Kulko v. Superior Court* reminds us, regardless of which long-arm statute is utilized in an effort to obtain personal jurisdiction over a nonresident defendant, the exercise of authority must satisfy the fairness requirement of the Due Process Clause of the Fourteenth Amendment.

Case Preview	*Kulko v. Superior Court*

Kulko addresses the issue of a state's ability to exercise personal jurisdiction over a nonresident parent for purposes of child support when that parent has permitted the children to reside out of state with the other parent. In this case, the parties, who had been married in California, lived in New York for more than ten years before they separated. They had two children, both born in New York.

At the time of the separation, Mother moved to California. The parties obtained a divorce in Haiti, but entered into a separation agreement in New York. Under the agreement, the children were to stay with Father during the school year, and would go with Mother during certain vacation times and during the summer. Father agreed to pay $3,000 per year in child support. Approximately a year later, the parties' daughter went to live with Mother during the school year, and thereafter, the parties' son also went to live with Mother. Mother then brought an action in California to modify custody to give her full custody and to increase her child support.

As you read *Kulko v. Superior Court*, look for the following:

1. What contacts did Mother argue Father had with the state of California that were sufficient to find personal jurisdiction?
2. What bearing did the fact that Mother had moved out of state and Father remained in the state of the marital domicile have on the Court's holding?
3. What effect did the fact Mother could assert her right for modification of child support in the state where Father resided have on the Court's holding?

Kulko v. Superior Court
436 U.S. 84 (1978)

Mr. Justice MARSHALL delivered the opinion of the Court.

The issue before us is whether, in this action for child support, the California state courts may exercise in personam jurisdiction over a nonresident, nondomiciliary parent of minor children domiciled within the State. For reasons set forth below, we hold that the exercise of such jurisdiction would violate the Due Process Clause of the Fourteenth Amendment.

I

[Father and Mother were married in 1959 in California during father's three-day stopover en route from a military base in Texas on his way to a tour of duty in Korea. At the time of the marriage both parties were domiciled in New York, where Mother returned after the marriage. After Father's tour of duty, he also returned to New York, where they had two children.] The Kulkos and their two children resided together as a family in New York City continuously until March 1972, when the Kulkos separated.

Following the separation, Sharon Kulko moved to San Francisco, Cal. A written separation agreement was drawn up in New York; in September 1972, Sharon Kulko flew to New York City in order to sign this agreement. The agreement provided, inter alia, that the children would remain with their father during the school year but would spend their Christmas, Easter, and summer vacations with their mother....

The children resided with [Father] during the school year and with their mother on vacations, as provided by the separation agreement, until December 1973. At this time, just before Ilsa [their daughter] was to leave New York to spend Christmas vacation with her mother, she told her father that she wanted to remain in California after her vacation. [Father] bought his daughter a one-way plane ticket, and Ilsa left, taking her clothing with her. Ilsa then commenced living in California with her mother during the school year and spending vacations with her father. In January 1976, appellant's other child, Darwin, called his mother from New York and advised her that he wanted to live with her in California. Unbeknownst to [Father], [Mother] sent a plane ticket to her son, which he used to fly to California where he took up residence with his mother and sister.

Less than one month after Darwin's arrival in California, [Mother] commenced this action against [Father] in the California Superior Court.... [Father] appeared specially and moved to quash service of the summons on the ground that he was not a resident of California and lacked sufficient "minimum contacts" with the State under *International Shoe Co. v. Washington,* 326 U.S. 310, 316, 66 S. Ct. 154, 158, 90 L. Ed. 95 (1945), to warrant the State's assertion of personal jurisdiction over him.

[The trial court denied his motion to quash and the appellate court affirmed the denial of the motion to quash reasoning that, by consenting to his children's living in California, appellant had "caused an effect in th[e] state" warranting the exercise of jurisdiction over him. The California Supreme Court affirmed the ruling.]

II

. . .

The parties are in agreement that the constitutional standard for determining whether the State may enter a binding judgment against appellant here is that set forth in this Court's opinion in *International Shoe Co. v. Washington, supra*: that a defendant "have certain minimum contacts with [the forum State] such that the maintenance of the suit does not offend 'traditional notions of fair play and substantial justice.' " 326 U.S., at 316, 66 S. Ct., 13, 418, 96 L. Ed. 485 (1952).

Like any standard that requires a determination of "reasonableness," the "minimum contacts" test of *International Shoe* is not susceptible of mechanical application; rather, the facts of each case must be weighed to determine whether the requisite "affiliating circumstances" are present. We recognize that this determination is one in which few answers will be written "in black and white. The greys are dominant and even among them the shades are innumerable." *Estin v. Estin*, 334 U.S. 541, 545, 68 S. Ct. 1213, 1216, 92 L. Ed. 1561 (1948). But we believe that the California Supreme Court's application of the minimum-contacts test in this case represents an unwarranted extension of *International Shoe* and would, if sustained, sanction a result that is neither fair, just, nor reasonable.

A.

. . . [T]he California Supreme Court did not rely on [Father]'s glancing presence in the State some 13 years before the events that led to this controversy, nor could it have. [Father] has been in California on only two occasions, once . . . for a three-day military stopover on his way to Korea, . . . and again in 1960 for a 24-hour stopover on his return from Korean service. To hold such temporary visits to a State a basis for the assertion of in personam jurisdiction over unrelated actions arising in the future would make a mockery of the limitations on state jurisdiction imposed by the Fourteenth Amendment. Nor did the California court rely on the fact that appellant was actually married in California on one of his two brief visits. We agree that where two New York domiciliaries, for reasons of convenience, marry in the State of California and thereafter spend their entire married life in New York, the fact of their California marriage by itself cannot support a California court's exercise of jurisdiction over a spouse who remains a New York resident in an action relating to child support.

Finally, in holding that personal jurisdiction existed, the court below carefully disclaimed reliance on the fact that [Father] had agreed at the time of separation to allow his children to live with their mother three months a year and that he had sent them to California each year pursuant to this agreement. . . .

The "purposeful act" that the California Supreme Court believed did warrant the exercise of personal jurisdiction over [Father] in California was his "actively and fully consent[ing] to Ilsa living in California for the school year . . . and . . . sen[ding] her to California for that purpose." We cannot accept the proposition that [Father's] acquiescence in Ilsa's desire to live with her mother conferred jurisdiction over [Father] in the California courts in this action. A father who agrees, in the interests of family harmony and his children's preferences, to allow them to spend more time in California than was required under a separation agreement can hardly be said to have "purposefully availed himself" of the "benefits and protections" of California's laws. . . .

Nor can we agree with the assertion of the court below that the exercise of in personam jurisdiction here was warranted by the financial benefit appellant derived from his daughter's presence in California for nine months of the year. This argument rests on the premise that, while [Father]'s liability for support payments remained unchanged, his yearly expenses for supporting the child in New York decreased. But this circumstance, even if true, does not support California's assertion of jurisdiction here. Any diminution in [Father]'s household costs resulted, not from the child's presence in California, but rather from her absence from [Father]'s home. . . .

B

In light of our conclusion that [Father] did not purposefully derive benefit from any activities relating to the State of California, it is apparent that the California Supreme Court's reliance on [Father]'s having caused an "effect" in California was misplaced. . . .

The circumstances in this case clearly render "unreasonable" California's assertion of personal jurisdiction. . . .

Finally, basic considerations of fairness point decisively in favor of [Father]'s State of domicile as the proper forum for adjudication of this case, whatever the merits of appellee's underlying claim. It is appellant who has remained in the State of the marital domicile, whereas it is appellee who has moved across the continent. . . .

. . .

Reversed.

Mr. Justice BRENNAN, with whom Mr. Justice WHITE and Mr. Justice POWELL join, dissenting.

The Court properly treats this case as presenting a single narrow question. That question is whether the California Supreme Court correctly "weighed" "the facts," of this particular case in applying the settled "constitutional standard," that before state courts may exercise in personam jurisdiction over a nonresident, nondomiciliary parent of minor children domiciled in the State, it must appear that the nonresident has "certain minimum contacts [with the forum State] such that the maintenance of the suit does not offend 'traditional notions of fair play and substantial justice.' " *International Shoe Co. v. Washington*, 326 U.S. 310, 316, 66 S. Ct. 154, 158, 90 L. Ed. 95 (1945). The Court recognizes that "this determination is one in which few answers will be written 'in black and white,' " *ante*, at 92. I cannot say that the Court's determination against state-court in personam jurisdiction is implausible, but, though the issue is close, my independent weighing of the facts leads me to conclude, in agreement with the analysis and determination of the California Supreme Court, that appellant's connection with the State of California was not too attenuated, under the standards of reasonableness and fairness implicit in the Due Process Clause, to require him to conduct his defense in the California courts. I therefore dissent.

Post-Case Follow-Up

Although arising in the context of a child support modification, the Court goes back to the basic principles that to be bound by a judgment a defendant must have certain minimum contacts with the state attempting to exercise jurisdiction so that the suit does not offend " 'traditional notions of fair play and substantial justice.' " The mere fact that a parent may permit a child to reside with the other parent out of state is not enough to confer jurisdiction over the parent. Nor is the fact that there may be some financial benefit to the parent by having the child live out of state sufficient to confer jurisdiction.

Instead, when the action arises from an agreement that was entered into in another state, and modification is sought in the state where the parent objecting to jurisdiction has had virtually no contact, it is unreasonable for a state to exercise personal jurisdiction over that parent.

Kulko v. Superior Court: Real Life Applications

1. After Margaret and Tom divorced, Tom moved to Illinois. The two minor children remained in Kansas with Margaret during the school year and spent their summers in Illinois with Tom. The parties followed the parenting plan for three years until the older son, Charlie, age 12, asked to reside with his father during the school year. Margaret consented, and at the end of the summer, the younger son, Garrett, returned to Margaret in Kansas and Charlie remained with his father in Illinois. The following summer, Garrett also asked if he could remain in Illinois for the school year with Father. The parents agreed informally between them that the parenting plan would be revised in order to permit the boys to go to school in Illinois and to spend their summers with Mother in Kansas. Tom now wants to serve Margaret in Illinois with a complaint for modification in which he is seeking to end his child support obligation and to have Margaret pay child support to him now that the children are living with him for a significantly greater portion of the year.

   a. Does the Illinois court have jurisdiction over Margaret based upon *Kulko*?
   b. What additional facts would you need to give an informed opinion?
   c. Assuming Tom files for modification of child support, what would you recommend that Margaret do if she objects to jurisdiction?

2. Until the time of divorce, Robert and Jill live in Connecticut where they were both born and raised, and went to school and married. They have one child, Bobby, age 3. Although they lived in Connecticut, Robert and Jill worked in New York and commuted to work on the train. The parties have shared custody. Jill comes to your office and states that she would like to move to New York. She indicates that Robert has agreed she may take Bobby with her to New York. Robert will arrange to see Bobby two nights a week after work and take him

home with him every other weekend. Jill asks you if it will be possible for her to file an action in New York to modify child support, or if that is something she needs to do before she moves. She is afraid if she asks to modify the support before she moves, Robert may not be agreeable to her moving with Bobby. What do you advise Jill?

D. DOES THE COURT HAVE JURISDICTION TO DIVIDE PROPERTY?

The jurisdictional rules regarding property distribution are more complex than they are with respect to support and will be set out as a series of general principles:

1. As a foundational matter, jurisdiction is not premised upon domicile as it is for the divorce itself.
2. If the court has personal jurisdiction over the defendant, it may effectuate a division of all property located within its borders.
3. Even if it has personal jurisdiction over the defendant, a court cannot directly affect title to property that is located outside the state. However, it may be able to accomplish this result indirectly by ordering the defendant to convey title to the property. In short, based on its authority over the defendant, a court can require him or her to take actions that affect how the property is held, even though the court is unable to affect title directly.
4. Even if a court lacks personal jurisdiction over a defendant, it may be able to effectuate a division of property based on its authority over property located within its borders. This is known as *in rem* **jurisdiction**. As a general rule, to satisfy due process requirements, *in rem* jurisdiction requires a connection between the underlying cause of action and the claims to the property—a connection that would be satisfied in the divorce context.

    It should, however, be noted that many commentators have challenged the fairness of this approach given the direct lack of connection between the defendant and the forum state, and have called for its replacement by the minimum contacts standard. Accordingly, when it comes to effectuating a division of property involving a nonresident defendant, the applicable jurisdictional standards may well be in a state of flux.

E. DOES THE COURT HAVE JURISDICTION TO DETERMINE CUSTODY?

Traditionally, most states exercised jurisdiction over child custody matters based on the physical presence of the child within its borders. Although this rule usually meant that the court that granted the divorce had jurisdiction over the initial custody determination, it also served to encourage a dissatisfied spouse to remove his or her children to a new state in order to relitigate the issue in the hope of a more favorable outcome. In addition to encouraging parental removals, this approach often resulted in multiple and frequently conflicting decrees resulting in an enforcement nightmare.

In 1968, prompted by this jurisdictional morass, the National Conference of Commissioners on Uniform State Laws (NCCUSL) approved the Uniform Child Custody Jurisdiction Act (UCCJA) in the hope that consistent jurisdictional standards would deter the removal or kidnapping of children, eliminate interstate jurisdictional competition, and prevent states from relitigating custody decisions from other states. Although states responded favorably to the adoption of the UCCJA, loopholes in the law kept interstate jurisdictional tensions alive. In 1997, in an effort to address these ongoing problems, the National Conference adopted the Uniform Child Custody Jurisdiction and Enforcement Act (UCCJEA), which replaces the UCCJA. Currently, all states except for Massachusetts have adopted the UCCJEA.[5] In the meantime, at the federal level, in 1980, Congress enacted the Parental Kidnapping Prevention Act (PKPA) in an effort to address the ongoing and interrelated problems of parental removals and interstate jurisdictional conflicts that had clearly not been fully resolved by the UCCJA. 28 U.S.C. §1738A (1994).

Before turning our attention to these Acts, it is important to bear in mind that interstate (and international) custody cases are among the most complex in the family law field and contain many traps for the unwary. This section will provide you with a basic overview of key jurisdictional rules; however, you should be aware that these Acts contain many other important rules, such as those pertaining to notice and disclosure, which are not addressed here. Moreover, it also does not discuss other laws that might come into play in an interstate custody case, such as the full faith and credit provisions of the Violence Against Women Act[6] or the laws governing conflicts involving Native American children.[7] So by way of a caution, when handling a divorce case, it is imperative that you elicit a complete and detailed narrative from your client regarding the present and past locations of both parties and the children as this information can have important jurisdictional implications.

1. Jurisdictional Requirements Under the UCCJEA

In this section, we consider the four jurisdictional bases for initial custody determinations under the UCCJEA: (1) home state, (2) significant connection, (3) emergency, and (4) last resort.[8] We then look at when a state may assume modification jurisdiction under these Acts and the full faith and credit requirement of PKPA. An important consideration underlying this Act is that in contrast to the traditional

---

[5]The text of the UCCJEA can be found at http://www.uniformlaws.org/shared/docs/child_custody_jurisdiction/uccjea_final_97.pdf (accessed June 8, 2016).

[6]18 U.S.C. §2265. Although our focus here is on custody disputes that arise in the context of divorce actions, it should be noted that the UCCJEA and PKPA apply to a wide range of child custody determinations including, for example, those arising in a proceeding for neglect, abuse, dependency, and protection from domestic violence.

[7]In this situation, reference must also be made to the Indian Child Welfare Act of 1978, 25 U.S.C. §§1901 et seq., the Indian Civil Rights Act of 1968, 25 U.S.C. §§1301 et seq., and the appropriate Tribal Code.

[8]*See* UCCJEA Section 201, available online at http://www.uniformlaws.org/ (accessed Mar. 5, 2015).

approach, the mere physical presence of a child in a state is not sufficient to confer jurisdiction; in fact, with the exception of emergency jurisdiction, the physical presence of a child, although preferred, is not an essential prerequisite to a state's assumption of jurisdiction.

UCCJEA DEFINITIONS

§102. Definitions

. . .

(2) "Child" means an individual who has not attained 18 years of age.

(3) "Child-custody determination" means a judgment, decree, or other order of a court providing for the legal custody, physical custody, or visitation with respect to a child. The term includes a permanent, temporary, initial, and modification order. The term does not include an order relating to child support or other monetary obligation of an individual.

(4) "Child-custody proceeding" means a proceeding in which legal custody, physical custody, or visitation with respect to a child is an issue. The term includes a proceeding for divorce, separation, neglect, abuse, dependency, guardianship, paternity, termination of parental rights, and protection from domestic violence, in which the issue may appear. The term does not include a proceeding involving juvenile delinquency, contractual emancipation, or enforcement. . . .

. . .

(7) "Home State" means the State in which a child lived with a parent or a person acting as a parent for at least six consecutive months immediately before the commencement of a child-custody proceeding. In the case of a child less than six months of age, the term means the State in which the child lived from birth with any of the persons mentioned. A period of temporary absence of any of the mentioned persons is part of the period.

(8) "Initial determination" means the first child-custody determination concerning a particular child.

(9) "Issuing court" means the court that makes a child-custody determination for which enforcement is sought under this [Act].

(10) "Issuing State" means the State in which a child-custody determination is made.

(11) "Modification" means a child-custody determination that changes, replaces, supersedes, or is otherwise made after a previous determination concerning the same child, whether or not it is made by the court that made the previous determination.

Home State Jurisdiction

A state that is or has been the child's home may assert "home state" jurisdiction over a custody dispute. A home state is the state in which a child has lived for six continuous months or, if the child is younger than six months, has lived in from birth. Temporary absences from the state do not stop the running of the clock but are included in the time computation.

A state may exercise jurisdiction if it is the child's home state at the commencement of the custody proceeding or if it was the child's home state within six months prior to the commencement of the proceeding. Once a state acquires "home state" status, it can retain that status for six months after the departure of the child so long as a parent or a parent substitute remains in that state.

Significant Connection Jurisdiction

A state may exercise "significant connection" jurisdiction in situations where it has a significant connection with the child and at least one contestant, and substantial evidence is available in that state that is relevant to the merits of the custody determination.

In contrast to the UCCJA, which did not prioritize between home state and significant connection jurisdiction thus potentially leaving open the possibility of a conflict between two states, under the UCCJEA, a state may only exercise significant connection jurisdiction if there is no home state, or the home state has declined jurisdiction. In short, the Act plugs this hole by prioritizing home state over significant connection jurisdiction (as discussed below, PKPA does the same).

Emergency Jurisdiction

A state may exercise emergency jurisdiction where the child is physically present in the state and has been abandoned or needs emergency protection from abuse or neglect or it is necessary in an emergency "to protect the child because the child, or a sibling or parent of the child, is subjected to or threatened with mistreatment or abuse." 28 U.S.C. §1738A (1994.) Although the child must be physically present, the endangerment need not have occurred within that state. Courts are generally cautious when proceeding under this section and will generally assume emergency jurisdiction only in "extraordinary circumstances." Also, most courts will assume emergency jurisdiction only on a temporary basis to stabilize the situation and will then refer the case back to the state with either home state or significant connection jurisdiction.

UCCJEA EMERGENCY JURISDICTION

§204. Temporary Emergency Jurisdiction

(a) A court of this State has temporary emergency jurisdiction if the child is present in this State and the child has been abandoned or it is necessary in an emergency to protect the child because the child, or a sibling or parent of the child, is subjected to or threatened with mistreatment or abuse.

(b) If there is no previous child-custody determination that is entitled to be enforced under this [Act] and a child-custody proceeding has not been commenced in a court of a State having jurisdiction [under this Act] a child-custody determination made under this section remains in effect until an order is obtained from a court of a State having jurisdiction [under this Act]. If a child-custody proceeding has not been or is not commenced in a court of a State having jurisdiction [under this Act], a child-custody determination made under this section becomes a final determination, if it so provides and this State becomes the home State of the child.

(c) If there is a previous child-custody determination that is entitled to be enforced under this [Act], or a child-custody proceeding has been commenced in a court of a State having jurisdiction under [this Act], any order issued by a court of this State under this section must specify in the order a period that the court considers adequate to allow the person seeking an order to obtain an order from the State having jurisdiction under [this Act]. The order issued in this State remains in effect until an order is obtained from the other State within the period specified or the period expires.

(d) A court of this State which has been asked to make a child-custody determination under this section, upon being informed that a child-custody proceeding has been commenced in, or a child-custody determination has been made by, a court of a State having jurisdiction under Sections 201 through 203, shall immediately communicate with the other court. A court of this State which is exercising jurisdiction pursuant to Sections 201 through 203, upon being informed that a child-custody proceeding has been commenced in, or a child-custody determination has been made by, a court of another State under a statute similar to this section shall immediately communicate with the court of that State to resolve the emergency, protect the safety of the parties and the child, and determine a period for the duration of the temporary order.

Modification Jurisdiction

An important goal of the UCCJA was to limit the ability of states to modify custody determinations of other states to prevent the proliferation of potentially conflicting orders. Accordingly, under the Act, a state could modify the custody order of another state only if it appeared that the decree state no longer had jurisdiction and the new state could assert jurisdiction in accordance with the UCCJA. This means that the initial decree state should have exclusive **modification jurisdiction**, sometimes referred to as exclusive **continuing jurisdiction**, until such time as it could no longer satisfy the jurisdictional requirements of the UCCJA.

However, as with initial custody determination, it was also possible that two states could simultaneously assert modification jurisdiction. For example, let's say that state A makes an initial determination giving custody to Mom, with visitation rights to Dad. Mom then moves to state B with the child, but the child visits Dad regularly in state A. What happens if Dad files a modification action in state A ten months after Mom's departure? At this point in time, home state status has shifted to state B, but state A still has a connection to the child and one parent and could thus claim significant connection jurisdiction. But if Mom then filed a modification action in state B, that court could decide that A's connection is not significant enough to retain authority over the case and that modification jurisdiction had shifted to state B, the child's present home state.

To address this problem, the UCCJEA (as well as PKPA) provides for continuing, exclusive modification jurisdiction in the initial state (subject to the emergency jurisdiction exception) until one of two determinations are made: (1) the initial state determines that it no longer has jurisdiction because it lacks a significant connection to the case and substantial evidence is no longer available there, or (2) it is established that neither the child nor either parent still lives there. UCCJEA §201.2. Returning to our example, under the UCCJEA, state *B* could not modify the initial order based on its status as the home state, unless state *A* first determined that it no longer had a significant connection to the case. Given the facts, this is unlikely, as the dad still lives there, the child left the state only ten months earlier, and the child still visits there on a regular basis.

UCCJEA MODIFICATION

§203. Jurisdiction to Modify Determination

Except as otherwise provided in Section 204, a court of this State may not modify a child-custody determination made by a court of another State unless a court of this State has jurisdiction to make an initial determination under Section 201(a)(1) or

(2) and:

(1) the court of the other State determines it no longer has exclusive, continuing jurisdiction under Section 202 or that a court of this State would be a more convenient forum under Section 207; or

(2) a court of this State or a court of the other State determines that the child, the child's parents, and any person acting as a parent do not presently reside in the other State.

Declining Jurisdiction

In addition to determining when a state may properly assume jurisdiction over a custody dispute, the UCCJEA also encourages states to decline jurisdiction under certain circumstances. Based on the doctrine of *forum non conveniens*, states are encouraged to decline jurisdiction if it is an inconvenient forum and another state is in a better position to hear the case. *Id.* §207. Further, based on the "clean hands" doctrine, states are urged to refuse jurisdiction where the petitioner has engaged in wrongful conduct such as improperly removing a child from the home state. *Id.* §208. However, as the comments to the Act make clear, a parent who has fled a state with a child for good cause, such as to escape from violence, should not be penalized by this provision even if her conduct is "technically illegal."[9]

---

[9]Uniform Child Custody Jurisdiction and Enforcement Act (1997), 43. http://www.uniformlaws.org/shared/docs/child_custody_jurisdiction/uccjea_final_97.pdf (accessed June 8, 2016).

Case Preview

Welch-Doden v. Roberts

This case involves an attempt to determine "home state" jurisdiction when the child has moved between states in the six months immediately prior to commencement of an action. Under the UCCJEA, the home state of the child is the state where the child has lived with a parent or a person acting as a parent for at least six consecutive months immediately before commencement of a child custody proceeding. However, what happens if the child has not been in the state in which a proceeding is filed for the six consecutive months prior to that time? The Arizona Court of Appeals in *Welch-Doden* examines this question in determining whether Arizona or Oklahoma is the home state of the minor child.

As you read *Welch-Doden v. Roberts*, look for the following:

1. What is the time frame the court finds important for determining jurisdiction?
2. Why was Mother trying to obtain jurisdiction in Arizona?
3. Why does the court look to the purposes behind adoption of the UCCJEA?
4. What does the court say about the "best interest" standard in determining jurisdiction?

Welch-Doden v. Roberts
42 P.3d 1166 (Ariz. Ct. App. 2002)

This special action arises from the trial court's dismissal of a petition for dissolution of marriage, with a minor child, due to lack of jurisdiction. [Mother and Father were married in Arizona in November 1996 and thereafter moved to Oklahoma where the child was born on April 28, 1999. Mother and the child moved back and forth between Arizona and Oklahoma. They were in Oklahoma for seven and a half months after the birth, then Arizona for three months, Oklahoma for six months, and then Arizona for the four months prior to Mother filing a Petition for Dissolution of Marriage in Arizona. After being served, Father filed a petition for divorce and custody in Oklahoma. He then appeared specially to contest jurisdiction in the Arizona action.]

After hearing from both sides and conferring with the Oklahoma trial judge, the trial judge ruled that Oklahoma had home state jurisdiction pursuant to UCCJEA....

[After ruling that Arizona did not have jurisdiction, the Oklahoma court granted Father's divorce petition and awarded custody to Father, thereby requiring the child, who was living with Mother in Arizona, to be transferred to Father's custody. Mother filed this special action requesting a stay of the Arizona order dismissing her action.]

. . .

We consider several issues: First, does the UCCJEA provide that home state jurisdiction is based on a child residing in a state (a) for a six-month period immediately prior to the filing of a custody petition, or (b) for a six-month period that is completed at any time within six months of the filing?

[The second issue is whether a state without home state jurisdiction may consider the child's best interest for jurisdiction purposes. The final issue is whether a state with home state jurisdiction has priority when a petition is filed first in another state.]

All of the issues pertain to the question of jurisdiction to make an initial custody determination. . . .

THE RELEVANT STATUTES AND THE STATUTORY CONFLICT

[Under the UCCJEA §201 as adopted by Arizona, the Arizona court has] jurisdiction when Arizona qualifies as a home state. If a state is the "home state" under this section, it has jurisdiction. There is no further factual inquiry on the jurisdictional issue. Paragraphs (2)-(4) of subsection A provide the circumstances whereby Arizona may have jurisdiction when it does not qualify as the home state. Paragraph 2, in particular, requires the court to consider whether the child has a significant connection to the state (as well as other factors) before jurisdiction may be found. Subsection C clarifies that the presence of the child is neither necessary nor sufficient to establish jurisdiction.

. . . [A]s it relates to the present case, we must also take into account the statutory definition of "home state." [The UCCJEA] defines "home state" as follows:

> The state in which a child lived with a parent or a person acting as a parent for at least six consecutive months immediately before the commencement of a child custody proceeding, including any period during which that person is temporarily absent from that state.

> . . .

Specifically, . . . a state has jurisdiction if the "home state" qualifier is met under either one of two elements:

> This state is the [1] home state of the child on the date of the commencement of the proceeding, or [2] was the home state of the child within six months before the commencement of the proceeding and the child is absent from this state but a parent or person acting as a parent continues to live in this state.

The definition of "home state" provides, however, that a state is a "home state" only when "a child lived with a parent . . . for *at least six consecutive months immediately before the commencement of a child custody proceeding.*" [Emphasis added.]

Thus, applying literally the definition of "home state" from [§102(7)] to element one of §201(a)(1) renders superfluous the language . . . that says jurisdiction lies when a state is the home state "on the date of the commencement of the proceeding." That latter phrase merely restates what is already required by the definition of "home state." . . .

Element two of [§201(a)(1)] poses a more significant problem in statutory construction when the home state definition [§102] is applied: the two statutes directly conflict. Element two . . . provides that a state has jurisdiction if it is the "home state . . . within six months before" the commencement of the child custody proceeding.

Section [102,] as noted above, requires that in order to be a "home state" at all, a child must have lived in a state for six consecutive months "immediately before" the child custody proceeding. Thus, if a child's home state two months before a proceeding was commenced is different from the state to which a child has permanently moved (and in which the proceeding was commenced), §[102(7)] would indicate there is no home state at all. Initial jurisdiction would then be determined based on substantial connections to the state and other factors. . . . On the other hand, under the same facts, element two . . . would declare the prior state the home state because it was the home state within six months of the filing. Initial jurisdiction would then be in the prior state regardless of any significant connections to the state in which the filing was made.

The statutory conflict is directly at issue here. The child lived in Oklahoma for six consecutive months ending in September 2000. The child then resided in Arizona for the next four months, immediately before the petition was filed in January 2001. Thus, under father's (and the trial judge's) reading of the statute, Oklahoma is the home state as a matter of law. . . . Oklahoma, under this view, was the home state (from March to September 2000) within six months of the filing of the petition in January 2001 and thus has initial jurisdiction.

Under mother's reading of the statute, however, neither Oklahoma nor Arizona is the home state as neither state meets the requirement of [the definition of home state under the UCCJEA] that the child live in the state "for at least six consecutive months immediately before the commencement" of the proceeding. Under that scenario, Oklahoma does not have initial jurisdiction. The trial court would be required to hold a hearing to determine whether there were significant connections with Arizona and other factors . . . to determine whether Arizona should have initial jurisdiction. Thus, depending upon how one resolves the conflict between these competing interpretations, the outcome may differ.

STANDARDS FOR STATUTORY CONSTRUCTION

In construing statutes, we have a duty to interpret them in a way that promotes consistency, harmony, and function. The primary purpose "is to determine and give effect to the legislative intent behind the statute, considering among other things the context of the statute, the language used and the spirit and purpose of the law." *Midland Risk Management Co. v. Watford*, 179 Ariz. 168, 171, 876 P.2d 1203, 1206 (App. 1994).

To appropriately resolve the conflict here, it is critical to examine the stated purposes behind the changes in home state jurisdiction brought about by the UCCJEA.

THE PURPOSE BEHIND HOME STATE JURISDICTION UNDER THE UCCJEA

The original drafters of the UCCJA (the predecessor to the UCCJEA) had assumed that home state jurisdiction was the most appropriate factor in demonstrating the best interests of the child. They also thought that a state should be able to proceed without delay and, therefore, should find jurisdiction on any acceptable basis. Thus, the drafters included the four separate bases for jurisdiction. However, state courts were split as to whether the four bases were equal or whether home state was preferred.

Additionally, in 1981 a significant federal statute was passed by the United States Congress. That statute, the Parental Kidnapping Prevention Act ("PKPA"), 28 U.S.C. §1738A, was aimed at interstate custody problems that continued to exist after the adoption of the UCCJA. It mandated states to apply full faith and credit to interstate custody decisions. Importantly, it did not allow for full faith and credit on the four bases as set forth in the UCCJA. Instead, enforceability under the PKPA was based on the priority of home-state jurisdiction:

> A child custody or visitation determination made by a court of a State is consistent with the provisions of this section *only if such State (i) is the home State of the child on the date of the commencement of the proceeding, or (ii) had been the child's home State within six months* before the date of the commencement of the proceeding and the child is absent from such State because of his removal or retention by a contestant or for other reasons, and a contestant continues to live in such State.

28 U.S.C. §1738A(c)(2)(A) (emphasis added).

In 1997, the National Conference of Commissioners on Uniform State Laws, which had authored the UCCJA, drafted the UCCJEA. The main purposes for revising the UCCJA were uniformity and the need to avoid disputes between competing jurisdictions. . . .

The UCCJEA drafters dealt specifically with the conflict created by differing jurisdictions taking contrary views of the four bases of jurisdiction. They reconciled the jurisdictional provisions of the UCCJA with the PKPA:

> The UCCJA, however, specifically authorizes four independent bases of jurisdiction without prioritization. Under the UCCJA, a significant connection custody determination may have to be enforced even if it would be denied enforcement under the PKPA [which prioritizes home state jurisdiction]. *The UCCJEA prioritizes home state jurisdiction*[.]

9 U.L.A. 650-51 (emphasis added). The drafters made it clear that the new act was to give priority to a finding of home state jurisdiction over any other jurisdictional provisions.

Furthermore, the UCCJEA completely eliminates a determination of "best interests" of a child from the jurisdictional inquiry. These changes advance a more efficient and "bright line" jurisdictional rule consistent with the UCCJEA's purpose. . . .

It is clear from the drafters' intent that the UCCJEA should be construed to promote one of its primary purposes: avoiding the jurisdictional competition and conflict that flows from hearings in competing states when each state substantively reviews subjective factors (such as "best interests") for purposes of determining initial jurisdiction. With this fundamental purpose in mind, when there is a statutory conflict in the application of home state jurisdiction, the conflict should be resolved to strengthen (rather than dilute) the certainty of home state jurisdiction. This course is consistent with the UCCJEA's statutory purpose.

. . .

Given the fundamental purpose of the UCCJEA . . . [w]e hold that "home state" for purposes of determining initial jurisdiction . . . is not limited to the time period of "six consecutive months immediately before the commencement of a child custody proceeding[.]" Instead, the applicable time period to determine "home state" in such circumstances is "within six months before the commencement of the [child custody] proceeding." This interpretation promotes the priority of home state jurisdiction that the drafters specifically intended. To adopt the reading that mother supports would result in narrowing home state jurisdiction. It would increase the number of potentially conflicting jurisdictional disputes in competing jurisdictions. This is contrary to the UCCJEA's purpose.

. . .

Thus, we conclude that the trial court did not err in rejecting mother's position and concluding that Oklahoma had home state jurisdiction.

[Mother also contended that even if Arizona is not the home state of the child, the court is still required to determine if the exercise of jurisdiction by Arizona is in the child's best interest. However, the "best interests" analysis does not take place in determining jurisdiction. "Best interests" may be fully explored and considered in the context of a request that the home state not exercise jurisdiction because it is an "inconvenient forum" but that motion must be made in Oklahoma. Similarly, Mother's first in time argument fails because the first in time filing must be in a state having jurisdiction under the UCCJEA.]

For the foregoing reasons, the trial court did not err in determining that it was without jurisdiction to consider mother's child custody request. Therefore, we deny mother's requested relief.

Post-Case Follow-Up

Mother had contended that it was in the best interest of the minor child to stay with her in Arizona. However, the court makes clear that while the best interest test is the appropriate substantive standard in custody disputes, it cannot be used to confer jurisdiction on a court. Rather, as *Welch-Doden* makes clear, jurisdictional priority goes to the home state under the UCCJEA. However, a home state may decide to decline jurisdiction because another jurisdiction is more convenient or has a more substantial connection to the child.

Welch-Doden v. Roberts: Real Life Applications

1. Lilly and Ralph were married in 2013 and had a child in December 2014. The family lived in North State until March 2015, when Lilly and the child moved to South State. Mother allowed Father to have regular visits with the child until November 2015 when she stopped the visits and all contact with Father. Mother filed a petition for dissolution and sought sole custody of the minor child in December 2015. Which state has jurisdiction over the custody determination under the UCCJEA?

2. Assume that Lilly moved back to North State in December 2015 and stayed until February 2016 and then moved back to South State. Lilly files her petition for dissolution of marriage seeking sole custody of the minor child in South State when she returns to South State in February 2016. Does South State have home state jurisdiction?

3. Assume the same facts in Question 1 except that Ralph, upon learning that Lilly has moved to South State, files his own action in North State in August 2015 but does not serve it until after he learns of Lilly's filing in December 2015. Which state is the home state of the minor child?

4. Melody and Jorge are the parents of Stefani, age 13, and Jacob, age 10. The parties decided to divorce and Jorge moved to East State to take a temporary employment position that was to last one year. Melody and the children remained in West State. Neither party filed a divorce or custody action, as the parties decided they would wait until Jorge returned to West State before proceeding with the divorce. Two months after Jorge moved, Melody had to take care of her mother who had recently had a stroke. She suggested that Jorge temporarily take the children to reside with him in East State until he came back to West State. The children immediately went to stay with Jorge. Six months after the children went to live with Jorge in East State, he filed for dissolution of the marriage and custody of the minor children. Does East State have jurisdiction over the minor children under the UCCJEA?

5. Assume you represent Melody in Question 4. What arguments can you make on behalf of Melody that East State is not the home state of the minor children?

2. Jurisdictional Requirements of PKPA

In 1980, in an effort to resolve the ongoing problem of interstate jurisdictional conflicts left open by the UCCJA, Congress enacted the Parental Kidnapping and Prevention Act (PKPA), which requires states to give full faith and credit to the custody decrees of other states if they conform to PKPA's jurisdictional requirements. Like the UCCJEA, PKPA has four jurisdictional bases: home state, significant connection, emergency, and last resort, with priority being given to the home state.

Accordingly, in order for its decree to be enforceable under PKPA, a state can assume significant connection jurisdiction only if no other state qualifies as the home state; the two are not alternative jurisdictional bases. If a state does assume jurisdiction based on its connection with the case where another state qualifies as the home state, the decree will not be entitled to interstate recognition in other states. PKPA also vests exclusive, continuing jurisdiction in the initial state so long as a parent or the child remains there, and the state has jurisdiction under its own laws. So long as this state has jurisdiction, no other state may modify its decree. Modification jurisdiction shifts only when everyone has moved away from the decree state (or it declines jurisdiction) and another state can satisfy PKPA's jurisdictional requirement.

Uniform Deployed Parents Custody and Visitation Act (UDPCVA)

In 2012, the National Conference of Commissioners on Uniform State Laws approved the Uniform Deployed Parents Custody and Visitation Act (UDPCVA) to address the "wide variability in the ways that states handle child custody and visitation issues that arise when service members are deployed" — a problem that is made more complicated by the fact that these cases often involve two states due to the "mobile nature of military service."[10] In addition to a number of substantive provisions, including, for example, that a parent's past or future deployment should not be taken into account when determining best interest absent a showing that it has a "material effect" on his or her wellbeing, the Act seeks to avoid jurisdictional conflicts by declaring that deployment does not alter a service member's residence under the UCCJEA. To date, only a handful of states have adopted the UDPCVA, although legislation to adopt it is pending in a number of states.

In sum, the hope is that PKPA (and now also the UCCJEA), by giving priority to the home state and vesting continuing jurisdiction in a single state, will eliminate the final vestiges of interstate competition in the custody arena. However, due to the complex legal and factual nature of these cases, true interstate harmony is unlikely in the foreseeable future.

3. International Child Custody Disputes

In addition to the complex jurisdictional issues that are raised by custody disputes involving two or more states, the process of globalization with the corresponding increase in transnational migration makes it more likely that disputes over children will be played out on the global stage. Accordingly, in addition to controlling the jurisdictional rules in interstate cases, the UCCJEA is also applicable to cases involving child custody determinations from other counties. Under the Act, courts are directed to treat a foreign country "as if it were a State of the United States" and are accordingly to recognize and enforce a "child-custody determination made in a foreign country under factual circumstances in substantial compliance with jurisdictional standards" of the UCCJEA. UCCJEA §105(a) & (b).

The only exception to this requirement is if the "child custody law of a foreign country violates fundamental principles of human rights." *Id.* §105(c).

On an international level, in 1980, the Hague Conference on Private International Law approved a multilateral treaty, known as the Hague Convention on the Civil Aspects of International Child Abduction. (The **Hague Conference** is an intergovernmental organization whose primary purpose is "to work for the progressive unification of the rules of private international law.") The Abduction Convention "seeks to protect children from the harmful effects of abduction and retention across international boundaries by providing a procedure to bring about their prompt return." The United States is a signatory to the Convention and its provisions have been implemented in this country through the International Child Abduction Remedies Act. 42 U.S.C. §11601.

---

[10]Why States Should Adopt the Uniform Deployed Parents Custody and Visitation Act, http://www.uniformlaws.org/Shared/Docs/Deployed_Parents/UDPCVA%20Why%20States%281%29.pdf (accessed June 8, 2016).
[11]Uniform Deployed Parents Custody and Visitation Act §107.

Similar to PKPA and the UCCJEA, the Abduction Convention seeks to deter parents from removing a child to another jurisdiction with the hope of obtaining a more favorable custody outcome. This is particularly important in the global context as the return process of wrongly removed children has historically been particularly haphazard. To this end, for the purpose of determining custody, jurisdictional priority is vested in the country that is a child's "habitual residence"—a concept that is doctrinally similar to that of "home state" jurisdiction.

Accordingly, in brief, if a parent removes a child to another country in violation of the "left-behind" parent's custodial rights, the left-behind parent can file a legal action seeking the return of the child. If the court determines that the child was removed from a country that is his or her place of "habitual residence," it can order the prompt return of the child, unless the parent who took the child can justify the removal based upon the limited exceptions provided in the Convention, such as that the left-behind parent consented to the removal, or that the child "objects to being returned and has attained an age and degree of maturity at which it is appropriate to take account of its views." A parent may also seek to establish that "there is a grave risk that his or her return would expose the child to physical or psychological harm or otherwise place the child in an intolerable situation."[12]

It is important to be aware that a hearing held pursuant to the Abduction Convention is intended to address the narrow question of whether the removal was wrongful and thus whether the child should be returned home. Under the terms of the Convention, the court making this determination is precluded from deciding the merits of the custody case, unless it determines that the removal was not wrongful, and that the child may remain in that country.

Chapter Summary

- Subject matter jurisdiction refers to the authority of a court to hear specific types of cases, while personal jurisdiction refers to a court's authority over a defendant.
- Personal jurisdiction can be based on domicile, minimum contacts, consent, or physical presence.
- Long-arm statutes allow states to assert personal jurisdiction over nonresident defendants who have sufficient minimum contacts with the forum state. The assertion of personal jurisdiction must satisfy the fairness requirement of the Due Process Clause.
- Jurisdiction to dissolve the marriage is usually based on domicile; personal jurisdiction over the defendant is not required.
- A court cannot order a defendant to pay support if it does not have personal jurisdiction over him or her. Personal jurisdiction may be asserted over a nonresident through the long-arm provisions of UIFSA or state jurisdictional statute.

---

[12]Article 13, Hague Convention on the Civil Aspects of International Child Abduction. This latter exception is most commonly invoked by women who have fled to another country in order to escape an abusive partner.

▧ Where property is concerned, a distribution can be effectuated based either on personal jurisdiction over the defendant or on the court's in rem authority over property located within its borders.

▧ Jurisdiction over child custody disputes is determined by the UCCJA, the UCCJEA, and PKPA. These Acts establish four jurisdictional bases for when a state may assert jurisdiction over a custody dispute: home state, significant connection, emergency, and last resort.

▧ The UCCJA does not prioritize between these bases; thus, it is possible for two states to claim authority over a case at the same time; however, both PKPA and the UCCJEA prioritize home state jurisdiction.

▧ In the global arena, the Hague Convention on the Civil Aspects of International Child Abduction likewise seeks to deter the wrongful removal of children and to ensure their prompt return to their place of "habitual residence," absent extenuating circumstances.

Applying the Rules

1. Steven and Shreya were married in California. For the next 20 years, the couple lived outside of the United States. In 2001, while living in Indonesia, the couple purchased land near Kalispell and built a house. In 2010, Shreya moved to Florida, and Steven remained in Indonesia. Shreya files for divorce in Montana. In Montana, for the court to have subject matter jurisdiction at least one party must have resided in the state for at least 90 days preceding the filing of the complaint. Steven moved to dismiss the petition for lack of subject matter jurisdiction because Shreya neither resided in nor was domiciled in Montana for the 90 days preceding her petition for dissolution. Shreya admits she was not domiciled in Montana for the 90 days prior to the filing of the divorce, but she has since moved there, and has filed an amended petition, based on her current domiciliary status. What should the trial court do? Should the petition be dismissed?

2. Karen and John, who are both residents of Kansas, marry and have two children in Kansas. They separate and Karen moves to Florida. John has never been to Florida. After meeting the domicile requirements, Karen files an action for dissolution of marriage in Florida. Does the court have jurisdiction to grant a divorce?

3. Assume in Question 2 that John objects and specially appears to contest jurisdiction. What can the court adjudicate? If John appears and does not contest jurisdiction, can the court adjudicate issues of property and alimony?

4. Delores and Hector were divorced seven years ago in Arizona. Delores was given primary custody of their two-year-old daughter, Katy, and Hector had visitation every other week. Two months later Delores moved with Katy to Michigan. Hector never objected, and Katy primarily came to visit Hector during the

summer. Katy is now nine years old, and Hector would like to move to modify custody so that he has additional parenting time. Hector would like to know in which state he must file his motion to modify custody and parenting time. What arguments might Delores raise?

5. Assume a client has come to your firm's office seeking a divorce. All you know at this point is that she and her husband and their children have moved frequently over the past five years, and she has recently moved to your state with the children. In preparation for the interview, develop a set of interview questions so that all facts bearing on jurisdiction will be covered when you meet with her. In developing the questions, make sure you think about all aspects of the case.

6. Assume the following statute is in place in your jurisdiction: "Residence requirement.—The plaintiff in action for the dissolution of the bonds of matrimony must have been an actual resident, in good faith, of the state for one (1) year next preceding the filing of his or her complaint." Perry comes to your office and informs you that he has lived in the state for the past 13 months and would like to file for divorce. What questions do you want to ask Perry to ensure that he is residing in the state in good faith? Assume that you file a petition for divorce on behalf of Perry. His wife, Julia, who lives out of state, files a motion to quash on the grounds that Perry does not have an intent to remain in your state because he has told friends he plans to move out of state as soon as the divorce is final. What evidence might you use to show that Perry is an actual resident? Assume the court denies the motion to quash by Julia and ultimately grants a divorce for Perry, who then moves out of state three weeks after the divorce is granted. Are there grounds for Julia to object to the granting of the divorce?

Family Law in Practice

1. Locate your state law concerning personal jurisdiction to determine support. How does your state law compare to the bases for personal jurisdiction under the UIFSA?

2. Locate your state law defining home state of a minor child. How does your state law compare to the definition under the UCCJEA?

3. Find two cases from your state that involve an interstate custody dispute. Analyze how the court made its decision. In the course of your analysis, refer back to the UCCJEA and make sure that you both understand and discuss all provisions relevant to the court's analysis in each case.

4. Find a case in your state that discusses modification of child support. What law does the court use? Be sure to compare your state law to the law under the UIFSA.

Domestic Violence

All states have laws that enable victims of **domestic violence** (also referred to as **intimate partner violence**) to obtain civil orders of protection from abuse. In addition, criminal laws also provide potential protection for acts of physical violence, criminal trespass, and criminal damage. In some jurisdictions, there are mandatory arrest policies for batterers involved in crimes of domestic violence. These laws came about largely as a result of the late twentieth-century women's movement that focused public attention on the extent and seriousness of violence directed toward women by their male partners. Insisting that partner violence was not simply a private matter, activists successfully campaigned for laws that would allow victims to seek legal protection from abuse. This chapter begins with a brief historical overview of these laws, and then focuses on the expanding nature of state and federal protections for victims of domestic violence, and the more newly established crime of stalking, including cyberstalking.

A. HISTORICAL OVERVIEW

To put the current legal approach to intimate partner violence into context, we first briefly examine the historical approach of the law. This history reveals an unsettling failure of the legal system to become involved in the personal lives of husbands and wives in the area of physical control, as well as the social acceptance of male physical authority over the female spouse.

The Roman law of marriage required that married women obey the will of their husbands, and the husband could use physical force to make his wife obey him. If a married woman drank, committed adultery, or engaged in other conduct that threatened his honor, her husband could use physical violence without inquiry or

Key Concepts

- Abuse protection laws
- Enforcement of protective orders
- Anti-stalking laws
- Specialized domestic violence courts
- The Violence Against Women Act

Domestic Abuse Statistics

Intimate partner violence remains a serious problem, accounting for 21 percent of all violent crime. Although overall rates have declined significantly since the 1990s, it is hard to pinpoint what this drop in domestic abuse actually means with regard to changing norms in intimate relationships, as the "overall pattern and size of the decline were similar to the decline in the overall violent crime rate." What remains unchanged is the gendered pattern of violence. According to the most recent Department of Justice (DOJ) statistics, between 2003 and 2012, 76 percent of the victims of nonfatal domestic violence were female, while 24 percent were male. Jennifer L. Truman and Rachel E. Morgan, Nonfatal Domestic Violence, 2004-2012, 1 (2014), U.S. Department of Justice, Office of Justice Programs, Bureau of Justice Statistics, http://www.bjs.gov/content/pub/pdf/ndv0312.pdf (accessed June 8, 2016). When it comes to violence resulting in death, recent DOJ statistics reveal that 70 percent of the victims are women. Shannon Catalano, Erice Smith, Howard Snyder, and Michael Rand, U.S. Department of Justice, Office of Justice Programs, Bureau of Justice Statistics (2009), http://www.bjs.gov/content/pub/pdf/fvv.pdf (accessed June 8, 2016).

punishment. This right of a husband to use physical force against his wife was carried forward into English common law. As the legal head of the household, a husband could physically discipline his wife to command her obedience both for its own sake and because he was legally responsible for her misconduct. He was directed to use the same moderation in physically chastising his wife as he would use when disciplining his apprentices or children.

In the United States, acceptance of the doctrine of marital unity (see Chapter 1) implied acceptance of a husband's right of "moderate chastisement" — although this was not without challenge. In the early days of the nation, a husband, as head of the household, was generally thought entitled to use the degree of force necessary to make his wife obey.

By the 1960s, the women's rights movement helped to focus public attention on the issue of domestic violence. Reformers challenged the prevailing understanding that intimate partner violence was a private matter that resulted from the interpersonal dynamics of an individual relationship and instead located its roots in the history of male authority over women in the domestic realm. As part of a broader effort to reallocate this historical imbalance of power, legal reform efforts focused on the enactment of abuse prevention laws. Now in effect in all states, these laws enable victims of domestic violence to obtain protective orders through a simplified court procedure.

B. ABUSE LAWS

In understanding how abuse protection laws work, it is helpful to consider a number of basic questions, as follows:

- What kinds of relationships qualify for a court to issue a protective order to prohibit contact between two persons?
- What kinds of harm entitle a victim of abuse to obtain a protective order in court?
- What kinds of protection are available to the victim?
- What is the process for obtaining a protective order in court?

These questions will guide our discussion, but, as always, keep in mind that the laws vary significantly from state to state.

1. Qualifying Relationships

Abuse prevention laws are generally intended to provide protection to persons who are being abused by someone with whom they have an intimate, family, or family-like relationship. When parties are in a more distant relationship, such as that of neighbor or co-worker, protection cannot usually be obtained through an abuse prevention law, although other remedies, such as a criminal action or injunctions against harassment, may be available. The discussion in this chapters centers on the intimate, family, or family-like relationships that qualify for an order of protection.

The statutes in some states are fairly comprehensive and allow someone to seek protection from abuse by a range of persons with whom they have a "special" relationship. See the sample statute below from the State of Washington. An inclusive statute might permit someone to seek protection from

- a spouse or former spouse;
- a cohabiting partner or former cohabiting partner (but some statutes frame this category more broadly to include all household members even if there is no family or intimate relationship);
- the parent of a child in common (statutes in a few states permit a pregnant woman to seek an order before the birth of the "child in common");
- family members related by blood and possibly by marriage; or
- a dating or an intimate partner.

DOMESTIC VIOLENCE PREVENTION — DEFINITIONS

Wash. Rev. Code §26.50.010

Under the State of Washington statute the terms Domestic Violence and the required relationships are defined as follows:

(1) "Domestic violence" means: (a) Physical harm, bodily injury, assault, or the infliction of fear of imminent physical harm, bodily injury or assault, between family or household members; (b) sexual assault of one family or household member by another; or (c) stalking as defined in RCW 9A.46.110 of one family or household member by another family or household member.

(2) "Family or household members" means spouses, domestic partners, former spouses, former domestic partners, persons who have a child in common regardless of whether they have been married or have lived together at any time, adult persons related by blood or marriage, adult persons who are presently residing together or who have resided together in the past, persons sixteen years of age or older who are presently residing together or who have resided together in the past and who have or have had a dating relationship, persons sixteen years of age or older with whom a person sixteen years of age or older has or has had a dating relationship, and persons who have a biological or legal parent-child relationship, including stepparents and stepchildren and grandparents and grandchildren.

(3) "Dating relationship" means a social relationship of a romantic nature. Factors that the court may consider in making this determination include: (a) The length of time the relationship has existed; (b) the nature of the relationship; and (c) the frequency of interaction between the parties.

Although the trend is in favor of increasing inclusivity, most state statutes are not this broad, and many impose specific eligibility qualifications on certain categories of individuals. For example, although all statutes include spouses and most, if not all, include former spouses, some exclude spouses who are in the process of getting a divorce or a legal separation (although as discussed in Chapter 4, a party may be able to seek protection from abuse within the framework of the divorce/separation proceeding). And although virtually all statutes cover unmarried cohabiting partners, some exclude former cohabiting partners. This is an unfortunate omission because research shows that battered spouses are at increased risk of abuse when they leave a relationship. Some cohabitation provisions specify that a couple must live together in a spousal-like relationship, which (as discussed below) has been used, until recently, to deny coverage to victims in a same-sex relationship, and many provisions exclude other householders unless they are family members.

Many states now permit an individual to seek protection from a person with whom he or she has had a child, even if they do not have any kind of ongoing relationship. These are often referred to as "child in common" provisions. In states that have such a provision, an issue that has come up is whether a woman can seek protection while she is pregnant but has not yet given birth. In recognition of the fact that where there is a history of violence, a pregnant woman may be at high risk of abuse, some "child in common" provisions expressly extend coverage to pregnant women. Where the statute is silent, case law is divided. Some courts have held that battered pregnant women come within the purpose and intent of the "child in common" provision, while other courts have denied coverage based on a narrow reading of the statutory language holding that birth is a condition precedent to eligibility.

In *Woodin v. Rasmussen*, 455 N.W.2d 535 (Minn. Ct. App. 1990), the trial court was faced with the issue of whether, under Minnesota's Domestic Abuse Act, it could issue a protective order "when the parties have never been married, have never lived together, have no children in common, yet do have an unborn child claimed to be in common[.]" The Minnesota statute provided, in part, that a trial court may issue a protective order prohibiting "family or household members" from committing acts of domestic abuse. In turn, "family or household members" are defined as "spouses, former spouses, parents and children, persons related by blood, and persons who are presently residing together or who have resided together in the past, and persons who have a child in common regardless of whether they have been married or have lived together at any time." While the trial court granted the protective order, reasoning that the natural extension of the "child in common" refers as well to an unborn child in common between the parties, the Court of Appeals reversed. Since the statute was silent as to the definition of "child," the court was unwilling to supply one that included an "unborn child." The court explained: "The legislature may wish to extend the Act to include unborn children in common as a basis for protection under the Act. This, however, is a legislative determination and not an extension which can be reached by judicial interpretation." *Id.* at 537.

In addition to the above relationships, some states permit an individual who is assisting a victim of violence to seek an order of protection. In effect, this person is regarded as being in a "special" relationship with the abuser based on the connection with the victim, as this connection may place the aider in direct risk of harm. Further exemplifying this expansive trend, a few states have eliminated the relationship requirement to specifically account for the violence that sometimes accompanies the dissolution and formation of new relationships. For example, following the highly publicized murder of a Texas woman by her boyfriend's former wife, Texas amended its abuse prevention law to allow a party to obtain a protective order against a person who was previously married to or in a dating relationship with the victim's current spouse or dating partner, while in Oklahoma, abuse victims may seek a restraining order against "present spouses of ex-spouses." Texas Stat. Ann., tit. 4, §71.0021(1)(B) (2012), and Okla. Stat. Ann. tit. 22, §60.1 (2012).

A few states have gone considerably further and eliminated the relationship requirement altogether. However, the available protections may be more limited if the parties are not in a "qualifying" type of relationship. Accordingly, the first step in determining whether an order of protection is possible is to consult the applicable state statute and determine if the relationship between the perpetrator and victim qualifies for such an order.

Case Preview

Turner v. Lewis

In the following case, the court looks to two important legal trends — the increasing attempt to protect victims of domestic violence and the expanding concept of family. In this case, the issue arose whether, based upon a Massachusetts statute, a paternal grandmother could seek an order of protection against the mother of the grandchild she was raising. While the statute was not clear that the paternal grandmother would definitively fall within the concept of "related by blood" when the paternal grandmother was not related by blood to the child's mother, the court looked to public policies and social trends in arriving at a conclusion.

As you read *Turner v. Lewis*, look for the following:

1. What were the facts that formed the basis for the grandmother to seek a restraining order against the child's mother?
2. Why did the trial court deny her request for an order?
3. What was the definitional issue that the court was confronted with?
4. What public policies did the court look to in reaching its decision?

Turner v. Lewis
749 N.E.2d 122 (Mass. 2001)

This appeal raises the question whether the paternal grandparent of a child whose parents were not married is "related by blood" to the child's mother, and thus, has a right to invoke protection from domestic abuse under G. L. c. 209A. . . . The grandmother has custody of the child, and the child resides with her. . . .

The grandmother makes the following allegations. On September 2, 1999, the mother entered the grandmother's home unannounced and without permission while the grandmother and the child were upstairs. The mother, who appeared "obviously high," yelled for the child and demanded that she come downstairs. The grandmother told her that the child was not at home. When the grandmother then attempted to descend the stairs, the mother blocked her, and punched and pushed her, saying, "You know what I want to do to you, don't you?" The mother then punched the grandmother again and pushed her up against the wall, causing the grandmother's head to hit a windowsill. After hitting the grandmother once more, the mother fled the scene in a van. The grandmother telephoned the police.

The grandmother subsequently filed a . . . complaint against the mother for protection from abuse. . . . Although a Probate and Family Court judge granted the grandmother an emergency protective order, another Probate and Family Court judge declined to extend that order, because [the judge] found that the "parties are [not] related by blood, marriage or household membership" as required by the statute. . . .

In 1978, Massachusetts enacted G. L. c. 209A to address the problem of domestic violence through the provision of judicial remedies. . . . Under G. L. c. 209A, a person "suffering from abuse from an adult or minor family or household member may file a complaint in the court requesting protection from such abuse." . . .

The question in this case is whether the abuse was perpetrated by a "family or household member." Under G. L. c. 209A, §1, "family or household members" include persons who, among other categories, . . . "(c) are or were related by blood or marriage. . . ." The grandmother claims that the parties are "related by blood" and have a "child in common," and thus, she qualifies for protection under the statute. . . .

Here we conclude that the parties are "related by blood." The paternal grandmother, through her son, is "related by blood" to the child. Likewise, the child and her mother are "related by blood." Thus, the child is "related by blood" to both parties, making the mother and grandmother "related by blood" through that child.

Interpreting the term "related by blood" to include the relationship between the grandmother and the mother would be consistent with the Legislature's purpose in enacting c. 209A. We note first that, in light of the grandmother's custody of the child and the mother's visitation rights with the child, there will likely be significant, albeit unwanted, contact between the mother and the grandmother, a fact particularly evidenced by the events that precipitated this appeal. . . .

Our conclusion is supported by sound public policy. We take judicial notice of the social reality that the concept of "family" is varied and evolving and that, as a result, different types of "family" members will be forced into potentially unwanted contact with one another. The recent increases in both single parent and grandparent headed households are two examples of this trend. . . .

These trends require that "domestic violence statutes [such as G. L. c. 209A] offer coverage to a wide range of extended family relationships to fully reflect the reality of American family life [and] . . . the definition of 'family members' embraced by civil protection order statutes must be equally applicable to all concepts of family as they exist in the reality of our diverse family relationships." Klein, Providing Legal Protection for Battered Women: An Analysis of State Statutes and Case Law, 21 Hofstra L. Rev. 801, 818-820 (1993). The relationship here meets the definition of "family," carrying with it all the risks and problems inherent in domestic violence. It is within that familial setting that this grandmother was exposed to violence and the threat of future violence.

For these reasons, we conclude that the grandmother and the defendant are "related by blood," and that the Probate and Family Court's ruling contravenes "the Commonwealth's public policy against domestic abuse — preservation of the fundamental human right to be protected from the devastating impact of family violence." *Champagne v. Champagne, supra* at 327. Accordingly, we vacate the denial of the extension of the protective order. . . .

COWIN, J. (dissenting, with whom SOSMAN, J., joins). I respectfully dissent. In my view, the legislative history indicates that the phrase "related by blood" was not intended to encompass persons such as the paternal grandmother and mother in this case.

The court's decision ignores legislative history and bases its decision on social policy. . . .

. . . I do not believe that it is the court's function to interpret a statute in accordance with the most recent "trend" or judicial perception of what "is best" as a matter of social policy, particularly when such interpretation is not consistent with the statutory language. . . . I recognize that the violence alleged in this case would, in common parlance, be viewed as a form of "domestic" violence, and that the unique remedies of G. L. c. 209A would seem suitable to the situation. However, it is not for this court to engraft G. L. c. 209A onto any dispute that is, in some sense, a "domestic" dispute. The appropriate procedure for protecting a person such as the paternal grandmother in this case is by legislative, not judicial, amendment to G. L. c. 209A.

Post-Case Follow-Up

The grandmother's ability to obtain a protective order in this case hinged on the court's interpretation of the term "related by blood." While the paternal grandmother was not a direct blood relation to the mother, the court found that the grandmother was related by blood to her son, the father. The child was therefore related by blood to both parties. Thus, according to the majority, the technical terms of the statute are met.

The court also finds that for public policy reasons the grandmother should be permitted to obtain a protective order in furtherance of the fundamental human right to be protected from familial violence. However, the dissent has a strong argument that the legislature must precisely say what it means.

As a result of interpretations like that of the dissent in *Turner v. Lewis*, many state statutes that failed to give protection against the parents of a child being raised by grandparents or third parties have been amended. For example, the Oklahoma statute provides a broad definition of "family and household members" and includes "spouses, ex-spouses, present spouses of ex-spouses, parents, including grandparents, stepparents, adoptive parents and foster parents, children, including grandchildren, stepchildren, adopted children and foster children, persons otherwise related by blood or marriage, persons living in the same household or who formerly lived in the same household, and persons who are the biological parents of the same child, regardless of their marital status, or whether they have lived together at any time. This shall include the elderly and handicapped." Okla. Stat. Ann. tit. 22, §60.1 Definitions (Oklahoma Statutes (2015 edition)).

Turner v. Lewis: Real Life Applications

1. Lilly is three years old, and the child of Tom and Ellen. Tom and Ellen were never married. Lilly resides with Ruby, her paternal grandmother. Ellen has recently has been granted day-time visits with Lilly to try to establish a relationship with Lilly since she has spent very little time with the child since her birth. Ellen has four hours of visitation each Saturday, and picks Lilly up from Ruby's house at 10:00 A.M. and returns her at 2:00 P.M. When arriving for the visit one Saturday, Ellen became angry at Ruby because Lilly was not ready. She yelled at Ruby, pushed her out of the doorway, and went up the stairs to get Lilly. Ruby suffered a bruised shoulder. On the way out, Ellen told Ruby, "If you ever try to avoid my visit with Lilly again, next time it will be more than just a push." Can Ruby obtain an order of protection against Ellen based upon a statute similar to the one used in *Turner v. Lewis*? Why?

2. Assume the same facts as in Question 1, but Tom was adopted. Can Ruby obtain an order of protection against Ellen? What arguments would you make for Ellen? What arguments would you make for Ruby?

3. Kevin and Tonya are the biological parents of Sam and recently divorced. On a recent visit by Kevin to Tonya's home, he found Sam being watched by Parker, Tonya's new boyfriend. Tonya was not home. Kevin was extremely upset that Tonya would allow someone he did not know to watch Sam in her absence. He grabbed Parker by the shirt and told him that he better tell Tonya that if Kevin ever finds out that she has left Sam with Parker when she is not at home, he is going to take her to court and change the custody arrangement. Can Parker obtain an order of protection? Would it make it difference if Parker and Tonya were married?

Dating Relationships

Initially, abuse prevention laws did not offer relief to victims of dating violence, which was not considered to be a serious or common problem. However, with time it became increasingly apparent that intimate partner abuse is not limited to marital or cohabiting relationships and also occurs within the context of dating relationships. For instance, research reveals that women are at greatest risk of being abused when they are between the ages of 16 and 24 and that approximately one in three to one in five young women in high school have been physically and/or sexually abused by someone they were dating. Compounding the seriousness of the problem, young women who are in abusive dating relationships are at particular risk for other serious health problems, including eating disorders, drug and alcohol abuse, and suicidality.

Today, a majority of states have amended their abuse protection laws to include individuals in dating or engagement relationships. Some statutes refer simply to dating relationships, while other specifically impose qualifying conditions. For example, the Massachusetts abuse prevention law, which was one of the first in the country to include dating relationships, requires a petitioner to establish the existence of a "substantial dating or engagement relationship." Mass. Gen. Laws Ann. ch. 209A, §1.

In evaluating substantiality, a judge is to consider the duration and type of the relationship and the frequency of the parties' interaction. If the relationship has ended, the judge must consider how much time has elapsed since termination. In some states, the question of whether the parties are sexually intimate may also be relevant to determining if they are in a qualifying dating relationship.

The inclusion of various qualifying elements, such as that a relationship be substantial or sexually intimate, was intended to allay concerns that the inclusion of dating partners would open the floodgates to a wide range of petitioners who were not in a "special" relationship with the party who was harming them. Another approach has been to specifically write an exclusion into law. Thus, for example, New York's Expanded Access to Family Court Act of 2008, which enables persons who "are or have been in an intimate relationship" to seek a restraining order, makes clear that "neither a casual acquaintance nor ordinary fraternization between two individuals in business or social contexts shall be deemed to constitute an 'intimate relationship.'" Ch. 326, §7, §812(1) 2008 N.Y. Laws 326 (codified as amended at N.Y. Fam. Ct. Act §812(1)(e)).

However, those working in the domestic violence field have raised a number of important concerns about statutory limitations on what constitutes a dating relationship for purposes of seeking protection. One potential concern is that qualifying conditions — such as that the relationship be substantial or that the parties be sexually intimate — give judges considerable discretion to decide if a petitioner qualifies for protection. If the judge's standard is not met, the petitioner may end up a greater risk because she has brought the perpetrator into court but then leaves without a protective order in place. Another important concern is that these kinds of requirements may mean that abuse cannot be addressed early on in a relationship. Since violence often escalates in frequency and severity over time, a victim of dating violence may have to wait until there is a risk of serious injury, or actual injury before being eligible for protection. Criminal laws can punish for the injury that occurs in the past, but often cannot protect against the risk of future injury in the same way that the victim is protected by obtaining a protective order.

Teen Dating Relationships

Teen dating violence raises some particular concerns. One concern is that although it is often difficult for any victim of domestic violence to disclose his or her situation to others (see Section G, below), disclosure can be especially difficult for teens, who are struggling to establish their autonomy and adult sense of self.

Teens in relationships may also face legal barriers that adults usually do not have to contend with. First, in a handful of states, it is possible that a teen will not be eligible to seek an order of protection from a dating partner due to her minority status. A more common potential barrier, however, is the fact that many statutes do not permit a minor to seek a protective order on his or her own, but require that it be filed on the minor's behalf by a parent or other responsible adult. For example, under Chapter 455 of Missouri's Revised Statutes, the petition for a child protection order must be filed by a parent or guardian of the victim, a guardian ad litem or court-appointed special advocate appointed for the victim, or the juvenile officer.

Alternatively, a statute might permit a minor to file for a protective order on his or her own, but then require the court to notify the minor's parents that the minor has done so. Although the involvement of a parent or other caring adult can provide a minor with much-needed support, these adult involvement requirements may deter some teens from seeking help due to a sense of shame or the desire to keep a dating relationship secret.

Moreover, even if a minor is comfortable having a parent participate in the court process, his or her presence may inhibit her from revealing certain information in court, such as that she is sexually active. Another potential barrier is that statutes do not permit a party to obtain an order of protection from an abuser who is under the age of 18, thus significantly limiting the availability of protection to teens who are in peer dating relationships.

Same-Sex Couples

Intimate partner violence is not limited to heterosexual couples; however, the law has been slower to respond to victims who experience violence within the context of same-sex relationships. However, with the recognition of same-sex marriages, these barriers are now being removed.

As it currently stands, abuse prevention laws take three basic approaches toward same-sex couples. A minority of statutes expressly limit the availability of protections to opposite-sex couples. However, the Supreme Court's decision in *Obergefell v. Hodges* casts the validity of this approach into doubt, particularly with respect to laws that differentiate between same-sex and heterosexual couples. At the other end of the continuum, a few statutes expressly extend protections to same-sex couples, thus formally equalizing the treatment of same-sex and heterosexual relationships.

In most states, however, the abuse prevention law does not either expressly include or expressly exclude same-sex couples. Accordingly, where an abuse victim can demonstrate that he or she is in a qualifying relationship, there should be no doubt about the applicability of the law.

2. Covered Conduct

As a general matter, there is not as much variability with respect to the types of conduct that are covered by abuse prevention laws as there is with regard to who is entitled to seek protection. While some statutes are more comprehensive than others, conduct that is usually not covered by abuse prevention laws includes malicious destruction of property and false imprisonment. These actions are generally covered by criminal law statutes. Accordingly, the following discussion focuses on the kinds of behaviors that are covered in most states.

Most often petitioners are seeking protection from physical abuse, and all states authorize the issuance of protective orders in this situation. **Physical abuse** includes acts such as slaps or pushes as well as potentially life-threatening conduct such as physical beatings with an object or a fist; the throwing of objects that hit a person will be considered physical abuse as well. Protection can also be sought for **attempted physical harm**, such as where someone throws a rock or other object but misses.

Most statutes also cover **threatened physical harm**. Generally, a petitioner must show that he or she was placed in fear of imminent bodily harm — the definition of **criminal assault**. However, as a practical matter, some courts are reluctant to issue orders for threats of harm in the absence of any history of physical abuse. This reluctance can put a victim at risk because threats often escalate into violence. Some research indicates that up to 50 percent of battered women who are murdered by their partners had previously been threatened with death. *See* Catherine F. Klein and Leslye E. Orloff, Providing Legal Protection for Battered Women: An Analysis of State Statutes and Case Law, 21 Hofstra L. Rev. 801, 859 (1993).

Some states also authorize relief for **emotional abuse** or **verbal abuse**, which does not involve threats of physical harm, although these provisions are not common. Courts tend to interpret these provisions narrowly, and may, for instance, grant relief only where there has been a prior history of abuse or where an intent to harm can be inferred from accompanying conduct. An order may also be based on **stalking** (see Section D, below) either as a distinct behavior or as tied to some other category of recognized harm, such as threatened physical harm.

Orders also may be granted based on harassment or **interference with an individual's liberty**, although most states do not recognize these as separate qualifying behaviors, but subsume them into another category of harm such as threatened physical harm. **Harassment** has been defined to include a range of conduct, such as preventing a person from leaving a room, pulling the telephone out of the wall or cutting the wires, or slashing the tires of someone's car. Based on an understanding of domestic violence as an expression of power, some state statutes take an expanded recognition of these types of harms in order to fully account for the complex array of strategies that abusers use to gain control over a partner's or former partner's life.

Many statutes also expressly authorize the granting of protective orders based on sexual assault. In states where sexual assault is not specifically mentioned, judges are likely to include this conduct in their working definition of physical abuse. **Sexual assault** is generally understood to involve coercing someone to engage in sexual relations against that person's will through force, threats of force, or possibly duress, such as where someone says, "If you do not have sex with me you'll never see your children again." In such cases, the consent is negated by the coercion.

3. Available Remedies

Most abuse prevention laws authorize a fairly broad range of specific remedies, and typically have a "catchall" provision that allows a judge to tailor the remedy to the circumstances of the case before him or her. Before looking at generally available remedies, a brief word is in order about a supplemental approach that has slowly been gaining traction in some states, namely, the use of tort law as a way of obtaining compensation for injuries caused by domestic violence beyond what may be awarded under a state's abuse prevention law. In this regard, the ability to seek compensation for emotional pain and suffering may be of particular value to abuse victims.

A number of traditional tort actions are potentially available to domestic violence victims, depending, of course, on the circumstances of the case. These include assault and battery, false imprisonment, and the intentional infliction of emotional distress. In addition, a few states now recognize domestic violence as a distinct form of tortious conduct. This approach often provides a more generous statute of limitations than is typically available in tort actions, which can be particularly beneficial to domestic violence victims who, due to the fear of reprisal, may well delay the initiation of legal proceedings beyond the usual time limits.

Refraining from Further Abuse

Judges in all states can enjoin the abusive party from engaging in conduct that places the victim at risk of harm. This is often expressed as a requirement that the abuser refrain from committing any further acts of abuse as defined by the applicable abuse prevention law. This provision is commonly referred to as a **restraining order**. By itself, a restraining order does not usually prohibit contact between the parties; it simply prohibits abusive behavior.

Vacate and Stay-Away Orders

The most common order in a situation where the parties are married or are living in a shared home is a **vacate order**, which requires the abuser to leave the parties' home. In many instances, removal of the perpetrator is an important step in securing the safety of the abuse victim. However, the remedy is not fail safe because it leaves the victim living in a place that is known to the abuser. Thus, despite the fact that the law may require the perpetrator to depart the premises, safety concerns may force the victim to vacate the shared premises.

The issuance of a vacate order does not affect the vacated party's title to the property, or how the property is divided. The order merely gives exclusive possession, during the terms of the protection order, to the victim of abuse.

If the parties are not living together, the court can issue a **stay-away order**, which requires the abuser to stay away from the victim's home. Regardless of whether the order is a vacate order or a stay-away order, the order may include language that also requires the abuser to stay away from places such as the victim's place of work, or school, or to maintain a certain distance.

No-Contact Orders

Most abuse prevention laws expressly authorize a judge to issue a **no-contact order**. Where not expressly authorized, a no-contact order can issue under a law's "catchall" provision. When drafted with care and specificity, no-contact orders can greatly enlarge the scope of available protection because they can be used to prohibit the abusive party from seeking any contact with the victim through any means or in any place. No-contact orders also can be drafted to prevent individuals who are acting on the abuser's behalf from contacting the victim. Accordingly, no-contact may include not just telephone calls, but e-mails and text messages.

Custody and Visitation

When an order of protection is sought by someone who has children in common with the abuser, different precautions must be taken. While most abuse prevention laws authorize judges to include temporary custody awards of minor children in a protective order, there is often a reluctance to do so unless the abuse is directed toward the children, or likely to result in harm to the children. The judge must be careful to guard against someone coming into court and alleging abuse in order to gain an unfair advantage regarding custody in a pending family law case. For example, if a divorce action is pending, and the parties have children in common, even if the judge finds abuse or a threat of abuse by the father against the mother, the judge may leave to the family court judge the determination of whether visitation or contact should be withheld from the father. Otherwise, the obtaining of an order of protection, which is often done initially without notice by the victim to the perpetrator, will affect custody without a full hearing.

If an order of protection is in place, there may be some presumptions that arise in the family law case. In some states, custody can be awarded only to the victim of the abuse, leaving the abuser with no right to custody. Other states employ a rebuttable presumption against awarding custody to the perpetrator of violence.

In cases where the judge determines that some visitation with the children by the abuser is appropriate, a judge may fashion a visitation order with certain limitations. For example, supervised visitation may be ordered, which requires that visitations take place only during the day and in the presence of a third party, often court appointed. Other orders may require that drop-off and pick-up of the children occur at the home of a third party or other neutral location, such as a police station or social service agency. By structuring visitations in this way, the need for contact between the parties is minimized, which, in turn, reduces the risk of continued abuse.

It is important to be aware that before a final hearing on custody and parenting time, the custody and visitation orders are temporary in nature. Thus, the orders may be superseded by orders entered in a subsequent divorce, custody, or separation proceeding. If you are assisting someone who is seeking a restraining order, it is important to be aware of how the various statutory provisions governing custody and visitation interact in your jurisdiction. The interactive patterns are often complex and can potentially result in conflicting orders that must be properly prioritized so the controlling order can be determined. The failure to do this can leave a client unprotected and at risk of violating a court order that has been superseded by a subsequent one.

Protection of Pets

A number of studies have documented substantial rate of co-occurrence between domestic violence and cruelty to animals. In some instances, harm or threatened harm to a pet may be a deliberate strategy for the purpose of controlling or intimidating a victim. Here, the harm that is caused to the animal is not the real intent. Rather, the act is committed primarily to cause psychological trauma due to the ultimate victim seeing the suffering of the animal. There has also been a growing awareness of the fact that, just like when the parties have children in common, a victim of intimate partner violence may be reluctant to leave an abusive relationship based on fears for the safety of the pets he or she may be forced to leave behind.

Responding to these realities, a rapidly growing number of jurisdictions have amended their abuse protection laws to provide for the safety and well-being of household pets. Typically, these laws include provisions for the protection of pets and for the preservation of the relationship between the pet and the domestic violence victim within the remedies section of the law. These types of measures enable a judge to order a defendant to stay away from and to refrain from abusing or injuring a pet and/or to grant the exclusive care, custody, and possession of the pet to the petitioner.

Support and Monetary Compensation

Most states authorize the inclusion of a temporary child support and/or a temporary spousal support award in a protective order. However, even where allowed, some judges are reluctant to make support awards, perhaps believing that financial matters are best addressed in the family law proceeding. The failure to provide financial support, whether through a statutory exclusion or a judicial omission, can compromise the victim's safety. If victims are unable to provide for themselves or their children, they may feel that they have no choice but to return to their abusers.

Distinct from support, most statutes enable a judge to order the abuser to compensate the victim for any financial loss suffered due to the abuse. Compensation might include out-of-pocket medical expenses, the repair or replacement of damaged property, lost wages, and moving costs. However, frequently fearful that the court action will provoke retaliation, many victims are reluctant to request relief not directly related to securing their safety and the safety of their children.

Treatment/Counseling

A judge often can order an abuser to participate in a treatment or counseling program that works specifically with batterers. A growing number of states have adopted mandatory guidelines that **Batterer Intervention Programs**, as they are generally called, must follow. These guidelines allow for state oversight of the quality and effectiveness of the program. Guidelines often relate to matters such as staff qualifications, intake and discharge procedures, and the intervention approach.

A judge may only have the authority to order a party into a batterer intervention program after a violation of the protective order has occurred. However, a judge may be able to *recommend* that an abuser seek help as part of the initial order. Where intervention is ordered rather than just recommended, the abuser's attendance is monitored, often by having the program send periodic reports back to the judge; if sessions are missed, the judge can impose sanctions.

Relinquishment of Firearms

The use of a firearm significantly increases the chance of a violent death. Accordingly, given these potentially deadly consequences, many abuse prevention laws now include gun (and other weapon) possession provisions that restrict an abuser's access to firearms and ammunition. In some states, the entry of a protective order based on specific criteria, such as that the abuser poses a credible threat to the safety of the petitioner, results in a mandatory prohibition on the possession of a firearm. More commonly, however, a judge is given the discretion to enter an order prohibiting the abuser from possessing a firearm. Additionally, some abuse prevention laws allow a judge to revoke the abuser's license to carry a firearm for the duration of the protective order.

Supplementing these state law provisions, in 1994, based on a recognition of the increased risk of lethality when domestic violence involves firearms, Congress amended the Federal Gun Control Act of 1968 to criminalize the possession of a firearm or ammunition by a party who is already subject to a qualifying restraining order. This law contained an exception for certain government employees, such as police officers and military personnel, who are required to carry a weapon as part of their official duties. 18 U.S.C. §922(g)(8).

In 1996, Congress further amended the Gun Control Act by approving the "Domestic Violence Offender Gun Ban." This law is codified at 18 U.S.C. §924(g)(9). Frequently referred to as the Lautenberg Amendment, after its Senate sponsor, this provision makes it illegal for any person who has been convicted of a misdemeanor crime of domestic violence to possess a firearm. Unlike the 1994 Act, which provides limited exceptions to the possession ban for certain governmental employees, such as police officers and military personnel who are required to carry a weapon as part of their official duties, the Lautenberg Amendment does not contain any such exceptions.

In *United States v. Castleman*, 134 S. Ct. 1405 (2014), the Supreme Court explained that 18 U.S.C. §922(g)(9) was enacted to close a loophole. "While felons had long been barred from possessing guns, many perpetrators of domestic violence are convicted only of misdemeanors." And, while there was no ban preventing domestic abusers from possessing firearms, there is a "sobering" connection between domestic violence and homicide. *Id.* Thus, the purpose of the Lautenberg Amendment was to remedy this "potentially deadly combination" of "[f]irearms and domestic strife." *United States v. Hayes*, 555 U.S. 415, 426-427 (2009). Thus, it is against federal law for *any* person "who has been convicted in any court of a misdemeanor crime of domestic violence" to "possess in or affecting commerce[ ] any firearm or ammunition." A "misdemeanor crime of domestic violence" is defined as an offense that (1) is a misdemeanor under federal, state, or tribal law, and (2) "has, as an element, the use or attempted use of physical force . . . committed by a current or former spouse, parent, or guardian of the victim" or by a person in a similar domestic relationship with the victim.

Statutory Obligations of Police Officers

Although not technically a form of relief, most abuse prevention laws impose specific obligations on police officers to assist victims of domestic violence. An officer may be required to provide a victim with information about obtaining an order, to arrange or provide transportation to a hospital or shelter, to remain on the scene until the threat of immediate danger has passed, and to assist the victim to collect his or her belongings. In some states, the police may be able to seize a batterer's weapons where the police officer has cause to believe that continued possession exposes the victim to the risk of serious injury. As discussed below in Enforcement of Protective Orders, the police also have an important role in serving and enforcing protective orders.

4. The Court Process

Due to the frequently urgent nature of domestic violence cases, the court process for obtaining protective orders is simpler and quicker than it is in most other kinds of cases. Filing a petition does not require a lawyer. However, in many instances, it can be very useful for a petitioner to have a lawyer (or other advocate) in court, as unanticipated issues can arise, particularly if minor children are involved. It can also be very frightening and possibly dangerous for a victim to face an abuser in court, especially where the perpetrator has threatened to take revenge if a court action is filed. A lawyer (or advocate) can accordingly provide much-needed support and help ensure that the victim is not pressured into abandoning the action.

The court process for obtaining a protective order usually takes place in two distinct stages. The first hearing is most commonly on an *ex parte* basis due to the potential risk to the petitioner if notice is given to the other side without the prior entry of temporary protective orders. Some statutes limit the relief that is available at this stage to restraining and eviction orders and postpone consideration of matters such as custody, support, and counseling until the second hearing. In some states, the date for the second hearing, which is typically between 10 to 20 days later, is also set at this time. In others, the alleged abuser must specifically request a hearing to vacate the order of protection.

Because abuse frequently takes place on weekends or in the evening when courts are closed, most states have a procedure in place for obtaining after-hour emergency orders. An emergency judge might be available on a 24-hour on-call basis, or an official, such as a magistrate, might be empowered to issue after-hour orders. These orders generally are good only until the next business day.

After service is made on the other side, which many states require to be personally served by a police officer, sheriff, or authorized process server, unless the court authorizes an alternative means of service, the case then proceeds to the second hearing if ordered by the court or requested by the alleged abuser. The person who obtained the order of protection has the burden to prove to the judge that the order of protection must stay in place due to the fact that there was an act or series of acts of domestic violence in the past and there is the risk that there will be future acts of domestic violence. Assuming the victim meets this burden, the alleged abuser has an opportunity to respond and provide a defense. A defense might include evidence to demonstrate that the abuse did not happen or is made up in order to gain exclusive possession of the shared residence or temporary custody of the minor children.

After evaluating the evidence, the judge can either extend or decline to extend the original orders for an additional period of time. Most states allow orders to be extended for up to at least one year, although in some states, the limit is six months at a time. Still others no longer impose any durational limits based on the recognition that abusers can use the court system to control and intimidate their victims, and also because the need to continually renew a protective order can expose a victim to an increased risk of harm.

Although the practice has drawn considerable criticism and is prohibited in a number of jurisdictions, some judges are inclined to grant mutual orders of protection at the second hearing whereby each party is ordered to refrain from harming the other, despite the fact that only one party has requested relief. By suggesting that both persons are responsible for the violence, mutual orders are criticized for not holding abusers accountable for their behavior. They can also create enforcement problems for police responding to a call for assistance because each party can claim that he or she is the protected one and that the other should be arrested. Additionally, a mutual order can adversely impact the petitioner in a subsequent custody or visitation dispute in which the court is directed to consider the existence of prior protective orders when making an award because both parties will appear to be equally responsible for the violence.

C. ENFORCEMENT OF PROTECTIVE ORDERS

Although the orders themselves are civil in nature, violations can be prosecuted in the criminal justice system. In most states, the act of violating an order is a separate and independent crime. This is particularly valuable in situations where the violating behavior may not itself be an independent crime, such as where a party continually telephones the petitioner in violation of a no-contact order. However, most acts committed in violation of a protective order are themselves crimes (e.g., trespass, assault, battery, and false imprisonment), and a party can thus be prosecuted for any specific criminal acts as well as for violating the order.

Most states have adopted mandatory arrest policies that require police officers to arrest a suspect, without having to first obtain a warrant, whenever there is probable cause to believe an act of domestic violence has occurred, regardless of whether the officer witnessed the incident or not. By requiring arrest, these laws are intended to remove police discretion. However, in 2005, the U.S. Supreme Court held in *Gonzales v. Castle Rock* that the right to enforcement of a restraining order does not amount to a constitutionally protected right.

Case Preview

Castle Rock v. Gonzales

Jessica Gonzales obtained a restraining order against her estranged husband in conjunction with her divorce proceedings. The restraining order provided that he was not to molest or disturb the peace of Jessica or of any child, and to remain at least 100 yards from the family home at all times. Ms. Gonzales sued the town of Castle Rock and the local police department after they ignored her calls that her husband had taken the couple's three daughters in violation of a restraining order and unfortunately tragically murdered the three children.

Jessica Gonzales
AP Photo/Craig F. Walker, Denver Post

The sole issue was whether an individual who obtains a state-law restraining order has a constitutionally protected property interest under the Due Process Clause of the Fourteenth Amendment in having the police enforce the restraining order when they have probable cause to believe it has been violated. As you read *Castle Rock v. Gonzales*, look for the following:

1. What was the state law that Jessica Gonzales relied upon to argue that she had a due process right to have the law enforced?
2. How does the Court distinguish an "entitlement" from a "benefit"?
3. Why did the Court think that the deference the Court of Appeals gave to Colorado's state law was inappropriate?

Castle Rock v. Gonzales
545 U.S. 748 (2005)

Justice SCALIA delivered the opinion of the Court.

. . .

Respondent Jessica Gonzales alleges that petitioner, the town of Castle Rock, Colorado, violated the Due Process Clause of the Fourteenth Amendment to the United States Constitution when its police officers, acting pursuant to official policy or custom, failed to respond properly to her repeated reports that her estranged husband was violating the terms of a restraining order.

[The restraining order obtained by Ms. Gonzales had a "Notice to Law Enforcement Officials" preprinted on the back of the form, which read in part:]

"YOU SHALL USE EVERY REASONABLE MEANS TO ENFORCE THIS RESTRAINING ORDER. YOU SHALL ARREST, OR, IF AN ARREST WOULD BE IMPRACTICAL UNDER THE CIRCUMSTANCES, SEEK A WARRANT FOR THE ARREST OF THE RESTRAINED PERSON WHEN YOU HAVE INFORMATION AMOUNTING TO PROBABLE CAUSE THAT THE RESTRAINED PERSON HAS VIOLATED OR ATTEMPTED TO VIOLATE ANY PROVISION OF THIS ORDER AND THE RESTRAINED PERSON HAS BEEN PROPERLY SERVED WITH A COPY OF THIS ORDER OR HAS RECEIVED ACTUAL NOTICE OF THE EXISTENCE OF THIS ORDER."

[Pursuant to the restraining order as modified, Husband had parenting time with the three daughters (ages 10, 9, and 7) on alternate weekends, for two weeks during the summer, and, a mid-week dinner visit upon reasonable notice with advanced arrangements made by the parties. He was permitted to come to the home to take the children for his parenting time. On June 22, 1999, Husband took the three girls while they were playing outside the family home. No advance arrangements had been made. Ms. Gonzales called the police and requested that the children be immediately returned to her. The police advised her to wait until 10:00 P.M. to see if he returned the children.]

At approximately 8:30 P.M., respondent talked to her husband on his cellular telephone. He told her "he had the three children [at an] amusement park in Denver." She called the police again and asked them to "have someone check for" her husband or his vehicle at the amusement park and "put out an [all-points bulletin]" for her husband, but the officer with whom she spoke "refused to do so," again telling her to "wait until 10:00 P.M. and see if" her husband returned the girls.

At approximately 10:10 P.M., respondent called the police and said her children were still missing, but she was now told to wait until midnight. She called at midnight and told the dispatcher her children were still missing. She went to her husband's apartment and, finding nobody there, called the police at 12:10 A.M.; she was told to wait for an officer to arrive. When none came, she went to the police station at 12:50 A.M. and submitted an incident report. The officer who took the report "made no reasonable effort to enforce the TRO or locate the three children. Instead, he went to dinner."

At approximately 3:20 A.M., respondent's husband arrived at the police station and opened fire with a semiautomatic handgun he had purchased earlier that evening. Police shot back, killing him. Inside the cab of his pickup truck, they found the bodies of all three daughters, whom he had already murdered.

. . .

[The district court granted the town of Castle Rock's motion to dismiss finding that it failed to state a claim upon which relief could be granted. The Court of Appeals affirmed the rejection of a substantive due process claim but found that Ms. Gonzales had a "protected property interest in the enforcement of the terms of her restraining order" and that the town had deprived her of due process because "the police never 'heard' nor seriously entertained her request to enforce and protect her interests in the restraining order."] We granted certiorari.

II

The Fourteenth Amendment to the United States Constitution provides that a State shall not "deprive any person of life, liberty, or property, without due process of law." Amdt. 14, §1. In 42 U.S.C. §1983 Congress has created a federal cause of action for "the deprivation of any rights, privileges, or immunities secured by the Constitution and laws." Respondent claims the benefit of this provision on the ground that she had a property interest in police enforcement of the restraining order against her husband; and that the town deprived her of this property without due process by having a policy that tolerated nonenforcement of restraining orders.

. . .

The procedural component of the Due Process Clause does not protect everything that might be described as a "benefit": "To have a property interest in a benefit, a person clearly must have more than an abstract need or desire" and "more than a unilateral expectation of it. He must, instead, have a legitimate claim of entitlement to it." *Board of Regents of State Colleges v. Roth*, 408 U.S. 564, 577 (1972). Such entitlements are " 'of course, . . . not created by the Constitution. Rather, they are created and their dimensions are defined by existing rules or understandings that stem from an independent source such as state law.' " *Paul v. Davis*, 424 U.S. 693, 709 (1976) (quoting *Roth*, supra, at 577).

A

Our cases recognize that a benefit is not a protected entitlement if government officials may grant or deny it in their discretion. See, e.g., *Kentucky Dept. of Corrections v. Thompson*, 490 U.S. 454, 462-463 (1989).

We have said that a "presumption of deference [is] given the views of a federal court as to the law of a State within its jurisdiction." That presumption can be overcome, however, and we think deference inappropriate here. The Tenth Circuit's opinion, which reversed the Colorado District Judge, did not draw upon a deep well of state-specific expertise, but consisted primarily of quoting language from the restraining order, the statutory text, and a state-legislative-hearing transcript. These texts, moreover, say nothing distinctive to Colorado, but use mandatory language that (as we shall discuss) appears in many state and federal statutes. As for case law:

the only state-law cases about restraining orders that the Court of Appeals relied upon were decisions of Federal District Courts in Ohio and Pennsylvania and state courts in New Jersey, Oregon, and Tennessee. Moreover, if we were simply to accept the Court of Appeals' conclusion, we would necessarily have to decide conclusively a federal constitutional question (i.e., whether such an entitlement constituted property under the Due Process Clause and, if so, whether petitioner's customs or policies provided too little process to protect it). We proceed, then, to our own analysis of whether Colorado law gave respondent a right to enforcement of the restraining order.

B

The critical language in the restraining order came not from any part of the order itself (which was signed by the state-court trial judge and directed to the restrained party, respondent's husband), but from the preprinted notice to law-enforcement personnel that appeared on the back of the order. That notice effectively restated the statutory provision describing "peace officers' duties" related to the crime of violation of a restraining order. At the time of the conduct at issue in this case, that provision read as follows:

> "(a) Whenever a restraining order is issued, the protected person shall be provided with a copy of such order. A peace officer shall use every reasonable means to enforce a restraining order.
>
> "(b) A peace officer shall arrest, or, if an arrest would be impractical under the circumstances, seek a warrant for the arrest of a restrained person when the peace officer has information amounting to probable cause that:
>
>> "(I) The restrained person has violated or attempted to violate any provision of a restraining order; and
>>
>> "(II) The restrained person has been properly served with a copy of the restraining order or the restrained person has received actual notice of the existence and substance of such order.
>
> "(c) In making the probable cause determination described in paragraph (b) of this subsection (3), a peace officer shall assume that the information received from the registry is accurate. *A peace officer shall enforce a valid restraining order whether or not there is a record of the restraining order in the registry.*" Colo. Rev. Stat. §18-6-803.5(3) (Lexis 1999) (emphases added).

The Court of Appeals concluded that this statutory provision . . . established the Colorado Legislature's clear intent "to alter the fact that the police were not enforcing domestic abuse retraining orders," and thus its intent "that the recipient of a domestic abuse restraining order have an entitlement to its enforcement." Any other result, it said, "would render domestic abuse restraining orders utterly valueless."

This last statement is sheer hyperbole. Whether or not respondent had a right to enforce the restraining order, it rendered certain otherwise lawful conduct by her husband both criminal and in contempt of court. . . . The creation of grounds on which he could be arrested, criminally prosecuted, and held in contempt was hardly "valueless" — even if the prospect of those sanctions ultimately failed to prevent him from committing three murders and a suicide.

We do not believe that these provisions of Colorado law truly made enforcement of restraining orders mandatory. A well established tradition of police discretion has long coexisted with apparently mandatory arrest statutes.

. . .

Respondent does not specify the precise means of enforcement that the Colorado restraining-order statute assertedly mandated — whether her interest lay in having police arrest her husband, having them seek a warrant for his arrest, or having them "use every reasonable means, up to and including arrest, to enforce the order's terms." . . . Such indeterminacy is not the hallmark of a duty that is mandatory.

. . .

The creation of a personal entitlement to something as vague and novel as enforcement of restraining orders cannot "simply g[o] without saying." Post, at 17, n.16 (Stevens, J., dissenting). We conclude that Colorado has not created such an entitlement.

. . .

III

We conclude, therefore, that respondent did not, for purposes of the Due Process Clause, have a property interest in police enforcement of the restraining order against her husband. . . .

The judgment of the Court of Appeals is Reversed.

Post-Case Follow-Up

Although the police ignored Colorado's mandatory arrest law, the Court concluded that Ms. Gonzales did not have a recognized "property" interest in the restraining order because, despite the "seemingly mandatory legislative command," police apparently maintained some discretion over the arrest decision. In short, as long as the police were able to exercise discretion, the Court would not hold their failure to enforce the restraining order a violation of procedural due process.

It should be noted that the Supreme Court's ruling in *Castle Rock v. Gonzales* was not the end of the matter. Following her loss at the nation's highest court, Jessica Lenahan (formerly Jessica Gonzales) became the first domestic violence survivor from the United States to bring her case before the Inter-American Court on Human Rights (IACHR). In a landmark ruling, the IACHR held that the failure of the government to protect Jessica and her children constituted a violation of their human rights. In addition to recommending that Ms. Lenahan and her family receive "full reparations" for their loss, the IACHR also recommended that the United States "adopt multifaceted legislation at the federal and state levels, or to reform existing legislation making mandatory the enforcement of protection orders and other precautionary measures to protect women [and children in the context of domestic violence] from imminent acts of violence, and to create effective implementation mechanisms." *Jessica Lenahan (Gonzales) v. United States*, Report No. 80/11 (2011), p. 53.

Castle Rock v. Gonzales: Real Life Applications

1. Assume the same facts as in *Castle Rock v. Gonzales*, but instead the restraining order prohibited the husband from having any contact with the minor children until further court order. Would the decision of the Court be different under those circumstances?

2. As part of her divorce decree, Phyllis obtained a restraining order against David that prohibited him from having any contact with the minor children until he completed 40 hours of an anger-management course and provided proof of completion to the court. Upon completion, David was entitled to every other weekend of parenting time. David advised Phyllis he had completed the course but that since it was a Saturday when he completed the course he did not have the ability to provide the notice of completion immediately to the court. David advised Phyllis that he would like to begin his parenting time that weekend. Phyllis refused but David threatened to take the children anyway. Phyllis called the police, and they arrived just as David was putting the children in his car. They advised him that he could not take the children with him due to the restraining order and advised that they would arrest him if he attempted to take the children before he provided proof of completion to the court. David tried to show his completed certificate but the police refused to review it. David then proceeded to take the children, and the police arrested him for violating the temporary restraining order. Does David have a claim that the police violated his right to due process by refusing to recognize he had a right to parenting time?

3. Gary, a ten-year veteran of the local police department, shot and seriously injured his wife, Jackie, and then shot and killed himself. There is no dispute that Gary had emotionally and physically abused Jackie for years prior to the shooting. Although she reported numerous incidents of abuse to the police over the years, obtained several restraining orders over their 15-year marriage, including one just days before the shooting, and told police that her husband continued threatening her despite the orders, the police failed to arrest him. There is also no dispute that Gary's superiors at the police department knew he had emotional issues in the past and that he had been off work for a period of time because of an attempt to commit suicide after he was involved in a shooting of a suspect, even thought it was ultimately found that the shooting was justified and Gary had returned to work. The trial court held that the police officers had a constitutional obligation to protect Jackie from her husband's abuse. The police department has appealed. How should the Court of Appeals rule?

Many states have also adopted mandatory prosecution (or no-drop) policies that enable a prosecutor to pursue a domestic violence case even if the victim does not want to proceed. Some states maintain what is often referred to as a "soft-drop" approach, which means that there is no consequence to the victim if he or she chooses not to cooperate with the prosecution. In contrast, in states with a "hard-drop" approach, a victim may face contempt proceedings if he or she opts not to testify against the abuser.

D. SUPPLEMENTING THE ENFORCEMENT PROCESS: CRIMINAL ANTI-STALKING LAWS

Rebecca Schaeffer
Everett Collection

In 1990, California enacted the nation's first anti-stalking law following the murder of actress Rebecca Schaeffer, the star of a popular sitcom, by a fan who had pursued her for over two years. Since then, all states have enacted criminal anti-stalking laws.

As indicated by the rapid proliferation of these laws, stalking has come to be recognized as a serious problem. Although the precise contours vary from state to state, stalking is generally defined as harassing or threatening behavior that an individual engages in on a repeated and often escalating basis that causes the victim to fear for his or her safety. Because stalking laws do not contain a "special relationship" requirement, in addition to supplementing the protections of abuse prevention laws, they can also fill an important gap in coverage for those who fall outside the scope of these statutes.

Stalking is typically defined to include a variety of unwanted behaviors, such as following or spying on someone, repeatedly showing up uninvited at a person's home or work, making repeated phone calls, and repeatedly waiting in places for the victim (see Section D.2, below). Recognizing that behavior that may seem fairly innocent at the start frequently escalates in both frequency and severity, and may result in serious physical harm or even death if not stopped, most statutes provide for the escalation of penalties for repeat violations. Additionally, in many states, stalking in violation of a protective order may be considered "aggravated" stalking and carry additional penalties.

In 2006, Congress enacted the Interstate Stalking Punishment and Prevention Act, which makes it a federal crime to travel across state lines for the purpose of stalking someone. 18 U.S.C. §2261A(1) (2012). See the excerpt below.

STALKING LAW

18 U.S.C. §2261A — Stalking

Whoever —

(1) travels in interstate or foreign commerce or is present within the special maritime and territorial jurisdiction of the United States, or enters or leaves Indian country, with the intent to kill, injure, harass, intimidate, or place under surveillance with intent to kill, injure, harass, or intimidate another person, and in the course of, or as a result of, such travel or presence engages in conduct that —

(A) places that person in reasonable fear of the death of, or serious bodily injury to —

(i) that person;

(ii) an immediate family member (as defined in section 115) of that person; or

(iii) a spouse or intimate partner of that person; or

(B) causes, attempts to cause, or would be reasonably expected to cause substantial emotional distress to a person described in clause (i), (ii), or (iii) of subparagraph (A); or

(2) with the intent to kill, injure, harass, intimidate, or place under surveillance with intent to kill, injure, harass, or intimidate another person, uses the mail, any interactive computer service or electronic communication service or electronic communication system of interstate commerce, or any other facility of interstate or foreign commerce to engage in a course of conduct that—

(A) places that person in reasonable fear of the death of or serious bodily injury to a person described in clause (i), (ii), or (iii) of paragraph (1) (A); or

(B) causes, attempts to cause, or would be reasonably expected to cause substantial emotional distress to a person described in clause (i), (ii), or (iii) of paragraph (1)(A),

shall be punished as provided in section 2261(b) of this title.

1. Protection from Harassing and Threatening Behavior

Despite common threads, state laws vary quite a bit with respect to stalking laws. For example, some jurisdictions require proof of a credible threat of bodily harm, while others treat the stalking itself as criminal behavior. Some statutes also require proof that the stalker intended to induce fear in the victim. However, because it can be difficult to prove what a person's specific intent was, many states have made stalking a "general intent" crime. This means that intent to cause harm does not need to be established, only that the defendant intentionally engaged in a prohibited act.

2. Cyberstalking

When stalking laws were first enacted in the 1990s, it was not possible to foresee how the use of social media, electronic communications, websites, cell phones, GPS tracking devices, and the like could be used to stalk an individual. Social networking profiles provide stalkers with an easy way to track and monitor the whereabouts of their intended victims based upon updating posts designed to keep family and friends abreast of current activities. In addition, spyware may be remotely installed on someone's computer as a way to gain access to the intended victim's e-mail, passwords, and computer activities. Today, however, what is commonly referred to as "cyberstalking" is a significant problem that the law is slowly catching up with. Like "offline" stalkers, most "online" stalkers "are motivated by a desire to control their victims," and they use a wide range of techniques to accomplish this. As indicated in the U.S. Department of Justice, Office of Justice Program, 2001 report on stalking and domestic violence:

[A] [c]yberstalker may send repeated, threatening, or harassing messages by the simple push of a button. More sophisticated cyberstalkers use programs to send messages at

Cyberstalking Laws

In order to keep up with the technology of stalking on the Internet, many states have amended their laws to clarify that stalking includes electronic communications. California's amendment to its civil code is an example:

Cal. Civ. Code §1708-1725

SECTION 1. It is the intent of this act to clarify that electronic communications are included in the actions that can constitute the crimes of harassment and stalking. It is not the intent of the Legislature, by adoption of this act, to restrict in any way the types of conduct or actions that can constitute harassment or stalking.

regular or random intervals without being physically present at the computer terminal. . . . In addition, a cyberstalker can dupe other Internet users into harassing or threatening a victim by, for example, posting a victim's name, telephone number, or e-mail addresses on a bulletin board or chat room.

Although the technology has clearly outpaced the law, the law is beginning to catch up. A number of states have either enacted specific cyberstalking laws, or amended their existing stalking laws to specifically include cyberstalking.

In addition, the Interstate Stalking Law makes it a federal crime to use an "interactive computer service . . . to engage in a course of conduct that causes serious emotional distress" or that places a person in "reasonable fear of the death of, or serious injury to" him or herself, an immediate family member, or his/her spouse or intimate partner. 18 U.S.C. §2261A(2)(A and B) (2013). The constitutionality of this statute was challenged in the 2014 case of *United States v. Sayer*.

Case Preview

United States v. Sayer

United States v. Sayer involved a challenge to the constitutionality of 18 U.S.C. §2261A, the federal cyberstalking statute. Sayer pled guilty to one count of cyberstalking and was sentenced to the maximum penalty of 60 months in prison. Sayer appealed on the grounds that the statute allegedly violated his constitutional right of free speech, and that the statute was further overbroad and void for vagueness. The case looked at the important principle of whether as applied to the defendant, the statute was unconstitutional since it criminalized protected speech.

As you read *United States v. Sayer*, look for the following:

1. What provisions of the federal cyberstalking statute did the court rely upon in reaching its decision?
2. How did the defendant violate the statute?
3. What did the defendant claim were his rights under the First Amendment that would allow him to post items on the Internet about Jane Doe?
4. What does the court say about speech that also involves criminal conduct?

United States v. Sayer
748 F.3d 425 (1st Cir. 2014)

. . .

The facts are not disputed on appeal. Sayer and the victim in this case, Jane Doe, had dated in Maine starting some time in 2004 until Jane Doe ended their relationship in January 2006. After their break-up, Sayer persistently stalked and harassed Jane Doe for over four years. [This harassment included Sayer showing up at stores and other places where he knew she would be. After Jane Doe obtained an order of protection, Sayer started using the Internet to induce anonymous third parties to harass her.] . . .

Specifically, several unknown men came to Jane Doe's house in Maine one day in October 2008 claiming that they had met her online and were seeking "sexual entertainment." . . . She later discovered an online ad in the "casual encounters" section of Craigslist, a classified advertisements website, that had pictures of her in lingerie that Sayer had taken while they were dating. The ad gave detailed directions to her home and described a list of sexual acts she was supposedly willing to perform. Jane Doe did not place these ads nor did she authorize Sayer to place them. The unwanted visits from men seeking sex persisted for eight months until June 2009, when Jane Doe changed her name and moved to her aunt's house in Louisiana to escape from Sayer and this harassment.

[The harassment continued when an unknown man came to her home in Louisiana who knew her new name and said he met her online and was seeking sexual encounters.] When Jane Doe later searched the internet, she found videos of herself and Sayer engaged in consensual sexual acts from when they were dating on at least three pornography sites. Several of the websites included Jane Doe's name and then-current Louisiana address. One site encouraged viewers to write to Jane Doe and tell her what they thought of the videos. Jane Doe contacted the police again in late September 2009 because someone had posted a fraudulent account in her name on Facebook, a social networking site, which included sexually explicit pictures of her.

. . .

Forensic analysis of a laptop computer they seized [from Sayer's home] showed that Sayer had created "numerous fake profiles" through Yahoo! Messenger, an online chat service, using some variation of Jane Doe's name, between June and November 2009. All of the profiles had sexually suggestive or explicit pictures of Jane Doe and in many cases directed viewers to sex videos of her on adult pornography sites. In many instances, Sayer, posing as Jane Doe, chatted with men online and encouraged them to visit Jane Doe at her home in Louisiana. Jane Doe said Sayer did not stop sending men to her home until he was arrested by state police in July 2010 for violating a protection order she had against him.

. . .

Sayer initially pled not guilty to both counts on July 19, 2011. On February 16, 2012, in a pre-trial motion to dismiss the cyberstalking count, Sayer made three constitutional arguments: (1) the cyberstalking statute is unconstitutional as applied to him because it imposes criminal sanctions on protected speech; (2) the statute is overbroad in violation of the First Amendment; and (3) the statute is unconstitutionally vague in violation of the Fifth Amendment.

. . .

Under §2261A(2)(A), a defendant must first have the intent "to kill, injure, harass, or place [a victim] under surveillance with intent to kill, injure, harass, or intimidate, or cause substantial emotional distress." Second, the defendant must engage in a "course of conduct" that actually "causes substantial emotional distress . . . or places [the victim] in reasonable fear of . . . death . . . or serious bodily injury. . . ." 18 U.S.C. §2261A(2)(A). Sayer argues that because his course of conduct involved speech, or online communications, it cannot be proscribed in accord with the First Amendment. This argument is meritless. "[I]t has never been deemed an abridgement of freedom of speech or press to make a course of conduct illegal merely because the conduct was in part initiated, evidenced, or carried out by means of language, either spoken, written, or printed." *Giboney v. Empire Storage & Ice Co.*, 336 U.S. 490, 502, 69 S. Ct. 684, 93 L. Ed. 834 (1949). For example, in *Giboney* the Court held that enjoining otherwise lawful picketing activities did not violate the First Amendment where the sole purpose of that picketing was to force a company to enter an unlawful agreement restraining trade in violation of a state criminal statute. Id. at 501-02. Speech integral to criminal conduct is now recognized as a "long-established category of unprotected speech." *Stevens*, 559 U.S. at 471, 130 S. Ct. 1577. Sayer's online communications fall in this category.

Sayer does not claim that his acts of creating false online advertisements and accounts in Jane Doe's name or impersonating Jane Doe on the internet constitute legal conduct. In fact, he has admitted that his conduct, which deceptively enticed men to Jane Doe's home, put Jane Doe in danger and at risk of physical harm. To the extent his course of conduct targeting Jane Doe involved speech at all, his speech is not protected. Here, as in *Giboney*, it served only to implement Sayer's criminal purpose. . . . The Eighth Circuit rejected a similar First Amendment challenge to §2261A(2)(A) in *United States v. Petrovic*, 701 F.3d 849 (8th Cir. 2012). There, the defendant had created a website with links to images of his ex-wife "in the nude or engaging in sex acts" with him. Id. at 853. The defendant also sent sexually explicit pictures of his ex-wife to her work, her boss, and her relatives. Id. The court held that these "communications," which resulted in the defendant's §2261A(2)(A) conviction, were integral to criminal conduct and unprotected under *Giboney*, as they carried out the defendant's extortionate threats to harass and humiliate his ex-wife if she terminated their sexual relationship. Id. at 855. . . . Sayer points to no lawful purpose of the communications at issue here that would take them outside the *Giboney* exception. . . . Nor can we surmise any on this record. Rather, his conduct lured potentially dangerous men to Jane Doe's doorstep, men whom Jane Doe was not free to ignore. As a result, §2261A(2)(A) has been constitutionally applied to Sayer.

[The court also dismissed challenges by Sayer on the grounds of overbreath and void for vagueness.]

For these reasons we affirm.

Post-Case Follow-Up

Had Sayer shown up at the doorstep of Jane Doe there would be no doubt that he had violated the restraining order. However, instead of his personal presence, he used online communications to entice others to come near her. Sayer admits that enticing men to Jane Doe's home put her in danger and at risk of physical harm. However, he argued that although his conduct was illegal under the statute, the statute is unconstitutional because it violated his right to free speech.

The court, relying on its previous holding in *Giboney*, finds that lawful activity, such as picketing, can be enjoined without violating free speech when the sole purpose of the speech is to encourage criminal conduct. Thus, speech that is integral to criminal conduct is unprotected speech and the defense is not available in response to a charge for violation of the cyberstalking statute.

United States v. Sayer: Real Life Applications

1. Melissa has obtained a restraining order against Kevin as part of her decree of dissolution. Kevin knows he cannot go near Melissa, but instead has installed a GPS tracking device on her car so he at least knows where she has been going.

   a. Is Kevin's conduct a violation of Section 2261A of the Interstate Stalking Punishment and Prevention Act?
   b. What if Melissa did not know the GPS was placed on her car until after Kevin removed it?
   c. What if Melissa knew about the GPS and told a friend that she purposefully went places to throw Kevin off track?
   d. What facts would be important to know in determining whether Kevin could be found guilty of violating Section 2261A?

2. Perry and Denise met on an Internet dating site and dated for three months before Denise broke it off. Perry became upset when he saw that Denise was back on the Internet dating site. Accordingly, he developed an online profile for Denise under a different name and engaged in "chats" with several men. He then asked the men to meet "her" at her house and gave detailed directions to her home. Does Denise have a claim under the court's analysis in *United States v. Sayer*? Would it make a difference if it was Denise who had created a profile for Perry and sent women to Perry's house?

E. SPECIALIZED DOMESTIC VIOLENCE COURTS

Intimate partner violence is a pervasive and multidimensional problem, and in contrast to other types of family law matters, abuse prevention cases are both civil and criminal in nature. Adding to the complexity and potential fragmentation of the legal response to intimate partner violence, a couple may also be involved in separate legal proceedings, such as a divorce or custody action, in which domestic violence is a central consideration.

To address this reality, a growing number of jurisdictions have established specialized courts to address the problems inherent in the traditionally fragmented approach to domestic violence cases. Although the models vary, most use a carefully coordinated approach to the handling of the civil and criminal components of these actions at its core. Thus, the specialty domestic violence courts will often provide victim advocates, support groups, and assistance with navigating the legal system. Another important advantage is that civil and criminal jurisdiction may be combined in a single court, thus enabling the court to both issue protective orders and prosecute criminal violations.

F. THE FEDERAL RESPONSE TO DOMESTIC VIOLENCE: THE VIOLENCE AGAINST WOMEN ACT

In 1994, Congress enacted the Violence Against Women Act (VAWA) as part of a national effort to combat intimate partner violence against women. Pub. L. No. 103-322, 108 Stat. 1902 (1994). In addition to establishing federal protections and remedies for abuse victims, VAWA provides grants to states to enable them to better meet the needs domestic violence victims, by, for example, training police officers, supporting community anti-violence initiatives, providing victims with legal advocacy services, and assisting victims with immigration matters.

1. The Extension of Full Faith and Credit to Abuse Prevention Orders

Demonstrations in support of VAWA
Associated Press

Prior to VAWA, states often did not recognize protective orders from other states and required domestic violence victims who had left their home states to obtain new orders. VAWA fills a significant enforcement gap by requiring states to give full faith and credit to protective orders from other states that meet the basic requirements of the Act — including that the court had jurisdiction over the parties and provided the defendant with reasonable notice and an opportunity to be heard — and to enforce these orders as if they were issued by a court in that state. VAWA makes it clear that states must now also give full faith and credit to custody, visitation, and support provisions that are included in protective orders.

2. Protections for Battered Immigrant Women

VAWA recognizes that battered immigrant women are a particularly vulnerable population. The fear of deportation or the dependence on a spouse for obtaining lawful permanent resident status may prevent immigrant women from seeking protection from or filing criminal charges against an abuser. VAWA therefore permits a battered immigrant to self-petition for lawful permanent resident status, which can free her from reliance on an abusive spouse to obtain this status. The Act also provides battered immigrant women with expanded opportunities to petition for relief from deportation proceedings.

3. Recent Amendments

VAWA has been reauthorized and expanded several times since 1994, with the most recent reauthorization of the Act being signed into law in 2013. Pub. L. No. 113-4, §1-1264, 127 Stat. 54. VAWA 2013 fills two historic gaps in the Act as follows.

First, in recognition of the fact that American Indian and Alaska Native women suffer from a higher rate of intimate partner violence than any other population of women, the previous reauthorization of VAWA increased funding for and improved the delivery of services to Native women. However, a continued problem was that tribal courts lacked criminal jurisdiction over non-Indian perpetrators of domestic and dating violence, even if the acts were committed on Indian lands. VAWA 2013 addressed this problem by clarifying the authority of tribal courts to issue and enforce civil orders of protection against non-Indians as well as Indians.

Second, VAWA 2013 includes a strong antidiscrimination provision that bars any program or activity that receives VAWA funds from discriminating against any person seeking access to assistance or services on the basis of gender orientation or sexual orientation. This provision also ensures that the term "victim" as used in the Act includes someone who has been injured by a same-sex intimate partner.

G. WORKING WITH VICTIMS OF DOMESTIC VIOLENCE

Although there is no easy formula for how to work with victims of partner violence, the following considerations will contribute to effective and supportive interactions with clients who have been abused:

- Victims often feel a tremendous sense of shame and may be reluctant to acknowledge the violence in their lives. Listen carefully for clues that may suggest an abusive relationship — for example, a woman who says, "Well, I don't get out much; my husband doesn't approve of my friends." Inquire further in a sensitive manner. You might, for example, respond to such statements with the following questions: "Why doesn't your husband approve of your friends?" and "What might happen if you went out with someone he doesn't approve of?" With a client who is not quite ready to open up, these questions work more effectively than do more direct questions such as "So, is your husband abusive?"

■ Trust the client's assessment of the danger; too often, professionals minimize the potential risks that victims face.

■ You should fully inform clients about the abuse prevention laws in your state. If your office does not assist clients in obtaining protective orders, then provide referrals.

■ Understand that it can be very difficult for persons to extricate themselves from an abusive relationship. For example, a client may have no money and be unable to find housing that she can afford. She may fear greater harm if she leaves. She may fear community or family disapproval, or she may worry about taking the children away from their father. It is not your job to criticize her for failing to leave or take action. She should know that your services are available if and when she does decide to leave or seek a court order.

■ Make certain you have information available regarding local shelters, hotline numbers, and battered women's support groups. These are invaluable resources. Many shelters, hospitals, and police departments have developed materials on "safety plans" that help domestic violence victims think through how best to extricate themselves from a dangerous situation. You should also make these available.

■ If you are assisting an abuse victim who is an immigrant to this country, you should be aware that certain protections may be available under the federal Violence Against Women Act. In this situation, it may be appropriate for the client to also meet with an immigration law specialist (see the discussion above on VAWA, Section F).

Chapter Summary

■ All states have abuse prevention laws that enable domestic violence victims to obtain civil orders of protection. In some states, the statutes are broad and cover most intimate and family relationships; in other states, the scope of coverage is narrower, and many individuals may not be able to obtain protection. A few states also expressly exclude same-sex couples from the reach of their statutes.

■ Protection can be obtained from a wide range of abusive behaviors, including physical abuse, attempted physical abuse, sexual assaults, and threats of harm and harassment.

■ Many types of relief can be included in a protective order, such as ordering the respondent to refrain from further acts of abuse, to vacate the premises, to avoid any contact with the petitioner, and to relinquish any firearms.

■ A protective order is usually obtained in two stages. First, the petitioner appears before the court in an *ex parte* proceeding at which temporary relief may be ordered. At the second hearing, both parties are given the opportunity to present their version of events.

▨ Specialized domestic violence courts that provide integrated legal and social services are a recent innovation designed to eliminate the disjointed approach to domestic abuse cases.

▨ Effective enforcement procedures are essential to ensure the safety of abuse victims, and much effort has been devoted to increasing the responsiveness of the criminal justice system, including the adoption of mandatory arrest and prosecution policies.

▨ All states now have anti-stalking laws that criminalize qualifying harassing or threatening behavior, and many now also treat cyberstalking, which is a rapidly growing problem, as a crime.

▨ At the federal level, VAWA has increased protections for domestic violence victims by criminalizing interstate acts of violence and requiring states to give full faith and credit to protective orders. The Act also provides relief to battered immigrants, such as by allowing them to self-petition for lawful permanent resident status, thus avoiding reliance on the batterer and expanding anti-deportation protections.

Applying the Rules

1. Jeremy and Shelley have never been married; however, they do have a child in common, five-year-old Natalie. Shelley only permits Jeremy to exercise parenting time with Natalie at Shelley's home. On a recent visit, Jeremy and Shelley began arguing about whether Natalie should be permitted to go to a birthday party at a friend's home that has an unfenced pool. Shelley became angry at Jeremy and raised her voice. Jeremy, concerned that the neighbors would hear Shelley screaming, told her to "shut up" and went toward her to cover her mouth to stop her from screaming. Shelley backed away and told Jeremy if he came any closer she would call the police. Jeremy, upset with the entire incident, left the house. Protective orders are available in your state for acts of domestic violence that include physical assault, such as hitting or kicking; threatening words or conduct; and intimidation. Shelley has obtained an *ex parte* order of protection. The hearing is set in one week and Jeremy has sought your legal advice. What arguments can you make on behalf of Jeremy to quash the order of protection?

2. Patty and Diego are married, but Diego has recently moved out of the family residence and intends to file for a divorce. Diego seeks your advice as to whether he can obtain an order of protection against Patty. He claims that one of the reasons he left the family residence is that Patty was constantly yelling at him for what he considered to be small things such as leaving dishes in the sink or socks on the floor. When she would yell he often would try to retreat to the bedroom, but she would often come after him and continue yelling until he would lock the door. Eventually, she would calm down, but he always feared that one day she would cause physical harm to him. Assume protective orders are available for acts of domestic violence that include physical assault, such as hitting or

kicking; threatening words or conduct; and intimidation. Can Diego seek an order of protection? What arguments would you make on behalf of Diego to obtain an order of protection?

3. Chris and Jane Doe began a romantic relationship. Several months later, Jane Doe attempted to break all ties with Chris. Chris threatened that if she attempted to leave him he would make sure no other person wanted to date her. Based on these statements, Jane Doe obtained an order of protection. However, in violation of the protection order, Chris continued to make contact with Jane Doe. These contacts included leaving a handwritten note and flowers on her car, hang-up calls over a three-day weekend, trying to make personal contact through a mutual friend, and damaging her automobile tires when she was inside a store shopping. Has Chris violated any laws? What potential violations might he be charged with?

4. Howard was married to his now ex-wife Tabatha in 2013. After a brief and stormy marriage, they separated in 2015. Tabatha instituted divorce proceedings; moved into her own apartment; was granted temporary custody of their son Evan, then two years old; and received an order of protection that required Howard to stay away from Tabatha except for purposes of picking up Evan for visitations. Howard began visiting Tabatha's apartment, ostensibly to see Evan, sometimes showing up without invitation or notice. The parenting time order required that he advise Tabatha 48 hours in advance when he planned to have visitation with his son. During one of the unannounced visits, Howard took Evan over Tabatha's objections and threatened not to bring him back. Tabatha called the police, asking them to go to Howard's home and retrieve her son. The police told her to wait until evening and see if Howard voluntarily returned him. When he did not she called again, and the police advised her they would to Howard's home the next morning. When they went there the next morning, neither Howard nor Evan was at the house. It has now been three months and neither of them have been found. Tabatha would like to sue the police department. Does she have a claim?

5. Heather is 35 years old and lives in a house with her six-year-old son, Noah. Two months ago the home was flooded and she sought temporary housing while she was involved in negotiations with her insurance company. She met Sam through an online roommate matching service. She rented a room from him for her and Noah for three months and then moved back to her home. She continued to maintain a friendship with Sam because Noah had started to look to Sam as a father figure, and Sam, not having any children of his own, took a liking to Noah. For the next several months, Sam often took Heather and Noah to amusement parks and the zoo, or they would go to the park where Sam would play catch with Noah. Unfortunately, Sam wanted to have a romantic relationship with Heather, but she told him she was not interested and that it would be too uncomfortable for her to have him continue these visits. Despite being told not to come to the house, Sam still comes to her home occasionally and leaves

small gifts, flowers, or toys for Noah on her front doorstep. Even though Sam usually does this when she is not home or after she has gone to bed, Heather finds it creepy. She wants Sam to stop. What are Heather's potential remedies to stop this behavior from Sam?

6. Amy and Anne have been domestic partners for the past six years. Two months ago, Amy moved out of the residence they shared. Anne became very angry and threatened violence against Amy. Amy obtained an order of protection and moved out of state. Anne has now followed Amy to the state where Amy lives. Anne has confronted Amy and told her that there is nothing she can do because the order of protection is from an out-of-state court. Does Amy have any remedies against Anne? What should Amy do?

7. Peter is the father of Jade, age 16. He is very disturbed because Jade has fallen in with a crowd that he does not approve of. In particular, he is concerned about Jade's new boyfriend, Thomas. Jade claims she loves Thomas and she is continually sneaking out of the house to meet him. Peter does not want Jade to see Thomas anymore but knows of no way to stop them. He recently transferred Jade to a different school from Thomas, but he knows that she is still sneaking out of the house at night or making arrangements to meet him. Peter would like to obtain an order of protection to stop Thomas from coming near Jade. Does Peter have the ability to obtain an order of protection under these circumstances on behalf of Jade?

Family Law in Practice

1. Find the abuse prevention act for your state and determine the following:
   - What court(s) are these cases heard in?
   - Who can petition the court for relief?
   - Are dating partners eligible? If so, are there any qualifications?
   - Is a person in a same-sex relationship eligible to seek relief under the statute?
   - What kinds of protection are available?

2. Using the abuse prevention act located for Question 1, trace the court procedure from start to finish. Make sure you include all relevant time frames.

3. Assume that you are serving as a legal advocate at a local battered women's shelter. They have asked you to develop a brochure that sets out the basic elements of your state's abuse prevention law and explains the court process so women coming to the shelter will know what their legal rights are. The key here is to make sure the brochure is complete, accurate, and comprehensible to the layperson.

4. Assume that you are a legislative aide in a state that is considering adopting a mandatory arrest and prosecution law. In an advisory memo, evaluate the arguments in favor of and against such an approach, and then develop a persuasive position in which you argue in favor of or against such a law.

5. A number of women are presently serving time for killing their batterers. A controversial question is whether, as part of their defense cases, expert testimony can be admitted regarding the "battered women's syndrome." Assume you are a trial judge who has been asked to rule on the admissibility of such evidence. Research and then write a legal memorandum setting out your conclusion.

6. Determine if your state court has specialized courts for issuing orders of protection. If so, find a time to sit in for at least one hour during the court proceedings. Write a courtroom observation memorandum that includes the following: date, time, and judge or hearing officer that presided over the proceedings, as well as the number of orders of protection sought during the one-hour proceeding. For each order of protection sought, indicate the basis upon which the plaintiff was seeking to obtain an order of protection, whether the judge or hearing officer granted the order of protection, and whether any conditions were placed on the order of protection.

Determining Parentage

Historically, the legal relationship between parent and child was determined by the marital status of the parents. Children were considered "legitimate" if born to married parents and "illegitimate" if born to unwed parents. Gradually, the law moved away from strict reliance on marital status as the legal determinant of the parent-child relationship, and the traditional distinction between children of married parents and those of unmarried parents has been virtually eliminated. However, unwed parents do not always have the same rights and status that both unwed mothers and married parents have.

We begin this chapter by tracing the evolution of the legal status of children of unmarried parents. We then consider the constitutional rights of unwed fathers, followed by a discussion of paternity establishment and a look at the relatively new topic of paternity disestablishment. We conclude with a discussion about sperm donation and parental rights.

A. HISTORICAL OVERVIEW OF CHILDREN OF UNMARRIED PARENTS

English common law drew a sharp distinction between children born to married parents and those born to unmarried parents. A child of unmarried parents was considered a "filius nullius"—a child of no one. These rules were designed to deter sexual promiscuity, reinforce the institution of marriage, and protect family lineage by ensuring that a father's property, name, and status passed to his legitimate sons in an orderly manner. Following the English tradition, our early laws also

Key Concepts

- Historical overview of the legal status of children of unmarried parents
- Factors in determining paternity
- Factors in paternity disestablishment
- Sperm donation and paternity

placed children of unmarried parents outside the connective threads of family relations.

By the beginning of the nineteenth century, attitudes toward children of unwed mothers had begun to soften, resulting in some legal reforms. This shift in views reflected two broader trends. First, as discussed in Chapter 6, attitudes toward children changed as we moved from an agrarian to an early industrial nation. Children were no longer seen as embodiments of original sin in need of harsh corrective measures but as innocent creatures in need of love and nurturance. Second, the post-Revolutionary emphasis on individual rights and responsibilities raised questions about the fairness of the rules that stigmatized children based on the conduct of their parents.

Creating Limited Family Rights

A central reform was the extension of legal recognition to the mother-child unit. No longer a child of no one, a nonmarital child was now formally recognized as the child of its mother; as a result, mothers were entitled to custody and obligated to provide support. Mothers were favored over fathers both because, unlike paternal identity, maternal identity was readily established, and because a maternal preference was consistent with the prevailing emphasis on female domesticity and the belief in women's superior nurturing capabilities. Thus, by the middle of the nineteenth century, children were considered "legitimate" in relationship to their mothers regardless of their mothers' marital status, although, as discussed below, states maintained clear legal distinctions between children of married parents and those of unmarried parents.

Legitimation

A significant reform was the gradual rejection of the harsh common law rule that a child's status was fixed permanently at birth. Beginning with Virginia in 1823, most states amended their laws to allow for legitimation where parents married each other after the birth of a child. A few states went further than this and were willing to recognize a father-child relationship based on an acknowledgment of paternity.

B. CONSTITUTIONAL DEVELOPMENTS

Although these nineteenth-century reforms mitigated some of the harsh common law rules, children of unmarried parents remained a distinct legal category of persons. Referred to as "bastards" or "illegitimates," they suffered a variety of legal disabilities, particularly in relationship to their fathers. For example, they were frequently excluded as beneficiaries under statutory benefit programs, such as workers' compensation; they lacked inheritance rights under state intestacy laws; and they were denied standing in wrongful death actions for the loss of a parent. Additionally, unwed fathers had few legal rights in relationship to their children. Beginning in the 1960s, a number of lawsuits were brought challenging this differential treatment of children of unmarried parents and the denial of rights to unwed fathers. In the following sections, we will look at the Supreme Court's response to these challenges.

1. The Equal Protection Challenge to Differential Treatment

In 1968, in *Levy v. Louisiana*, 391 U.S. 68 (1968), the Supreme Court held that the state of Louisiana had violated the Equal Protection Clause by denying children the right to recover for the death of their mother under the state's wrongful death law because of their "illegitimate" status. As explained by the Court:

> Legitimacy or illegitimacy of birth has no relation to the nature of the wrong allegedly inflicted on the mother. These children, though illegitimate, were dependent on her; she cared for them and nurtured them; they were indeed hers in the biological and spiritual sense; in her death they suffered wrong in the sense that any dependent would.

Id. at 72. The Court thus recognized that the significance of the parent-child relationship does not depend on the marital status of the parents and further that children should not be discriminated against based on parental conduct over which they had no control.

Since *Levy*, the Court has decided a number of cases involving similar equal protection challenges to laws that discriminated against children born to unmarried parents by, for example, denying or limiting their ability to obtain statutory benefits or to inherit under state intestacy laws. Unfortunately, these decisions are not always clear and consistent with one another; nonetheless, some general principles do emerge from them.

First, a court must carefully review any law that classifies children based on the marital status of their parents. Central to this review, the court must evaluate the reason for the statutory classification. If its purpose is to deter nonmarital sexual relations or promote the state's interest in marriage, the classification is invalid because these goals do not justify the discriminatory treatment of children. Children may not be disadvantaged based on circumstances over which they have no control. Moreover, states may not deprive children of benefits based on the assumption that there cannot be a meaningful parent-child relationship outside the marital family unit.

Second, although a law may not discriminate against children of unmarried parents in order to promote marriage or regulate sexual behavior, all legal distinctions between children of unmarried parents and children of married parents are not necessarily unconstitutional. Most important, if a distinction is carefully drawn for the purpose of preventing fraudulent claims, it is likely to withstand constitutional scrutiny. For example, although a state may not deprive nonmarital children of paternal inheritance rights under its intestacy statute in order to encourage marriage, it probably can condition these rights upon a prior adjudication of paternity in order to prevent fraudulent claims. Thus, a state may be able to exclude a child from receiving a statutory share of benefits where the father-child relationship had not been formally established prior to the father's death.

2. The Legal Status of the Unwed Father

As developed above, the differential treatment of children of unmarried parents is impermissible for the purpose of discouraging nonmarital sexual relations or promoting marriage. However, what if it is the unwed father rather than the child who is singled out for differential treatment? Should the law treat him in the same manner that it treats an unwed mother or a married father, or does he occupy a distinct legal position in relationship to his child? Are the cases involving the interests of unwed fathers the flip side of the cases involving children, or are different considerations at stake? To consider these questions, we turn to a series of landmark United States Supreme Court cases focusing on the rights of unwed fathers.

Challenging the Exclusion of Unwed Fathers

In 1972, in *Stanley v. Illinois*, 405 U.S. 645 (1972), the Court considered whether it was unconstitutional for a state to presume that all unwed fathers were unfit parents. Peter and Joan Stanley had lived together on an intermittent basis for 18 years. During this time, they had three children together. When Joan Stanley died, the state of Illinois initiated a dependency proceeding. The children were declared wards of the state for lack of a surviving parent and placed in the care of a court-appointed guardian. Peter Stanley was not provided with an opportunity to challenge the removal of his children because the state of Illinois presumed that all unwed fathers were unfit to raise their children. In contrast, married parents and unwed mothers could not be deprived of their children without a hearing on the issue of fitness.

Stanley challenged the presumption of unfitness, which effectively severed his tie with his children without inquiry into their actual circumstances, and argued that, like other parents, he too was entitled to a hearing on the question of fitness. Although acknowledging, as argued by the state, that most unwed fathers may in fact be "unsuitable and neglectful" parents, the Court nonetheless agreed with Stanley that he could not be deprived of custody without a hearing. In supporting Stanley's claim, the Court recognized the potential for meaningful relationships between unwed fathers and their children and made clear that paternal rights do not merit protection only when developed within a marital family unit. *Id.* at 654-658.

Following *Stanley*, it appeared as if the Court might be moving in the direction of eliminating all distinctions between unwed fathers and other parents. However, the Court did not make clear why it was protecting Stanley's rights. Would a mere biological connection to these children have entitled him to a hearing, or was he entitled to a hearing because, in the words of the Court, he had both "sired and raised" them? *Id.* at 651.

What Makes an Unwed Father a Father?

After *Stanley*, a number of unwed fathers brought lawsuits challenging state laws that permitted the adoption of nonmarital children based solely on the consent of the mother. Building on *Stanley*, they argued (1) that an unwed father has a constitutionally protected liberty interest in maintaining a parental relationship with his child that cannot be abrogated without his consent absent proof of unfitness; and (2) that differential treatment of unwed fathers and unwed mothers violates the Equal Protection Clause.

In responding to these challenges, the Court answered the question left open in *Stanley.* In particular, in the 1983 case of *Lehr v. Robertson,* 463 U.S. 248 (1983), the Court clarified that the rights of unwed fathers do not spring into being based solely on the biological link between father and child.

Case Preview

Lehr v. Robertson

In *Lehr v. Robertson,* Jessica M. was born out of wedlock on November 9, 1976. Her biological father was Jonathan Lehr. However, her mother, Lorraine, married Richard Robertson eight months after Jessica's birth. When Jessica was two years old, Lorraine and her husband Richard filed an adoption petition, which was approved by the court. Jonathan, after learning of the adoption, filed this action claiming that he was the putative father and that since he had never been given notice of the adoption, the adoption was invalid. He argued that the Due Process and Equal Protection Clauses gave him an absolute right to notice and an opportunity to be heard before the child could be adopted.

The issue before the Court was whether the state of New York sufficiently protected an unmarried father's undeveloped relationship with his two-year-old child whom he had never financially supported and had rarely seen since birth.

As you read *Lehr v. Robertson,* look for the following:

1. Although the father admitted he did not fall into any of the classes of possible fathers entitled to notice of adoption proceedings, why did he nonetheless believe he was entitled to notice of the proceeding?
2. What was the gender-based classification that the father claimed denied him the right to consent to the adoption?
3. What reasons did the Court give for denying the father's due process claim?
4. On what basis did the Court distinguish this case from previous cases involving the constitutional claims of unwed fathers vis-à-vis their children?
5. According to the Court, what steps would the father have needed to take in order to prevail on his due process claim?

Lehr v. Robertson
463 U.S. 248 (1983)

STEVENS, Justice.

The question presented is whether New York has sufficiently protected an unmarried father's inchoate relationship with a child whom he has never supported and rarely seen in the two years since her birth. The appellant, Jonathan Lehr, claims that the Due Process and Equal Protection Clauses of the Fourteenth Amendment, as interpreted in *Stanley v. Illinois*, 405 U.S. 645, 92 S. Ct. 1208, 31 L. Ed. 2d 551 (1972), and *Caban v. Mohammed*, 441 U.S. 380, 99 S. Ct. 1760, 60 L. Ed. 2d 297 (1979), give him an absolute right to notice and an opportunity to be heard before the child may be adopted. We disagree.

Jessica M. was born out of wedlock on November 9, 1976. Her mother, Lorraine Robertson, married Richard Robertson eight months after Jessica's birth. On December 21, 1978, when Jessica was over two years old, the Robertsons filed an adoption petition in the Family Court of Ulster County, New York. The court heard their testimony and received a favorable report from the Ulster County Department of Social Services. On March 7, 1979, the court entered an order of adoption. In this proceeding, appellant contends that the adoption order is invalid because he, Jessica's putative father, was not given advance notice of the adoption proceeding.

The State of New York maintains a "putative father registry." A man who files with that registry demonstrates his intent to claim paternity of a child born out of wedlock and is therefore entitled to receive notice of any proceeding to adopt that child. Before entering Jessica's adoption order, the Ulster County Family Court had the putative father registry examined. Although appellant claims to be Jessica's natural father, he had not entered his name in the registry.

In addition to the persons whose names are listed on the putative father registry, New York law requires that notice of an adoption proceeding be given to several other classes of possible fathers of children born out of wedlock—those who have been adjudicated to be the father, those who have been identified as the father on the child's birth certificate, those who live openly with the child and the child's mother and who hold themselves out to be the father, those who have been identified as the father by the mother in a sworn written statement, and those who were married to the child's mother before the child was six months old. Appellant admittedly was not a member of any of those classes. He had lived with appellee prior to Jessica's birth and visited her in the hospital when Jessica was born, but his name does not appear on Jessica's birth certificate. He did not live with appellee or Jessica after Jessica's birth, he has never provided them with any financial support, and he has never offered to marry appellee. Nevertheless, he contends that the following special circumstances gave him a constitutional right to notice and a hearing before Jessica was adopted.

[One month after the adoption proceedings were filed in Ulster County, the appellant, not realizing the adoption proceedings had been filed, filed an action for paternity and visitation in Westchester County. Appellee was served with notice of that action. Upon learning of the action, appellee's attorneys advised the Ulster County judge of the paternity proceeding. The Ulster County judge entered an order staying the paternity action until he could rule on a motion to change venue of that proceeding to Ulster County. Appellant received notice of the change of venue, which is how he learned of the adoption proceedings. Four days after receiving notice, appellant's attorney telephoned the Ulster County judge to inform him that he planned on filing a motion to stay the adoption proceedings. The judge stated that he had signed the adoption order the day before and that he was aware of the pending paternity petition but did not believe he was required to give notice to appellant prior to the entry of the order of adoption. The Family Court in Westchester County then granted appellee's motion to dismiss the paternity action. A motion to vacate the order of adoption was denied. The Appellate Division of the Supreme Court of New York affirmed the adoption, as did the New York Court of Appeals.]

Appellant . . . offers two alternative grounds for holding the New York statutory scheme unconstitutional. First, he contends that a putative father's actual or potential relationship with a child born out of wedlock is an interest in liberty which may not be destroyed without due process of law; he argues therefore that he had a constitutional right to prior notice and an opportunity to be heard before he was deprived of that interest. Second, he contends that the gender-based classification in the statute, which both denied him the right to consent to Jessica's adoption and accorded him fewer procedural rights than her mother, violated the Equal Protection Clause.

THE DUE PROCESS CLAIM

The Fourteenth Amendment provides that no State shall deprive any person of life, liberty, or property without due process of law. . . . We therefore first consider the nature of the interest in liberty for which appellant claims constitutional protection and then turn to a discussion of the adequacy of the procedure that New York has provided for its protection.

I

The intangible fibers that connect parent and child have infinite variety. They are woven throughout the fabric of our society, providing it with strength, beauty, and flexibility. It is self-evident that they are sufficiently vital to merit constitutional protection in appropriate cases. In deciding whether this is such a case, however, we must consider the broad framework that has traditionally been used to resolve the legal problems arising from the parent-child relationship.

In the vast majority of cases, state law determines the final outcome. . . . In some cases, however, this Court has held that the Federal Constitution supersedes state law and provides even greater protection for certain formal family relationships. In those cases, as in the state cases, the Court has emphasized the paramount interest in the welfare of children and has noted that the rights of the parents are a counterpart of the responsibilities they have assumed. Thus, the "liberty" of parents to control the education of their children that was vindicated in *Meyer v. Nebraska*, 262 U.S. 390, 43 S. Ct. 625, 67 L. Ed. 1042 (1923), and *Pierce v. Society of Sisters*, 268 U.S. 510, 45 S. Ct. 571, 69 L. Ed. 1070 (1925), was described as a "right, coupled with the high duty, to recognize and prepare [the child] for additional obligations." Id., at 535. . . .

There are also a few cases in which this Court has considered the extent to which the Constitution affords protection to the relationship between natural parents and children born out of wedlock. . . . This Court has examined the extent to which a natural father's biological relationship with his illegitimate child receives protection under the Due Process Clause in precisely three cases: *Stanley v. Illinois*, 405 U.S. 645, 92 S. Ct. 1208, 31 L. Ed. 2d 551 (1972), *Quilloin v. Walcott*, 434 U.S. 246, 98 S. Ct. 549, 54 L. Ed. 2d 511 (1978), and *Caban v. Mohammed*, 441 U.S. 380, 99 S. Ct. 1760, 60 L. Ed. 2d 297 (1979).

. . .

The difference between the developed parent-child relationship that was implicated in *Stanley* and *Caban*, and the potential relationship involved in *Quilloin* and this case, is both clear and significant. When an unwed father demonstrates a full commitment to the responsibilities of parenthood by "com[ing] forward to participate in the rearing of his child," *Caban*, 441 U.S., at 392, 99 S. Ct., at 1768, his interest in personal contact with his child acquires substantial protection under the due process clause. At that point it may be said that he "act[s] as a father toward his children." Id., at 389, n.7. But the mere existence of a biological link does not merit equivalent constitutional protection. . . .

The significance of the biological connection is that it offers the natural father an opportunity that no other male possesses to develop a relationship with his offspring. If he grasps that opportunity and accepts some measure of responsibility for the child's future, he may enjoy the blessings of the parent-child relationship and make uniquely valuable contributions to the child's development. If he fails to do so, the Federal Constitution will not automatically compel a state to listen to his opinion of where the child's best interests lie.

In this case, we are not assessing the constitutional adequacy of New York's procedures for terminating a developed relationship. Appellant has never had any significant custodial, personal, or financial relationship with Jessica, and he did not seek to establish a legal tie until after she was two years old. . . .

II

The most effective protection of the putative father's opportunity to develop a relationship with his child is provided by the laws that authorize formal marriage and govern its consequences. But the availability of that protection is, of course, dependent on the will of both parents of the child. Thus, New York has adopted a special statutory scheme to protect the unmarried father's interest in assuming a responsible role in the future of his child.

. . .

[The Court rejected the father's argument that he was entitled to special notice because he had filed this argument as an indirect attack on the notice provisions of the New York statute.] Since the New York statutes adequately protected appellant's inchoate interest in establishing a relationship with Jessica, we find no merit in the claim that his constitutional rights were offended because the Family Court strictly complied with the notice provisions of the statute.

THE EQUAL PROTECTION CLAIM

The concept of equal justice under law requires the State to govern impartially. . . .

The legislation at issue in this case . . . is intended to establish procedures for adoptions. Those procedures are designed to promote the best interests of the child, to protect the rights of interested third parties, and to ensure promptness and finality. To serve those ends, the legislation guarantees to certain people the right to veto an adoption and the right to prior notice of any adoption proceeding. The mother of an illegitimate child is always within that favored class, but only certain putative fathers are included. Appellant contends that the gender-based distinction is invidious.

As we have already explained, the existence or nonexistence of a substantial relationship between parent and child is a relevant criterion in evaluating both the rights of the parent and the best interests of the child. In *Quilloin v. Walcott*, we noted that the putative father, like appellant, "ha[d] never shouldered any significant responsibility with respect to the daily supervision, education, protection, or care of the child. Appellant does not complain of his exemption from these responsibilities. . . ."

We therefore found that a Georgia statute that always required a mother's consent to the adoption of a child born out of wedlock, but required the father's consent only if he had legitimated the child, did not violate the Equal Protection Clause. Because appellant, like the father in *Quilloin*, has never established a substantial relationship with his daughter, . . . the New York statutes at issue in this case did not operate to deny appellant equal protection.

Jessica's parents are not like the parents involved in *Caban*. Whereas appellee had a continuous custodial responsibility for Jessica, appellant never established any custodial, personal, or financial relationship with her. If one parent has an established custodial relationship with the child and the other parent has either abandoned or never established a relationship, the Equal Protection Clause does not prevent a state from according the two parents different legal rights.

The judgment of the New York Court of Appeals is Affirmed.

Post-Case Follow-Up

According to the Court, the significance of the biological connection is that it provides a father with the unique opportunity to develop a relationship with his offspring. If he grasps that opportunity and assumes some responsibility for the child, he may be entitled to some of the benefits and rights that attach to the parent-child relationship; however, if he fails to grasp this opportunity, he cannot claim a constitutionally protected right to participate in the adoption decision. In short, outside of the marital context, biology alone does not a father make. Instead, a man must act like a father to be legally recognized as one and thus entitled to an equal say regarding adoption. This "biology-plus" approach drew harsh criticism from the dissent, who argued that the biological tie itself merits protection because it is the nature rather than the weight of the interest that is important.

Lehr v. Robinson: Real Life Applications

1. Jason and Jenny met three years ago. They lived together for approximately six months and then Jason moved out. Shortly thereafter Jenny advised Jason she

was pregnant. Jason visited Jenny infrequently, but he did give her $500 to help cover the cost of prenatal vitamins and unreimbursed medical expenses for her prenatal check-ups. When the baby, Laurie, was born, Jason came to visit Laurie and Jenny in the hospital. When Jenny checked out of the hospital, she did not go back to her previous home and appeared to just disappear with the baby. For over 18 months Jason tried to locate Jenny. With the aid of a private investigator, he found her living about two hours away. She was married to Ben Anderson and had assumed the last name Anderson. Laurie was enrolled in a day care and also used the last name Anderson. Jason discovered that adoption proceedings were pending to allow Ben to adopt Laurie. Does Jason have any legal rights?

2. Assume the same facts as in Question 1, but adoption proceedings have not yet started. After Jason found Jenny and Laurie, his lawyer wrote to Jenny asking if Jason could have visitation rights. Jenny ignored the request and instead started the adoption proceedings. Jason intervened in the adoption proceedings and requested parenting rights. The trial court denied the request relying upon *Lehr v. Robinson*. How should the appellate court rule?

3. Hideki and Carolyn had a one-night stand that resulted in the birth of a baby boy. Carolyn assured Hideki he would always have parenting rights and there was no need to do anything as she intended on keeping the baby. Hideki liked this arrangement because he knew as long as nothing was formalized he would not have to pay child support. He exercised informal parenting time approximately once every week, sometimes more, when he would come over to visit with Carolyn and the baby. Oftentimes Carolyn would leave Hideki and the baby alone together while she ran errands. This arrangement went on for eight months. However, one afternoon when Hideki came to the house, Carolyn answered the door and said that she was really sorry but she found motherhood was too stressful for her at this time and she had decided to give the baby up for adoption. Hideki did some checking and confirmed that Carolyn had put the baby up for adoption. The baby was now placed with another couple, although the adoption was not yet final. Hideki has come to you to find out his rights. The state that Hideki resides in has a putative father registry, but Hideki did not know about its existence. What rights, if any, does Hideki have?

In the 2001 case of *Nguyen v. Immigration and Naturalization Services*, 533 U.S. 53 (2001), the Court reaffirmed its support of the "biology-plus" approach. In *Nguyen*, the Court upheld the constitutionality of a provision of the Immigration and Naturalization Act that treated unwed fathers and mothers differently with respect to the citizenship of children born outside the United States where only one parent was a citizen. Under the Act, if the citizen parent is the mother, then the child was automatically considered a U.S. citizen (assuming the mother met very liberal residency requirements); however, if the father is the citizen parent, citizenship was not automatic. Among other requirements, the father had to formally establish paternity and agree in writing to support the child.

The Court reasoned that this differential treatment was justifiable because motherhood is established by birth, whereas fatherhood, in both its biological and relational dimensions, is not. As expressed by the Court:

> Fathers and mothers are not similarly situated with respect to biological parenthood. . . . Given the proof of motherhood that is inherent in birth itself, it is unremarkable that Congress did not require the same affirmative steps of mothers. . . . In the case of a citizen mother and a child born overseas, the opportunity for a meaningful relationship between citizen parent and child inheres in the very event of birth. . . . [T]he same opportunity does not result from the event of birth, as a matter of biological inevitability, in the case of the unwed father.

Id. at 64-66. Interestingly, the Court did not require proof of an actual relationship but was satisfied that the establishment of paternity created the opportunity for the development of a relationship.

Again, the dissent was critical, chastising the majority for relying "on the generalization that mothers are significantly more likely than fathers . . . to develop caring relations with their children," and called for the use of gender-neutral criteria. *Id.* at 90, citing *Miller v. Albright*, 523 U.S. 420, 482-483 (1998) (dissenting opinion of Justice O'Connor, joined by Justices Souter, Ginsburg, and Breyer).

The Biology-Plus Approach Confronts the Presumption of Paternity

Unfortunately, the matter is a bit more complex than presented so far. In 1989, after *Lehr* but before *Nguyen*, the Court rendered a very important decision, which appears to limit the scope of the biology-plus approach—at least where it bumps up against the presumption of paternity. We now turn to the case of *Michael H. v. Gerald D.*

Case Preview

Michael H. v. Gerald D.

This case involves the issue of whether the presumption that a child born during marriage is the biological child of the husband is constitutional. In 1981, a baby girl named Victoria was born to Carole. At the time, Carole was married to Gerald, who was listed as the father on the birth certificate. However, subsequent blood tests showed a 98.7 percent probability that a man named Michael was actually Victoria's father. At times, Victoria, Carole, and Gerald made up a household; at other times, Victoria, Carole, and Michael made up a household.

To secure his relationship with Victoria, Michael filed a paternity action seeking formal legal recognition as her father. Gerald opposed the paternity action claiming that under California law he was Victoria's presumed father based on his marriage to Carole and that Michael lacked standing to assert paternal rights. Michael argued that the presumption was unconstitutional.

As you read *Michael H. v. Gerald D.*, look for the following:

1. What relief did Michael request from the court in California?
2. Why was Michael denied visitation rights by the lower court?
3. What was the basis for Michael's substantive due process challenge?
4. What role did the marital presumption play in the Court's decision?
5. Why did the Court state that Michael's argument distorted the rationale of the previous unwed father cases?

Michael H. v. Gerald D.
491 U.S. 110 (1989)

Justice SCALIA announced the judgment of the Court and delivered an opinion, in which THE CHIEF JUSTICE joins, and in all but footnote 6 of which Justice O'CONNOR and Justice KENNEDY join.

. . .

The facts of this case are, we must hope, extraordinary. On May 9, 1976, in Las Vegas, Nevada, Carole D., an international model, and Gerald D., a top executive in a French oil company, were married. The couple established a home in Playa del Rey, California, in which they resided as husband and wife when one or the other was not out of the country on business. In the summer of 1978, Carole became involved in an adulterous affair with a neighbor, Michael H. In September 1980, she conceived a child, Victoria D., who was born on May 11, 1981. Gerald was listed as father on the birth certificate and has always held Victoria out to the world as his daughter. Soon after delivery of the child, however, Carole informed Michael that she believed he might be the father.

In the first three years of her life, Victoria remained always with Carole, but found herself within a variety of quasi-family units. In October 1981, Gerald moved to New York City to pursue his business interests, but Carole chose to remain in California. At the end of that month, Carole and Michael had blood tests of themselves and Victoria, which showed a 98.07% probability that Michael was Victoria's father. In January 1982, Carole visited Michael in St. Thomas, where his primary business interests were based. There Michael held Victoria out as his child. In March, however, Carole left Michael and returned to California, where she took up residence with yet another man, Scott K. Later that spring, and again in the summer, Carole and Victoria spent time with Gerald in New York City, as well as on vacation in Europe. In the fall, they returned to Scott in California.

In November 1982, rebuffed in his attempts to visit Victoria, Michael filed a filiation action in California Superior Court to establish his paternity and right to visitation. In March 1983, the court appointed an attorney and guardian ad litem to represent Victoria's interests. Victoria then filed a cross-complaint asserting that if she had more than one psychological or de facto father, she was entitled to maintain her filial relationship, with all of the attendant rights, duties, and obligations, with both. In May 1983, Carole filed a motion for summary judgment. During this period, from March through July 1983, Carole was again living with Gerald in New York. In August, however, she returned to California, became involved once again with Michael, and instructed her attorneys to remove the summary judgment motion from the calendar.

For the ensuing eight months, when Michael was not in St. Thomas he lived with Carole and Victoria in Carole's apartment in Los Angeles and held Victoria out as his daughter. In April 1984, Carole and Michael signed a stipulation that Michael was Victoria's natural father. Carole left Michael the next month, however, and instructed her attorneys not to file the stipulation. In June 1984, Carole reconciled with Gerald and joined him in New York, where they now live with Victoria and two other children since born into the marriage.

In May 1984, Michael and Victoria, through her guardian ad litem, sought visitation rights for Michael pendente lite. To assist in determining whether visitation would be in Victoria's best interests, the Superior Court appointed a psychologist to evaluate Victoria, Gerald, Michael, and Carole. The psychologist recommended that Carole retain sole custody, but that Michael be allowed continued contact with Victoria pursuant to a restricted visitation schedule. The court concurred and ordered that Michael be provided with limited visitation privileges pendente lite.

On October 19, 1984, Gerald, who had intervened in the action, moved for summary judgment on the ground that . . . there were no triable issues of fact as to Victoria's paternity. This law provides that "the issue of a wife cohabiting with her husband, who is not impotent or sterile, is conclusively presumed to be a child of the marriage." Cal. Evid. Code Ann. §621(a) (West Supp. 1989). The presumption may be rebutted by blood tests, but only if a motion for such tests is made, within two years from the date of the child's birth, either by the husband or, if the natural father has filed an affidavit acknowledging paternity, by the wife. §§621(c) and (d).

On January 28, 1985, having found that affidavits submitted by Carole and Gerald sufficed to demonstrate that the two were cohabiting at conception and birth and that Gerald was neither sterile nor impotent, the Superior Court granted Gerald's motion for summary judgment, rejecting Michael's and Victoria's challenges to the constitutionality of §621. The court also denied their motions for continued visitation pending the appeal. . . . It found that allowing such visitation would "violat[e] the intention of the Legislature by impugning the integrity of the family unit."

On appeal, Michael asserted, inter alia, that the Superior Court's application of §621 had violated his procedural and substantive due process rights. Victoria also raised a due process challenge to the statute, seeking to preserve her de facto relationship with Michael as well as with Gerald. She contended, in addition, that as §621 allows the husband and, at least to a limited extent, the mother, but not the child, to rebut the presumption of legitimacy, it violates the child's right to equal protection. Finally, she asserted a right to continued visitation with Michael. [The California Court of Appeal affirmed the judgment. The California Supreme Court denied discretionary review.]

II

The California statute that is the subject of this litigation is, [in its present form,] as follows:

"§621. Child of the marriage; notice of motion for blood tests

"(a) Except as provided in subdivision (b), the issue of a wife cohabiting with her husband, who is not impotent or sterile, is conclusively presumed to be a child of the marriage.

"(b) Notwithstanding the provisions of subdivision (a), if the court finds that the conclusions of all the experts, as disclosed by the evidence based upon blood tests performed pursuant to Chapter 2 (commencing with Section 890) of Division 7 are that the husband is not the father of the child, the question of paternity of the husband shall be resolved accordingly.

"(c) The notice of motion for blood tests under subdivision (b) may be raised by the husband not later than two years from the child's date of birth.

"(d) The notice of motion for blood tests under subdivision (b) may be raised by the mother of the child not later than two years from the child's date of birth if the child's biological father has filed an affidavit with the court acknowledging paternity of the child."

. . .

III

We address first the claims of Michael. At the outset, it is necessary to clarify what he sought and what he was denied. California law, like nature itself, makes no provision for dual fatherhood. Michael was seeking to be declared the father of Victoria. The immediate benefit he evidently sought to obtain from that status was visitation rights. . . . But if Michael were successful in being declared the father, other rights would follow—most importantly, the right to be considered as the parent who should have custody. . . . All parental rights, including visitation, were automatically denied by denying Michael status as the father. . . .

[Michael first asserted that] requirements of procedural due process prevent the State from terminating his liberty interest in his relationship with his child without affording him an opportunity to demonstrate his paternity in an evidentiary hearing. We believe this claim derives from a fundamental misconception of the nature of the California statute. While §621 is phrased in terms of a presumption, that rule of evidence is the implementation of a substantive rule of law. California declares it to be, except in limited circumstances, irrelevant for paternity purposes whether a child conceived during, and born into, an existing marriage was begotten by someone other than the husband and had a prior relationship with him. As the Court of Appeal phrased it: "The conclusive presumption is actually a substantive rule of law based upon a determination by the Legislature as a matter of overriding social policy, that given a certain relationship between the husband and wife, the husband is to be held responsible for the child, and that the integrity of the family unit should not be impugned." . . .

Of course the conclusive presumption not only expresses the State's substantive policy but also furthers it, excluding inquiries into the child's paternity that would be destructive of family integrity and privacy.

. . .

A conclusive presumption does, of course, foreclose the person against whom it is invoked from demonstrating, in a particularized proceeding, that applying the presumption to him will in fact not further the lawful governmental policy the presumption is designed to effectuate. But the same can be said of any legal rule that establishes general classifications, whether framed in terms of a presumption or not. In this respect there is no difference between a rule which says that the marital husband shall be irrebuttably presumed to be the father, and a rule which says that the adulterous natural father shall not be recognized as the legal father. . . . We therefore reject Michael's procedural due process challenge and proceed to his substantive claim.

Michael contends as a matter of substantive due process that, because he has established a parental relationship with Victoria, protection of Gerald's and Carole's marital union is an insufficient state interest to support termination of that relationship. This argument is, of course, predicated on the assertion that Michael has a constitutionally protected liberty interest in his relationship with Victoria.

. . .

Michael reads the landmark case of *Stanley v. Illinois*, 405 U.S. 645, 92 S. Ct. 1208, 31 L. Ed. 2d 551 (1972), and the subsequent cases of *Quilloin v. Walcott*, 434 U.S. 246, 98 S. Ct. 549, 54 L. Ed. 2d 511 (1978), *Caban v. Mohammed*, 441 U.S. 380, 99 S. Ct. 1760, 60 L. Ed. 2d 297 (1979), and *Lehr v. Robertson*, 463 U.S. 248, 103 S. Ct. 2985, 77 L. Ed. 2d 614 (1983), as establishing that a liberty interest is created by biological fatherhood plus an established parental relationship—factors that exist in the present case as well. We think that distorts the rationale of those cases. As we view them, they rest not upon such isolated factors but upon the historic respect—indeed, sanctity would not be too strong a term—traditionally accorded to the relationships that develop within the unitary family. . . .

Thus, the legal issue in the present case reduces to whether the relationship between persons in the situation of Michael and Victoria has been treated as a protected family unit under the historic practices of our society, or whether on any other basis it has been accorded special protection. We think it impossible to find that it has. In fact, quite to the contrary, our traditions have protected the marital family (Gerald, Carole, and the child they acknowledge to be theirs) against the sort of ·claim Michael asserts.

We have found nothing in the older sources, nor in the older cases, addressing specifically the power of the natural father to assert parental rights over a child born into a woman's existing marriage with another man. Since it is Michael's burden to establish that such a power (at least where the natural father has established a relationship with the child) is so deeply embedded within our traditions as to be a fundamental right, the lack of evidence alone might defeat his case. But the evidence shows that even in modern times—when, as we have noted, the rigid protection of the marital family has in other respects been relaxed—the ability of a person in Michael's position to claim paternity has not been generally acknowledged. . . .

Moreover, even if it were clear that one in Michael's position generally possesses, and has generally always possessed, standing to challenge the marital child's legitimacy, that would still not establish Michael's case. As noted earlier, what is at issue here is not entitlement to a state pronouncement that Victoria was begotten by Michael. It is no conceivable denial of constitutional right for a State to decline to declare facts unless some legal consequence hinges upon the requested declaration.

What Michael asserts here is a right to have himself declared the natural father and thereby to obtain parental prerogatives. What he must establish, therefore, is not that our society has traditionally allowed a natural father in his circumstances to establish paternity, but that it has traditionally accorded such a father parental rights, or at least has not traditionally denied them.

. . .

IV

We have never had occasion to decide whether a child has a liberty interest, symmetrical with that of her parent, in maintaining her filial relationship. We need not do so here because, even assuming that such a right exists, Victoria's claim must fail. Victoria's due process challenge is, if anything, weaker than Michael's. . . .

The judgment of the California Court of Appeal is affirmed.

Post-Case Follow-Up

Although there was little doubt that Michael met the biology-plus standard, the Court chose to focus its attention elsewhere. Zooming in on the adulterous relationship between Michael and Carole, the Court determined that the bond between Michael and Victoria was not deserving of recognition because it did not take root within the sanctity of a "unitary family." The Court thus concluded that when faced with a choice between an "adulterous natural father" and a marital father who parents within "the integrity of the traditional family unit," the Constitution does not compel recognition of the "irregular" relationship over one that conforms to traditional standards.

According to the decision, the federal constitution does not require states to provide unwed fathers with the opportunity to challenge the marital presumption; however, they are not prohibited from doing so. However, many states do permit unwed fathers to challenge the presumption and assert their own claim to fatherhood, although many impose a threshold requirement that a father must meet before he can proceed, such as that rebuttal of the presumption would be in the child's best interest and/or that he has a substantial relationship with the child. A few states do not impose these limitations and permit a challenge in almost all situations; in these jurisdictions, the interests of unwed fathers may be afforded heightened protection under the state constitution.

The *Michael H.* Dissent

In a biting dissent, it was argued that the unwed father cases had nothing to do with protecting "unitary families" and everything to do with protecting unwed fathers who, like Michael, had developed a relationship with their children. From the dissenter's perspective, the relevant inquiry should have been whether the "relationship under consideration is sufficiently substantial to qualify as a liberty interest under our prior cases," without reference to the constellation of household arrangements. In short, according to the dissent, the goal of protecting the marital unit does not justify overriding the interests of a biological father who seeks to maintain a relationship with his child.

Michael H. v. Gerald D: Real Life Applications

1. Jacinda and Aran have been married for five years. However, Aran has been in the armed services for the majority of this time and only home for brief furloughs. Approximately three years ago, Jacinda began an adulterous relationship with Jaime, and conceived a child, Nevana. Jacinda told Aran that she believed Jaime was the father, and given the date of birth, there was no chance that Aran was the father. After the birth, a blood test was done and showed a 99 percent probability that Jaime was the father. Jaime, not wanting to disturb the family relationship, did not do anything to assert his rights of fatherhood at that time, but did continue to see Nevana on occasion and was referred to by both parties as Uncle Jaime. Jaime now comes to you and wants to know if he can file for paternity. Assuming the statute is the same as the statute in *Michael H. v. Gerald D.*, what would you tell Jaime?

2. Assume the statute in your state provides the following presumptions: "A man is presumed to be the father of the child if (1) he and the mother were married anytime within ten months immediately preceding the birth of the child or the child is born within ten months after the marriage is terminated; or (2) a birth certificate is signed by the mother and father of a child born out of wedlock. Any presumption shall be rebutted by clear and convincing evidence." Sally is three months pregnant when she meets Sam. Sally advises Sam that the baby is actually that of her previous boyfriend Ted.

   a. Two months after the baby is born, Sally and Sam marry. There was no father listed on the birth certificate. Who is the presumed father?

   b. Assume that Sally and Ted sign the birth certificate. Sally and Sam marry two months after the baby is born. Who is the presumed father? Should one presumption take precedence over the other?

   c. Assume that Sally does not tell Ted about the pregnancy and Sally and Sam sign the birth certificate and marry shortly after the birth. When the child is five years old, Sally and Sam decide to divorce. Both are seeking full custody of the minor child. Sally then locates Ted on his Facebook page and sends him a message that he is actually the father and he should do something if he does not want Sam to have custody of his child. Ted is thrilled to learn he may be a father, and a blood test is arranged that shows that Ted is indeed the biological father. Ted attempts to intervene in the divorce proceeding asserting his rights as father. What should the trial court do? Would it make a difference if the divorce was final and the trial court had ruled that Sam was the father and established parenting rights for Sam in advance of Ted learning that he was the biological father?

C. ESTABLISHING PATERNITY

When parents are unmarried, paternity must be established in order for a man to be recognized as the legal father of a child. The two primary approaches to establishing paternity are adjudication and acknowledgment. As we have seen, it may also be established through the marital presumption.

In 1973, when Congress entered the child support arena, it also sought to upgrade state procedures for paternity establishment so that more support awards could be established for the benefit of children of unmarried parents. Accordingly, the aptly named Child Support Enforcement and Establishment of Paternity Act (see Chapter 6) directed states to conform their paternity laws to the new federal requirements or risk loss of federal funding. These federal requirements (which have since been strengthened by subsequent Acts) apply to both the adjudication and the acknowledgment of paternity.

1. The Adjudication of Paternity

Establishing Paternity by DNA Testing

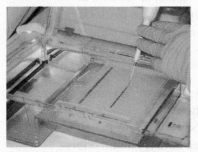

DNA testing
Rio Carb/Shutterstock.com

When paternity is contested, federal law insists that states have procedures in place to require the parties and the child to submit to genetic testing if requested by either party. If the case is being handled by the IV-D agency, the agency must pay for the testing; however, it is entitled to recoup the funds from the father if paternity is established. Unlike in years past, when testing required the drawing of blood and was unreliable, DNA-based identity testing today can be done through a cheek swab and can prove or disprove paternity with virtual certainty. Unless an objection is made, the tests must be admissible without foundation testimony or proof of authenticity.

The modern-day paternity action evolved from the colonial era bastardy proceeding, which was criminal in nature and intended to punish the "fornicator." The goal of punishing sexual misconduct has dropped by the historical wayside, and today, paternity actions are brought to identify a man as the legal father of a child based on his biological connection to him or her.

Most paternity actions are initiated by mothers or an IV-D agency (recall from Chapter 6 that in order to receive TANF benefits, a mother must assign her child support rights to the state and cooperate in establishing paternity, unless she can show good cause for noncooperation) so that the child can receive support as well as other potential benefits that flow from an established parent-child relationship. Although far less common, men may also initiate paternity proceedings in order to secure custody and visitation rights. Here, in a historical shift, the father seeks to affirm rather than to deny his paternity. However, as discussed above, if the mother is married to someone else, the presumption of paternity may bar the action, or a man may first have to satisfy a threshold requirement, such as that he has a substantial relationship with the child.

Under federal law, states must have rules in place that create a rebuttable presumption of paternity if the genetic tests indicate that the man is the father of the child within a threshold degree of probability. Once the presumption is triggered, the burden shifts to the man in question to prove nonpaternity by, for example, establishing "nonaccess" or that he is sterile. States also have the option of making the presumption conclusive, in which case it would operate like a court judgment and could be challenged only under very limited circumstances.

2. The Voluntary Acknowledgment of Paternity

Paternity can also be established voluntarily. This approach has gained favor, and under federal law all states must have a simple procedure in place that enables parents to acknowledge paternity by completing a notarized paternity affidavit. See Exhibit 12.1 on the next page. States must offer paternity establishment services at hospitals and at the state agency responsible for maintaining birth records. States may also offer paternity establishment services at other locations where children and parents receive services or care, such as at pediatricians' offices and Head Start programs.

Before signing the paternity acknowledgment form, a parent must be provided with information regarding the legal consequences of establishing paternity. Some states have developed separate materials for mothers and fathers in recognition of the different concerns that each may have regarding, for example, child support obligations and custody and visitation rights. Although most state materials emphasize the benefits of acknowledging paternity, some address the concerns that victims of violence may have and may recommend against signing if the mother fears for her own safety or the safety of the child. Typically, the parties are told about the availability of genetic testing; such notification is not required, however, thus creating the possibility that the acknowledged father, either knowingly or unknowingly, may not necessarily be the biological father. (See Section D, below.)

The parties have a set window of time within which to rescind the acknowledgment and thereby disestablish paternity. Thereafter, if the acknowledgment is not rescinded, it operates as a legal finding of paternity and is entitled to full faith and credit in other states. However, a subsequent challenge may be permitted on the limited grounds of fraud, duress, or mistake of fact.

3. Following the Determination of Paternity

Once paternity is established, the formerly putative father is now the legal father of the child with the rights and responsibilities that this status entails. He can be required to pay child support and can seek court-ordered custody and visitation rights.

If paternity is established in court, a child support order can usually be established at the same time. The fact that the parties are not married should not impact the support amount. As far as custody and visitation are concerned, if the court is one of limited jurisdiction without broad authority over family matters, the father may need to bring a separate action in family court. Moreover, unlike with child support, some states use different substantive standards where unmarried parents of children, as distinct from divorcing parents, are involved. Although the focus remains the best interest of the child, some states employ a rebuttable presumption that it is in the child's best interest to remain with the parent who has been the

EXHIBIT 12.1   **Voluntary Acknowledgment of Paternity**

Illinois Voluntary Acknowledgment of Paternity

File Date for ACU use only

PLEASE READ ALL PARTS OF THIS FORM INCLUDING YOUR RIGHTS AND RESPONSIBILITIES AND INSTRUCTIONS ON THE OTHER SIDE BEFORE COMPLETING THE FOLLOWING INFORMATION. ALL ITEMS MUST BE ANSWERED.

Child's Information as shown on Birth Certificate   Print all requested information

Child's First Name	Middle Name	Last Name (same as on birth certificate)	Suffix (Jr, II, III)

Gender ☐ M ☐ F	Date of Birth (mm/dd/yy)	Place of Birth – Hospital Name	City/State of Birth

Biological Father's Name (first/middle/last) Suffix (Jr, II, III, IV, V)		Date of Birth (mm/dd/yy)	Place of Birth (city/state or foreign co.)
Address	City/State/Zip		Social Security Number

Were you married to or in a civil union with the biological mother when this child was conceived and/or born?   Yes☐   No ☐
If yes, you are presumed to be the biological father.

Biological Mother's Name (first/middle/last)	Maiden Name	Date of Birth (mm/dd/yy)	Place of Birth (city/state or foreign co.)
Address	City/State/Zip		Social Security Number

Were you married to or in a civil union with a person other than the father when this child was conceived and/or born?   Yes☐   No ☐
If yes, provide the presumed parent's name (first/middle/last) _____ . A Denial of Parentage must also be completed by the biological mother and presumed parent to place the biological father's name on this child's birth certificate.

By signing I acknowledge that I have read the rights and responsibilities and instructions on the other side of this form. I have been provided an oral explanation about the VAP and understand my rights and responsibilities created and waived by signing this form.

I UNDERSTAND THAT I CAN REQUEST A GENETIC TEST REGARDING THE CHILD'S PATERNITY. BY SIGNING THIS FORM I GIVE UP MY RIGHT TO A GENETIC TEST.

BIOLOGICAL FATHER: Under the penalties of perjury provided by Section 1-109 of the Illinois Code of Civil Procedure, I certify that my statements in this document are true and correct and that there is no other presumed, acknowledged or adjudicated parent for this child. I understand that the acknowledgment is the equivalent of a judicial adjudication of parentage of the child and that a challenge to the acknowledgment is permitted only under limited circumstances and is generally barred after 2 years.

Biological Father's Signature _____

Witness Information

Signature _____   Printed Name _____

Address _____

Phone Number _____   Date Parties Signed _____

BIOLOGICAL MOTHER: Under the penalties of perjury provided by Section 1-109 of the Illinois Code of Civil Procedure, I certify that my statements in this document are true and correct and that there is no other presumed, acknowledged or adjudicated parent for this child. I understand that the acknowledgment is the equivalent of a judicial adjudication of parentage of the child and that a challenge to the acknowledgment is permitted only under limited circumstances and is generally barred after 2 years.

Biological Mother's Signature _____

Witness Information

Signature _____   Printed Name _____

Address _____

Phone Number _____   Date Parties Signed _____

HFS 3416B (R-1-16) To request a certified copy of the VAP go to www.ChildSupportIllinois.com and complete and follow instructions on HFS 3416H, Request for a Certified copy of the Voluntary Acknowledgment of Paternity and/or Denial of Parentage.

For Official Use Only _____

Case #	Docket #	CP RIN	NCP RIN	Child RIN

child's primary caretaker or with whom the child has lived continuously for a certain period of time. This standard often favors the mother, who, especially where parents are unmarried, is likely to be the primary care parent.

D. PATERNITY DISESTABLISHMENT

A controversial issue that courts are deeply divided on is whether a father should be permitted to "disestablish" his paternity—that is, to undo a determination that he is the child's biological father. In large part, the ready availability of reliable genetic testing has prompted this push for biological certainty, even if the quest threatens to disrupt a well-established father-child relationship.

Like joint custody, **paternity disestablishment** is closely identified with the fathers' rights movement, which, as noted in Chapter 5, emerged in the 1970s to address a perceived anti-male bias in the family courts. In this context, the ability to disavow fatherhood is seen as necessary to vindicate the rights of men who have been "duped" by women, often with the aid of the legal system. However, "exoneration" in the family law domain does not simply undo a mistake; it also serves to dismantle an established parent-child relationship with potentially devastating emotional consequences for a child. Disestablishment is also likely to have an adverse financial impact on a child, as termination of the legal parent-child relationship typically operates to terminate a man's duty to provide support, which, of course, is often a primary motivating consideration behind the quest to disestablish paternity.

Paternity disestablishment cases once again present us with important questions regarding the weight and meaning of fatherhood. Is it a genetic link that makes a man a father? Is it grasping the opportunity presented by a genetic link to develop a relationship with a child, or can fatherhood be achieved in the absence of a biological link by assuming the role of a father in a child's life? How should the competing interests of a father who wishes to disavow his misidentified status be balanced with the needs of the child? As noted in a leading monograph on the subject, other critical questions include the following:

> At what point should the truth about genetic parentage outweigh the consequences of leaving a child fatherless? Is a child better off knowing his/her genetic heritage or maintaining a relationship with his/her father and his family that provides both emotional and financial support? Should it matter who brings the action or should the rules be the same for men trying to disestablish paternity, women seeking to oust a father from the child's life, and third parties trying to assert their paternity of a child who already has a legal father?

Paula Roberts, Truth and Consequences: Part I—Disestablishing the Paternity of Non-Marital Children 2 (2003), http://www.clasp.org/resources-and-publications/publication-1/0111.pdf (accessed June 14, 2016).

Broadly speaking, paternity disestablishment cases fall into one of two categories. First, following the establishment of paternity through either a voluntary acknowledgment or a court action, an unmarried father begins to doubt whether he is the biological father and thus seeks to disestablish his paternity. Depending on the state, it may also be possible for the action to be initiated by a mother who seeks to limit or end the involvement of this man in her child's life or by another man who believes that he is the child's biological father. The second category of cases involves an attempt to disestablish the paternity of a man who is the presumed father of a child based on his marriage to the child's mother. The presumed father may seek to disestablish paternity based on doubts about his biological relationship to the child; a man who believes he might be a child's biological father might wish to challenge the paternity of the husband; or the mother herself, often in connection with a pending divorce action, may seek the disestablishment in order to end her husband's formal relationship with the child.

If disestablishment is allowed, a question arises as to what impact this has on the child support obligation. As a general matter, disestablishment ends the father's obligation to pay present and future child support. However, courts have been less willing to forgive support arrearages for a number of reasons, including the hardship that this would impose on children, and that forgiveness would reward the father who had been remiss in making support payments. Likewise, most courts do not permit a father to recoup payments made prior to the disestablishment of paternity, although this is not an absolute rule, and some statutes permit recoupment under carefully delineated circumstances.

States have begun addressing the issue of when to allow paternity disestablishment through both statutory enactments and judicial decisions. For example, some states have passed laws allowing men who have been adjudicated fathers to reopen the court decision to disprove their paternity through the introduction of genetic evidence. In other states, either the mother or the father can seek judicial relief where paternity has been adjudicated or acknowledged. Courts have expressed a dizzying array of opinions on the matter. In part, this reflects differences in underlying fact patterns; however, it also reflects deeply divided views on how the competing interests should be accommodated. We turn now to two paternity disestablishment decisions that weigh the best interest of the child in the decisional calculus very differently.

1. Considering Best Interest: Conflicting Approaches

In *Paternity of Cheryl*, 746 N.E.2d 488 (Mass. 2001), the Massachusetts Supreme Judicial Court (SJC) refused to permit an unmarried father to disestablish paternity. Briefly, the facts are as follows. Cheryl was born in 1993. Shortly thereafter, the parents, who were not married, signed a voluntary acknowledgment, which was entered as a court judgment. The father participated in Cheryl's life as a father, and she referred to him as "Daddy." When Cheryl was six, the state's IV-D agency sought an increase in child support. Five days later, the father raised doubts about his paternity, and genetic tests revealed that he was not the girl's biological father. In rejecting his request to vacate the paternity judgment, the SJC focused on the impact this would have on Cheryl:

> Where a father challenges a paternity judgment, courts have pointed to the special needs of children that must be protected, noting that consideration of what is in a child's best interest will often weigh more heavily than the genetic link between parent and child. . . . [C]hildren benefit psychologically, socially, educationally and in other ways

from stable and predictable parental relationships. . . . [W]here a father and child have a substantial parent-child relationship, an attempt to undo a determination of paternity is "potentially devastating to a child who has considered the man to be the father."

Id. at 496-497, quoting *Hackley v. Hackley*, 426 Mich. 582, 598 n.11, 395 N.W.2d 906 (1986).

In contrast to this child-centered focus, the Court of Appeals of Maryland in *Langston v. Riffe*, 754 A.2d 389 (Md. 2000), concluded that the best interest of the child has no place in a paternity disestablishment action. In this consolidated action, three men were seeking to set aside a paternity judgment based on new evidence indicating in each case that another man might be the child's biological father. At issue was whether, in seeking reconsideration of a paternity judgment, the fathers had an automatic statutory right to blood or genetic testing as they would at the time of paternity establishment or, as argued by the state on behalf of the mothers, whether in this context, the court must first consider the best interest of the children. In reviewing the legislative history, the court concluded that the "'best interests of the child' standard generally has no place in a proceeding to reconsider a paternity declaration. . . . To not allow testing now would violate . . . the Legislature's intent . . . to provide relief to putative fathers seeking review of potentially false paternity declarations entered against them." *Id.* at 405, 428.

Underlying these decisions is the familiar struggle to arrive at an understanding of what makes a man a father. The two cases embody different understandings of the role that biology plays in determining fatherhood. By focusing on the developed relationship between Cheryl and her father, the SJC downgraded the importance of the biological link between a father and child in favor of relational considerations. However, it is possible that the court would have paid less attention to this connection if Cheryl's biological father had been standing in the wings, ready, willing, and able to assume a role in her life. In contrast, the Maryland court, in focusing on the vindication of the father's interest without regard to the impact of disestablishment on the children of these men, elevated the biological dimension of fatherhood over relational considerations.

E. DETERMINING LEGAL FATHERHOOD WHEN THE GENETIC "FATHER" IS A SPERM DONOR

In this section, we consider how questions of paternity are addressed in situations where conception has been accomplished through donor insemination rather than through sexual intercourse. The involvement of a donor potentially adds another layer of complexity to the determination of legal parentage, thus injecting a greater element of unpredictability and variability from state to state.

1. Sperm Donation and Heterosexual Couples

Where a married woman and her husband are unable to conceive due to his infertility (or possibly the wish to avoid a genetic condition), they may opt for donor insemination. Here, although she is married, the child is actually the biological offspring of two persons who are not married to each other. Under these circumstances, who is entitled to legal recognition as the father?

Under the marital presumption, the husband is regarded as the resulting child's legal father. However, it is possible that where permitted by law a sperm donor might seek to rebut the presumption. To address this situation, the Uniform Parentage Act (UPA) makes it clear that a "donor is not a parent of a child conceived by assisted reproduction," and that the consenting husband is the presumed father. UPA §702-704 (last amended or revised in 2002). Importantly, the updated 2002 UPA has dropped the marriage requirement. As a result, the cut-off provision will apply regardless of a woman's marital status, and her consenting male partner steps into the shoes of the presumed father. *Id.* The UPA further provides that the absence of a signed consent does not preclude a finding of paternity where the couple resided together during the first two years of the child's life and the father holds the child out as his own. *Id.* §704(b).

If a state has not adopted the 2002 UPA or a similar provision, a court is nonetheless likely to hold that a consenting husband is the presumed legal father (this presumption may well not be extended to an unmarried man in the absence of a statute). For instance, in the case of *People v. Sorenson*, 437 P.2d 495 (Cal. 1968), which is an early and still influential decision on this issue, a husband who had consented to the insemination of his wife and had held himself out as the child's father argued upon divorce that he should not have to pay child support because the sperm donor, not he, was the child's legal father. In rejecting this position, the court stated:

> [W]here a reasonable man who because of his inability to procreate, actively partici-pates and consents to his wife's artificial insemination in the hope that a child will be produced whom they will treat as their own, knows that such behavior carries with it the legal responsibilities of fatherhood. . . . One who consents to the production of a child cannot create a temporary relation to be assumed and disclaimed at will. . . . [I]t is safe to assume that without defendant's active participation and consent, the child would not have been procreated.

Id. at 499.

Accordingly, the father's consent was deemed to bind him to the child, and he was not permitted to disavow the relationship. Courts have similarly relied on the doctrine of equitable estoppel to reach the same result, finding that where a husband consents to the insemination of his wife and then treats the child as his own, he may be estopped from denying his paternity in order to avoid paying child support in the event of a separation or a divorce.

2. Sperm Donation and Same-Sex Couples and Single Women

As we have just seen, the law in this area is fairly well settled when it comes to the married heterosexual couple, and unmarried couples in states that have adopted the 2002 UPA or a cognate provision. In this section, we consider the somewhat more variable and complex rules when the intended mother is partnered with another woman (or single).

The UPA Approach

Under the 1973 version of the UPA, the sperm donor "cut-off" provision was only triggered when the intending mother was married to a consenting husband (and the insemination was done under the supervision of a licensed physician). However, the 2002 UPA has done away with the marriage requirement. Accordingly, in states that have adopted this version of the Act or otherwise enacted a similar rule, the cut-off rule should apply without regard to the marital status of the woman who conceived the child with the donated sperm. However, under the UPA and UPA-like laws, the parties may have the statutory option of opting out of the cut-off provision and entering into an agreement embodying their intent that the donor will assume the rights and responsibilities of legal parenthood.

Insemination with an Unknown Donor

A single woman or lesbian couple may decide to obtain sperm from a sperm bank. This essentially forecloses the possibility of a future legal conflict over the establishment of paternal rights as most facilities promise the donors anonymity and maintain their records in such a way as to make the subsequent matching of sperm donor and birth mother difficult. Moreover, it is unlikely that the donor was motivated by the desire to become a parent, but was instead may have provided the donation as a result of the desire to earn extra money, or possibly by an altruistic wish to assist others who were unable to bear children on their own; thus his participation cannot be read as a sign of intended parenthood.

However, it should be noted that there is a growing push for greater openness in the process, and many programs now provide sperm donors with an identity-release option that allows children conceived with their sperm to obtain certain information about their biological fathers when they reach adulthood. Moreover, in 2000, a California appeals court, in a case involving a genetically transmitted disease, concluded that the donor's right to preserve his anonymity was outweighed by the state's compelling interest in protecting the health and welfare of minor children, including those born by artificial insemination. Accordingly, the court ordered the disclosure of the donor's identity so that needed medical information could be obtained. *Johnson v. The Superior Court of Los Angeles County*, 80 Cal. App. 4th 1050, 95 Cal. Rptr. 2d 864 (2000). Although perhaps signaling a growing awareness that a blanket guarantee of anonymity may not be in the interest of children conceived through donor insemination, this is, however, a far cry from extending paternal rights to men who donate their sperm to a sperm bank.

Insemination with a Known Donor

Rather than relying on a sperm bank, a couple (or an individual) may prefer to use a known donor. This approach provides the recipient with more control over the process and a greater knowledge of the child's origins. It also allows for the possibility that the donor can play a continuing role in the child's life.

Given the potential uncertainty of the legal status of the donor in jurisdictions that do not have an applicable cut-off statute, it is particularly important that parties enter into an agreement setting out their intent regarding the future role of the sperm donor. One option is for them to agree that the donor will relinquish his parental rights in exchange for a commitment from the mother not to seek child support. Alternatively, they may agree that the donor will have to be recognized as the legal father of the child with all the rights and responsibilities that this status entails. Another option would be to settle for something in between these two poles that allows the donor to be involved in the child's life without casting him as a legal parent.

However, particularly in the context of a waiver of parental rights, parties may subsequently change their mind. A father may decide that he wishes to establish a relationship with the child, or the mother may decide that she wishes to obtain child support from him. Although we consider two basic approaches that courts have taken in these cases, it is important to be aware that the law is far more unsettled and variegated than presented here.

Some courts have refused to enforce an agreement in which the donor waives his parental rights based largely on the public policy view that it is in a child's best interest to have an identifiable legal father. Also potentially relevant here is the legal principle that parents are generally deemed incapable of waiving rights that ostensibly belong to a child. In effect, this approach serves to privilege the donor's biological link to the child over the express intent of the parties, with some courts making clear that, absent proof of unfitness, they will not cut off the rights of a biological "parent," even if his initial intended status was simply that of a sperm donor.

On the other hand, courts may be willing to enforce such an agreement based on the recognition that to do otherwise would be to discourage this form of assisted reproduction. As the Supreme Court of Pennsylvania observed in the 2007 case of *Ferguson v. McKiernan* where the mother sought to revoke a prior agreement in which the father waived his paternal rights so she could obtain child support, the non-enforcement of the these kinds of agreements "would mean that a woman who wishes to have a baby but is unable to conceive through intercourse could not seek sperm from a man she knows and admires, while assuring him that he will never be subject to a support order and being herself assured that he will never be able to seek custody of the child." 596 Pa. 78, 940 A.2d 1236, 1247 (2007). The court went on to remark that she would accordingly have no choice but to "resort to anonymous donation or abandon her desire to be a biological mother, notwithstanding her considered personal preference to conceive using the sperm of someone familiar, whose background, traits, and medical history are not shrouded in mystery." *Id.*

F. DETERMINING LEGAL MOTHERHOOD

In this section, we consider whether the kinds of rules that operate to vest legal paternity in the husband of a married heterosexual woman, namely, the marital presumption and the UPA approach (the latter of which may vest paternal rights in an unmarried father), are likewise applicable to a lesbian couple. In this regard, keep in mind that, as discussed in Chapter 9, another possible approach that some jurisdictions have adopted is to treat the non-biologically related co-parent as a de facto parent, although, recall that this approach does not always result in full legal equality. (Disputes over legal motherhood in the surrogacy context will be discussed Chapter 15.)

1. Presuming Maternity Based Upon State Parentage Laws

As we have seen, if a married heterosexual couple uses donor insemination to conceive a child, it is fairly settled law in all jurisdictions that the rights of the donor are cut off and a consenting husband is considered the legal father of the resulting child (although some states have retained the requirement that the insemination be done under the supervision of a licensed physician). Moreover, in keeping with the recommended approach of the 2002 UPA, a number of states have extended this same rule to unmarried couples. Absent a formal agreement, this result may be accomplished where the parties lived together during the first two years of the child's life and the father held the child out as his own.

By logical extension, a few courts have considered the question of whether a same-sex partner or spouse can rely on the operative UPA principles to establish her status as the other legal parent of the child born to her partner — a result that is certainly consistent with the UPA's unequivocal statement that "[p]rovisions of this [Act] relating to determination of paternity apply to determinations of maternity." UPA §106.

Leading the way, in 2005, courts in both California and New Jersey used the approach to recognize the reality of two-mother households. In the case of *Elisa B. v. Emily B.*, the California court concluded that under the UPA, as adopted by California, just as a similarly situated man would be the presumed legal father, a woman who consents to the insemination of her partner, and then receives the child into her home and openly holds the child out as her own, is the presumed legal mother of that child. *Elisa B. v. Emily B.*, 117 P.3d 660 (Cal. 2005). Likewise, a New Jersey court ruled that the state's sperm donor law, which treats a husband who consents to his wife's insemination as the child's legal father, was equally available to committed same-sex partners, thus allowing the names of both women to be placed on their child's birth certificate as her legal parents. *In re Parentage of the Child of Kimberly Robinson*, 383 N.J. Super. 165, 890 A.2d 1036 (2005).

Case Preview

Chatterjee v. King

Bani Chatterjee and Taya King were two women in a long-term committed domestic relationship. They agreed to adopt a child, and, because same-sex partners could not jointly adopt a child, King adopted a child from Russia. However, despite the fact that only King was the child's adopted parent, Chatterjee supported both the child and King and co-parented the child in the family home for a number of years. When their relationship dissolved, King moved to Colorado and attempted to prohibit Chatterjee from having contact with the child.

Chatterjee filed an action to be recognized as a parent with parenting rights. The issue that was addressed by the Supreme Court of New Mexico was whether Chatterjee had standing to pursue a claim for joint custody on the grounds that she could be considered the natural mother of the child even though she was neither the biological parent nor the adoptive parent.

As you read *Chatterjee v. King*, look for the following:

1. What did Chatterjee argue were the grounds that gave her standing to assert a claim for joint custody as a natural mother of the child in question?
2. What specific language in the New Mexico Uniform Parentage Act did the court rely upon in addressing the issue of Chatterjee's standing?
3. What public policy did the court rely upon to justify its decision?

Chatterjee v. King
280 P.3d 283 (N.M. 2012)

CHÁVEZ, Justice.

The question in this case is whether Chatterjee has pleaded sufficient facts in her Petition to give her standing to pursue joint custody of Child under the Dissolution of Marriage Act. Whether Chatterjee has standing to pursue joint custody depends on whether Chatterjee has pleaded facts sufficient to establish that she is an interested party under Section 40-11-21 of the New Mexico Uniform Parentage Act (UPA). Her pleading sets forth facts, which, if true, establish that she has a personal, financial, and custodial relationship with Child and has openly held Child out as her daughter, although she is neither Child's biological nor adoptive mother.

We hold that a natural mother is an interested party who has standing to pursue joint custody of a child. We conclude, based on the facts and circumstances of this case, that the facts pleaded by Chatterjee are sufficient to confer standing on her as a natural mother. . . .

I. SECTION 40-11-21 ESTABLISHES A BASIS FOR STANDING FOR "ANY INTERESTED PARTY"

Chatterjee argues that she has standing to establish parentage as an interested party under Section 40-11-21 of the UPA because she has held Child out as her child pursuant to Section 40-11-5(A)(4). Section 40-11-21 provides that "[a]ny interested party may bring an action to determine the existence or nonexistence of a mother and child relationship. Insofar as practicable, the provisions of the Uniform Parentage Act applicable to the father and child relationship apply."

While there is no case law in New Mexico holding that a person alleging a natural parent relationship under the UPA is per se an interested party, our courts have recognized that the Legislature "clearly intended" that the UPA have broad application.

We agree that a case-by-case analysis is the best way to determine whether an action is appropriate under the UPA. Chatterjee claims that she openly held out Child as her natural child from the moment that she and King brought Child to New Mexico from Russia and therefore that she should be able to establish a parent and child relationship under Section 40-11-5(A)(4), which creates a presumption of paternity. Section 40-11-5(A)(4), which we refer to as the "hold out provision," provides that "[a] man is presumed to be the natural father of a child if . . . he openly holds out the child as his natural child and has established a personal, financial or custodial relationship with the child." Any person who is able to establish presumed natural parenthood under Section 40-11-5(A)(4) would qualify as an interested party. Therefore, we must now determine whether Chatterjee, as a woman, can establish a presumed natural parent and child relationship under Section 40-11-5(A)(4).

II. THE UPA REQUIRES COURTS TO APPLY PROVISIONS RELATING TO THE FATHER AND CHILD RELATIONSHIP TO WOMEN WHEN IT IS PRACTICABLE TO DO SO

Chatterjee argues that the Court of Appeals erred in holding that none of the UPA provisions relating to the father and child relationship may be applied to women. She claims that this holding directly contradicts the plain language of Section 40-11-21. King responds that the UPA provisions establishing paternity should not be applied to women because the UPA expressly provides the ways in which maternity can be established. We agree with Chatterjee. We find support for Chatterjee's argument not only in the plain language of the statute itself, but also in the purpose of the UPA, the application of paternity provisions to women in jurisdictions with similar UPA provisions, and in public policy that encourages the love and support of children from able and willing parents.

A. The Plain Language of Sections 40-11-4(A) and 40-11-21, Read Together, Requires This Court to Apply the Hold Out Provision of Section 40-11-5(A)(4) to Alleged Mothers

We begin our analysis with Section 40-11-2 of the UPA, which states that a "'parent and child relationship' means the legal relationship existing between a child and his natural or adoptive parents incident to which the law confers or imposes rights, privileges, duties and obligations. It includes the mother and child relationship and the father and child relationship." For a mother, Section 40-11-4(A) provides that "the natural mother may be established by proof of her having given birth to the child, *or as provided by Section [40-11-21 NMSA 1978]*." (Emphasis added.) Section 40-11-21 states that "[a]ny interested party may bring an action to determine the existence or nonexistence of a mother and child relationship. Insofar as practicable, the provisions of the Uniform Parentage Act applicable to the father and child relationship apply."

. . .

Because the presumption is based on a person's conduct, not a biological connection, a woman is capable of holding out a child as her natural child and establishing a personal, financial, or custodial relationship with that child. This is particularly true when, as is alleged in this case, the relationship between the child and both the presumptive and the adoptive parent occurred simultaneously.

In addition, by limiting proof of natural motherhood to biology under Section 40-11-4(A), the Court of Appeals renders meaningless the clear instruction in Section 40-11-4(A) that a "natural mother may [also] be established . . . as provided by Section 21 [40-11-21 NMSA 1978]." . . . A straightforward reading of Section 40-11-4(A) is that motherhood may be established by giving birth, by adoption, and in any other way in which a father and child relationship may be established when it is practicable to do so. Because it is practicable for a woman to hold a child out as her own, the plain language instructs us to recognize that Section 40-11-5(A)(4) relating to the father and child relationship also applies to the mother and child relationship.

B. The Drafters of the Original UPA Intended That Provisions Relating to the Father and Child Relationship Apply to Women in Appropriate Situations

The authors of the Uniform Parentage Act of 1973 (the original UPA), anticipating situations such as this case, provided in a comment that masculine terminology was used for the sake of simplicity and not to limit application of its provisions to males. . . .

. . .

Consistent with the underlying policy-based rationale of the New Mexico UPA that equality in child welfare requires laws that achieve equality in parentage, Child's need for love and support is no less critical simply because her second parent also happens to be a woman. Experts in child psychology recognize that sometimes the law is too limiting when it comes to actually addressing what is in the child's best interests. The attachment bonds that form between a child and a parent are formed regardless of a biological or legal connection. . . . Indeed, New Mexico courts have long recognized that children may form parent-child bonds with persons other than their legal parents. . . . It is inappropriate to deny Chatterjee the opportunity to establish parentage, when denying Chatterjee this opportunity would only serve to harm both Child and the state. In our view, it is against public policy to deny parental rights and responsibilities based solely on the sex of either or both of the parents.

. . .

Assuming that all of her allegations are true, Chatterjee would then have standing to seek joint custody as a natural parent under Section 40-4-9.1 of the Dissolution of Marriage Act. We reverse the Court of Appeals and remand this case to the district court for further proceedings consistent with this opinion.

It Is So Ordered.

Post-Case Follow-Up

The court concluded that Chatterjee had pled sufficient facts to give her standing to at least raise the issue of whether she should be able to have joint custody as a natural parent. The court reasoned that the plain language of the UPA statute as adopted by New Mexico instructs courts to apply the presumption of parentage to men and women. Thus, in addition to a man, a woman also can hold a child out as her own by providing, among other things, emotional and financial support. This reasoning is also in accordance with the public policy of considering the child's best interest.

Chatterjee v. King: Real Life Applications

1. Isidora and Amalia were domestic partners. They both were foster parents and, although only one of them was technically the foster parent, they both would care for the children who resided with them in the home. Approximately three years into their relationship, a baby boy, Mateo, for whom Isidora was the foster mother, became available for adoption. Isidora decided that since she had been the foster mother she now wanted to adopt Mateo. Isidora and Amalia decided that if Isidora adopted Mateo, they would raise him jointly. The adoption was complete and Isidora, Amalia, and Mateo lived as a family unit for the next five years until they decided to end their relationship. Isidora moved out of the family residence with Mateo and attempted to block any visitation of Mateo by Amalia. Under a statute similar to the one at issue in *Chatterjee*, does Amalia have any remedies? How should a court rule?

2. Ian and Bao are domestic partners. Ian decides to adopt a child that both men agree to raise. Bao has heard about the *Chatterjee* case and comes to your office to ask if there is anything he can do in advance to avoid costly litigation over custody of the child that Bao intends to adopt in the event the parties separate in the future. What would you tell Bao?

3. Alice and Paul are husband and wife and have one child, Cyndi. When Cyndi is four, Paul is unfortunately killed in a car accident. Alice becomes involved two years later with a woman named Marsha, and they take up residency together as domestic partners. For the next two years, they raise Cyndi together, until the relationship ends and Marsha moves out, attempting to take Cyndi with her because she claims Alice has severe mental issues and is not a fit parent. Alice is able to stop Marsha from taking Cyndi, but Marsha files an action for custody. Alice files a motion to dismiss in which she claims Marsha has no rights since Cyndi is her biological child. Can Marsha state sufficient facts to withstand a motion to dismiss for custody of Cyndi? What are Marsha's best arguments? What are Alice's best arguments? How should a court rule?

2. Presuming Parenthood Based Upon Marriage

Now that the United States Supreme Court has held that same-sex marriages must be recognized in all states, a child born into the marriage should be regarded as the legal child of that union as in a heterosexual marriage based upon the marital presumption. The parallel application of the marital presumption means that a spouse would not have to prove that she is a de facto parent in order to maintain a relationship with the child in the event of a divorce or separation; rather, this status and the correlative rights would flow from the existence of marriage itself.

As previously discussed, pursuant to the common law marital presumption, a woman's husband is presumed to be the father of any child born during the marriage. By logical extension, the same presumption should arguably also control parentage determinations in the context of a lesbian marriage, thus making a woman's wife the presumed parent of any child born to her during the marriage. However, despite the Supreme Court's ruling in *Obergefell*, some jurisdictions appear to be resisting the application of the marital presumption to lesbian spouses. Accordingly, while this issue sorts itself out, the non-biologically related spouse should not rely on marriage alone to secure parental rights by way of the marital presumption, but should instead secure her status by way of an adoption or other court judgment of parentage.

Case Preview

Madrone v. Madrone

Madrone involves the rather unique issue of whether an unmarried same-sex couple should be treated the same as a married opposite-sex couple under Oregon's parentage statute. Oregon's Revised Statute Section 109.243 provided that the husband of a woman who conceives by artificial insemination with the husband's consent is automatically considered the father. There is no need for any filings or a judicial hearing.

In interpreting the statute, the Oregon Court of Appeals had previously extended the statute to include registered same-sex partners. Thus, the statute applied to married opposite-sex couples and same-sex domestic partners. However, *Madrone* was different because this case involved parties that were not married at the time of the insemination because at that time Oregon did not recognize same-sex marriages or permit domestic partners to register their partnership. Thus, the court had to address the issue of whether the statute should once again be extended but this time to same-sex couples who were neither married nor registered as same-sex domestic partners at the time of insemination but would have married or registered as partners if given the option.

As you read *Madrone v. Madrone*, look for the following:

1. What was the basis of Petitioner's claim that she was entitled to a declaration that she was a legal parent of her partner's child?

2. What was Respondent's counterargument?
3. What did the court conclude and why?

Madrone v. Madrone
350 P.3d 495 (Or. Ct. App. 2015)

HADLOCK, J.

. . .

During the parties' relationship, respondent gave birth to a daughter, R, who was conceived by artificial insemination. Shortly thereafter, the Oregon Family Fairness Act took effect, allowing same sex couples to register domestic partnerships, which petitioner and respondent then did. They later separated, and petitioner brought this action for dissolution of the domestic partnership. Among other claims, petitioner sought a declaration that she is R's legal parent by operation of ORS 109.243. The trial court granted summary judgment for petitioner on that claim based on our analysis in *Shineovich* [the previous case extending the statute to same-sex domestic partners]. Respondent appeals. For the reasons set out below, we conclude that ORS 109.243 applies to unmarried same-sex couples who have a child through artificial insemination if the partner of the biological parent consented to the insemination *and* the couple would have chosen to marry had that choice been available to them. The record in this case includes evidence creating a genuine dispute on the latter point. Accordingly, the trial court erred in entering summary judgment, and we reverse.

. . .

In *Shineovich*, we explained that "ORS 109.243 grants a privilege—legal parentage by operation of law—to the husband of a woman who gives birth to a child conceived by artificial insemination, without regard to the biological relationship of the husband and the child, as long as the husband consented to the artificial insemination." 229 Or App 685. We held that the statute violates Article I, section 20, of the Oregon Constitution: "Because same-sex couples may not marry in Oregon, that privilege is not available to the same-sex domestic partner of a woman who gives birth to a child conceived by artificial insemination, where the partner consented to the procedure with the intent of being the child's second parent. We can see no justification for denying that privilege on the basis of sexual orientation, particularly given that same-sex couples may become legal coparents by other means—namely, adoption. There appears to be no reason for permitting heterosexual couples to bypass adoption proceedings by conceiving a child through mutually consensual artificial insemination, but not permitting same-sex couples to do so. Thus, we conclude that ORS 109.243 violates Article I, section 20." Id. at 686. We went on to hold that the appropriate remedy for the violation was to "extend the statute so that it applies when the same-sex partner of the biological mother consented to the artificial insemination." Id. at 687.

In her motion, petitioner argued that, under *Shineovich*, "there are two requirements for application of the statute to [R's] situation: that the parties be domestic partners and that [petitioner] consent to the insemination." She asserted that both requirements were satisfied and, thus, that the court should grant summary judgment in her favor.

In response to the motion, respondent argued that *Shineovich* is distinguishable from this case. She asserted that, there, the parties were registered domestic partners before their children were born, whereas she and petitioner did not become domestic partners until nearly two months after R was born. Respondent contended that "the protections afforded in ORS 109.243 apply to domestic partners, not simply people in a relationship." According to respondent, "[i]f petitioner were male, the situation at hand would be that of a boyfriend trying to assert parental rights over a child who was born before the marriage and is undisputedly not the biological father." Respondent also argued that she had never consented to petitioner being considered her "husband equivalent" and that "to presume such consent now would be to deprive Respondent of significant due process rights to consent or withhold consent to the biological and/or legal paternity of a child born of her body." Respondent argued that this case is further distinguishable from *Shineovich* because, in that case, "the parties were unable to have both parties' names on the birth certificate, but in this case the parties were able, but chose not, to add Petitioner's name to the birth certificate. This gives insight into the parties' intent. . . ."

. . .

Respondent's argument that this case is factually distinguishable from *Shineovich* misses the mark, as we addressed a different question in *Shineovich* than we address in this case. In *Shineovich*, we analyzed only whether ORS 109.243 violates Article I, section 20, because it denies a privilege to the same-sex partner of a woman who conceives a child through artificial insemination and, having concluded that the statute does violate Article I, section 20, held that the appropriate remedy was to extend the statute "so that it applies when the same-sex partner of the biological mother consented to the artificial insemination." 229 Or App at 687. Beyond addressing those broad points, we did not have reason to articulate a precise standard by which to determine whether the same-sex partner of a mother who conceived by artificial insemination comes within the reach of ORS 109.243. We attempt to draw the line more precisely here.

. . .

In *Shineovich*, we held that ORS 109.243 violates Article I, section 20, because it creates a privilege that "is not available to the same-sex domestic partner of a woman who gives birth to a child conceived by artificial insemination, where the partner consented to the intent of being the child's second parent." 229 Or App at 686. In rejecting respondent's contention that the statute does not apply in this case because the parties did not establish a legal relationship before R was born, the trial court noted our reference to intent in *Shineovich*. The court stated that we had "focused on the parties' intent, not upon their legal status."

. . .

We therefore conclude that choice is the key to determining whether ORS 109.243 applies to a particular same-sex couple. Ultimately, the distinction between married and unmarried heterosexual couples is that the married couples have chosen to be married while the unmarried couples have chosen not to be. And, as we have explained, that choice determines whether ORS 109.243 applies. Given that same-sex couples were until recently prohibited from choosing to be married, the test for whether a same-sex couple is similarly situated to the married opposite-sex couple contemplated in ORS 109.243 cannot be whether the same-sex couple chose to be married or not. Rather, the salient question is whether the same-sex partners would have chosen to marry before the child's birth had they been permitted to.

Whether a particular couple would have chosen to be married, at a particular point in time, is a question of fact. . . .

Reversed and remanded.

Post-Case Follow-Up

In *Madrone*, the court was faced with a statute that did not directly apply to the situation before it. Thus, the court had to determine whether a statute that automatically recognizes a husband as a parent who consents to his wife's conception of a child by artificial insemination applies to a mother's same-sex partner. In resolving this question, the court concluded that it was unconstitutional to exclude same-sex partners who would have married had that choice been available to them from the operation of this law.

The *Madrone* case is a good example of how courts are grappling with the potential unconstitutionality of parentage statutes based on the historic denial of legal rights to same-sex couples.

Madrone v. Madrone: Real Life Applications

1. Peggy and Sue were in a domestic partnership at a time when same-sex marriages were not recognized in their state. Peggy had a child through donor insemination, and the two of them raised the child together. Two years after the child was born, same-sex marriage became legal in their state. The parties talked about doing a formal marriage ceremony but decided that it was not something they wanted to do at that time. Unfortunately, they then decided to separate when the child was three years old. Sue now wants to establish her legal rights as a parent. The state in which they reside has a statute that is the same as the Oregon statute in *Madrone*. Sue filed an action and the court granted summary judgment for Peggy. On appeal, how should the appellate court rule?

2. Assume the same facts as in Question 1 except that Peggy has filed an action seeking to establish Sue as a second parent and hold her responsible for child support. How should the trial court rule?

3. Tom and Henry are domestic partners. Tom adopted a child who the two of them raised together. The state in which they reside does not recognize second-parent adoptions unless the parties are legally married, and at the time of the adoption, the state also did not permit marriages between same-sex partners. Shortly after

the state legalized same-sex marriages, Tom and Henry were married. However, Henry did not go through the formal steps of adopting their child because he did not believe this was necessary now that they were married. Tom and Henry are now going through a divorce. Under a statute similar to the Oregon statute, does Henry have any parental rights?

Chapter Summary

- Laws that differentiate children based on the marital status of their parents are unconstitutional if the underlying purpose is deterrence of nonmarital sexual relations or the promotion of an idealized family type. However, laws that differentiate for the narrow purpose of preventing fraud are generally allowed.
- Although biology alone does not give a man a protected interest in maintaining a relationship with his child, his rights cannot be unilaterally terminated where he has sought to develop a relationship with his child. However, where the mother is married to another man, the presumption of paternity may preclude the unwed father from seeking paternal rights.
- Paternity must be established either through a court proceeding (i.e., adjudication) or a voluntary acknowledgment of paternity.
- In determining paternity, states must now comply with federal requirements or risk the loss of federal funds. A court must order genetic testing if requested by one party, and states must have rules that create a rebuttable presumption of paternity if the tests establish that the man is the father of the child within a threshold degree of probability. States must also have simplified procedures in place, such as the availability of paternity affidavits, for the voluntary acknowledgment of paternity.
- In regard to disestablishing paternity, some states focus on the effect that disestablishment will have on the child and take best interest into account in determining whether a father can disavow his legal relationship with the child. Other states take the position that best interest is irrelevant, and focus on the rights and status of the man who is seeing to disavow his paternity.
- The presumption of paternity and sperm donor laws generally operate to make the husband who consents to the insemination of his wife the legal father of the child despite the lack of a biological connection, and the rights of the sperm donor are terminated.
- In the case of a single woman or a lesbian couple who uses a sperm donor to conceive a child, the allocation of parental rights is more variable, and may turn on the existence and enforceability of a contract between the parties. However, some jurisdictions may rely on state parentage laws or the marital presumption to secure the parental rights of a same-sex partner or spouse.

Applying the Rules

1. Kelly and Griffin are not married when Kelly becomes pregnant. Kelly does not believe that Griffin should have any rights with respect to the child and does nothing to establish paternity as she would rather Griffin be completely out of the child's life. Griffin has come to your office and asked what rights he has as to the child. What do you advise Griffin about his ability to have equal rights with respect to the child? Would it make a difference if Kelly and Griffin were in a serious long-term relationship or if the pregnancy resulted from a casual fling?

2. Midori and Ray were married when they had a baby, Grace. Three years after the birth, Midori told Ray that he was not the biological father of Grace. Ray is not sure, but he is now having doubts about whether the child he has been raising is his and wishes to have genetic testing done to determine if he is in fact the biological father. Can Ray have the testing done to show he is not the father? If it shows he is not, does he have grounds to disestablish paternity? What considerations do you think are important here?

3. Sarah and Doug were married and had two children. After ten years of marriage Sarah indicated she was considering a divorce, and the two agreed a trial separation was appropriate. Sarah moved out of state where she met Bob. After six months of living out of state and seeing Bob fairly frequently, she found out she was pregnant. Scared that this would upset Doug and recognizing that Bob was not someone she would want to be the father of her children, Sarah went back to Doug and told him she wanted to reconcile. Eight months later she gave birth to twins, a boy and a girl. Doug assumed the children were his, and his name is on the birth certificate. When Bob found out that Sarah had given birth to twins, he immediately filed an action for paternity. Sarah objects on the grounds that Doug is the presumptive father. Should the court order a paternity test? What rights does Doug have in the proceedings? Are there any non-legal issues that should influence the court's decision? Would it matter if the action by Bob was filed when the twins were five years old, versus a few months old?

4. Anne and Cathy are married and have chosen to have a child by using a known sperm donor, Tom. The parties all enter into an agreement under which Tom agrees not to seek any parental rights or to see the child, and Anne and Cathy agree not to hold him responsible for child support. The child is now two years old. Tom changes his mind and wants to establish his paternity and see the child. Tom seeks your legal advice. What do you tell Tom? Is there additional information you need to know? Are there policy reasons that favor Tom asserting such rights? Are there policy reasons against Tom asserting any rights?

Family Law in Practice

1. For your state, locate the applicable paternity statute (and custody statute, if separate) and determine the following:

   a. What court are the proceedings held in?
   b. With respect to the use of genetic tests, at what percentage of probability of paternity is a man presumed to be the father?
   c. Does your state employ a rebuttable or a conclusive presumption of paternity?
   d. What is the legal standard for determining custody? Are there any differences in the treatment of married and unmarried parents?

2. Find online the form your state uses for voluntary paternity acknowledgments. If explanatory information is not contained on the form, contact the appropriate agency to determine whether any supplementary documents are required. Now, assume that your office has a client who is contemplating executing the acknowledgment. You have been asked to send him the relevant documents with a cover letter explaining the process and its significance. In writing the letter, assume the client is young and has no familiarity with legal concepts.

3. Assume you are representing an unmarried woman who is planning to be inseminated with the sperm of a known donor. You need to draft an agreement between the parties to memorialize their intent. They have agreed on the following:

   - The donor waives all potential parental rights.
   - The donee agrees not to pursue any child support or other claims.
   - The donor may see the child as a friend of the family but agrees not to disclose his true relationship to the child or to anyone else.
   - The child is to have no established relationship with the donor's extended family.

   After drafting the agreement, draft a cover letter to the client explaining the legal provisions contained in the agreement.

13

Child Abuse and Neglect

In this chapter, we look at the difficult topic of child abuse and neglect. Each year there are countless stories that make headlines demonstrating the enormity of the problem of abuse inflicted upon children by not just parents, but also third-party caretakers.

While in some cases the abuse and neglect are criminal in nature, where the actions do not rise to the criminal level, the legal system must confront the tension that exists between respecting family autonomy and protecting children from potential harm. As touched on in Chapter 1, the Due Process Clause of the Fourteenth Amendment protects the fundamental right of parents to the care and custody of their children — a protection that is grounded in the assumption that parents are in the best position to love and nurture their children. However, this right is not absolute, and at some point, the state may step in to shield children from maltreatment; of course, the challenging question to consider as you read this chapter is at what point should the right of family privacy yield to the ultimate oversight authority of the state?

Although it is clear that protection of children is an important social goal, it is far less clear how the law should respond to concerns about parental non-criminal maltreatment. For example, assume two parents are ice skating with their ten-year-old child. The child looks cold and tired. When the child asks if he can leave the ice, the father insists that the child continue skating until he learns the basics. Eventually, the child begins stumbling from fatigue and begs to leave the ice, but the father does not permit him to stop skating. The father does not raise his voice or strike the child, but it is clear the child feels as if he has no choice but to continue. During this time, the mother is aware of what is going on but appears to ignore it as she continues to skate. Is this abuse? Alternatively, can it possibly

Key Concepts

- Historical recognition of child abuse and neglect
- Legislative measures for addressing child abuse and neglect
- The role and processes of the child protective system
- Reporting abuse and neglect

be characterized as an effective parenting technique — teaching a child how to push beyond obstacles and strive for perfection? Should something be said to the father? Should this conduct be reported to authorities? Would outside intervention be helpful? Intrusive? Destructive? By whose standards are these determinations to be made? These are concepts that will be explored in this chapter.

A. HISTORICAL OVERVIEW

In the early days of our nation, the family was regarded as the essential building block of a well-ordered society and was responsible for the moral character, education, discipline, religious training, and economic well-being of its members. Thus, while this is still true today, in the early days this domestic regime was presided over solely by the husband. The husband, as the household governor, was vested with broad authority over his wife and children. Correspondingly, the other members of the household were expected to defer to the husband's authority.

Parental authority, however, was not absolute, and the community had the right to intervene where a parent either engaged in excessive cruelty or failed to properly discharge his or her child-rearing responsibilities. In practice, though, intervention was rare due to deference to parental authority. When it did occur, the primary goal was preservation of the social order rather than the protection of the child. Considered a greater threat to the cohesion of the community, most interventions were triggered by parental neglect, such as exposing children to drunkenness or immorality or failing to provide them with basic necessities, rather than by physical cruelty.

1. The Emergence of the Privatized Family

As we have seen, industrialization helped to usher in a new family ideal. No longer the locus of production, the individual household became less tightly bound to the wider community. The home was accordingly reconceptualized as a place of refuge from the harshness of the external world. In keeping with emerging middle class norms, it was instead cast as a private domain in which household members would be encouraged to flourish under the gentle guidance of women's newly exalted domestic role.

Childhood was reconceived as a time of innocence during when individual potential could flourish under the nurturance of the sentimentalized maternal figure. As the home came to be viewed as a sanctuary from the public realm, family relations were increasingly sealed off from community scrutiny. Family privacy was enshrined as a cherished value, and future generations of reformers would have to struggle against this ideal as they sought to protect children from parental harm.

2. Child Rescue: Preventing Cruelty to Children

In 1874, a New York charitable worker's attention was drawn to the plight of Mary Ellen Wilson, a ten-year-old who was being brutalized by her foster mother, Mrs.

Connolly. Not knowing where to turn, the worker appealed to the American Society for the Prevention of Cruelty to Animals (ASPCA), in the belief that the society had the authority to intercede on behalf of maltreated children as well as maltreated animals. Moved by Mary Ellen's plight, the ASPCA decided to help. Lacking an obvious legal approach, the ASPCA's attorney petitioned to have Mary Ellen brought before the court under the authority of an old English writ that permitted a magistrate to remove a person from the custody of another. In court, Mary Ellen recounted the horrors she had suffered, including being gashed on the face with a large pair of scissors and almost daily beatings. Mrs. Connolly was convicted of assault and battery, and Mary Ellen was committed to an orphanage and subsequently entrusted to a new family.[1]

Mary Ellen's case led to the creation of the New York Society for the Prevention of Cruelty to Children. *American Humane Society*

Mary Ellen's case built on reforms that had taken place in the early part of the century when a number of states had expanded their neglect laws to encompass grounds beyond parental poverty. Motivated by fear that children would become public charges or turn to a life of crime, removal became sanctioned in cases of parental immorality, drunkenness, or where a child was living in idleness. In upholding the constitutionality of these laws against claims that they abrogated family rights, the courts relied on the English common law doctrine of *parens patriae*, which gives the state, as the sovereign power, the authority to protect those unable to care for themselves.

Mary Ellen's case penetrated the barrier of domestic privacy and helped to usher in an era of intense concern for the maltreated child. It also generated a public awareness that while many societies existed to help mistreated animals, none existed for child victims. Within a year of Mrs. Connolly's conviction, the ASPCA attorney who had helped Mary Ellen founded the New York Society for the Prevention of Cruelty to Children (NYSPCC), the first organization dedicated to child cruelty work. Similar societies soon emerged in other cities and towns.

In general, these child protection agencies regarded themselves as an arm of the police and were committed to seeing that existing laws were vigorously enforced. Agents could arrest offending parents, search homes for evidence of abuse or neglect, remove children, and initiate prosecutions. The focus of the agents was on the offending parent rather than on the child, and punishment rather than assistance was the likely result.

The societies reached the peak of their influence in the 1920s. The Depression brought a loss of funding and a shift in societal emphasis from concern about family violence to family economic survival. Protection of children from parental harm would not surface again as a significant social issue until the 1960s.

---

[1]For more on this case, see Elizabeth Pleck, Domestic Tyranny: The Making of American Social Policy Against Family Violence from Colonial Times to the Present, ch. 4 (1987); Mason P. Thomas, Jr., Child Abuse and Neglect, Part 1: Historical Overview, Legal Matrix, and Social Perspectives, 50 N.C. L. Rev. 293, 307-313 (1972).

B. THE REDISCOVERY OF CHILD ABUSE AND THE INITIAL LEGISLATIVE RESPONSE

In the late 1950s, child abuse was "rediscovered" as a social problem. As discussed in this section, this rediscovery paved the way for the inauguration of a coordinated federal and state response to the problem of child maltreatment.

1. The Battered Child Syndrome

Based mainly on advances in x-ray technology, doctors came to identify patterns of injuries in children that were inconsistent with parental explanations of accidental occurrences. Doctors were also faced with parents who disclaimed a history of past injuries, yet x-rays revealed old fractures in various stages of healing. In 1962, a major study entitled The Battered Child Syndrome was published; based on medical findings, the study detailed the harms that children suffer at the hands of their caretakers. C. Henry Kempe et al., The Battered Child Syndrome, 181 JAMA 17 (1962). As with the case of Mary Ellen Wilson nearly a century earlier, this study triggered a public outcry and paved the way for a major reworking of abuse and neglect laws.

Within a few years of the publication of The Battered Child Syndrome, all states had enacted **abuse reporting laws**. Initially narrow in scope, these laws focused on physical abuse and generally only imposed reporting requirements on doctors. A variety of agencies — including the police, juvenile courts, and child protection agencies — were designated to receive reports, but, unfortunately, most of the reporting laws did not specify who was to assume responsibility once a report had been made. As a result, reports often fell into a void and were passed from agency to agency without any clear lines of accountability. This fragmentary approach resulted in the loss of vital information and a gross inattention to the children who had been identified as possible abuse victims.

2. The Child Abuse and Prevention Act of 1974

Frustrated by the state's fragmented approach to child maltreatment, reformers pushed for greater coordination of protective services. In 1974, Congress responded to these concerns by enacting the Child Abuse Prevention and Treatment Act (CAPTA). *See* Pub. L. No. 93-247, 88 Stat. 4 (codified as amended in scattered sections of 42 U.S.C.). Since 1974, CAPTA has been reauthorized and amended multiple times in order to refine and expand the scope of the law, and it remains at the center of the child protective system.

Under CAPTA, states that developed a coordinated child protective system in accordance with federal requirements became eligible for federal funding to help them defray the costs of implementing such a program. In response, all states revised their existing laws and centralized responsibility in a single **child protection agency**. These agencies now stand at the forefront of what is intended to be a coordinated system to protect children from harm by parents or other caretakers. They are charged with responsibility for receiving and investigating reports of abuse or neglect, providing services to families, taking children into emergency custody, and initiating court dependency and termination proceedings. In some states, protection agencies are also obligated to refer certain cases, such as those in which a child has been raped, has suffered serious physical injury, or has died, to the district attorney's office for possible prosecution.

C. THE CHILD PROTECTIVE SYSTEM

In most cases, a family comes to the attention of a child protection agency when a report of suspected abuse or neglect is filed. The reporting triggers a complex responsive process that may ultimately result in a termination of parental rights.

1. Defining Abuse and Neglect

CAPTA "provides guidance to States by identifying a minimum set of acts or behaviors that define child abuse and neglect,"[2] as follows:

- "Any recent act or failure to act on the part of a parent or caretaker which results in death, serious physical or emotional harm, sexual abuse or exploitation"; or
- "An act or failure which presents an imminent risk of serious harm."

The Federal Child Abuse Prevention and Treatment Act (CAPTA) (42 U.S.C.A. §5106g), as amended by the CAPTA Reauthorization Act of 2010.

With these minimal definitions serving as the operative floor for the receipt of federal CAPTA funding, states are responsible for developing their own definition of abuse and neglect (however, CAPTA includes definitions of sexual abuse and forms of medical neglect). In turn, some state statutes provide broad definitions and speak generally about conduct that poses a threat to a child's well-being, while others provide considerable definitional detail regarding the behaviors that come within the purview of the law.

Determining which behaviors meet the statutory definitions of "abuse" and "neglect" is a powerful act as it mediates the boundary between family autonomy and permissible state intervention. Once parental behavior is defined as coming within the statute, the door is opened to ongoing state involvement. Accepting the premise that family autonomy is worth protecting, how do we decide when it must yield in order to protect children? What if one family's notion of acceptable punishment is a social worker's idea of abuse? What if the family's view is shaped by cultural values that differ from the social worker's? What if lack of food or inappropriate clothing is due to poverty rather than lack of parental concern? These are

---

[2]Definitions of Child Abuse and Neglect in Federal Law, https://www.childwelfare.gov/topics/can/defining/federal/?hasBeenRedirected=1 (accessed June 8, 2016).

delicate questions that highlight the pervasive tension between the need to protect children and the privacy rights of families.

Physical Abuse

Physical abuse is generally defined as conduct that causes physical injury or endangers the health of a child. This definition clearly leaves room for some physical "correction." For example, slapping a child's hand would not support a finding of abuse, but submerging the hand in boiling water would. Between these acts, however, lies a range of behaviors that are more difficult to categorize, and a determination whether a child is being abused may involve multiple factors such as the frequency of punishment and the state of mind of the parent. For example, a parent who occasionally spanks a child in accordance with his or her understanding of the appropriate boundaries of parental authority is not likely to be considered abusive, whereas a parent who frequently spanks a child, especially if an instrument is used, may well be considered abusive.

Physical abuse can be difficult to prove. Often there are no witnesses, and parents may be able to provide a plausible explanation for their child's injuries. For example, a cigarette burn on an arm may be the result of an intentional act or an accidental occurrence. Complicating matters in cases of intentional injuries, the victim may be too young or too afraid to tell anyone what really happened.

Case Preview

Department of Human Resources v. Howard

This case involved the question of whether the actions of the mother involved physical discipline, which was appropriate, versus physical abuse, which was considered "child abuse" under Maryland statutory law. The facts were not in dispute. Mother decided to impose corporal punishment on her son in response to what she viewed as disrespectful behavior. She intended to strike the back of his head with her knuckles, but when he turned just as she was striking him she ended up hitting him in the eye. The injury left a bruised and swollen left eye. The case came to the attention of the Department of Social Services when the school reported the case as possible child abuse.

The department investigated the incident and concluded that mother was responsible for indicated abuse. A person found responsible for child abuse or neglect is identified ("indicated") in a central registry as having committed an act of child abuse.

Mother appealed and the Administrative Law Judge affirmed the decision concluding that the department had established that Mother's actions were a form of indicated child abuse. Mother appealed to the circuit court. The circuit court ruled in favor of Mother holding that the facts did not warrant such a finding. Rather, this was a form of corporal punishment designed to change behavior. While injury did occur, this was not Mother's intent and it was not reasonably predictable that the result would follow from the action of trying to rap the back of the child's head. The department appealed.

As you read *Department of Human Resources v. Howard*, look for the following:

1. What does the court say is required to find that the corporal punishment is not appropriate?
2. How does the parent's "intent" affect a finding of child abuse?
3. Does a finding of "reckless indifference" affect a finding of abuse?

Department of Human Resources v. Howard
897 A.2d 904 (Md. Ct. Spec. App. 2006)

MURPHY, C.J.

This appeal from the Circuit Court for Anne Arundel County presents the question of whether an administrative finding that the mother of a 13-year old boy committed an act of "indicated child abuse" is "appropriate" based upon factual findings that the mother (1) decided to impose corporal punishment on her son in response to his disrespectful behavior towards her, (2) intended to strike the back of her son's head with her knuckles, as she was looking at the back of his head when she moved her hand towards him, and (3) caused an injury to her son's eye when he suddenly turned his head and was therefore struck in the face. For the reasons that follow, we hold that the answer to this question is "no," and we shall therefore affirm the judgment of the circuit court.

[After reviewing the procedural history, statutes, and law, the court explained its decision.]

We are persuaded that the following principles have been established by the statutes, regulations, and cases set forth above:

1. The Maryland General Assembly has expressly codified the parent's common law right to impose "reasonable corporal punishment, in light of the age and condition of the child."

2. A finding of "indicated child abuse" is not "appropriate" when the evidence establishes that the child's parent imposed corporal punishment that left the child with an injury unless "[t]he nature, extent, and location of the injury indicate that the child's health or welfare was harmed or was at substantial risk of harm."

3. Under COMAR 07.02.07.12(C), a finding of "ruled out child abuse" would be "appropriate" even though an observable injury has resulted from corporal punishment that was intentionally imposed. This regulation expressly requires the consideration of other "reasons," such as (1) the reasonableness of the alleged abuser's expectation that no injury would result from the punishment, (2) the fact that the child's injury did not require medical treatment, and (3) the lack of expert testimony on the issue of whether the observable injury caused either "harm" or "substantial risk of harm" to the child's "health or welfare."

4. A finding of "indicated child abuse" may be "appropriate" when the evidence establishes that the child's parent imposed corporal punishment that left the child

with an injury "[t]he nature, extent, and location of [which] indicate that the child's health or welfare was harmed or was at substantial risk of harm."

(a) [*Taylor v. Harford County Dept. of Social Services*, 384 Md. 213 (2004)] made it clear that an "indicated" finding is certainly appropriate when the parent intended to cause such an injury.

(b) [*Charles County Dept. of Social Services v. Vann*, 382 Md. 286 (2004)] makes it clear that an "indicated" finding is also appropriate when, even though the parent did not intend to cause such an injury, the parent imposed corporal punishment under circumstances in which it is likely that such an injury would result from the punishment imposed.

(c) *Taylor*, supra, also makes it clear that an "indicated" finding is appropriate when, even though the parent did not intend to cause such an injury, the parent imposed corporal punishment with reckless indifference to the issue of whether the punishment would produce such an injury.

Applying these principles to the ALJ's factual findings in the case at bar, we begin with the *Taylor* Court's "threshold question," which requires a determination of "whether the act causing injury to [appellee's] child was done with an intent to injure or was done recklessly and injury resulted." A review of the record makes it clear that appellee did not swing at the back of her son's head (1) with intent to injure him, or (2) with knowledge that the likely result of her action would be an injury "[t]he nature, extent, and location of [which] indicate that the child's health or welfare was harmed or was at substantial risk of harm," or (3) with reckless indifference to the issue of whether her action would cause such an injury. We therefore agree with the circuit court that appellee's conduct on the occasion at issue did not constitute "indicated child abuse."

Judgment Affirmed; Appellant to Pay the Costs.

Post-Case Follow-Up

The Maryland statute defined "abuse" of a minor as "physical injury sustained by a minor as a result of cruel or inhumane treatment or as a result of malicious act under circumstances that indicate that the minor's health or welfare is harmed or threated by the treatment or act." This statute, though, had to be read with the codified common law right in Maryland of a parent to impose "reasonable corporal punishment." Since the mother did not intend to injure the child, and her actions were not done with knowledge that they would result in the injury sustained, nor with reckless indifference, her actions could not be considered child abuse that would require her to be indicated as such in the central registry. In reaching its decision, the court also took account of the fact that the child did not need medical attention.

Department of Human Resources v. Howard: Real Life Applications

1. Adrian and Leah are divorced and share equal parenting time with their daughter, Isabella, age 8. During one of his parenting times, Adrian was attempting to take a nap on his sofa when Isabella approached him and asked him to help her with a homework assignment. Adrian told her she would have to wait until he was finished with his nap. Isabella approached Adrian a second time 30 minutes later. Adrian again told her he had to finish his nap. When 30 minutes more passed, she again approached Adrian, this time waking him up from his nap. Adrian, angry he had been woken up, kicked the footstool next to the couch with the intent of kicking it into the sofa. Unfortunately, the thrust of the kick propelled the footstool in the direction that Isabella was standing and hit her in the face, causing her nose to bleed and her jaw to be bruised. Leah has now come to you and asked if you believe these are grounds to report Adrian under the same statute as in *Howard*. Are Adrian's actions likely to be considered child abuse?

2. Tim and Sheila are the parents of six-year-old Adam. The facts are not in dispute: Tim and Sheila have had many calls from the day care center where Adam goes after school. The calls are mainly about how uncontrollable Adam is at times and how he bullies the other children. The parents have been advised if this continues Adam will not be able to stay at the day care. On the occasion in issue, the day care called Sheila and advised her to pick up Adam because he had just punched a teacher in the stomach. The teacher was thought to be pregnant and potentially could have suffered serious injuries. Sheila picked up Adam, and when Tim came home that evening she discussed the situation with him. They both decided that the situation warranted corporal punishment. Using his belt, Tim struck at his son. However, Adam attempted to avoid the blows by running away. Tim struck him two to three times. One of the blows was with the buckle and left a mark on Adam's back. The following day while at school, Adam complained of back pain. The teacher, observing the injury, contacted social services, and after an investigation Tim was found to have engaged in child abuse under a statute like the one in *Howard*. What arguments can be made for Tim that this is not child abuse? How should an appellate court rule?

3. Father is accused of disciplining his three children with a yard stick whenever they, in his opinion, misbehaved. Although the yard stick often left very light marks on their bodies, they usually disappeared within a day or two. When questioned by a social service representative who was investigating a complaint, Father indicated that he did not intend to injure his children, but he did intend to leave marks believing that if the children were embarrassed enough by the marks on their body they would behave to avoid discipline. Father explains that his religion advises that if you spare the rod, you spoil the child. Is this child abuse? Do Father's religious beliefs affect whether it should be considered child abuse or proper corporal punishment?

4. Kristy is a single mom. Her 16-year-old, Penelope, has a job at a local fast food restaurant. Penelope told her mother she would be home a little late after her shift ended at 9:00 P.M. because she needed to drop a book off at a friend's home. When it was 10:00 P.M., Kristy tried calling Penelope and her phone was off. Worried, Kristy called all of Penelope's friends but no one had heard from her. Penelope came home at 11:00 P.M. and Kristy lashed out at Penelope with her fists, more from worry than in anger, causing Penelope to fall against a table resulting in a gash over her right eye. Worried that she might need stitches, Kristy takes Penelope to the emergency hospital where she is questioned about what occurred. Is this abuse?

Sexual Abuse

Child sexual abuse encompasses a range of actions from inappropriate touching to actual penetration. Unlike sexual assaults by strangers, incest by a family member often begins with nonspecific sexualized touching and gradually evolves into more overt sexual acts. The child is usually sworn to secrecy and may be threatened with great harm if disclosure is made.

To provide additional guidance to the states, CAPTA defines sexual abuse to include the following:

> A. the employment, use, persuasion, inducement, enticement, or coercion of any child to engage in, or assist any other person to engage in, any sexually explicit conduct or simulation of such conduct for the purpose of producing a visual depiction of such conduct; or
>
> B. the rape, and in cases of caretaker or inter-familial relationships, statutory rape, molestation, prostitution, or other form of *sexual exploitation* of children, or incest with children.

42 U.S.C. §5106(g), §111(4)(A) & (B). In turn, most states have defined sexual exploitation to include acts such as allowing or inducing a child to engage in prostitution or the production of child pornography.

Emotional Abuse and Neglect

Emotional abuse and emotional neglect are more recently recognized forms of child maltreatment, and many statutes now include them as distinct categories of behavior that can trigger state intervention. These terms are difficult to define, and many statutes refer generally to parental conduct that is causally linked to mental or emotional injuries in a child, such as depression, self-destructive impulses, acute anxiety, withdrawal, and uncontrollable aggression.

Emotional abuse frequently involves subjecting a child to intense and recurring anger or hostility. The child may constantly be belittled, scapegoated, threatened, insulted, and verbally assaulted. Prolonged isolation or acts such as locking a child in a closet can also constitute emotional abuse. **Emotional neglect** usually refers to the withdrawal of love and affection. The boundary between emotional abuse and neglect is often blurry, and both may be present simultaneously.

State intervention is rarely based solely on emotional maltreatment for a number of reasons: (1) it usually co-exists with other kinds of abuse or neglect; (2) the symptoms identified with emotional harm are difficult to identify and tend to emerge gradually over time; (3) it is difficult to establish a causal link between parental conduct and a child's emotional suffering; and (4) it is difficult to determine the standard that parents should be held to. More generally, it is difficult to determine what constitutes good enough parenting and when a parent's failure to provide a secure, loving environment slides into destructive behavior. These determinations require tremendous sensitivity and respect for a diversity of parenting styles so that an idealized vision of the "good" parent is not imposed on nonconforming families.

Neglect

More children suffer from neglect than from any other form of parental maltreatment. According to a 2012 governmental report, 78 percent of the cases of child maltreatment that came to the attention of child protective services involved neglect.[3]

Speaking generally, neglect is the failure to provide for a child's basic needs. More specifically, it has been defined to include a range of acts, such as the failure to provide food, the provision of unsanitary or unsafe housing, the lack of supervision, neglect of personal hygiene, and educational neglect. Failing to provide a child with necessary medical care may likewise constitute neglect, although both CAPTA and many state statutes specify that the failure to obtain medical care that violates a parent's religious beliefs does not constitute medical neglect. However, this religious exemption will not necessarily preclude a court from ordering medical treatment for a child if the child is in imminent danger. Moreover, if the child dies, a parent is still subject to criminal prosecution.

To support a finding of neglect, most states require some degree of parental willfulness. Accordingly, a parent's inability to meet a child's needs because of poverty should not be considered neglect. However, most statutes do not contain an express exemption from a finding of neglect due to financial exigencies. Accordingly, advocates for the poor have raised serious concerns about whether poverty is too readily equated with neglect, as the overt manifestations may be similar. For example, a child might go to school hungry because a parent spent the last of his or her income on rent, or it might be because of a willful failure to feed a child as a form of punishment. An additional concern in this regard is that if a child is removed from the home, a family's poverty may influence a social worker's decision not to return the child, particularly if the family lacks adequate shelter. Thus, identifying the basis for neglect, and providing the services and resources to a family

---

[3]Child Maltreatment 2012, http://www.acf.hhs.gov/sites/default/files/cb/cm2012.pdf (accessed June 8, 2016).

to remedy the neglect are important social policy determinations that overlap the legal determinations.

Establishing neglect usually requires evidence that the child has been harmed or faces a risk of serious harm due to the deprivation. In making this determination, the frequency of the neglectful act may be relevant. An infrequent parental slipup, such as occasionally sending a child to school in the winter without a hat is not neglect, whereas a consistent failure to provide a child with warm clothing during the winter may well be, although again, poverty should provide an exemption from a finding of neglect. Also, where the risk of injury is great, such as where a child is left alone in an apartment with exposed wires, a single incident may constitute neglect.

A parent may also be considered neglectful for the failure to protect a child in his or her care from abuse; most commonly, in these situations, the abuse is committed by the parent's partner or the other parent. In short, although the parent is not directly harming the child, the failure to prevent maltreatment may support the finding of neglect. It is not uncommon in these situations for the "passive" parent to also be a victim of abuse; in these cases, some courts are less likely to find that the parent was neglectful, recognizing that her ability to take action may be impaired by the abuse she is experiencing. Moreover, it would hold the wrong person accountable for the harms to the children.

Taking this practice a step further, some courts have supported findings of neglect when a battered spouse or partner "exposes" his or her children to acts of domestic violence. In these situations, the neglect lies in the failure to protect a child from *witnessing* acts of violence, rather than in failing to protect him or her from actual physical injury. The characterization of failing to protect children from witnessing abuse as neglect, which can lead to the removal of children from the parent who was subjected to abuse, has emerged as the serious consequences of witnessing domestic violence (see Chapter 11).

The practice of removing children from parents for neglect based on their failure to shield their children from exposure to domestic violence is quite controversial. Some argue that this approach is necessary to push victims to leave their abusers. Others believe that this approach serves to punish the victim, by holding him or her, rather than the abuser, responsible for the impact of the abuse. It also ignores the fact that often the victim may be at greater risk when he or she decides to leave. Moreover, the punitive nature of this approach may deter battered spouses or partners from seeking the services they need to safely extricate themselves from an abusive environment.

Case Preview

Nicholson v. Scoppetta

This action was brought by several women on behalf of themselves and their children who had been removed from them solely because they had witnessed the domestic abuse of their mothers. For that reason, the children were deemed neglected by their mothers.

In relevant part, the New York Court of Appeals addressed the question certified to it by the lower court: Whether "the definition of a 'neglected child' under N.Y. Family Ct. Act §1012(f), (h) include[s] instances in which the sole allegation of neglect is that the parent or other person legally responsible for the child's care allows the child to witness domestic abuse against the caretaker?"

As you read *Nicholson v. Scoppetta*, look for the following:

1. What are the two prerequisites the court requires for a determination of child neglect under New York law?
2. How does the court interpret the statutory term "minimum degree of care"?
3. How might a child be considered "neglected" when the child has witnessed domestic violence?

Nicholson v. Scoppetta
820 N.E.2d 840 (N.Y. 2004)

. . .

Family Court Act §1012(f) is explicit in identifying the elements that must be shown to support a finding of neglect. As relevant here, it defines a "neglected child" to mean:

> "a child less than eighteen years of age
> "(i) whose physical, mental or emotional condition has been impaired or is in imminent danger of becoming impaired as a result of the failure of his parent or other person legally responsible for his care to exercise a minimum degree of care. . . .

. . .

Thus, a party seeking to establish neglect must show, by a preponderance of the evidence . . . first, that a child's physical, mental or emotional condition has been impaired or is in imminent danger of becoming impaired and second, that the actual or threatened harm to the child is a consequence of the failure of the parent or caretaker to exercise a minimum degree of care in providing the child with proper supervision or guardianship. The drafters of Article 10 were "deeply concerned" that an imprecise definition of child neglect might result in "unwarranted state intervention into private family life." . . .

The first statutory element requires proof of actual (or imminent danger of) physical, emotional or mental impairment to the child. This prerequisite to a finding of neglect ensures that the Family Court, in deciding whether to authorize state intervention, will focus on serious harm or potential harm to the child, not just on what might be deemed undesirable parental behavior. "Imminent danger" reflects the Legislature's judgment that a finding of neglect may be appropriate even when a child has not actually been harmed; "imminent danger of impairment to a child is an independent and separate ground on which a neglect finding may be based." Imminent danger, however, must be near or impending, not merely possible.

In each case, additionally, there must be a link or causal connection between the basis for the neglect petition and the circumstances that allegedly produce the child's impairment or imminent danger of impairment. In *Dante M.*, for example, we held that the Family Court erred in concluding that a newborn's positive toxicology for a controlled substance alone was sufficient to support a finding of neglect because the report, in and of itself, did not prove that the child was impaired or in imminent danger of becoming impaired (87 NY2d at 79). We reasoned, "[r]elying solely on a positive toxicology result for a neglect determination fails to make the necessary causative connection to all the surrounding circumstances that may or may not produce impairment or imminent risk of impairment in the newborn child" (id.). The positive toxicology report, in conjunction with other evidence — such as the mother's history of inability to care for her children because of her drug use, testimony of relatives that she was high on cocaine during her pregnancy and the mother's failure to testify at the neglect hearing — supported a finding of neglect and established a link between the report and physical impairment.

The cases at bar concern, in particular, alleged threats to the child's emotional, or mental, health. The statute specifically defines "impairment of emotional health" and "impairment of mental or emotional condition" to include

> "a state of substantially diminished psychological or intellectual functioning in relation to, but not limited to, such factors as failure to thrive, control of aggressive or self-destructive impulses, ability to think and reason, or acting out or misbehavior, including incorrigibility, ungovernability or habitual truancy" (Family Ct Act §1012[h]).

Under New York law, "such impairment must be clearly attributable to the unwillingness or inability of the respondent to exercise a minimum degree of care toward the child" (id.). Here, the Legislature recognized that the source of emotional or mental impairment — unlike physical injury — may be murky, and that it is unjust to fault a parent too readily. The Legislature therefore specified that such impairment be "clearly attributable" to the parent's failure to exercise the requisite degree of care.

Assuming that actual or imminent danger to the child has been shown, "neglect" also requires proof of the parent's failure to exercise a minimum degree of care. As the Second Circuit observed, "a fundamental interpretive question is what conduct satisfies the broad, tort-like phrase, 'a minimum degree of care.' The Court of Appeals has not yet addressed that question, which would be critical to defining appropriate parental behavior."

"[M]inimum degree of care" is a "baseline of proper care for children that all parents, regardless of lifestyle or social or economic position, must meet" (*Besharov*, at 326). Notably, the statutory test is "minimum degree of care" — not maximum, not best, not ideal — and the failure must be actual, not threatened (see e.g. *Matter of Hofbauer*, 47 NY2d 648, 656 [1979] [recognizing, in the context of medical neglect, that the court's role is not as surrogate parent and the inquiry is not posed in absolute terms of whether the parent has made the "right" or "wrong" decision]).

Courts must evaluate parental behavior objectively: would a reasonable and prudent parent have so acted, or failed to act, under the circumstances then and there. The standard takes into account the special vulnerabilities of the child, even where general physical health is not implicated. . . . Thus, when the inquiry is whether a mother—and domestic violence victim—failed to exercise a minimum degree of care, the focus must be on whether she has met the standard of the reasonable and prudent person in similar circumstances.

As the Subclass A members point out, for a battered mother—and ultimately for a court—what course of action constitutes a parent's exercise of a "minimum degree of care" may include such considerations as: risks attendant to leaving, if the batterer has threatened to kill her if she does; risks attendant to staying and suffering continued abuse; risks attendant to seeking assistance through government channels, potentially increasing the danger to herself and her children; risks attendant to criminal prosecution against the abuser; and risks attendant to relocation. Whether a particular mother in these circumstances has actually failed to exercise a minimum degree of care is necessarily dependent on facts such as the severity and frequency of the violence, and the resources and options available to her (see *Matter of Melissa U.*, 148 AD2d 862 [3d Dept 1989]; *Matter of James MM. v June OO.*, 294 AD2d 630 [3d Dept 2002]).

Only when a petitioner demonstrates, by a preponderance of evidence, that both elements of section 1012(f) are satisfied may a child be deemed neglected under the statute. When "the sole allegation" is that the mother has been abused and the child has witnessed the abuse, such a showing has not been made. This does not mean, however, that a child can never be "neglected" when living in a household plagued by domestic violence. Conceivably, neglect might be found where a record establishes that, for example, the mother acknowledged that the children knew of repeated domestic violence by her paramour and had reason to be afraid of him, yet nonetheless allowed him several times to return to her home, and lacked awareness of any impact of the violence on the children, as in *Matter of James MM.* 294 AD2d at 632; or where the children were exposed to regular and continuous extremely violent conduct between their parents, several times requiring official intervention, and where caseworkers testified to the fear and distress the children were experiencing as a result of their long exposure to the violence (*Matter of Theresa CC.*, 178 AD2d 687 [3d Dept 1991]).

In such circumstances, the battered mother is charged with neglect not because she is a victim of domestic violence or because her children witnessed the abuse, but rather because a preponderance of the evidence establishes that the children were actually or imminently harmed by reason of her failure to exercise even minimal care in providing them with proper oversight.

Post-Case Follow-Up

The court addressed the question of whether it is possible to find a parent responsible for neglect based on "evidence of two facts only: that the parent has been the victim of domestic violence, and that the child has been exposed to that violence." Although recognizing that witnessing violence can have a negative impact on children, the court ruled that a parent's failure to protect her children from exposure to such violence is not enough to establish, as required under New York law, that she failed to exercise a "minimum degree of care" and thus neglected her children.

Nicholson v. Scoppetta: Real Life Applications

1. Sarah is a single mother of three-year-old Samantha and two-year-old Brooke. Robby, the children's biological father, often comes to the house to visit the children. He is always very gentle with the children; however, Sarah is afraid of Robby because of his violent temper toward her. She has often been subjected to physical abuse by him, but she has been afraid to say anything because Robby has claimed that if she does he'll take the children away from her. One day, a co-worker, tired of seeing the bruises on Sarah's arms, reports the abuse to the authorities. Will Sarah have the children taken away from her if an investigation shows that the children were exposed to the violence? Would it matter if the children were age 13 and 12 versus 3 and 2?

2. Assume the same facts as in Question 1, but Samantha has started becoming afraid whenever she sees another man, and starts to cry and shake uncontrollably. When Sarah mentioned it to Samantha's pediatrician, the pediatrician advised Sarah to immediately get counseling help for Samantha. Sarah refuses to do so, as she is afraid that Robby will be prohibited from seeing the girls, which will only make him angrier. Can Samantha be deemed to be a neglected child?

3. Perry and Kristen are husband and wife. Perry is never physically abusive with Kristen, but he is often verbally abusive, calling her demeaning names. One time when she accidentally dropped a plate of food while bringing it to the dinner table, he made her get down on her hands and knees and told her to pick it up with her hands. This was all done in front of their seven-year-old son, Buddy. Perry told Buddy that this is what you have to do in order to have control over your household and your wife or they will never respect you as the head. Perry often encourages Buddy to shout orders to his mother and has told Buddy that his mother must never discipline him because that is a man's job. A neighbor was recently at the house and heard Buddy shouting orders to Kristen. Appalled, she asked Kristen about it, who confided in the neighbor everything that has been going on for the past couple of years. If the neighbor reports the incident, what arguments can be made that Kristen is guilty of neglect of Buddy? What arguments can be made that she does not meet the statutory definition?

Another controversial issue that a few courts have recently grappled with is whether state intervention is appropriate in cases where a child is morbidly obese and the parents do not appear to be willing or able to take steps to address the situation. Given the serious comorbidities of obesity, which include "type two diabetes, obstructive sleep apnea, asthma, nonalcoholic fatty liver disease, cardiovascular conditions, such as hypertension and atherosclerosis, and psychological problems such as depression," a handful of courts have begun to regard this type of situation as a form of medical neglect that justifies state intervention, including the possible removal of a child from his or her home. *See* Melissa Mitgang, Childhood Obesity and State Intervention: An Examination of the Health Risks of Pediatric Obesity and When They Justify State Involvement, 44 Colum. J. L. & Soc. Probs. 553, 555 (2011).

In re Brittany T.

In re Brittany T. involved the issue of whether it was in the best interest of a child to permanently remove her from her parents. The child was, as described by the court, morbidly obese. The child also suffered from numerous comorbidities. The parents failed to address the medical concerns or to ensure the child's attendance in school. At the time of the petition, the child was 12 years old. However, there had been other encounters with the Department of Social Services prior to that time.

In 2003, when the child was nine years old, the department had placed the child with the maternal aunt through a kinship foster care program. The court had granted the placement because of the failure of the parents to address the child's morbid obesity and lack of commitment in addressing the child's mental and physical needs. At various times over a three-year period, the child was returned to the parents and then removed. The child's weight ranged from 237 pounds in October 2002 to 266 pounds at the time of the petition in 2006.

As you read *In re Brittany T.*, look for the following:

1. What was the law that the parents violated?
2. What does the court indicate the parents failed to do in managing the minor child's weight?
3. What do the parents need to do in order to have the minor child returned to them?

In re Brittany T.

835 N.Y.S.2d 829 (N.Y. Fam. Ct. 2007)

FAMILY COURT

DAVID M. BROCKWAY, J.

[The parents are accused of having violated certain terms of the previous court order, which included ensuring the child attend school on a regular basis and on time, taking the child to a gym two to three times per week, and actively and honestly attending and participating in nutrition and education programs.]

[G]enerally testifying on behalf of the department, and probably most compelling, was Dr. William J. Cochran. Cochran is a board certified pediatric gastroenterologist and nutritionist. . . .

Cochran had first started working with the child and respondents by doing an evaluation in November 2004. Extensive testing, interviewing and teaching has been done with Brittany [the minor child], and he has been monitoring her weight management program. Genetic and psychiatric disease syndromes were ruled out by Cochran; rather, he deemed the obesity as simply due to excessive caloric intake and a sedentary lifestyle.

Cochran credibly testified that the child currently suffers from morbid obesity and associated comorbidities. One is considered morbidly obese in medical literature and by practitioners when one's body mass index (BMI) exceeds 40. An ideal BMI is 18-25; Brittany's BMI is 50. Comorbidities are other disorders or diseases accompanying a primary diagnosis. In Brittany, these include those typically found with morbid obesity: gallstones, excessive fat in her liver with resultant fatty liver disease (which, he said, could eventually develop into nonalcoholic cirrhosis of the liver), sleep apnea, intermittent high blood pressure, pain in her knee joints, insulin resistance (indicating an increased risk of developing diabetes) and acanthosis nigricans (darkening and thickening of the skin around her neck associated with insulin resistance). Additionally, he testified as to the significant social and psychological impact such morbidity has. . . .

. . .

THE RESPONDENTS' CASE

. . .

The respondents testified on their own behalf. Court records indicate the father (date of birth 1966) is now approaching 41 years of age. He is confined to a wheelchair and, he testified, suffers from cardiomyopathy, muscular dystrophy, arthritis and scoliosis. He asserted that "all" the family follow a dietary regime. He further testified that Brittany bowls weekly, has attended school dances and has walked to school once. . . .

The mother, according to court records, is soon to be 32 years of age (date of birth 1972). The court has observed throughout the past four years that Mrs. T. herself is very obese (436 pounds). Moreover, at least fairly recently, the court has observed that the mother suffers from some very audible breathing difficulties. The mother expressed during testimony (as she had to Dr. Cochran several years earlier) a seeming understanding of caloric intake, the keeping of accurate food logs, the importance of exercise and the like. She offered that there were numerous difficulties during the period of supervision including such things as weather and transportation troubles and a hospital stay for herself for gallstones. She was aware that Brittany often had snacks after school and after dinner in the evening and that the child was known to "sneak food" at home. She also attributed some of the compliance difficulties to Brittany getting "frustrated" at "all she needs to do" and that the child "hates all of what the court has ordered the parents to do." On a positive note, the mother indicated that Brittany was now enjoying and doing better in school, to which she or her husband regularly drive her the half mile.

Distilled to its essence, the parents disagreed with particular dates and times, but did not refute that there have been missed appointments, missed school days and numerous tardies. While not disputing that they have not thoroughly complied with the court's dispositional order, they indicated they had tried their best. Essentially, however, they each offered numerous excuses for their noncompliance and argued that the child has not been negatively impacted by their noncompliance. The court frankly finds the respondents' explanations regarding their inability to comply with the terms to be spurious, unpersuasive and largely lacking credibility.

LAW ON VIOLATION

A petition alleging a violation of an order of supervision can be sustained if the court is satisfied by competent proof that the violation was done "willfully and without just cause." . . .

Additionally, it is well established that terms to be enforced must sufficiently apprise a respondent what is required of him, her or them. Here, the terms are very clear. Moreover, it is equally clear that a willful violation is supported by one's failure to regularly attend and meaningfully participate in programs, as it indicates an unwillingness or inability to take the steps necessary to assume responsibility for one's children.

DISCUSSION AND CONCLUSIONS AS TO VIOLATION

With respect to the alleged violation [for failure to actively and honestly attend and participate in a nutrition program and education program approved by the department,] the court finds that several of the missed appointments at the nutrition clinic may have been with just cause and thus so much of the violation . . . as is based thereon, is not sustained. With respect to the rest of [the terms] and all of the other terms, however, their willful violation is sustained by competent, credible evidence which is ample, clear and convincing. The respondents' failures regarding those established to have been violated are further found, by equally clear and convincing evidence, to have been without just cause. All of this has convincingly and patently had a very negative physical, emotional and mental impact on Brittany. (*Nicholson v Scoppetta*, 3 NY3d 357 [2004].)

In arriving at these conclusions, it is startling to read the original neglect petition of February 21, 2003 (when Brittany was about to turn nine). That petition alleged, inter alia, that

> "Brittany T. has a severe weight problem and weighs in excess of 240 pounds. Brittany has been seen by a variety of doctors and all of the physicians involved are very concerned about her health due to the fact that she is morbidly obese. Despite these doctors' concerns, Mr. and Mrs. T. have been uncooperative with service providers and have shown a lack of follow through with these services. [Physicians] have made numerous recommendations to Mr. and Mrs. T. in the past and none of these recommendations were ever followed through with. . . . It has been determined by [the physicians] involved that Brittany's weight problems are not organic in nature and are the result of poor parental modeling and control of food intake. Physicians have seen a pattern of alarming behavior on the part of Mr. and Mrs. T. regarding their attitude toward Brittany's morbid obesity and her extremely poor attendance in school. Brittany has had attendance problems at school ever since she began kindergarten. Many of these absences have been unexcused absences and the family refuses to ensure that Brittany attend school, even [on] a semi regular basis. . . . When Robert and Shawna have enrolled Brittany in programs in the past, they have not continued with these programs and have multiple excuses as to why they do not continue. . . ."

Shockingly, it is truly as if nothing (except weight gain) has changed in the past three-plus years. This court on many, many occasions has expressed its concern with respect to the lack of commitment and motivation demonstrated by the respondents in effectively and wholeheartedly addressing their daughter's school issues (at least until the eve of trial) and her morbid obesity. The latter concern continues unabated, along with its concomitant health complications. It is inconceivable to this court that the respondents continue to disregard the medical and other advice of their experts. This is despite the myriad services which the department has actively and repeatedly urged. Furthermore, CASA, too, has been intimately involved with and assisted the family since its assignment in October 2004. Even more incredible is that this has continued in spite of respondents' knowing that their jailing and/or their daughter's removal from home were more immediate likelihoods than Brittany's probable premature death.

The long history of this unfortunate case demonstrates that the respondents have unequivocally evinced an unwillingness to follow doctors' and others' advice, so as to justify a finding that they willfully violated the terms of the order of disposition. The respondents' continued noncompliance in ensuring Brittany's regular school attendance and in assuring their active and diligent cooperation with, and participation in, programs designed to aggressively address the child's morbid obesity, only amplifies the willfulness of their violation. The court recognizes the physical limitations of the respondents but finds that this neither excuses nor prohibits them from executing their parental and court-ordered responsibilities.

. . .

DISCUSSION AND CONCLUSIONS AS TO DISPOSITION

It is clear in New York that a child is neglected when his or her "physical, mental or emotional condition has been impaired . . . as a result of the failure of his or her parent to exercise a minimum degree of care in supplying the child with adequate . . . education . . . or medical . . . care, though financially able to do so." . . . The respondents, due to their continued failures with respect to Brittany's educational and medical needs, have not provided that minimum degree of care, which is measured against the behavior of reasonable and prudent parents faced with the same circumstances. . . .

. . .

In so deciding, of course, the court notes that less drastic remedies should generally be attempted first. In the instant matter, as noted above, absolutely every thing and every effort has been attempted — not for months, but for years. The court finds that Brittany's continued residency in the home is contrary to her health, welfare and safety and that the best interest of the child warrants her removal from the care and custody of the parents and placement once again with the department. The court finds that the department has employed not only reasonable but, indeed, extraordinary efforts to prevent or eliminate this need.

Therefore, it is hereby ordered that the respondents are found in willful violation of this court's dispositional order dated April 24, 2003 (as subsequently extended by this court); and it is further ordered that the child Brittany T. shall, pursuant to section 1055 of the Family Court Act, be placed in the custody of the Commissioner of the Chemung County Department of Social Services within seven court days of the entry of this order; and it is further ordered that the parents shall be authorized to jointly visit the child at the Human Resources Building, or where the child might be placed, or other fitting place chosen by the department, twice per week, totaling no less than four hours per week, provided it is in keeping with the department's service objectives and placement goals; and it is further ordered that the respondents, pursuant to Social Services Law §409-e(3), shall be notified of any and all planning conferences, of their right to attend the conference(s), and of their right to have counsel or another representative or companion with them; and it is further ordered that the court specifically prohibits any trial discharge without court leave; and it is further ordered that, subject to future petitions or hearings, return to parents is the permanency goal, provided that the child obtains and maintains a healthy weight and lifestyle before returning home and further provided that one or both parents can actually demonstrate an ability to provide appropriate home, school and community supports so as to so maintain the child, including indicia of consistently affording an environment conducive to healthy eating habits, exercise regimens and to meeting educational attendance requirements; and it is further ordered that the prior disposition is revoked, but the same terms and conditions of supervision are hereby reimposed on this violation, for a period of 12 months.

Post-Case Follow-Up

The family court in New York concluded that the willful failure by the parents of a morbidly obese daughter to take affirmative steps to address her obesity constituted the neglectful failure to "exercise a minimum degree of care," thus exposing her to "severe life-limiting dangers."

It should be noted that the court was also concerned with the parents' failure to ensure that their daughter attended school on a regular basis. Accordingly, the court ordered that the daughter be placed in state custody until such time as "one or both parents [could] actually demonstrate an ability to provide appropriate home, school and community supports . . . including indicia of consistently affording an environment conducive to healthy eating habits [and] exercise regimens." *Id.* at 840-841.

In re Brittany T.: Real Life Applications

1. Sophia and Jackson are the parents of nine-year-old Emily. Emily is 200 pounds overweight. Previous court orders have temporarily placed Emily in foster care where she successfully loses weight. When she is returned to her parents, they promise to monitor her diet and ensure she attends classes at the gym three days a week. However, every time Emily is returned to their care she gains even more weight than she lost. The parents take Emily to a few of the gym classes when she returns to them but they do not force her to attend if she does not want to go. They also have not seriously monitored her calorie intake and believe that life is short and you should eat what you want. What order should the court impose?

2. Olivia and Aiden are the parents of 12-year-old Liam. They have tried to teach Liam good eating habits, but both parents work and they know that Liam must be sneaking food when they are not at home, because he continues to gain weight and is currently approaching morbid obesity. They have enrolled him in fitness classes, but they can tell he does not put his heart into the classes and does not engage in any activity he finds too strenuous. The department of social services is attempting to remove Liam temporarily from their home due to his continued weight gain. What should a court do?

3. Isabella and Lucas are the parents of Mason, age 15. Mason is approximately 50 pounds overweight for his age and height. However, wanting to lose weight, Mason has asked his parents if he can join a gym. His parents have refused claiming gyms are a waste of money. Mason also objects to the food his parents provide at home because of the high caloric intake. His parents have told him if he does not like it he can just not eat. Mason's grades have begun to suffer, and he has become emotionally depressed over his weight. Are his parents guilty of neglect under the statute in *Brittany T.*?

4. Caden and Madelyn are the parents of 12-year-old Lily. Both Caden and Madelyn decided for their New Year's resolutions they were going to lose weight. Although Lily is not overweight, they decided it would be a good idea for her to get in the habit of also staying fit and losing weight. They have enrolled as a family in a local gym, and have taken to the outdoors by running and hiking. They also have instituted a strict calorie intake at home. When Lily had her annual check-up with her pediatrician, the pediatrician was alarmed at how much weight Lily had lost since the last check-up. The pediatrician recommended that Lily start eating foods higher in calories to put on weight. The parents ignored the recommendation. When school personnel noticed the extreme weight loss, they attempted to discuss the situation with the parents. Both Caden and Madelyn felt the school was overreacting. Is this a possible issue of neglect?

Drug Use by Pregnant Women

In the mid-1980s, the plight of babies born to women who used drugs, most notably crack cocaine, while pregnant attracted much public attention. Of concern was the fact that these drug-exposed infants are frequently born at low birth weights, may exhibit painful withdrawal symptoms, and suffer from a host of serious medical and developmental complications.

In response to these concerns, a number of states expanded the concept of abuse and neglect to include prenatal drug exposure — based on either the actual physical impairment caused by the exposure or the risk of future harm the mother is thought to pose to the child.[4] As a result, some states specifically require health care professionals to report suspected prenatal drug abuse to child protective services,

---

[4]In some states, prenatal drug exposure may also expose a woman to criminal prosecution on a number of grounds including child endangerment, manslaughter, and the delivery of illegal substances — in this case through the umbilical cord.

and a handful of states mandate testing for exposure if there are indications that the woman used drugs during her pregnancy. Positive results must then be reported to child protective services. The consequences of determined drug use during pregnancy vary from state to state: In some states, there may be an evaluation of parenting ability and the determination of the need for social services. In other states, the positive results may trigger a presumption of neglect. In still others, it may itself be the basis of a parental termination proceeding. Regardless of approach, the immediate consequence is most likely to be the separation of mother and newborn and the placement of the infant into foster care.

Treating prenatal drug exposure as a form of child abuse or neglect is quite controversial. Supporters of this approach point to the potentially devastating effect of prenatal drug exposure and to the need to hold women accountable for their conduct during pregnancy. Many speak of a duty of care that a woman owes to her unborn child once she elects to carry a pregnancy to term, and reject the idea that a woman's constitutional right of privacy bars the state from scrutinizing her conduct in order to protect the unborn.

On the other hand, critics of this approach argue that it is unduly punitive and ignores the complex social reality of drug addiction. Rather than recognizing the often desperate situation of these women, it is argued that this approach portrays them as the purposeful destroyers of their unborn children. By blaming the individual, it avoids social responsibility for ensuring that pregnant women have access to adequate educational, prenatal, and drug treatment services. In this regard, it is noted that many pregnant drug users do not have ready access to treatment programs because many of them do not serve pregnant women. Seeking to remedy this historical exclusion, a number of states have established drug treatment programs specifically for pregnant women, or now provide them with priority access to state funded services. Critics also express the concern that, in addition to shifting attention away from the need to provide pregnant women with essential services, reporting laws will deter them from utilizing whatever services are available based on the fear that this will result in the loss of their babies.

D. THE REPORTING OF SUSPECTED ABUSE OR NEGLECT

Most families come to the attention of a child protection agency following a report of suspected child abuse or neglect. In the cases of separated or divorced families, the reporting may be done by one parent when they see signs of abuse after the child returns from parenting time with the other parent. In these cases, judges must attempt to guard against a parent using the legal system to gain custody by making false child abuse reports. Many states will use a false report of child abuse against one parent as a factor in denying custody to that parent.

1. Mandatory versus Permissive Reporters

The reporting laws in most states distinguish between mandatory and permissive reporters. Mandatory reporters are specifically designated as such by statute and are usually professionals who are likely to encounter children in the course of their work, such as dentists, social workers, therapists, teachers, and physicians. Mandatory reporters are legally obligated to report suspected instances of abuse or neglect and may be subject to criminal sanctions for the failure to do so, although prosecutions tend to be rare. Generally, these statutes abrogate professional privileges so that a reporter can disclose information without violating any duty of confidentiality. Most, if not all, reporting laws also protect a reporter from liability for reporting the suspected abuse, so long as the report was made in good faith.

Attorneys are not identified as mandated reporters in many states. Of course, even if not legally required, a report can always be made on a permissive basis. However, the attorney-client privilege may not be abrogated in this situation, which raises ethical considerations regarding the duty to preserve client confidentiality.

Any person not specifically identified as a mandatory reporter is considered a permissive reporter. Permissive reporters can, but are not obligated to, report suspected cases of abuse or neglect. To encourage these reports, most states permit them to be made on an anonymous basis. Because permissive reporters have no duty to report, the failure to act will not result in sanctions. However, as discussed above, parents may be legally responsible for failing to protect their children from harm inflicted by the other parent or caretaker. Accordingly, even where not required by statute, the duty to protect may effectively impose a reporting obligation on a parent. But again, the report must be made on a good faith basis that abuse is suspected to avoid having the false report used against the reporting parent.

A number of states do not distinguish between mandatory and permissive reporters. Accordingly, in these jurisdictions, any person who has reasonable grounds to believe a child is being harmed has a duty to report his or her concerns to child protective services.

Reports are generally made directly to the child protection agency. In specific circumstances, such as where a child has been killed, a reporter may be *required* to also notify a law enforcement agency. As a rule, reports must be made immediately or as soon as practicable after the harm comes to the reporter's attention. Due to this timeliness requirement, reports are usually made by telephone and then followed up on in writing.

2. Screening and Investigation

When a report is received, it is either screened in for investigation or screened out because the case does not meet the statutory definition of abuse or neglect, such as where the suspected perpetrator is not a parent or caretaker. Cases may also be screened out for a variety of other reasons, such as when the child cannot be identified with reasonable certainty, or because the family is already involved with protective services.

If a case is screened in, a social worker (or allied professional) must promptly initiate an investigation to determine if the allegations can be substantiated. In most states, the required time frames and nature and scope of the investigation will vary based upon the initial assessment of the risk to the child. In short, many states have adopted a two-track investigative process based on the seriousness of the allegations. Where the child is not considered to be at imminent risk of harm, most states require that the investigation be initiated no later than 72 hours after receipt of the report. Where the risk to the child is great, protective services may be required to launch the investigation within as few as two hours after receiving the report.

If the investigator cannot substantiate the allegations contained in the report, the case is closed, and no further action is taken, although voluntary services such as parenting classes or day care referrals may be offered to the family. If, however, the investigator has reasonable cause to believe that the child is being abused or neglected, the case will remain open and under the authority of the protection agency.

If the investigator has cause to believe that a child is in immediate danger of serious harm, he or she may remove the child without a court order or prior notice to the parents. Emergency removal is not a preferred approach and is generally limited to situations where there is no other way to ensure a child's safety while the investigation is pending. Following removal, the agency must immediately initiate court proceedings. The parents are entitled to a hearing (usually within 72 hours of removal), at which time they can challenge the state's actions. The court may decide the removal was in error and return the child to the home, or it may decide to keep temporary custody in the agency.

Case Preview

Ohio v. Clark

In the recent case of *Ohio v. Clark*, the United States Supreme Court had an opportunity to examine under what circumstances the statements of a child made out of court to a teacher could be used against the defendant. The child was three years old, and not old enough to testify in court. However, when questioned about the injuries by a teacher at school, the child had made statements implicating the defendant.

The defendant argued that these out-of-court statements could not be used by the prosecutor since they were hearsay and would violate the defendant's rights under the Sixth Amendment Confrontation Clause.

As you read *Ohio v. Clark*, look for the following:

1. What was the testimony that the lower court was concerned about?
2. What does the Confrontation Clause prohibit?
3. Why did the Court find a difference between speaking to a teacher and speaking to the police?

Ohio v. Clark
576 U.S. ___ (2015)

Justice ALITO delivered the opinion of the Court.

Darius Clark sent his girlfriend hundreds of miles away to engage in prostitution and agreed to care for her two young children while she was out of town. A day later, teachers discovered red marks on her 3-year-old son, and the boy identified Clark as his abuser. The question in this case is whether the Sixth Amendment's Confrontation Clause prohibited prosecutors from introducing those statements when the child was not available to be cross-examined. Because neither the child nor his teachers had the primary purpose of assisting in Clark's prosecution, the child's statements do not implicate the Confrontation Clause and therefore were admissible at trial.

I

[After noting marks on the child, a teacher asked,] " '[w]hat happened,' " and he initially said nothing. Eventually, however, he told the teacher that he " 'fell.' " When they moved into the brighter lights of a classroom, [the teacher] noticed " '[r]ed marks, like whips of some sort,' " on L.P.'s face She notified the lead teacher, Debra Jones, who asked L.P., " 'Who did this? What happened to you?' " Id. According to Jones, L.P. " 'seemed kind of bewildered' " and " 'said something like, Dee, Dee.' " Jones asked L.P. whether Dee is "big or little," to which L.P. responded that "Dee is big." Jones then brought L.P. to her supervisor, who lifted the boy's shirt, revealing more injuries. [The teacher] called a child abuse hotline to alert authorities about the suspected abuse.

When Clark later arrived at the school, he denied responsibility for the injuries and quickly left with L.P. The next day, a social worker found the children at Clark's mother's house and took them to a hospital, where a physician discovered additional injuries suggesting child abuse. . . .

At trial, the State introduced L.P.'s statements to his teachers as evidence of Clark's guilt, but L.P. did not testify. Under Ohio law, children younger than 10 years old are incompetent to testify if they "appear incapable of receiving just impressions of the facts and transactions respecting which they are examined, or of relating them truly." Ohio Rule Evid. 601(A) (Lexis 2010). After conducting a hearing, the trial court concluded that L.P. was not competent to testify. But under Ohio Rule of Evidence 807, which allows the admission of reliable hearsay by child abuse victims, the court ruled that L.P.'s statements to his teachers bore sufficient guarantees of trustworthiness to be admitted as evidence.

[The trial court convicted Clark. The appellate court reversed based on the ground that the out-of-court statements of L.P. violated the Confrontation Clause. The Ohio Supreme Court affirmed.]

II

A

The Sixth Amendment's Confrontation Clause, which is binding on the States through the Fourteenth Amendment, provides: "In all criminal prosecutions, the accused shall enjoy the right . . . to be confronted with the witnesses against him." In *Ohio v. Roberts*, 448 U.S. 56, 66 (1980), we interpreted the Clause to permit the admission of out-of-court statements by an unavailable witness, so long as the statements bore "adequate 'indicia of reliability.'" Such indicia are present, we held, if "the evidence falls within a firmly rooted hearsay exception" or bears "particularized guarantees of trustworthiness." Ibid.

In *Crawford v. Washington*, 541 U.S. 36 (2004), we adopted a different approach. We explained that "witnesses," under the Confrontation Clause, are those "who bear testimony," and we defined "testimony" as "a solemn declaration or affirmation made for the purpose of establishing or proving some fact." Id., at 51 (internal quotation marks and alteration omitted). The Sixth Amendment, we concluded, prohibits the introduction of testimonial statements by a nontestifying witness, unless the witness is "unavailable to testify, and the defendant had had a prior opportunity for cross-examination." Id., at 54. Applying that definition to the facts in *Crawford*, we held that statements by a witness during police questioning at the station house were testimonial and thus could not be admitted. But our decision in *Crawford* did not offer an exhaustive definition of "testimonial" statements. Instead, *Crawford* stated that the label "applies at a minimum to prior testimony at a preliminary hearing, before a grand jury, or at a former trial; and to police interrogations." Id., at 68.

Our more recent cases have labored to flesh out what it means for a statement to be "testimonial." In *Davis v. Washington* and *Hammon v. Indiana*, 547 U.S. 813 (2006), which we decided together, we dealt with statements given to law enforcement officers by the victims of domestic abuse. The victim in *Davis* made statements to a 911 emergency operator during and shortly after her boyfriend's violent attack. In *Hammon*, the victim, after being isolated from her abusive husband, made statements to police that were memorialized in a "'battery affidavit.'" Id., at 820.

We held that the statements in *Hammon* were testimonial, while the statements in *Davis* were not. Announcing what has come to be known as the "primary purpose" test, we explained: "Statements are nontestimonial when made in the course of police interrogation under circumstances objectively indicating that the primary purpose of the interrogation is to enable police assistance to meet an ongoing emergency. They are testimonial when the circumstances objectively indicate that there is no such ongoing emergency, and that the primary purpose of the interrogation is to establish or prove past events potentially relevant to later criminal prosecution." Id., at 822.

. . .

Thus, under our precedents, a statement cannot fall within the Confrontation Clause unless its primary purpose was testimonial. "Where no such primary purpose exists, the admissibility of a statement is the concern of state and federal rules of evidence, not the Confrontation Clause." Id., at 359. . . .

In this case, we consider statements made to preschool teachers, not the police. We are therefore presented with the question we have repeatedly reserved: whether statements to persons other than law enforcement officers are subject to the Confrontation Clause. Because at least some statements to individuals who are not law enforcement officers could conceivably raise confrontation concerns, we decline to adopt a categorical rule excluding them from the Sixth Amendment's reach.

Nevertheless, such statements are much less likely to be testimonial than statements to law enforcement officers. And considering all the relevant circumstances here, L.P.'s statements clearly were not made with the primary purpose of creating evidence for Clark's prosecution. Thus, their introduction at trial did not violate the Confrontation Clause.

. . .

There is no indication that the primary purpose of the conversation was to gather evidence for Clark's prosecution. On the contrary, it is clear that the first objective was to protect L.P. At no point did the teachers inform L.P. that his answers would be used to arrest or punish his abuser. L.P. never hinted that he intended his statements to be used by the police or prosecutors.

. . .

[A]lthough we decline to adopt a rule that statements to individuals who are not law enforcement officers are categorically outside the Sixth Amendment, the fact that L.P. was speaking to his teachers remains highly relevant. Courts must evaluate challenged statements in context, and part of that context is the questioner's identity. Statements made to someone who is not principally charged with uncovering and prosecuting criminal behavior are significantly less likely to be testimonial than statements given to law enforcement officers. It is common sense that the relationship between a student and his teacher is very different from that between a citizen and the police.

We reverse the judgment of the Supreme Court of Ohio and remand the case for further proceedings not inconsistent with this opinion. It is so ordered.

Post-Case Follow-Up

The U.S. Supreme Court reversed the judgment of the Ohio Supreme Court. The Court held that the introduction of L.P.'s statements that were made to the teacher did not violate the Confrontation Clause of the Sixth Amendment.

The Court based its decision on the grounds that the statements made by L.P. were not for the primary purpose of giving testimony against the defendant. Rather, no one advised L.P. that his statements would be used as evidence against the defendant, nor, given L.P.'s age, could that have been a consideration as it is extremely unlikely L.P. would have understood that concept. The Court did not go so far as to say that all testimony to individuals outside law enforcement will not be considered testimony — rather, only that statements to individuals who are not principally charged with uncovering and prosecuting criminal behavior are less likely to be considered testimony.

Ohio v. Clark: Real Life Applications

1. Cindy was tried on several charges related to her alleged abuse of a six-year-old child. The child had made statements about the abuse to a teacher. The child

did not testify at trial, but the teacher testified, telling the court that when questioned about the bruise on her arm, the child told the teacher that Cindy had caused the bruise. Cindy seeks to overturn her conviction on the grounds that the statements of the child should not have been admitted. What result?

2. Pedro is on trial for child abuse. The prosecutor asks the judge to receive evidence from the eight-year-old victim by one-way closed circuit television because the child's courtroom testimony would result in the child suffering serious emotional distress if required to face the defendant. Pedro's attorney objects on the grounds that this violates the Confrontation Clause. What result?

3. Tami, age 5, was removed from her mother Alyssa's home because of suspected abuse by Alyssa's live-in boyfriend. Tami was temporarily placed in foster care with Melissa. Melissa, concerned that Tami could be reunited with her mother Alyssa and that Alyssa would not watch out for Tami, tried to coax Tami into telling her about abuse by any of her mother's friends. Finally, after days of coaxing, Tami confided, "Sometimes Mommy's boyfriend hits me really hard, but I can't tell anyone because then he will hurt Mommy." The prosecutors wish to use this statement by Tami at trial. What result?

E. SUBSTANTIATED CASES

If the allegations of abuse or neglect are substantiated, the child protection agency must, subject to limited exceptions, make "reasonable efforts" to keep the family together before it can seek to remove a child from the home and place him or her in foster care. If a child is removed, the agency must again, in most cases, make a reasonable effort to reunite the child with his or her family before it can seek to terminate the rights of the parents in order to free the child for adoption.

1. The Federal Statutory Framework: The Adoption Assistance and Child Welfare Act (CWA) and the Adoption and Safe Families Act (ASFA)

The reasonable efforts requirement has been a cornerstone of the child protective system since the passage of the federal Adoption Assistance and Child Welfare Act of 1980 (CWA). Pub. L. No. 96-272, 94 Stat. 500 (codified in scattered sections of 42 U.S.C.). CWA was enacted in response to concerns that children who were removed from their homes ended up spending much of their youth adrift in the foster care system. By emphasizing family preservation, the Act replaces the costly and disruptive out-of-home placements and attempts to emphasize instead prevention and reunification.

This required emphasis on family preservation and reunification soon came under increasing criticism for two primary reasons. First, several high-profile and tragic cases involving children who had been killed by a parent following an agency decision to either leave a child with or return a child to his or her parents focused attention on the fact that family preservation is not necessarily in the child's best interest. The second concern was the lack of permanency in children's lives as many spent extended periods of time in the foster care system while child protection agencies attempted to rehabilitate parents that were unlikely to ever be rehabilitated.

In 1997, in response to these dual concerns, Congress passed the Adoption and Safe Families Act (ASFA), which shifted the emphasis of the child protective system from family preservation to child safety and permanency planning. Pub. L. No. 105-89, 111 Stat. 2115 (1997) (codified in scattered sections of 42 U.S.C.). Although ASFA preserves the reasonable efforts requirement, it makes the "health and safety" of the child the paramount consideration in determining if the state has done enough to try to keep the family together or to enable a child who has been removed to return home. Closely related, to avoid having children languish in foster care while ongoing efforts were being made to "rehabilitate" the parents, the Act "fast-tracks" the permanency planning process so that children can be returned home or parental rights terminated in order to free the child for adoption.

As a result, parents now have considerably less time in which to try to remedy the difficulties that brought them into the child protective system in the first place, which, as noted below, has raised serious concerns that ASFA unduly penalizes parents who may need more time to resolve an often complex myriad of problems, such as drug addiction and mental illness, which impair their ability to care for their children.

Like CWA, ASFA is a federal funding law. Accordingly, rather than directly imposing substantive requirements on states, ASFA instead establishes the standards that a state must comply with in order to receive federal funding for its child protective program; in short, if a state fails to comply with federal mandates, it is at risk of being sanctioned by way of a reduction in federal support.

Reasonable Efforts Prior to Removal

When allegations of abuse or neglect have been substantiated, subject to the exceptions discussed below, ASFA requires states to make reasonable efforts to keep a family together in order to eliminate the need for removing a child from his or her home. Accordingly, supportive services, such as day care, parenting education classes, counseling, and respite care, are typically offered to parents in order to strengthen their ability to care for their children. In determining if reasonable efforts have been made prior to the decision to remove a child from his or her home, ASFA makes clear that considerations of a child's health and safety are paramount.

EXHIBIT 13.1   **ASFA Exceptions**

Seeking to redress the concern that the reasonable efforts requirement under CWA privileged family preservation over child safety, ASFA contains specific exceptions to the reasonable efforts requirement, and permits states to adopt additional exceptions. Accordingly, under ASFA, an agency is exempted from the reasonable effort requirement when

- a parent has subjected a child to "aggravating circumstances," as defined by state law. Federal examples of aggravating circumstances include abandonment, torture, and sexual abuse;
- a parent has
  - committed murder of another child of the parent;
  - committed voluntary manslaughter of another child of the parent; aided or abetted, attempted, conspired, or solicited to commit murder of voluntary manslaughter of another child of the parent; or
  - committed felony assault that resulted in serious bodily injury to the child or another child of the parent.
- Parental rights with respect to a sibling have been terminated involuntarily. 42 U.S.C. §671(a)(15).

Removal of a Child: Reasonable Efforts and Permanency Planning

In some instances, the child protection agency may decide that despite its efforts to keep a family together (which, of course, is not a consideration where exempted from the reasonable efforts requirement in the first place) a child's health and safety requires his or her removal from the home and placement in foster care. This is done through the filing of a dependency proceeding, in which the agency seeks to have the child adjudicated dependent or in need of care and protection. Essentially, the state is asking the court to find that the parents are currently unable to care for their child and that alternative arrangements for the child must be made. If the court agrees that the parents cannot presently care for the child, the child is adjudicated dependent. With this determination, custody is usually transferred to the agency, which then assumes primary responsibility for making decisions involving the child, and the child is placed in foster care.

If a child is adjudicated dependent, the case then moves into the dispositional phase during which time a plan is developed that sets out the reasonable efforts that must be made in order to try to reunite the child with his or her family, subject to the same exceptions that exempted the agency from having to make reasonable efforts to keep the family together in the first instance. Reasonableness is again determined in light of the child's health and safety needs. A reunification case plan — which usually includes services to help the parents address the problems that led to the removal in the first place — is developed. Unless contraindicated, visitation arrangements are usually also incorporated into the plan in the hope that the maintenance of family connections will increase the likelihood of reunification.

To prevent a child from languishing in the foster care system, once a child has been removed from his or her home, ASFA requires that a permanency plan be developed within an expedited time frame. If the agency has been able to bypass the reasonable efforts requirement based on one of the permitted exceptions, the

Terminating Parental Rights

Reinforcing ASFA's focus on expedition, a state is also required to initiate (or join) proceedings to terminate parental rights if a child has been in foster care for 15 of the previous 22 months unless the child is being cared for by a relative, initiation proceedings would not be in the child's best interest, or where the state has failed to provide services that would have enabled the child to return home safely.

permanency hearing is held within 30 days of this determination. Otherwise, the hearing is to be held no later than 12 months after a child has entered into foster care, although states are free to set a shorter time frame for this hearing, and a number have done so.

The primary purpose of the hearing is to develop a "permanency plan" so the child is not left in limbo. By far the two most common outcomes are either a determination that the child can safely be reunited with his or her family or if this is deemed not to be possible, the agency will seek to terminate the rights of the parents so the child can be freed for adoption. Both options can be pursued concurrently so the child is not left hanging if the preferred goal of reunification fails.

This fast-tracking of cases may be the most significant change that ASFA has made to the child protective system. However, this change has also been criticized for not providing many parents with enough time to remedy the difficulties that brought them into the child protective system in the first place.

Termination of parental rights is a drastic measure because it permanently severs the parent-child relationship. Upon termination, the child is freed up for adoption and can thus be permanently incorporated into a new family. Because termination results in an irrevocable change in parental status, it must be based on clear and convincing proof of parental unfitness. *See Santosky v. Kramer*, 455 U.S. 745 (1982).

2. The Federal Statutory Framework: The Indian Child Welfare Act (ICWA)

In 1978, Congress enacted the Indian Child Welfare Act in order to "address the Federal, State, and private agency policies and practices that resulted in the 'wholesale separation of Indian children from their families.'" Bureau of Indian Affairs, Guideline for State Courts and Agencies in Indian Child Custody Proceedings, 80 Fed. Reg. 10146, 10147 (2015), quoting H. Rep. 95-1978 at 9.

More specifically, congressional hearings revealed that "cultural ignorance and biases within the child welfare system" had resulted in the alarming failure of courts and administrative bodies to "recognize the essential tribal relations of Indian people and the cultural and social standards prevailing in Indian communities and families." 25 U.S.C. §1901(4) and (5).

Due to the risk that a high number of children could be placed with non-Indian families, thus losing their cultural identity, the ICWA established specialized rules for the removal and placement of children who are members of or are eligible for membership in a federally recognized Indian tribe.[5]

---

[5]ICWA does not apply in custody cases between parents.

First, ICWA requires states to employ "active efforts," in order to prevent removal of a child or to reunify the family if a child is removed. This is a more robust standard than ASFA's reasonable efforts requirement. For example, while "a referral for services" might satisfy ASFA, under the active efforts standard, a state might be obligated to "arrange for the best-fitting service and help families engage in those services."[6]

Second, subject to very limited exceptions, ICWA also vests exclusive jurisdiction over any state custody proceeding involving an Indian child (as defined by the Act) who resides or is domiciled on the reservation lands of the tribe, or is a ward of the tribe, in the tribal court. In other instances, state courts are expected to transfer jurisdiction when asked to do so by a parent, the tribe, or the tribal custodian, absent an objection by the parent. 25 U.S.C. §1911(a) & (b).

Third, in the absence of good cause to the contrary, foster care, pre-adoption, and adoption placements are to be made, in order of preference, with (1) a member of the child's extended family; (2) other members of the child's tribe; or (3) other Indian families. 25 U.S.C. §1915(a) and (b). See Section (b) for other applicable considerations in pre-adoption and foster care placements.

Chapter Summary

- A systematic legal response to child abuse and neglect emerged in the latter half of the twentieth century following medical evidence revealing the seriousness and scope of the problem.
- Following the enactment of the federal Child Abuse Prevention and Treatment Act in 1974, all states enacted abuse reporting laws and established a coordinated child protective system under the authority of a single state agency.
- A family usually comes to the attention of a protective agency when a report of suspected abuse or neglect is filed. If, after an investigation, the allegations are substantiated, the family remains under the authority of the agency.
- Subject to limited exceptions, reasonable efforts must be made to prevent the need to remove the child from the home; reasonableness is determined in light of the child's health and safety needs.
- If removal becomes necessary, a dependency proceeding is initiated, in which the state seeks a determination that the parents are presently unable to care for the child and that the child should be removed and placed in foster care. Following removal, reasonable efforts at reunification must be made, subject, again, to limited exceptions.

---

[6]FAC, National Indian Child Welfare Association, http://www.nicwa.org/Indian_Child_Welfare_Act/faq/ (accessed Mar. 26, 2015).

▨ In most cases, a permanency hearing must be held within 12 months of the time the child enters foster care to decide if the child can return home or whether the rights of the parents should be terminated.

▨ The termination of parental rights is the most drastic form of intervention because it permanently severs the parent-child relationship. Once parental rights have been terminated, the child can be adopted by another family.

Applying the Rules

1. Assume you represent a state agency charged with child protective services. Katrina, a new case worker, has come to you because she is concerned about a report that has been made regarding the Smith family: A neighbor knocked on the door of the Smith residence to see if anyone there had seen her missing cat. Upon being admitted to the home, she observed that the house was filthy. Garbage was piled all over, and rotten food was covering the counters. Both the mother and her four-year-old child were dirty, although no symptoms of illness or injury were apparent. The neighbor departed after about five minutes and promptly called the state protective service agency to report what she had seen, and the case was assigned to Katrina. Katrina visited the home and saw the same things. Both mother and child appeared in dirty clothes and the entire house reeked. Katrina inquired about whether any services were needed, but the mother politely declined, saying that she receives enough in child support from her ex-husband, Katrina's father, to pay the bills and get by and they do just fine on their own. Based on the above facts, Katrina asks you if anything else should be done. She does not want the agency to be liable for leaving the child in the mother's care, but wonders if this is neglect and also whether intervention is warranted. What do you tell Katrina?

2. You represented Rocco several years ago in his divorce action. He and his former wife Sophia have one child, Desiree, in common. Sophia is now married to Cade, who has one son, Patrick, age 10, from an earlier marriage. Rocco tells you that he recently went to pick up Desiree for the start of his parenting time at the local outdoor skating rink. He arrived early and saw Sophia, Desiree, Cade, and Patrick skating. Patrick looked miserable. He was cold, tired, and wanted to get off the ice. When Patrick asked to leave the rink, Cade indicated that he had to continue skating — that he must master the basics before sitting down. Eventually, Patrick began stumbling from fatigue and begged to leave the ice, but Cade would still not permit him to stop skating. Cade did not raise his voice or strike the child, but it was clear that Patrick felt he had no choice but to continue. During this time, Sophia must have been aware of what was going on, but she continued to skate as if all was fine. Sophia then noticed Rocco and brought

Desiree over to him, and he promptly took Desiree's skates off, put her shoes on, and got ready to leave. When Rocco left, Patrick was still on the ice despite his exhaustion and abject misery. Rocco is not concerned that Cade would ever do such a thing to Desiree, but he wonders if this is abuse that should be reported. Or, is it teaching a child how to push beyond obstacles and strive for perfection? Based on the readings in the chapter, how do you respond to Rocco?

3. Fran and Brett are the parents of three-year-old Eloise. A teacher at her day care center noticed small red bumps on Eloise's arms and legs, and asked Fran about the bumps when she came to pick up Eloise. Fran said that they were bed bug bites and that they have had a terrible bed bug infestation at the house. Over the next few weeks, the teacher notices that the marks have gotten worse and that Eloise is constantly itching them and crying about how much they hurt. You are the attorney for the day care center and you are asked what can be done in this situation. What do you advise? Is this neglect on the part of Fran and Brett?

4. Assume the same facts as in Question 3, but instead you are the attorney for the social service agency that investigates abuse. A case worker investigates and discovers the house is a mess and that there is trash and soiled laundry throughout the house. The case worker strongly suspects that the bumps are not from bed bugs, but possibly bites from rats or other rodents. Would you recommend filing a removal order?

5. A state statute provides that "the Department of Child Services shall request an Order of Temporary Custody when there is reasonable cause to believe that the child is in immediate physical danger, or the child is suffering from serious physical illness or physical injury, and the conditions or circumstances surrounding the care of said child require that custody be immediately assumed to safeguard the child." Leland is six years old. He has reported to his teacher that his mother sometimes stays out really late at night and leaves him to watch his three-year-old sister. The teacher has never known Leland to lie and finds him to be a very honest child. Based solely on Leland's statements, does the department have grounds to seek an order of temporary custody?

6. Mateo and Stephanie are divorced. The parties have an eight-year-old daughter, Shelley. Mateo knows that Stephanie has no relationship with her biological mother, as she was removed from her custody due to abuse when Stephanie was young. Mateo has recently learned the whereabouts of Stephanie's biological mother and has decided that whatever issues Stephanie had with her mother, it should not affect Shelley. Stephanie has just learned that Mateo has set up several visits between Shelley and Stephanie's mother. She is concerned that by the time she goes to court to try to obtain an order to prevent the visits that Shelley could be in grave danger. What do you advise Stephanie to do? Assuming the same state statute governs as in Question 5, are there grounds for Stephanie to ask the department to remove Shelley from the care of Mateo on an emergency basis?

Family Law in Practice

1. Locate the statute in your state that governs child abuse and neglect cases as well as the applicable regulations. Answer the following questions:

   a. Who are mandated reporters?
   b. What are the sanctions for failing to report suspected abuse or neglect?
   c. What kinds of services must be offered to families?

2. Develop a set of questions and interview a person who is involved with child protection work, such as an attorney, a judge, or a protective service worker. Ask this person to describe his or her role in the system. Ask about some of the most difficult situations he or she has encountered and his or her perceptions of the major strengths and weaknesses of the protective system, and write a memorandum of the interview.

3. Assume you are representing a child who was removed from her home at age 3 because of extreme neglect. At the time, the parents had serious drug and alcohol problems. The child has been in foster care for 12 months. During this time, the parents have tried to get their act together, but until recently their efforts had fallen short. However, they have recently both completed intensive treatment programs. The father has been at a new, steady job for about three months, and the mother is working hard toward her high school degree. Both have completed a parenting class. The agency is pushing termination so the child can be adopted by her foster parents. The child has bonded with them and is thriving. The judge has asked you to submit a memorandum outlining your position on behalf of the child. In doing do, you should research relevant case law to determine how your state approaches this kind of case and incorporate the results of your research into the memo.

Adoption

14

Adoption allows for the formal establishment of a parent-child relationship in the absence of a biological connection. This chapter examines the two major methods of adoption — agency adoption and independent or private placement adoption — and also briefly considers safe haven laws. We then turn to the adoption process both generally and in particularized contexts, such as where a same-sex couple seeks to adopt a baby, although in light of the recent federalized constitutional right of same-sex couples to marry, this area of the law is likely to expand and be redefined over time. This chapter does not address the issue of international adoption, and you should be aware that other policy and legal considerations come into play when the adoption process crosses national borders. Finally, we consider what happens when adoptive parents are unhappy with the child they have adopted and wish to abrogate or undo the adoption.

A. HISTORICAL OVERVIEW

In ancient Rome, adoptions were for the benefit of the adopting family rather than the adopted child. A family approaching the end of its bloodline might adopt a male child or adult who could perform the sacred rites of ancestor worship as well as save the family from extinction. Or, as with Julius Caesar, who adopted his nephew, adoption could be used for political ends by enabling rulers to handpick their successors. With the emergence of Christianity, adoption fell into disrepute due to its association with pagan religious practices and its utilitarian nature.

Key Concepts

- Historical framework for adoption
- Differences between agency and private placement
- Process for adoption
- Unsealing court records in adoption
- Terminating parents' rights
- Adoptions under special circumstances
- Revoking consent and rights of unwed fathers

569

Unlike many other Roman legal practices, adoption did not find its way into English common law. Beyond being associated with paganism, adoption was regarded as incompatible with the English emphasis on blood lineage in establishing family ties and ensuring the orderly succession of property. Many English children, however, spent portions of their childhood living with families other than their family of origin.

As in England, the children of many American colonists were sent to live with other families, most commonly as servants or apprentices. Apprenticeships were formal arrangements by which a child was indentured to an individual who was to teach the child a trade and provide him or her with a place to live in exchange for the child's labor. This person stood *in loco parentis* and assumed the rights and responsibilities of a parent for the duration of the apprenticeship. These arrangements were found in all social classes, with children from middle and upper classes being indentured to persons from similar backgrounds in which they could complete their social and professional training. Accordingly, in the early part of our nation's history, it was not uncommon for children to spend part, or even most, of their youth living apart from their family of origin.

Adoption was accepted earlier in this country than in England, perhaps because there was less historical emphasis on blood lineage, class distinction, and the orderly succession of property. In 1851, Massachusetts passed the nation's first general adoption statute. It quickly became a model, and similar laws were enacted in a majority of states.

The Massachusetts law, which framed the modern approach, placed adoption under judicial control and made clear that adoption was intended to benefit the child in need of a home rather than the parents in search of an heir. Under the law, each prospective adoptive family was to be scrutinized to ensure they were fit and proper parents and had the ability to raise the child. Upon approval by the court, the rights of the child's natural parents were severed and the child became the legal child of the adoptive parents.

These newly enacted adoption laws were prompted by a number of considerations. First, the laws were passed to ensure that children living in de facto adoptive relationships would be able to receive a share of the parental estate if the parents died intestate. Second, related to child welfare reforms, these statutes responded to a growing criticism of the common practice of placing poor and orphaned children in institutions and perhaps indenturing them. Corresponding to the emphasis on domestic nurture, placement in homes became the preferred alternative for children not in the care of their parents.

Although placement in a family was generally a humane alternative to institutionalization, many children were initially "put out" by their parents because of desperate poverty or taken from them because the family did not conform to the emerging middle class view of the proper family. Moreover, families sometimes lost control of the process, and what was initially intended as a temporary arrangement would evolve into a permanent separation.

B. TYPES OF ADOPTIONS

Adoption usually takes place in one of two ways. It can be accomplished either by an agency (agency adoption) or by the parents themselves acting with or without the assistance of a third-party intermediary (independent, private, or direct placement adoption). Agency adoptions are permitted in all states; however, due to some of the concerns discussed below, a few states prohibit independent adoptions except where a stepparent or a close relative is the adopting parent. In addition to providing a comparative overview of these two types of adoption, this section also takes a brief look at "safe haven" laws, which are intended to address the problem of infant abandonment.

1. Agency Adoptions

In an **agency adoption**, a state-licensed agency arranges the adoption and oversees the process. An adoption agency can be either public, in that it is part of the state's child protective system, or private. In either instance, an agency can obtain custody of a child for purposes of adoption either following an involuntary termination of parental rights (see Chapter 13) or following a voluntary surrender. Before accepting a voluntary surrender, an agency will typically provide the parents with counseling to help them understand their options and make sure their decision is fully informed. A range of other services, such as legal referrals and financial assistance for basic legal and medical services, may also be available. Once the agency assumes custody of a child, it is then responsible for finding him or her a suitable adoptive home.

Before placing a child with prospective adoptive parents, the agency will conduct a home study to determine the appropriateness of the placement. Once a placement has been made, the agency maintains some degree of supervisory responsibility to ensure the placement meets the needs of the child. State rules often require an agency to make a certain number of home visits at specified intervals and to take remedial action, including removal, if the child is not adjusting well. In some states, the agency remains legally responsible for the child until the adoption is finalized.

2. Independent Adoptions

In contrast, in an **independent adoption** (also known as **private** or **direct placement adoptions**), a child is placed directly with the adoptive parents without a prior surrender to a licensed adoption agency. Most involve healthy newborns who are placed with the adoptive parents immediately after birth. Accordingly, adoption arrangements are usually made during pregnancy, often after an extensive search for an adoptable baby. If state law permits, searching parents may even launch a public outreach, which can include advertising in the classified section of a local paper, to help them locate a potential birth mother and demonstrate their qualifications as parents.

Some prospective adoptive parents hire an intermediary, who is often an attorney, to help them to find a child and arrange the placement. Where this is the case, the child may initially be transferred to this third party; however, unlike in an agency adoption, this is not a formal surrender — rather, the intermediary is simply serving as a conduit between the birth and the adoptive parents.

Unlike with agency adoptions, the birth parents are not usually provided with counseling prior to the relinquishment of the baby, and the prospective adoptive parents are not required to undergo a pre-placement home study, although some states now require adoptive parents to be certified before they can accept a child into their home. In further contrast, once a baby is placed, the placement is not usually supervised, although a post-placement home study must be done before a court can approve the adoption.

Although as discussed below, birth parents must consent to the adoption, a number of concerns have been raised about the potential for exploitation that exists when adoptions occur without the involvement of a state-licensed agency, and a few states accordingly prohibit independent adoptions. Other states have instead opted for increased control of the process, particularly with respect to the often closely related role of intermediaries and the payment of the birth mother's expenses.

EXAMPLE OF A LAW WITH LIMITATION OF EXPENSES

Kan. Stat. Ann. §59-2121. Payment for adoption; limitation; approval by court; criminal penalties.

(a) Except as otherwise authorized by law, no person shall request, receive, give or offer to give any consideration in connection with an adoption, or a placement for adoption, other than:

(1) Reasonable fees for legal and other professional services rendered in connection with the placement or adoption not to exceed customary fees for similar services by professionals of equivalent experience and reputation where the services are performed, except that fees for legal and other professional services as provided in this section performed outside the state shall not exceed customary fees for similar services when performed in the state of Kansas;

(2) reasonable fees in the state of Kansas of a licensed child-placing agency;

(3) actual and necessary expenses, based on expenses in the state of Kansas, incident to placement or to the adoption proceeding;

(4) actual medical expenses of the mother attributable to pregnancy and birth;

(5) actual medical expenses of the child; and

(6) reasonable living expenses of the mother which are incurred during or as a result of the pregnancy.

(b) In an action for adoption, a detailed accounting of all consideration given, or to be given, and all disbursements made, or to be made, in connection with the adoption and the placement for adoption shall accompany the petition for adoption. Upon review of the accounting, the court shall disapprove any such consideration which the court determines to be unreasonable or in violation of this section and, to the extent necessary to comply with the provisions of this section, shall order reimbursement of any consideration already given in violation of this section.

(c) Knowingly and intentionally receiving or accepting clearly excessive fees or expenses in violation of subsection (a) shall be a severity level 9, nonperson felony. Knowingly failing to list all consideration or disbursements as required by subsection (b) shall be a class B nonperson misdemeanor.

With regard to intermediaries, a primary concern is that because they stand to gain financially from facilitating adoptions, they may resort to unscrupulous means to help prospective parents procure adoptable children. In response, many states have enacted laws imposing restrictions on intermediaries, such as by limiting the fees they can charge and requiring a strict accounting to the court. A few states have gone further and prohibit the use of intermediaries altogether, or only permit licensed adoption agencies to function in this capacity.

Applicable to both intermediaries and prospective adoptive parents, a potentially worrisome means of attempting to persuade a pregnant woman to relinquish her child is through the promise of generous payments to cover all of her needs in exchange for a commitment to give up her child — an inducement that can be particularly coercive in certain situations such as, for example, where a young teen has been kicked out of her home and is facing living on the streets or in a shelter. Intending to draw a clear line between baby-selling, which is illegal in all states, and adoption, most states accordingly limit the kinds of payments that be offered to a birth mother by the prospective adoptive parents in order to help ensure that her choice is not distorted by her economic circumstances. Thus, for example, although most states allow the prospective adoptive parents to pay some of the birth mother's living expenses, the trend is to place limits on these expenditures, by, for example, specifically delineating what can be included, and/or by setting a dollar cap on the expenditures, or imposing a durational restriction that is usually linked to a specific time period prior to delivery.

3. Infant Safe Haven Laws

In response to several highly publicized cases involving newborn babies who had been abandoned in dumpsters, garbage cans, and toilets, since 1999, all states as well as the District of Columbia and Puerto Rico have enacted infant **safe haven laws** (sometimes referred to as "Baby Moses laws"), which permit birth parents, or in some states only the birth mother, to leave a baby at a designated safe location, such as a hospital or fire station, as an alternative to abandonment. Some states also permit a party acting with the express consent of the birth parent(s) to surrender the child at the safe haven, with some of these states requiring that this person have legal custody of the infant. Intended to prevent the abandonment of newborns, all laws contain an express limit on how much time can elapse between birth and the surrender of the child. Limits usually range from 72 hours to a month after birth, although a few states provide longer periods of time.

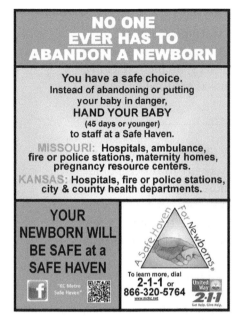

Safe haven laws permit birth parents to leave a baby at a designated safe location as an alternative to abandonment.
Mother & Child Health Coalition

Several common statutory features are designed to encourage parents to surrender their babies to a designated safe haven location rather than abandoning them. First, these laws are structured to protect parental anonymity, and accordingly permit a parent to surrender a child without having to provide any identifying information. Some laws, however, do require that inquiry be made of the baby's medical and family history, but the parent is not required to provide this information. Second, a majority of states offer parents who *safely* relinquish a child immunity from prosecution for child abandonment or neglect. In other states, however, the protection is not as comprehensive, and the statute simply gives parents the right to raise safe relinquishment in accordance with the law as an affirmative defense to criminal charges. However, these protections may be forfeited if there is evidence that the child was abused or neglected.

Following relinquishment, the safe haven provider turns the infant over to the appropriate child protection agency. In some states, a parent is given a brief window of opportunity within which to change his or her mind and reclaim the child. This usually must be done prior to the formal termination of parental rights. In other states, the relinquishment effectively serves to terminate parental rights and there is no change-of-heart provision. The agency is then responsible for making an adoption plan for the child. A potentially complicating factor is that it is not always clear what steps must be taken by the agency in order to terminate the rights of the parents — the safe haven law may have specialized provisions, or it might reference the applicable provisions of the child protection law — and a number of cases have arisen over whether the agency had done enough to provide notice to the birth parents regarding the termination of their rights. This is most likely to be an issue with regard to the father, who may not have participated in or known about the decision to relinquish the baby, as it is usually the mother who avails herself of the safe haven option. To address this situation, a few states require the protection agency to check the putative father registry prior to the filing of a petition to terminate parental rights. (See Section F.3, below.)

C. THE ADOPTION PROCESS

In this section, we will look at the stages of the adoption process. First, we will look at adoption based on parental consent or relinquishment, which is a necessary requirement in a private placement adoption. We will also examine what happens when a parent who previously consented wants to revoke his or her consent to a placement. Next, we will examine the adoption process for involuntary terminations. As we saw in Chapter 13, there are times, based upon the findings of child abuse or neglect, that a child will be removed from the care and custody of a parent. In these cases, if it is not in the child's best interest to be returned to a parent, the parent's rights may be involuntarily terminated and the child placed with an adoption agency. Finally, we will examine the steps that are needed in order to complete the adoption process.

1. Adoption Based on Parental Consent or Relinquishment

Unless the rights of parents have been involuntarily terminated, an adoption cannot proceed without their consent. (See, however, the discussion below regarding unwed fathers, Section F.3.) In some states, the consent of the child also becomes necessary once he or she reaches a certain age, which is generally set somewhere between age 10 and 14. Although this section generally speaks in terms of the birth parents, it is important to recognize that the parents may not be participating in the adoption as a unit and that each may play a different role in the process.

Parental Consent to a Private Placement Adoption

Parental consent is an essential requirement in a private placement adoption. To be valid, consent must be fully informed and free from duress, fraud, or undue influence and given in a manner that conforms with all applicable state regulations, such as that it is in writing and signed before a public official.

In some situations, it can be difficult to determine if the consent was truly voluntary. For example, a young birth mother who is under pressure from her parents and friends to give up the child may be ambivalent but feel as if she has no choice but to give up her baby to a married couple who appear to be in a better position to raise the child. Although there may not be undue influence or duress in a strictly legal sense, under some circumstances, it may be difficult to characterize a decision to give up a child as a purely voluntary one.

In most, if not all, states, a mother's pre-birth consent is not binding, and a legally valid consent cannot be obtained until some time after the birth of the child; a typical waiting period is 48 or 72 hours after birth. This rule recognizes the impact of giving birth and the fact that it may be impossible to fully comprehend the import of a decision to give up a child until the child is actually born. Interestingly, in many states, a father's pre-birth consent is binding. This differential treatment reflects both conventional views about fathers as less impacted by the birth process and thus less likely to regret a prior decision to give up a child, as well as the practical concern that a father might not be around to give consent at the time of birth.

By itself, the consent does not actually terminate the rights of the birth parents or transfer them to the adoptive parents. In effect, by executing a consent, the birth parents are authorizing the court to proceed with the adoption.

Relinquishment to an Agency

In an agency adoption, the operative legal act is the relinquishment of the child to the agency, rather than the giving of consent to the adoption itself. By relinquishing their child, parents are effectively transferring their right to consent to the adoption to the agency. In many states, the act of relinquishment automatically terminates the rights of the birth parents. In other states, this result is not automatic, but relinquishment enables an agency to seek an immediate court order terminating parental rights. (Note: Keep in mind that these adoptions begin with a voluntary act and are thus different from adoptions that result from an involuntary termination of parental rights — these adoptions are discussed below.)

Revocation of Consent

What happens if, after either consenting to an adoption or relinquishing a child to an agency, a parent changes his or her mind about going forward with the adoption? Although this occurs only in a small number of cases, it can result in bitter litigation that pits the birth parents against the prospective adoptive parents.

In private placement adoptions, most states allow parents to revoke their consent within a specified time period, such as up until the time the adoption is approved by the court. Thereafter, consent is deemed irrevocable. In some jurisdictions, however, irrevocability is limited to validly obtained consents. This leaves open the possibility that even after the adoption has been finalized, a birth parent could seek to revoke his or her consent by establishing that it was improperly obtained.

In most states, the revocation of consent (including those within the applicable time period) requires court approval. The standards for determining whether to allow a revocation vary widely from state to state. Some states are fairly tolerant of parental changes of heart and give judges considerable discretion. In other states, judges can approve revocations based only on specific statutory factors, which typically address the validity of the consent and do not allow for changes of heart that are not bound up with considerations of duress and the like. In these states, a birth mother who experiences profound regret about her decision would not be permitted to revoke her consent even if requested within the statutory time frame. But a young birth mother who could establish that the prospective adoptive parents in concert with her own parents repeatedly pressured her to give up the child might be allowed to revoke her consent. For example, under the Arizona statute, "consent is irrevocable" unless obtained by "fraud, duress or undue influence." Ariz. Rev. Stat. §8-106(D).

Where a parent seeks to revoke his or her consent, the prospective adoptive parents may respond by asking the court to dispense with the parental consent requirement. In effect, the adoptive parents are asking the court to terminate the parental rights of the birth parents so the adoption can proceed without their consent. In evaluating this request, the court may treat the consent as evidence of an intent to abandon the child and count it against the biological parents in evaluating their fitness. Thus, what began as a voluntary process may result in litigation and a possible involuntary termination of parental rights. (See Section C.2, below, for greater detail on involuntary termination.)

Most states are stricter about revocations where a relinquishment has been made to an agency, and in many states the relinquishment becomes irrevocable once the child has been placed with the prospective adoptive parents for a specified period of time. This stricter standard reflects the fact that greater safeguards, such as pre-relinquishment counseling for the birth parents, are built into the agency process.

Case Preview

In re Adoption of D.N.T.

In this case the minor child, Diane, was born to Camille, who at the time of Diane's birth was 16 years old. Approximately a year after Diane was born, Camille and Diane moved in with a couple, Carol and Rick. Carol and Rick often cared for Diane when Camille was out with friends. A few months later, Carol and Rick decided to adopt Diane and filed a sworn complaint for adoption that was signed under oath by Camille. However, two months later, Camille filed an objection to the adoption proceedings asking that the documents she signed be set aside and canceled. The Chancery Court entered a temporary judgment of custody in favor of Rick and Carol. A few days later, Camille, and her mother Sally, filed a complaint to revoke consent and for custody of the minor child.

As you read *In re Adoption of D.N.T.*, consider the following:

1. What was the basis for Camille's claim that she should be allowed to revoke her consent to the adoption?
2. How does the court treat Camille's claim that she was under "undue influence, duress and intimidation" of the adoptive parents?
3. What effect does the fact that Camille was under age when she gave her consent to adopt have on the court's decision?

In re Adoption of D.N.T.
843 So. 2d 690 (Miss. 2003)

CARLSON, Justice, for the Court:

Aggrieved by the Clarke County Chancery Court's dismissal of their complaint to revoke consent and for custody of minor child and its judgment granting a permanent adoption of the minor child to the adoptive parents, the natural mother and maternal grandmother of the adopted child have appealed to this Court seeking relief. Finding no error by the chancellor, we affirm.

. . .

Miss. Code Ann. §93-15-103(2) (Supp. 2002) states:

(2) The rights of a parent with reference to a child, including parental rights to control or withhold consent to an adoption, and the right to receive notice of a hearing on a petition for adoption, may be relinquished and the relationship of the parent and child terminated by the execution of a written voluntary release, signed by the parent, *regardless of the age of the parent.*

(Emphasis added).

Camille originally joined in the adoption complaint, as evidenced by her signature on the document. The chancellor found this act on the part of Camille constituted an abandonment by her of Diane and found that the appropriate Mississippi court had jurisdiction pursuant to Miss. Code Ann. §93-23-5(1)(c)(i).

In *Grafe v. Olds*, 556 So. 2d 690, 694 (Miss. 1990), we stated that: "a written voluntary release, or consent by the parent, [§93-15-103(2)] terminates the parental rights and thereafter, no objection to the adoption from the natural parent may be sustained.

Miss. Code Ann. §93-17-7 states in pertinent part:

No infant shall be adopted to any person if either parent, after having been summoned, shall appear and object thereto before the making of a decree for adoption, unless it shall be made to appear to the court from evidence touching such matters that the parent so objecting had abandoned or deserted such infant or is mentally, or morally, or otherwise unfit to rear and train it. . . .

Returning to *Grafe*, after the inquiry under Miss. Code Ann. §93-17-7, we must next determine whether the consent was voluntary and abandonment was both physical and legal. *C.C.I. v. Natural Parents*, 398 So. 2d 220 (Miss. 1981). "Absent a showing by the parent(s) establishing either fraud, duress, or undue influence by clear and convincing evidence, surrenders executed in strict compliance with the safeguard provision of §93-17-9, supra, are irrevocable." Id. at 226. . . .

In *C.C.I.*, we also stated:

[U]ndue influence is one of several grounds demonstrating a lack of voluntary consent on the part of the parents. Several of the means which may constitute undue influence include over-persuasion, threat of economic detriment or promise of economic benefit, the invoking of extreme family hostility both to the child and mother, and undue moral persuasion. Because undue influence is such a broad concept, cases must be resolved upon their particular facts. General law is that the party asserting undue influence has the heavy burden to show that the consent was obtained by undue influence. Such a burden must be met by clear and convincing evidence, and there is no presumption that a party has exercised undue influence upon another. A mere preponderance of evidence on the issue of undue influence is not sufficient.

. . .

Turning to the facts of this case . . . Camille testified that she had no intention of putting Diane up for adoption until Carol brought it up "jokingly"; that she never initiated any conversations about adoption; that Carol also confided in her that she had considered "cheating on Rick to get pregnant"; . . . that Rick and Carol were providing food and shelter and spending money for her and that she was not working at all; that when she told her mother (Sally) of her second thoughts about the adoption on March 18 or 19, Sally immediately left Arizona to come for Camille in Mississippi; that she was afraid to tell Rick and Carol of her change of heart until her mother was close by; that as soon as she told Carol she wanted to withdraw her consent to the adoption, Carol began crying; and, that when Rick found out, he told Camille to get the "f___ out of his house" and that "no one was going to take this baby from them — that he would hurt anyone that tried."

At the close of the case-in-chief as presented by Sally and Camille, Rick and Carol, through counsel, made an ore tenus motion to dismiss pursuant to Miss. R. Civ. P. 41(b), which was granted by the chancellor, but only after a detailed finding of fact which consumed approximately seven pages of the trial record. The chancellor found:

> [Camille] knew for a substantial amount of time prior to the time that the adoption papers were drawn up that the adoption was in the works. She knew when Rick and Carol went to the attorney's office; she knew that the adoption papers were being drawn up, and she went without Rick and Carol to the lawyer's office.
>
> She could have called her father or her mother at any time during the time that she remained with Rick and Carol. She was not under Rick and Carol's direct control at all times. She spent substantial periods of time with her boyfriend, Calvin, and could have called either parent at any time.
>
> She had a contemporary with her when she went to the lawyer's office to sign the papers and that contemporary told her she wouldn't sign adoption papers, she wouldn't give up her child, and yet Camille made the decision to go in to the lawyer's office and complete the process of signing the consent forms.
>
> At the time that she signed the consent forms she was in a relationship with her boyfriend who had asked her to marry [him] and even offered to raise the minor child as his own.

The chancellor's findings of fact are amply supported by the record. Camille admitted that she and Carol began talking about the adoption in February before the adoption papers were prepared and signed in early March. Neither Carol nor Rick was with Camille when she went to the lawyer's office to sign the adoption papers, and in fact, Denise, Carol's college-age sister, accompanied Camille to the lawyer's office. Additionally, Camille readily admitted that Carol's own sister, Denise, told Camille that same day that Camille did not have to sign the adoption papers. In fact, Camille admitted that Denise "always told me that if I didn't want to do it (sign the consent), I didn't have to. That she wouldn't have done it." Camille testified that she and Carol talked about the adoption "probably over ten times." Camille also stated that she and Calvin, her boyfriend, talked about Rick and Carol's proposed adoption of Diane. Calvin tried to talk Camille out of consenting to the adoption and offered to marry Camille and take care of Diane "as his own." Finally, Camille admitted that when she was in the lawyer's office to sign the adoption papers, she read the entire document, and when asked on cross-examination if it were her choice to sign the adoption papers, she replied "yes."

The record clearly reveals that Camille signed the original complaint for adoption, though she later changed her mind and attempted to withdraw her consent. Under Miss. Code Ann. §93-15-103(2), [as well as case law] the chancellor was eminently correct in finding that upon joining in the sworn complaint for adoption and requesting, *inter alia*, that Diane be permanently adopted to Rick and Carol, Camille had in effect relinquished her parental rights to Diane. The record likewise clearly supports the chancellor's finding that Camille (and Sally) failed to prove by clear and convincing evidence that Camille's consent to the adoption was procured by Rick and Carol's exercise of "undue influence or fraud."

. . .

Our adoption statutes state specifically that age does not matter when it comes to voluntarily releasing the child for adoption: "the rights of a parent . . . *may be relinquished and the relationship of the parent and child terminated by the execution of a written voluntary release, signed by the parent, regardless of the age of the parent.*" Miss. Code Ann. §93-15-103(2) (emphasis added). See Miss. Code Ann. §93-17-7, which refers to §§93-15-101, et seq.

Camille was competent to waive process and has, under our case law and statutes, effectively done so. Additionally her actions, under Mississippi law, constituted an abandonment of Diane, and the chancellor was eminently correct in so ruling.

. . .

Accordingly, we affirm the various rulings of the chancellor which denied the efforts of Camille and Sally to revoke Camille's consent to Diane's adoption by Rick and Carol and which granted the permanent adoption of Diane to Rick and Carol.

Post-Case Follow-Up

The attorney for Camille and Sally also raised the argument that a minor should not be allowed to consent to an adoption and identified a number of things that a minor cannot do, such as vote, enter into binding contracts, and consent to an abortion. However, the chancellor in the lower court disregarded the comparisons, finding instead that a minor who is contemplating an abortion has not yet become a parent. However, once the minor is a parent, the lower court saw no problem with finding that the capacity to consent to an adoption should be treated differently.

In re Adoption of D.N.T.: Real Life Applications

1. Angela and her husband Cho have four children. After the birth of their fifth child, Brianna, Angela and Cho decided they just could not afford to raise so many children and wanted to give Brianna a better life. Accordingly, shortly after Brianna's birth, they executed documents relinquishing Brianna for adoption by a couple (Harry and Charlie) who they had agreed to through a private adoption arranged by a lawyer for Harry and Charlie. Assume the same statutes govern as in *In re Adoption of D.N.T.* Two months after signing the papers, Angela and Cho receive notice of the adoption proceedings. Angela comes to you and asks if she can object. She indicates that she only signed the papers

because Cho threatened to leave her if she did not agree to give Brianna up for adoption because he did not want any more children. What do you tell Angela? If she were to pursue an objection to the proceedings and attempt to revoke her consent, why kind of facts might be persuasive to the judge?

2. Adele comes to your office and advises you of the following facts: Ten months ago she signed adoption papers to allow her newborn son (J.B.) to be placed with his godmother, Zelda, who initially agreed to adopt him. As part of the adoption proceedings, Adele signed documents entitled: "Final and Irrevocable Consent to Adoption," which provided that she did "consent and agree to the adoption" of her son. However, shortly after signing the papers, Zelda changed her mind and that adoption did not proceed. At that time, J.B. was taken from Zelda's home and placed in a foster home. Approximately eight months after Adele signed the original consent, she learned that J.B. was going to be adopted by a single father, Lesly. Adele did not want J.B. being raised by a single father and asks you if she can file a motion to void her original consent. Does Adele have grounds to revoke her consent?

3. Assume the same facts as in Question 2, except that Adele is 15 years old when she signs the consent papers. Adele tells you that she only signed the papers at the urging of Zelda who assured Adele that Zelda would raise J.B. until Adele finished school and then would give J.B. back to Adele to raise. Does this give Adele grounds to successfully revoke her consent?

---

2. Adoption Based on the Involuntary Termination of Parental Rights

If the rights of parents have been involuntarily terminated because of abuse or neglect, an adoption can proceed without their consent because the termination frees the child for adoption. Following termination, custody is generally transferred to the state or, more specifically, to a public adoption agency, which must then try to find an appropriate adoptive home for the child.

If the rights of both parents have been terminated, the placement is virtually risk-free because they have been divested of any say in the matter. If, however, the rights of both parents have not been terminated, such as where one parent has vanished, the agency may not be able to proceed with the adoption until that parent's status is resolved. In some cases, if allowed by state law, an agency may choose to make an at-risk placement. These placements are subject to the risk of disruption if a parent whose rights have not been terminated subsequently seeks to assert his or her right to the child.

Many children who are available for adoption following the termination of parental rights have been in the protective services system for considerable periods of time. Few are infants, and many have experienced severe abuse or neglect and have lived in a variety of foster homes and institutional settings. Although desperate for homes, these children are often passed over in favor of infants who are generally more available through the independent or private agency adoption route.

In most states, parental rights can also be terminated within the context of the adoption proceeding itself. Unlike a separate termination proceeding, which is almost always initiated by the state, here the request, generally referred to as "a request to dispense with parental consent," is usually initiated by a private party. These requests are made under a variety of circumstances. For example, a child may be living with relatives who then decide they want to adopt him or her, but the parents are opposed. The relatives would file an adoption petition and ask the court to dispense with the need for parental consent. Or an unmarried mother who places her newborn with prospective adoptive parents might seek to have the court dispense with the father's right of consent. Similarly, if a child was relinquished to an agency by one birth parent, the agency might seek to dispense with the consent of the other parent. In order to prevail, it must be shown that the parent is unfit; otherwise his or her consent is legally required.

3. The Adoption Placement

Before an adoption can be finalized, a child must live with the prospective parents in a pre-adoption placement; however, many states exempt close relative, stepparent, and co-parent adoptions from this requirement. The pre-adoption placement requirement applies to both agency and independent adoptions; however, as discussed below, important differences typically exist in the placement process.

The Home Study

Perhaps the most significant distinction in the placement process between agency and independent adoptions is the home study. Home studies, which are intended to weed out potentially unsuitable parents, are generally not required in independent adoptions, whereas an agency cannot place a child until a home study has been completed. During the home study, prospective parents are usually asked about the following:

- religious beliefs and practices;
- approaches to child rearing and discipline;
- child-rearing skills;
- the nature of relationships with extended family members;
- history of prior intimate relationships;
- career plans and how the child will be cared for;
- ability to provide for the child financially;
- history of criminal convictions; and
- emotional stability and maturity.

Most adoption professionals regard the home study as essential to protect the well-being of adoptive children. While recognizing its potential intrusiveness, it is widely believed that in the absence of a biological connection from which affective bonds are thought to naturally flow, prospective parents must be evaluated to determine their capacity for developing a loving relationship with an adoptive child.

However, the home study process has also been subject to criticism. One concern is that the process may serve as a thinly disguised effort to rank prospective parents based on how closely they conform to an idealized vision of the perfect family. Through the use of highly subjective evaluative criteria, "nonconforming" adults, including single parents, same-sex couples, and low-income parents, may be placed at the bottom of waiting lists or are offered only children no one else wishes to adopt.

Configuration of Relationships During the Placement

With **private placement adoptions**, parental rights are usually not terminated until the adoption is approved by the court. This makes these placements somewhat riskier than agency placements because the possibility exists that a biological parent will change his or her mind and seek the return of the child. As discussed earlier, states vary in their approach to post-placement revocations — some are very strict, while others are more flexible and may permit a change of mind unless harm to the child can be shown.

Because the rights of the biological parents are not terminated until the adoption is approved, the authority of the prospective adoptive parents to make decisions on behalf of the child during the placement needs to be established. This is usually done through a voluntary transfer of temporary custody from the birth parents to the adoptive parents.

With adoption through an agency, unless it is an at-risk placement, the rights of both parents will have been terminated by the time the placement is made; accordingly, the agency usually has legal custody of the child, although it may delegate some decision-making authority to the prospective parents. As the repository of legal authority, the agency retains supervisory control over the placement, and a social worker will make periodic visits to evaluate how the placement is working out. The agency has the right to remove the child if it determines that the placement is not in the child's best interest. Most states place some limits on the authority of an agency to revoke a placement, and aggrieved adoptive parents may have a form of redress, such as the right to an administrative hearing.

4. The Social Study

Although pre-placement home studies are characteristic of agency adoptions, a post-placement **social study** must be completed in both private placement and agency adoptions before an adoption can be finalized, although the requirement may be waived in certain situations, such as where a close relative or a stepparent is the adopting parent. These studies are intended to provide the judge with information to help him or her decide whether or not to approve the adoption. In some states, the evaluator must also make a specific recommendation in favor of or against the adoption. Although important, these studies tend to be less comprehensive than the initial pre-placement home study.

5. The Adoption

All adoptions must be approved by a judge, and proper notice of the proceeding must be given to all persons with an interest in the child, including, for example, foster parents, pre-adoptive parents, and relatives who have been caring for the child. To protect the validity of the adoption, it is critical that notice rules be carefully followed.

The rights of the parents must be terminated before the adoption can be approved. As has been discussed elsewhere in this chapter, parental rights may already have been terminated in a separate proceeding, such as where the child has been in foster care, or termination may occur as part of the adoption proceeding itself. In a private placement adoption, termination is usually a formality, as the court is simply being asked to approve what the parties have agreed to; however, when a party is requesting that the court dispense with the parental consent requirement, the termination phase of the hearing may well be contested.

Once parental rights are terminated, the court determines whether the adoption is in the best interest of the child. If approved, the court may also at the same time approve an open adoption agreement, allowing for post-adoption contact between the birth parents, the child, and the adoptive parents (see below). If the court concludes the adoption is not in the child's best interest, it is not approved. If it is an agency adoption, the underlying relinquishment remains in effect, and the agency can attempt a subsequent placement. However, in a private placement adoption, parents usually consent to an adoption by a specific person or couple, and if the adoption fails, the consent is nontransferable. This is a difficult situation, as the prospective adoptive parents lose the child they were hoping to adopt, and the birth parents may find themselves with custody of a child they were planning to relinquish.

D. OPEN ADOPTIONS

Once the adoption is approved (subject to any rights of appeal or post-judgment challenges), a child's legal ties with his or her family of origin are severed, and the child is now legally incorporated into a new family. In most states, the records of the proceeding are sealed along with the original birth certificate, and a new birth certificate is issued, naming the adoptive parents as the child's parents, thus completing this transformation. The sealing of the records and the issuance of the new birth certificate exemplify the secrecy in which adoptions have typically been shrouded. As a rule, no information was shared either before or after an adoption, and adoptive parents were counseled not to disclose the fact of adoption to the child. This secrecy was thought necessary to protect the interests of all participants; birth mothers would be protected from the taint of immorality or shame, adopted children could grow up with unquestioned ties to their adoptive parents, and adoptive parents would not be threatened with the lurking presence of a child's biological parent.

However, this began to change in the 1960s in large part because secrecy was no longer thought to be in an adoptive child's best interest. Rather, knowing one's biological parents did not necessarily disrupt the stability of the adoptive families, and in fact in many cases the family was strengthened by the adoptee having answers to a major question of why he or she had been placed for adoption. Adult adoptees began to speak out about how damaging and confusing the silence about their origins had been and of their deep longing to know about their past. Other considerations, such as the lessening of the stigma of unwed motherhood, also contributed to a lifting of the shroud of secrecy, and today, many states facilitate an open adoption process and increased access to adoption records.

The central feature of an open adoption is that it anticipates some degree of continued contact between the birth parents and the adopted child, despite the severance of their legal bond. Open adoptions are generally associated with private placement adoptions and those in which parents voluntarily relinquish a child to an agency; however, in some states, an open adoption may be an option even if the rights of a parent have been involuntarily terminated, if continued contact is determined to be in the best interest of the child.

Historically, most state laws were silent on the issue of post-adoption contact between the birth parents and the adopted child. Accordingly, if the birth and the adoptive parents entered into an agreement giving the birth parents rights of contact with the child, the contract would not have been judicially enforceable. However, a growing number of states have adopted open adoption laws that permit birth parents and adoptive parents to enter into judicially enforceable agreements regarding post-adoption contact, if such contact is deemed to be in the best interest of the child. Some states further extend this right to other birth relatives; however, they may impose a threshold showing before a contact agreement will be enforceable, such as that the relative had enjoyed a substantial relationship with the child prior to the adoption. In addition to laws recognizing the validity of contracts for post-adoption contacts, in some cases judges are authorized to order post-adoption visits even where not expressly agreed to by the adoptive parents. In some states, the option of post-adoption contact is not available to parents whose rights were involuntarily terminated.

Although increasingly common and accepted, open adoption remains controversial. Proponents firmly believe that children will feel a greater sense of security and wholeness if they are permitted to retain a connection with their birth parents and that this will obviate the sense of longing and loss that some adopted children experience. But others believe that this continued contact will interfere with the ability of children to fully integrate into their new families; as a result, they may feel caught between two worlds and never wholly part of either. As always, there are no right or wrong answers, and the choice depends on individual facts and circumstances.

Parameters of Open Adoption

Although the term "open adoption" is usually identified with post-adoption arrangements, in a broader sense the term also applies to pre-adoption processes in situations where the birth parents and the prospective adoptive parents meet, share information, and, if the placement is agreed upon, determine how the post-adoption contact is to be structured. For example, contact might simply consist of a yearly exchange of letters and photographs with no direct interaction between the child and his or her birth parents. On the other hand, it might consist of regular telephone calls or even regular visits. Where visits are involved, they are often arranged through an intermediary so there is no direct contact between the birth and the adoptive parents.

Case Preview

Monty S. v. Jason W.

Monty S. v. Jason W. involves the issue of whether biological parents have the right to revoke their consent for an adoption where they were under the mistaken belief that the adoption would be "open." Under Nebraska law, open adoptions were specifically provided for in cases of agency adoptions but not private adoptions. At the time of the adoption, both the biological parents and the adoptive parents were under the belief that the adoption would be considered "open" and that the biological parents would be able maintain a relationship with the child.

The adoptive parents, Rebecca and Jason W., were unable to conceive a child. Their friends, Teresa and Monty S., agreed they would conceive a child and give it up for adoption to Rebecca and Jason through a private placement. Both couples agreed that the biological parents, Teresa and Monty, would be part of the child's life. In July 2013, Teresa gave birth to a baby boy. The baby was given to Rebecca and Jason, who took the baby home from the hospital. Two days later, Teresa and Monty signed papers in their lawyer's office relinquishing their parental rights and consenting to the adoption. However, the specific forms that must be signed by biological parents to seal the record were torn up by Rebecca in the lawyer's office since all parties agreed that the adoption was to be "open."

In May 2014, Teresa and Monty filed a petition seeking a return of the child claiming the consent was invalid. After a best interest hearing, the trial court awarded custody to Teresa and Monty and ordered the return of the child.

As you read *Monty S. v. Jason W.*, look for the following:

1. What did the Nebraska statute indicate about open adoptions?
2. Did the court consider the reasons for revoking consent?
3. What part of the statute did the court find controlling in making its ruling?
4. Why did the court reject any public policy reasons for a judicial extension of the statute?

Monty S. v. Jason W.
863 N.W.2d 484 (Neb. 2015)

This case presents a private adoption. In this situation, the child is relinquished directly into the hands of the prospective adoptive parents without interference by the state or a private agency.

A natural parent who relinquishes his or her rights to a child by a valid written instrument gives up all rights to the child at the time of the relinquishment. A valid relinquishment is irrevocable. The only right retained by the natural parents is the "right to commence an action seeking . . . to be considered as a prospective parent if the best interests of the child so dictate. The natural parent's rights are no longer superior to those of the prospective adoptive family."

Where the relinquishment of rights by a natural parent is found to be invalid for any reason, a best interests hearing is nevertheless held: "The court shall not simply return the child to the natural parent upon a finding that the relinquishment was not a valid instrument."

Such relinquishments are generally upheld. We have held repeatedly that a change of attitude subsequent to signing a relinquishment is insufficient to invalidate the relinquishment. Rather, as we noted above, in the absence of threats, coercion, fraud, or duress, a properly executed relinquishment of parental rights and consent to adoption signed by a natural parent knowingly, intelligently, and voluntarily is valid. [Under Nebraska law, once the decree of adoption is entered, the natural parents have no rights over the child.]

In this case, the district court explicitly found that there were no threats, fraud, or duress involved in the execution of Teresa and Monty's relinquishments. But the district court, relying on this court's decision in *McCormick v. State*, concluded that the relinquishments were conditioned upon the retention of some parental rights and were therefore invalid.

[*McCormick* involved a case where the natural parents relinquished rights to the child and the child was placed in foster care. However, at the time of the relinquishment, their case worker had told them that if the adoptive parents were cooperative, they might be able to have an "open" adoption. The McCormicks signed the relinquishment, but after the adoption, they were not permitted visitation with their son. After being denied rights to visitation the court found that the McCormicks' signatures on the relinquishment forms were coerced by the promise of the open adoption.] We noted that "[a] relinquishment conditioned upon the retention of some parental rights is invalid."

[After *McCormick*, the Nebraska Legislature passed a law that provided for exchange-of-information contracts in cases involving children in temporary foster care.] The legislative intent states:

> The Legislature finds that there are children in temporary foster care situations who would benefit from the stability of adoption. It is the intent of the Legislature that such situations be accommodated through the use of adoptions involving exchange-of-information contracts between the department and the adoptive or biological parent or parents.
>
> [Thus, when the agency decides that adoption involving an exchange of information is in a child's best interest, it can enter into contract with the proposed adoptive parents to exchange information with the natural parents such as letters by the adoptive parent or parents at specified intervals providing information regarding the child's development or photographs of the child at specified intervals. The Legislature subsequently amended the law further to provide for communication or contact agreements if the prospective adoptee is in the custody of the Department of Health and Human Services.]

. . .

While there is not a single definition of an "open" adoption, in our view, it is clear that these statutorily-provided-for agreements would fit within the general understanding of such an adoption.

The enactment of the exchange-of-information contracts and communication or contact agreements shows us that the Legislature clearly responded to this court's decision in *McCormick*. However, it did so in a limited way: as is noted above, these contracts are available only in foster care situations. Not included in these statutes or covered by other statutes are private adoptions such as the one presented by these facts.

Adoption was unknown to the common law and is a creature of statute. As such, adoptions are permissible only when done in accordance with statute. . . . Thus, the central holdings of *McCormick* — that the effect of an open adoption acts as the retention of some parental rights and, further, that the retention of some parental rights renders a relinquishment invalid — remain intact.

In this case, the record is clear, and the parties do not dispute, that an open adoption was planned. But this retention of parental rights, however slight, is sufficient to invalidate Teresa's and Monty's relinquishments.

We are not unsympathetic to the plight of adoptive and biological parents as they navigate through the highly emotional process of adoption. And it may be that in some situations, benefit could result from open arrangements such as those endorsed by the Legislature in the foster-adopt situation. At the same time, it is not this court's place to make such policy judgments. Until the Legislature acts to approve of these open adoption arrangements in a private adoption context, this court will not recognize them and will instead continue to hold that relinquishments signed with the promise of such an open adoption are invalid.

Rebecca and Jason's second assignment of error is without merit.

CONCLUSION

The decision of the district court is affirmed.

Post-Case Follow-Up

The Nebraska Supreme Court concluded that a biological parent who relinquishes his or her rights to a child by a valid written agreement gives up all rights. A valid relinquishment is irrevocable. Thus, a change of one's mind is not sufficient to invalidate the relinquishment. However, the legislature had provided for open adoptions in the context of prospective adoptees in foster care. Although open adoptions were provided in such agency placements, the court could not extend it to private placement adoptions. Thus, the mistaken intent by all parties to make the private placement an open adoption was not authorized by statute and therefore sufficient to invalidate the relinquishment.

Monty S. v. Jason W.: Real Life Applications

1. Eddie and Emma are best friends with Charlie and Chloe. When they learned that Charlie and Chloe could not conceive a child, they offered to have a child

for them. They agreed that Charlie and Chloe could adopt the baby, but they wanted to be able to visit with the child and to have the child know that Eddie and Emma were his or her biological parents. Charlie and Chloe agreed, and when the baby was born, they adopted her through a private adoption.

For the first two years of the child's life, Eddie and Emma regularly visited with her. Now, however, Charlie has learned he is being transferred to Australia for his job and Charlie and Chloe have indicated that they no longer wish for the child to have any further contact with Eddie and Emma as visitations would be too far away. Assume the same statutory scheme as in *Monty S. v. Jason W.* Eddie and Emma seek your legal advice on whether they can do anything to stop Charlie and Chloe from relocating with the child. What do you tell them?

2. Assume the same facts as in Question 1, except that there is no statute that governs open adoptions in your state. Is there any basis for Eddie and Emma to stop the relocation? What other factors would you need to know?

3. Assume the same facts as in Question 1, except that the state statute governing private placement adoptions allows for open adoptions. Without giving notice to Eddie and Emma, Charlie and Chloe move. Eddie and Emma hire a private investigator who tells them they have moved to another city approximately 100 miles away. Eddie and Emma try to contact Charlie and Chloe, but they have refused to return any telephone calls. What remedies do Eddie and Emma have to enforce their agreement? Can they revoke their relinquishment?

4. Assume you have been asked to rewrite the Nebraska law to avoid the consequences of the *Monty S. v. Jason W.* case. How would you rewrite the law?

E. ACCESS TO ADOPTION RECORDS

Beginning in the 1970s, adult adoptees began to call for the opening of sealed birth adoption records, both so that they could fill in the missing pieces of their past and possibly also search for their birth parents. Asserting a right to know about their past, adult adoptees brought several class action suits challenging the constitutionality of state laws requiring the sealing of adoption records. They argued that these laws violated their right to privacy, including a right to know one's identity, and their right to equal protection of the law by conditioning access to birth information upon one's adoptive status. Courts weighed these claims against the interests of the other parties in the "adoption triangle," namely, the privacy rights of birth parents and the interest of adoptive parents in safeguarding the integrity of their newly constituted families, and generally concluded that the sealed record laws served valid state interests.

Alma Society, Inc. v. Mellon

The following case is an important decision involving the constitutionality of a sealed records law. The case highlights the difficulty of sorting out the potentially conflicting interests of parties in what is often referred to as the "adoption triangle." While state laws regarding the access to records have evolved over the years, the case still gives a good overview of the issues that face adult adoptees, the potential constitutional challenges, and the interpretation of statutes by courts.

The plaintiffs are all adult adoptees who argue that the New York statutes that require the sealing of adoption records violated the Fourteenth Amendment Due Process and Equal Protection Clauses, as well as the Thirteenth Amendment. The District Court dismissed the complaint and the Second Circuit Court of Appeals affirmed.

As you read *Alma Society, Inc. v Mellon*, look for the following:

1. What statute did the plaintiffs challenge in this case? What harms did the plaintiffs say were caused by this law? What relief were they seeking?
2. What constitutional arguments did the plaintiffs make in challenging this statute?
3. What competing interests does the court identify? How does the court balance these considerations?

Alma Society, Inc. v. Mellon
601 F.2d 1225 (2d Cir. 1979)

This appeal presents the question whether adopted persons upon reaching adulthood ("adult adoptees") are constitutionally entitled, irrespective of a showing of cause, to obtain their sealed adoption records, including the names of their natural parents. . . .

[Plaintiffs] argue that adult adoptees should be given access to the records of their adoptions with no showing of cause whatsoever. Their supporting affidavits . . . indicate that lack of access to such records causes some of them serious psychological trauma and pain and suffering, may cause in them or their children medical problems or misdiagnoses for lack of history, may create in some persons a consciousness of danger of unwitting incest, and in others a "crisis" of religious identity or what they feel is an impairment of religious freedom because they are unable to be reared in the religion of their natural parents. . . .

The attack upon the New York statutes is three-fold. [Plaintiffs] first argue that the interests of an adult adoptee in learning from the State (or from agencies acting under compulsion of state law) the identity of his natural family is a fundamental right under the Due Process clause of the Fourteenth Amendment. . . .

Second, [plaintiffs] argue that adult adoptees constitute a suspect or "quasi-suspect" classification under the Equal Protection clause of the Fourteenth Amendment. . . .

Finally, [plaintiffs] argue that the Thirteenth Amendment also applies to this case because the statutes that require sealing of the adoption records as to adults constitute the second of the five incidents of slavery namely, the abolition of the parental relation. . . . Under [plaintiffs'] view, the rights that the Thirteenth Amendment guarantees are not subject to balancing but are instead protected absolutely. We will discuss each of [plaintiffs'] three arguments in turn.

SUBSTANTIVE DUE PROCESS

What [plaintiffs] assert is a right to "personhood." They rely on a series of Supreme Court cases involving familial relationships, rights of family privacy, and freedom to marry and reproduce. As they put it, "an adoptee is someone upon whom the State has, by sealing his records, imposed lifelong familial amnesia . . . injuring the adoptee in regard to his personal identity when he was too young to consent to, or even know, what was happening." . . .

[W]e must look to the nature of the relationships and [recognize] that choices made by those other than the adopted child are involved. . . . [T]he State may take these choices into consideration and protect the natural mother's choice of privacy which not all have forsaken even if [plaintiffs] are correct, as we are told, that many mothers would be willing in this day and age to have their adult adopted children contact them. So, too, a state may take into account the relationship of the adopting parents, even if, as [plaintiffs] assert, many of them would not object to or would even encourage the adopted child's seeking out the identity of or relationship with a natural parent.

EQUAL PROTECTION

[Plaintiffs] begin their equal protection analysis with the argument that adult adoptees are a suspect classification (and the correlative argument that the State has no compelling interests to support the validity of the sealed records laws). Even assuming that the classification here were subject to intermediate scrutiny, it would not violate equal protection; for we conclude that it is substantially related to an important state interest. . . .

[T]he New York sealed record statutes do not want constitutional validity. The statutes, we think, serve important interests. [T]he purpose of [the statute] was to erase the stigma of illegitimacy from the adopted child's life by sealing his original birth certificate and issuing a new one under his new surname. And the major purpose of adoption legislation is to encourage natural parents to use the process when they are unwilling or unable to care for their offspring. . . . These significant legislative goals clearly justify the State's decision to keep the natural parents' names secret from adopted persons but not from non-adopted persons.

To be sure, once an adopted child reaches adulthood, some of the considerations that apply at the time of adoption and throughout the child's tender years no longer apply or apply with less force. Illegitimacy might stigmatize an adult less than a child, and the goal of encouraging adoption of unwanted and uncared for children might not be significantly affected if adult adoptees could discover their natural parents' identities. But the state does have an interest that does not wane as the adopted child grows to adulthood, namely, the interest in protecting the privacy of the natural parents. . . .

THIRTEENTH AMENDMENT

[Plaintiffs] make the novel argument . . . that the Thirteenth Amendment's prohibition of slavery and involuntary servitude gives them an absolute right to release of their adoption records. . . . The argument is that in abolishing slavery and involuntary servitude the Framers also intended to abolish five "necessary incidents of slavery." We address only the second point because we find that the Amendment is entirely inapplicable to this case.

. . . Although it is doubtless true that an "incident" of slavery (in the original sense) was the abolition of the parental relation, i.e., the offspring of a slave was deprived of the care and attention of parents, . . . the New York sealed records laws do not deprive appellants of their parental relation. It is the New York adoption laws themselves and not the sealed records laws that recognize the divestment by natural parents of their guardianship because of formal surrender, abandonment, or forfeiture by unfitness or jeopardy of the child's best interests; and it is the adoption laws that create a new parent-child relationship between appellants and their adoptive parents. [Plaintiffs] do not challenge the constitutionality of the adoption laws; thus their challenge to the sealed records laws, even if cognizable under the Thirteenth Amendment in the absence of congressional legislation, is misdirected. [Plaintiffs] are left to their remedies under the New York statute or with the New York legislature.

Post-Case Follow-Up   The New York statutes provide a mechanism for unsealing of records when there is "good cause" shown. However, the mere fact that an adult adoptee wants to obtain the information concerning his or her natural parents is not sufficient cause. Had the court overturned the statute, then in every case an adult adoptee would have access to the records. The court was not willing to go that far. Having found that the sealed records statutes are not unconstitutional, the remedy then lies with the New York Legislature to make changes in the law.

Alma Society, Inc. v. Mellon: Real Life Applications

1. Shelley is a 35-year-old woman living in New York. She has recently discovered that she has leukemia and needs a bone marrow transfer. She was adopted by her parents when she was five years old. She has no recollection of her birth

parents but remembers she use to live in a house with at least two younger siblings until one day a woman from an agency came and took her and her siblings away. She would now like to try to find her birth parents and the whereabouts of her siblings to see if they are a match for her. Absent finding a match, Shelley has been told her condition is life threatening. Does Shelley have good cause for unsealing her adoption records?

2. Katy is 23 years old. She has been suffering from depression and anxiety after her adoptive parents, who were the only family she ever knew, were killed in a car accident two years ago. Her psychologist has suggested that if she tried to find her birth parents, it might give a sense of family connection and help her emotionally. Does Katy have good cause to unseal her adoption records?

3. Ron is 67 years old. His wife Bea, whom he had married when they were both 22, recently passed away. While going through her things, he discovered a letter she had written to him to be opened after her death. In the letter, she explained that she had become pregnant with his child when they were 17 and going into their senior year of high school. She reminded him about how she had gone away to live with her aunt out of state and did not come back until the very end of their senior year. She said that she had given the baby up for adoption. She had always thought that she would tell him at some point, but after they graduated from college, were married, and had children she felt it better for the family to just put what had happened in the past. Ron is devastated to think that he has a child out there who does not know his or her biological mother and father and that he or she has siblings and nieces and nephews. He wants to have the adoption records opened and try to find the child who was given up for adoption. Assuming the same statute as in *Alma Society, Inc.*, does Ron have constitutional grounds to find the child that was given up for adoption?

4. Pablo is a 54-year-old man who was adopted by his parents when he was an infant. He feels very strongly that adult adoptees have an absolute right to know who their birth parents are regardless of whether the records are sealed. He has asked for your assistance in coming up with arguments he can use to help lobby the legislature to change the law in *Alma Society, Inc.* What policy reasons can you give him for changing the law? What objections from biological parents do you foresee being made? What objections from adoptees do you see being made?

Unable to gain results in court, reform efforts for unsealing adoption records have shifted to the legislative arena, with considerably more success. Today, all states allow the release of nonidentifying information about the birth parents to the parents or guardian of an adopted person who is a minor, and most also permit an adopted person to access this information upon turning 18, although the procedures governing the release of such information vary from state to state. In addition, many states also allow the birth parents to obtain nonidentifying information about the child, which usually addresses his or her "health and social history." This information may also be available to adult birth siblings.[1] Depending on the state, nonidentifying information may include medical information; information about the birth parents, such as their age, race, and religion; and information about the birth and the adoption process.

The pattern is considerably more complex when it comes to information that "may lead to the positive identification of birth parents, the adoptee, or other birth relatives," such as "current or past names of the person, addresses, employment, or other similar records or information."[2] Some of this information can usually be found in the adoption records, and at least some of this information is typically contained in sealed birth records.

States differ in the ease with which they permit adoptees to access their adoption records. At one end of the spectrum, a handful of states allow children who have been adopted to access their birth records once they reach adulthood, without needing either the consent of the birth parents or proof of good cause or best interest. Most of these states give birth parents who do not want to be contacted the option of filing a "contact veto," and states providing this option also subject adoptees who violate the veto to civil or criminal penalties. At the other end of the spectrum, many states do not allow individuals who have been adopted to access their birth records without a court order, which typically must be premised upon proof of good cause or that disclosure is in the adoptee's best interest. In the middle of the spectrum, many states have created various kinds of registry systems through which adult adoptees and birth parents (and sometimes birth siblings and adoptive parents) may be able to access identifying information. Some states use a "passive" registry system, which requires that both parties register their consent to the release of information before a match can be attempted. In other states, search efforts can be initiated based on the request of one party. If the other party is located and gives his or her consent, identifying information can be released to the person initiating the search.[3]

F. ADOPTION IN SPECIFIC SITUATIONS

The sections above traced the general stages of the adoption process. However, given the myriad of family arrangements, certain situations involve more specialized rules or raise unique issues. In this section, we consider some, although certainly not all, of these situations.

1. Stepparent Adoptions

Many of the adoptions that take place each year involve stepparents. Typically, this occurs when a divorced custodial parent remarries, and the couple wishes

---

[1] Access to Adoption Records, Child Welfare Information Gateway, http://www.childwelfare.gov (accessed June 8, 2016).

[2] *Id.*

[3] For further detail, including the approaches that individual states take, see Access to Adoption Records, https://www.childwelfare.gov/topics/systemwide/laws-policies/statutes/infoaccessap/?hasBeenRedirected=1 (accessed June 8, 2016).

to establish a formal parent-child relationship between the new spouse and the children from the previous marriage. Most states have a "streamlined" procedure that allows a judge to waive the home study requirement; however, in some states, the adoption cannot be approved until the parties have been married for at least a year.

The custodial parent must consent to the adoption, as must the noncustodial parent. If the noncustodial parent refuses to consent, the adoption can proceed only if there are grounds for dispensing with his or her consent (see above). Some states have relaxed the requirements for the dispensing of consent in the stepparent adoption context by either statute or judicial decision. Thus, for example, the failure of a parent to maintain communication with his or her children, although not usually by itself considered unfitness, may be enough in the stepparent context to allow the adoption to proceed over the objection of the noncustodial parent.

Case Preview

In re Adoption of K.A.H.

This case involves the right of a biological father to object to the adoption of his biological children by their stepfather even though he did not pay child support or have extensive contact with the minor children.

Mother and Father were divorced in 2009. The divorce decree provided that the parties would have a shared parenting plan and that Father would pay no child support. Mother was a physician and her income was much higher than Father's income. Shortly after the divorce, Father moved to England. During the period of time Father was away, he called several times and sent some cards and gifts.

Mother remarried, and in 2013 the stepfather petitioned for adoption. Under Ohio law, consent to an adoption is not required from the parent who "has failed without justifiable cause to provide more than de minimis contact with the minor or to provide for the maintenance and support of the minor as required by law or judicial decree for a period of at least one year immediately preceding" the filing of the adoption petition.

As you read *In re Adoption of K.A.H.*, look for the following:

1. Why did Stepfather believe he had grounds to adopt the minor children without seeking the biological father's consent?
2. What contacts did the court find persuasive in saying that there was at least de minimis contact?
3. If there is a common law duty to support a child, why did the court find that support was not required in this case?

In re Adoption of K.A.H.

2015 Ohio 1971 (Ohio App. 2015) Ohio Court of Appeal

Appellant, W.J.H., is appealing the decision of the Franklin County Probate Court which required that P.C.'s consent be obtained before his children can be adopted by their step-father. For the following reasons, we affirm the probate court's decision.

. . .

[Stepfather] petitioned to adopt two minor children, K.A.C. and P.C.C. Both children were born to [Mother] formerly while she was married to [Father]. In 2011, Mother and the petitioner were married. In April 2013, [Stepfather] petitioned to adopt the children. Father received notice of the adoption petition on or about June 13, 2013 and filed a written objection on July 26, 2013. The petition for adoption alleged that [Stepfather's] consent to the adoption was not necessary due to the provisions of [state statute], which reads:

Consent to adoption is not required of any of the following:

(A) A parent of a minor, when it is alleged in the adoption petition and the court, after proper service of notice and hearing, finds by clear and convincing evidence that the parent has failed without justifiable cause to provide more than de minimis contact with the minor or to provide for the maintenance and support of the minor as required by law or judicial decree for a period of at least one year immediately preceding either the filing of the adoption petition or the placement of the minor in the home of the petitioner.

After a hearing, the probate court's magistrate found that the consent of [Father] was required. This finding was based upon a factual finding that between July 1, 2012 and March 24, 2013, [Father] placed calls to his children totaling 91 minutes at a cost of 112 British Pounds Sterling, the equivalent of roughly $174 U.S.D. Because of the phone calls and because of an undetermined number of cards and gifts which were provided during the relevant time frame, the magistrate found [Stepfather] failed to demonstrate by clear and convincing evidence that [Father] did not have more than de minimis contact with his children. [Stepfather appeals.]

The Supreme Court of Ohio has articulated a two-step analysis for probate courts to employ when applying R.C. 3107.07(A). . . . The first step involves the factual question of whether the petitioner has proved by clear and convincing evidence that the parent willfully failed to have more than de minimis contact with the minor child and failed to provide maintenance and support. . . . The second step occurs if a probate court finds a failure to have more than de minimis contact and provide the required maintenance and support, the court then determines the issue of whether there is justifiable cause for the failure. . . .

[Stepfather] argues that [Father's] 91 minutes of phone calls and a few cards do not amount to more than de minimis contact with the children. There is evidence that many of these minutes were spent waiting for the maternal grandparents, who [Father] would call to put the children on the phone. There is also evidence that, on some phone calls, P.C. was unable to speak to the children.

We review the probate determination of the significance of these facts under an abuse of discretion standard. . . .

Comparing examples of when other courts have found that no more than de minimis contact existed, we see that the standard has not been raised higher by Ohio courts: *In re Adoption of A.L.C.*, 7th Dist. No. 14 BE 4, 2014-Ohio-4045 (father did not contact the child for over one year but argued he had a justifiable cause); *In re Adoption of R.L.H.*, 2d Dist. No. 25734, 2013-Ohio-3462 (mother voluntarily suspended her agreed upon court-ordered parenting time, and mother did not see, speak, or correspond with the child); *In re Adoption of K.D.*, 6th Dist. No. L-09-1302, 2010-Ohio-1592 (father's only effort to contact the child was through an internet site and a visit to a clerk's office, and the father's limited cognition and bi-polar disorder did not provide justifiable cause); *In re M.F.*, 9th Dist. No. 27166, 2014-Ohio-3801 (father failed to contact the child, but was prevented by court order and later by the mother ignoring his email requests); *In re Adoption of J.A.C.*, 4th Dist. No. 14CA3654, 2015-Ohio-1662 (father only performed a single two-hour visitation during the year). Contrasting these examples where courts found that there was no more than de minimis contact with the children with P.C.'s short but regular phone calls, we cannot find that the probate court's decision is unreasonable, arbitrary or unconscionable.

We note the well-established law that the right to parent one's children is a fundamental right. *Troxel v. Granville*, 530 U.S. 57, 66, 120 S. Ct. 2054, 147 L. Ed. 2d 49 (2000). . . . In recognition of the significance of that fundamental interest, the Supreme Court of Ohio has described the permanent termination of parental rights as "the family law equivalent of the death penalty in a criminal case." *In re Hayes*, 79 Ohio St. 3d 46, 48, 679 N.E.2d 680 (1997). Therefore, parents "must be afforded every procedural and substantive protection the law allows." Id.

We find that the probate court did not abuse its discretion in determining that W.J.H. failed to prove by clear and convincing evidence that P.C. did not provide more than de minimis contact with his children.

[Stepfather also] argues that the existence of a zero support order does not negate [Father's] common law duty of support. [Father] argues that the existence of a zero support order is justifiable cause to not have provided financial support for his children. A probate court's decision on whether justifiable cause exists will not be disturbed on appeal unless the determination is against the manifest weight of the evidence. M.B. at ¶24; Masa at paragraph two of the syllabus. Decisions supported by competent, credible evidence going to all the essential elements of the case will not be reversed as being against the manifest weight of the evidence. *Melvin v. Ohio State Univ. Med. Ctr.*, 10th Dist. No. 10AP-975, 2011-Ohio-3317, ¶34; see *C.E. Morris Co. v. Foley Const. Co.*, 54 Ohio St. 2d 279, 376 N.E.2d 578 (1978).

Examining the nature of the duty of support and maintenance . . . Ohio has long recognized that a biological parent's duty to support his or her children is a "principle of natural law" that is "fundamental in our society." . . .

However, when a husband and wife are divorced, their obligation to support a minor child is governed by the domestic relations child support statute. . . . The probate court, in the case at bar, determined that the shared parenting plan which set [Father's] child support payments as $0 was incorporated into the divorce decree. The probate court reasoned that, when no support order is issued at the time of the custody award, the custodial parent is not entitled to support payment. . . .

To additionally compel [support] when there is already a valid judicial order in existence would be to incorrectly interpret [the law]. . . . [W]e find that the child support order of zero dollars that was incorporated into the divorce decree governs in this case. P.C.'s common-law duty to support, which is reduced to statute R.C. 3103.03(A), is now governed by the domestic relation's child support statute, R.C. 3109.05.

[A third assignment of error was also overruled.]

Judgment affirmed.

Post-Case Follow-Up

The Ohio court found a common law duty of support, but given the fact that the parents had agreed no support was owed, the court relied on the parenting plan that had been adopted by the parties. This is because dissolution of marriages is governed by statute, and if the statute is followed, common obligations of support will not prevail in the case. Otherwise, the statute would be completely nullified, and parents could not rely on the decree that has been entered. In this case, since there was a zero support order, the father had "justifiable cause" not to pay support.

In re Adoption of K.A.H.: Real Life Applications

1. Monica and David were divorced three years ago. David was a wealthy physician and Monica was a stay-at-home mom. Monica was so anxious to move out of state with the children to get away from David after the divorce that she agreed that no support would be owed if she were allowed to move out of state with the children. The decree adopted their parenting plan and provided a zero support order. Monica moved with the two children and has now remarried. Monica's spouse, Rob, wants to adopt the children. For the past year, David has not seen the children and has not paid any support. However, he does call once a month and sends the children postcards whenever he travels. Does Rob need to obtain David's consent to adopt the children?

2. Beth and Hugh were divorced five years ago. They had one child in common, Brittney, who was an infant when they divorced. Hugh was ordered to pay minimum child support of $100 a month, which he paid until approximately two years ago when Beth married Zack. Because Zack and Beth did not want to take any money from Hugh, Beth told Hugh that now that she was remarried Hugh did not have to pay support. Hugh happily stopped paying support, although neither party modified the order with the court. Through the years, even though Hugh does not live far away, he has seen very little of Brittney, except at Christmas for a couple of hours and for her birthday where he generally attends her party for a few hours. Brittney calls him Daddy Hugh but otherwise has no relationship with him. Zack now wants to adopt Brittney. When Hugh received

the petition, he immediately consulted a lawyer and was told to pay all the back support owed. Hugh tendered a check to Beth for the full amount of support over the past two years, which Beth refused to accept. How should the trial court rule on the petition for adoption?

3. Assume the same facts as in Question 2, except that Hugh never paid child support, and, not wanting to cause any problems, Beth never sought to enforce the child support obligation. How should the trial court rule on the petition for adoption?

4. Susan and Bill are the sister and brother-in-law of Lynn, who is unmarried and has a daughter Shayna. Lynn does not know who the biological father is. When Shayna was two years old, Lynn received a job offer that would take her to Europe for six months after which she would return home. Susan and Bill agreed to care for Shayna for the six months. While she was gone, Lynn would call Susan occasionally to check in on Shayna, but never spoke to Shayna because Lynn said she did not want Shayna to miss her and it would be too heartbreaking for Lynn to hear her voice. At the end of six months, Lynn indicated her job had been extended for another six months. The calls from Lynn became less frequent, and approximately two months ago stopped all together. It has now been 14 months since Lynn left for Europe and other than postcards sent to Susan and Bill from various places promising to be home soon, there has been no word from Lynn. Susan has an address for Lynn but wants to know whether she should seek out Lynn or if she and Bill can at this stage petition to adopt Shayna without obtaining Lynn's consent. What would you tell Susan?

5. Assume the same facts as in Question 4, but upon receiving the petition to adopt, Lynn immediately comes home and objects. Lynn has asked you to represent her. What are Lynn's best arguments to oppose the adoption?

As you are now aware, adoption typically severs the legal rights of the birth parents. Thus, in a "regular" adoption situation, the custodial parent, by consenting to the adoption, is agreeing to a termination of his or her legal status. However, given that the entire point of a stepparent adoption is to create a new parental unit consisting of the custodial parent and his or her new spouse, it would make no sense to apply the **"cut-off" rule** in this situation. In recognition of the absurdity of this potential outcome, most statutes include an explicit exception to the cut-off rule for stepparent adoptions, making it clear that the parental rights of the biological spouse continue in full force and effect following the adoption.

As far as the noncustodial parent is concerned, adoption by a stepparent does result in the termination of that parent's rights. However, questions have been raised as to whether severing all ties with this parent makes sense in every situation, and courts appear increasingly willing to grant post-adoption rights to the noncustodial parent even though legal parenthood now resides in the adopting parent. These rights can range from a yearly exchange of letters and photographs to regularly scheduled visitation.

In support of this open adoption model, some judges and commentators believe that it is important for a child's sense of well-being to provide the child with a continued connection to a parent with whom he or she previously enjoyed a relationship, and that severing this relationship cuts the child off from a vital sense of continuity with the past. In contrast, others fear that this more flexible, open arrangement will jeopardize the ability of the new family to develop a coherent identity and will subject the child to competing loyalty claims and uncertainty about the stability of the family.

2. Adoption by Same-Sex Couples

As discussed in earlier chapters, over the past few decades, gay men and lesbians have struggled to secure legal recognition of their family relationships, including the right to become parents through adoption, both as individuals and as couples. While express bans on adoptions by "couples of the same gender" are essentially a relic of the past, there is still the issue of laws and policies that give preference to adoptions by married couples of the opposite sex. However, it is anticipated that with marriage equality now the law of the land, the historic bias that many adoption agencies have shown toward same-sex couples seeking to adopt will continue to weaken as the culture continues to become increasingly accepting of same-sex households.

Single-Parent and Joint Adoption

All states generally permit single parents to adopt. However, many agencies and birth parents prefer to place a child with a married couple, thus potentially making it more difficult for any unmarried individual — straight or gay — to adopt. Although no state currently has an express ban on adoption by single parents, this tilt toward married couples sometimes makes it more difficult for unmarried individuals to adopt.

In a **joint adoption**, a couple, whether same-sex or heterosexual, seeks to adopt a child who is not related to either party. Although all states allow unmarried individuals to adopt a child, many do not permit adoption by unmarried couples, regardless of sexual orientation. Rather, the adoption is treated as a single-parent adoption. This creates an issue when parties terminate their relationship. Although they have raised the child together, only the adoptive parent will have rights.

Co-Parent Adoption

Co-parent adoption, or as it is sometimes known, **second-parent adoption**, involves a situation where a couple is raising a child together, but only one is recognized as the child's legal parent (through birth or a prior adoption). Accordingly, the couple seeks to have the second parent (or co-parent) adopt the child so both partners are fully recognized as his or her legal parents.

In seeking adoptive rights for co-parents, the stepparent adoption cases have been drawn on as analogous since, as with a stepparent, legal recognition is being sought for an established parent-child relationship that exists within the frame-work of a committed relationship with the child's legal parent. Recognizing this structural similarity, a number of courts have recently approved co-parent adoptions as being in a child's best interest. *In re Adoption of Evan*, 153 Misc. 2d 844, 583 N.Y.S.2d 997, 998-999 (Sur. Ct. 1992), was one of the first cases to allow a second-parent adoption. The court explained:

> It seems clear that the proposed adoption is in Evan's best interest. He is part of a family unit that has been functioning successfully. . . . The adoption would bring no change or trauma to his daily life; it would serve only to provide him with important legal rights which he does not presently possess. It would afford him additional economic security because Diane would become legally obligated to support him. . . . He would also be entitled to inherit from Diane and her family under the law of intestate succession and be eligible for Social Security benefits in the event of her disability or death. He would also be able to participate in the medical and educational benefits provided by her employment. . . .
>
> Even if, as anticipated, the petitioners remain together, there is a significant emotional benefit to Evan from adoption which is perhaps even more crucial than the financial.

As with stepparent adoptions, in approving these adoptions, courts have agreed that it would be absurd to apply the cut-off provisions to terminate the rights of the legal parent. To avoid this result, courts have either read in a statutory exception based on the absurdity of the result or extended the stepparent exception to the cut-off rule by analogy.

As discussed in Chapter 13, it is possible that a co-parent might be able to rely upon either a state's parentage laws or the marital presumption in order to establish a formal parent-child relationship, thus obviating the need for a formalized adoption. However, given the current uncertainty of the law in this arena, as we saw, experts are still advising married co-parents to go the adoption route rather than rely on legal presumptions in order to secure their relationships with the children they are parenting.

3. Unwed Fathers

Historically, many jurisdictions permitted the adoption of a child born to unmarried parents based solely on the consent of the mother. Although the legal status of unwed fathers has improved, they do not have the same adoption consent rights as unmarried mothers. For women, consent rights vest automatically at the time of birth, whereas, as we saw in Chapter 12, under the "biology-plus" rule, men must take some steps to demonstrate their parental commitment to the child. This differential treatment reflects a number of considerations:

■ Because the mother is always present at birth, maternal identity is readily determined and a maternal consent requirement does not introduce delays into the process. In contrast, if the consent of the father were always required, many adoptions would be delayed until the father could be located and his paternity established.

▓ The automatic vesting of rights in women may also reflect the asymmetrical involvement of men and women during pregnancy. Since only women are directly involved in the gestational process, social motherhood is seen as taking root during this time; at birth, the mother may be regarded as already having demonstrated a commitment to being a parent, thus making her consent essential. This difference may be less significant where the father is involved with the pregnancy; on the other hand, the difference may be even more pronounced where the pregnancy resulted from a casual sexual encounter. A related consideration is the generally operative assumption that the mother is most likely to be the one to care for the infant, thus giving her a more direct and immediate stake in the decision-making process.

▓ Third, this differential treatment is also rooted in the recognition that women may become pregnant in the context of an abusive relationship or as a result of rape and that exclusive consent rights may be necessary to protect her safety and ensure that paternal rights do not automatically spring forth from an act of coerced sexual intercourse.

Within these parameters, states have been sorting out, with inconsistent results, how to provide a meaningful role for unwed fathers in light of potentially competing maternal interests and the goal of providing children who are to be adopted with immediate homes. At the simplest level, all states now provide consent rights to unwed fathers who have taken steps to actualize a relationship with their children. Once the right to consent attaches, an adoption cannot proceed over the father's objection unless he is proved unfit—at this point, he is legally indistinguishable from either an unmarried mother or a married father. Note that even if an unwed father has not demonstrated enough of a parental commitment to become a consenting party, he may still be entitled to receive notice of the adoption hearing as an interested party. As an interested party, although he lacks authority to approve or veto the adoption, he most likely will be permitted to give testimony on the issue of whether the adoption is in the best interest of the child.

States take a variety of approaches with respect to what an unwed father must do to acquire consent rights. Over half of the states have established what are known as **putative father registries** that enable men who are or believe they may be the father of a child to register with the state in order to protect their potential interest in the child. Registration must usually be accomplished within a statutorily prescribed time period following a child's birth; once registered, a man is entitled, at a minimum, to notice of any adoption proceeding involving the child. See Exhibit 14.1. In some states, the failure to register cuts off the father's rights. Exceptions may be included, though for situations in which a man did not have a reasonable opportunity to comply with the statutory requirements, such as where the mother moved to another state before he knew she was pregnant, or where he did not know about the birth of the child under circumstances that do not suggest abandonment.

Some states employ a more open-ended approach and look to see whether an unwed father has demonstrated a substantial commitment to developing a

EXHIBIT 14.1   **Putative Father Registration**

PUTATIVE FATHER REGISTRY - REGISTRATION FORM
STATE OF GEORGIA

USE A SEPARATE FORM FOR EACH CHILD.   PRINT OR TYPE ALL INFORMATION.

My name is: _____
               first   middle   last

My current address is: _____
            street number, name, apartment number, P.O. box

_____
       city   state   zip code

My date of birth is: _____
                month, day, year

My social security number is: _____

I hereby indicate the possibility of paternity of the child described below without acknowledging paternity.

The name of the mother of the child is: _____
                     first   middle   last

The mother's social security number is: (if known) _____

The mother's address is: _____
         street number, name, apartment number, P.O .box

_____
       city   state   zip code

The child's name is: (if known) _____
             first   middle   last

The child **(select one)**   (   ) was born on _____ sex of child _____
                                  month, day, year   male or female

                                   _____

OR   city   state

        (   ) is estimated to be born in _____
                                   month   year

As detailed above, I hereby register on the Putative Father Registry as provided by law. I do so to indicate the possibility of my paternity of the child, but I understand I am not formally acknowledging paternity of this child.

Signature of Registrant: _____ *Date Signed:* _____

SEE INFORMATION AND INSTRUCTIONS ON REVERSE

Form 3960 (Rev. 9-2014) Vital Records/Georgia Department of Public Health relationship with his child. Just what is meant by a substantial commitment, however, is far from clear. In some states, a minimal level of involvement seems to be enough, while in others, the father must demonstrate that he participates in his child's life in a consistent, meaningful manner.

When the child is a newborn, there is considerable divergence over what constitutes the demonstration of a substantial parenting commitment. Some states will evaluate the father's conduct during pregnancy to determine if he demonstrated a commitment to becoming a parent through the financial and emotional support of the mother. A lack of involvement during the pregnancy may deprive him of consent rights, while an active, involved role may serve as the basis for finding a demonstrated commitment to the assumption of parental responsibilities. In other jurisdictions, the father's conduct during pregnancy is less important, and the focus is more on his conduct immediately following the birth of the child, and whether he acted in a timely manner to demonstrate his commitment to assuming the responsibilities of parenthood.

Difficult questions arise in situations where the father has not been able to take advantage of the "opportunity interest" in developing a relationship with his child either because the mother has prevented him from developing a relationship with the child or because he did not know about the pregnancy. If he then somehow learns about the proposed adoption, will he be given the opportunity to consent or object to it going forward?

Most courts have permitted a father to participate in the adoption proceeding in the absence of an established relationship with the child where he can show that he sought to establish a relationship in a timely manner, even if his efforts failed. Thus, his rights will generally not be defeated in situations where the mother actively prevented the relationship from developing, absent countervailing considerations, such as a history of intimate partner abuse. Even less clear is what the result should be in situations where the putative father has no knowledge of the pregnancy and thus made no attempt to establish a relationship with the child. If he has no idea, should that be regarded as evidence of a lack of interest in or commitment to parenting? As one court concluded, a biological father who was "not interested enough in the outcome of his sexual encounter . . . to even inquire about the possibility of . . . pregnancy" should not acquire constitutionally protected rights to participate in an adoption proceeding. *In re Adoption of A.A.T.*, 287 Kan. 590, 196 P.3d 1180, 1195 (2008), citing *In re Adoption of S.J.B.*, 294 Ark. 598, 600, 745 S.W.2d 606 (1988).

On the other hand, is it really fair to expect someone to grasp an opportunity that he knows nothing about? Should courts really impose an affirmative duty on men to inquire about pregnancy, or should they instead focus on protecting the opportunity itself even if not known about and therefore not acted upon?

These kinds of questions can also arise in the context of the safe haven laws (discussed earlier) if the father does not know either of the pregnancy or of the mother's decision to avail herself of this option. Many safe haven laws do not have clear notice provisions, and as a result, some courts have refused to terminate the father's rights. Others do include specific notice provisions, such as that a search be made for the father using any information that might be available; that service be made through publication in the paper, which includes any possible identifying information about the baby; and that a search be done of the putative father registry.

Last, and perhaps raising the most difficult questions, is what should happen in a situation where an unwed father does not learn about the child until after an adoption has been approved by a court? Should the adoption be set aside in order to vindicate a father's right to develop a relationship with his child? Does this approach elevate the biological claims of fatherhood over the best interests of the child? What weight should be given to the adoptive parents? Should the outcome turn on the conduct of the mother, in terms of whether or not she lied to the father about the existence of the child? Is her conduct relevant from the perspective of the child's needs? Should the outcome turn on the conduct of the father — whether he did what he could to learn about and connect with the child?

These are agonizing questions to which there are no simple answers, and these cases highlight the tension between the long-cherished rights of biological parenthood and the need to secure stable adoptive homes for children where there does not appear to be a birth parent who is ready and able to assume the responsibilities of parenthood. Some courts have focused on the harm to the father and have been willing to set an adoption aside to vindicate his right to develop a relationship with his child. Here, his underlying biological connection to the child is given priority in determining which parenting relationships will be permitted to continue. In contrast, other courts have refused to set aside an adoption in this situation if it determines that it is in the best interest of the child to maintain the continuity of the adoptive relationships. The much publicized 1993 *"Baby Richard"* case exemplifies both judicial approaches.[4]

| **Case Preview**  | *In re Doe ("Baby Richard")* |

In this case, an unwed mother placed her newborn for adoption without informing the father. During her pregnancy, the father had returned to Czechoslovakia to care for his dying grandmother. While he was away, the mother received a call from his aunt informing her that he had resumed a former romantic relationship with another woman. As a result of this news, the mother moved out of their shared home and gave birth in a different hospital than the couple had decided on.

Upon the father's return, the mother informed him that the child had died. He did not believe this and made a number of attempts to find out what had happened to the child, including checking with the hospital they had planned to use, checking birth and death certificates, and going through the garbage at the mother's house for signs that a baby was living there. About six months later, the parties married

---

[4]The name of the case is actually *In re Doe.*

and subsequently sought the return of the child based on the fact that the father had not consented to the adoption.

In evaluating Richard's best interest, the Illinois Appellate Court found that he should remain with his adoptive parents with whom he had lived since four days after his birth.

The Illinois Supreme Court had a radically different view of the situation. It disagreed that the father's actions to discover what had happened to the child had been inadequate in light of the mother's dishonesty, which was compounded by the fact that the lawyer for the adoptive parents had also encouraged concealment of the truth. Finding that the father had been wrongfully deprived of an opportunity to express his interest in the child, the court focused on the "preemptive rights" of a natural parent in his own children. It held that these rights had to be considered apart from the best interest of the child.

Excerpts from both cases are given to demonstrate the contrasting views taken by the courts.

As you read *In re Doe*, look for the following:

1. What standard did the Illinois Appellate Court use in deciding the adoption petition?
2. Why did the Illinois Supreme Court refuse to look at the best interest of the child?
3. Was the supreme court concerned about the fact that three years had passed while this case was pending?
4. Is there any concern about the child's best interest by the supreme court?

In re Doe

627 N.E.2d 648 (Ill. App. Ct. 1993)
[Illinois Appellate Court decision]

[The trial court held that the father was unfit because he had failed to demonstrate a reasonable degree of interest, concern, or responsibility during the first 30 days of the child's life as required by state law, and his consent to the adoption was therefore not required. The appellate court was similarly unimpressed with the father's efforts to determine what had happened to the baby and agreed that he had failed to demonstrate a reasonable degree of interest, concern, or responsibility for the child. However, in upholding the adoption, the appellate court's primary focus was on the best interest of the child rather than on the rights of the father.]

Fortunately, the time has long past when children in our society were considered the property of their parents. Slowly, but finally, when it comes to children even the law has rid itself of the *Dred Scott* mentality that a human being can be considered a piece of property "belonging" to another human being. To hold that a child is the property of his parents is to deny the humanity of the child. Thus, in the present case we start with the premise that Richard is not a piece of property with property rights belonging to either his biological or adoptive parents. Richard "belongs" to no one but himself. . . .

. . . A child's best interest is not part of an equation. It is not to be balanced against any other interest.

If it were otherwise, few parents would be secure in the custody of their own children. If best interests of the child were a sufficient qualification to determine child custody, anyone with superior income, intelligence, education, etc., might challenge and deprive the parents of their right to their own children.

In re Doe
638 N.E.2d 181 (Ill. 1994)
[Illinois Supreme Court decision]

Otakar and Daniella began living together in the fall of 1989, and Daniella became pregnant in June of 1990. For the first eight months of her pregnancy, Otakar provided for all of her expenses.

In late January 1991, Otakar went to his native Czechoslovakia to attend to his gravely ill grandmother for two weeks. During this time, Daniella received a phone call from Otakar's aunt saying that Otakar had resumed a former romantic relationship with another woman.

Because of this unsettling news, Daniella left their shared apartment, refused to talk with Otakar on his return, and gave birth to the child at a different hospital than where they had originally planned. She gave her consent to the adoption of the child by the Does, telling them and their attorney that she knew who the father was but would not furnish his name. Daniella and her uncle warded off Otakar's persistent inquiries about the child by telling him that the child had died shortly after birth.

Otakar found out that the child was alive and had been placed for adoption 57 days after the child was born. He then began the instant proceedings by filing an appearance contesting the Does' adoption of his son. As already noted, the trial court ruled that Otakar was an unfit parent under section 1 of the Adoption Act (the Act) (750 ILCS 50/1) because he had not shown a reasonable degree of interest in the child within the first 30 days of his life. Therefore, the father's consent was unnecessary under section 8 of the Act (750 ILCS 50/8).

The finding that the father had not shown a reasonable degree of interest in the child is not supported by the evidence. In fact, he made various attempts to locate the child, all of which were either frustrated or blocked by the actions of the mother. Further, the mother was aided by the attorney for the adoptive parents, who failed to make any effort to ascertain the name or address of the father despite the fact that the mother indicated she knew who he was. Under the circumstances, the father had no opportunity to discharge any familial duty.

In the opinion below, the appellate court, wholly missing the threshold issue in this case, dwelt on the best interests of the child. Since, however, the father's parental interest was improperly terminated, there was no occasion to reach the factor of the child's best interests. That point should never have been reached and need never have been discussed.

Unfortunately, over three years have elapsed since the birth of the baby who is the subject of these proceedings. To the extent that it is relevant to assign fault in this case, the fault here lies initially with the mother, who fraudulently tried to deprive the father of his rights, and secondly, with the adoptive parents and their attorney, who proceeded with the adoption when they knew that a real father was out there who had been denied knowledge of his baby's existence. When the father entered his appearance in the adoption proceedings 57 days after the baby's birth and demanded his rights as a father, the petitioners should have relinquished the baby at that time. It was their decision to prolong this litigation through a lengthy, and ultimately fruitless, appeal.

The adoption laws of Illinois are neither complex nor difficult of application. Those laws intentionally place the burden of proof on the adoptive parents in establishing both the relinquishment and/or unfitness of the natural parents and, coincidentally, the fitness and the right to adopt of the adoptive parents. In addition, Illinois law requires a good-faith effort to notify the natural parents of the adoption proceedings. These laws are designed to protect natural parents in their preemptive rights to their own children wholly apart from any consideration of the so-called best interests of the child. If it were otherwise, few parents would be secure in the custody of their own children. If best interests of the child were a sufficient qualification to determine child custody, anyone with superior income, intelligence, education, etc., might challenge and deprive the parents of their right to their own children. The law is otherwise and was not complied with in this case.

Accordingly, we reverse.

Post-Case Follow-Up

Wholly apart from any considerations of best interest, the adoption was overturned, and the child returned to his birth parents based on the primacy of the biological link and the potentiality it embodies. The supreme court is concerned that if the best interest standard is used for adoptions, that wealthier parties, those with more education, or those who could provide a child with a "better" lifestyle would always prevail in these kinds of contests. Rather, there appears to be a presumption that, absent other circumstances, it is in the child's best interest to be united with his or her biological parents.

In re Doe: Real Life Applications

1. The state law provides that a parent who is deemed unfit to care for a child does not need to give consent to an adoption. The law also provides that a parent is deemed unfit if the parent has had no contact with the child for the first 30 days of the child's life. Sheila became pregnant with Miguel's child, but she told Miguel that the child was not his. Upset that Sheila had cheated on him with

someone else, Miguel left Sheila, who subsequently gave birth to a baby boy. Sheila gave the child up for adoption, saying she knew the name of the father but refused to give his name. Forty-five days after the birth, Sheila told Miguel the baby was his but that she had given the baby up for adoption. Miguel filed an action to revoke the adoption because he had not given his consent and his failure to have contact with the child during the first 30 days was justified. How should the trial court rule?

2. Assume the same facts as in Question 1, except Miguel contacts Sheila shortly after the birth of the baby and Sheila tells him the baby is his. She suggests a DNA test to confirm paternity so that Miguel will believe her. Miguel says he believes her but he is out of town on business and will not be back for at least six weeks. During this time, he sends Sheila money for the baby as well as some things for the baby. When he returns several weeks later, he learns that Sheila has given the baby up for adoption. Is Miguel an unfit parent under the statute? Should his consent have been required?

3. Tyler is informed by his girlfriend Rosie that she is expecting and it is his child. Tyler seeks your legal advice and you advise him about the putative father registry and give him the form to fill out. Tyler unfortunately gets sidetracked and fails to fill out the form. However, immediately after the birth, Tyler spends a great deal of time with Rosie and his infant son. Unbeknownst to Tyler, Rosie had signed papers to place the child for adoption. For the next three months, Rosie makes excuses as to why Tyler cannot see the baby. The revocation period for a child placed for adoption is 30 days. Finally, after 90 days had passed, Rosie advised Tyler that the baby was placed for adoption. What are Tyler's options, if any?

4. Transracial Adoption

Significant controversy surrounds the issue of the role that race should or should not play in the creation of families by adoption. Until the 1950s, many states had laws prohibiting the placement of children across racial lines, and, even where not expressly prohibited, most agencies had explicit policies against such placements. Similar to laws banning interracial marriage, this prohibition reflected racial animus and a belief in the desirability of maintaining white racial purity. As courts began to strike down racial classifications in the late 1950s, these laws were eventually declared unconstitutional.

This constitutional direction, combined with other factors — including the increased numbers of children in the foster care system, the decline in the number of white infants available for adoption, and a greater societal acceptance of interracial relationships — led to an upsurge in the number of transracial adoptions. An additional contributing factor was that social workers had also begun to question their generally held assumption that children should be placed in families

The Multiethnic Placement Law (MEPA), along with other enactments, prohibits agencies that receive federal funding from denying or delaying adoption (or foster care) placements based on considerations of race, color, or national origin.
DNF Style/Shutterstock.com

that most closely matched their families of origin based on the belief that children would do best if they blended into their adoptive families.[5]

In 1994, Congress passed the Multiethnic Placement Law (MEPA), which was amended in 1996 by the Interethnic Placement Provisions. Multiethnic Placement Act of 1994, Pub. L. No. 103-382, 108 Stat. 405, as amended by the Removal of Barriers to Interethnic Adoption Provisions of the Small Business Job Protection Act of 1996, Pub. L. No. 104-188, 110 Stat. 1755, §1808. Together, these enactments prohibit agencies that receive federal funding from denying or delaying adoption (or foster care) placements based on considerations of race, color, or national origin, and also requires states to make diligent efforts to recruit a diverse pool of potential foster and adoptive families that reflects the race and ethnicity of children needing out-of-home placements. Violations of MEPA also violate Title VI of the Civil Rights Act of 1964, which prohibits discrimination based on race, color, or national origin in programs and activities that receive federal funding, and the Office of Civil Rights is responsible for receiving and investigating complaints regarding MEPA violations.

MEPA's ban is not absolute. Consistent with the strict scrutiny standard that is deployed in constitutional cases involving discrimination on the basis of race, color, or national origin, consideration of these factors is permissible in individual cases where necessary to achieve the compelling governmental interest of promoting the best interest of a particular child.

G. ADOPTION ABROGATION AND THE TORT OF WRONGFUL ADOPTION

Like any other parents, most adoptive parents are prepared to handle the daily vicissitudes that come with raising children. However, what happens if they come to regret their decision due to the fact that the experience proves far more difficult than expected because, for example, unbeknownst to them, the child had previously experienced severe physical and sexual abuse or is genetically predisposed to a debilitating disease. Should they be permitted to abrogate or undo the adoption?

The majority view is that children cannot be sent back — that once finalized, adoptions cannot be undone based on parental dissatisfaction with the child. Underlying this position is the recognition that children are not goods that can be

---

[5]For additional discussion, see Cynthia G. Hawkins-Leon & Carla Bradley, Mid-Atlantic People of Color Legal Scholarship Conference: Race and Transracial Adoption: The Answer Is Neither Simply Black Nor White or Wrong, 51 Cath. U. L. Rev. 1227 (2002); Valerie Phillips Herman, Transracial Adoption: "Child-Saving" or "Child-Snatching," 13 Natl. Black L.J. 147 (1993).

returned if they later are viewed as "damaged." However, this position is not universal. A few states, either by statute or judicial decision, permit parents to undo an adoption in what are deemed extraordinary circumstances, such as where a child is facing a lifetime of institutional care; however, most judges are wary of these actions because they effectively orphan the child. Note, however, that as with any parent, if adoptive parents cannot care for their child, they may eventually lose their parental rights due to abuse or neglect.

However, in contrast to situations involving an attempt to abrogate an adoption based upon the adoptive parents' dissatisfaction with the child or their concerns that they cannot provide the child with the kind of care needed, the law tends to be somewhat more lenient where the abrogation is premised upon procedural defects in the adoption proceeding. Most commonly in this category of case are claims by the adoptive parents that the agency engaged in fraud or deliberate misrepresentation by, for example, telling them that a child had no history of mental disorders when it knew the child had been institutionalized for mental illness in order to induce them to adopt a child that they might not have otherwise taken into their home. In this situation, some courts are willing to undo an adoption based upon their authority to vacate court judgments for fraud in accordance with the rules of civil procedure.

However, based on the recognition that this approach disregards the interests of the adopted child, a number of states no longer permit adoptive parents to set aside an adoption based upon fraud or misrepresentation, but instead permit them to sue the agency for "wrongful adoption" in order to recover damages for unanticipated expenses, which might include, for example, residential care or extraordinary medical treatments. In allowing these damage suits, courts have been careful to make clear that adoption agencies cannot be expected to guarantee that adopted children develop as happy and healthy children. At the same time, they have emphasized that adoptive parents are entitled to rely on the accuracy of the information they obtain from an agency when seeking to make an informed choice about whether or not they wish to proceed with the adoption of a particular child.

Chapter Summary

- Through adoption, a child acquires new parents who assume all of the rights and responsibilities previously vested in the biological parents, and the child's legal relationship with his or her birth parents is extinguished. This cut-off rule is subject to limited exceptions, most commonly in stepparent and co-parent adoptions.
- Adoptions can be accomplished through an agency or by the parents themselves acting with or without the assistance of a third-party intermediary.
- Most states now have safe haven laws, which permit birth parents to anonymously drop a newborn off at a designated location without fear of being prosecuted for abandonment.

- An adoption cannot proceed without the consent of the birth parents, subject to a limited exception for some unwed fathers, unless parental rights have been terminated or the court has approved a request to dispense with parental consent.

- In private placement adoptions, the consent attaches to the adoption itself; in an agency adoption, the consent attaches to the relinquishment of the child to the agency, which in turn acquires the right of consent.

- Most states allow a birth parent to revoke consent under specific circumstances; some states give birth parents considerable latitude, while others are quite strict; however, in all jurisdictions, it is harder to revoke a relinquishment to an agency.

- In most situations, the child must live with the prospective adoptive parents in a pre-adoption placement before the adoption can be finalized.

- In an agency adoption, placement will not be made until a home study has been completed, and the placement is supervised by the agency. Post-placement social studies are done in both agency and private placement adoptions in order to assist the judge in deciding whether to approve the adoption. This decision is based on the best interest standard.

- Many states now allow open adoptions, which permit post-adoption contact between the adopted child and the birth parent. Additionally, most states now permit the release of nonidentifying information to adopted children, and many now permit the release of identifying information in accordance with specific procedures, which may result in communication between an adult adoptee and his or her birth parents.

- Stepparent adoptions account for a considerable number of yearly adoptions. Here, in a significant exception to the cut-off rule, the parental rights of the custodial spouse survive the adoption.

- While many states prohibit joint adoption by same-sex couples, now that same-sex couples can marry, married same-sex couples are likely to enjoy the same rights as heterosexual married couples.

- Unwed fathers now have considerably more rights in the adoption arena than they had in the past and may be entitled to consent rights based on a substantial parenting commitment or an acknowledgment of paternity or the filing of notice in a putative father registry.

- Presently, federal law prohibits delays in or denials of adoption placements based on considerations of race, color, or national origin.

- When an adoption does not live up to parental expectations, most courts will not permit the parents to abrogate or undo the adoption, although abrogation has been permitted by some courts under extraordinary circumstances. Where the agency has breached its obligation to properly disclose information, parents may be able to sue the agency in tort for wrongful adoption.

Applying the Rules

1. Cassie and Karen are a same-sex couple and live together, but they have decided not to get married. They would, however, like to adopt Sasha, a two-year-old foster child of Cassie. Cassie has been Sasha's foster mother for the past eight months. Cassie and Karen come to you to ask what challenges they might face in doing a joint adoption of Sasha. What do you tell Cassie and Karen?

2. Assume the same facts as in Question 1, but Cassie and Karen are married. Cassie and Karen come to you because they have been advised by the local adoption agency that a state law allows the agency to give adoption preference to heterosexual couples over same-sex couples. Based only on the readings in this chapter, are there any arguments you can make for Cassie and Karen to help them build a case that they should be given preference to adopt Sasha?

3. Tom and Prisha would like to adopt Dustin, who is of their same racial and religious background. Equally qualified to adopt Dustin are Bob and Patty. However, Bob and Patty are of a different racial and religious background than Dustin but have been on the prospective parent adoption list for twice as long as Tom and Prisha. The agency that is in the process of placing Dustin for adoption has come to you and asked whether they should place Dustin with Tom and Prisha, or Bob and Patty. What do you tell them?

4. A state law provides that "[e]xcept where a husband and wife adopt jointly, no person shall be adopted by more than one person." Beth and Virginia are legally married. They would like to adopt Ben, who is currently in their foster care. What arguments can be made for Beth and Virginia to allow them to adopt Ben? What objections might they face?

5. Danny and Alma were divorced when their son Ian was five years old, and Danny was awarded primary physical and legal custody of Ian. Danny married Sally three years after his divorce from Alma, and Ian has lived with the two of them. Now Sally wants to adopt Ian. A state law provides that notice of a stepparent adoption must be given to the biological parent and the biological parent has 30 days to file a written objection to the adoption. Alma was properly served with notice of the stepparent adoption. She did not file a notice of objection, but she did show up at the hearing where the adoption was to be finalized and objected to the adoption. What should the trial court do?

6. A state law provides that a man who believes he may have fathered a child must register his name in the putative father's registry anytime within 30 days after the birth of the child. Steve believes that his girlfriend Delia is pregnant with his child, but he is unsure, and he would rather not have to pay child support if it turns out that it is not his child. Unfortunately, Steve had not considered that Delia might give the baby up for adoption, but was under the impression that

he could still see the child but not have to pay child support by not claiming the child as his. After the birth of the child, Delia and Steve attempted to live together, but things did not work out, and one day Delia took off with the baby and did not come back. It has now been six months and Steve, through a private investigator, found Delia, but she no longer had the baby with her. Delia told Steve that, unable to care for the child on her own, she gave the baby up for adoption. Steve asks you what remedies he may have. What do you tell Steve?

Family Law in Practice

1. Determine whether private placement adoptions are permitted in your jurisdiction. If they are, determine the following by consulting the relevant statutory and/or regulatory provisions:

   a. Are prospective adoptive parents subject to a certification requirement?
   b. Is the use of intermediaries allowed?
   c. If so, are they subject to any legal requirements, such as limitations of fees and costs or accounting requirements?

2. Determine what the rules are in your jurisdiction governing when a parent can revoke his or her consent to an adoption. In developing your answer, detail both the substantive standards as well as the procedural requirements. To do this, you may need to consult both the relevant statutory and regulatory provisions as well as case law.

3. Locate an adoption agency in your area and interview someone who works there and write a memorandum. In your interview, see if you can determine the following:

   a. Does the agency specialize in a particular type of adoption?
   b. How does it screen parents who want to adopt?
   c. What is the cost of a typical adoption?
   d. How long does the typical adoption take?
   e. What areas of inquiry are of particular importance when conducting a home study?
   f. Does the agency ever revoke placements? Under what circumstances?

4. Assume that you are the judge in a *Baby Richard* situation. Write your opinion setting out how you would decide the case and why.

5. Assume you have a client seeking a co-parent adoption and you need to file a petition on his behalf. As there is no law in your jurisdiction on co-parent adoptions, locate rulings from other jurisdictions that both permit and deny second-parent adoptions. Carefully read and analyze the cases you have located, and prepare a memorandum setting out the essential reasons behind the court decisions.

Assisted Reproductive Technologies

This chapter introduces you to some of the complex legal and ethical issues that are raised in achieving pregnancy through the use of assisted reproduction technologies (ART). The Centers for Disease Control (CDC) defines ART to include

> all fertility treatments in which both eggs and sperm are handled. In general, ART procedures involve surgically removing eggs from a woman's ovaries, combining them with sperm in the laboratory, and returning them to the woman's body or donating them to another woman. They do NOT include treatments in which only sperm are handled.[1]

This definition is used for the purpose of the mandatory reporting of clinic-specific pregnancy success rates pursuant to the 1992 Fertility Clinic Rate and Certification Act of 1992, which was adopted in order to provide potential ART users with "an idea of their average chance of success" in response to concerns about false advertising.[2] Thus, the definition excludes sperm donations. However, ART can include all procedures including artificial insemination, in vitro fertilization, and surrogacy.

This chapter does not focus on the establishment of parental rights in the context of sperm donation outside of the surrogacy context as this topic is addressed in Chapter 12. Rather, the chapter focuses on topics in the family law context related to gestational surrogacy law and disposition of frozen embryos.

Key Concepts

- Definitional expansion of assisted reproductive technology
- Validity of surrogacy contracts
- The rights of gestational carriers
- The disposition of frozen embryos

---

[1] CDC, What Is Assisted Reproductive Technology?, http://www.cdc.gov/art/whatis.html (accessed June 8, 2016).
[2] CDC, National ART Surveillance, http://www.cdc.gov/art/nas/index.html (accessed June 8, 2016).

A. GENERAL OVERVIEW

Noted above is the definition of assisted reproductive technology by the CDC. However, state laws sometimes define the term more expansively to include any process by which a pregnancy is accomplished by means other than sexual intercourse. This expansive definition brings donor insemination within the definitional boundaries of assisted reproduction under some state laws. However, given the lack of extensive case law in this area, definitional challenges often arise.

Bruce v. Boardwine, 770 S.E.2d 774 (Va. Ct. App. 2015), is an example of the definitional challenges sometimes faced by the courts. The Virginia statute in issue provided that unless the sperm donor is the husband of the gestational mother, the donor is "not the parent of a child conceived through assisted conception." The purpose was to allow married couples to obtain sperm donations without the fear that the donor would come back and attempt to claim parental rights. "Assisted conception" in turn was defined as "a pregnancy resulting from any intervening medical technology. . . ." *Id.* at 776. Joyce Bruce wanted to raise a child on her own and believed that if "she became pregnant in a way that did not involve sexual intercourse the biological father would not have a claim to any parental rights." *Id.* at 775. She asked a long-time friend of hers, Robert Boardwine, to be a sperm donor. However, the parties did not go through a doctor's office or medical facility for the insemination. Rather, on several different occasions, Robert came to Joyce's home, went to a separate room, and then he would give her a plastic container with his sperm before leaving the house. After he left, Joyce would use an "ordinary turkey baster to inseminate herself." *Id.* Joyce conceived a child and after the birth of the child, Robert sought legal recognition as the child's father. *Id.* The trial court ruled in favor of declaring Robert the father of the child and entitled to parental rights. The Court of Appeals agreed reasoning that "the plain meaning of the term 'medical technology' does not encompass a kitchen implement such as a turkey baster." *Id.* at 777. As a result, Robert was entitled to establish his parental rights based upon evidence of genetic paternity. *Id.* at 778.

Although not addressed by the appeals court, the trial court made clear that biology alone was not enough to establish Bruce's paternal rights, but that he was also required to prove by "clear and convincing evidence" that the parties intended for him to be the legal father. *See Boardwine v. Bruce*, 22-29 (Va. Cir. Ct. May 6, 2014). This is similar to the legal standard we saw in Chapter 12 in discussion of a father's rights.

B. SURROGACY

At its core, surrogacy is an arrangement in which a woman (the surrogate) agrees to become pregnant and bear a child for an individual or a couple (the intended parent[s]), and to relinquish the child together with her parental rights to them at the time of birth. As it has been the primary site of legal contestation, our focus here is on commercial, as distinct from "altruistic," surrogacy. In contrast to an altruistic arrangement, which typically involves a woman who agrees to bear a child to help out an infertile friend or relative without any expectation of compensation beyond perhaps pregnancy-related expenses, participants in a commercial arrangement are usually strangers who are bound by a formal contractual agreement in which the intended parents promise to compensate the surrogate in exchange for her promise to carry and relinquish the child to them. Surrogacy arrangements can also be distinguished in terms of whether the surrogate has both a genetic and a gestational connection to the child (traditional surrogacy) or only has a gestational link (gestational surrogacy) to the child by being inseminated with both a donor egg and donor sperm.

There is no uniform or federal law on surrogacy contracts. Therefore, the definitions and legality of surrogacy contracts have been left up to the states to adopt and define either by state statute or case law. Traditionally, states have taken a variety of approaches with respect to the validity of surrogate parenting contracts. A handful of states have banned surrogacy by way of statute or case law, which, of course, means that surrogacy contracts are void and unenforceable; in a few of these states, parties may also be subject to the risk of a fine or imprisonment.

Other states permit surrogacy; however, they may have specific requirements that must be met in order for a surrogate parenting agreement to be enforceable, including, for example, that the intending parents be a married couple, or that one or both of them have a genetic link to the child. As a general rule, if these requirements are met, the intending parents can petition the court for a pre-birth parentage order, which identifies them as the legal parents of the child born to the surrogate. This provides them with immediate access to and control of the baby when born. It also allows their names to be placed on the birth certificate. Still other states have no law on the subject. Arguably, surrogacy is therefore allowed since it is not formally prohibited, and intending parents may accordingly be able to obtain a pre-birth parentage order.

With marriage equality now the law of the land as a result of the *Obergefell v. Hodges* case, there has been renewed emphasis in surrogacy legislation on ensuring that same-sex married couples have the same rights as heterosexual married couples. In states that permitted surrogacy for married intended parents prior to *Obergefell*, after this Supreme Court decision, these laws were applied equally to all married couples regardless of sexual orientation. Today, with the exception of Mississippi, in states that permit surrogacy contracts, both married heterosexual couples and same-sex couples are treated the same for commercial surrogacy.

1. Traditional Surrogacy

Traditional surrogacy is when the surrogate agrees to become pregnant by artificial insemination in order to give birth to a child that will be given to the intended parents. The woman uses her own eggs and is therefore biologically related to the child. The donor sperm may be from an unknown donor or from one of the intended parents. This traditional surrogacy in the context of parties that are not related and not engaging in surrogacy for an altruistic purpose is considered commercial surrogacy. As seen below in *In re Baby M*, 537 A.2d 1227 (1988), and *Johnson v. Calvert*, 851 P.2d 776, *cert. denied*, 510 U.S. 874 (1993), commercial surrogacy is a controversial practice with legal ramifications that may not have been considered at the time of the initial surrogacy contract.

We start the analysis with the *Baby M* case (in which the initial M was used to protect the identity of the baby later known to be named "Melissa"), one of the earliest litigated commercial surrogacy cases. The case is an important backdrop to understanding the future of surrogacy contracts as the case directly shaped the first wave of surrogacy laws in the country.

Case Preview

In re Baby M

The iconic *Baby M* case involved a dispute over the enforceability of a surrogate parenting contract pursuant to which Mary Beth Whitehead (the surrogate) agreed to be inseminated with the sperm of William Stern (one of the intended parents) and, if a pregnancy resulted, to relinquish the resulting child to Mr. Stern and his wife, Elizabeth, and to further relinquish to Mr. Stern her parental rights in exchange for payment in

William and Elizabeth Stern, who entered into a surrogate parenting agreement with Mary Beth Whitehead
AP Photo/Peter Cannata

the amount of $10,000. Mary Beth's husband, Richard Whitehead, was also made a party to the contract in order to secure his commitment to relinquishing any claims to the child based upon the marital presumption. In contrast, Elizabeth Stern, who was without either a genetic or a presumptive path to parenthood, was deliberately not made a party to the contract in order to avoid the suggestion that this was an agreement for the sale of a child from one woman to another, which would be illegal under New Jersey law.

As you read the *Baby M* case, look for the following:

1. What were the terms of the contract between the Whiteheads and the Sterns?
2. What terms, or lack of terms, did the contract have that violated New Jersey statutory law?
3. What role did the best interest of the minor child have in the court's decision?

In re Baby M
537 A.2d 1227 (N.J. 1988)

. . .

In February 1985, William Stern and Mary Beth Whitehead entered into a surrogacy contract. It recited that Stern's wife, Elizabeth, was infertile, that they wanted a child, and that Mrs. Whitehead was willing to provide that child as the mother with Mr. Stern as the father.

The contract provided that through artificial insemination using Mr. Stern's sperm, Mrs. Whitehead would become pregnant, carry the child to term, bear it, deliver it to the Sterns, and thereafter do whatever was necessary to terminate her maternal rights so that Mrs. Stern could thereafter adopt the child. Mrs. Whitehead's husband, Richard, was also a party to the contract; Mrs. Stern was not. Mr. Whitehead promised to do all the acts necessary to rebut the presumption of paternity [under New Jersey law]. Although Mrs. Stern was not a party to the surrogacy agreement, the contract gave her sole custody of the child in the event of Mr. Stern's death. Mrs. Stern's status as a nonparty to the surrogate parenting agreement presumably was to avoid the application of the baby-selling statute to this agreement.

[The Sterns agreed to pay Mrs. Whitehead $10,000 after the child's birth, and $7,500 to the Infertility Center of New York for bringing the parties together.]

. . .

The pregnancy was uneventful and on March 27, 1986, Baby M was born. . . . [Mrs. Whitehead] turned her child over to the Sterns on March 30 at the Whiteheads' home. [However, later that evening] Mrs. Whitehead became deeply disturbed, disconsolate, stricken with unbearable sadness. She had to have her child. She could not eat, sleep, or concentrate on anything other than her need for her baby. The next day she went to the Sterns' home and told them how much she was suffering.

[Mrs. Whitehead told the Sterns she could not live without the baby and that she needed to have the baby back at least for one week and after that she would return the child to them. The Sterns were afraid that Mrs. Whitehead might commit suicide, and believing she would indeed return the child, they let Mrs. Whitehead take the baby home with her. Mrs. Whitehead did not return the baby, and it was discovered that Mary Beth Whitehead, Richard Whitehead, their ten-year-old daughter, and the baby had disappeared. Their whereabouts remained unknown to the Sterns for 87 days, when it was finally discovered that they were living in Florida in a home owned by Mary Beth Whitehead's parents. The Sterns received an order for return of the child to them and an order to give the Sterns temporary custody pending final judgment. Mrs. Whitehead was awarded limited visitation with Baby M.]

The trial took thirty-two days over a period of more than two months. . . . [T]he trial court announced its opinion from the bench. It held that the surrogacy contract was valid; ordered that Mrs. Whitehead's parental right be terminated and that sole custody of the child be granted to Mr. Stern; and, after hearing brief testimony from Mrs. Stern, immediately entered an order allowing the adoption [of Baby M] all in accordance with the surrogacy contract. . . .

Although clearly expressing its view that the surrogacy contract was valid, the trial court devoted the major portion of its opinion to the question of the baby's best interests. The inconsistency is apparent. The surrogacy contract calls for the surrender of the child to the Sterns, permanent and sole custody in the Sterns, and termination of Mrs. Whitehead's parental rights, all without qualification, all regardless of any evaluation of the best interests of the child. As a matter of fact the contract recites (even before the child was conceived) that it is in the best interest of the child to be placed with Mr. Stern. In effect, the trial court awarded custody to Mr. Stern, the natural father, based on the same kind of evidence and analysis as might be expected had no surrogacy contract existed. . . .

On the question of best interest — we agree, but for different reasons, that custody was the critical issue. . . . We agree substantially with both its analysis and conclusions on the matter of custody. . . . The court's review and analysis of the surrogacy contract, however, is not at all in accord with ours.

The Sterns claim that the surrogacy contract is valid and enforced, largely for the reasons given by the trial court. They claim a right of privacy, which includes the right of procreation, and the right of consenting adults to deal with matters of reproduction as they see fit. As for the child's best interests, their position is factual: given all of the circumstances, the child is better off in their custody with no residual parental rights reserved for Mrs. Whitehead.

. . .

We have concluded that this surrogacy contract is invalid. Our conclusion has two bases: direct conflict with existing statutes and conflict with the public policies of this State. . . .

A. CONFLICT WITH STATUTORY PROVISIONS

The surrogacy contract conflicts with: (1) laws prohibiting the use of money in connection with adoptions; (2) laws requiring proof of parental unfitness or abandonment before termination of parental rights is ordered or an adoption is granted; and (3) laws that make surrender of custody and consent to adoption revocable in private placement adoptions. . . . Our statutes, and the cases interpreting them, leave no doubt that where there has been no written surrender to an approved agency [or state agency] termination of parental rights will not be granted in this state absent a strong showing of abandonment or neglect. . . . It is clear that a "best interests" determination is never sufficient to terminate parental rights; the statutory criteria must be proved. . . . The provision of the surrogacy contract stating Mary Beth Whitehead agrees to "surrender custody . . . and terminate all parental rights" contains no clause giving her a right to rescind.

B. PUBLIC POLICY CONSIDERATIONS

The surrogacy contract's invalidity, resulting from its direct conflict with the above statutory provisions, is further underlined when its goals and means are measured against New Jersey's public policy. The contract's basic premise, that the natural parents can decide in advance of birth which one is to have custody of the child, bears no relationship to the settled law that the child's best interests shall determine custody. . . . The surrogacy contract guarantees permanent separation of the child from one of its natural parents. Our policy, however, has long been that to the extent possible, children should remain with and be brought up by both of their natural parents.

. . .

In sum, the harmful consequences of this surrogacy arrangement appear to us all too palpable. In New Jersey the surrogate mother's agreement to sell her child is void. Its irrevocability infects the entire contract, as does the money that purports to buy it.

. . .

We have found that our present laws do not permit the surrogacy contract used in this case. Nowhere, however, do we find any legal prohibitions against surrogacy when the surrogate mother volunteers, without any payment, to act as a surrogate and is given the right to change her mind and to assert her parental rights. . . .

The judgment is affirmed in part, reversed in part, and remanded for further proceedings consistent with this opinion.

Post-Case Follow-Up

On remand from the New Jersey Supreme Court, Mr. Stern was declared the father of Melissa (Baby M), and the trial court permitted liberal unsupervised visitations for Mary Beth. Mary Beth Whitehead went on to be an outspoken spokesperson against surrogacy and wrote a book about her ordeal. She appeared on television talk shows and was interviewed for magazines. A full-length movie was made based on the events.

When Melissa turned 18, she signed papers to allow Elizabeth Stern to formally adopt her. Melissa married in 2012, in a ceremony performed by Harvey M. Sorkow, the trial court judge in the original case. Melissa and her husband are reportedly living in London where Melissa works as a medical writer.

Under current New Jersey law, "[u]nless the donor of semen and the woman have entered into a written contract to the contrary, the donor of semen provided to a licensed physician for use in artificial insemination of a woman other than the donor's wife is treated in law as if he were not the father of a child thereby conceived and shall have no rights or duties stemming from the conception of a child." N.J. Stat. Ann. §9:17-44 Artificial insemination (New Jersey Statutes (2016 edition)).

In re Baby M: Real Life Applications

1. Dereck is an unmarried male lawyer who wanted to become a parent by having a child that was his biological child. He asked his friend, Shayna, an unmarried female actress, if she would agree to carry his child and give sole custody to him, and in exchange he would take full responsibility for the child with no financial commitment from Shayna. Shayna said she was in between movie roles and could use a little extra money and asked that Dereck pay all the medical expenses and provide her with an additional $10,000. She also wanted to make sure that Dereck was serious that she would have no responsibility for the child. Dereck agreed and Shayna went through an artificial insemination process at a local fertility clinic with Dereck's sperm. The process was successful and Shayna gave birth to twin girls. Dereck was identified as the father on the birth certificate, and the parties agreed that Dereck could obtain a court order terminating Shayna's parental rights to the girls. However, shortly after the birth

Shayna became distraught over the thought of losing custody of the children and objected to Dereck's attempt to terminate her parental rights. Under the *Baby M* case, what result?

2. Assume the same facts as in Question 1, but there is no compensation paid as Shayna was doing a movie role in which she is pregnant and thought it would be easier if she were actually pregnant for the role. Under the *Baby M* case, what result?

3. Assume the same facts as in Questions 1 and 2, but in addition, the parties sign a contract with the fertility clinic in which Shayna is advised in the contract that she will give up her parental rights to any resulting child to the sperm donor, Dereck. Under the *Baby M* case, what result?

4. If Dereck came to your office and showed you the contract as set forth in Question 3, is there anything you would want Dereck to make sure is included in the contract so that his right to obtain sole custody of any resulting children is protected?

---

2. Gestational Surrogacy

Although the court in the *Baby M* case faced the difficult and novel issue of whether a surrogate parenting contract is enforceable, it did not have to address the equally difficult question of who Baby M's mother was, as it was clear that Mary Beth Whitehead, who had both a genetic and gestational relationship with her, was the child's legal mother. However, the advent of gestational surrogacy, which is now the preferred arrangement as it weakens the surrogate's claim that she is the legal mother of the resulting child due to the lack of a genetic connection between them, has interwoven the vexing question of how maternity is to be determined when more than one woman claims the status of legal mother into the already potent ethical and legal debates about surrogacy.

Gestational surrogacy involves the extracorporeal creation of embryos through a procedure known as in vitro fertilization (IVF). Very briefly, this is a multistep process in which the intended mother (or an egg donor) typically injects herself with fertility drugs over approximately a two-week period to stimulate the production of multiple ripe eggs, rather than the single mature egg that is naturally produced in the course of a woman's monthly menstrual cycle, in order to increase the likelihood of an eventual successful pregnancy. Egg maturation is carefully monitored, and when they are at the correct stage of development, they are surgically aspirated using a hollow needle. The aspirated eggs are then mixed with the intending father's (or a donor's) sperm, and one or more resulting embryos are transferred into the uterus of the surrogate whose cycle has been managed with hormonal injections in order to suppress her natural ovulation and ready her uterus for the transfer.

By its very nature, gestational surrogacy disaggregates the genetic component of motherhood from the gestational one, which, of course raises the profound question of how legal motherhood is to be determined when these biological connections are allocated between two women. Moreover, if an egg donor is used, three potential women may be able to assert a maternal claim based on the intent to become a parent, the genetic link to the child, or the gestational link to the child.

Johnson v. Calvert provides an example of the shift from traditional to gestational surrogacy. Although our primary interest is in the court's novel approach to determining maternity where one woman claims a genetic link to the child and the other a gestational one, we also consider its overall approach to the validity of surrogate parenting contracts, as it is at the opposite end of the spectrum from the New Jersey high court.

Case Preview

Johnson v. Calvert

Mark and Crispina Calvert entered into a gestational surrogate contract with Anna Johnson. In exchange for the sum of $10,000, Anna agreed that an embryo created from Mark's sperm and Crispina's egg would be transferred to her uterus, and that upon birth, she would relinquish the child and all parental rights to the Calverts. Eventually, the relationship between the parties soured, and Mark and Crispina sought a declaration from the court that they were the legal parents of the unborn child. Anna then filed her own action seeking to be declared the child's mother based on her gestational link to the child.

As you read *Johnson v. Calvert*, look for the following:

1. How did the court define "natural mother" of the child?
2. What were the terms of the agreement that the surrogate claimed were unenforceable?
3. Why did the court reject the analogy to artificial insemination? What is the difference in cases involving artificial insemination and this case?

Johnson v. Calvert
851 P.2d 776 (Cal. 1993)

In this case we address several of the legal questions raised by recent advances in reproductive technology. When, pursuant to a surrogacy agreement, a zygote formed of the gametes of a husband and wife is implanted in the uterus of another woman, who carries the resulting fetus to term and gives birth to a child not genetically related to her, who is the child's "natural mother" under California law? Does a determination that the wife is the child's natural mother work a deprivation of the gestating woman's constitutional rights? And is such an agreement barred by any public policy of this state?

We conclude that the husband and wife are the child's natural parents, and that this result does not offend the state or federal Constitution or public policy.

On January 15, 1990, Mark, Crispina, and Anna signed a contract providing that an embryo created by the sperm of Mark and the egg of Crispina would be implanted in Anna and the child born would be taken into Mark and Crispina's home "as their child." Anna agreed she would relinquish "all parental rights" to the child in favor of Mark and Crispina. In return, Mark and Crispina would pay Anna $10,000 in a series of installments, the last to be paid six weeks after the child's birth. Mark and Crispina were also to pay for a $200,000 life insurance policy on Anna's life.

The zygote was implanted on January 19, 1990. Less than a month later, an ultrasound test confirmed Anna was pregnant.

Unfortunately, relations deteriorated between the two sides. Mark learned that Anna had not disclosed she had suffered several stillbirths and miscarriages. Anna felt Mark and Crispina did not do enough to obtain the required insurance policy. She also felt abandoned during an onset of premature labor in June.

In July 1990, Anna sent Mark and Crispina a letter demanding the balance of the payments due her or else she would refuse to give up the child. The following month, Mark and Crispina responded with a lawsuit, seeking a declaration they were the legal parents of the unborn child. Anna filed her own action to be declared the mother of the child, and the two cases were eventually consolidated. The parties agreed to an independent guardian ad litem for the purposes of the suit.

The child was born on September 19, 1990, and blood samples were obtained from both Anna and the child for analysis. The blood test results excluded Anna as the genetic mother. The parties agreed to a court order providing that the child would remain with Mark and Crispina on a temporary basis with visits by Anna.

At trial in October 1990, the parties stipulated that Mark and Crispina were the child's genetic parents. After hearing evidence and arguments, the trial court ruled that Mark and Crispina were the child's "genetic, biological and natural" father and mother, that Anna had no "parental" rights to the child, and that the surrogacy contract was legal and enforceable against Anna's claims. The court also terminated the order allowing visitation. Anna appealed from the trial court's judgment. The Court of Appeal for the Fourth District, Division Three, affirmed. We granted review.

The Uniform Parentage Act (the Act) was part of a package of legislation introduced in 1975 as Senate Bill No. 347. The legislation's purpose was to eliminate the legal distinction between legitimate and illegitimate children. The Act followed in the wake of certain United States Supreme Court decisions mandating equal treatment of legitimate and illegitimate children. (See, e.g., *Levy v. Louisiana* (1968) 391 U.S. 68, 88 S. Ct. 1509, 20 L. Ed. 2d 436 [state could not deny illegitimate child right to bring tort action for wrongful death of parent if it gave legitimate child the same right]. . . .

Passage of the Act clearly was not motivated by the need to resolve surrogacy disputes, which were virtually unknown in 1975. Yet it facially applies to any parentage determination, including the rare case in which a child's maternity is in issue. We are invited to disregard the Act and decide this case according to other criteria, including constitutional precepts and our sense of the demands of public policy. We feel constrained, however, to decline the invitation. Not uncommonly, courts must construe statutes in factual settings not contemplated by the enacting legislature.

[The parties'] contentions are readily summarized. Anna, of course, predicates her claim of maternity on the fact that she gave birth to the child. The Calverts contend that Crispina's genetic relationship to the child establishes that she is his mother.

. . .

Anna's argument depends on a prior determination that she is indeed the child's mother. Since Crispina is the child's mother under California law because she, not Anna, provided the ovum for the in vitro fertilization procedure, intending to raise the child as her own, it follows that any constitutional interests Anna possesses in this situation are something less than those of a mother. . . .

Anna relies principally on the decision of the United States Supreme Court in *Michael H. v. Gerald D.* (1989) 491 U.S. 110, 109 S. Ct. 2333, 105 L. Ed. 2d 91, to support her claim to a constitutionally protected liberty interest in the companionship of the child, based on her status as "birth mother." In that case, a plurality of the court held that a state may constitutionally deny a man parental rights with respect to a child he fathered during a liaison with the wife of another man, since it is the marital family that traditionally has been accorded a protected liberty interest, as reflected in the historic presumption of legitimacy of a child born into such a family. (491 U.S. at pp. 124-125, 109 S. Ct. at pp. 2342-2343 (plur. opn. by Scalia, J.).) The reasoning of the plurality in *Michael H.* does not assist Anna. Society has not traditionally protected the right of a woman who gestates and delivers a baby pursuant to an agreement with a couple who supply the zygote from which the baby develops and who intend to raise the child as their own; such arrangements are of too recent an origin to claim the protection of tradition. To the extent that tradition has a bearing on the present case, we believe it supports the claim of the couple who exercise their right to procreate in order to form a family of their own, albeit through novel medical procedures.

. . .

Drawing an analogy to artificial insemination, Anna argues that Mark and Crispina were mere genetic donors who are entitled to no constitutional protection. That characterization of the facts is, however, inaccurate. Mark and Crispina never intended to "donate" genetic material to anyone. Rather, they intended to procreate a child genetically related to them by the only available means. . . .

Finally, Anna argues that the Act's failure to address novel reproductive techniques such as in vitro fertilization indicates legislative disapproval of such practices. Given that the Act was drafted long before such techniques were developed, we cannot agree. Moreover, we may not arrogate to ourselves the power to disapprove them. It is not the role of the judiciary to inhibit the use of reproductive technology when the Legislature has not seen fit to do so; any such effort would raise serious questions in light of the fundamental nature of the rights of procreation and privacy. Rather, our task has been to resolve the dispute before us, interpreting the Act's use of the term "natural mother" (Civ. Code, §7003, subd. (1)) when the biological functions essential to bringing a child into the world have been allocated between two women.

DISPOSITION

The judgment of the Court of Appeal is affirmed.

Post-Case Follow-Up

Two aspects of *Johnson v. Calvert* deserve additional attention in analyzing the California Supreme Court's treatment of the validity of a gestational surrogacy contract versus the unenforceability of a traditional surrogacy contract ruled upon by the New Jersey Supreme Court in the *Baby M* case. First, the California court acknowledged that acts such as the Uniform Parentage Act were enacted in a time when surrogacy contracts were virtually unknown. Thus, the court relied on language in the Act that states that a parent-child relationship "may be established by proof of [a person] giving birth to the child" as well as on provisions allowing for the establishment of a parent-child relationship based upon "genetic evidence derived from blood testing," in concluding that both women had "adduced evidence of a mother and child relationship as contemplated by the Act." *Id.* at 780-781. Finding no "clear legislative preference as between blood testing evidence and proof of having given birth," one possible outcome would have been to declare that both women had a legally cognizable parenting relationship with the child. The court, however, rejected this option stating that "for any child California law recognizes only one natural mother, despite advances in reproductive technology rendering a different outcome biologically possible." *Id.* at 782.

The court also gave rather short shrift to the kinds of legal and policy concerns that ultimately led the Supreme Court of New Jersey to hold that surrogacy parenting contracts are void and unenforceable due to their exploitative nature. The court was quite unsympathetic to Anna Johnson's concern that "surrogacy contracts tend to exploit or dehumanize women, especially women of lower economic status." Although acknowledging that "common sense suggests that women of lesser means serve as surrogate mothers more often than do wealthy women," it nonetheless discounted the potential for exploitation in light of a lack of proof that "surrogacy contracts exploit poor women to any greater degree than economic necessity in general exploits them by inducing them to accept lower-paid or otherwise undesirable employment." *Id.* at 780-781. In rejecting the exploitation argument, the court embraced the view that the failure to enforce such agreements would be a form of legal paternalism; the suggestion that "a woman cannot knowingly and intelligently agree to gestate and deliver a baby for intending parents carries overtones of the reasoning that for centuries prevented women from attaining equal economic rights and professional status under the law."

Finally, Anna fared no better with respect to the constitutional dimensions of the case. The court remarked that any recognition of a protected "liberty interest in the companionship of the child" would necessarily infringe the rights of the Calverts, whose interests as the "natural" parents of the child were entitled to protection from impairment of any kind.

Johnson v. Calvert: Real Life Applications

1. Elisa and Emily entered into a same-sex relationship and began living together six months later. They introduced each other to their friends as partners for life,

opened joint bank accounts, and told everyone they were in a committed relationship. Deciding to have children, but without the benefit of marriage, they each became artificially inseminated by donor sperm through a sperm bank and became pregnant at the same time. Elisa gave birth to a little boy named Chance, and Emily gave birth to twins, Mason and Mallory. Both parties took over responsibility for parenting the children; however, Elisa was the stay-at-home parent and Emily worked and provided the primary financial support. The parties have lived together for seven years, and the children refer to both Elisa and Emily as "Mom." The parties are now separating, and Elisa would like the right to adopt Mason and Mallory. Emily refuses claiming that Elisa has no biological ties to the children. Based upon your reading of *Johnson v. Calvert*, what arguments can be made for Elisa? For Emily?

2. Assume the same facts as in Question 1, but the events take place after the decision in *Obergefell v. Hodges* legalizing same-sex marriages. Elisa and Emily were married in a formal ceremony. Would your arguments for Elisa change? How should a judge rule?

3. Jake and Justin are a same-sex married couple. They have asked Ella to be a gestational carrier for them. Ella successfully becomes pregnant by a procedure in which she is inseminated with an embryo from a fertility clinic. Ella has no biological connection to the child she delivers. Ella would like to make an argument, however, that she should have visitation rights with the child because she is the "mother"; since Jake and Justin are both male, neither of them can be the mother and a child is entitled to have at least one mother. Ella asks you to advise her if her argument has any validity. What do you tell Ella?

SURROGACY PROHIBITION

Some states prohibit surrogacy and have taken the approach to deny enforcement of surrogacy contracts, and go so far as to make the surrogate the legal mother of the child born. An example is Arizona, which prohibits all types of surrogacy agreements.

Ariz. Rev. Stat. §25-218. Surrogate Parentage Contracts; Prohibition; Custody; Definition

A. No person may enter into, induce, arrange, procure or otherwise assist in the formation of a surrogate parentage contract.

B. A surrogate is the legal mother of a child born as a result of a surrogate parentage contract and is entitled to custody of that child.

C. If the mother of a child born as a result of a surrogate contract is married, her husband is presumed to be the legal father of the child. This presumption is rebuttable.

D. For the purposes of this section, "surrogate parentage contract" means a contract, agreement or arrangement in which a woman agrees to the implantation of an embryo not related to that woman or agrees to conceive a child through natural or artificial insemination and to voluntarily relinquish her parental rights to the child.

Case Preview

J.F. v. D.B.

This case highlights some of the complexity of the issues involving surrogate relationships and gestational carriers. Father lived with E.D., who was a widow with two grown children. Father had no children. The couple were not married but wanted to have children together. After unsuccessfully undergoing fertility treatments it was determined that E.D. could not conceive any additional children. Accordingly, Father and E.D. contracted with Surrogate Mothers, Inc. ("SMI"), a private surrogacy agency in Indiana. SMI matched the couple with gestational carrier, a married resident of Pennsylvania with three children of her own, and egg donor, a single woman residing in Texas. Under the contract, the gestational carrier agreed that she would not attempt to form a parent-child relationship with any child or children she might bear; that she would voluntarily relinquish any parental rights to any such child or children; and that Father would not be responsible for any lost wages, child care expenses for existing children, or any other expenses not expressly set forth in the contract. In the event that custody was somehow awarded to either the gestational carrier or the egg donor, each agreed to indemnify Father for any and all monies paid for child support, and reimburse him for any and all monies paid to either one pursuant to the surrogacy contract. Father agreed to assume legal responsibility for any child or children of his, born pursuant to the contract, and the contract also provided that any such child or children should be placed in the sole custody of E.D if Father were to die before the birth of the child or children.

Pursuant to the contract, the gestational carrier and the egg donor underwent a procedure whereby the egg donor's eggs were mixed with Father's sperm and then the resulting embryos were transferred to the gestational carrier, who was then to carry Father's child (or children) until birth at which time the child (or children) would be delivered to Father. After the birth of triplet boys, D.B. (the gestational carrier) took the boys home from the hospital and refused to give up custody to Father.

As you review the court's decision, consider the following:

1. Why did the gestational carrier believe she had standing to seek custody even though she was not biologically related to the children?
2. Why did the trial court find that the gestational carrier had standing to seek custody of the triplets?
3. Why did the appeals court conclude that this determination was in error?
4. What rights did the egg donor have?
5. Why did the court conclude that the trial court erred in its decision to void the surrogate parenting agreement?

J.F. v. D.B.

897 A.2d 1261 (Pa. Super. Ct. 2006)

Opinion by McCaffery, J.:

Appellant, J.F. ("Father"), asks us to determine whether the trial court erred in holding that D.B. ("gestational carrier") has standing to seek custody of the triplet boys she carried and delivered, after having taken them from the hospital against Father's wishes when they were eight days old. In a companion case, an action initiated by gestational carrier, Father appeals from the trial court's order terminating the parental rights of J.R. ("egg donor"). Following an exhaustive review of the record, the briefs of the parties and the pertinent law, we decline to comment on the validity of surrogacy contracts, either specifically in this case or generally in this Commonwealth. That task is for the legislature. Our holding today is limited to our conclusion that gestational carrier lacked standing to seek custody or challenge Father's custody of the triplets. As a result, gestational carrier also lacked standing to seek termination of egg donor's parental rights. Accordingly, we vacate the order of the trial court and remand the matter with directions.

. . .

[After the gestational carrier took the children home with her and refused to relinquish custody to Father, Father filed an action seeking legal custody and physical custody of the triplets.] . . .

The trial court held hearings on the issue of standing. . . . In an opinion filed April 2, 2004, the court, sua sponte, voided the surrogacy contract as against public policy for, among other things, failure to specifically name a "legal mother," "particularly if something were to happen to [intended parents], or if they were to decide not to take custody of the children." The court summarily eliminated both E.D. and egg donor as possible legal mothers, without sending either woman notice of her right to be heard or to intervene. The court further found gestational carrier was the "legal mother" of the triplets. Finally, the court concluded that gestational carrier "would most likely still have third[-]party standing in loco parentis" to seek custody, even if she were not the "legal mother" of the children.

The court then entered its order finding that gestational carrier had standing to pursue custody and child support based both on her court-conferred status as "legal mother" and her in loco parentis status. . . .

[The] gestational carrier commenced proceedings against egg donor, seeking termination of egg donor's parental rights to the triplets. Father intervened in the termination matter with the consent of all parties and asked that the case be stayed pending resolution of the custody matter. The trial court refused Father's request to put the termination matter on hold. . . .

Nearly six months after the custody trial had concluded and while the termination proceedings were ongoing, the court issued an order on January 7, 2005 ("Custody Order"), awarding primary physical custody to gestational carrier. The Custody Order also granted Father partial custody/visitation, and ordered that legal custody be shared between Father and gestational carrier. In addition, the court entered a stipulated order for child support. Father timely appealed the Custody Order.

[Following a hearing in April on] the termination matter . . . the court entered an order on June 21, 2005 ("Termination Order"), terminating egg donor's parental rights. Father timely appealed the Termination Order, as did egg donor. . . .

In his appeal . . . Father raises [among other issues] the [issue of whether the trial court erred in finding the gestational surrogate had standing to seek custody of children to which she has no genetic connection and had no intention of raising or parenting.]

. . .

As we noted above, our resolution of the custody matter necessarily resolves the termination matter. For this reason, we address first the issues Father raises in his brief challenging the Custody Order. For our purposes, Father's . . . claims can be condensed into two distinct issues. . . .

1) Whether the trial court erred in determining that gestational carrier had standing to challenge the natural father's custody of the triplets based on
a) her in loco parentis status, and/or
b) her status as the legal mother of the babies; and
2) Whether the trial court erred in granting primary physical custody to gestational carrier.

Because we find that gestational carrier has no standing to pursue custody of the children on either an in loco parentis basis or as the children's "legal mother," we do not reach the issue of whether the evidence presented at the custody hearings was sufficient to support the court's award of primary physical custody to gestational carrier.

STANDING BASED ON IN LOCO PARENTIS STATUS

Regarding the first part of the standing issue, Father contends that gestational carrier does not have in loco parentis status because she is a non-parent third party who took the children home from the hospital in defiance of his wishes. We agree.

. . .

Well-settled Pennsylvania law provides that persons other than a child's biological or natural parents are "third parties" for purposes of custody disputes. . . . "Except via dependency proceedings, third parties lack standing to seek custody as against the natural parents unless they can demonstrate a prima facie right to custody." . . . Even when standing to seek custody is conferred upon a third party, the natural parent has a "prima facie right to custody," which will be forfeited only if clear and "convincing reasons appear that the child's best interest will be served by an award to the third party. Thus, even before the proceedings start, the evidentiary scale is tipped, and tipped hard to the [biological] parents' side." *Jones v. Jones*, 884 A.2d 915, 917 (Pa. Super. 2005) (citation omitted).

. . .

The phrase "in loco parentis" refers to a person who puts oneself in the situation of a lawful parent by assuming the obligations incident to the parental relationship without going through the formality of a legal adoption. . . . The third party in this type of relationship, however, cannot place himself in loco parentis in defiance of the parents' wishes and the parent/child relationship.

. . .

When deciding the issue of standing in [under Pennsylvania law], the court must consider how the child came to be in the care of the third party, and whether the parental duties were discharged by the third party with the acquiescence of the natural parent.

. . .

There was no acquiescence or participation by Father in gestational carrier's unilateral decision to take custody of the triplets. The requirement of a natural parent's participation and acquiescence is critical to the determination of whether to accord a third party in loco parentis status. . . . The law simply cannot permit a third party to act contrary to the natural parent's wishes in obtaining custody and then benefit from that defiant conduct in a subsequent custody action. Here, the manner in which gestational carrier obtained custody of the children was fraught with impropriety, a fact completely overlooked by the trial court.

[In this case, Father and E.D. came to visit the triplets the day they were born, and E.D. made numerous calls while the babies were in the neonatal care unit to check on the health, status, and welfare of the triplets. The gestational carrier was discharged prior to the babies, and knew that Father and E.D. were taking steps to bring the babies home and that E.D. planned on adopting them. When the intended parents learned from the physicians that the triplets had to stay longer in the neonatal unit, they tried to exercise "nesting" and trained monitoring. At that point, they were told by hospital staff that the triplets had been discharged when in fact they were still in the hospital.]

. . .

Clearly, the facts of this case show unequivocally that Father at no time participated or acquiesced in gestational carrier's assuming custody of the triplets. Indeed, the very manner in which gestational carrier managed to secure custody establishes the complete lack of Father's participation and the knowledge that her actions were in defiance of Father's wishes. Hospital personnel lied to Father by telling him that the babies had been "discharged" to gestational carrier when, in fact, they were in the hospital at that moment and remained there for two more days. Our case law is very clear that there can be no finding of in loco parentis status where the third party obtains her status in defiance of the natural parent's wishes. See *B.A.*, supra; *Gradwell*, supra. Accordingly, gestational carrier's standing to pursue custody of the babies cannot be sustained on the basis of in loco parentis status and the trial court erred in ruling otherwise.

STANDING BASED ON "LEGAL MOTHER" STATUS

Father also asserts that the trial judge erred in granting gestational carrier standing on an alternate basis, namely, her status as "legal mother." Specifically, Father challenges the trial court's authority to void the Surrogacy Contract sua sponte and name gestational carrier as the "legal mother" of the babies without notice to the biological mother or the intended mother. We agree that these findings cannot be sustained and rely on multiple reasons why the court's actions do not withstand scrutiny.

First, it is clear from the pleadings in this case that neither Father nor gestational carrier sought invalidation of the Contract. The law of this Commonwealth provides that courts may not rule on matters not before them. . . .

In addition to assessing the validity of the Contract without a request that it do so, the trial court herein proceeded to declare the Contract void despite the absence of some of the parties to the Contract. . . . The court compounded its error by naming gestational carrier the "legal mother" without even notifying egg donor, the person all parties concede is the biological mother of the babies. Plainly, egg donor was an indispensable party in this action. Thus, not only was it necessary to notify egg donor because she was a party to the Contract, it was also imperative that she have notice because she is the biological mother of the triplets. In light of these facts, the court lacked jurisdiction to rule on the issue of who was the "legal mother." . . .

Even if we were to ignore the fact that the court sua sponte addressed the validity of the Contract without a request from the parties and without all indispensable parties present, we would conclude that the court's analysis of the issue was seriously flawed. . . . For example, in determining that gestational carrier was the "legal mother" of the triplets, the trial court treated egg donor as an anonymous biological donor who had signed her rights away by contract much like an anonymous sperm donor. . . .

Further, the trial court simply does not offer sufficient support or a reasoned basis for its decision to void the Surrogacy Contract and name gestational carrier the "legal mother" of the babies. "Generally, a clear and unambiguous contract provision must be given its plain meaning unless to do so would be contrary to a clearly expressed public policy [and we are mindful that] public policy is more than a vague goal which may be used to circumvent the plain meaning of the contract." *Eichelman v. Nationwide Ins. Co.*, 551 Pa. 558, 563, 711 A.2d 1006, 1008 (1998) (citations omitted). . . .

The trial court herein struck down the Contract primarily because the parties failed to name a legal mother. However, the designation of who is a "legal mother" is one ultimately determined by statute and/or judicial ruling. Had the parties named a legal mother in the Contract, that designation surely would not have been binding on the court. We find the trial court's basis for invalidating the Contract unsupportable.

. . .

This case involves a biological father seeking custody of his children from a third party gestational carrier who is not the children's biological mother, and who took the children from the hospital in direct defiance of Father's wishes after she completely changed her mind about how matters would proceed. There is no law in this Commonwealth that accords standing to a surrogate with no biological connection to the child she seeks to take into her custody. Today, on these facts, we decline to grant such a party standing.

In summary, we hold that, with regard to the custody matter, Father was entitled to obtain custody of his biological children from the third party gestational carrier who has no biological connection to the children and who took custody of the children in flagrant defiance of Father's wishes. The trial court erred in finding that gestational carrier had in loco parentis status to challenge Father's right to custody. Gestational carrier's defiant conduct precluded such a finding. Moreover, the trial court erred in sua sponte voiding the Surrogacy Contract as contrary to public policy and in naming gestational carrier as the "legal mother." None of the bases upon which the trial court relied for standing can be sustained.

Post-Case Follow-Up

The court was concerned about the lack of applicable law and, how, despite the lack of law the trial court would strike the surrogacy contract and name the gestational carrier the legal mother of the triplets. At the same time, though, there is a biological father seeking custody from a third party who is not the biological mother. Because the court did not find there was an in loco parentis standing, there was no standing for someone with no biological connection to the child to seek custody. Thus, it would be the task of the legislature to address this issue, not the court to redefine who is the "legal mother."

The holding by the court in the custody matter also controlled the outcome of the termination case. If the gestational carrier had no right to be named the legal mother, she had no standing to bring the termination action against egg donor.

J.F. v. D.B.: Real Life Applications

1. You are an attorney in a firm and the appeals court has just issued its decision in *J.F. v. D.B.* A client comes to you and tells you that he was the donor for a couple that used his sperm, the egg of the intended mother, and a gestational carrier. Under the surrogacy contract, he was to give up all rights to the child as was the gestational carrier. A child was born three weeks ago, but he has since learned that the gestational carrier has not relinquished the child to the intended parents. The intended mother (who is also the genetic mother) is seeking custody, and her husband intends to adopt the child once she has legal and physical custody. The client wants to know what rights he has as the sperm donor. Can he also decide at this point that he does not want to relinquish custody?

2. Katrina was the gestational carrier of twins born two months ago. Because the twins were born with some serious medical issues, the biological father decided he did not want to take custody of the children as he agreed to do in the surrogate parenting agreement. Can Katrina enforce the contract and require the biological father to assume all parenting obligations?

3. Suzanne agrees to be the gestational carrier for her friends Mark and Maddie, who are unable to have children. Mark acted as the sperm donor and his sperm was combined with the eggs of an anonymous donor. Unfortunately, by the time of the birth of the baby girl, Mark and Maddie had filed for divorce. Suzanne, feeling that she did not want the baby raised by a single dad, decided it would be better for her to keep the baby and raise it with her husband. Accordingly, when the baby was born, she did not tell Mark about the birth. She instead left the hospital with the baby, and Mark did not learn about the birth for several weeks. When he did find out, he attempted to enforce the surrogacy contract, which was similar to the one in *J.F. v. D.B.* What are Suzanne's best arguments for invalidating the contract? Who should prevail?

Reestablishing Relationships with a Parent

It undoubtedly takes time for court cases to reach a final non-appealable decision. The problem is that while the court case is proceeding, the children continue to grow up and, in the case of *J.F. v. D.B.*, the children remained in the custody of D.B. By the time of the decision, the triplet boys were almost three years old.

The court was not unmindful of this fact and stated:

> We cannot conclude this matter without recognizing the profound effect its resolution will have on the three persons who matter most in this case: Father's biological children. We reach our resolution here only after lengthy, serious reflection and concern. Due in part to troubling conduct on the part of gestational carrier and [hospital] personnel, and due also to the length of time it takes for matters to wend their way through our legal system, we have before us three small boys who no doubt face a challenging period of transition and change. In light of this, we urge the parties to act hereinafter with the utmost respect for the boys' right of privacy. Furthermore, we strongly recommend that the transfer of custody and the preparations therefor be conducted privately, in the presence of the parties and their immediate families only. Although it is likely unnecessary, we encourage all parties to put aside their personal positions in this case and instead place the emotional welfare of these children above all other concerns in the days ahead.

Id. at 1281.

C. THE DISPOSITION OF FROZEN EMBRYOS

In addition to being used to create embryos for transfer to a gestational surrogate, many infertile couples also turn to IVF in their effort to have a child that is genetically related to one or both of them. As the above brief overview of the process suggests, IVF is a rather invasive procedure; moreover, it is not without risk to the woman undergoing the procedure including the possibility of perforation, infection, and ovarian hyperstimulation, in which the ovaries become enlarged. An additional concern is that the process is quite expensive — with the average price per cycle estimated to be about $12,400. Many health insurance plans do not cover the costs of infertility treatments.

Compounding these potential difficulties, the pregnancy success rate using IVF is fairly low, which means that couples often attempt multiple cycles in an effort to conceive, without any guarantee of success. However, the more recently developed technological ability of fertility clinics to freeze embryos through cryopreservation — a technique whereby embryos are cooled and then stored at extremely low temperatures to preserve the embryos — enables couples to store excess embryos created in a single IVF cycle for future use in the event a pregnancy does not result or they subsequently decide they wish to have additional children.

The ability to cryopreserve and store excess embryos minimizes some of the burdens associated with IVF in the event a pregnancy is not achieved or a couple decides that they want more children in the future. However, a largely unanticipated problem is that a couple may subsequently end their relationship and disagree over what should happen to their stored embryos, resulting in litigation over their fate. Although, as developed below, the primary issue that courts have grappled with is a determination of the appropriate legal framework within which to resolve the competing claims of the parties, we begin our discussion of this topic with the threshold question that some courts have considered — namely, what legal niche do frozen embryos occupy?

1. Human Beings? Property? Or Deserving of "Special Respect?": The Legal Status of Frozen Embryos

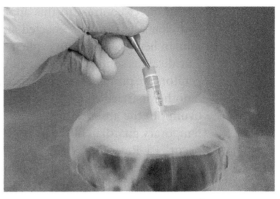

What is the legal status of frozen embryos?
dra_schwartz/iStockphoto

In seeking to resolve what have generally proven to be deeply bitter contests over the fate of frozen embryos in the wake of divorce, some courts have attempted to first determine their legal status — an inquiry that may be particularly pressing in cases where one spouse claims they are akin to children, and that their disposition should therefore be governed by the best interest standard.

Three basic categorical approaches are possible; namely, that frozen embryos are the moral equivalent of persons; that they are property; or that they occupy a middle position that entitles them to "special respect."

The courts that have directly addressed this issue have consistently concluded that frozen embryos are not the moral equivalent of children, and they have accordingly rejected the best interest standard as an appropriate guideline for resolving these disputes. In *Davis v. Davis* (included below), a seminal case of national first impression, the high court of Tennessee relied, among other legal authorities, upon the U.S. Supreme Court's statement in *Roe v. Wade* that the "the unborn have never been recognized in the law as persons in the whole sense," to repudiate the trial court's conclusion that the "four to eight cell pre-embryos" are "children in vitro" who are possessed of a "legal right to be born." 842 S.W.2d 588, 595 (Tenn. 1992), quoting *Roe v. Wade*, 410 U.S. 113, 162 (1973).

It accordingly rejected the wife's claim that she was entitled to custody of the embryos so that she could bring them into being through transplantation into her uterus. 842 S.W.2d at 594-595. The wife subsequently changed her position and instead sought to donate the embryos to a childless couple.

The Supreme Court of Iowa employed a somewhat different approach in its rejection of the wife's claim "that the embryos [were] children and that their best interest demand[ed] placement with her" in accordance with the state's custody statute. *In re Marriage of Whitten*, 672 N.W.2d 768, 774 (Iowa 2003).

Reasoning that the goal of the best interest standard is "to assure the child the opportunity for the maximum continuing physical and emotional contact with both parents" and to "encourage parents to share the rights and responsibilities of raising the child," it concluded that the standard was not accordingly "suited to the resolution of disputes over the control of frozen embryos" as these "do not involve maximizing physical and emotional contact between both parents and the child," but rather "involve the more fundamental decision of whether the parties will be parents at all." *Id.* at 775. The court further remarked that it was "premature to consider which parent can most effectively raise the child when the 'child' is still frozen in a storage facility." *Id.*

In direct contrast to this approach, at least two states, specifically Louisiana and New Mexico, have enacted statutes that effectively regard frozen embryos as human beings. The more explicit of the two, the Louisiana law deems them to be "juridical person[s]," and accordingly prohibits their intentional destruction. Progenitors are permitted to renounce their parental rights by "notarial act" in favor of "another married couple . . . who is willing and able to receive the in vitro fertilized ovum"; in the absence of such a couple, the "physician shall be deemed to be the temporary guardian of the in vitro fertilized ovum until adoptive implantation can occur." La. Rev. Stat. §9:121-132.

The New Mexico statute implicitly vests frozen embryos with personhood status by prohibiting their destruction by way of a statutory mandate that "each living . . . embryo [be] implanted in a human female recipient." N.M. Stat. Ann. §24-9A-1(D).

At least one court has characterized frozen embryos as property in the context of a dispositional dispute between divorcing spouses. Specifically, in *Dahl v. Angle*, the Oregon appellate court concluded that the "contractual right to dispose of 'frozen embryos'" comes within the definition of personal property as used in the state's equitable distribution provision. 222 Or. App. 572, 194 P.3d 834, 838-839 (2008).

Accordingly, the "right to dispose of the frozen embryos" was subject to a "just and proper" division under Oregon's equitable distribution law, which the court ruled should track the original intent of the parties. *Id.* at 839.

In keeping with their stated intent, it thus ruled that the embryos should be destroyed, although the husband was currently seeking to have them transferred to a third party based on his belief that they constituted life and should be permitted to "'develop their full potential as human beings.'" *Id.* As discussed below, this result is consistent with marked tendency of courts to rule in favor of the party seeking to avoid genetic parenthood.

Occupying a middle position, the most common judicial approach appears to lie somewhere between these two poles, positing that a frozen embryo is neither a person nor property, but rather is an entity that is entitled to "special respect." This position was first adopted by the *Davis* court, which, in addition to rejecting the personhood approach, also declined to sanction the suggestion of the appellate court that frozen embryos are property, characterizing its reliance on *York v. Jones*, in which the court held that a cryopreservation agreement between a couple and a fertility clinic "created a bailment relationship [that] obligated the [clinic] to return the subject of the bailment to the Yorks once the purpose of the bailment had terminated" as "troublesome." *Davis*, 842 S.W.2d at 596, discussing the result in *York v. Jones*, 717 F. Supp. 421 (E.D. Va. 1989).

In adopting this "special respect" position, the *Davis* court explained, based on the report of the Ethics Committee of the American Fertility Society, that

> a preembryo deserves respect greater than other human tissue because of its potential to become a person and because of its symbolic meaning for many people. Yet, it should not be treated as a person, because it has not yet developed the features of personhood, is not yet established as developmentally individual, and may never realize its biologic potential.

Id. at 597. Although dismissing the idea that frozen embryos are a type of property, the court nonetheless declared that the progenitors "have an interest in the nature of ownership, to the extent that they have decision-making authority concerning the disposition of the pre-embryos, within the scope of policy set by law." *Id.* This arguably raises questions about what "special respect" actually means, particularly in light of the fact that some courts that have adopted this view have nonetheless authorized the destruction of the parties' embryos as the preferred alternative to imposing unwanted genetic parenthood on one of the progenitors.

2. Dispositional Frameworks

The approaches that courts have taken in divorce disputes over the disposition of frozen embryos are generally identified as falling into one of three frameworks — the balancing of interests standard, the contractual ordering approach, and the mutual contemporaneous consent model. Each of these alternatives will be discussed in this section using a leading court decision to illuminate its contours. However, be aware that this organizational schema is not always so tidy, and that the lines between approaches can blur, or courts may combine or depart from these models.

The Balancing of Competing Interests

Case Preview

Davis v. Davis

Davis v. Davis is an example of the balancing of competing interests. The case involves the disposition of cryogenically preserved product of in vitro fertilization (IVF). Junior Lewis Davis filed a divorce action against his then wife, appellant Mary Sue Davis. The parties agreed on all terms of the dissolution action except the "custody" of the seven "frozen embryos" that were being stored in a Knoxville fertility clinic. The court was faced with balancing the interests between Mr. Davis, who did not want to father children at this time, and Mrs. Davis, who at first wanted to transfer the embryos to her own uterus, but during the course of the proceeding changed her mind and sought to have the embryos donated to another couple.

In resolving this dispute, the court sought to balance Mr. Davis's interest in avoiding unwanted procreation with Mrs. Davis's interest in donating the embryos to another couple for implantation, which would protect her considerable investment in the process and ensure that her genetic material would result in children.

Thus, the court's balance was between Junior Davis's express interest in avoiding parenthood with Mary Sue Davis's interest in donating the pre-embryos to another couple for implantation due to the burden of the lengthy IVF procedure she underwent and her knowledge that her contributed genetic material would never become children.

As you read *Davis v. Davis*, look for the following:

1. Why did Mr. Davis object to his wife's plan to donate the embryos to another couple for implantation?
2. Why did the court reject an "implied contract" approach to resolving the Davises' dispositional dispute?
3. What two interests of the parties did the court seek to balance?

Davis v. Davis

842 S.W.2d 588 (Tenn. 1992), cert. denied sub nom.
Stowe v. Davis, 507 U.S. 911 (1993)

DAUGHTREY, M:

. . .

I. INTRODUCTION

Mary Sue Davis originally asked for control of the "frozen embryos" with the intent to have them transferred to her own uterus, in a post-divorce effort to become pregnant. Junior Davis objected, saying that he preferred to leave the embryos in their frozen state until he decided whether or not he wanted to become a parent outside the bounds of marriage.

Based on its determination that the embryos were "human beings" from the moment of fertilization, the trial court awarded "custody" to Mary Sue Davis and directed that she "be permitted the opportunity to bring these children to term through implantation." The Court of Appeals reversed, finding that Junior Davis has a "constitutionally protected right not to beget a child where no pregnancy has taken place" and holding that "there is no compelling state interest to justify ordering implantation against the will of either party." The Court of Appeals further held that "the parties share an interest in the seven fertilized ova" and remanded the case to the trial court for entry of an order vesting them with "joint control . . . and equal voice over their disposition." . . .

We note, in this latter regard, that their positions have already shifted: both have remarried and Mary Sue Davis (now Mary Sue Stowe) has moved out of state. She no longer wishes to utilize the "frozen embryos" herself, but wants authority to donate them to a childless couple. Junior Davis is adamantly opposed to such donation and would prefer to see the "frozen embryos" discarded. The result is, once again, an impasse, but the parties' current legal position does have an effect on the probable outcome of the case, as discussed below. . . .

When the Davises signed up for the IVF program at the Knoxville clinic, they did not execute a written agreement specifying what disposition should be made of any unused embryos that might result from the cryopreservation process. . . .

We believe, as a starting point, that an agreement regarding disposition of any untransferred preembryos in the event of contingencies (such as the death of one or more of the parties, divorce, financial reversals, or abandonment of the program) should be presumed valid and should be enforced as between the progenitors. This conclusion is in keeping with the proposition that the progenitors, having provided the genetic material giving rise to the preembryos, retain decision-making authority as to their disposition. . . .

At the same time, we recognize that life is not static, and that human emotions run particularly high when a married couple is attempting to overcome infertility problems. It follows that the parties' initial "informed consent" to IVF procedures will often not be truly informed because of the near impossibility of anticipating, emotionally and psychologically, all the turns that events may take as the IVF process unfolds. Providing that the initial agreements may later be modified *by agreement* will, we think, protect the parties against some of the risks they face in this regard. But, in the absence of such agreed modification, we conclude that their prior agreements should be considered binding.

It might be argued in this case that the parties had an implied contract to reproduce using *in vitro* fertilization, that Mary Sue Davis relied on that agreement in undergoing IVF procedures, and that the court should enforce an implied contract against Junior Davis, allowing Mary Sue to dispose of the preembryos in a manner calculated to result in reproduction. The problem with such an analysis is that there is no indication in the record that disposition in the event of contingencies other than Mary Sue Davis's pregnancy was ever considered by the parties, or that Junior Davis intended to pursue reproduction outside the confines of a continuing marital relationship with Mary Sue. . . .

VI. THE RIGHT OF PROCREATIONAL AUTONOMY

[T]he essential dispute here is . . . whether the parties will become parents. . . . We conclude that the answer to this dilemma turns on the parties' exercise of their constitutional right to privacy. . . .

For the purposes of this litigation it is sufficient to note that whatever its ultimate constitutional boundaries, the right of procreational autonomy is composed of two rights of equal significance — the right to procreate and the right to avoid procreation. . . . The equivalence of and inherent tension between these two interests are nowhere more evident than in the context of *in vitro* fertilization. . . .

It is further evident that, however far the protection of procreational autonomy extends, the existence of the right itself dictates that decisional authority rests in the gamete-providers alone, at least to the extent that their decisions have an impact upon their individual reproductive status. . . .

Further, at least with respect to Tennessee's public policy and its constitutional right of privacy, the state's interest in potential human life is insufficient to justify an infringement on the gamete-providers' procreational autonomy. . . .

Certainly, if the state's interests do not become sufficiently compelling in the abortion context until the end of the first trimester, . . . after very significant developmental stages have passed, then surely there is no state interest in these preembryos which could suffice to overcome the interests of the gamete-providers. . . .

VII. BALANCING THE PARTIES' INTERESTS

Resolving disputes over conflicting interests of constitutional import is a task familiar to the courts. One way of resolving these disputes is to consider the positions of the parties, the significance of their interests, and the relative burdens that will be imposed by differing resolutions. . . . In this case, the issue centers on the two aspects of procreational autonomy — the right to procreate and the right to avoid procreation. We start by considering the burdens imposed on the parties by solutions that would have the effect of disallowing the exercise of individual procreational autonomy with respect to these particular preembryos.

Beginning with the burden imposed on Junior Davis, we note that the consequences are obvious. Any disposition which results in the gestation of the preembryos would impose unwanted parenthood on him, with all of its possible financial and psychological consequences. The impact that this unwanted parenthood would have on Junior Davis can only be understood by considering his particular circumstances, as revealed in the record.

Junior Davis testified that he was the fifth youngest of six children. When he was five years old, his parents divorced, his mother had a nervous break-down, and he and three of his brothers went to live at a home for boys run by the Lutheran Church. Another brother was taken in by an aunt, and his sister stayed with their mother. From that day forward, he had monthly visits with his mother but saw his father only three more times before he died in 1976. Junior Davis testified that, as a boy, he had severe problems caused by separation from his parents. He said that it was especially hard to leave his mother after each monthly visit. He clearly feels that he has suffered because of his lack of opportunity to establish a relationship with his parents and particularly because of the absence of his father.

In light of his boyhood experiences, Junior Davis is vehemently opposed to fathering a child that would not live with both parents. . . .

Balanced against Junior Davis's interest in avoiding parenthood is Mary Sue Davis's interest in donating the preembryos to another couple for implantation. Refusal to permit donation of the preembryos would impose on her the burden of knowing that the lengthy IVF procedures she underwent were futile, and that the preembryos to which she contributed genetic material would never become children. While this is not an insubstantial emotional burden, we can only conclude that Mary Sue Davis's interest in donation is not as significant as the interest Junior Davis has in avoiding parenthood. If she were allowed to donate these preembryos, he would face a lifetime of either wondering about his parental status or knowing about his parental status but having no control over it. He testified quite clearly that if these preembryos were brought to term he would fight for custody of his child or children. Donation, if a child came of it, would rob him twice — his procreational autonomy would be defeated and his relationship with his offspring would be prohibited.

The case would be closer if Mary Sue Davis were seeking to use the preembryos herself, but only if she could not achieve parenthood by any other reasonable means. We recognize the trauma that Mary Sue has already experienced and the additional discomfort to which she would be subjected if she opts to attempt IVF again. Still, she would have a reasonable opportunity, through IVF, to try once again to achieve parenthood in all its aspects — genetic, gestational, bearing, and rearing.

Further, we note that if Mary Sue Davis were unable to undergo another round of IVF, or opted not to try, she could still achieve the child-rearing aspects of parenthood through adoption. The fact that she and Junior Davis pursued adoption indicates that, at least at one time, she was willing to forego genetic parenthood and would have been satisfied by the child-rearing aspects of parenthood alone.

VIII. CONCLUSION

In summary, we hold that . . . [if] no prior agreement exists, then the relative interests of the parties in using or not using the preembryos must be weighed. Ordinarily, the party wishing to avoid procreation should prevail, assuming that the other party has a reasonable possibility of achieving parenthood by means other than use of the preembryos in question. If no other reasonable alternatives exist, then the argument in favor of using the preembryos to achieve pregnancy should be considered. However, if the party seeking control of the preembryos intends merely to donate them to another couple, the objecting party obviously has the greater interest and should prevail.

But the rule does not contemplate the creation of an automatic veto. . . .

Post-Case Follow-Up

After concluding that frozen embryos were neither persons nor property, but entities entitled to special respect, the *Davis* court expressed its view that an agreement between parties regarding the disposition of any untransferred embryos in the event of a future contingency such as death of one of the parties or divorce should "be presumed valid and should be enforced as between the progenitors." Although some commentators have accordingly classified *Davis* as a contracts case, its endorsement of this approach is, in fact, dicta as the parties had not entered into a contract embodying their intent regarding the disposition of any excess embryos in the event of divorce. In the absence of such an agreement, the court adopted what has become a highly influential balancing test.

Although the *Davis* court concluded that its balancing rule did not "contemplate the creation of an automatic veto" in favor of the party seeking to avoid procreation, courts following this approach have nonetheless generally adopted the position that "the party wishing to avoid procreation" should prevail in light of the comparatively greater burden of unwanted genetic parenthood as compared to the loss of a procreative opportunity. This result is the practical consequence of the contemporaneous mutual consent approach.

Davis v. Davis: Real Life Applications

1. Jason and Louise decided that at some point in the future they would like to have children. Accordingly, in order to preserve this option in the event that by

waiting it became more difficult for Louise to conceive, they elect to go through the IVF process. The resulting five embryos were frozen and held at a fertility clinic's storage facility for future use. Jason subsequently filed for divorce and asked that the embryos be destroyed or used for scientific purposes. Louise requested custody in the event she wanted children in the future and was unable to conceive. What arguments can you make for Jason? What arguments can you make for Louise? How should a trial court rule?

2. Assume the same facts as in Question 1, but Louise does not wish to utilize the embryos for herself, but to give them to another infertile couple. How should the court rule?

3. Assume the same facts as in Question 1, but Louise wants to have the embryos given to another infertile couple and Jason wants to obtain custody because he is fearful that he may not have the opportunity to father children and he accordingly wants to have the embryos implanted in a gestational carrier so he can become a parent. What arguments can Louise make in objection to Jason's custody request? How should a court rule using the balancing of interests test?

Although subsequent decisions that have employed the balancing test have certainly tilted toward the party seeking to avoid procreation, as indicated by the *Davis* court's remark that the "case would be closer if Mary Sue Davis were seeking to use the preembryos herself, but only if she could not achieve parenthood by any other reasonable means," the result is not a foregone conclusion. Accordingly, in *Reber v. Reiss* — a case of first impression in Pennsylvania — the superior court ruled in favor of the progenitor seeking to use the embryos to become a genetic parent. 42 A.3d 1131 (Pa. Super. Ct. 2012), *appeal denied*, 619 Pa. 680, 62 A.3d 380 (2012).

In this instance, the parties had turned to IVF in order to preserve the wife's ability to have a genetically related child after she underwent chemotherapy for breast cancer. However, the husband subsequently filed for divorce, and then developed a relationship with another woman with whom he had a child and planned to have more.

As part of the divorce, the wife requested an award of the parties' frozen embryos for implantation while the husband sought their destruction in order to avoid unwanted procreation. In light of the fact that the parties had not entered into a prior agreement regarding the disposition of the embryos in the event of divorce, and were unable to reach a contemporaneous mutual decision regarding their disposition, the court concluded that the balancing approach was the most appropriate way to resolve the dispute. Although the court recognized, as urged by the husband, that both foster parenting and adoption were available options to the wife, the court was sympathetic to the fact that implantation of the embryos was the only way for her to have a biological child, which, as she testified, was the reason she went through the IVF process in the first place. Accordingly, it reasoned that "simply because adoption or foster parenting may be available to Wife, it does not mean that such options should be given equal weight in a balancing test." *Id.* at 1138. Moreover the court also addressed the reality that adoption would not have been an easy path for her to follow, remarking that "especially for single older women, adoption is an expensive process fraught with the potential for protracted delay and ultimate disappointment." *Id.* at 1139, quoting Ellen Waldman, The Parent Trap: Uncovering the Myth of "Coerced Parenthood" in Frozen Embryo Disputes, 53 Am. U. L. Rev. 1021, 1055 (2004).

Accordingly, based on the reality that implantation of the embryos most likely represented the wife's only opportunity for biological parenthood, the court concluded that her procreational interests outweighed the husband's interest in avoiding procreation, and that she was therefore entitled to an award of the parties' frozen embryos for implantation in her uterus. *Id.* at 1142.

The Contractual Approach

Although the *Davis* court took the position that dispositional agreements regarding untransferred embryos were entitled to a presumptive validity, it did not elaborate on its support for this position in light of the fact that the progenitors in that case did not have such an agreement. However, in the 1998 case of *Kass v. Kass*, 696 N.E.2d 174 (N.Y. 1998), the New York high court had the opportunity to expound upon why reliance on an existing contract regarding the disposition of untransferred embryos is the appropriate approach for resolving disputes between progenitors, at least in situations where the document embodies the clear intent of the parties with regard to the contingency they are facing.

Case Preview	### *Kass v. Kass*

In this case, the parties had signed a contract with the IVF program in which they were enrolled agreeing that any remaining embryos (referred to in the case as pre-zygotes) would be examined by the hospital for biological research and disposed of for approved research investigation. Sixteen eggs were removed from Mrs. Kass resulting in nine pre-zygotes. Four were transferred to her sister, who was to be the surrogate mother, and the remaining five were cryopreserved. When the results came back negative, Mrs. Kass's sister indicated she was no longer willing to participate as a surrogate. The couple shortly thereafter decided to dissolve their marriage. As part of the divorce decree, the parties confirmed that the pre-zygotes should be disposed of in the manner outlined in their consent form and that "neither Maureen Kass, Steve Kass or anyone else will lay claim to custody of these pre-zygotes."

As you read *Kass v. Kass*, consider the following:

1. Why does the court decide that this dispositional dispute between divorcing spouses should be governed by contract principles?
2. According to the court, does the disposition of the frozen embryos implicate a woman's right to privacy and bodily integrity? Why or why not?

3. Why does the court ultimately decide against an order authorizing the implantation of the embryos?
4. Does the court take into consideration the structure of the family or policy considerations in arriving at a decision?
5. How does the notion of parental rights and family values play into the court's decision?

Kass v. Kass
696 N.E.2d 174 (N.Y. 1998)

KAYE, J:

FACTS

. . .

On May 20, 1993, doctors retrieved 16 eggs from appellant, resulting in nine pre-zygotes. Two days later, four were transferred to appellant's sister, who had volunteered to be a surrogate mother, and the remaining five were cryopreserved. The couple learned shortly thereafter that the results were negative and that appellant's sister was no longer willing to participate in the program. They then decided to dissolve their marriage. The total cost of their IVF efforts exceeded $75,000.

With divorce imminent, the parties themselves on June 7, 1993 — barely three weeks after signing the consents — drew up and signed an "uncontested divorce" agreement, typed by appellant, including the following:

> "The disposition of the frozen 5 pre-zygotes at Mather Hospital is that they should be disposed of [in] the manner outlined in our consent form and that neither Maureen Kass, Steve Kass or anyone else will lay claim to custody of these pre-zygotes."

On June 28, 1993, appellant by letter informed the hospital and her IVF physician of her marital problems and expressed her opposition to destruction or release of the pre-zygotes.

One month later, appellant commenced the present matrimonial action, requesting sole custody of the pre-zygotes so that she could undergo another implantation procedure. Respondent opposed removal of the pre-zygotes and any further attempts by appellant to achieve pregnancy, and counterclaimed for specific performance of the parties' agreement to permit the IVF program to retain the pre-zygotes for research. . . .

The Supreme Court granted appellant custody of the pre-zygotes and directed her to exercise her right to implant them within a medically reasonable time. The court reasoned that a female participant in the IVF procedure has exclusive decisional authority over the fertilized eggs created through that process, just as a pregnant woman has exclusive decisional authority over a nonviable fetus, and that appellant had not waived her right. . . .

While a divided Appellate Division reversed that decision, all five Justices unanimously agreed on two fundamental propositions. First, they concluded that a woman's right to privacy and bodily integrity are not implicated before implantation occurs. Second, the court unanimously recognized that when parties to an IVF procedure have themselves determined the disposition of any unused fertilized eggs, their agreement should control. . . .

   . . .

We now affirm, agreeing with the plurality that the parties clearly expressed their intent that in the circumstances presented the pre-zygotes would be donated to the IVF program for research purposes.

ANALYSIS

A. *The Legal Landscape Generally*

In the case law, only *Davis v Davis* . . . attempts to lay out an analytical framework for disputes between a divorcing couple regarding the disposition of frozen embryos. . . . Having declared that embryos are entitled to "special respect because of their potential for human life" [842 SW2d 588, 597], *Davis* recognized the procreative autonomy of both gamete providers, which includes an interest in avoiding genetic parenthood as well as an interest in becoming a genetic parent. In the absence of any prior written agreement between the parties — which should be presumed valid, and implemented — according to *Davis,* courts must in every case balance these competing interests, each deserving of judicial respect. In *Davis* itself, that balance weighed in favor of the husband's interest in avoiding genetic parenthood, which was deemed more significant than the wife's desire to donate the embryos to a childless couple. . . .

B. *The Appeal Before Us*

Like the Appellate Division, we conclude that disposition of these pre-zygotes does not implicate a woman's right of privacy or bodily integrity in the area of reproductive choice; nor are the pre-zygotes recognized as "persons" for constitutional purposes. . . . The relevant inquiry thus becomes who has dispositional authority over them. Because that question is answered in this case by the parties' agreement, for purposes of resolving the present appeal we have no cause to decide whether the pre-zygotes are entitled to "special respect." . . .

Agreements between progenitors, or gamete donors, regarding disposition of their pre-zygotes should generally be presumed valid and binding, and enforced in any dispute between them. . . . Indeed, parties should be encouraged in advance, before embarking on IVF and cryopreservation, to think through possible contingencies and carefully specify their wishes in writing. Explicit agreements avoid costly litigation in business transactions. They are all the more necessary and desirable in personal matters of reproductive choice, where the intangible costs of any litigation are simply incalculable. Advance directives, subject to mutual change of mind that must be jointly expressed, both minimize misunderstandings and maximize procreative liberty by reserving to the progenitors the authority to make what is in the first instance a quintessentially personal, private decision. Written agreements also provide the certainty needed for effective operation of IVF programs.

While the value of arriving at explicit agreements is apparent, we also recognize the extraordinary difficulty such an exercise presents. All agreements looking to the future to some extent deal with the unknown. Here, however, the uncertainties inherent in the IVF process itself are vastly complicated by cryopreservation, which extends the viability of pre-zygotes indefinitely and allows time for minds, and circumstances, to change. Divorce; death, disappearance or incapacity of one or both partners; aging; the birth of other children are but a sampling of obvious changes in individual circumstances that might take place over time.

These factors make it particularly important that courts seek to honor the parties' expressions of choice, made before disputes erupt, with the parties' overall direction always uppermost in the analysis. Knowing that advance agreements will be enforced underscores the seriousness and integrity of the consent process. Advance agreements as to disposition would have little purpose if they were enforceable only in the event the parties continued to agree. To the extent possible, it should be the progenitors — not the State and not the courts — who by their prior directive make this deeply personal life choice.

Here, the parties prior to cryopreservation of the pre-zygotes signed consents indicating their dispositional intent. While these documents were technically provided by the IVF program, neither party disputes that they are an expression of their own intent regarding disposition of their pre-zygotes. . . .

The conclusion that emerges most strikingly from reviewing these consents as a whole is that appellant and respondent intended that disposition of the pre-zygotes was to be their joint decision. The consents manifest that what they above all did not want was a stranger taking that decision out of their hands. Even in unforeseen circumstances, even if they were unavailable, even if they were dead, the consents jointly specified the disposition that would be made. That sentiment explicitly appears again and again throughout the lengthy documents. Words of shared understanding — "we," "us" and "our" — permeate the pages. The overriding choice of these parties could not be plainer: "*We have the principal responsibility to decide the disposition of our frozen pre-zygotes. Our frozen pre-zygotes will not be released from storage for any purpose without the written consent of both of us, consistent with the policies of the IVF Program and applicable law*" (emphasis added). . . .

Thus, only by joint decision of the parties would the pre-zygotes be used for implantation. And otherwise, by mutual consent they would be donated to the IVF program for research purposes. . . .

As they embarked on the IVF program, appellant and respondent — "husband" and "wife," signing as such — clearly contemplated the fulfillment of a life dream of having a child during their marriage. The consents they signed provided for other contingencies, most especially that in the present circumstances the pre-zygotes would be donated to the IVF program for approved research purposes. These parties having clearly manifested their intention, the law will honor it.

Accordingly, the order of the Appellate Division should be affirmed, with costs.

Post-Case Follow-Up

Invoking classical contract law principles, the *Kass* court stressed that an important benefit of this approach is that it encourages parties to think carefully about future contingencies in order to ensure that their wishes are carried out in accordance with their procreative intent. In the court's view, the memorialization of intent "promotes procreative liberty by reserving to the progenitors the authority to make what is in the first instance a quintessentially personal, private decision." Stressing the connection between contractual enforcement and procreative liberty, the court spoke of the "simply incalculable" costs of a judicially imposed resolution to these deeply private matters.

Kass v. Kass: Real Life Applications

1. Deanna and Randy have signed a consent agreement with an IVF facility that provides that any frozen embryos remaining after the initial insemination of Deanna will only be released and disposed of in a manner consistent with the joint instructions of Deanna and Randy. If Deanna and Randy cannot agree, "the IVF facility will store the embryos for a period of five years after which time the embryos will be donated to the IVF facility for research. Neither party will have unilateral right to dispose of the embryos." Randy has now filed for divorce and Deanna wishes to obtain custody of the embryos. Under the *Kass v. Kass* decision, what is the result?

2. Assume the same facts as in Question 1, but Deanna argues during the divorce proceeding, and proves to a reasonable degree of medical certainty, that she is unable to conceive a child and that she is no longer a candidate for egg retrieval. Thus, her only opportunity to have her a biological child is with the embryos that are stored. Randy objects claiming he has no desire to have a child with Deanna. What should the trial court do?

3. Assume the same facts as in Question 1, but it is Randy who wants to have the embryos and wishes to have the option to utilize a surrogate in order to have biological children of his own. What result?

Mutual Contemporaneous Consent

In the previous section, we examined the issue of consent provided in contracts that predetermined the disposition of embryos. In this section, we turn to a third approach, that of requiring mutual contemporaneous consent as a precondition of a dispositional award. This is a rather unique and complex approach that has been given a particularly thoughtful and well-developed treatment by the Supreme Court of Iowa in *In re Witten*, 672 N.W.2d 768 (Iowa 2003). *See also A.Z. v. B.Z.*, 431 Mass. 150, 725 N.E.2d 1051 (2000).

In re Witten

Arthur (known as Trip) and Tamera were married for seven and half years when Trip filed for divorce. The parties had undergone several unsuccessful attempts at in vitro fertilization using eggs retrieved from Tamera and fertilized by Trip's sperm. At issue in the case was the control of the resulting frozen embryos that were in storage at the University of Nebraska medical center.

As part of the IVF process, the parties had signed an agreement that provided the medical center would not release, discard, or transfer the embryos without the written authorization of both parties. At trial, Tamera indicated she wanted the embryos to be implanted in her or a surrogate mother and if the pregnancy was successful she would afford Trip the opportunity to exercise parenting rights. Trip argued that he did not want the embryos destroyed but was opposed to Tamera using them. He would agree to use by another couple and wanted the court to enter a permanent injunction prohibiting either party from releasing the embryos without written consent of both parties.

As you read *In re Witten*, look for the following:

1. Why did Tamera indicate that the storage agreement did not address the current situation of the parties?
2. Why does the court reject the contractual approach?
3. What standard does the court adopt?
4. What public policy rationale does the court provide for adopting this standard?
5. What does this standard have in common with the contractual approach? How does it depart from this approach?

In re Witten

672 N.W.2d 768 (Iowa 2003)

TERNUS, M:

. . .

III. DISPOSITION OF EMBRYOS

A. *Scope of Storage Agreement*

We first consider Tamera's contention that the storage agreement does not address the situation at hand. As noted earlier, the agreement had a specific provision governing control of the embryos if one or both parties died, but did not explicitly deal with the possibility of divorce. Nonetheless, we think the present predicament falls within the general provision governing "release of embryos," in which the parties agreed that the embryos would not be transferred, released, or discarded without "the signed approval" of both Tamera and Trip. This provision is certainly broad enough to encompass the decision-making protocol when the parties are unmarried as well as when they are married.

The only question, then, is whether such agreements are enforceable when one of the parties later changes his or her mind with respect to the proper disposition of the embryos. . . . [W]e have identified three primary approaches to resolving disputes over the disposition of frozen embryos, which we have identified as (1) the contractual approach, (2) the contemporaneous mutual consent model, and (3) the balancing test.

Tamera's argument that her right to bear children should override the parties' prior agreement as well as Trip's current opposition to her use of the embryos resembles the balancing test. As for Tamera's alternative argument, we have found no authority supporting a "best interests" analysis in determining the disposition of frozen embryos. . . .

C. Enforcement of Storage Agreement

We now consider the appropriateness of the trial court's decision to allow Tamera and Trip's agreement with the medical center to control the current dispute between them. As we noted above, there are three methods of analysis that have been suggested to resolve disputes over frozen embryos. We will discuss them separately.

1. Contractual approach

The currently prevailing view — expressed in three states — is that contracts entered into at the time of in vitro fertilization are enforceable so long as they do not violate public policy. . . .

This approach has been criticized, however, because it "insufficiently protects the individual and societal interests at stake":

> First, decisions about the disposition of frozen embryos implicate rights central to individual identity. On matters of such fundamental personal importance, individuals are entitled to make decisions consistent with their contemporaneous wishes, values, and beliefs. Second, requiring couples to make binding decisions about the future use of their frozen embryos ignores the difficulty of predicting one's future response to life-altering events such as parenthood. Third, conditioning the provision of infertility treatment on the execution of binding disposition agreements is coercive and calls into question the authenticity of the couple's original choice. Finally, treating couples' decisions about the future use of their frozen embryos as binding contracts undermines important values about families, reproduction, and the strength of genetic ties.

Carl H. Coleman, Procreative Liberty and Contemporaneous Choice: An Inalienable Rights Approach to Frozen Embryo Disputes, 84 Minn. L. Rev. 55, 88-89 (1999). . . .

2. Contemporaneous mutual consent

The contractual approach and the contemporaneous mutual consent model share an underlying premise: "decisions about the disposition of frozen embryos belong to the couple that created the embryo, with each partner entitled to an equal say in how the embryos should be disposed." Coleman, 84 Minn. L. Rev. at 81. Departing from this common starting point, the alternative framework asserts the important question is "at what time does the partners' consent matter?" *Id.* at 91. Proponents of the mutual-consent approach suggest that, with respect to "decisions about intensely emotional matters, where people act more on the basis of feeling and instinct than rational deliberation," it may "be impossible to make a knowing and intelligent decision to relinquish a right in advance of the time the right is to be exercised." *Id.* at 98. . . . One's erroneous prediction of how she or he will feel about the matter at some point in the future can have grave repercussions. "Like decisions about marriage or relinquishing a child for adoption, decisions about the use of one's reproductive capacity have lifelong consequences for a person's identity and sense of self":

> When chosen voluntarily, becoming a parent can be an important act of self-definition. Compelled parenthood, by contrast, imposes an unwanted identity on the individual, forcing her to redefine herself, her place in the world, and the legacy she will leave after she dies. For some people, the mandatory destruction of an embryo can have equally profound consequences, particularly for those who believe that embryos are persons. If forced destruction is experienced as the loss of a child, it can lead to life-altering feelings of mourning, guilt, and regret.

Coleman, 84 Minn. L. Rev. at 96-97. To accommodate these concerns, advocates of the mutual-consent model propose "no embryo should be used by either partner, donated to another patient, used in research, or destroyed without the [contemporaneous] mutual consent of the couple that created the embryo." *Id.* at 110. Under this alternate framework

> advance instructions would not be treated as binding contracts. If either partner has a change of mind about disposition decisions made in advance, that person's current objection would take precedence over the prior consent. If one of the partners rescinds an advance disposition decision and the other does not, the mutual consent principle would not be satisfied and the previously agreed-upon disposition decision could not be carried out.
>
> . . .
>
> When the couple is unable to agree to any disposition decision, the most appropriate solution is to keep the embryos where they are — in frozen storage. Unlike the other possible disposition decisions — use by one partner, donation to another patient, donation to research, or destruction — keeping the embryos frozen is not final and irrevocable. By preserving the status quo, it makes it possible for the partners to reach an agreement at a later time.

Id. at 110-12. . . . Although this model precludes one party's use of the embryos to have children over the objection of the other party, the outcome under the contractual approach and the balancing test would generally be the same. . . .

3. Balancing test

The New Jersey Supreme Court appears to have adopted an analysis regarding the disposition of frozen human embryos that incorporates the idea of contemporaneous decision-making, but not that of mutual consent. In *J.B.* [*v. M.B.*,] the New

Jersey court rejected the *Kass* and *Davis* contractual approach, noting public policy concerns in "enforcement of a contract that would allow the implantation of preembryos at some future date in a case where one party has reconsidered his or her earlier acquiescence." 783 A.2d 707, 718 (2001). The court stated:

> We believe that the better rule, and the one we adopt, is to enforce agreements entered into at the time in vitro fertilization is begun, *subject to the right of either party to change his or her mind about disposition up to the point of use or destruction of any stored preembryos.*

Id. at 719 (emphasis added).

D. Discussion

With these alternative approaches in mind, we turn to the present case. Trip asks that the contractual provision requiring mutual consent be enforced; Tamera claims this agreement is against the public policy of Iowa because it allows Trip to back out of his prior agreement to become a parent. We first consider whether there is any merit to Tamera's public policy argument. . . .

Tamera contends the contract at issue here violates public policy because it allows a person who has agreed to participate in an in vitro fertilization program to later change his mind about becoming a parent. . . . The public policy evidenced by our law relates to the State's concern for the physical, emotional, and psychological well being of children who have been born, not fertilized eggs that have not even resulted in a pregnancy.

Nor can we say that the "morals of the times" are such that a party participating in an in vitro fertilization process has the duty to use or facilitate the use of each fertilized egg for purposes of pregnancy. . . . Thus, we find no public policy that requires the use of the frozen embryos over one party's objection.

That brings us to the more complex issue: are prior agreements regarding the future disposition of embryos enforceable when one of the donors is no longer comfortable with his or her prior decision? We first note our agreement with other courts considering such matters that the partners who created the embryos have the primary, and equal, decision-making authority with respect to the use or disposition of their embryos. We think, however, that it would be against the public policy of this state to enforce a prior agreement between the parties in this highly personal area of reproductive choice when one of the parties has changed his or her mind concerning the disposition or use of the embryos.

Our statutes and case law evidence an understanding that decisions involving marital and family relationships are emotional and subject to change. For example, Iowa law imposes a seventy-two hour waiting period after the birth of a child before the biological parents can release parental rights. . . . In addition . . . the court will not force a party to actually consummate the marriage. . . . It has also long been recognized in this state that agreements for the purpose of bringing about a dissolution of marriage are contrary to public policy and therefore void. . . .

This court has also expressed a general reluctance to become involved in intimate questions inherent in personal relationships. . . .

We have considered and rejected the arguments of some commentators that embryo disposition agreements are analogous to antenuptial agreements and divorce stipulations, which courts generally enforce. . . . Whether embryos are viewed as having life or simply as having the potential for life, this characteristic or potential renders embryos fundamentally distinct from the chattels, real estate, and money that are the subjects of antenuptial agreements. Divorce stipulations are also distinguishable. While such agreements may address custody issues, they are contemporaneous with the implementation of the stipulation, an attribute noticeably lacking in disposition agreements.

In addition to decisional and statutory authority supporting a public policy against judicial enforcement of personal decisions concerning marriage, family, and reproduction, our statutes also anticipate the effect of a couple's dissolution on their prior decisions. For example, Iowa Code section 633.271 provides that if a testator is divorced after making a will, "all provisions in the will in favor of the testator's spouse" are automatically revoked. . . .

We think judicial decisions and statutes in Iowa reflect respect for the right of individuals to make family and reproductive decisions based on their current views and values. They also reveal awareness that such decisions are highly emotional in nature and subject to a later change of heart. For this reason, we think judicial enforcement of an agreement *between a couple* regarding their future family and reproductive choices would be against the public policy of this state.

Our decision should not be construed, however, to mean that disposition agreements *between donors and fertility clinics* have no validity at all. We recognize a disposition or storage agreement serves an important purpose in defining and governing the relationship between the couple and the medical facility, ensuring that all parties understand their respective rights and obligations. . . .

In view of these competing needs, we reject the contractual approach and hold that agreements entered into at the time in vitro fertilization is commenced are enforceable and binding on the parties, "subject to the right of either party to change his or her mind about disposition up to the point of use or destruction of any stored embryo." *J.B.*, 783 A.2d at 719. This decisional model encourages prior agreements that can guide the actions of all parties, unless a later objection to any dispositional provision is asserted. It also recognizes that, *absent a change of heart by one of the partners*, an agreement governing disposition of embryos does not violate public policy. Only when one person makes known the agreement no longer reflects his or her current values or wishes is public policy implicated. Upon this occurrence, allowing either party to withdraw his or her agreement to a disposition that person no longer accepts acknowledges the public policy concerns inherent in enforcing prior decisions of a fundamentally personal nature. In fairness to the medical facility that is a party to the agreement, however, any change of intention must be communicated in writing to all parties in order to reopen the disposition issues covered by the agreement.

That brings us, then, to the dilemma presented when one or both partners change their minds and the parties cannot reach a mutual decision on disposition. We have already explained the grave public policy concerns we have with the balancing test, which simply substitutes the court as decision maker. A better principle to apply, we think, is the requirement of contemporaneous mutual consent. Under that model, no transfer, release, disposition, or use of the embryos can occur without the signed authorization of both donors. If a stalemate results, the status quo would be maintained. The practical effect will be that the embryos are stored indefinitely unless both parties can agree to destroy the fertilized eggs. Thus, any expense associated with maintaining the status quo should logically be borne by the person opposing destruction. . . .

Turning to the present case, we find a situation in which one party no longer concurs in the parties' prior agreement with respect to the disposition of their frozen embryos, but the parties have been unable to reach a new agreement that is mutually satisfactory. Based on this fact, under the principles we have set forth today, we hold there can be no use or disposition of the Wittens' embryos unless Trip and Tamera reach an agreement. Until then, the party or parties who oppose destruction shall be responsible for any storage fees. Therefore, we affirm the trial court's ruling enjoining both parties from transferring, releasing, or utilizing the embryos without the other's written consent.

Post-Case Follow-Up

In rejecting the contractual approach, the *Witten* court relied upon the conclusion of the New Jersey Supreme Court that "agreements entered into at the time in vitro fertilization is commenced are enforceable and binding on the parties, 'subject to the right of either party to change his or her mind about disposition up to the point of use or destruction of any stored embryo.'" Importantly, in adopting this approach, the court expressed its support for the view that "the partners who created the embryos have the primary, and equal, decision-making authority with respect to the use or disposition of their embryos"—a philosophical stance that resulted in its ultimate determination that it violated public policy to impose a prior agreement on a party who had since changed his or her mind about such an intimate and personal matter.

Although in accord with the New Jersey court's view that the disposition of frozen embryos requires "contemporaneous decision-making," the *Witten* court took strong issue with its adoption of a balancing test to resolve the dispute in the absence of mutual consent between the parties. In its view, the substitution of the court as the ultimate decision maker in this highly personal realm would constitute an even more egregious breach of public policy than would the enforcement of a prior agreement in light of a party's subsequent change of mind. Departing from what might be considered the hybrid approach of the New Jersey court in its rejection of the contractual model in favor of a contemporaneous decision making requirement coupled with a judicially determined balancing of interests (hence, as noted above, the difficulty of imposing a strict organizational schema on these cases), the court instead concluded that the embryos would remain frozen until and unless the parties reached a new mutual agreement regarding their fate.

In re Witten: Real Life Applications

1. Trevor and Beth signed a contract before undergoing IVF procedures at their local hospital, which also had a storage facility for frozen embryos. The consent decree provided that any embryos stored at the facility would be released only with the signed consent of both parties. It further stated that in the event there was no disposition of the embryos after ten years the hospital was free to destroy the embryos or use them for research and investigation. Fifteen eggs were removed from Beth and fertilized with Trevor's sperm. Four fertilized eggs were transferred to Beth's uterus. The procedure worked and Beth gave birth to a healthy baby girl. The other 11 embryos were frozen and held at the hospital's storage facility. Trevor has now filed for divorce. Trevor does not want to release the embryos to Beth, who is arguing for custody. How should the court rule?

2. Assume the same facts as in Question 1, but the contract the parties sign says that the embryos will be released with the signed consent of both parties or by a court order. Does that addition to the contract change the result?

3. Gilbert and Jillian have signed a contract to have their unused embryos frozen. The contract provides that they must agree on the release of the embryos or else the embryos will remain frozen. Just before Jillian was to undergo her last round of insemination, Gilbert dies. In his will, Gilbert left the decision of what to do with the embryos "in the hands of my brother as executor who has my authority to make the decision to release the embryos to Jillian if he believes it is the best thing to do at the time." Gilbert's brother declines and indicates that Gilbert would never have wanted to have children who never knew their father and that he will not give consent to the release. What should the result be?

Although the *Witten* court did not address this issue, it should be noted that the contemporaneous mutual consent approach gives a clear edge to the party wishing to avoid procreation as it requires the embryos to remain frozen unless both parties can agree that they should be used for the purpose of bringing children into the world. Accordingly, although vastly different in approach from the balancing test, the result is likely to be the same given the balancing test's tilt away from requiring procreation over a progenitor's objection, although, as we saw, this expressed wish is not tantamount to veto power.

Chapter Summary

- Under a commercial surrogacy arrangement, a woman (the surrogate) agrees to become pregnant and bear a child for an individual or a couple and to relinquish the child together with her parental rights to the child for an agreed-upon fee.
- The use of the surrogacy contract came under attack in the *Baby M* case where the state of New Jersey had no law governing the enforcement. The trial court

upheld the contract, but the New Jersey Supreme Court reversed holding that the contract was void and unenforceable due to its exploitative nature and could thus not be relied upon to terminate the biological mother's rights.

- In response to the *Baby M* case, many states enacted laws governing surrogacy contracts. In some states, surrogacy contracts are void and unenforceable, and may even subject the parties to fines or imprisonment. Other states permit surrogacy; however, they may have specific requirements that must be met in order for a surrogate parenting agreement to be enforceable, including that the intending parents be a married couple, or that one or both parents have a genetic link to the child.

- In the case of *Johnson v. Calvert*, the California Supreme Court concluded that in the context of a gestational surrogacy arrangement where two women assert claims to motherhood based either upon a gestational or genetic link to the child, the woman who intended to procreate the child should be regarded as the legal mother.

- In cases where disputes arise over disposition of frozen embryos, the courts take one of three approaches: the balancing of interests standard, the contractual ordering approach, and the mutual contemporaneous consent model.

Applying the Rules

1. Raphael and Cindy signed a contract with the medical center where Cindy was undergoing egg removal with the intent that the eggs would someday be fertilized with Raphael's sperm and transferred to her uterus or they would utilize a gestational carrier. In the meantime, the eggs were to be frozen until both Raphael and Cindy decided to begin the IVF process. The contract specifically indicated that both parties must agree to the release of any resulting embryos that are frozen. Shortly after the eggs were frozen, Raphael died. Cindy now wants the eggs returned to her. The medical center has sought a declaratory action in the trial court to determine what to do with the eggs because the contract is silent as what to do with the eggs if one party dies. You are the law clerk working for the trial judge who must decide the issue of what do with the eggs. Utilizing the cases discussed in this chapter, how should the judge rule on the issue?

2. Katy agreed to be a surrogate for Tony and Wendy. The surrogate contract provided that Katy would be inseminated with Tony's sperm and that she would then relinquish all rights to the child. The contract provided that Katy had 72 hours after giving birth to rescind her agreement to terminate her parental rights. Katy's husband Dennis and Tony both signed the contract. Wendy did not sign. Katy gave birth to a baby girl, Baby S, and Tony and Wendy took the baby home from the hospital. After one week, the parties met in the lawyer's office, where Katy indicated she did not believe she could go forward with the contract and asks to terminate the agreement. What is the result?

3. Stan and Ellen used Barbara as a gestational surrogate. The contract provided that she would carry a child to term that was created with Stan's sperm and a donor egg through IVF, and that she would transfer the child to Stan and Ellen and relinquish all of her rights to the child. Barbara was artificially inseminated and gave birth to a little girl, Shellie. Barbara gave up all parental rights and Shellie has been raised by Stan and Ellen. Shellie is now eight years old and Stan has filed for divorce. Ellen did not legally adopt Shellie. Ellen comes to you and asks if she has any rights. Specifically, she would like to know if she is the presumed mother, if she has an in loco parentis claim, and, if Stan objects, can he seek to terminate her rights?

4. A state law makes surrogacy contracts void and unenforceable. It further stipulates that if parties do hire a surrogate, she is considered the legal mother and, if she is married, her husband is presumed to be the father assuming that they were married at the time of the conception. In an attempt to avoid the state law, Paul and Patty make an oral contract with Jenny to act as a surrogate using Paul's sperm. Jenny used a turkey baster to inseminate herself and after two failed attempts, Jenny became pregnant. Jenny gave birth to a baby boy and attempted to give the baby to Paul and Patty to adopt. However, Jenny's husband, Kevin, objects. Kevin comes to you and wants to know if he has a valid right to object. What do you tell Kevin?

5. Emma and Marco entered into a gestational surrogacy contract with Caitlin (a surrogate) and Caitlin's husband, Rob. The contract provided that Caitlin would carry a child to term who was created through IVF with the sperm of Marco and a donor egg, and upon giving birth would relinquish the child to the intended parents. Seventeen days prior to the birth of the child, the court issued a parentage order that declared Emma and Marco to be the legal parents of the child and terminated the parental rights of Caitlin and Rob. After giving birth, Caitlin filed a court action asking that the order be vacated and the surrogacy contract considered void. There is no state law governing surrogacy contracts. Emma and Marco have come to you for advice. What do you tell them?

6. David and Marcia were friends with Monica and Cory. David and Marcia were unable to have children of their own, so Monica agreed to be a surrogate for them under a parentage agreement that provided that "David and Marcia shall be considered the legal parents of the child born to Marcia. The child's best interests will be served by being in David and Marcia's legal custody and physical placement," and that "[t]he parties will cooperate fully in any parentage proceedings to determine David and Marcia are the child's legal parents, . . . including but not limited to termination of parental rights and adoption." Monica became pregnant through artificial insemination using her egg and David's sperm. Monica gave birth to Baby R. Shortly before Baby R's birth, Monica informed David and Marcia that she longer wanted to give up her parental rights. She further sought custody and placement of Baby R. David responded by seeking enforcement of the parentage agreement. How should the court analyze the parentage agreement?

Family Law in Practice

1. Research the law in your state regarding surrogacy contracts. Are there any laws that prohibit surrogacy contracts? If there is a law, are there any limitations imposed on surrogacy contracts?

2. Assume you are asked to write a law that voids surrogacy contracts as a violation of public policy. Write the proposed law and include the penalties that exist. Include a list of pros and cons for adoption of the law.

3. You are working for the general counsel of a large medical facility that stores frozen embryos for parties going through the IVF process. The contract that all parties sign before going through treatment states: "We understand that the embryos are subject to our joint disposition and, therefore, all future decisions about their disposal must be joint decisions." The contract also specifies alternatives for disposition of the embryos in the event that the parties divorced, including donation to another couple, donation for research, or thawing and discarding. Mary Jane and her husband Trey checked the box marked "thawed and discarded." Mary Jane and Trey made several attempts at IVF, but each was unsuccessful. Now, five years after their last attempt, the parties are in the process of getting a divorce. Trey wants the embryos destroyed pursuant to the contract. Mary Jane, who is now 46 years old, would like to take possession of the embryos as she is fearful that at her age the embryos are her only chance of being able to conceive a biological child. You have decided to file an action in court to have the trial judge make a determination of disposal of the embryos. What arguments do you expect from each party? Based on the law in your state, how should the judge rule?

4. As seen in the cases, the best interests of the children who are born as a result of the IVF process do not come into play in determining parentage. A local news program has asked to do an interview with you about whether the best interest standard should be used in determining parentage in such cases. Prepare an outline of the talking points you would like to make during your interview.

5. Mike and Leonard are married but do not have children. They have come to your office to talk to the partner you work with to learn more about the possibility of surrogacy parenting. The partner has asked you to research the law in your state and write a memorandum on whether surrogacy contracts for same-sex married couples are permissible.

Glossary

abuse reporting laws   Laws that establish a mechanism for the reporting of suspected cases of child abuse and/or neglect to a state protective agency. (Ch. Thirteen)

active appreciation   Appreciation where the gain is due to the investment of marital funds or efforts; considered marital property. (Ch. Eight)

active listening   An engaged way of listening, involving reflection back of informational and emotional content. (Ch. Nine)

adjusted gross income   One method of calculating income for child support based on an adjusted amount. Believed to be more fair, as it is a more accurate measure of the obligor's available income. (Ch. Six)

adultery   Voluntary sexual intercourse between a married person and someone who is not his or her spouse; a fault divorce ground. (Ch. Four)

age of capacity   The minimum age below which a young person may not marry — commonly set at age 14. (Ch. Two)

age of consent   The age at which a young person becomes eligible to consent to his or her own marriage — usually set at the age of majority. (Ch. Two)

agency adoption   As distinct from an independent adoption, an adoption that is handled by a state or private agency. A key component of these adoptions is that a home study is done prior to the placement of a child with a prospective adoptive family. (Ch. Fourteen)

alimony   Spousal support; an allowance paid to one spouse by the other for support pending or after legal separation or divorce. Sometimes referred to as spousal maintenance. (Ch. Seven)

alimony in gross   Sometimes referred to as a *lump-sum support payment*. Unlike permanent alimony, it involves the payment of a sum certain; it is generally paid in a single installment, although it can also be made payable in periodic installments until the full amount of the order is reached. (Ch. Seven)

alimony pendente lite   Temporary support paid to one spouse by the other during the pendency of a divorce. (Ch. Seven)

all property approach   Allows a couple's accumulated assets to be distributed at divorce without a formal distinction between separate property and marital property. (Ch. Eight)

analytical approach   Concerns damage awards; approach where an award is divided into component parts and allocated between the separate and marital estates in accordance with general classification principles. (Ch. Eight)

annulment   A decree establishing that a husband and wife were never actually married because an impediment existed at the time the marriage was celebrated. (Ch. Four)

arbitration   A dispute resolution mechanism whereby parties agree to submit their disagreement to a neutral decision maker. The arbitrator's authority derives from the party's agreement, and his or her decision is usually binding subject to a limited right of court review. (Ch. Nine)

attempted physical harm   Occurs when physical abuse is intended, but not inflicted. (Ch. Eleven)

attributed income   See *imputed income*.

bankruptcy   The filing of a court action in which a party seeks to be discharged from responsibility for paying his or her debts. (Ch. Seven)

Batterer Intervention Programs   A treatment or counseling program that works specifically with batterers. (Ch. Eleven)

best interest attorney   In contested custody cases, an attorney appointed to advocate a position that will serve the child's best interests even if this is contrary to the child's expressed objectives. (Ch. Five)

best interest of the child   The predominant legal standard for resolving custody disputes between parents; the standard is child-centered, focusing on the needs of the child rather than on the rights of the parents. (Ch. Five)

change in circumstances   A future event that arguably makes an existing order unfair and serves as the basis for a request for modification. (Ch. Seven)

child custody   Broadly, the care of and responsibility for a child. (Ch. Five)

child protection agency   Usually a state agency with responsibility for handling cases of child abuse and neglect. (Ch. Thirteen)

child's attorney   An attorney appointed by the court to express the child's preferences rather than making an independent determination of what is in the minor child's best interest. (Ch. Five)

civil contempt   A contempt action can be brought where an obligor fails to comply with a court order of support. The purpose of a civil contempt proceeding is to secure compliance with the support order. (Ch. Six)

civil union   A formal status that was used to provide same-sex couples with the rights, benefits, protections, and responsibilities that are available to married heterosexual couples under state (but not federal) law. (Ch. Two)

clean-break approach   Approach where there is no long-term duty of spousal support. (Ch. Seven)

collaborative law   An approach to the dissolution of marriage that stresses cooperation and the avoidance of litigation. (Ch. Nine)

collusion   Agreement by a couple to obtain a divorce in avoidance of the fault principle that requires a guilty and an innocent spouse. (Ch. Four)

common law   A body of law that has evolved from judicial decisions in cases that do not involve the application of constitutions, statutes, or administrative regulations; law created by the courts. (Ch. One)

community property   A system of property ownership between husband and wife in civil law jurisdictions in which each spouse has a vested one-half ownership interest in all marital property regardless of title; excluded is all property classified as separate property. (Ch. One)

comparative rectitude   A doctrine that ameliorates the harsh effects of the traditional divorce defense of recrimination by allowing a divorce when one party's marital fault is regarded as less serious than the other party's. (Ch. Four)

complaint   In a civil case, the pleading filed by the plaintiff to initiate a lawsuit; includes factual allegations, a statement of legal claims against the defendant, and a request for relief; called *petition* in some states. (Ch. Nine)

condonation   A divorce defense, the essence of which is that the plaintiff has forgiven the acts of marital misconduct upon which his or her complaint for divorce is based. (Ch. Four)

connivance   Occurs when one spouse sets up or consents to a situation involving the other spouse committing a wrongdoing that is the reason for divorce. (Ch. Four)

consideration   The bargained-for exchange that underlies the formation of an enforceable contract; consideration serves to distinguish a contract from a promise. (Ch. Three)

constructive desertion   Imputes the act of desertion to the spouse responsible for the other's departure. (Ch. Four)

contempt   Violation of a court order. (Ch. Seven)

contempt proceeding   A proceeding against a party who is in violation of a court order; contempt proceedings can be either civil or criminal in nature. The purpose of a civil contempt action is to obtain compliance with a court order, while the purpose of a criminal contempt action is to punish a party for his or her noncompliance. (Ch. Six)

continuing jurisdiction   In the custody context, the continuation of the initial decree state's authority to modify a decree to the exclusion of other states. (Ch. Ten)

co-parent   A parent who shares the raising of a child with his or her partner in the absence of a formally recognized parent-child relationship. (Ch. Fourteen)

co-parent adoption   Adoption by a co-parent. The adoption does not extinguish the rights of the biological parent. (Ch. Fourteen)

cost approach   Method of valuation; entails an assessment of what it would cost to replace the asset if necessary. (Ch. Eight)

covenant marriage Developed in response to concerns about the prevalence and impact of divorce, covenant marriage laws emphasize the permanency of marriage and limit the availability of divorce. (Ch. Four)

credit reporting In the child support context, the provision of information to a credit agency about a party's failure to make child support payments. (Ch. Six)

criminal assault Occurs when someone is placed in fear of imminent bodily harm. (Ch. Eleven)

criminal contempt A contempt action can be brought where an obligor fails to comply with a court order of support. The purpose of a criminal contempt proceeding is to punish the support obligor for violating the court order. (Ch. Six)

criminal nonsupport The willful failure to pay child support when one has the ability to do so; may also apply to the willful failure to pay spousal support. (Ch. Six)

cruelty A fault ground for divorce based on mistreatment of a relatively serious nature; cruelty generally can include either physical or emotional wrongdoing. (Ch. Four)

cut-off rule Principle that operates to extinguish the parental rights of the biological parents at the time of adoption; may not be applied when a stepparent or a co-parent is adopting the child. (Ch. Fourteen)

declaration of indigency Filed by divorce petitioners to request a fee waiver in cases of financial hardship. (Ch. Nine)

defined benefit plan Pension plans funded solely by employer contributions that will pay out a set amount over a period of time. (Ch. Eight)

defined contribution plan Pension plans funded solely by employee contributions that will pay out a set amount over a period of time. (Ch. Eight)

desertion A fault ground for divorce; involves the voluntary, nonconsensual departure of one spouse without justification for a period of time defined by statute. (Ch. Four)

direct placement adoption See *independent adoption*. (Ch. Fourteen)

divorce The legal dissolution of a marital relationship, such that the parties are no longer husband and wife. (Ch. Four)

divorce *a mensa et thoro* A common law term meaning a "divorce from board and bed" this is a decree of separation that permits a husband and wife to live apart without dissolving the marital relationship. (Ch. Four)

domestic violence Abusive behavior toward someone with whom one is in a dating, familial, household, or intimate relationship. See also *intimate partner violence*. (Ch. Eleven)

domicile A person's permanent home; the place to which the person intends to return when away. (Ch. Ten)

dual property approach The division of property at divorce based principally on considerations of fairness and contribution rather than title. (Ch. Eight)

e-discovery Discovery of electronic information. (Ch. Nine)

electronically stored information (ESI) Electronic information that includes emails, voicemails, instant messages, text messages, documents and spreadsheets, file fragments, digital images and video. (Ch. Nine)

e-mediation See *online dispute resolution.* (Ch. Nine)

emotional abuse Acts such as isolation, verbal assault, humiliation, intimidation, or any other treatment which may diminish the sense of identity and self-worth. In the context of child abuse, frequently involves subjecting a child to intense and recurring anger or hostility. (Chs. Eleven, Thirteen)

emotional neglect Refers to the withdrawal of love and affection. (Ch. Thirteen)

equal distribution approach Distribution standard where courts must divide marital property equally between the spouses. (Ch. Eight)

equitable distribution approach The division of property at divorce based principally on considerations of fairness and contribution rather than title. (Ch. Eight)

extraordinary expenses Large, discrete expenditures that do not recur on a regular basis, as distinct from the day-to-day expenses of raising a child. (Ch. Six)

fair market value The price that a willing buyer would pay to a willing seller when neither party is under compulsion to buy or sell. (Ch. Eight)

family and probate court See *family court.* (Ch. Ten)

family court In most states, exclusive subject matter jurisdiction over divorce actions—including all collateral issues such as support, property, and custody—is vested in this specialized court. Sometimes called *family and probate court.* (Ch. Ten)

Federal Parent Locator Service Service operated by the Office of Child Support Enforcement (OCSE); requires each state IV-D agency to establish its own parent locator service. (Ch. Six)

financial affidavit A document that discloses income and assets, which parties must complete in family court proceedings where property or support is at issue. Sometimes called Affidavit of Financial Information (Ch. Six)

for-profit child support collection agency Collection agencies that promise to fill the existing gap in enforcement services that IV-D agencies seem unable to meet. (Ch. Six)

freedom of contract The right of each individual to freely structure his or her own affairs. (Ch. Three)

gestational surrogacy involves the extracorporeal creation of embryos through a procedure known as in vitro fertilization (IVF). The aspirated eggs are then mixed with the intending father's (or a donor's) sperm, and one or more resulting embryos are transferred into the uterus of the surrogate whose cycle has been managed with hormonal injections in order to suppress her natural ovulation and ready her uterus for the transfer. (Ch. Fifteen)

ghostwriting Assistance with drafting pleadings; often offered as part of unbundled legal services. (Ch. Nine)

gift   A voluntary transfer of property made with donative intent, meaning that the gift-giver (donor) simply wishes to give the recipient something without requiring anything in exchange. For a gift to be effective, the transfer must be complete — the donor must fully relinquish all vestiges of ownership and control. (Ch. Eight)

goodwill   An intangible asset; the good reputation of a business in the community that generates future patronage. (Ch. Eight)

gross income   One method of calculating income for child support; advantage is simplicity and the fact that income cannot be manipulated because no deductions are taken before the support amount is calculated. (Ch. Six)

guardian ad litem   A person who is appointed by a court to conduct a custody investigation; may also refer to a person appointed to provide legal representation to a child. (Ch. Nine)

Hague Conference   An intergovernmental organization whose primary purpose is "to work for the progressive unification of the rules of private international law." (Ch. Ten)

harassment   Aggressive pressure or intimidation. Includes a range of conduct, such as preventing a person from leaving a room, pulling the telephone out of the wall or cutting the wires, or slashing the tires of someone's car. (Ch. Eleven)

home study   An evaluation of a person or couple seeking to adopt a child to determine potential suitability, usually done only in agency adoptions. (Ch. Fourteen)

hotchpot of assets approach   *See all property approach.* (Ch. Eight)

if, as, and when approach   When used to value pensions, awards the non-employee spouse a share of pension funds "if, as, and when" the employee spouse receives them. (Ch. Eight)

imputed income   The attribution of income to a party who is deliberately un- or underemployed, based on earning capacity, for the purpose of establishing the amount of his or her support obligation. (Ch. Six)

in rem jurisdiction   The authority of a court to resolve a case based on the presence of property within its borders. (Ch. Ten)

inception of title rule   A rule fixing title at the time an asset is acquired. (Ch. Eight)

income approach   Method of valuation; a determination is made of the amount of income that an asset may produce over a certain period of time, which is then capitalized over the life expectancy of the asset and discounted to present day value. (Ch. Eight)

independent adoption   An adoption that is accomplished without an agency; parents can either place the child directly or utilize an intermediary. (Ch. Fourteen)

indissoluble   In reference to marriage, the belief that the legal relationship between a husband and wife is permanent and can never be terminated. (Ch. Four)

innocent spouse   Pertaining to fault divorce, the requirement that the petitioning spouse not have engaged in marital misconduct. (Ch. Four)

intangible assets   Assets that lack a physical presence and cannot be ascertained by the senses. (Ch. Eight)

intimate partner violence   Violence between partners who are in a same-sex or heter-sexual relationship, including dating relationships. See also *domestic violence.* (Ch. Eleven)

irreconcilable differences   A no-fault divorce ground, the essence of which is that the parties are no longer compatible and there is no hope of reconciliation. (Ch. Four)

IV-D Agency   Under Title IV-D of the Federal Code, the agency in each state responsible for administering that state's child support program. (Ch. Six)

joint adoption   When a couple, whether same-sex or heterosexual, seeks to adopt a child who is not related to either party. (Ch. Fourteen)

joint custody   As distinct from sole custody, the sharing of parental rights and responsibilities — can apply to legal or physical custody, or both. (Ch. Five)

joint petitions   Pleadings filed in a no-fault divorce action by co-petitioners to initiate the divorce. (Ch. Nine)

legal custody   The parent responsible to make decisions for the minor child regarding health, education and religion. (Ch. Five)

legal separation   A judicial decree permitting parties to live apart, usually for cause, without dissolving the legal relationship of husband and wife. (Ch. Four)

license   An intangible asset that permits a person to engage in some activity. (Ch. Eight)

limited task representation   See *unbundled legal services.* (Ch. Nine)

long-arm statutes   A statute that spells out when a state may assert personal jurisdiction over a nonresident. (Ch. Ten)

lump-sum support   A future event that arguably makes an existing order unfair and serves as the basis for a request for modification. (Ch. Seven)

marital breakdown   See *irreconcilable differences.* (Ch. Four)

marital fault   Acts of wrongdoing by one spouse toward the other that serve as the basis of a fault divorce. (Ch. Four)

marital property   As distinct from separate property, assets acquired during the marriage as a result of marital efforts or funds, which are subject to division at divorce. (Ch. Eight)

marital unity   A common law principle espousing that upon marriage a husband and wife become one, resulting in the suspension of the wife's legal identity. (Ch. One)

Married Women's Property Acts   The series of statutory reforms that gradually improved the legal status of married women, principally through extending rights of property ownership and control that had been denied at common law. (Ch. One)

mechanistic approach   Concerns damage awards; approach that classifies the entire personal injury award as marital. (Ch. Eight)

metadata   Data hidden in documents that is generated during the course of creating and editing electronic documents. It may include fragments of data from files that were previously deleted, overwritten or worked on simultaneously. (Ch. Nine)

minimum contacts   A jurisdictional concept enabling a state to assert personal jurisdiction over a nonresident when he or she has a sufficiently developed relationship with that state. (Ch. Ten)

modification   The alteration of an existing order based on a change in circumstances. (Ch. Seven)

modification jurisdiction   The authority of a court to modify a custody or support decree. (Ch. Ten)

net income   One method of calculating income for child support; allows for further deductions than the adjusted gross income base. Might be the most accurate method, but can be manipulated to show a reduced income, thus limiting the support base. (Ch. Six)

nexus approach   As distinct from the per se approach, this approach requires that parental conduct have a demonstrated detrimental impact on a child before it will be taken into account in a custody determination. (Ch. Five)

no-contact order   A protective order that prohibits someone from having any contact with the party he or she has abused. (Ch. Eleven)

online dispute resolution (ODR)   Virtual approach to mediation where, in domestic abuse situations, the physical separation of the parties can serve to neutralize the power advantage that an abuser typically has over the victim. (Ch. Nine)

opportunity cost   The loss of earning potential attributable to a lack of a sustained relationship with the labor force, often due to a spouse's primary investment in the domestic realm. (Ch. Seven)

ordinary expenses   Relatively small, predictable, and fairly consistent expenses in families of the same size and income level. (Ch. Six)

parens patriae   The authority of the state, as a sovereign power, to protect those who cannot protect themselves, most notably children. (Ch. Thirteen)

parenting coordinators   In some states, the person who has the responsibility of helping parties to successfully implement their parenting plan. (Ch. Five)

parenting plan   A written agreement in which the parents detail how they intend to care for their children following a divorce. (Ch. Five)

passive appreciation   Appreciation where the increase is unrelated to spousal efforts and is due to causes such as inflation or market conditions, it is usually considered the separate property of the spouse who owns the asset. (Ch. Eight)

paternity disestablishment   The undoing/revocation of a determination that a man is a child's legal father. (Ch. Twelve)

per se approach   As distinct from the nexus approach, the idea that some behaviors are so inherently harmful that they should be the basis for denying custody to a parent without proof of actual harm. (Ch. Five)

percentage-of-income approach   Sets the support amount as a fixed percentage of the noncustodial parent's income. (Ch. Six)

permanent alimony   An ongoing support award to a spouse who is unlikely to become economically self-sufficient; the award is subject to modification and is generally terminable upon death of either spouse or remarriage of the recipient. (Ch. Seven)

personal jurisdiction   The authority of a court over the person of a defendant. (Ch. Ten)

petitions   See *complaint*. (Ch. Nine)

physical abuse   Abuse involving acts such as slaps or pushes as well as potentially life-threatening conduct such as physical beatings with an object or a fist, and the throwing of objects that hits a person. (Ch. Eleven)

physical custody   As distinct from legal custody, physical custody refers to where a child lives; a parent with physical custody usually maintains a home for the child and is responsible for the child's day-to-day care. Physical custody can be either sole or joint. (Ch. Five)

premarital counseling   Using incentives such as a reduced marriage license fee, some states now encourage potential to participate in counseling as a way to reduce the divorce rate. (Ch. Four)

present value approach   When used to value pensions, determines the present value of the pension and then assigns the non-employee spouse an offsetting share of property. (Ch. Eight)

private adoption   See *independent adoption*. (Ch. Fourteen)

private placement adoptions   See *independent adoption*. (Ch. Fourteen)

problem-solving model   Approach of mediation where the goal is to arrive at a solution that "solves tangible problems on fair and realistic terms. (Ch. Nine)

procedural fairness   Fairness of the parties in their treatment of one another in the process of negotiating an agreement, as distinct from fairness in the resulting terms (substantive fairness). (Ch. Three)

putative father registries   Enable men who are or believe they may be the father of a child to register with the state in order to protect their potential interest in the child. (Ch. Fourteen)

Qualified Domestic Relations Order (QDRO)   A court order that allows the distribution of pension benefits to a non-employee spouse. (Ch. Eight)

Qualified Medical Child Support Order (QMCSO)   A qualified medical child support order; requires every employer group health plan to provide coverage to the children named by the court or a qualified administrative agency to facilitate coverage of children. (Ch. Six)

recapture   The recomputation of a support obligor's gross income to include amounts that had been improperly deducted as spousal support payments, and the readjustment of his or her tax obligation. (Ch. Seven)

recrimination   A divorce defense that prevents a divorce from being granted on the basis that both parties are guilty of marital misconduct; may be ameliorated by the doctrine of comparative rectitude.(Ch. Four)

rehabilitative support   Time-limited support intended to enable a spouse to obtain the education or training necessary to become economically self-sufficient. (Ch. Seven)

res judicata   Legal principle that prevents a court from reexamining an issue that already has been litigated. (Ch. Five)

restraining order   Court order issued by judges in all states. Enjoins the abusive party from engaging in conduct that places the victim at risk of harm. Often expressed as a requirement that the abuser refrain from committing any further acts of abuse as defined by the applicable abuse prevention law.

revival   The restoration of certain rights deriving from a prior marriage following the annulment of a subsequent marriage. (Ch. Four)

safe haven laws   These laws allow a birth parent, or an agent of the parent, to leave a baby at a safe location, such as a hospital or fire station, without fear of being prosecuted for child abandonment or neglect. (Ch. Fourteen)

second-parent adoption   See *co-parent adoption*. (Ch. Fourteen)

separate property   As distinct from marital property, property that belongs to the acquiring spouse and is not subject to distribution at divorce. It usually consists of gifts, inheritances, and premarital acquisitions. (Ch. Eight)

separation agreement   A contract between divorcing spouses in which they set out the terms of their agreement relative to all collateral matters, such as custody, support, and the distribution of property. (Ch. Nine)

sexual assault   Involves coercing someone to engage in sexual relations against their will through force, threats of force, or duress. (Ch. Eleven)

social study   A post-placement study that must be completed in both private placement and agency adoptions before an adoption can be finalized, although the requirement may be waived in certain situations. Intended to provide the judge with information to help him or her decide whether or not to approve the adoption. (Ch. Fourteen)

sole custody   The vesting of custodial rights in one parent — can apply to legal or physical custody, or both. (Ch. Five)

source of funds rule   As distinct from the inception of title rule, an approach that ties the time of acquisition of an asset to the contribution of funds and permits the dual characterization of an asset as both marital and separate in proportion to contribution. (Ch. Eight)

special equity rule A rule giving a spouse who contributed purchase funds to an asset titled in the name of the other an interest in the asset, which is reachable at divorce; was relevant in jurisdictions that divided property according to title. (Ch. Eight)

stalking The malicious, willful, and repeated tracking down and following of another person; stalking is often a precursor to acts of serious bodily harm. (Ch. Eleven)

statute of frauds A rule requiring that certain kinds of contracts be in writing in order to be enforceable. (Ch. Three)

stay-away order A court order, pursuant to an abuse prevention law, requiring the perpetrator to keep away from the victim's home or from other places where the victim regularly goes (e.g., work). (Ch. Eleven)

subject matter jurisdiction The authority of a court to hear a particular kind of case. (Ch. Ten)

substantive fairness Fairness of the actual terms of an agreement, as distinct from procedural fairness. (Ch. Three)

tangible property Property with a physical presence, which is capable of being felt and seen. (Ch. Eight)

temporary alimony Support awarded during the pendency of the divorce action intended to assist a spouse during this interim period. Sometimes referred to as temporary support or temporary maintenance. (Ch. Seven)

tender years presumption The traditional custodial assumption that children of a young age should be raised by their mothers. (Ch. One)

threatened physical harm Most domestic abuse statutes cover threats; generally, a petitioner must show that he or she was placed in fear of imminent bodily harm. (Ch. Eleven)

title The right of exclusive ownership and control of an asset. (Ch. Eight)

Title IV-D Law that amends the Social Security Act to establish a cooperative federal-state program for the obtaining and enforcement of child support orders. (Ch. Six)

traditional surrogacy When the surrogate agrees to become pregnant by artificial insemination in order to give birth to a child that will be given to the intended parents. The woman uses her own eggs and is therefore biologically related to the child. The donor sperm may be from an unknown donor or from one of the intended parents. (Ch. Fifteen)

transformative model Approach where the primary goal of mediation is not problem solving, but changing the interactional patterns between the parties. (Ch. Nine)

transitional support See *rehabilitative support*.

transmutation   The post-acquisition change in the classification of an asset from marital to separate or vice versa. Transmutation can occur through agreement, commingling, the taking of title in joint name, or use. (Ch. Eight)

unallocated support   Child and spousal support awards combined in a single support amount without designation. (Ch. Six)

unbundled legal services   Also referred to as *limited task representation*. An attorney agrees to provide a client with limited assistance from a menu of options instead of providing the client with comprehensive representation. Typically, rather than entering into a retainer agreement, the client pays for each separate service at the time it is rendered. Unbundled services include the giving of legal advice, coaching on how to handle the case, assistance with drafting pleadings, and representation in court. (Ch. Nine)

unconscionability   When a contract is grossly unfair to one side, usually involves parties with a significant disparity in bargaining power. (Ch. Three)

vacate order   A court order requiring a perpetrator of domestic violence to move out of the home he or she shares with the party who has been abused; vacate orders do not affect title to property. (Ch. Eleven)

valuation   The determination of what an asset is worth, most commonly by ascertaining its fair market value; usually done by an expert. (Ch. Eight)

verbal abuse   Language or behavior that seeks to coerce its victim to doubt their abilities and submit to the abuser. (Ch. Eleven)

void   A marriage that is without any legal effect from its inception; a void marriage does not require a decree of annulment to invalidate it. See also *voidable*. (Ch. Four)

voidable   A marriage that is without any legal effect from its inception; a void marriage does not require a decree of annulment to invalidate it. See also *void*. (Ch. Four)

Table of Cases

Index